COMMERCIAL TRANSACTIONS

SALES, LEASES AND LICENSES

Second Edition

By

Richard E. Speidel

Beatrice Kuhn Professor of Law Emeritus
Northwestern University School of Law
Distinguished Visiting Professor
University of San Diego School of Law

Linda J. Rusch

Professor of Law
Hamline University School of Law

AMERICAN CASEBOOK SERIES®

Mat # 40274723

TEXT IS PRINTED ON 10% POST
CONSUMER RECYCLED PAPER

To Liz with thanks for the present and to Reeve, Connor and Nancy Jean with hope for the future.

RES

To Doug, Kari, and Anna.

LJR

PREFACE TO THE SECOND EDITION

This book revises Commercial Transactions, Sales, Leases and Licenses (West 2001) which was based upon the sales materials in Speidel, Summers, & White, Sales and Secured Transactions (West 1993). We thank Bob Summers and Jim White for their contribution to those earlier materials.

The materials draw on, among other things, our experience as reporter and associate reporter (until July, 1999) to the Article 2 revision process. We learned much from our friends and colleagues in that process. The amendments to Articles 2 and 2A are noted and discussed throughout the book.

The materials consist of original text, problems, cases, and limited reprinted material. The focus is on the problems, which require students to work with UCC Articles 2 and 2A and the United Nations Convention on Contracts for the International Sale of Goods. In addition, the Uniform Electronic Transactions Act (UETA) and the Uniform Computer Information Transactions Act (UCITA) are also discussed. Given the lack of action in state legislatures on UCITA, coverage of that act has been reduced in this edition.

It is unwise to teach the law of sales in isolation from other Articles of the UCC and changes in the commercial world around the UCC. We have tried, however, to be selective in the integration of other materials and to provide options for the teacher.

There is more than enough material here for a three hour course.

ACKNOWLEDGMENTS

Professor Speidel acknowledges the help of his long time assistant at Northwestern, Shirley Scott, and the suggestions of students in classes over a five year period at the University of San Diego School of Law for ways to clarify and sharpen the materials..

Professor Rusch acknowledges the help and suggestions of students concerning improvements in the book. Of course responsibility for any mistakes remains with the authors.

The authors thank Joan Vogel and the Arizona State Law Journal for granting permission to reprint portions of their material in this book.

Vogel, Joan, Squeezing Consumers: Lemon Laws, Consumer Warranties, and a Proposal for Reform, 1985 Ariz. St. L.J. 589. Copyright © 1985 by Arizona State Law Journal and Joan Vogel. Reprinted by permission of the author and the Arizona State Law Journal.

Summary of Contents

Preface v

Acknowledgments vii

Table of Cases xxvii

Table of Statutes and Regulations xxxvii

Table of Secondary Authorities xlvii

Part One: Nature and Scope of Commercial Codes 1

Chapter One The Nature and Sources of Commercial Law 1

  Section 1.   Introduction to Commercial Law 1

    A.   Types of Commercial Transactions 1

    B.   Functions of Commercial Law 1

    C.   Role of the Commercial Lawyer 5

  Section 2.   The Uniform Commercial Code: History,

    Structure, and Purpose 6

    A.   A Brief History of the Uniform Commercial Code 6

    B.   What Does the UCC Cover? 9

    C.   What Transactions Does This Book Cover? 14

    D.   Interpreting the UCC: Some Notes on Methodology 15

  Section 3.   Commercial Law Not in the Uniform Commercial Code .. 20

  Section 4.   International Commercial Law 22

  Section 5.   An Exercise in UCC Methodology 24

Chapter Two Scope: What Law Applies to the Transaction 43

  Section 1.   A Roadmap to the Sales and Leases Articles

    of the UCC 43

    A.   The Agreement Stage 43

    B.   The Post-Agreement–Pre-Shipment Stage 45

    C.   The Stage of Getting the Goods or Documents

    Therefor to the Buyer or Lessee 47

    D.   The Receipt-Inspection Stage 49

    E.   The Payment Stage 53

    F.   Finance Leases 55

    G.   Special Problems of Third Party Rights in a Lease Transaction 56

    H.   Conclusion 56

  Section 2.   Determining What Law Applies 57

    A.   Analysis of the Scope of Article 2 and Article 2A 57

    B.   Mixed Transactions 65

    C.   United Nations Convention on Contracts for the

International Sale of Goods (CISG) 73

D. Choice of Law and Choice of Forum Clauses 74

SECTION 3.   SOME BASIC CONCEPTS IN ARTICLE 2 76

A. Introduction 76

B. Agreement, Not Promise, as the Foundation Stone 78

C. The Article Two "Merchant" Concept 79

D. Legal Controls on Contractual Behavior: Unconscionability
and Good Faith 82

PART TWO: FORMATION AND TERMS OF THE CONTRACT 95

Chapter Three Contract Formation and Enforcement 95

SECTION 1.   INTRODUCTION; ELECTRONIC CONTRACTING 95

SECTION 2.   CONTRACT FORMATION: THE BASICS 98

SECTION 3.   CONTRACT FORMATION: BATTLE OF THE FORMS 108

A. Under Former UCC 2-207 108

B. The Reform (?) of UCC 2-207 124

C. The "Gateway" Problem 127

SECTION 4.   THE STATUTE OF FRAUDS 128

A. History and Purposes 128

B. Satisfying the Statute of Frauds 130

Chapter Four Terms of the Agreement: Sources and Meaning 147

SECTION 1.   "GAP FILLERS" AS TERMS OF THE CONTRACT 147

A. The Scope of Agreement in Fact: A Reprise 147

B. "Gap Fillers" as Terms of the Contract 148

SECTION 2.   OPEN TERMS 153

A. Quantity 154

B. Price 166

C. Delivery Terms and Payment of the Price 179

SECTION 3.   PRE-CONTRACT FACTS WHICH VARY, SUPPLEMENT,
OR GIVE MEANING TO THE AGREEMENT 179

A. Introduction 179

B. Effect of Usage of Trade and Course of Dealing 181

C. The Parol Evidence Rule 189

Chapter Five Breach of Warranty as to the Quality of the Product Sold . . . 203

SECTION 1.   INTRODUCTION 203

A. Warranty Theory: Some History 203

B. Warranties Under the Code: An Introduction 207

C. Warranties under the CISG and UCITA 209

SECTION 2.   EXPRESS WARRANTIES 209

SECTION 3. IMPLIED WARRANTIES 241
    A. Introduction 241
    B. Merchantability 242
    C. Overlap Between Merchantability and Strict Tort Liability 258
    D. Fitness for Particular Purpose 266
    E. Finance Leases 274
    F. Proof of Breach: Effect of Lack of Causation and Plaintiff's
        Contributory Behavior 283
SECTION 4. DISCLAIMERS AND LIMITATIONS OF WARRANTIES 292
SECTION 5. EXTENSION OF WARRANTY OBLIGATIONS 301

PART THREE: PERFORMANCE OF THE CONTRACT 305
Chapter Six Delivery and Payment 305
SECTION 1. TENDER, INSPECTION, AND PAYMENT 305
    A. The Basic Scenario 305
    B. The Seller's Shipment of Goods to the Buyer 308
    C. Goods in the Hands of a Bailee and Delivery
        Without Moving the Goods 313
    D. The Documentary Draft Transaction 314
    E. The Letter of Credit Transaction 315
SECTION 2. REJECTION, ACCEPTANCE, AND REVOCATION
    OF ACCEPTANCE 320
    A. Rejection or Acceptance 320
    B. Revocation of Acceptance 348
    C. The Right to Cure 352
SECTION 3. TERMINATION 359
SECTION 4. PUTTING IT ALL TOGETHER 359

Chapter Seven Excuse from or Adjustment of the Contract
for Changed Circumstances 363
SECTION 1. RELIEF FROM CHANGED CIRCUMSTANCES 363
    A. Loss of Identified Goods 364
    B. Failure of Delivery or Payment Mechanisms 364
    C. The Basic Assumption Test: Force Majeure Events 365
    D. Relief From Non-Force Majeure Events 380
SECTION 2. MODIFICATION OF THE CONTRACT 395
    A. Agreed Modifications 395
    B. Modification or Rescission by Waiver 403

Chapter Eight Risk of Loss and Insurance 421
SECTION 1. GROUND RULES 421

SECTION 2.   RISK OF LOSS IN THE ABSENCE OF BREACH 423
    A.   Goods in Possession of Seller 423
    B.   Goods in the Possession of a Bailee to be Delivered
        Without Being Moved 425
    C.   Seller Authorized or Required to Ship Goods by Carrier 428
SECTION 3.   EFFECT OF BREACH ON RISK OF LOSS 439

Chapter Nine Property Rights **447**
SECTION 1.   TITLE AND IDENTIFICATION 447
SECTION 2.   SELLER OR LESSOR IN POSSESSION OF THE GOODS 450
    A.   Introduction 450
    B.   Buyer's or Lessee's Rights to Obtain the Goods
        From the Seller or Lessor 451
    C.   The Buyer's or Lessee's Right to Obtain Possession As Against
        Third Persons with Claims to the Goods 455
    D.   Seller's or Lessor's Ability to Stop or Withhold Delivery
        of the Goods From the Buyer or Lessee 459
    E.   Security Interests Arising Under Article 2: Seller's Right to
        Retain Title or Ship Under Reservation 460
        Note: Retaining Control of the Product Under UCITA 460
    F.   Claims to the Goods Asserted by the Buyer's or Lessee's
        Creditors or Transferees When the Seller or Lessor
        in Possession of the Goods 461
SECTION 3.   BUYER OR LESSEE IN POSSESSION OF THE GOODS 462
    A.   Introduction 462
    B.   Seller's or Lessor's Right to Regain Possession of the Goods
        From Buyer or Lessee 463
    C.   Priority of Seller's or Lessor's Right to Possession Against
        Buyer's or Lessee's Creditors or Transferees 467
    D.   Priority of Buyer's or Lessee's Claim to the Goods Against Persons
        Claiming Pre-existing Ownership 471
    E.   Buyer's and Lessee's Rights as Against Seller's or
        Lessor's Creditors 480
SECTION 4.   WARRANTY OF TITLE, NON-INTERFERENCE, AND
        AGAINST INFRINGEMENT 482
SECTION 5.   ASSIGNMENT AND DELEGATION 490

PART FOUR: BREACH OF CONTRACT AND REMEDIES **495**
Chapter Ten Remedies: Breach When Product Not Accepted **495**
SECTION 1.   INTRODUCTION 495
SECTION 2.   INSECURITY AND REPUDIATION 497

A.   Insecurity and Prospective Inability 497
B.   Repudiation 511
C.   Right to Cancel 516
SECTION 3.   REMEDIES OF SELLER AND LESSOR 526
A.   Availability and Cumulative Effect 526
B.   Action for the Price, Rent, or Specific Performance 527
C.   Resale, Release, or Substitute Transactions 532
D.   Contract-Market Damages 540
E.   Lost Profit 543
F.   Remedial Choice 555
G.   Incidental and Consequential Damages 563
SECTION 4.   REMEDIES OF BUYER OR LESSEE 564
A.   Introduction 566
B.   Cover 566
C.   Market-Contract Damages 574
D.   Consequential and Incidental Damages 577

Chapter Eleven Non-conforming Performance and Accepted Products:
Damages for Breach 581
SECTION 1.   REPRISE OF REJECTION, ACCEPTANCE AND
REVOCATION OF ACCEPTANCE 581
SECTION 2.   ACCEPTING A NON-CONFORMING PERFORMANCE; NOTICE 582
SECTION 3.   DAMAGES FOR ACCEPTED PERFORMANCE 591
A.   Direct Damages 591
B.   Incidental and Consequential Damages 595
SECTION 4.   PRODUCTS LIABILITY LAW 612
A.   Injury to Person and Property 612
B.   The "Economic Loss" Doctrine 617

Chapter Twelve Limitations on Remedies for Breach of Contract 629
SECTION 1.   AGREED LIMITATIONS ON REMEDIES 629
A.   Liquidated Damages 629
B.   Limited Remedies 639
SECTION 2.   CONSUMER PROTECTION LAW 652
A.   Federal Law: FTC and the Magnuson-Moss Warranty Act 654
B.   State Law: "Lemon" Laws 666
SECTION 3.   THE STATUTE OF LIMITATIONS 670

INDEX 681

TABLE OF CONTENTS

———

PREFACE v
ACKNOWLEDGMENTS vii
TABLE OF CASES xxvii
TABLE OF STATUTES AND REGULATIONS xxxvii
TABLE OF SECONDARY AUTHORITIES xlvii

PART ONE: NATURE AND SCOPE OF COMMERCIAL CODES 1
Chapter One The Nature and Sources of Commercial Law 1
   SECTION 1. INTRODUCTION TO COMMERCIAL LAW 1
     A. Types of Commercial Transactions 1
     B. Functions of Commercial Law 1
     C. Role of the Commercial Lawyer 5
   SECTION 2. THE UNIFORM COMMERCIAL CODE: HISTORY,
   STRUCTURE, AND PURPOSE 6
     A. A Brief History of the Uniform Commercial Code 6
     B. What Does the UCC Cover? 9
     C. What Transactions Does This Book Cover? 14
     D. Interpreting the UCC: Some Notes on Methodology 15
   SECTION 3. COMMERCIAL LAW NOT IN THE UNIFORM COMMERCIAL CODE .. 20
   SECTION 4. INTERNATIONAL COMMERCIAL LAW 22
   SECTION 5. AN EXERCISE IN UCC METHODOLOGY 24
     B & W Glass, Inc. v. Weather Shield Mfg., Inc. 26
     Blue Valley Cooperative v. National Farmers Organization 36
     Problem 1-1 41
     Problem 1-2 41

Chapter Two Scope: What Law Applies to the Transaction 43
   SECTION 1. A ROADMAP TO THE SALES AND LEASES ARTICLES
   OF THE UCC 43
     A. The Agreement Stage 43
     B. The Post-Agreement–Pre-Shipment Stage 45
     C. The Stage of Getting the Goods or Documents
     Therefor to the Buyer or Lessee 47
     D. The Receipt-Inspection Stage 49
     E. The Payment Stage 53
     F. Finance Leases 55
     G. Special Problems of Third Party Rights in a Lease Transaction 56
     H. Conclusion 56

SECTION 2.   DETERMINING WHAT LAW APPLIES 57

    A.   Analysis of the Scope of Article 2 and Article 2A 57

        1.   Article 2: Sales 57

        2.   Article 2A: Leases 60

        Problem 2-1 61

    B.   Mixed Transactions 65

        Coakley & Williams, Inc. v. Shatterproof Glass Corp. 65

        Problem 2-2 72

    C.   United Nations Convention on Contracts for the

        International Sale of Goods (CISG) 73

        Problem 2-3 73

    D.   Choice of Law and Choice of Forum Clauses 74

SECTION 3.   SOME BASIC CONCEPTS IN ARTICLE 2 76

    A.   Introduction 76

    B.   Agreement, Not Promise, as the Foundation Stone 78

    C.   The Article Two "Merchant" Concept 79

        Problem 2-4 80

    D.   Legal Controls on Contractual Behavior: Unconscionability

        and Good Faith 82

        Zapatha v. Dairy Mart, Inc. 82

        Problem 2-5 93

PART TWO: FORMATION AND TERMS OF THE CONTRACT 95

Chapter Three   Contract Formation and Enforcement 95

    SECTION 1.   INTRODUCTION; ELECTRONIC CONTRACTING 95

    SECTION 2.   CONTRACT FORMATION: THE BASICS 98

        Flanagan v. Consolidated Nutrition, L.C. 99

        Problem 3-1 105

        Problem 3-2 105

        Problem 3-3 105

        Problem 3-4 106

        Problem 3-5 107

        Problem 3-6 108

        Note: UCITA and Contract Formation Principles 108

    SECTION 3.   CONTRACT FORMATION: BATTLE OF THE FORMS 108

    A.   Under Former UCC 2-207 108

        Daitom, Inc. v. Pennwalt Corp. 110

        Note: Arbitration and the Battle of the Forms 121

        Problem 3-7 123

    B.   The Reform (?) of UCC 2-207 124

        Problem 3-8 124

Note: Battle of the Forms Under the UNIDROIT Principles 125
Note: UCITA and Standard Form Contracting 126
C. The "Gateway" Problem 127
Problem 3-9 128
SECTION 4.   THE STATUTE OF FRAUDS 128
A. History and Purposes 128
B. Satisfying the Statute of Frauds 130
Casazza v. Kiser 130
General Trading International, Inc. v. Wal-mart Stores, Inc. 138
Problem 3-10 144
Problem 3-11 145
Problem 3-12 145
Problem 3-13 145

Chapter Four Terms of the Agreement: Sources and Meaning 147
SECTION 1.   "GAP FILLERS" AS TERMS OF THE CONTRACT 147
A. The Scope of Agreement in Fact: A Reprise 147
B. "Gap Fillers" as Terms of the Contract 148
1. "Gap Fillers" Supplied by the UCC 148
2. The Content of "Gap Fillers" 150
Problem 4-1 151
Problem 4-2 152
Note: UCITA and Default Rules 153
Note: The CISG and Default Rules 153
SECTION 2.   OPEN TERMS 153
A. Quantity 154
Orange & Rockland, Etc. v. Amerada Hess Corp. 155
Problem 4-3 163
Note: Best Efforts in Exclusive Dealing Relationships 165
B. Price 166
Mathis v. Exxon Corporation 168
Problem 4-4 177
Problem 4-5 177
Problem 4-6 178
C. Delivery Terms and Payment of the Price 179
SECTION 3.   PRE-CONTRACT FACTS WHICH VARY, SUPPLEMENT,
OR GIVE MEANING TO THE AGREEMENT 179
A. Introduction 179
B. Effect of Usage of Trade and Course of Dealing 181
Columbia Nitrogen Corp. v. Royster Co. 181
C. The Parol Evidence Rule 189

Alaska Northern Development, Inc. v. Alyeska
Pipeline Service Co. 189
Problem 4-7 199
Note: Contract Interpretation Under the UCC 199
Note: Effect of "Usage" and "Practice" Under the CISG 201

Chapter Five Breach of Warranty as to the Quality of the Product Sold ... 203
  SECTION 1.   INTRODUCTION 203
    A.   Warranty Theory: Some History 203
    B.   Warranties Under the Code: An Introduction 207
    C.   Warranties under the CISG and UCITA 209
  SECTION 2.   EXPRESS WARRANTIES 209
    Sessa v. Riegle 212
    Keith v. Buchanan 216
    Problem 5-1 222
    Note: The "Basis of the Bargain" Test 223
    Rogath v. Siebenmann 226
    Downie v. Abex Corp. 233
    Note: Express Warranties and Privity 239
    Problem 5-2 239
    Note: Express Warranties Under the CISG 240
    Problem 5-3 241
    Note: Express Warranties Under UCITA 241
  SECTION 3.   IMPLIED WARRANTIES 241
    A.   Introduction 241
    Problem 5-4 242
    B.   Merchantability 242
    Agoos Kid Co., Inc. v. Blumenthal Import Corp. 243
    Valley Iron & Steel Co. v. Thorin 245
    Delano Growers' Cooperative Winery v. Supreme Wine Co., Inc. . 250
    Note: Merchantability and Used Goods 257
    Problem 5-5 258
    C.   Overlap Between Merchantability and Strict Tort Liability 258
    Castro v. QVC Network, Inc. 258
    D.   Fitness for Particular Purpose 266
    Lewis v. Mobil Oil Corp. 266
    Note: Implied Warranties Under the CISG 273
    Note: Implied Warranties Under UCITA 273
    E.   Finance Leases 274
    Problem 5-6 274
    Mercedes-Benz Credit Corp. v. Lotito 275

Note: Finance Licenses Under UCITA 282

F. Proof of Breach: Effect of Lack of Causation and Plaintiff's
Contributory Behavior 283

Chatfield v. Sherwin-Williams Co. 284

SECTION 4. DISCLAIMERS AND LIMITATIONS OF WARRANTIES 292

Martin v. Joseph Harris Co., Inc. 292

Problem 5-7 299

Problem 5-8 300

Note: Disclaimers of Warranty Under the CISG 300

Note: Disclaimers of Warranty Under UCITA 301

SECTION 5. EXTENSION OF WARRANTY OBLIGATIONS 301

Problem 5-9 302

Problem 5-10 303

PART THREE: PERFORMANCE OF THE CONTRACT 305

Chapter Six Delivery and Payment 305

SECTION 1. TENDER, INSPECTION, AND PAYMENT 305

A. The Basic Scenario 305

Problem 6-1 306

Problem 6-2 308

B. The Seller's Shipment of Goods to the Buyer 308

Problem 6-3 312

Problem 6-4 312

C. Goods in the Hands of a Bailee and Delivery
Without Moving the Goods 313

Problem 6-5 314

D. The Documentary Draft Transaction 314

E. The Letter of Credit Transaction 315

Note: Delivery, Inspection, and Payment Under Article 2A 317

Note: Delivery, Inspection, and Payment Under the CISG 317

Note: Delivery, Inspection, and Payment Under UCITA 319

SECTION 2. REJECTION, ACCEPTANCE, AND REVOCATION
OF ACCEPTANCE 320

A. Rejection or Acceptance 320

1. The Rightfulness of the Rejection 320

Problem 6-6 322

*Midwest Mobile Diagnostic Imaging v. Dynamics
Corp. of America* 324

Problem 6-7 332

2. Procedural Requirements of Effective Rejection 333

Problem 6-8 334

3. What Constitutes Acceptance of the Goods 334
Plateq Corp. of North Haven v. Machlett Laboratories, Inc. 335
Problem 6-9 343
4. Duties Regarding Rejected Goods 344
Borges v. Magic Valley Foods, Inc. 344
B. Revocation of Acceptance 348
Problem 6-10 351
C. The Right to Cure 352
Problem 6-11 356
Note: "Fundamental Breach" and "Avoidance" of the Contract
in International Sales 356
Note: Rejection, Acceptance, Revocation of Acceptance, and
Cure Under UCITA 358
SECTION 3. TERMINATION 359
SECTION 4. PUTTING IT ALL TOGETHER 359
Problem 6-12 360
Problem 6-13 361

**Chapter Seven Excuse from or Adjustment of the Contract
for Changed Circumstances** 363
SECTION 1. RELIEF FROM CHANGED CIRCUMSTANCES 363
A. Loss of Identified Goods 364
Problem 7-1 364
B. Failure of Delivery or Payment Mechanisms 364
Problem 7-2 364
C. The Basic Assumption Test: Force Majeure Events 365
Wickliffe Farms, Inc. v. Owensboro Grain Co. 365
*Specialty Tires of America, Inc. v. The CIT Group/Equipment
Financing, Inc.* 370
D. Relief From Non-Force Majeure Events 380
1. Increased Costs of Performance 380
2. Buyer's Excuse 382
3. Effect of Agreement on Excuse 383
International Minerals & Chemical Corp. v. Llano, Inc. 383
Problem 7-3 393
SECTION 2. MODIFICATION OF THE CONTRACT 395
A. Agreed Modifications 395
1. Agreed Modifications in Good Faith 395
Problem 7-4 395
Roth Steel Products v. Sharon Steel Corp. 396
2. Agreed Modifications and the Statute of Frauds 402

B. Modification or Rescission by Waiver 403
    BMC Industries, Inc. v. Barth Industries, Inc. 404
    Cloud Corporation v. Hasbro, Inc. 411
    Problem 7-5 419

Chapter Eight Risk of Loss and Insurance **421**
    SECTION 1.   GROUND RULES 421
    SECTION 2.   RISK OF LOSS IN THE ABSENCE OF BREACH 423
    A. Goods in Possession of Seller 423
        Problem 8-1 423
        Problem 8-2 424
        Problem 8-3 424
        Problem 8-4 424
    B. Goods in the Possession of a Bailee to be Delivered
        Without Being Moved 425
        Silver v. Wycombe, Meyer & Co., Inc. 425
        Problem 8-5 428
    C. Seller Authorized or Required to Ship Goods by Carrier 428
        Windows, Inc. v. Jordan Panel Systems Corp. 429
        Problem 8-6 435
        Note: Risk of Loss and Insurance 435
        Note: Liability of Overland Carrier for Goods
        Lost or Damaged in Shipment 437
    SECTION 3.   EFFECT OF BREACH ON RISK OF LOSS 439
        Problem 8-7 440
        Note: Risk of Loss Under the CISG 441
        BP Oil International, Ltd. v. Empresa Estatal Petroleos
        De Ecuador (Petroecuador) 442
        Note: Risk of Loss Under UCITA 446

Chapter Nine Property Rights **447**
    SECTION 1.   TITLE AND IDENTIFICATION 447
        Problem 9-1 448
        Note: Title and Identification Under the CISG 449
        Note: Title and Identification Under UCITA 450
    SECTION 2.   SELLER OR LESSOR IN POSSESSION OF THE GOODS 450
    A. Introduction 450
    B. Buyer's or Lessee's Rights to Obtain the Goods
        From the Seller or Lessor 451
        1. Pre-paying Buyer or Lessee 451
        Problem 9-2 451

2.   Specific Performance and Replevin 452
Problem 9-3 454
Note: Rights of a Buyer to Obtain the Goods Under the CISG 454
Note: Rights of a Licensee to Obtain the Product Under UCITA . . 455

C. The Buyer's or Lessee's Right to Obtain Possession As Against
    Third Persons with Claims to the Goods 455
    1.   Lien Creditors 455
    Problem 9-4 455
    2.   Secured Creditors 456
    Problem 9-5 457
    3.   Buyers or Lessees from the Seller or Lessor 458
    Problem 9-6 458

D. Seller's or Lessor's Ability to Stop or Withhold Delivery
    of the Goods From the Buyer or Lessee 459
    Problem 9-7 460

E. Security Interests Arising Under Article 2: Seller's Right to
    Retain Title or Ship Under Reservation 460
    Note: Retaining Control of the Product Under UCITA 460

F. Claims to the Goods Asserted by the Buyer's or Lessee's
    Creditors or Transferees When the Seller or Lessor
    in Possession of the Goods 461
    Problem 9-8 462

Section 3.   Buyer or Lessee in Possession of the Goods 462
A. Introduction 462
B. Seller's or Lessor's Right to Regain Possession of the Goods
    From Buyer or Lessee 463
    1.   Seller's Security Interest in Goods 463
    2.   Seller's Right to Reclaim When no Security Interest in Goods 463
    3.   Consignments 464
    4.   Lessor's Right to Possession of Goods from Lessee 466
    Note: Licensor Reclamation Under UCITA 466

C. Priority of Seller's or Lessor's Right to Possession Against
    Buyer's or Lessee's Creditors or Transferees 467
    1.   Seller's Security Interest or a Consignor's Interest in Goods . . 467
    Problem 9-9 467
    2.   Seller's Right to Reclaim 468
    Problem 9-10 469
    3.   Lessor's Right to Reclaim Against the Lessee's
        Creditors or Transferees 470

D. Priority of Buyer's or Lessee's Claim to the Goods Against
    Persons Claiming Pre-existing Ownership 471

       1.   Buyer Against Persons Claiming Pre-existing
           Ownership of the Goods 471
       Inmi-Etti v. Aluisi 471
       Note: Certificates of Title and the BFP of Motor Vehicles 476
       Problem 9-11 477
       Problem 9-12 477
       Problem 9-13 478
       Problem 9-14 478
       Problem 9-15 478
       2.   Lessee Against Person Asserting Previously Created
           Right in the Goods Obtained from the Lessor 479
       Note: Ownership Claims Under UCITA and the CISG 480
    E. Buyer's and Lessee's Rights as Against Seller's or
       Lessor's Creditors 480
       Problem 9-16 482
       Note: Licensee's Rights as Against Licensor's Creditors
       Under UCITA 482
  SECTION 4.   WARRANTY OF TITLE, NON-INTERFERENCE, AND
  AGAINST INFRINGEMENT 482
       Sumner v. Fel-Air, Inc. 483
       Note: Fifty Ways to Breach the UCC 2-312 Warranty of Title ... 488
       Problem 9-17 489
       Note: Title and Infringement Claims Under the CISG 490
       Note: Title and Infringement Claims Under UCITA 490
  SECTION 5.   ASSIGNMENT AND DELEGATION 490
       Problem 9-18 493

PART FOUR: BREACH OF CONTRACT AND REMEDIES 495
Chapter Ten Remedies: Breach When Product Not Accepted 495
  SECTION 1.   INTRODUCTION 495
  SECTION 2.   INSECURITY AND REPUDIATION 497
    A. Insecurity and Prospective Inability 497
       Top of Iowa Cooperative v. Sime Farms, Inc. 499
       Problem 10-1 509
       Problem 10-2 510
    B. Repudiation 511
       Problem 10-3 514
       Problem 10-4 514
       Note: Insecurity and Anticipatory Repudiation under the CISG ... 515
       Note: Insecurity and Repudiation under UCITA 516
    C. Right to Cancel 516

1.   Grounds for and Effect of Cancellation 516
2.   Cancellation Under Installment Contracts 517
Plotnick v. Pennsylvania Smelting & Refining Co. 519
Note: Avoidance for Breach of Installment Contract
Under the CISG 525
Note: Cancellation Under UCITA 526
SECTION 3.   REMEDIES OF SELLER AND LESSOR 526
A.   Availability and Cumulative Effect 526
B.   Action for the Price, Rent, or Specific Performance 527
Problem 10-5 528
Problem 10-6 530
Note: Action for the Price Under the CISG 531
Note: Action for the Price Under UCITA 531
C.   Resale, Release, or Substitute Transactions 532
Problem 10-7 532
Afram Export Corp. v. Metallurgiki Halyps, S.A. 533
Note: Disposition by Lease of Goods under Article 2A 538
Note: Substitute Transactions Under the CISG 539
Note: Substitute Transactions Under UCITA 540
D.   Contract-Market Damages 540
Problem 10-8 541
Note: Market Price Damages Under the CISG 542
Note: Market Price Damages Under UCITA 543
E.   Lost Profit 543
R.E. Davis Chemical Corp. v. Diasonics, Inc. 544
Problem 10-9 554
Note: Lost Profits Under the CISG 555
Note: Lost Profits Under UCITA 555
F.   Remedial Choice 555
Trans World Metals, Inc. v. Southwire Co. 556
Problem 10-10 562
G.   Incidental and Consequential Damages 563
Note: Consequential Damages Under the CISG 564
Note: Consequential Damages Under UCITA 564
SECTION 4.   REMEDIES OF BUYER OR LESSEE 564
A.   Introduction 566
B.   Cover 566
Problem 10-11 567
Problem 10-12 567
Fertico Belgium S.A. v. Phosphate Chemicals 568
Note: Other Sources of Cover 572

Note: Cover Under the CISG 573
Note: Cover Under UCITA 574
C. Market-Contract Damages 574
Problem 10-13 574
Problem 10-14 575
Note: Market Price Damages Under the CISG 576
Note: Market Price Damages Under UCITA 577
D. Consequential and Incidental Damages 577
Problem 10-15 578
Note: Consequential Damages Under the CISG 578
Note: Consequential Damages Under UCITA 579
Note: Punitive Damages for Breach by Repudiation
or Non-delivery 579

Chapter Eleven Non-conforming Performance and Accepted Products:
Damages for Breach **581**
SECTION 1. REPRISE OF REJECTION, ACCEPTANCE AND
REVOCATION OF ACCEPTANCE 581
SECTION 2. ACCEPTING A NON-CONFORMING PERFORMANCE; NOTICE 582
Aqualon Company v. Mac Equipment, Inc. 582
Problem 11-1 589
Problem 11-2 590
Note: Notice of Breach Under the CISG 591
Note: Notice of Breach Under UCITA 591
SECTION 3. DAMAGES FOR ACCEPTED PERFORMANCE 591
A. Direct Damages 591
Problem 11-3 592
Problem 11-4 593
Problem 11-5 593
Note: Damages for Breach When Goods Accepted
Under the CISG 594
Note: Damages for Breach When Product Accepted
Under UCITA 595
B. Incidental and Consequential Damages 595
Hydraform Products Corp. v. American Steel & Aluminum Corp. . 596
Nezperce Storage Co. v. Zenner 602
Delano Grower's Co-op. Winery v. Supreme Wine Co. 607
Problem 11-6 609
Problem 11-7 609
Problem 11-8 610
Note: Consequential and Incidental Damages Under the CISG 612

Note: Consequential and Incidental Damages Under UCITA 612

SECTION 4.   PRODUCTS LIABILITY LAW 612

A. Injury to Person and Property 612

   Problem 11-9 615

B. The "Economic Loss" Doctrine 617

   Note: Leases and Licenses 619

   Note: The CISG 619

   Note: Status of Consumers 620

   Fieldstone Co. v. Briggs Plumbing Products, Inc. 621

Chapter Twelve Limitations on Remedies for Breach of Contract 629

SECTION 1.   AGREED LIMITATIONS ON REMEDIES 629

A. Liquidated Damages 629

   Metlife Capital Financial Corp. v. Washington

   Avenue Associates L.P. 629

   In re Baldwin Rental Centers, Inc. 632

   Problem 12-1 638

   Note: Liquidated Damages Under the CISG 639

   Note: Liquidated Damages Under UCITA 639

B. Limited Remedies 639

   Problem 12-2 640

   Cayuga Harvester, Inc. v. Allis-Chalmers Corp. 640

   Note: Effect When Agreed Remedy Fails of its Essential Purpose . 649

   Note: Contracting Out of Tort Liability 651

SECTION 2.   CONSUMER PROTECTION LAW 652

A. Federal Law: FTC and the Magnuson-Moss Warranty Act 654

   Ventura v. Ford Motor Corp. 655

   Problem 12-3 665

B. State Law: "Lemon" Laws 666

   Joan Vogel, Squeezing Consumers: Lemon Laws,

   Consumer Warranties, and a Proposal for Reform 667

   Note: Informal Dispute Resolution 670

SECTION 3.   THE STATUTE OF LIMITATIONS 670

   Problem 12-4 671

   Standard Alliance Indus., Inc. v. Black Clawson Co. 672

   Problem 12-5 679

INDEX 681

TABLE OF CASES

The principal cases are in bold type. Cases cited or discussed in the text
are roman type. References are to pages. Cases cited in principal
cases and within other quoted materials are not included.

Aceros Prefabricados, S.A. v. Tradearbed, Inc., 122

Advent Systems, Ltd. v. Unisys Corp., 15, 58

Afram Export Corp. v. Metallurgiki Halyps, S.A., 533, 563

Agoos Kid Co., Inc. v. Blumenthal Import Corp., 243

Ajax Tool Works, Inc. v. CanEng. Mfg., Ltd., 75

AKA Distributing Co. v. Whirlpool Corp., 71

Alaska Northern Development, Inc. v. Alyeska Pipeline Co., 189, 196, 197

Alimenta (U.S.A.), Inc. v. Anheuser-Busch Companies, Inc., 341

Alimenta (U.S.A.), Inc. v. Cargill, Inc., 369

Alimenta (U.S.A.), Inc. v. Gibbs Nathaniel (Canada) Ltd., 369

Alloway v. General Marine Industries, L.P., 617

ALOFS Manufacturing Co. v. Toyota Manufacturing Kentucky, Inc., 447

Aluminum Company of America v. Essex Group, Inc., 380, 381, 382, 393

American Bumper & Manufacturing Co. v. Transtechnology Corp., 582

American Fertilizer Specialists, Inc. v. Wood, 290

American Nursery Products, Inc. v. Indian Wells Orchards, 651

American Tobacco Co., Inc. v. Grinnell, 256

Anchor Glass Container Corp., In re, 165

Anthony Pools v. Sheehan, 70

Apex Oil Co. v. Belcher Co. of New York, Inc., 537

Aqualon Company v. Mac Equipment Inc., 582

ARB, Inc. v. E-Systems, Inc., 197

Arlco, Inc., In re, 470

Au Rustproofing Center, Inc. v. Gulf Oil Corp., 167

Austin Instrument, Inc. v. Loral Corp., 402

Avedon Engineering, Inc. v. Seatex, 121

Axion Corp. v. G.D.C. Leasing Corp., 271

B & R Textile Corp. v. Paul Rothman Indus. Ltd, 561

B & W Glass, Inc. v. Weather Shield Mfg., Inc., 26, 144

BAAN U.S.A. v. USA Truck, Inc., 76

Baker v. DEC International, 671

Baldwin Rental Centers, Inc., In re, 632

Balog v. Center Art Gallery-Hawaii, Inc., 679

Barco Auto Leasing Corp. v. PSI Cosmetics, Inc., 60

Bartlett & Co., Grain v. Merchants Co., 309

Basselen v. General Motors Corp., 349

Bead Chain Manufacturing Co. v. Saxton Products, Inc., 333

Belleville Toyota Inc. v. Toyota Motor Sales, U.S.A., Inc., 91

Betaco, Inc. v. Cessna Aircraft Co., 197

Billings Cottonseed, Inc. v. Albany Oil Mill, Inc., 164

Bill's Coal Co., Inc. v. Board of Public Utilities of Springfield, Mo., 512

Birwelco-Monenary Inc. v. Infilco Degremont, Inc., 58

Bishop Logging Co. v. John Deere Indus. Equip., 651

Bloor v. Fallstaff Brewing Corp., 166

Blue Valley Cooperative v. National Farmers Organization, 36

BMC Industries, Inc. v. Barth Industries, Inc., 404

BP Oil International Ltd. v. Empresa Estatal Petroleous De Ecuadar (Petroecuador), 442

Bocre Leasing Corp. v. General Motors Corp., 618

Bogner v. General Motors Corp., 663

Borges v. Magic Valley Foods, Inc., 344

Boud v. SDNCO, Inc., 222

Bowen v. Foust, 354

Braden v. Stem, 350

Brandeis Machinery and Supply Co. v. Capital Crane Rental, Inc., 529

Brandt v. Boston Scientific Corp., 70

Brewster of Lynchburg, Inc. v. Dial Corp., 162

Brower v. Gateway 2000, Inc., 93, 128

Buettner v. R.W. Martin & Sons, Inc., 223

C.F. Sales, Inc. v. Amfert, Inc., 489

C.I.C. Corp. v. Ragtime, Inc., 552

Campbell Farms v. Wald, 200

Canusa Corp. v. A & R Lobosco, Inc., 163

Casazza v. Kiser, 130, 144

Cassidy Podell Lynch, Inc. v. SnyderGeneral Corp., 524

Castro v. QVC Network, Inc., 258, 614

Cate v. Dover Corp., 298

Cates v. Morgan Portable Building Corp., 595

Catlin Aviation Co. v. Equilease Corp., 488

Cayuga Harvestor, Inc. v. Allis-Chalmers Corp., 640, 648, 651

Chateau Des Charmes Wines Ltd. v. Sabate USA Inc., 125

Chateaugay Corp, In re, 513

Chatfield v. Sherwin-Williams Co., 284, 290, 291

Cherwell-Ralli, Inc. v. Rytman Grain Co., Inc., 524

Cipollone v. Liggett Group, Inc., 223, 291

Circuit City Stores Inc. v. Commissioner of Revenue, 422

Cives Corp. v. Callier Steel Pipe & Tube, Inc., 573

Clark v. Wallace County Cooperative Equity Exchange, 369

Cliffstar Corp. v. Elmar Industries Inc., 343

Cline v. Prowler Industries of Maryland, 613

Cloud Corporation v. Hasbro, Inc., 411, 418

Coakley & Williams, Inc. v. Shatterproof Glass Corp., 65

Coast Trading Co. v. Cudahy Co., 562

Cognitest Corp. v. Riverside Publishing Co., 651

Cole v. Keller Industries, Inc., 582

Cole v. Melvin, 561

Colton v. Decker, 488

Columbia International Corp. v. Kempler, 465

Columbia Nitrogen Corp. v. Royster Co., 181, 187, 188, 189

Comark Merchandising, Inc. v. Highland Group, Inc., 254

Commonwealth Petroleum Co. v. Petrosol

Int'l, Inc., 427

ConAgra, Inc. v. Bartlett Partnership, 369

Concord General Mut. Ins. Co. v. Sumner, 447

Condon Bros., Inc. v. Simpson Timber Co., 61

Conister Trust Ltd. v. Boating Corp. of America, 461

Controlled Environments Construction, Inc. v. Key Industrial Refrigeration Co., 237

Cook Specialty Co. v. Schrlock, 436

Cosden Oil v. Karl O. Helm Aktiengesellschaft, 574

Costco Wholesale Corp. v. World Wide Licensing Corp., 402

Ctkovic v. Boch, Inc., 567

Cuesta v. Classic Wheels, Inc., 350

Custom Automated Machinery v. Penda Corp., 649

D.C. Leathers, Inc. v. Gelmart Indus., Inc., 308

D.P. Technology Corp. v. Sherwood Tool, Inc., 321

Dartmouth Motor Sales, Inc. v. Wilcox, 477

Davidson Oil Country Supply Co. v. Klockner, Inc., 290

Dekalaito v. Nissan Motor Corp., 653

Delano Growers' Cooperative Winery v. Supreme Wine Co., Inc., 250, 254, 607, 609

Delchi Carrier, SpA v. Rotorex Corp., 612

Denny v. Ford Motor Co., 616

DeWeldon, Ltd. v. McKean, 476

Diatom, Inc. v. Pennwalt Corp., 110, 119, 120, 123

DiCintio v. Daimler Chrysler Corp, 653

Dienes Corp. v. Long Island Railroad Co., 162

Diversified Energy Inc. v. Tennessee Valley

Authority, 541

Diversified Food Service Distributors, Inc., In re, 469

Doe v. Travenol Laboratories, Inc., 256

Dorton v. Collins & Aikman Corp., 121

Dotts v. Bennett, 249

Downie v. Abex Corp., 233

Drennan v. Star Paving, 36

Dura-Wood Treating Co. v. Century Forest Indus., Inc., 572, 573

E. Clemens Horst Co. v. Biddell Bros., 318

Echo, Inc. v. Whitson Co., Inc., 99

El Paso Refinery, L.P., In re, 552

Elias v. Dobrowolski, 488

Ellsworth v. Worthey, 476

Empire Gas Corp. v. American Bakeries Co., 162

Employers Ins. of Wausau v. Suwanee River SPA Lines, Inc., 649

Ernst Steel Corp. v. Horn Construction Division, 537

Essco Geometric v. Harvard Industries, 165

Evans ex rel Husted v. General Motors Corp., 671

Federal Pants, Inc. v. Stocking, 370

Federal Signal Corporation v. Safety Factors, Inc., 41

Feld v. Henry S. Levy & Sons, Inc., 163

Ferragamo v. Massachusetts Bay Transportation Authority, 249

Fertico Belgium S.A. v. Phosphate Chemicals Export Assoc., Inc., 568

Fidelity & Deposit Co. of Maryland v. Krebs Engineers, 650

Fieldstone Co. v. Briggs Plumbing Products, Inc., 621, 628

Figgie Intern., Inc. v. Destileria Serralles,

Inc., 649

Firwood Mfg. Co. v. General Tire, Inc., 537

Fiske v. MacGregor, Div. of Brunswick, 291

Flanagan v. Consolidated Nutrition, L.C., 99

Flowers Baking Co. of Lynchburg, Inc. v. R-P Packaging, Inc., 167

Fode v. Capital RV Center, Inc., 352

Ford Motor Co. v. General Accident Insurance Co., 290

Forest River, Inc. v. Posten, 593

Forms World of Illinois, Inc. v. Magna Bank N.A., 81

Foxco Indus., Ltd. v. Fabric World, Inc., 529

Frank Arnold Contractors, Inc. v. Vilsmeier Auction Co., Inc., 488

Franklin v. Lovitt Equipment Co., 197

Fred J. Moore, Inc. v. Schinmann, 249

Freeman & Mills, Inc. v. Belcher Oil Co., 580

Frigaliment Importing Co. v. B.N.S. Int'l Sales Corp., 201

Gardiner v. Gray, 241

General Aviation, Inc. v. Cessna Aircraft Co., 198

General Plumbing & Heating, Inc. v. American Air Filter Co., 198

General Trading International, Inc. v. Wal-Mart Stores, Inc., 138

Geneva Pharmaceuticals Technology Corp. v. Barr Laboratories, Inc., 22

Gerard v. Almouli, 166

Gibson v. Methodist Hospital, 256

Glen Distributors Corp. v. Carlisle Plastics, Inc., 528

Gochey v. Bomardier, Inc., 664

Godfrey v. Gilsdorf, 476

Gold Kist, Inc. v. Citizens & Southern

National Bank of South Carolina, 298

Goldstein v. Stainless Processing Co., 517

Golsen v. ONG Western, Inc., 391

Hadley v. Baxendale, 496

Hampton Bank v. River City Yachts, Inc., 481

Hansen v. Firestone Tire & Rubber Co., 211

Hanson v. Funk Seeds International, 298

Harriscom Svenska, AB v. Harris Corp., 392

Harrison v. Nissan Motor Corp. in U.S.A., 670

Havird Oil Co. v. Marathon Oil Co., 168

Hawaiian Telephone Co. v. Microform Data Systems, Inc., 650

HCI Chemicals (USA), Inc. v. Henkel KGaA, 308

Herrick v. Monsanto Co., 298

Hess Energy Inc. v. Lightening Oil Co., 574

Hessler v. Crystal Lake Chrysler-Plymouth, Inc., 566

Hill v. Gateway 2000, Inc., 127

HML Corporation v. General Foods Corporation, 163

Hollingsworth v. Queen Carpet, Inc., 290

Homeplace Stores, Inc., In re, 64

Homestake Mining Co. v. Washington Public Power Supply System, 163

Horizons, Inc. v. Avco Corp., 596

Horn Waterproofing Corp. v. Bushwick Iron & Steel Co., 18

House of Lloyd, Inc. v. Director of Revenue, 422

HRN, Inc. v. Shell Oil Co., 177

Huff v. Hobgood, 679

Hunt Foods, Inc. v. Phillips, 166

Hutcherson v. Sears Roebuck & Co., 93

Hutchinson Utilities Commission v.

Curtiss-Wright Corp., 290

Hydraform Products Corp. v. American Steel & Aluminum Corp., 596, 601, 602

Hyosung America, Inc. v. Sumagh Textile Co., Ltd., 99

Hyundai Motor Co. v. Rodriguez, 266

I. Lan Systems Inc. v. Netscout Services Level Corp., 97

Ide Jewelry Co, In re, 465

Impossible Electronic Techniques, Inc. v. Wackenhut Protective Systems, Inc., 146

Infocomp, Inc. v. Electra Products, Inc., 99

Ingle v. Circuit City Stores, Inc., 93

Ingram River Equipment, Inc. v. Pott Industries, Inc., 27

Inmi-Etti v. Aluisi, 461, 471

Integrated Circuits Unlimited v. E.F. Johnson Co., 333

Intermet Corp. v. Financial Federal Credit Inc., 481

International Minerals & Chemical Corp. v. Llano, Inc., 383, 390, 391, 392

International Petroleum Services, Inc. v. S & N Well Service, Inc., 257, 595

Interpetrol Bermuda Ltd. v. Kaiser Aluminum International Corp., 378

Intershoe, Inc. v. Bankers Trust Co., 196

Intervale Steel Corp. v. Borg & Beck Div., Borg-Warner Corp., 341, 342

Iowa Elec. Light and Power Co. v. Atlas Corp., 382

Islamic Republic of Iran v. Boeing Co., 553

Island Creek Coal Co. v. Lake Shore, Inc., 651

J.O. Hooker & Sons, Inc. v. Roberts Cabinet Co., Inc., 70

Jackson v. Nestle-Beich, Inc., 255

Jackson Hole Traders, Inc. v. Joseph, 71

Jacobs v. Rosemount Dodge-Winnebago South, 663

James River Equipment Co. v. Beadle County Equipment, Inc., 211

Jason's Foods, Inc. v. Peter Eckrich & Sons, Inc., 425, 436

Jeanneret v. Vichey, 488

Jefferson v. Jones, 488

JHC Ventures, L.P. v. Fast Trucking, Inc., 592

Jimenez v. The Superior Court of San Diego County, 627, 628

Johannsen v. Minnesota Valley Ford Tractor Co., 350, 351

Johnson Enterprises of Jacksonville, Inc. v. FPL Group, Inc., 71

Johnson & Johnson Prod. v. Dal Intern. Trading, 475

Jom, Inc. v. Adell Plastics, Inc., 121

Jones v. Mitchell, 476

Joswick v. Chesapeake Mobile Homes, Inc., 680

Kaiser-Francis Oil Co. v. Producer's Gas Co., 391, 512

Keck v. Wacker, 351

Keith v. Buchanan, 216, 221, 223

Kellstrom Industries, Inc., In re, 461

Kelly v. Miller, 519

Kelsey-Hayes Co. v. Galtaco Redlaw Castings Corp., 402, 572

Keppelon v. W.M. Ritter Flooring Corp., 499

Klocek v. Gateway, Inc., 127

Krieger v. Nick Alexander Imports, Inc., 678

Kumar Corp. v. Nopal Lines, Ltd, 437

Kunkel v. Sprague Nat'l Bank, 462

Larsen v. Pacesetter Systems, Inc., 614

Leininger v. Sola, 649

Leitchfield Development Corp. v. Clark, 354

Lenape Resources Corp. v. Tennessee Gas Pipeline Co., 165

Leopold v. Rock-Ola Mfg. Corp., 499

Lewis v. Mobil Oil Corp., 266, 270

Linc Equipment Services Inc. v. Signal Medical Devices, Inc., 538

Lindemann v. Eli Lilly & Co., 298, 651

Louis Dreyfus Corp. v. Brown, 512

Louisiana Power & Light v. Allegheny Ludlum Industries, 382

Maddux Supply Co. v. A-C Electric Co., Inc., 499

Madrid v. Bloomington Auto Co., 476

Marjam Supply Co. v. BCT Walls & Ceilings, Inc., 179

Marlow v. Conley, 477

Martin v. Joseph Harris Co., Inc., 292, 298, 611

Martin v. Nager, 476

Martin Imports v. Courier-Newsom Exp., Inc., 438

Mathis v. Exxon Corporation, 168, 176, 177

Mattek v. Malofsky, 476

Mattoon v. City of Pittsfield, 70

MCC-Marble Ceramic Center, Inc. v. Cermaica Nuova D'Agostino, S.P.A., 198

McDonald's Chevrolet, Inc. v. Johnson, 479

McFarland v. Newman, 210

McIntosh v. Magna Systems, Inc., 579

McKenzie v. Olmstead, 424

McLaughlin v. Michelin Tire Corp., 290

McNally Wellman Co. v. New York State Elec. & Gas Corp., 639

McNeir v. Greer-Hale Chinchilla Ranch, 210

McPherson v. Buick Motor Company, 206

Mercedes-Benz Credit Corp. v. Lotito, 275, 282

Mercury Marine v. Clear River Construction Co., 353

Messer v. Averill, 476

Metlife Capital Financial Corp. v. Washington Avenue Associates L.P., 629

Mexicali Rose v. Superior Court, 255

MG Refining & Marketing, Inc. v. Knight Enterprises, Inc., 392

Micro Data Base Systems, Inc. v. Dharma Systems Inc., 58

Midwest Mobile Diagnostic Imaging v. Dynamics Corp. of America, 324, 355

Milgard Tempering, Inc. v. Selas Corp. of America, 650

Minnesota Mining & Mfg. Co. v. Nishika Ltd., 303

Miron v. Yonkers Raceway, Inc., 344

Mississippi Chemical Corp. V. Dresser-Rand Co., 678

Missouri P.R. Co. v. Elmore & Stahl, 438

Missouri Public Serv. Co. v. Peabody Coal Co., 382, 396

Mitchell v. BBB Services Co., 255

Mitchell Motors Inc. v. Barnett, 478

Mix v. Ingersoll Candy Co., 255

Moncrief v. Williston Basin Interstate Pipeline Co., 391

Mott Equity Elevator v. Svihovec, 517

Moulton Cavity & Mold, Inc. v. Lyn-Flex Indus., Inc., 321

Multi-Tech Systems Inc. v. Floreat, Inc., 58

Nanakuli Paving & Rock Co. v. Shell Oil

Co., Inc., 188, 189

National Crane Corp. v. Ohio Steel Tube Co., 488

National Farmer's Org. v. Bartlett and Company Grain, 512

National Utility Service, Inc. v. Whirlpool Corp., 404

Neal v. SMC Corp., 352

Nebraska Popcorn, Inc. v. Wing, 680

Nelson v. McGoldrick, 92

Nevada Contract Services, Inc. v. Squirrel Companies, Inc., 290

Nezperce Storage Co. v. Zenner, 602

Nissho-Iwai Co., Ltd. v. Occidental Crude Sales, Inc., 378

Nobs Chemical, U.S.A., Inc. v. Koppers Co., Inc., 560

North River Homes, Inc. v. Bosarge, 350

Northern Illinois Gas Co. v. Energy Cooperative, Inc., 382, 383

Northern Indiana Public Service Co. v. Carbon County Coal Company, 383

Northern Nat. Gas Co. v. Conoco, Inc., 91

Nowalski v. Ford Motor Co., 678

Oak Hall Cap and Gown Co. v. Old Dominion Freight Line, Inc., 438

Oglebay Norton Co. v. Armco, Inc., 178

Olcott Intern. & Co. v. Micro Base Systems, Inc., 71

Old Kent Bank v. Kal Kustom, Inc., 589

Orange & Rockland, Etc. v. Amerada Hess Corp., 155, 162, 163

Overstreet v. Norden Laboratories, Inc., 596

Pacific Gas and Elec. Co. v. G.W. Thomas Drayage & Rigging Co., 200

Painter v. General Motors Corp., 680

Paper Magic Group, Inc. v. J.B. Hunt Transport, Inc. 310

Paramount Aviation Corp. v. Agusta, 618

Pearl Investments LLC v. Standard I/O Inc., 58

Pester Refining Co., In re, 469

Peterson v. Bendix Home Systems, Inc., 291

Phelps v. Spivey, 196

Phillips v. Town of West Springfield, 255

Phipps v. General Motors Corp., 613

Pierce v. Catalina Yachts, Inc., 650

Piotrowski v. Southworth Products Corp., 614

Pisano v. American Leasing, 254

Pittsburgh-Des Moines Steel Co. v. Brookhaven Manor Water Co., 510

Plas-Tex, Inc. v. U.S. Steel Corp., 290

Plateq Corp. of North Haven v. Machlett Laboratories, Inc., 335

Plotnick v. Pennsylvania Smelting & Refining Co., 513, **519**, 524, 525

PMC Corp. v. Houston Wire & Cable Co., 154, 164

Poli v. Daimler Chrysler Corp., 678

Polytop Corp. v. Chipsco, Inc., 110

Potter v. Chicago Pneumatic Tool Co., 265

Power Engineering v. Krug International, 382

Powers v. Coffeyville Livestock Sales Co., Inc., 249

PPG Indus. Inc. v. Shell Oil Co., 378

Prenalta Corp. v. Colorado Interstate Gas Co., 391

Price Brothers Co. v. Philadelphia Gear Corp., 254

Princess Cruises, Inc. v. General Electric Co., 71

ProCD, Inc. v. Zeidenberg, 127

Purina Mills, L.L.C. v. Less, 554, 560

QDS Components, Inc., In re, 61

Quest Diagnostics, Inc. v. MCI Worldcom, Inc., 619

R.E. Davis Chemical Corp. v. Diasonics, Inc., 544, 552
R.I. Lampus Co. v. Neville Cement Products Corp., 595
R.W. Murray Co. v. Shatterproof Glass Corp., 678
Ralph's Distributing Co. v. AMF, Inc., 198
Ramirez v. Autosport, 663
Randy Knitwear, Inc. v. American Cyanamid Co., 205
Ready Trucking, Inc. v. BP Exploration & Oil Co., 81
Reliance Insurance Co. v. Market Motors, Inc., 476
Rheem Manuf. Co. v. Phelps Hearing & Air Conditioning Co., 650
Rheinberg-Kellerei GMBH v. Vineyard Wine Co., Inc., 436
Richards v. Lloyd's of London, 75
Richardson v. Union Carbide Corp., 120
Rockdale Cable T.V. Co. v. Spadora, 489
Rockland Industries, Inc. v. E+E (US), Inc., 377
Rodriguez v. Learjet, Inc., 552
Rogath v. Siebenmann, 226
Roger Edwards LLC v. Fiddes & Sons Ltd., 165
Romy v. Picker International, Inc., 350
Rosen v. Spanierman, 679
Roth Steel Products v. Sharon Steel Corp., 370, **396**, 401, 402
Rothe v. Malony Cadillac, Inc., 664
Royal Business Machines, Inc. v. Lorraine Corp., 221, 254
Royal Typewriter Co. v. Xerographic Supplies Corp., 222
Rudd Construction Equipment Co., Inc. v. Clark Equipment Co., 649

Ruffin v. Shaw Industries, Inc., 222

Saber v. Dan Angelone Chevrolet, Inc., 488
Sagent Technology Inc. v. Micros Systems Inc., 71
Sally Beauty Products, Inc. v. Nexxus, 91
Salt River Project Agr. v. Westinghouse Electric Co., 652
Salve Regina College v. Russell, 611
Sam and Mac, Inc. v. Treat, 451
Saturn of Kings Automall, Inc. v. Mike Albert Leasing Inc., 476
Schulze & Burch Biscuit Co. v. Tree Top, Inc., 122
Schumann v. Levi, 528
Schwak, Inc. v. Donruss Trading Cards Inc., 162
S-Creek Ranch, Inc. v. Monier & Co., 310
Security Pacific Nat'l Bank v. Goodman, 481
Seely v. White Motor Co., 653
Seibel v. Lyne & Bowler, Inc., 197
Seixas v. Woods, 209
Sessa v. Riegle, 212, 215
Sibcoimtrex, Inc. v. American Foods Group, Inc., 110
Sierra Diesel Injection Service, Inc. v. Burroughs Corp., Inc., 197
Silver v. Wycombe, Meyer & Co., Inc., 425
Simcala, Inc. v. American Coal Trade, Inc., 162
Simpson v. Widger, 215
Sipco, Inc. v. Director of Revenue, 422
Smith v. Navistar Intern. Transp. Corp., 650
Smith v. Stewart, 249
Solar Kinetics Corp. v. Joseph T. Ryerson & Son, Inc., 350
Sons of Thunder, Inc. v. Borden Inc., 92

Soo Line Railroad Company v. Fruehauf Corp., 606

Southern Illinois Riverboat Casino Cruises, Inc. v. Triangle Insulation and Sheet Metal Co., 110

Specht v. Netscape Communications, 64

Specialty Tires of America, Inc. v. The CIT Group/Equipment Financing, Inc., 370

Spirit of Excellence, Ltd. v. Intercargo Inc. Co., 437

Spoon v. Herndon, 489

Standard Alliance Indus., Inc. v. Black Clawson Co., 672

Standard Bent Glass Corp. V. Glassrobots Oy, 110

Stanley-Bostitch, Inc. v. Regenerative Environmental Equipment Co., Inc., 122

Starmakers Pub. Corp. v. Acme Fast Freight, Inc., 439

Steiner v. Mobil Oil Co., 120

Step-Saver Data Systems, Inc. v. Wyse Technology, 71, 298

Stinnes Interoil, Inc. v. Apex Oil Co., 517

Sumner v. Fel-Air, Inc., 483, 488

Superior Bank, FSB v. Human Services Employees Credit Union, 481

Superior Boiler Works, Inc. v. R.J. Sanders, Inc., 119

Szajna v. General Motors Corp., 664

T.W. Oil, Inc. v. Consolidated Edison Co. of New York, Inc., 353

Tarling v. Baxter, 427

TCP Industries, Inc. v. Uniroyal, Inc., 167

Teeman v. Jurek, 511

Terrell v. R & A Manufacturing Partners, Ltd., 300

Tesoro Petroleum Corp. v. Holborn Oil Co., Ltd, 560, 561

Tex Enterprises, Inc. v. Brockway Standard, Inc., 239

TexPar Energy, Inc. v. Murphy Oil USA, Inc., 576

Textile Unlimited v. AbmH & Co., 122

The Corner v. Pinnacle, Inc., 544

Thomas, In re, 424

Thomas G. Faria Corp. v. Dama Jewelry Technology Inc., 343

Thompson-Starrett Co. v. La Belle Iron Works, 322

Thunder Basin Coal Co. v. Southwestern Public Service Co., 512

Tigg Corp. v. Dow Corning Corp., 166

Tittle v. Steel City Oldsmobile, Inc., 678

Tolmie Farms, Inc. v. J.R. Simplot, Inc., 223

Tom-Lin Enterprises, Inc. v. Sunoco, Inc., 177

Tongish v. Thomas, 575

Top of Iowa Cooperative v. Sime Farms, Inc., 499, 510

Torres v. Northwest Engineering Co., 223

Toyota Motor Credit Corp. v. C.L. Hyman Auto Wholesale, Inc., 481

Trans World Metals, Inc. v. Southwire Co., 556, 561

Transamerica Equip. Leasing Corp. v. Union Bank, 147

Transamerica Oil Corp. v. Lynes, Inc., 648

Travelers Indemnity Co. v. Maho Machine Tool Corp., 354

Trico Steel Co, In re, 461

True North Composite Services LLC v. Trinity Industries, 71

U.S. Tire-Tech, Inc. v. Boeran, B.V., 239, 589

Union Carbide Corporation v. Consumers Power Co., 560

United Services Auto Ass'n. v. Schlang, 165

United States v. Great Plains Gasification Assoc., 512

United States v.Westside Bank, 469

Universal C.I.T. Credit Corp. v. State Farm Mut. Auto. Ins. Co., 490

Universal Resources Corp. v. Panhandle Eastern Pipe Line Co., 390, 391, 512

Usinor Industeel v. Leeco Steel Products, 449, 450

Valley Iron & Steel Co. v. Thorin, 245, 248, 249

Ventura v. Ford Motor Corp., 655, 663

Vince v. Broome, 249

Vista St. Clair, Inc. v. Landry's Commercial Furnishings, Inc., 606

Viva Vino Import Corp. v. Farnese Vina S.r.l., 91

Vulcan Automotive Equip. Ltd. v. Global Marine Engine & Parts, Inc., 110

Walker v. American Cyanamid Co., 298

Walker v. Keith, 147

Wal-Mart Stores, Inc. v. Wheeler, 588

Walton v. Rose Mobile Homes LLC, 664

Waste Stream Environmental, Inc. v. Lynn Water and Sewer Commission, 162

Waters v. Massey-Ferguson, Inc., 650

Wayman v. Amoco Oil Co., 168

Welken v. Conley, 348

Weng v. Allison, 223

Westendorf v. Gateway 2000, Inc., 127

Wickliffe Farms, Inc. v. Owensboro Grain Co., 365

Wilhelm Lubrication Co. v. Brattrud, 147

Wilk Paving, Inc. v. Southworth-Milton, Inc., 351

Williams v. Western Surety Co., 481

Wilson v. Scampoli, 354

Wilson Trading Corp. v. David Ferguson, Ltd., 590

Windows, Inc. v. Jordan Panel Systems Corp., 429

Wisconsin Knife Works v. National Metal Crafters, 411

Wright v. Vickaryous, 488

Zabriskie Chevrolet, Inc. v. Smith, 340, 354

Zapatha v. Dairy Mart, Inc., 82, 91, 92, 359

Zemco Manufacturing Inc. v. Navistar Int'l Transportation Corp., 402

Zeta Consumer Products Corp., In re, 469

Zidell Explorations, Inc. v. Conval International, Ltd., 377

TABLE OF STATUTES AND REGULATIONS

Uniform Commercial Code

Revised Article 1

1-102 57
1-103 . . . . . 15, 19, 20, 23, 25, 26, 41,
          45, 59, 82, 96, 197, 470,
          538, 579, 679
1-201 . . . . 79, 310, 313, 458, 469,
          470, 471, 479, 480
1-201(b)(3) 96, 147, 152, 180, 207
1-201(b)(8) 201
1-201(b)(9) 456, 475, 476, 480
1-201(b)(12) 96, 148, 152
1-201(b)(13) 456
1-201(b)(20) 91, 177
1-201(b)(23) 498, 509
1-201(b)(35) 62, 448, 463, 465
1-203 . . . . 10, 60, 61, 62, 64, 448
1-204 . . . . 458, 470, 471
1-205 . . . . 514, 590
1-206 196
1-301 . . . . 24, 57, 75, 76
1-302 . . . . . 20, 24, 25, 57, 64, 76, 150
1-303 . . . . 2, 45, 107, 147, 152,
          180, 181, 187, 188,
          198, 200, 202, 419
1-304 . . . . 3, 82, 91, 149,
          202, 321, 396, 560
1-305 . . . . 5, 46, 526, 538, 541,
          552, 560, 562, 575,
          579, 591, 594, 632
1-306 . . . . 404, 517
1-308 . . . . 18, 161
1-309 527

Former Article 1

1-102 . . . . 15, 19, 20, 24, 25, 45,
          57, 59, 64, 76, 150
1-103 249
1-105 . . . . 24, 57, 75, 76
1-106 . . . . . 5, 46, 130, 526, 538, 541,
          552, 560, 562, 575, 579,
          591, 594, 632
1-107 . . . . 404, 517
1-201 458
1-201(3) 96, 152, 207
1-201(11) 96, 148
1-201(19) 82
1-201(31) 196
1-201(37) 10, 60, 62, 64, 448,
          463, 465
1-203 . . . . . . 3, 82, 91, 149, 202, 321,
          396, 560
1-204 . . . . 514, 590
1-205 . . . . . . 2, 45, 96, 107, 147, 152,
          180, 181, 187, 188, 189,
          198, 200, 202
1-207 . . . . 18, 161
1-208 527

Amended Article 2

2-101 447
2-102 . . . . 13, 21, 57, 59, 61, 62
2-103 . . . . 57, 61, 72, 96, 210,
          423, 463, 653
2-104 . . . . 79, 81, 242, 248, 315
2-105 . . . . 58, 61, 323, 447
2-106 . . . . 9, 58, 59, 61, 321,
          359, 447, 516, 517
2-107 . . . . 57, 61, 62
2-108 . . . . 13, 21, 60, 97, 477
2-201 . . . . . . 25, 44, 59, 61, 73, 79,80,
          81,129,130,144,145,146,
          152, 154, 248, 402, 418

2-202 .... 2, 44, 59, 180, 181,196,
                197, 198, 199, 200, 208
2-203 44
2-204 ..... 41, 44, 96, 105, 107, 128,
                148, 152, 153, 166
2-205 ... 15, 44, 59, 79, 105, 106, 128
2-206 .... 44, 59, 105, 106, 107,
                        124, 128
2-207 .... 44, 121, 124, 126,
                    127, 128, 201
2-209 .... 25, 44, 79, 128, 144,
                363, 395, 396, 401,
                402, 404, 411, 419
2-210 .... 56, 492, 498
2-211 98
2-212 .... 59, 98
2-213 .... 59, 98
2-301 .... 305, 498
2-302 ...... 3, 82, 209, 298, 590, 651
2-304 148
2-305 .... 44, 82, 91, 148, 150,
                152, 166, 167, 177, 179
2-306 .... 44, 91, 148, 154, 155,
                162, 163, 165, 166
2-307 .... 44, 47, 148, 179, 305,
                319, 323, 517
2-308 .... 44, 47, 148, 152, 153,
                179, 305, 319, 423, 425
2-309 .... 44, 47, 82, 149, 152,
                179, 359, 411, 514
2-310 ..... 44, 50, 53, 149, 179, 306,
                311, 312, 314, 517
2-311 .... 44, 149, 179
2-312 ..... 50, 59, 79, 149, 208, 448,
                483, 488, 489, 490, 491
2-313 .... 3, 50, 51, 59, 79, 149, 205,
                206, 207, 208, 209, 210, 211,
                222, 223, 224, 239, 241
2-313A 3, 50, 51, 149, 205, 239,
                240, 301, 352, 589, 620
2-313B 3, 50, 51, 149, 205,

                            226, 239, 240, 300,
                            301, 352, 589
2-314 ...... 3, 13, 50, 51, 59, 70, 79,
                80, 81, 149, 205, 208, 223,
                241, 242, 248, 249, 254,
                255, 257, 258, 265, 266,
                273, 616, 664
2-315 .... 3, 50, 51, 59, 149, 151,
                205, 208, 241, 242, 266,
                270, 271, 273, 594
2-316 .... 3, 51, 149, 208, 242,
                292, 298, 299, 301, 663
2-317 .... 51, 149, 208
2-318 .... 25, 51, 149, 301,
                302, 303, 483, 613
2-325 315
2-326 468
2-327 .... 79, 468
2-401 ..... 9, 58, 62, 421, 427, 440,
                447, 448, 449, 459,
                460, 461, 463, 476
2-402 .... 46, 56, 79, 453,
                455, 456, 477, 481
2-403 ..... 9, 20, 25, 52, 56, 79, 422,
                448, 458, 460, 461, 468,
                469, 471, 475, 476,
                477, 479, 480, 481
2-501 .... 58, 307, 369, 436,
                437, 449, 451, 459
2-502 ..... 25, 46, 47, 451, 452, 453,
                455, 456, 457, 499, 516
2-503 .... 44, 47, 48, 49, 51, 305,
                308, 309, 311, 313, 314,
                318, 423, 425, 448, 542
2-504 .... 44, 47, 309, 310, 318,
                323, 436, 440
2-505 .... 311, 312, 460, 461
2-506 315
2-507 .... 44, 47, 52, 305, 319,
                464, 468, 469, 527
2-508 .... 50, 51, 318, 332, 334,

349, 352, 353, 354, 355,
357, 440, 581

2-509 .... 48, 61, 364, 422, 423,
425, 427, 428, 435, 436,
439, 442, 446, 448, 529

2-510 .... 48, 334, 422, 437, 439,
440, 442, 446, 529

2-511 .... 44, 52, 305, 308, 319

2-512 .... 50, 311, 313, 317, 319, 320

2-513 ..... 49, 50, 51, 306, 308, 309,
310, 311, 312, 313,
314, 317, 319, 320

2-514 .... 314, 315

2-515 .... 51, 351

2-601 .... 50, 208, 307, 320, 321,
322, 323, 333, 348,
353, 440, 581

2-602 .... 50, 52, 333, 334, 341, 344,
348, 351, 352, 529, 581

2-603 .... 51, 52, 79, 344,
348, 352, 581

2-604 .... 51, 52, 344, 348, 352

2-605 .... 50, 79, 208, 311, 317,
333, 343, 350, 352, 355

2-606 .... 51, 52, 306, 307, 333,
334, 341, 351, 440, 529

2-607 ..... 21, 41, 51, 208, 283, 307,
320, 333, 334, 342, 343, 348,
350, 351, 581, 582, 589, 592

2-608 .... 51, 208, 307, 320, 333,
334, 341, 342, 344, 348,
349, 350, 351, 352, 353,
355, 441, 529, 581, 663, 664

2-609 .... 46, 79, 497, 498,
499, 509, 511, 512,
513, 516, 524, 525

2-610 .... 45, 511, 513, 514, 518,
519, 531, 533, 542, 560

2-611 .... 498, 511, 513, 514, 542

2-612 ..... 47, 50, 52, 208, 305, 320,
321, 323, 332, 348, 349, 354,

355, 498, 513, 517, 518, 519,
524, 525, 531, 533, 581

2-613 ..... 20, 47, 48, 363, 364, 365,
369, 393, 421, 428

2-614 .... 20, 47, 323, 363, 364, 365,
393

2-615 .... 20, 48, 363, 365, 369, 370,
377, 378, 381, 382, 391,
392, 393, 395, 396, 421, 513

2-616 .... 25, 48, 363, 365, 369, 370,
393

2-702 ..... 25, 47, 53, 459, 463, 464,
468, 469, 470, 498,
499, 509, 516, 519, 527

2-703 .... 45, 52, 152, 320, 421, 459,
462, 514, 516, 517, 518,
526, 527, 533, 540, 555, 560

2-704 .... 45, 540, 562, 563

2-705 .... 48, 459, 498, 516

2-706 .... 45, 46, 496, 526, 527,
532, 533, 537, 540, 542,
543, 555, 560, 561, 562,
563, 565, 566

2-707 315

2-708 .... 45, 46, 152, 391, 496,
526, 527, 533, 537, 540,
541, 542, 543, 552, 554,
555, 560, 561, 562, 563,
574, 602

2-709 ..... 41, 45, 52, 343, 350, 361,
391, 421, 441, 495, 518,
519, 526, 527, 528, 530,
531, 540, 543, 555, 562

2-710 .... 46, 361, 526, 538, 563, 564

2-711 ...... 45, 47, 51, 61, 152, 208,
307, 323, 342, 344, 348,
354, 421, 516, 518, 519,
565, 581, 663, 664

2-712 .... 45, 46, 50, 177, 342,
353, 496, 565, 566,
567, 572, 573, 577, 591

2-713 . . . . 25, 45, 46, 50, 61, 152,
                    307, 342, 496, 565, 566,
                    568, 573, 574, 575, 576,
                    577, 591
2-714 . . . . 25, 51, 208, 307, 320,
                    342, 490, 581, 590, 591,
                    592, 593, 594, 595, 606,
                    609, 610, 611, 650
2-715 . . . . . 41, 46, 51, 150, 204, 208,
                    255, 342, 490, 538, 563,
                    565, 566, 573, 577, 581,
                    590, 591, 592, 595, 596,
                    606, 609, 612, 613, 650
2-716 . . . . 46, 51, 391, 452, 453,
                    454, 455, 456, 457, 495,
                    499, 516, 526, 528, 566
2-717 . . . . 320, 342, 581, 592, 594
2-718 . . . . 25, 50, 209, 292, 321,
                    532, 541, 543, 629,
                    632, 638, 639, 640
2-719 . . . . 25, 50, 150, 209, 292,
                    298, 321, 353, 590, 610,
                    613, 639, 640, 649, 650, 651
2-720 46
2-722 . . . . 428, 437, 449
2-723 . . . . 541, 542
2-724 541
2-725 . . . . 25, 41, 208, 238, 254,
                    581, 670, 671, 678, 679

Former Article 2
2-103(1)(b) 82
2-103(1)(d) 249
2-105 . . . . 57, 58, 447
2-202 . . . . 181, 198, 200
2-207 . . . 44, 108, 109, 110, 120, 121,
                    123, 124, 125, 126, 127, 128
2-208 . . . . . . 2, 45, 96, 147, 152, 180,
                    181, 419
2-210 498
2-316 . . . . 298, 301

2-318 . . . . 17, 302
2-319 through 2-324 . . . 149, 309, 311,
                    428
2-326 . . . . 465, 466
2-508 . . . . 353, 355, 358
2-509 . . . . 423, 425
2-602 350
2-606 350
2-607 . . . . 588, 589
2-608 . . . . 350, 355
2-612 . . . . 323, 332, 349, 519
2-703 . . . . 45, 560, 518
2-708 . . . . 541, 552, 561
2-709 518
2-710 . . . . 538, 563
2-711 . . . . 45, 323, 519, 664
2-713 574
2-718 632
2-723 . . . . 541, 561
2-725 671

Amended Article 2A
2A-102 . . . . 60, 62
2A-103(1) 55, 56, 57, 60, 62, 79,
                    96, 210, 274, 320, 359,
                    448, 456, 479, 481, 516,
                    539
2A-103(3) 79, 248
2A-104 . . . . 60, 97
2A-106 76
2A-108 . . . . 3, 82, 92, 209
2A-201 . . . . 44, 129, 130, 144,
                    151, 152, 154
2A-202 . . . . 2, 44, 180, 196,
                    197, 198, 208
2A-203 44
2A-204 . . . . 44, 96, 105, 148, 152, 153
2A-205 . . . . 44, 79, 105
2A-206 . . . . 44, 105, 107
2A-208 . . . . 44, 79, 363, 395, 402,
                    404, 419

2A-209 . . . . 55, 56, 144, 149, 274

2A-210 . . . . . 3, 50, 51, 149, 205, 208, 209, 210, 211, 239, 241, 274

2A-211 . . . . . 50, 55, 80, 149, 208, 483

2A-212 . . . . 3, 50, 51, 56, 80, 149, 205, 208, 241, 242, 248, 249, 254, 257, 266, 274

2A-213 . . . . . . 3, 50, 51, 56, 149, 205, 208, 241, 242, 266, 274

2A-214 . . . . 3, 51, 149, 208, 242, 292, 301

2A-215 . . . . 51, 149, 208

2A-216 . . . 51, 149, 301, 302, 303, 483

2A-217 . . . . 62, 449, 451, 459

2A-218 . . . . 437, 449, 451

2A-219 . . . . 48, 56, 364, 423, 428, 459

2A-220 . . . . 49, 56, 423

2A-221 . . . . 47, 48, 56, 363, 364, 365, 369, 392

2A-222 98

2A-223 98

2A-224 98

2A-301 . . . . 56, 449

2A-302 . . . . 423, 447, 449

2A-303 . . . . 56, 449, 492

2A-304 . . . . 56, 80, 449, 458, 479, 480

2A-305 . . . . 52, 56, 80, 449, 458, 462, 470, 479, 480

2A-306 . . . . 56, 449

2A-307 . . . . 46, 52, 53, 56, 449, 455, 456, 460, 461, 470, 481

2A-308 . . . . 46, 56, 449, 455, 456

2A-309 . . . . 56, 449

2A-310 . . . . 56, 449

2A-311 449

2A-401 . . . . . . 46, 497, 510, 511, 512, 516

2A-402 . . . . 45, 511, 519

2A-403 . . . . 511, 513

2A-404 . . . . 48, 363, 364, 365, 392

2A-405 . . . . 48, 56, 363, 365, 369,

370, 377, 380, 392

2A-406 . . . . 48, 56, 363, 365, 369, 370, 392

2A-407 . . . . . . 56, 274, 282, 283, 317, 352, 363, 392

2A-501 152

2A-503 . . . . 50, 209, 292, 321, 353, 639, 651

2A-504 . . . . . 50, 209, 292, 321, 532, 541, 543, 629, 632, 638, 639

2A-505 . . . . 46, 359, 517

2A-506 . . . . . 208, 254, 581, 670, 678

2A-507 541

2A-507A 46, 51, 452, 453, 456, 457, 516, 526, 528

2A-508 . . . . 45, 48, 51, 152, 208, 323, 344, 354, 516, 519, 565, 581, 592

2A-509 . . . . 50, 52, 208, 320, 322, 333, 344, 581

2A-510 . . . . 48, 50, 52, 208, 320, 321, 323, 517, 519, 581

2A-511 . . . . 51, 52, 80, 344, 581

2A-512 . . . . 50, 51, 52, 344, 581

2A-513 . . . . 50, 51, 352, 353, 581

2A-514 . . . . 50, 208, 333

2A-515 . . . . . 50, 51, 52, 317, 333, 334

2A-516 . . . . 51, 56, 208, 320, 334, 581, 582, 592

2A-517 . . . . 51, 56, 208, 320, 334, 352, 581

2A-518 . . . . . 45, 46, 50, 353, 565, 567

2A-519 . . . . 45, 50, 51, 208, 320, 565, 574, 581, 592, 595

2A-520 . . . 46, 51, 208, 538, 563, 565, 577, 578, 595, 596, 606

2A-522 . . . . 46, 47, 451, 452, 456, 457, 516

2A-523 . . . . 45, 52, 152, 320, 459, 516, 519, 526

2A-524 . . . . 45, 562

2A-525 . . . . . 47, 52, 53, 62, 459, 463,
                466, 516, 527, 538
2A-526 . . . . 48, 459, 516
2A-527 . . . . 45, 46, 526, 532,
                539, 561, 565
2A-528 . . . . 45, 46, 526, 539, 541,
                544, 561
2A-529 . . . . 45, 52, 526, 527, 528
2A-530 . . . . 46, 526, 538, 563

Former Article 2A

2A-103(4) 82
2A-207 . . . . 2, 45, 147, 180, 181
2A-508 . . . . 45, 344
2A-513 353
2A-521 . . . . 46, 51, 452, 453, 456, 516
2A-523 45
2A-528 544
2A-530 . . . . 538, 563

Article 3

3-102 13
3-103 91
3-104 . . . . 53, 313, 314
3-301 53
3-302 54
3-305 . . . . 53, 54
3-310 53
3-401 54
3-402 20
3-403 20
3-406 55
3-408 54
3-409 315
3-413 315
3-414 54
3-415 54
3-416 54
3-418 54
3-420 54

Article 4

4-102 13
4-210 315
4-401 . . . . 54, 55
4-501 . . . . 55, 314, 315
4-502 55
4-503 . . . . 55, 314, 315
4-504 315

Article 4A

4A-108 12

Article 5

5-102 316
5-104 316
5-106 316
5-107 316
5-108 316
5-109 317
5-111 317

Revised Article 7

7-102 437
7-103 439
7-104 310
7-106 310
7-204 428
7-301 . . . . 48, 49
7-306 49
7-309 . . . . 48, 310, 428, 439
7-403 . . . . 48, 437, 459
7-501 49
7-502 . . . . 49, 310
7-503 49
7-601 49

Article 8

8-103 13

Revised Article 9

9-102 482

9-102(a)(20) 466
9-102(a)(23) 653
9-102(a)(44) 59
9-103 . . . . 52, 466, 467
9-109 . . . . . . 13, 21, 59, 64, 448, 466
9-110 . . . . . . 13, 459, 460, 461, 462,
463, 565
9-201 . . . . 21, 52, 56
9-202 447
9-203 . . . . 457, 462
9-308 467
9-315 . . . . 467, 469, 480
9-317 . . . . 56, 456, 457, 462,
467, 470, 480, 482
9-320 . . . . 52, 56, 456,
457, 467, 480, 481
9-321 . . . . 56, 456, 480, 481, 482
9-322 462
9-323 56
9-324 467
9-333 56
9-334 56
9-335 56
9-403 491
9-404 491
9-405 491
9-406 491
9-407 . . . . 56, 491
9-408 491
9-409 491
9-601 . . . . 20, 62, 463, 466
9-609 . . . . 454, 463
9-610 463
9-615 463
9-625 519

Former Article 9
9-114 465

UETA
3 97

5 . . . . 97, 98
7 98
9 98
14 97

UCITA (2002)
102 . . . . 58, 79, 80, 93, 126, 241,
273, 283, 359, 450,
564, 579, 612
103 . . . . 58, 71, 72, 482
105 . . . . 72, 127
106 24
109 76
110 76
111 93
112 126
113 126
115 24
116 . . . . 26, 93
201 . . . . 80, 130, 154
202 . . . . 108, 153
203 108
204 . . . . 80, 126
207 126
208 126
209 126
210 126
301 198
302 198
303 . . . . 80, 419
305 . . . . 153, 177
306 153
307 . . . . 153, 155
308 153
401 . . . . 80, 153, 490
402 . . . . 153, 241
403 . . . . 80, 153, 273
404 . . . . 80, 153, 273
405 . . . . 153, 273
406 . . . . 153, 301
407 . . . . 153, 301

408 153
409 . . . . 153, 303
410 153
501 450
502 450
503 . . . . 450, 493
504 . . . . 450, 493
505 . . . . 450, 493
506 . . . . 450, 493
507 283
508 283
509 283
510 283
511 283
601 . . . . 319, 358
602 319
603 359
604 . . . . 319, 320, 359, 532
606 319
607 319
608 . . . . 319, 320
609 . . . . 319, 320, 358
610 . . . . 319, 358, 591, 595
611 320
612 320
613 . . . . 80, 359
614 446
615 393
616 359
617 359
618 359
701 358
702 . . . . 80, 358, 419
703 358
704 . . . . 320, 358
707 . . . . 320, 358
708 . . . . 80, 516
709 516
710 516
801 540
802 . . . . 460, 461, 526

803 651
804 639
805 679
807 540
808 . . . . 531, 540, 543, 555, 564
809 . . . . 574, 577, 579, 595, 612
810 595
811 455
812 562
815 . . . . 461, 466
816 466

UCITA (2000)
104 24

Uniform Sales Act
12 . . . . 211, 224
18 421
19 421
22 421
45 323
49 342
53 499
54 499

Iowa Stat.
554D.104 24

Mass. Gen. Laws Ann.
106 § 2-316A 665

Minn. Stat.
525.9221 256
604.01 291

Federal Statutes

United States Warehouse Act
7 U.S.C. 241 12

Federal Seed Act
7 U.S.C. 1551 298

Arbitration Act
9 U.S.C. 1 121
9 U.S.C. 2 121
9 U.S.C. 201 75

Bankruptcy Code
11 U.S.C. 544 . . . . 468, 470
11 U.S.C. 545 468
11 U.S.C. 546 . . . . 468, 469, 470
11 U.S.C. 547 468
11 U.S.C. 549 468

Expedited Funds Availability Act
12 U.S.C. 4001 . . . . 11, 21

Robinson-Patman Act
15 U.S.C. 13a, 13b, 21a 21

Consumer Protection Act
15 U.S.C. 1601 21

Electronic Funds Transfer Act
15 U.S.C. 1693 12

Magnuson-Moss Warranty Act
15 U.S.C. 2301 . . . . . 21, 621, 654, 663
15 U.S.C. 2302 654
15 U.S.C. 2303 654
15 U.S.C. 2304 . . . . 654, 663
15 U.S.C. 2308 654
15 U.S.C. 2310 655

Consumer Leases Act
15 U.S.C. 1667 653

E-Sign
15 U.S.C. 7001 . . . . 97, 98
15 U.S.C. 7002 97

15 U.S.C. 7003 97

Food, Drug and Cosmetic Act
21 U.S.C. 301 21

Ship Mortgage Act
46 U.S.C. 31321 21

Carriage of Goods by Sea Act
46 U.S.C. App. 1300 . . . . 12, 438

Bills of Lading Act
49 U.S.C. 80101 . . . . 21, 48

Interstate Commerce Commission Act
49 U.S.C. 11707 438

CFR
12 CFR Part 205 12
12 CFR Part 210 . . . . 11, 12
12 CFR Part 229 . . . . 11, 21
16 CFR Part 433 282
16 CFR 700.1 654
16 CFR 700.3 654
16 CFR 701 654
16 CFR 702 654
16 CFR 703 . . . . 655, 670
16 CFR 703.1 670
16 CFR 703.5 670

CISG
Art. 1 . . . . 22, 73, 74, 94, 449, 619
Art. 2 73
Art. 3 . . . . 22, 71, 73, 94
Art. 4 . . . . 73, 94, 449, 480, 639
Art. 5 . . . . 73, 619
Art. 6 . . . . 23, 24, 41, 73, 74, 153, 639
Art. 7 . . . . 23, 94, 202, 273
Art. 8 . . . . 198. 202, 240, 273
Art. 9 . . . . 198, 201, 202, 240
Art. 10 . . . . 73, 74

Art. 11 . . . . . . 73, 129, 198, 240, 418

Art. 12 . . . . 41, 73, 129, 240

Art. 14 . . . . 105, 108

Art. 15 105

Art. 16 . . . . 105, 106

Art. 17 105

Art. 18 . . . . 105, 107, 122

Art. 19 . . . . 105, 109, 122, 125

Art. 20 105

Art. 21 105

Art. 22 105

Art. 23 105

Art. 24 105

Art. 25 . . . . 357, 515, 525, 539

Art. 26 . . . . 357, 516, 525, 539

Art. 28 . . . . 454, 531

Art. 29 . . . . 94, 393, 418

Art. 30 . . . . 240, 317, 441, 490

Art. 31 . . . . 153, 317, 318, 441

Art. 32 . . . . 317, 318, 441

Art. 33 . . . . 153, 317, 318, 441

Art. 34 . . . . 317, 318, 441

Art. 35 . . 153, 240, 273, 300, 619, 620

Art. 37 . . . . 357, 591

Art. 38 . . . . 318, 356

Art. 39 . . . . . 318, 356, 525, 591, 594

Art. 40 . . . . 318, 591

Art. 41 . . . . 480, 490

Art. 42 490

Art. 45 . . . . 356, 454, 490, 612

Art. 46 . . . . 357, 454, 525

Art. 47 357

Art. 48 . . . . 357, 525, 591, 594

Art. 49 . . . . . . 357, 516, 573, 576, 594

Art. 50 . . . . 356, 594, 595

Art. 53 . . . . 318, 531

Art. 55 . . . . 108, 153, 177

Art. 57 . . . . 153, 318

Art. 58 . . . . 153, 318, 531

Art. 59 . . . . 153, 531

Art. 60 153

Art. 61 . . . . 531, 612

Art. 62 531

Art. 63 . . . . 531, 539

Art. 64 . . . . 516, 531, 539

Art. 65 531

Art. 66 441

Art. 67 . . . . 441, 442

Art. 68 . . . . 441, 442

Art. 69 . . . . 441, 442

Art. 70 . . . . 441, 442

Art. 71 515

Art. 72 . . . . 515, 516, 573

Art. 73 . . . . 525, 539

Art. 74 . . . . 356, 539, 542, 555, 564,
578, 595, 612, 619, 639

Art. 75 . . . . . . 357, 525, 539, 542, 573

Art. 76 . . . . 357, 525, 542, 576

Art. 77 . . . . 564, 612

Art. 79 . . . . . . 364, 365, 377, 392, 393

Art. 81 . . . . 357, 525

Art. 82 . . . . 357, 525

Art. 83 . . . . 357, 525

Art. 84 . . . . 357, 525

Art. 85 357

Art. 86 357

Art. 87 357

Art. 88 357

Art. 95 . . . . 73, 74

Art. 96 73

Convention on the Limitation
Period in the International
Sale of Goods

1 through 27 . . . . 23, 679

TABLE OF SECONDARY AUTHORITIES

RESTATEMENTS
Contracts (Second)

1	78, 95
5	579
3	95
17	95
21	96
22	95
24	95
50	95
58	108
59	108
71	95
84	403
87	35, 106
89	401
139	35, 36, 144
201	200
202	200
203	200
205	91, 579
208	91
209	196
210	180, 196
215	196
216	197
219	200
220	200
221	200
222	200
223	200
235	579
250	45
264	392
317	491
318	492
321	491
327	491
328	492
333	491
336	491
337	491
338	492
342	492
351	538, 577
355	579

Torts (Second)

402A	206, 582, 613, 614

Torts (Third) Products Liability

1	618
2	265, 614
18	582, 652
21	618, 652

UNIDROIT Principles of International Commercial Contracts

2.1	125
2.6	125
2.11	125
2.19	125
2.20	125
2.21	125
2.22	125
6.2.1	393
6.2.2	393
6.2.3	393
7.1.6	393
7.1.7	393

UCP 500

Generally	12, 315

ISP 98

Generally	12

ARTICLES AND BOOKS

Adame, Jorge, The UNIDROIT Principles and NAFTA, 4 Ann. Surv. Int'l & Comp. L. 56 (1997), 23

Alces, Peter A., W(h)ither Warranty: The B(l)oom of Products Liability Theory in the Case of Deficient Software Design, 87 Calif. L. Rev. 269 (1999), 303, 619

Alces, Peter A. & Frisch, David, Commenting on "Purpose" in the Uniform Commercial Code, 58 Ohio St. L.J. 419 (1997), 19

Alder, Barry E., The Questionable Ascent of Hadley v. Baxendale, 51 Stan. L. Rev. 1547 (1999), 577

Allen, Ronald J. & Hillman, Robert A., Evidentiary Problems In–And Solutions For–the Uniform Commercial Code, 1984 Duke L.J. 92, 201

Anderson, Roy Ryden, Damages Under the Uniform Commercial Code (2003), 46, 496

Anderson, Roy Ryden, In Support of Consequential Damages for Sellers, 11 J.L. & Com. 123 (1992), 563

Anderson, Roy Ryden, Of Hidden Agendas, Naked Emperors, And a Few Goods Soldiers: The Conference's Breach of Promise . . . Regarding Article 2 Damage Remedies, 54 SMU L. Rev. 795 (2001), 497

Ausness, Richard C., Replacing Strict Liability with a Contract-Based Products Liability Regime, 71 Temp. L. Rev. 171 (1998), 620

Ausness, Richard C., "Waive" Goodbye to Tort Liability: A Proposal to Remove Paternalism from Product Sales Transactions, 37 San Diego L. Rev. 293 (2000), 652

Ayres, Ian & Gertner, Robert H., Filling Gaps in Incomplete Contracts: An Economic Theory of Default Rules, 99 Yale L.J. 87 (1989), 151

Barnes, David W., The Meaning of Value in Contract Damages and Contract Theory, 46 Am. U. L. Rev. 1 (1996), 496

Barnes, David W., The Net Expectation Interest in Contract Damages, 48 Emory L.J. 1137 (1999), 562

Bates, John R., Continued Use of Goods After Rejection or Revocation of Acceptance: The UCC Rule Revealed, Reviewed, and Revised, 25 Rutgers L.J. 1 (1993), 349

Berger, Klaus Peter, The Lex Mercatoria Doctrine and the UNIDROIT Principles of International Commercial Contracts, 28 Law & Pol'y Int'l Bus. 943 (1997), 23

Bernstein, Lisa, Merchant Law in a Merchant Court: Rethinking the Code's Search for Immanent Business Norms, 144 U. Pa. L. Rev. 1765 (1996), 78, 189

Bernstein, Lisa, The Questionable Empirical Basis of Article 2's Incorporation Strategy: A Preliminary Study, 66 U. Chi. L. Rev. 710 (1999), 189

Bollas, Jacqueline S., Note, Use of the Comparative Negligence Doctrine in Warranty Actions, 45 Ohio St. U. L.J. 763 (1984), 291

Bonell, Michael Joachim, Policing the International Commercial Contract Against Unfairness Under the Unidroit Principles, 3 Tul. J. Int'l & Comp. L. 73 (1995), 93

Boss, Amelia H., Electronic Commerce and the Symbiotic Relationship Between International and Domestic Law Reform, 72 Tul. L. Rev. 1931 (1998), 98

Boss, Amelia H., The History of Article 2A: A Lesson for Practitioner and Scholar Alike, 39 Ala. L. Rev. 575 (1988), 43

Boss, Amelia H., The Jurisdiction of Commercial Law: Party Autonomy in Choosing Applicable Law and Forum Under Proposed Revisions to the Uniform Commercial Code, 32 Int'l Law. 1067 (1998), 76

Boss, Amelia H., Searching for Security in the Law of Electronic Commerce, 23 Nova L. Rev. 585 (1999), 98

Braucher, Jean, An Informal Resolution Model of Consumer Product Warranty Law, 1985 Wis. L. Rev. 1405, 654

Braucher, Jean, When Your Refrigerator Orders Groceries Online and Your Car Dials 911 After an Accident: Do We Really Need New Law for the World of Smart Goods, 8 Wash. U. J.L. & Pol'y 241 (2002), 58

Braucher, Robert, The Legislative History of the Uniform Commercial Code, 58 Colum. L. Rev. 798 (1958), 15

Breen, John M., The Lost Volume Seller and Lost Profits Under UCC § 2-708(2): A Conceptual and Lilnguistic Critique, 50 U. Miami L. Rev. 779 (1996), 553

Breen, John M., Statutory Interpretation and the Lessons of Llewellyn, 33 Loy. L.A. L. Rev. 263 (2000), 18, 19

Brennan, Lorin, Why Article 2 Cannot Apply to Software Transactions, 38 Duq. L. Rev. 459 (2001), 58

Bruckel, Caroline N., Consideration in Exclusive and Nonexclusive Open Quantity Contracts Under the U.C.C.: A Proposal for a New System of Validation, 68 Minn. L. Rev. 117 (1983), 164

Bruckel, Caroline N., The Weed and the Web: Section 2-201's Corruption of the Code's Substantive Provisions–The Quantity Problem, 1983 U. Ill. L. F. 811, 154

Buggs, David C., Crop Destruction and Forward Grain Contracts: Why Don't Sections 2-613 and 2-615 of the UCC Provide More Relief?, 12 Hamline L. Rev. 669 (1989), 369

Burnham, Scott J., Why Do Law Students Insist that Article 2 of the Uniform Commercial Code Applies Only to Merchants and What Can We Do About It?, 63 Brook. L. Rev. 1271 (1997), 80

Burton, Steven J., Breach of Contract and the Common Law Duty to Perform in Good Faith, 94 Harv. L. Rev. 369 (1980), 163

Caggiano, Joe, Understanding Natural Gas Contracts, 38 Oil & Gas Tax Q. 267 (1989), 391

Casebeer, Kenneth M., Escape from Liberalism: Fact and Value in Karl Llewellyn, 1977 Duke L.J. 671, 77

Caselton, Paul E., Note, Lost-Profits Damage Awards Under Uniform Commercial Code Section 2-708(2), 37 Stan. L. Rev. 1109 (1985), 543

Chalmers, M.D., Codification of Mercantile Law, 19 Law Q. Rev. 10 (1903), 6

Charney, David, Hypothetical Bargains: The Normative Structure of Contract Interpretation, 89 Mich. L. Rev. 1815 (1991), 150

Childres, Robert, Buyer's Remedies: The Danger of Section 2-713, 72 Nw. U. L. Rev. 837 (1978), 566

Clifford, Donald F., Express Warranty Liability of Remote Sellers: One Purchase, Two Relationships, 75 Wash U. L.Q. 413 (1997), 301

Clifford, Donald F., Non-UCC Statutory Provisions Affecting Warranty Disclaimers and Remedies in Sales of Goods, 71 N.C. L. Rev. 1011 (1993), 299

Coffinberger, Richard E. & Samuels, Linda B., Legislative Responses to the Plight of New Car Purchasers, 18 U.C.C. L.J. 168 (1985), 654

Comment, And Then There Were None: Requirements Contracts and the Buyer Who Does Not Buy, 64 Wash. L. Rev. 871 (1989), 163

Comment, The Statute of Frauds and the Business Community: A Re-Appraisal in Light of Prevailing Practices, 66 Yale L.J. 1038 (1957), 129

Comment, UCC Section 2-305(1)(c): Open Price Terms and the Intention of the Parties in Sales Contracts, 1 Valpo. L. Rev. 381 (1967), 167

Corbin on Contracts (1993) & (2003), 391, 498

Corbin, Arthur L., The Interpretation of Words and the Parol Evidence Rule, 50 Cornell L.Q. 161 (1965), 200

D'Angelo, Christopher Scott, The Economic Loss Doctrine: Saving Contract Warranty Law From Drowning in a Sea of Torts, 26 U. Tol. L. Rev. 591 (1995), 618

Danzig, Richard, A Comment on the Jurisprudence of the Uniform Commercial Code, 27 Stan. L. Rev. 621 (1975), 25, 77, 78

Devience, Jr., Alex, The Developing Line Between Warranty and Tort Liability Under the Uniform Commercial Code: Does 2-318 Make a Difference?, 2 DePaul Bus. L.J. 295 (1990), 302

Dimatteo, Larry A., A Theory of Efficient Penalty: Eliminating the Law of Liquidated Damages, 38 Am. Bus. L. J. 633 (2001), 632

Diamond, Thomas A. & Foss, Howard, Consequential Damages for Commercial Loss: An Alternative to Hadley v. Baxendale, 63 Fordham L. Rev. 665 (1994), 596

Dicker, E. Carolyn Hochstadter and Campo, John P., FF & E and the True Lease Question: Article 2A and Accompanying Amendments to UCC Section 1-201(37), 7 Am. Bankr. Inst. L. Rev. 517 (1999), 64

Dobie, Armistead Mason, Bailments and Carriers (1914), 437, 438

Dolan, John F., Changing Commercial Practices and the Uniform Commercial Code, 26 Loy. L.A. L. Rev. 579 (1993), 78

Dowling, Alan G., Note, A Right to Adequate Assurance of Performance in All Transactions: UCC § 2-609 Beyond Sales of Goods, 48 S. Cal. L. Rev. 1358 (1975), 498

Dunham, Allison, A History of the National Conference of Commissioners on Uniform State Laws, 30 Law & Contemp. Probs. 233 (1965), 7

Eddy, Jonathon A., On the "Essential" Purposes of Limited Remedies: The Metaphysics of U.C.C. Section 2-719(2), 65 Calif. L. Rev. 28 (1977), 648

Effross, Walter A., The Legal Architecture of Virtual Stores: World Wide Web Sites and the Uniform Commercial Code, 34 San Diego L. Rev. 1263 (1997), 98

Eisenberg, Melvin Aron, The Emergence of Dynamic Contract Law, 88 Cal. L. Rev. 1743 (2000), 147

Elofson, John, The Dilemma of Changed Circumstances in Contract Law: An Economic Analysis of the Forseeability and Risk Bearer Tests, 30 Colum. J. of Law & Soc. Prob. 1 (1996), 363

Eno, Lawrence R., Price Movement and Unstated Objections to the Defective Performance of Sales Contracts, 44 Yale L. J. 782 (1935), 322, 333

Epstein, Richard A., Confusion About Custom: Disentangling Informal Customs from Standard Contractual Provisions, 66 U. Chi. L. Rev. 821 (1999), 184

Farnsworth, E. Allan, Contracts (4th ed. 2004), 492

Farnsworth, E. Allan, Documentary Drafts Under the Uniform Commercial Code, 22 Bus. Law. 479 (1967), 315

Farnsworth, E. Allan, "Meaning" in the Law of Contracts, 76 Yale L.J. 939 (1967), 200

Ferrari, Franco, The Relationship Between the UCC and CISG and the Construction of Uniform Law, 29 Loy. L.A. L. Rev. 1021 (1996), 22

Ferrill, A. Michael & Japhet, Charles A., Deceptive Trade Practices--Consumer Protection Act, 52 SMU L. Rev. 971 (1999), 667

Festschrift to Charles J. Goetz and Robert E. Scott, 6 Va. J. 6 (2003), 151

Finberg, Dana J., Note, Blood Bank and Blood Products Manufacturer Liability in Transfusion-Related AIDS Cases, 26 U. Rich. L. Rev. 519 (1992), 257

Flechtner, Harry M., Enforcing Manufacturers' Warranties, "Pass Through" Warranties, and the Like: Can the Buyer Get a Refund?, 50 Rutgers L. Rev. 397 (1998), 301

Flores, Robert L., Risk of Loss in Sales: A Missing Chapter in the History of the U.C.C.: Through Llewellyn to Williston and A Bit Beyond, 27 Pac. L.J. 161 (1996), 422, 440

Foss, Howard, The Seller's Right to Cure When the Buyer Revokes Acceptance: Erase the Line in the Sand, 16 S. Ill. U. L.J. 1 (1991), 349

Frier, Bruce W., Interpreting Codes, 89 Mich. L. Rev. 2201 (1991), 19

Frisch, David, Remedies as Property: A Different Perspective on Specific Performance Clauses, 35 Wm. & Mary L. Rev. 1691 (1994), 452

Gabriel, Henry D., The Battle of the Forms: A Comparison of the United Nations Convention for the International Sale of Goods and the Uniform Commercial Code,

49 Bus. Law. 1053 (1994), 125

Gabriel, Henry D., The Inapplicability of the United Nations Convention on the International Sale of Goods as a Model for the Revision of Article Two of the Uniform Commercial Code, 72 Tul. L. Rev. 1995 (1998), 22

Gabriel, Henry D., A Primer on the United Nations Convention on the International Sale of Goods: From the Perspective of the Uniform Commercial Code, 7 Ind. Int'l & Comp. L. Rev. 279 (1997), 23

Gabriel, Henry D., The Revisions of the Uniform Commercial Code–Process and Politics, 19 J. L. & Comm. 125 (1999), 8

Galligan, Thomas C., Contortions Along the Boundary Between Contracts and Torts, 69 Tul. L. Rev. 457 (1994), 617

Garvin, Larry T., Adequate Assurance of Performance: Of Risk, Duress, and Cognition, 69 U. Colo. L. Rev. 71 (1998), 499

Garvin, Larry T., Credit, Information, and Trust in the Law of Sales: The Credit Seller's Right of Reclamation, 44 UCLA L. Rev. 247 (1996), 464

Garvin, Larry T., Disproportionality and the Law of Consequential Damages: Default Theory and Cognitive Reality, 59 Ohio St. L.J. 339 (1998), 577

Garvin, Larry T., Uncertainty and Error in the Law of Sales: The Article 2 Statute of Limitations, 83 B.U.L. Rev. 345 (2003), 671

Gedid, John L., U.C.C. Methodology: Taking a Realistic Look at the Code, 29 Wm. & Mary L. Rev. 341 (1988), 19

Gergen, Mark P., The Use of Open Terms in Contract, 92 Colum. L. Rev. 997 (1992), 150

Gillette, Clayton P., Harmony and Stasis in Trade Usage in International Sales, 39 Va. J. Int'l L. 707 (1999), 189

Gilmore, Grant, Article 9: What it Does for the Past, 26 La. L. Rev. 285 (1966), 25

Gilmore, Grant, On the Difficulties of Codifying Commercial Law, 57 Yale L.J. 1341 (1948), 17

Gilmore, Grant, Security Interests in Personal Property (1965), 19

Goetz, Charles J., & Scott, Robert E., The Limits of Expanded Choice: An Analysis of the Interactions Between Express and Implied Terms, 73 Cal. L. Rev. 261 (1985), 150

Goetz, Charles J., & Scott, Robert E., Measuring Seller's Damages: The Lost-Profits Puzzle, 31 Stan. L. Rev. 323 (1979), 553

Geotz, Charles J. & Scott, Robert E., Principles of Relational Contracts, 67 Va. L. Rev. 1089 (1981), 166

Goldberg, Victor P., Discretion in Long-Term Quantity Contracts: Reining in Good Faith, 35 U. C. Davis L. Rev. 319 (2002), 163

Goldberg, Victor P., Price Adjustment in Long-Term Contracts, 1985 Wis. L. Rev. 527, 154, 177

Goldman, Lee, My Way and the Highway: The Law and Economics of Choice of Forum Clause in Consumer Form Contracts, 86 Nw. U. L. Rev. 700 (1992), 76

Greenberg, Harold, Specific Performance Under Section 2-716 of the Uniform Commercial

Code: "A More Liberal Attitude" in the "Grand Style," 17 N. Eng. L. Rev. 321 (1982), 452

Greenfield, Michael M., The Role of Assent in Article 2 and Article 9, 75 Wash. U. L.Q. 289 (1997), 620

Gregory, John D., The Proposed UNCITRAL Convention on Electronic Contracts, 59 Bus. Law. 313 (2003), 98

Grewal, Shivbir S., Risk of Loss in Goods Sold During Transit: A Comparative Study of the U.N. Convention on Contracts for the International Sale of Goods, the U.C.C., and the British Sale of Goods Act, 14 Loy. L.A. Int'l & Comp. L.J. 93 (1991), 441

Grunfeld, C., Law Reform (Enforcement of Contracts) Act, 1954, 17 Mod. L. Rev. 451 (1954), 129

Hagen, Daniel C., Note, Sections 2-719(2) and 2-719(3) of the Uniform Commercial Code: The Limited Warranty Package & Consequential Damages, 31 Val. U. L. Rev. 111 (1996), 650

Hamilton, Walton H., The Ancient Maxim Caveat Emptor, 40 Yale L. J. 1133 (1931), 203, 204

Hannaway, Sean M., Note, The Jurisprudence and Judicial Treatment of the Comments to the Uniform Commercial Code, 75 Cornell L. Rev. 962 (1990), 16

Harrington, William A., The Law of Consignments: Antitrust and Commercial Pitfalls, 34 Bus. Law. 431 (1979), 465

Harris, Robert A., A Radical Restatement of the Law of Seller's Damages: Sales Act and Commercial Code Results Compared, 18 Stan. L. Rev. 66 (1965), 552, 553

Harris, Steven L., Using Fundamental Principles of Commercial Law to Decide UCC Cases, 26 Loy. L.A. L. Rev. 637 (1993), 458

Hawkland, William D., The Proposed Amendments to Article 9 of the UCC-Part 5: Consignments and Equipment Leases, 77 Com. L.J. 108 (1972), 465

Hawkland, William D., Uniform Commercial Code Series (2003), 19

Heckman, Charles A., 'Reliance' or 'Common Honesty of Speech': The History and Interpreation of Section 2-313 of the Uniform Commercial Code, 38 Case W. Res. L. Rev. 1 (1987-88), 225

Henderson, James & Twerski, Aaron, Achieving Consensus on Defective Product Design, 83 Cornell L. Rev. 867 (1998), 616, 617

Henderson, James & Twerski, Aaron, What Europe, Japan and Other Countries Can Learn from the New American Restatement of Products Liability, 34 Tex. Int'l L.J. 1 (1999), 207

Herbert, Michael J., Unconscionability under Article 2A, 21 U. Tol. L. Rev. 715 (1990), 92

Hillinger, Ingrid M., The Article 2 Merchant Rules: Karl Llewellyn's Attempt to Achieve the Good, The True, The Beautiful in Commercial Law, 73 Geo. L.J. 1141 (1985), 81

Hillinger, Ingrid M., The Merchant of Section 2-314: Who Needs Him?, 34 Hastings L. Rev. 747 (1983), 204

Hillman, Robert A., et al, Common Law and Equity Under the Uniform Commercial Code (1985), 26

Hillman, Robert A., Contract Modification Under the Restatement (Second) of Contracts, 67 Cornell L. Rev. 680 (1982), 402

Hillman, Robert A., Debunking Some Myths about Unconscionability: A New Framework for U.C.C. Section 2-302, 67 Cornell L. Rev. 1 (1981), 93

Hillman, Robert A., Rolling Contracts, 71 Fordham L. Rev. 743 (2002), 127

Hillman, Robert A. & Rachlinski, Jeffrey J., Standard-Form Contracting in the Electronic Age, 77 N.Y.U. L. Rev. 429 (2002), 98

Holdych, Thomas J. & Mann, Bruce D., The Basis of the Bargain Requirement: A Market and Economic Based Analysis of Express Warranties–Getting What You Pay For and Paying For What You Get, 45 DePaul L. Rev. 781 (1996), 223

Honnold, John, Buyer's Right of Rejection, 97 U. Pa. L. Rev. 457 (1949), 49

Honnold, John, Uniform Law for International Sales Under the 1980 United Nations Convention (Kluwer, 3d ed. 1999), 22, 319, 356

Howard, Margaret, Allocation of Risk of Loss Under the UCC: A Transaactional Evaluation of Sections 2-509 and 2-510, 15 UCC L.J. 334 (1983), 422, 440

Huddleson, Edwin E., Old Wine in New Bottles: UCC Article 2A-Leases, 39 Ala. L. Rev. 615 (1988), 61

Jackson, Thomas H., "Anticipatory Repudiation" and the Temporal Element of Contract Law: An Economic Inquiry into Contract Damages in Cases of Prospective Nonperfomance, 31 Stan. L. Rev. 69 (1978), 513

Jackson, Thomas H. & Kronman, Anthony T., A Plea for the Financing Buyer, 85 Yale L.J. 1 (1975), 454

Jenkins, Sarah Howard, Preemption and Supplementation Under Revised 1-103: The Role of Common Law and Equity in the New UCC, 54 SMU L. Rev. 495 (2001), 26

Johnson, Jason S., The Statute of Frauds and Business Norms: A Testable Game-Theoretic Model, 144 U. Pa. L. Rev. 1859 (1996), 129

Johnston, Jason Scott, Default Rules/Mandatory Principles: A Game Theoretic Analysis of Good Faith and the Contract Modification Problem, 3 S. Cal. Interdisciplinary L.J. 335 (1993), 395

Jones, William K., Product Defects Causing Commercial Loss: The Ascendancy of Contract over Tort, 44 U. Miami L. Rev. 731 (1990), 204

Kamp, Allen R., Between-the-Wars Social Thought: Karl Llewellyn, Legal Realism, and the Uniform Commercial Code in Context, 59 Alb. L. Rev. 325 (1995), 7

Kamp, Allen R., Uptown Act: A History of the Uniform Commercial Code: 1940-49, 51 SMU L. Rev. 275 (1998), 7

Kastley, Amy H., Stock Equipment for the Bargain in Fact: Trade Usage, "Express Terms," and Consistency Under Section 1-205 of the Uniform Commercial Code, 64 N. Car.

L. Rev. 777 (1986), 188

Kathrein, Reed R., Class Actions in Year 2000 Defective Software and Hardware Litigation, 18 Rev. Litig. 487 (1999), 619

Kavass, Igor I., Uniform Commercial Code Research: A Brief Guide to the Sources, 88 Com. L.J. 547 (1983), 15

Keating, Daniel, Explaining the Battle of the Forms in Action, 98 Mich. L. Rev. 2678 (2000), 110

Keating, Daniel, Measuring Sales Law Against Sales Practice: A Reality Check, 17 J.L. & Com. 99 (1997), 78

Kelly, Elizabeth Slusser, Uniform Commercial Code Drafts (1984) (Vols. I & II), 15, 76, 225

Kennedy, Andrew J., Recent Developments: Nonconforming Goods Under the CISG–What's A Buyer to Do?, 16 Dick. J. Int'l L. 319 (1998), 240, 241

King, Jr., F. Carlton, UCC Section 2-510–A Rule Without Reason, 77 Com. L.J. 272 (1972), 440

Kincaid, Peter M. and Stuntz, William J., Note, Enforcing Waivers in Products Liability, 69 Va. L. Rev. 1111 (1983), 652

Kirst, Roger W., Usage of Trade and Course of Dealing: Subversion of the UCC Theory, 1977 U. Ill. L.F. 811, 187

Kniffen, Margaret H., A New Trend in Contract Interpretation: The Search for Reality as Opposed to Virtual Reality, 74 Or. L. Rev. 643 (1995), 200

Kraus, Jody S., Decoupling Sales Law from the Acceptance-Rejection Fulcrum, 104 Yale L.J. 129 (1994), 321

Kronman, Anthony T., Paternalism and the Law of Contracts, 92 Yale L.J. 763 (1983), 653

Kunz, Christina L., et al, Browse-Wrap Agreements: Validation of Implied Assent in Electronic Form Agreements, 59 Bus. Law. 279 (2003), 98

Kunz, Christina L., et al, Click-Through Agreements: Strategies for Avoiding Disputes on Validity of Assent, 57 Bus. Law. 401 (2001), 97

Kunz, Christina L., Frontispiece on Good Faith: A Functional Approach Within the UCC, 16 Wm. Mitch. L. Rev. 1105 (1990), 91

Kunz, Christina L., Motor Vehicle Ownership Disputes Involving Certificate-of-Title Acts and Article Two of the UCC, 39 Bus. Law. 1599 (1984), 477

Kwestel, Sidnay, Express Warranty as Contractual–The Need for a Clear Approach, 53 Mercer L. Rev. 557 (2002), 211

Lannetti, David W., Toward a Revised Definition of "Product" Under the Restatement (Third) of Torts: Product Liability, 55 Bus. Law. 799 (2000), 619

Leff, Todd & Pinto, Joseph V., Comparative Negligence in Strict Products Liability: The Courts Render the Final Judgment, 89 Dick. L. Rev. 915 (1985), 291

Lemley, Mark A., Beyond Preemption: The Law and Policy of Intellectual Property Licensing, 87 Calif. L. Rev. 111 (1999), 127

Linzer, Peter, The Comfort of Certainty: Plain Meaning and the Parol Evidence Rule, 71 Fordham L. Rev. 799 (2002), 200

Llewellyn, Karl N., On Warranty of Quality and Society, 36 Colum. L. Rev. 699 (1936), 204

Llewellyn, Karl N., Through Title to Contract and A Bit Beyond, 25 N.Y.U. L.Q. Rev. 158 (1938), 528

Llewellyn, Karl N., What Price Contract? An Essay in Perspective, 40 Yale L.J. 704 (1931), 129

Llewellyn, Karl N., Why a Commercial Code?, 22 Tenn. L. Rev. 779 (1953), 17

Louderbach, Charles M. & Jurika, Thomas W., Standards for Limiting the Tort of Bad Faith Breach of Contract, 16 U.S.F. L. Rev. 187 (1982), 580

Lousin, Ann, Cases on the Scope of Article 2, 46 Bus. Law. 1855 (1991), 71

Lylles, Keven D., Note UCC Section 2-725: A Statute Uncertain in Application and Effect, 46 Ohio St. U. L.J. 755 (1985), 671

Macaulay, Stewart, Non-Contractual Relations in Business: A Preliminary Study, 28 Am. Sociol. Rev. 55 (1963), 496

Macintosh, Kerry Lynn, Liberty, Trade, and the Uniform Commercial Code: When Should Default Rules Be Based on Business Practices?, 38 Wm. & Mary L. Rev. 1465 (1997), 78, 151

MacNeil, Ian R., Contracts: Adjustment of Long-term Economic Relations Under Classical, Neoclassical and Relational Contract Law, 72 Nw. U. L. Rev. 854 (1978), 154

MacNeil, Ian R., Relational Contract: What We Do and Do Not Know, 1985 Wis. L. Rev. 483, 147

Madison, Michael J., Legal-Ware: Contract and Copyright in the Digital Age, 67 Fordham L. Rev. 1025 (1998), 127

Mann, Bruce & Holdych, Thomas J., When Lemons are Better Than Lemonade: The Case Against Mandatory Used Car Warranties, 15 Yale L. & Pol'y Rev. 1 (1996), 666

Mann, Richard A. & Phillips, Michael J., Section 546(c) of the Bankruptcy Reform Act: An Imperfect Resolution of the Conflict Between the Reclaiming Seller and the Bankruptcy Trustee, 54 Am. Bankr. L.J. 239 (1980), 469

Maxeiner, James R., Standard-Terms Contracting in the Global Electronic Age: European Alternatives, 28 Yale J. Int'l L. 109 (2003), 126

McClain, Emlin, Implied Warranties in Sales, 7 Harv. L. Rev. 213 (1903), 204

McCormick, C., Evidence (5th ed. 1999 & 2003 Supp.), 201

McDonnell, Julian B., The Floating Lienor as Good Faith Purchaser, 50 S. Cal. L. Rev. 429 (1977), 469

McDonnell, Julian B., Purposive Interpretation of the Uniform Commercial Code: Some Implications for Jurisprudence, 126 U. Pa. L. Rev. 795 (1978), 19

McElhaney, James W., Expert Witnesses and the Federal Rules of Evidence, 28 Mercer L. Rev. 463 (1977), 201

McLaughlin, Gerald T., The Evolving Uniform Commercial Code: From Infancy to Maturity to Old Age, 26 Loy. L.A. L. Rev. 691 (1993), 8

McNichols, William J., Who Says That Strict Tort Disclaimers Can Never Be Effective? The Courts Disagree, 28 Okla. L. Rev. 494 (1975), 651

Mentschikoff, Soia, The Uniform Commercial Code: An Experiment in Democracy in Drafting, 36 A.B.A. J. 419 (1950), 7

Miller, Fred H., Realism Not Idealism in Uniform Laws - Observations from the Revision of the UCC, 39 S. Tex. L. Rev. 707 (1998), 8

Miller, Fred H., The Uniform Commercial Code: Will the Experiment Continue?, 43 Mercer L. Rev. 799 (1992), 8

Miller, Rachel & Kanter, Lawrence, Litigation Under Manguson-Moss: New Opportunities in Private Actions, 13 U.C.C. L.J. 10 (1980), 654

Mirzaian, Aristotle G., Y2K Who Cares? We Have Bigger Problems: Choice of Law in Electronic Contracts, 6 Rich. J.L. & Tech. 20 (1999-2000), 98

Monserud, Gary L., Judgment Against a Non-Breaching Seller: The Cost of Outrunning the Law to do Justice Under Section 2-608 of the Uniform Commercial Code, 70 N.D. L. Rev. 809 (1994), 352

Monserud, Gary L., The Privileges of Suretyship for Delegating Parties Under UCC Section 2-210 in Light of the New Restatement of Suretyship, 37 Wm. & Mary L. Rev. 1307 (1996), 492

Muris, Timothy J., Opportunistic Behavior and the Law of Contracts, 65 Minn. L. Rev. 521 (1981), 163

Murray, Daniel, E., Risk of Loss of Goods In Transit: A Comparison of the 1990 Incoterms with Terms from Other Voices, 23 U. Miami Inter-Am. L. Rev. 93 (1991), 429

Murray, Daniel E., Under the Spreading Analogy of Article 2 of the Uniform Commercial Code, 39 Fordham L. Rev. 447 (1971), 59

Murray, Jr., John E., The Article 2 Prism: The Underlying Philosophy of Article 2 of the Uniform Commercial Code, 21 Washburn L.J. 1 (1981), 96

Murray, Jr., John E., Products Liability vs. Warranty Claims: Untangling the Web, 3 J.L. & Com. 269 (1983), 613

Newell, Douglas K., Cleaning up UCC Section 2-209, 27 Idaho L. Rev. 487 (1990), 404

Nimmer, David, et al, The Metamorphosis of Contract into Expand, 87 Cal. L. Rev. 17 (1999), 72

Nimmer, Raymond T., Breaking Barriers: The Relation Between Contract and Intellectual Property Law, 13 Berkeley Tech. L.J. 827 (1998), 127

Nimmer, Raymond T., Electronic Contracting: Legal Issues, 14 J. Marshall J. Computer & Info. L. 211 (1996), 98

Nimmer, Raymond T., Images and Contract Law–What Law Applies to Transactions in Information, 36 Hous. L. Rev. 1 (1999), 72

Note, 111 U. Pa. L. Rev. 132 (1962), 109

Note, Requirements Contracts, "More or Less," Under the Uniform Commercial Code, 33

Rutgers L. Rev. 105 (1980), 163

Note, Requirements Contracts: Problems of Drafting and Construction, 78 Harv. L. Rev. 1212 (1965), 154

Note, Risk of Loss in Commercial Transactions: Efficiency Thrown Into the Breach, 65 Va. L. Rev. 557 (1979), 422

Nowicki, Phillip R., State Lemon Law Coverage Terms: Dissecting the Differences, 11 Loy. Consumer L. Rep. 39 (1999), 666

O'Hara, Erin Ann, The Jurisprudence and Politics of Forum-Selection Clauses, 3 Chi. J. Int. L. 301 (2003), 76

O'Rourke, Maureen A., Drawing the Boundary Between Copyright and Contract: Copyright Preemption of Software License Terms, 45 Duke L.J. 479 (1995), 127

O'Rourke, Maureen A., Progressing Towards a Uniform Commercial Code for Electronic Commerce or Racing Towards Nonuniformity, 14 Berkeley Tech. L.J. 635 (1999), 98

Patterson, Edwin, W., 1 N.Y. Law Revision Commission Report 56 (1955), 21

PEB Study Committee, An Appraisal of the March 1, 1990, Preliminary Report of the Uniform Commercial Code Article 2 Study Group, 16 Del. J. of Corp. L. 981 (1991), 9, 321

PEB Study Group, Uniform Commercial Code, Article 2 Executive Summary, 46 Bus. Law. 1869 (1991), 321

Perillo, Joseph M., UNIDROIT Principles of International Commercial Contracts: The Black Letter Text and a Review, 63 Fordham L. Rev. 281 (1994), 23

Peters, Ellen A., Remedies for Breach of Contracts Relating to the Sale of Goods Under the Uniform Commercial Code: A Roadmap for Article Two, 73 Yale L.J. 199 (1963), 46, 496, 524

Phelan, Richard J. & Falkof, Bradley B., Proving a Defect in a Commercial Products Liability Case, 24 Trial Law. Guide 10 (1980), 283

Piche, Catherine, The Convention on Contracts for the International Sale of Goods and the Uniform Commercial Code Remedies in Light of Remedial Principles Recognized Under U.S. Law: Are the Remedies of Granting Additional Time to the Defaulting Parties and of Reduction of Price Fair and Efficient Ones?, 28 N.C. J. Of Int'l Law and Comm. Reg. 519 (2003), 358

Pinzur, Robert S., Insurable Interest: A Search for Consistency, 46 Ins. Counsel J. 109 (1979), 437

Poe, Stephen L. & Conover, Teresa L., Pulling the Plug: The Use and Legality of Technology-Based Remedies by Vendors in Software Contracts, 50 Alb. L. Rev. 609 (1993), 466

Posner, Erice A., Economic Analysis of Contract Law After Three Decades: Success or Failure?, 112 Yale L.J. 829 (2003), 151

Posner, Eric A., The Parol Evidence Rule, the Plain Meaning Rule, and the Principles of Contract Interpretation, 146 U. Penn. L. Rev. 533 (1998), 200

Prince, Harry G., Overprotecting the Consumer? Section 2-607(3)(a) Notice of Breach in NonPrivity Contexts, 66 N.C. L. Rev. 107 (1987), 343

Prince, Harry G., Unconscionability in California: A Need for Restraint and Consistency, 46 Hastings L.J. 459 (1995), 93

Prosser, William L., The Assault Upon the Citadel (Strict Liability to the Consumer), 69 Yale L. J. 1099 (1960), 205

Prosser, William L., The Implied Warranty of Merchantable Quality, 27 Minn. L. Rev. 117 (1943), 204, 241, 242, 245, 617

Prosser, William L., Open Price in Contracts for the Sale of Goods, 16 Minn. L. Rev. 733 (1932), 167

Rabel, Ernst, The Nature of Warranty of Quality, 24 Tul. L. Rev. 273 (1950), 203

Rapson, Donald J., Deficiencies and Ambiguities in Lessors' Remedies Under Article 2A: Using Official Comments to Cure Problems in the Statute, 39 Ala. L. Rev. 875 (1988), 46

Reichman, J.H. and Franklin, Jonathan A., Privately Legislated Intellectual Property Rights: Reconciling Freedom of Contract with Public Good Uses of Information, 147 U. Pa. L. Rev. 875 (1999), 72

Reitz, Curtis R., Consumer Product Warranties Under Federal and State Laws (2d ed. 1987), 653

Reitz, Curtis R., Manufacturers' Warranties of Consumer Goods, 75 Wash. U. L.Q. 357 (1997), 301

Remington, Clark A., Llewellyn, Antiformalism and the Fear of Transcendental Nonsense: Codifying the Variability Rule in the Law of Sales, 44 Wayne L. Rev. 29 (1998), 25

Ribstein, Larry E., From Efficiency to Politics in Contractual Choice of Law, 37 Ga. L. Rev. 363 (2003), 76

Rice, David A., Product Quality Laws and the Economics of Federalism, 65 B.U. L. Rev. 1 (1985), 204, 654

Ritter, Jeffrey B., Software Transactions and Uniformity: Accommodating Codes Under the Code, 46 Bus. Law. 1825 (1991), 71

Robertson, Jr., R.J., The Right to Demand Adequate Assurance of Due Performance: UCC Section 2-609 and Restatement (Second) of Contracts Section 251, 38 Drake L. Rev. 305 (1988-89), 498

Rohner, Ralph J., Leasing Consumer Goods: The Spotlight Shifts to the Uniform Leases Act, 35 Conn. L. Rev. 647 (2003), 654

Rowley, Keith A., A Brief History of Anticipatory Repudiation in American Contract Law, 69 U. Cinn. L. Rev. 565 (2001), 513

Rusch, Linda J., A History and Perspective of Revised Article 2: The Never Ending Saga of a Search for Balance, 52 SMU L. Rev. 1683 (1999), 9

Rusch, Linda J., Products Liability Trapped by History: Our Choice of Rules Rules Our Choices, 76 Temple L. Rev. 739 (2003), 204, 207, 618

Rusch, Linda J., Property Concepts in the Revised U.C.C. Articles 2 and 9 Are Alive and Well, 54 SMU L. Rev. 947 (2001), 448

Russell, Irma S., Reinventing the Deal: A Sequential Approach to Analyzing Claims for Enforcement of Modified Sales Contract, 53 Fla. L. Rev. 49 (2001), 395

Schlesinger, Rudolph, The Uniform Commercial Code in the Light of Comparative Law, 1 Inter-Am. L. Rev. 11 (1959), 3

Schlesinger, Rudolph, The Uniform Commercial Code in the Light of Comparative Law, 1 N.Y. Law Review Commission (1955), 8

Schlinsog, Jr., Allen C., Advent Systems Ltd. v. Unisys Corp.: UCC Governs Software Transactions, 4 Software L.J. 611 (1991), 71

Schmedemann, Deborah A., Beyond Words: An Empirical Study of Context in Contract Creation, 55 S.C. L. Rev. 145 (2003), 189

Schnader, William A., A Short History of the Preparation and Enactment of the Uniform Commercial Code, 22 U. Miami L. Rev. 1 (1967), 77

Schoenfeld, Steven R., Commercial Law: The Finance Lease under Article 2A of the Uniform Commercial Code, 1989 Ann. Surv. Am. L. 565, 55, 274

Schroeder, Jeanne L., Death and Transfiguration: The Myth that the U.C.C. Killed "Property", 69 Temp. L. Rev. 1281 (1996), 422, 448

Schwartz, Allan & Wilde, Louis L., Imperfect Information in Markets for Contract Terms: The Examples of Warranties and Security Interests, 69 Va. L. Rev. 1387 (1983), 653

Scott, Robert E., The Case for Formalism in Relational Contract, 94 Nw. U. L. Rev. 847 (2000), 189

Scott, Robert E., The Case for Market Damages: Revisiting the Lost Profits Puzzle, 57 U. Chi. L. Rev. 1155 (1990), 496, 543

Scott, Robert E., The Rise and Fall of Article 2, 62 La. L. Rev. 1009 (2002), 9

Scott, Robert E., A Theory of Self-Enforcing Indefinite Agreements, 103 Colum. L. Rev. 1641 (2003), 149

Sebert, John A., Rejection, Revocation and Cure Under Article 2 of the Uniform Commercial Code: Some Modest Proposals, 84 Nw. U. L. Rev. 375 (1990), 321

Sebert, John A., Remedies Under Article Two of the Uniform Commercial Code: An Agenda for Review, 130 U. Pa. L. Rev. 360 (1981), 496, 543, 553, 554

Shanker, Morris G., A Reexamination of Prosser's Products Liability Crossword Game; The Strict or Stricter Liability of the Commercial Code Sales Warranty, 29 Case W. L. Rev. 550 (1979), 613

Shapo, Marshall S., Products at the Millennium: Traversing a Transverse Section, 53 S.C. L. Rev. 1030 (2002), 204

Shapo, Marshall S., In Search of the Law of Products Liability: The ALI Restatement Project, 48 Vand. L. Rev. 631 (1995), 265, 617

Shinn, Jr., Allen M., Liabilities Under Article 42 of the U.N. Convention on the International Sale of Goods, 2 Minn. J. Global Trade 115 (1993), 490

Silkworth, Stacy A., Quantity Variation in Open Quantity Cases, 51 U. Pitt. L. Rev. 235 (1991), 162

Silverstein, Eileen, On Recovery in Tort for Pure Economic Loss, 32 U. Mich. J. of L. Reform 403 (1999), 618

Skilton, Robert H., Some Comments on the Comments to the Uniform Commercial Code, 1966 Wis. L. Rev. 597, 16

Snyder, David V., Language and Formalities in Commercial Contracts: A Defense of Custom and Conduct, 54 SMU L. Rev. 627 (2001), 78, 198

Snyder, David V., The Law of Contract and the Concept of Change: Public and Private Attempts to Regulate Modification, Waiver, and Estoppel, 1999 Wis. L. Rev. 607, 404

Snyder, David V., Private Lawmaking, 64 Ohio St. J. L. 371 (2003), 8

Sobelsohn, David C., Comparing Fault, 60 Ind. L.J. 413 (1985), 291

Sorkin, Saul, Changing Concepts of Liability, 17 Forum 710 (1982), 438

Speidel, Richard E., The Characteristics and Challenges of Relational Contracts, 94 Nw. U. L. Rev. 823 (2000), 79, 178

Speidel, Richard E., Court-Imposed Price Adjustments Under Long-Term Supply Contracts, 76 Nw. U. L. Rev. 369 (1981), 382

Speidel, Richard E., Restatement Second: Omitted Terms and Contract Method, 67 Cornell L. Rev. 785 (1982), 77, 149

Speidel, Richard E., The Revision of UCC Article 2, Sales in Light of the United Nations Convention on Contracts for the International Sale of Goods, 16 Nw. J. Int'l L. & Bus. 165 (1995), 22

Speidel, Richard E., Warranty Theory, Economic Loss, and the Privity Requirement: Once More Into the Void, 67 B.U. L. Rev. 9 (1987), 204, 618

Stallworth, William L., An Analysis of Warranty Claims Instituted by Non-Privity Plaintiffs in Jurisdictions that Have Adopted Uniform Commercial Code Section 2-318 (Alternative A), 20 Pepp. L. Rev. 1215 (1993), 302

Stallworth, William L., An Analysis of Warranty Claims Instituted by Non-Privity Plaintiffs in Jurisdictions that Have Adopted Uniform Commercial Code Section 2-318 (Alternatives B & C), 27 Akron L. Rev. 197 (1993), 302

Stockton, John M., An Analysis of Insurable Interest Under Article Two of the Uniform Commercial Code, 17 Vand. L. Rev. 815 (1964), 437

Stoljar, Samuel J., Conditions, Warranties and Descriptions of Quality in Sale of Goods, Part I, 15 Mod. L. Rev. 425 (1952), 210

Sullivan, L., Anti-Trust (1977), 166

Summers, Robert S., General Equitable Principles Under Section 1-103 of the Uniform

Commercial Code, 72 Nw. U. L. Rev. 906 (1978), 26

Summers, Robert S., "Good Faith" in General Contract Law and the Sales Provisions of the Uniform Commercial Code, 54 Va. L. Rev. 195 (1968), 91

Swanson, Carol B., Unconscionable Quandary: UCC Article 2 and the Unconscionability Doctrine, 31 N.M. L. Rev. 359 (2001), 93

Symposium, Ending the "Battle of the Forms": A Symposium on the Revision of Section 2-207 of the Uniform Commercial Code, 49 Bus. Law. 1019 (1994), 124

Symposium, Intellectual Property and Contract Law in the Information Age: The Impact of Article 2B of the Uniform Commercial Code on the Future of Transactions in Information and Electronic Commerce, 13 Berkley Tech. L.J. 809 (1998), 72

Symposium, Origins and Evolution: Drafters Reflect Upon the Uniform Commercial Code, 43 Ohio St. L.J. 537 (1982), 7

Symposium, Perspectives on the Uniform Laws Revision Process, 52 Hastings L.J. 603 (2001), 8

Symposium, Relational Contract Theory: Unanswered Questions, 94 Nw. U. L. Rev. 737 (2000), 147

Symposium, Ten Years of the United Nations Sales Convention, 17 J.L. & Com. 181 (1998), 23

Tabac, William Louis, Battle for the Bulge: The Reclaiming Seller vs the Floating Lien Creditor, 2001 Colum. Bus. L. Rev. 509, 470

Tabac, William L., The Unbearable Lightness of Title Under the Uniform Commercial Code, 50 Md. L. Rev. 408 (1991), 448

Threedy, Debora L., Liquidated and Limited Damages and the Revision of Article 2: An Opportunity to Rethink the U.C.C.'s Treatment of Agreed Remedies, 27 Idaho L. Rev. 427 (1990/91), 638

Titus, Herbert D., Restatement (Second) of Torts Section 402A and the Uniform Commercial Code, 22 Stan. L. Rev. 713 (1970), 204

Tourek, Steven C., et al, Bucking the "Trend": The Uniform Commercial Code, The Economic Loss Doctrine, and the Common Law Causes of Action for Fraud and Misrepresentation, 84 Iowa L. Rev. 875 (1999), 618

Twining, William A., Karl Llewellyn and the Realist Movement (1973), 77

Ulen, Thomas S., The Efficiency of Specific Performance: Toward a Unified Theory of Contract Remedies, 83 Mich. L. Rev. 341 (1984), 453

Van Alstine, Michael P., Consensus, Dissensus, and Contractual Obligation Through the Prism of Uniform International Sales Law, 37 Va. J. Int'l L. 1 (1996), 108

Van Alstine, Michael P., Of Textualism, Party Autonomy, and Good Faith, 40 Wm. & Mary L. Rev. 1223 (1999), 91

Vargo, John F., The Emperor's New Clothes: The American Law Institute Adorns a "New

Cloth" for Section 402A Products Liability Design Defects–A Survey of the States Reveals a Different Weave, 26 U. Mem. L. Rev. 493 (1996), 265

Vogel, Joan, Squeezing Consumers: Lemon Laws, Consumer Warranties, and a Proposal for Reform, 1985 Ariz. St. L.J. 589, 654, 667

Vold, Lawrence, The Application of the Statute of Frauds Under the Uniform Sales Act, 15 Minn. L. Rev. 391 (1931), 129

Wade, John W., Tort Liability for Products Causing Physical Injury and Article 2 of the U.C.C., 48 Mo. L. Rev. 1 (1983), 613

Walt, Steven, Expectations, Loss Distribution and Commercial Impracticability, 24 Ind. L. Rev. 65 (1990), 363

Walt, Steven, For Specific Performance Under the United Nations Sales Convention, 26 Tex. Int'l L.J. 211 (1991), 454

Wardrop, Jr., Lawrence B., Prospective Inability in the Law of Contracts, 20 Minn. L. Rev. 380 (1936), 498

Weiskop, Nicholas R., Frustration of Contractual Purpose–Doctrine or Myth?, 70 St. John's L. Rev. 239 (1996), 363

Whelan, Stephen T., et al, Leases, 50 Bus. Law. 1481 (1995), 207

White, James, Contract Law in Modern Commercial Transactions, An Artifact of Twentieth Century Business Life?, 22 Washburn L.J. 1 (1982), 496

White, James J., Default Rules in Sales and the Myth of Contracting Out, 48 Loy. L. Rev. 53 (2002), 127

White, James J., Good Faith and the Cooperative Antagonist, 54 SMU L. Rev. 679 (2001), 91

White, James J., Reverberations from the Collision of Tort and Warranty, 53 S.C. L. Rev. 1067 (2002), 204

White, James & Summers, Robert, The Uniform Commercial Code (5th ed. 2000), 19, 163

Williams, Chris, Book Review, 97 Harv. L. Rev. 1495 (1984), 77

Williams, Chris, The Statute of Limitations, Prospective Warranties, and Problems of Interpretation in Article Two of the UCC, 52 Geo. Wash. L. Rev. 67 (1983), 671

Willis, Hugh E., The Statute of Frauds–A Legal Anachronism, 3 Ind. L.J. 427 (1928), 129

Williston, Samuel, Representation and Warranty in Sales–Heilbut v. Buckleton, 27 Harv. L. Rev. 1 (1913), 204, 242

Williston, Samuel, Sales (5th ed. 1994), 19, 211

Wiseman, Zipporah B., The Limits of Vision: Karl Llewellyn and the Merchant Rules, 100 Harv. L. Rev. 465 (1987), 77

Wladis, John D., Impracticability as Risk Allocation: The Effect of Changed Circumstances Upon Contract Obligations for the Sale of Goods, 22 Ga. L. Rev. 503 (1988), 363

Woodward, Jr., William J., Neoformalism in a Real World of Forms, 2001 Wis. L. Rev. 971 (2001), 189

Woodward, Jr., William J., Private Legislation in the United States–How the Uniform

Commercial Code Becomes Law, 72 Temp. L. Rev. 451 (1999), 8

Woodward, Jr., William J., "Sale" of Law and Forum and the Widening Gulf Between "Consumer" and "Nonconsumer" Contracts in the UCC, 75 Wash. U. L.Q. 243 (1997), 76

Zamir, Eyal, The Inverted Hierarchy of Contract Interpretation and Supplementation, 97 Colum. L. Rev. 1710 (1997), 198

Ziegel, Jacob S., The Seller's Liability for Defective Goods at Common Law, 12 McGill L.J. 183 (1966), 223

Zollers, Frances E., et al, Consumer Protection in the European Union: An Analysis of the Directive on the Sale of Consumer Goods and Associated Guarantees, 20 U. Penn. J. of Int'l Econ. L. 97 (1999), 667

Zollers, Frances E., et al, Looking Backward, Looking Forward: Reflections on Twenty Years of Product Liability Reform, 50 Syracuse L. Rev. 1019 (2000), 204

COMMERCIAL TRANSACTIONS

SALES, LEASES AND LICENSES

Second Edition

*

PART ONE:
NATURE AND SCOPE
OF COMMERCIAL CODES

CHAPTER ONE

THE NATURE AND SOURCES
OF COMMERCIAL LAW

SECTION 1.   INTRODUCTION TO COMMERCIAL LAW

A. Types of Commercial Transactions

Millions of "deals" occur each day in the United States and around the world. Many are between business people and many are between business people and consumers. These deals and their performance are the stuff of commercial and consumer life to which these materials are addressed.

The deals involved vary greatly. Many involve sales of goods or intangibles. Many consist of leasing arrangements. Many involve loans or extensions of credit, with or without "security interests" (interests that give a creditor priority rights in a specific asset of the debtor). Many involve the rendition of services by insurers, carriers, bailees and the like. Many involve the licensing of intellectual property rights. Many involve the use of notes, checks and other "negotiable instruments." These deals are the "stuff" of domestic and international markets.

The overwhelming majority of these deals go through without incident. But when something does go wrong, there may be occasion to resort to law and to legal processes. What kinds of law? What kinds of processes? The answers to these questions turn on the nature of the real world problems which generate the need for laws and legal processes in the first place. We will illustrate some of this commercial law by references to the Uniform Commercial Code (UCC), primarily Article 2 on Sales of Goods and Article 2A on Leases of Goods.

B. Functions of Commercial Law

Suppose, for example, that one party to an alleged deal simply denies that a deal was ever made. It says, in effect, that under the law no binding relationship came into being. To determine whether that argument is correct, we resort to what might be called *rules of validity.* These rules specify the requisites of a valid contract of sale, or of a valid security interest, and so on. The legal need is for *such rules,* and for them to be clear, definite, accessible, and ascertainable, in advance of deals. Rules specifying *how* to "make it legal" are fundamental. Without them, private ordering under law could not exist. One of the primary functions of bodies of commercial and consumer law is to facilitate and sanction private ordering and private autonomy. In our system there is, we think, positive value in affording individuals extensive power to give their deals the force of law. *How* they must do this is the province of rules of validation. For example, UCC Article 2, Part 2, contains some rules validating contracts for the sale of goods and UCC Article 9, Part 2 contains some rules for validating security agreements.

Parties to a transaction may have sought, in writing, to specify their wants and expectations in Durer-like detail, only to find, at a later point, that they disagree over the interpretation or construction of some part of their agreement. Here the specific legal need is for rational and just *rules of interpretation and construction.* Such rules guide courts; they facilitate counseling; they may also lead parties to settle their differences without resort to courts. Unfortunately, UCC Article 2 in particular and the UCC in general say little about how to resolve disputes over the meaning of language. UCC 2-202, 2A-202, 1-303 [former 1-205, 2-208, 2A-207].

Assume the parties have not planned out their deal in detail. At some later stage, something goes wrong or some question arises on which their written agreement or their general understanding, as the case may be, is wholly silent. For example, goods contracted for are destroyed by fire while in transit. Or a pledgee of goods pledged to secure a loan decides he would like to repledge these same goods to a third party. Or a borrower wants to know if he has the right to pay back a loan without penalty. Or a lessee of goods wants to know if she can sublease the goods. Here the legal need is for *substantive suppletive rules* (or "default" rules), rules which presuppose and supplement the incomplete private transaction with specific "terms." To be generally fair and just, such rules should be based upon the likely commercial or consumer understanding of such matters. For, insofar as there is a standard understanding, it is not unreasonable to feed it into the skeletal deal. *See* UCC Article 2, Part 3 (examples of default rules in sale of goods transaction).

A variation on the immediately preceding problem is this: In many deals, parties do not specify their expected performances in detail. Here the legal need is for rationally conceived suppletive rules which specify the substance of the deal.

In modern law, "implied warranties" are perhaps the best example. In many simple sales of goods nothing is ever said at the time of the deal about the standard to which the goods must conform. Such warranty or warranties are left to be supplied by law. *See* UCC 2-313 through 2-315, 2A-210, 2A-212 and 2A-213. The very existence of such suppletive law gives rise to a further distinctive kind of legal need: a need for *rules of disclaimer,* rules which specify *how* the parties can modify or exclude altogether what the suppletive law would otherwise supply. These rules must also be clear, definite, and ascertainable in advance of the agreement. *See* UCC 2-316, 2A-214 which specify how parties may by their agreement disclaim or modify implied warranties.

[margin note: 4. Rules of Disclaimer]

People being what they are, and society being what it is, some parties will try to take advantage of others, and some will not always know what is in their own best interest. For example, a consumer may enter an entirely lopsided and unfair deal. The "real world" thus generates the problem of whether the terms of such deals should be enforced. And the law must then face another specific kind of legal need, a need for *regulatory policing rules.* It has been suggested that the "core task" of commercial and consumer law is "to determine the relatively few rules which are not subject to change by agreement, the rules which are designed to stake out the necessary minimum area of protection for parties whose bargaining power is inferior."[*] Extensive needs for policing rules to regulate exchanges have only recently been recognized in our system. Such rules plainly invade the province of private autonomy and limit freedom of contract. So far as possible, parties should know in advance what agreements cannot be enforced. The UCC, however, is not a regulatory statute. Apart from the policy against unconscionable contracts or clauses, UCC 2-302 and 2A-108, or the duty of good faith in performing and enforcing a contract, UCC 1-304 [former 1-203], the parties must look elsewhere for regulatory law.

[margin note: 5. Regulatory Policing rules]

Akin to regulatory policing rules are rules which may be designated *third party protection rules.* Many consumer and commercial transactions, occurrences, and events impinge directly or indirectly on the interests of third parties not privy to the transaction at hand. Some occur fraudulently, as where a seller of goods in his possession sells the same goods to two different parties and then absconds. But other such transactions are not necessarily dishonest, as where a creditor establishes a preferred position *vis a vis* other creditors of the same debtor. Here the specific

[margin note: 6. Third-Party Protection rules.]

---

[*] *See* Rudolph Schlesinger, *The Uniform Commercial Code in the Light of Comparative Law,* 1 INTER-AM. L. REV. 11, 33 (1959).

legal need is for rules that protect, as far as possible, the interests of all concerned. For example, in the creditor situation, the law might require that any creditor seeking such a preferred position must give public notice of this fact so that interested third parties may act accordingly. Like policing rules, third party protection rules limit freedom of contract, for to be effective they must not be subject to variation by agreement of the parties. *See* UCC Article 9, Part 3, Subpart 2 (perfection rules).

Within the world of commerce, the activities of selling, buying, leasing, licensing, lending, and borrowing are ubiquitous, and they are often intertwined. Buyer-debtors are actually more common than general debtors. Seldom is a debtor a debtor of only one person. Moreover, in a typical year, a significant minority of debtors fall into financial difficulty. Assuming such a debtor does not have enough assets to pay all of his debts, which creditors are to receive what? The specific legal need generated by such problems is for *rules of priority,* rules which, in circumstances of scarcity, determine who gets what. Prospective lenders, as well as sellers selling on credit, often want to know in advance the bearing such rules could have on their situations. The primary source of priority rules in the UCC is Article 9, Part 3, Subpart 3.

Failure to pay a debt when due is but one kind (and perhaps the simplest kind) of failure of promised performance known to the law. Among others are non-delivery or nonconforming delivery of goods; failure of a carrier or a bank to obey agreed instructions from the seller or the buyer; misconduct of a warehouser, and so forth. Here, the specific legal need is for *suppletive remedial rules and procedures.* Of course, the parties themselves might agree in advance on remedies and on the steps to be taken to perfect rights to such remedies. But in most transactions, remedies and remedial procedures are left to be supplied by the law. *See* UCC Article 2, Part 7; Article 2A, Part 5; Article 9, Part 6. "Remedies" is used here in an appropriately broad sense to include all of the permissible responses to breach of a deal: abandonment, specific relief, and damages. "Procedures" is used here to include the various hoops to be jumped through to perfect rights to particular remedies. Thus the law might, with reason, require a disgruntled buyer to notify the seller immediately of any specific defects in goods he wishes to reject for nonconformity. Similarly, the law might specify a whole series of steps that a creditor should take in order to walk off with some asset of a debtor against the protests of other similarly unpaid creditors. A lessor may be limited in what actions she can take in the event of default under a lease. The law must provide remedial rules and procedures if "making a deal legal" is to have any meaning at all in that vast majority of transactions in which the parties, assuming business will go forward as usual, say nothing of such matters in their agreement. To be fair, and to further one of the fundamental purposes of our law, such rules and procedures must provide remedies that protect the general expectations of parties similarly situated in deals of that kind. UCC 1-305 [former 1-106]. What such expectations are is a fact to be approximated, if not ascertained, and then embodied in the relevant legal doctrines.

Rules of validity, rules of interpretation and construction, substantive suppletive rules, rules of disclaimer, policing rules, third party protection rules, priority rules, and suppletive remedial rules and procedures: these, and others, are the kinds of rules that a legal system must introduce, through code law or case law, to meet legal needs arising out of commercial and consumer activities. One or more of these kinds of rules, in turn, furthers one or more of the varied general aims of such law, whether it be statutory or judge-made: to minimize the occasions for disputes in the course of commercial and consumer dealings; to facilitate *private* ordering of human relations; to protect justified expectations; to protect individuals from various forms of over-reaching and from their own improvidence; to safeguard the interests of third parties; and more.

There is one further type of legal need that consumer and commercial life generates, one which cuts across most of the others identified here. This is the need for rules, principles, and processes capable of accommodating and governing the *ever changing varieties* of transaction patterns that occur in the real world of commerce and business. Change and variety are now, have been, and certainly will continue to be distinctively dominant themes in this field, especially because of the use of computers and other electronic devices to transfer information and to create contracts.

C. Role of the Commercial Lawyer

A commercial lawyer needs a well developed understanding of all of these various types of legal rules and how those rules operate in the context of a wide variety of transactions. Her responsibility to a client includes at least three perspectives. A commercial lawyer needs to learn how to approach issues from a transactional perspective, a litigation perspective, and a dispute settlement perspective. A transactional perspective considers how to accomplish creatively the contracting parties' objectives within the boundaries of the applicable legal rules. A litigation perspective looks at the potential issues that may arise over the terms or performance of a contract and seeks to anticipate how those issues may be resolved in litigation. A dispute settlement perspective looks at ways that anticipated or actual disputes can be settled without litigation, such as including an arbitration clause in the contract or agreement to mediation after the dispute has arisen. All three perspectives are needed in order to facilitate the transaction.

SECTION 2. THE UNIFORM COMMERCIAL CODE: HISTORY, STRUCTURE, AND PURPOSE

A. A Brief History of the Uniform Commercial Code

The Uniform Commercial Code (UCC) codifies the law applicable to certain personal property transactions, such as the sale or lease of goods. Unlike codes in the civil law tradition, it does not purport to cover all commercial or consumer transactions. The UCC can trace its origins to the codification movement in 19th century England. Under the posthumous influence of proponents such as Jeremy Bentham and John Austin, a codification movement first in England and then in the United States began in the late 19th century. Some of these early efforts at codification were in fields of commercial law. The British Bills of Exchange Act of 1882 was the first successful attempt to codify a major branch of English commercial law. This Act was followed in 1893 by the British Sale of Goods Act. M.D. Chalmers, the principal drafter of these two codes, was invited to address the convention of the American Bar Association in 1902 on the desirability of codifying commercial law. He closed his speech by noting the challenges posed to uniform law by our federal system of government and the difficulties of accessing relevant law and concluded that "the only possible remedy that I can see for this state of affairs is codification."[*]

At the time Chalmers spoke, the movement to codify particular branches of commercial law in the United States was already underway. In the 1890's the National Conference of Commissioners on Uniform State Laws (NCCUSL) had been formed, with representatives from each state many of whom were dedicated to the cause of uniform codification. In 1896, NCCUSL promulgated the Negotiable Instruments Law, a code governing the rights and liabilities of parties to checks, promissory notes, and other kinds of commercial paper. Ultimately, the "NIL" was adopted by all state legislatures. In 1906, NCCUSL presented the

---

[*] *See* M.D. Chalmers, *Codification of Mercantile Law*, 19 LAW Q. REV. 10, 18 (1903).

Uniform Sales Act for adoption and more than two-thirds of the states enacted it. With this Act, American law professors entered the codification arena, and have been central figures there ever since. Professor Samuel Williston of the Harvard Law School drafted the Uniform Sales Act on behalf of NCCUSL, and also the Uniform Warehouse Receipts Act, promulgated in 1906, and the Uniform Bills of Lading Act promulgated in 1909 both of which became law in all states. Later, Professor Karl Llewellyn of the Columbia Law School drafted the Uniform Trust Receipts Act, which NCCUSL promulgated in 1933. Thirty-two states adopted it. Another uniform commercial act, dealing with "conditional" sales, was drafted by Professor Bogert, but it met with success in only ten state legislatures.*

In 1940, the idea of a single comprehensive commercial code covering all the foregoing branches of commercial law was conceived and proposed to NCCUSL. The foregoing uniform acts had become outdated in two ways: changes had occurred in the patterns of commercial activity extant when these laws were enacted, and wholly new patterns had emerged giving rise to new kinds of legal needs. Moreover, even with the uniform acts most widely enacted, uniformity no longer existed, because the various state legislatures and judiciaries had added their own distinctive amendments and glosses.

The American Law Institute (ALI) joined with NCCUSL to co-sponsor the "Uniform Commercial Code" (UCC) project. Professor Karl Llewellyn, then still at Columbia Law School, became chief architect, and his wife, Soia Mentschikoff, his principal assistant (designated, respectively, "Chief Reporter" and "Associate Chief Reporter").** In 1951, the sponsors promulgated the UCC, and, with minor revisions, it was enacted in Pennsylvania in 1953, effective July 1, 1954. Between

---

*   See Allison Dunham, *A History of the National Conference of Commissioners on Uniform State Laws*, 30 LAW & CONTEMP. PROBS. 233 (1965).

**   Ms. Mentschikoff described the drafting process in Soia Mentschikoff, *The Uniform Commercial Code: An Experiment in Democracy in Drafting*, 36 A.B.A. J. 419 (1950). The drafting process is also discussed extensively in a symposium to which five drafters contributed. *See Symposium, Origins and Evolution: Drafters Reflect Upon the Uniform Commercial Code*, 43 OHIO ST. L.J. 537-584 (1982). At least one author has argued that the UCC was a product of its historical era and the result of an intensely political process. Allen R. Kamp, *Downtown Code: A History of the Uniform Commercial Code 1949-54*, 49 BUFF. L. REV. 359 (2001); Allen R. Kamp, *Uptown Act: A History of the Uniform Commercial Code: 1940-49*, 51 SMU L. REV.275 (1998); Allen R. Kamp, *Between-the-Wars Social Thought: Karl Llewellyn, Legal Realism, and the Uniform Commercial Code in Context*, 59 ALB. L. REV. 325 (1995).

1953 and 1955, the New York Law Revision Commission dropped all other work and made a thorough study of the UCC, recommending many changes in the official text. During the hearings there were, from time to time, rather sharp conflicts between academicians defending the UCC and practitioners attacking it.

In 1956, the Editorial Board of the UCC made recommendations for revision of the 1952 Official Text, many of which were based on criticisms made at the New York Law Revision Commission Hearings. In 1957, a revised Official Text was promulgated incorporating recommended changes. Further Official Texts, with minor changes, were promulgated in 1958 and 1962. By 1968, the UCC had been enacted by all but one state in the United States. A "Permanent Editorial Board" (PEB) was established by the sponsoring organizations primarily to consider the wisdom of proposed amendments to the UCC.[*]

The ALI and NCCUSL have not left the UCC alone. In 1972, the new "1972" Official Text of the UCC was promulgated. That text left nearly all of the 1962 Official Text intact, except for secured transactions governed by Article 9. Article 9 was overhauled in 1972 without altering its basic theory, structure and scope. In 1978, Article 8 on investment securities was revised.

In the late 1980's, NCCUSL and the ALI started an extensive UCC revision process. That process has not been without controversy,[**] with concerns expressed that this unique "private" law making process may not always produce rules that are "consonant with democratic values."[***] Certainly, the revision of UCC Articles 2 and 2A was subject to extensive lobbying and political compromise.

---

[*] The idea for the PEB was set forth in Rudolf B. Schlesinger, *The Uniform Commercial Code in the Light of Comparative Law,* 1 N.Y. LAW REVISION COMMISSION 87 (1955). The PEB has made various reports and prepared careful commentaries on disputed questions. *See PEB Commentaries on the Uniform Commercial Code,* some of which are reprinted in THOMSON/WEST, SELECTED COMMERCIAL STATUTES issued every year for classroom use.

[**] *See* Fred H. Miller, *The Uniform Commercial Code: Will the Experiment Continue?,* 43 MERCER L. REV. 799 (1992); *see also* Gerald T. McLaughlin, *The Evolving Uniform Commercial Code: From Infancy To Maturity To Old Age,* 26 LOY. L.A. L. REV. 691 (1993); Fred H. Miller, *Realism not Idealism in Uniform Laws–Observations from the Revision of the UCC,* 39 S. TEX. L. REV. 707 (1998); William J.Woodward Jr., *Private Legislation in the United States–How the Uniform Commercial Code Becomes Law,* 72 TEMP. L. REV. 451 (1999); Henry D. Gabriel, *The Revisions of the Uniform Commercial Code–Process and Politics,* 19 J. L. & COMM. 125 (1999); Symposium, *Perspectives on the Uniform Laws Revision Process,* 52 HASTINGS L. J. 603-701 (2001).

[***] *See* David V. Snyder, *Private Lawmaking,* 64 OHIO ST. L.J. 371, 448 (2003).

B. What Does the UCC Cover?

What follows is a brief description of each article and its history over the course of the last fifteen to twenty years.

Article 1: General Provisions. Article 1 contains definitions and general principles applicable to transactions governed by other articles of the UCC. UCC 1-102.   Article 1, therefore, is not a free-standing Article. If the substantive transaction is not "code covered," Article 1 does not apply. In 2001, both the ALI and NCCUSL approved a revised Article 1. To date, revised Article 1 has been enacted in five states. The remaining states have former Article 1. These materials will cite to revised Article 1 and to former Article 1.

Article 2: Sales. Article 2, which replaced the Uniform Sales Act, deals primarily with the formation, adjustment, construction, performance and enforcement of contracts for the sale of goods. Although Article 2 defines a sale as passing title to goods for a price, UCC 2-106(1), Article 2 rejects the concept of title as a problem solving device. Nevertheless, when title passes in contracts for the sale of goods is stated in UCC 2-401 and that section is still important in disputes over when a seller can pass better title to a buyer than it has, *see* UCC 2-403, and in disputes outside of Article 2, such as the scope of insurance policies and the incidence of state and local personal property taxation. All states but Louisiana have enacted Article 2.

In 1991, following a two year study by the PEB, a drafting committee was appointed to consider amendments to Article 2. A reprint and appraisal of the PEB Preliminary Report on the revision of Article 2 is printed in 16 DEL. J. CORP. L. 981-1325 (1991). The revision was very controversial.[*] In 2002, NCCUSL approved a final version of a series of amendments to Article 2 and in 2003, the ALI approved those same amendments. To date no states have enacted the 2003 amendments. These materials will address Article 2 both prior to and after the 2003 amendments.

Article 2A: Leases. Article 2A was originally promulgated in 1987 and amended in 1990. This article covers all leases of goods, but is primarily concerned with equipment and finance leasing. The organization, similar to Article 2, contains five parts: General Provisions, Formation and Construction, Effect of Lease

---

[*] Linda J. Rusch, *A History and Perspective of Revised Article 2: The Never Ending Saga of a Search for Balance*, 52 SMU L. REV. 1683 (1999); Robert E. Scott, *The Rise and Fall of Article 2*, 62 LA. L. REV. 1009 (2002).

Contract, Performance, and Default. The differences from Article 2 arise where special principles are needed to deal with the transfer of a property interest for a limited period of time (the lease) as opposed to the transfer of ownership from a seller to a buyer (the sale). Note that a "true" lease, as defined in UCC 1-203 [former 1-201(37)], is neither a secured transaction nor a sale. All states but Louisiana have enacted Article 2A (although South Dakota has not enacted the 1990 amendments).

In 1994, the Article 2A Drafting Committee was appointed and charged with considering the Article 2 revision to the extent those revisions made sense for leasing transactions. The Article 2A amendments were also approved in 2002 by NCCUSL and in 2003 by the ALI. To date no state has enacted the 2003 amendments to Article 2A. These materials will address Article 2A both prior to and after the 2003 amendments.

Uniform Computer Information Transactions Act (UCITA). During the revision process of Articles 2 and 2A, much attention was devoted to software licensing. The original concept was that Article 2 would have a hub of general contracts principles with spokes for contracts of different types. There would have been a spoke for sale of goods, a spoke for leases of goods, and a spoke for software licensing. This idea was abandoned as too cumbersome and the software licensing "spoke" was spun off into its own drafting committee to develop another article of the UCC, tentatively entitled UCC Article 2B, Software Licensing. Eventually, the ALI decided that Article 2B should not be an article in the UCC. NCCUSL reincarnated Article 2B as a separate freestanding proposed uniform act, the Uniform Computer Information Transactions Act (UCITA). To date UCITA has been enacted in two states. In 2002, in response to vocal criticism of UCITA, NCCUSL adopted amendments to UCITA. Neither state has enacted the 2002 amendments. UCITA is one set of rules that may be used to govern licenses of "computer information." These materials will refer to UCITA as amended in 2002. As we study the contract principles from Articles 2 and 2A, we will compare views of the positions taken in UCITA. The choices between competing contract paradigms is a useful method of exploring the policy arguments that underlie the black letter rules in the statutory text.

Article 3: Negotiable Instruments. Article 3, which was extensively revised in 1990, deals with the negotiability, negotiation, rights and liabilities of the parties to, and the enforcement and discharge of commercial paper, including drafts, checks, certificates of deposit and notes. It does not apply to documents of title, Article 7, or investment securities, Article 8, even though these may be negotiable and negotiated for value. When issued, a negotiable note or check becomes the tangible and legal embodiment of the underlying obligation of the parties. Article 3 is designed to maximize the certainty and minimize the costs when that instrument is transferred. Revised Article 3 has been enacted in all but two states, New York and South Carolina. A small set of amendments to Article 3 were adopted in 2002. To date, one state has enacted the 2002 amendments. References in the materials will be to Revised Article 3 as amended by the 2002 amendments.

Article 4: Bank Deposits and Collections. Article 4, which was revised in 1990, deals with checks and other demand instruments that are drawn on a bank and collected through the banking system. Article 4 covers the contractual relationship between the drawer and the payor bank, the relationship between the payee and the depositary bank, and the relationship among the banks in the collection process, including the responsibilities of the payor bank when a check is presented for payment. Article 4 governs Article 3 to the extent that there are conflicts, but in many cases Article 3 supplements Article 4. Every state except New York and South Carolina has enacted Revised Article 4. A small set of amendments to Article 4 were adopted in 2002. To date one state has enacted the 2002 amendments. References in these materials will be to Revised Article 4 as amended by the 2002 amendments.

Article 4's provisions are supplemented and in some cases superseded by federal regulations. For example, Federal Reserve Regulation J, 12 CFR Part 210, governs check collection relationships among federal reserve banks. Similarly, the Federal Expedited Funds Availability Act, 12 U.S.C. 4001 et seq., and its accompanying Regulation CC, 12 CFR Part 229, preempts Article 4 on questions of when deposited funds are available for withdrawal as a matter of right and some of Article 4 on the check return process after a check presented for payment has been dishonored.

Article 4A: Funds Transfers. New Article 4A was promulgated in 1989 and governs commercial payment orders directing the transfer of funds from one bank account to another. The transfer is initiated by a payment order issued by a customer to its bank and concluded when the beneficiary's bank accepts the payment order for the benefit of the beneficiary. The payment order is usually communicated over the Federal Reserve wire transfer network (Fedwire) or, in international transfers, the New York Clearing House Interbank Payments Systems (CHIPS). Money, however, is not transferred by wire. Once a payment order is accepted, bank accounts are adjusted and settlements are made under Federal Reserve regulations or other applicable agreements. Federal Reserve Regulation

J, 12 CFR Part 210, governs payment orders through Fedwire. Article 4A does not govern transactions in which any part of the funds transfer is governed by the federal Electronic Fund Transfer Act, 15 U.S.C. 1693 et seq. (EFTA), and its implementing Regulation E, 12 CFR Part 205. UCC 4A-108. The EFTA and Regulation E govern many consumer electronic fund transfers. Article 4A has been enacted in every state.

Article 5: Letters of Credit. In a typical letter of credit transaction, a bank, at the buyer's request, issues a "letter" to the seller, providing that the bank will, under certain conditions, honor drafts drawn by the seller on the bank for payment of the purchase price. Article 5 governs this transaction and others, such as "standby" letters of credit, where a bank has agreed to pay if specified conditions are satisfied. In many instances, the parties agree that the letter of credit will be governed by the Uniform Customs and Practices (UCP) 500 or International Standby Practices (ISP) 98, both promulgated by the International Chamber of Commerce. Article 5 allows the parties to choose non-Article 5 principles. Article 5 was revised in 1995 in part to resolve the conflict between the provisions of Article 5 and the UCP. Revised Article 5 has been enacted in every state except Wisconsin. References in these materials will be to Revised Article 5.

Article 6: Bulk Sales. Article 6 deals with bulk transfers by a seller and, as such, emphasizes protection of the transferor's unsecured creditors. In light of strong criticism, NCCUSL and the ALI recommended that Article 6 be repealed and replaced, if at all, by a Revised Article 6. To date, 42 states have repealed Article 6 and four states have enacted the revised version.

Article 7: Documents of Title. Article 7 applies both to warehouse receipts and bills of lading, two types of documents of title. These documents were formerly governed by the Uniform Warehouse Receipts Act and the Uniform Bills of Lading Act. Federal law plays a role in governing documents of title through the United States Warehouse Act (codified at 7 U.S.C. 241 et seq.) and the Carriage of Goods by Sea Act (codified at 46 U.S.C. App. 1300 et seq.), among others. In 2000, a drafting committee to revise Article 7 was appointed and in 2003, the revision was approved. To date, eight states have enacted Revised Article 7. These materials will refer both to former Article 7 and Revised Article 7.

Article 8: Investment Securities. Article 8, often called the "negotiable instruments" law for investment securities, endows certain bonds, stocks and other securities with attributes of negotiability and defines the rights and liabilities of issuers, transferors, and transferees. Article 8, however, does not supersede state or federal regulatory laws governing the issuance of securities. The 1978 Official

Text revised Article 8 to cover more explicitly uncertificated investment securities. In attempting to keep abreast of new technology, Article 8 was revised again in 1994. The 1994 revision has been enacted in all states. References in the text will be to the 1994 revision of Article 8.

Article 9: Secured Transactions. Article 9 deals with the creation, perfection, priority and enforcement of security interests in personal property. It is the most innovative Article in that it substitutes a unitary security device for the plethora of security devices previously used. Terms such as "mortgagee," "pledgee," "conditional sale," and "trust receipt" do not appear in Article 9. Instead, its unitary security device is formulated in terms of four basic concepts: "secured party," "debtor," "collateral," and "security interest." Article 9 was revised for the 1972 Official Text. In 1998, a complete revision of Article 9 was approved and by 2001, every state had enacted the Revised Article 9. These materials will reference Revised Article 9.

The foregoing, then, represents the general structure of the UCC and demonstrates that its scope is broad. In terms of subject-matter, it applies to a wide range of transactions. There is not, in the UCC, a single "scope" provision which defines the *subject matter* to which the *entire* UCC applies. Instead, the UCC is divided into several articles as described above. The precise scope of each article must usually be determined by examining not merely a specific "scope" provision within the article (if there is one) but other provisions as well, some of which are definitional in nature. There is no general *de minimus* limitation on the UCC's application. Thus, for example, Article 2 would apply to the sale of a fifteen-cent hamburger. *See* UCC 2-314. At this point, the student should become familiar with the basic "scope" provisions of Articles 1 and 2. While many of the articles of the UCC can, in relation to some kinds of transactions, apply separately and alone, frequently provisions from more than one article will be applicable to the transaction at hand. The UCC recognizes the possibilities of conflict between Articles, and includes provisions governing such possibilities. *See, e.g.,* UCC 2-102, 2-108, 3-102, 4-102(a), 8-103(d), 9-109 and 9-110.

Each of the various revisions and amendments described above come complete with their own transition provisions which will determine whether the article as revised or amended will apply to transactions entered into before the effective date of the act. Careful attention to these transition provisions is critical to determining the parties' rights and obligations under the UCC.

C. What Transactions Does This Book Cover?

This book deals with contracts to transfer some interest in personal property. Transactions that transfer interests in goods can be sales, leases, or security agreements. Transactions that transfer limited rights in intellectual property are generally called licenses. As you have seen, sales of goods are governed by Article 2 of the UCC and leases of goods are governed by Article 2A of the UCC. Transactions which grant security interests in personal property are governed by Article 9 of the UCC. Licenses of intellectual property are covered by a mixture of state and federal law. UCITA proposes to cover licenses of computer information. Transfers of interests in investment property and financial assets are covered in part by Article 8 of the UCC.

To a lesser extent, the materials treat how the obligation to pay the price for the interest transferred is satisfied. Depending upon the method selected, payment is governed by Articles 3, 4, (payment by check), 4A (funds transfers), or 5 (letters of credit) of the UCC. These materials do not cover credit instruments, such as promissory notes, or secured transactions under Article 9, and provide limited coverage of payments by commercial paper.

The materials may be viewed, in part, as a kind of advanced course in contracts. Contract necessarily undergirds nearly the whole of the law school curriculum; we do not apologize for its reappearance here. Indeed, our own classroom experience tells us that a great many students would profit from an exact repetition of their first-year contracts course! But the materials we offer here will duplicate few of your first-year experiences. These materials will treat a few contracts topics to which you were exposed in your first year, but generally in greater depth or from a quite different angle. Further, we will take you into new and distinctive areas of advanced contracts including documents of title and commercial paper. In addition, here you will encounter far more regulatory law than is true in first-year contracts courses. As we shall see, in some branches of our subject there is a continuing tension between freedom of contract and regulatory law, although this tension has been reduced by recent trends in deregulation and privatization. Finally, and perhaps most important, the materials that follow afford students opportunities to develop skills in working with complex statutory schemes far beyond anything possible in the first year contracts course. We are now in the Age of the Statute.

D. Interpreting the UCC: Some Notes on Methodology

Using the UCC to help structure a transaction or to consider issues that may arise in litigation requires careful attention and has several recurring challenges.

First, you must identify the issue(s) posed by the dispute and find the statutory language that should be applied. Because the UCC is an integrated and interrelated body of law, that language may be found in more than one section of the UCC. For example, in UCC 2-205, there is a list of statutory cross-references after the comments. They must be consulted, but remember the list may not be exhaustive.

Second, the UCC includes more than the usual quota of definitions. Consider, for example, the first *line* of UCC 2-205. Some of the twenty-nine words in the first clause are defined in other provisions of the UCC and some are not. Which ones are defined in either Article 2 or Article 1? How is the researcher to know which words are defined and which are not? Look at the Definitional Cross References after the Comments. They purport to be exhaustive, but, as will be seen, they are not.

Third, UCC 1-103(a) [former UCC 1-102(1), (2)] states that the UCC "must be liberally construed and applied to promote its underlying purposes and policies which are: (1) to simplify, clarify, and modernize the law governing commercial transactions; (2) to permit the continued expansion of commercial practices through custom, usage, and agreement of the parties; and (3) to make uniform the law among the various jurisdictions." This direction may aid the courts in reaching a particular interpretation of statutory language.[*]

Fourth, there are several kinds of "legislative history" relevant to interpreting the UCC, each posing its own special problems. The four types of such history are: (1) Official Comments, (2) prior versions of the UCC, (3) legislative hearings and reports made prior to enactment in specific states, and (4) books and articles by the UCC drafters.[**]

Official Comments. As promulgated by the ALI and NCCUL, the Official

---

[*] *See e.g., Advent Systems Ltd. v. Unisys Corp.*, 925 F.2d 670 (3rd Cir. 1991) (contract to sell software contained on disk within scope of Article 2).

[**] *See generally* Robert Braucher, *The Legislative History of the Uniform Commercial Code,* 58 COLUM. L. REV. 798 (1958). An extensive treatment of the major research sources on the UCC is Igor I. Kavass, *Uniform Commercial Code Research: A Brief Guide to the Sources,* 88 COM. L.J. 547 (1983). *See also* ELIZABETH SLUSSER KELLY, UNIFORM COMMERCIAL CODE DRAFTS (1984), Vols. I & II.

Text of the UCC appears with comments on each section. State legislators, however, enact only the Official Text (with whatever amendments they make). In practice, the lawyer must consult the statute as enacted by the particular state, not the official text, to determine the law that applies to a given transaction. A state may have enacted non-uniform amendments to the text of the UCC. In many states the UCC with comments (and local annotations) is available to the bar through private publishing houses. A lawyer must bear in mind, however, that the Official Comments are not authoritative and do not cover a state's changes to the Official Text.

The Comment to each section usually contains four parts. The first, entitled "Prior Uniform Statutory Provision," lists provisions of prior Uniform Acts displaced by the section. The second part, designated "Changes," indicates the difference, if any, between the superseded law and the Official Text. The third part, called "Purposes of Changes" or "Purposes of Changes and New Matter," explains and in some instances illustrates the purposes of the particular Official Text. The fourth part, "Cross References," lists related UCC provisions. A list of definitional cross references appears in the last part.

The Official Comments do not stand in the same relation to the Official Text as true legislative history typically stands to the language of ordinary statutes. The Comments, or some of them, differ from such history in several ways. First, the Comments were not always laid before the enacting legislators when the legislature adopted the UCC. Some of the Comments were not yet written when the sections they comment on were enacted into law in some states. Some of the existing Comments appear to have been addressed to earlier drafts of sections of the UCC different from the sections later enacted into law. In some important parts of the UCC, the drafter of the Comments was not the same as the drafter of the section commented on.[*]

Still, the Comments have influenced many judicial decisions and will certainly continue to do so.[**] That they are not entitled to exactly the same weight as true legislative history may, therefore, be unimportant. But it is important to appreciate the special hazards and pitfalls in the use of the Comments. A detailed appreciation of these must await immersion in the processes of problem solving that lies ahead

---

[*] *See generally* Robert H. Skilton, *Some Comments on the Comments to the Uniform Commercial Code,* 1966 WIS. L. REV. 597.

[**] *See* Sean M. Hannaway, Note, *The Jurisprudence and Judicial Treatment of the Comments to the Uniform Commercial Code,* 75 CORNELL L. REV. 962 (1990).

in this book. For now, a general survey of the most common hazards and pitfalls must do.

Perhaps the principal hazard in using the Comments (apart from the inexhaustiveness of their cross references) is that they sometimes add to or vary the UCC language. Some insight into why this is so is revealed in the following passage from a speech made by the chief drafter of the UCC, Karl N. Llewellyn, who said: "I am ashamed of it in some ways; there are so many pieces that I could make a little better, there are so many beautiful ideas I tried to get in that would have been good for the law, but I was voted down * * * [W]hen we weren't allowed to put in where we wanted to go * * *, we at least got the thing set up so that we are allowed to state in accompanying comments where the particular sections are trying to go."[*]

The Comments are both expansive and restrictive in nature. Their expansiveness frequently takes the form of explicit rejection of negative implications from the text of the section. In view of such Comments, the maxim *expressio unius exclusio alterius est* (the expression of one thing is the exclusion of the other) loses some of its force. (See, for an example, the Comments to former 2-318.) On the restrictiveness of Comments, one drafter remarked that, "[i]t would not be difficult to cite examples where the draftsman has wisely left a breathing space, so to say, in the text to allow a free case-law development and then come back in the Comment to nail the coffin lid down tightly."[**] Of course, if the Comments are not *law* then perhaps the lid is not so tight as all that.

Earlier Versions of the UCC. We turn, now, to earlier versions of the UCC as a distinctive source of guidance and mis-guidance in resolving problems of interpretation and construction. The lawyer should know of the existence of such earlier drafts.[***]

---

[*] Karl N. Llewellyn, *Why A Commercial Code?*, 22 TENN. L. REV. 779, 782, 784 (1953).

[**] Grant Gilmore, *On the Difficulties of Codifying Commercial Law,* 57 YALE L. J. 1341, 1355 (1948).

[***] The main prior drafts are: 1945 Drafts and Redrafts of Parts of the Proposed Code (Unpublished); 1949 Proposed Draft with Comments; 1950 Proposed Final Draft with Comments; 1951 Final Text with Comments; Amendments in May, 1951; Amendments in September, 1951; 1952 Official Text with Comments; 1953 Changes Recommended by a Meeting of the Enlarged Editorial Board, Part A, Part B; 1956 Recommendations of the Editorial Board; 1957 Official Text with Comments; Supplement to the 1957 Official Edition

(continued...)

Inferences based on changes in the language of successive revisions of UCC sections are inherently unreliable. They are all the more unreliable because "frequently matters have been omitted as being implicit without statement and language has been changed or added solely for clarity." This quote comes from the comment to a section in the 1952 text of the UCC which read: "Prior drafts of text and comments may not be used to ascertain legislative intent." This section itself was eventually deleted from the Official Text of the UCC. It should have been left in.[*]

Legislative History of Enactment in Particular State. Another type of relevant material in resolving problems of UCC interpretation and construction consists of legislative hearings and official reports made by agencies of enacting states. These form the more immediate background of UCC enactment. Their status is somewhat uncertain in regard to the UCC, for it includes its own "legislative" history in the form of Comments. In the face of conflict, which is to control? For an excellent example, *see Horn Waterproofing Corp. v. Bushwick Iron & Steel Co.,* 488 N.E.2d 56 (N.Y. 2985), where the court, in holding that the original version of UCC 1-207 [now UCC 1-308] displaced the common law rules of accord and satisfaction, relied in part, on the conclusion of the New York Commission on Uniform State Laws as reported to the legislature.

Books and Other Commentary. A further type of material that has figured in UCC interpretation and construction consists of books and articles and

---

[***] (...continued)
of the Code; 1958 Official Text with Comments; 1962 Amendments to the Uniform Commercial Code, Permanent Editorial Board for the UCC, Report 1; 1962 Official Text with Comments; 1965 Report No. 2 of the Permanent Editorial Board for the Uniform Commercial Code; 1966 Report No. 3 of the Permanent Editorial Board for the Uniform Commercial Code; 1971 Review Committee for Article Nine, Final Report; 1972 Official Text with Comments; 1978 Official Text with Comments; 1987 Official Text with Comments; 1988 Official Text with Comments; 1990 Official Text with Comments; 1995 Official Text with Comments; 1998 Official Text with Comments; 2000 Official Text with Comments; 2002 Official Text with Comments; 2004 Official Text with Comments.

[*] For a view that the legislative history is critical to interpretation of the UCC, *see* John M. Breen, *Statutory Interpretation and the Lessons of Llewellyn*, 33 LOY. L.A. L. REV. 263 (2000). Access to prior versions of uniform acts as they go through a revision process is now facilitated by the internet. For example, earlier drafts of Article 2 as it went through the decades-long revision provision can be accessed through http://www.law.upenn.edu/bll/ulc/ulc_frame.htm. Final and close to final versions of the revised UCC articles may be obtained from the ALI or are available in commercially printed statutory compilations.

memoranda written by those who participated in drafting the UCC. The outstanding instance to appear to date is a two volume treatise: GRANT GILMORE, SECURITY INTERESTS IN PERSONAL PROPERTY (1965). In a footnote at p. 289 of the first volume of this treatise, Professor Gilmore confesses that he had a large hand in drafting Article 9 of the Code. His treatise has been justly acclaimed in reviews.

John Locke might have said that Professor Gilmore's treatise has a natural and inalienable right to be quoted and cited on any and all Article 9 problems. Actually such is not without parallel. After the Uniform Sales Act, promulgated in 1906, was widely enacted, its draftsman, Professor Samuel Williston, published a treatise, WILLISTON ON SALES, which explained what the Act was all about. Just as Williston's treatise influenced the law, so has Gilmore's.

Reliance by courts on academic commentary about the UCC has not been limited to commentary by those "present at the creation." Almost every dispute that reaches an appellate court is accompanied by citations to various treatises and law review articles expressing opinions on the issue at hand.[*]

This interpretation process does not always produce a satisfactory result. There are frequently questions that have not been resolved in your state or by the courts in other states. In these cases, you should look for a tie-breaker, a structuring policy that a court can resort to solve the issue. This policy might be found in the policies stated in UCC 1-103 [former 1-102] or those immanent in contemporary views of social welfare or justice.[**]

---

[*] For example, lawyers and judges regularly resort to the main treatise on the UCC, J. WHITE AND R. SUMMERS, THE UNIFORM COMMERCIAL CODE (5th ed. 2000), which will be cited as "White and Summers." Another fine place to look for analysis of UCC provisions is the loose leaf treatise prepared by William D. Hawkland, entitled UNIFORM COMMERCIAL CODE SERIES (2003).

[**] See Bruce W. Frier, *Interpreting Codes*, 89 MICH. L. REV. 2201 (1991) (suggesting such policies may be established by induction from a group of sections or a particular article of the UCC itself). For a sampling of the rich literature on statutory interpretation, you may wish to consult, John M. Breen, *Statutory Interpretation and the Lessons of Llewllyn*, 33 LOY. L.A. L. REV. 263 (2000) and Julian B. McDonnell, *Purposive Interpretation of the Uniform Commercial Code: Some Implications for Jurisprudence*, 126 U. PA. L. REV. 795 (1978). *See also* John L. Gedid, *U.C.C. Methodology: Taking a Realistic Look at the Code*, 29 WM. & MARY L. REV. 341 (1988); Peter A. Alces & David Frisch, *Commenting on "Purpose" in the Uniform Commercial Code*, 58 OHIO ST. L. J. 419 (1997).

SECTION 3. COMMERCIAL LAW NOT IN THE UNIFORM COMMERCIAL CODE

Despite its seemingly wide sweep, the UCC is far from comprehensive. There are some transactions it does not govern at all, and there are many aspects of many transactions to which its provisions might apply but, for various reasons, will not.

First and at the fore, the parties can generally make their own "law." They do so expressly through contract, implicitly through a course of dealing, and collectively through custom and resultant business understanding. By their own agreement, then, the parties to a commercial deal can vary the effect of many of the provisions of the UCC. *See* UCC 1-302 [former 1-102(3), (4)]. We will return to this topic in the last section of this chapter.

Second, the UCC by its own terms does not purport to control many types of transactions that can fairly be called commercial. For example, it does not apply to sales of commercial realty or to security interests therein. It does not apply to the formation, performance, and enforcement of insurance contracts. It does not apply to suretyship transactions (except where a surety is a party to a negotiable instrument or involved in a secured transaction). It does not encompass the law of bankruptcy. It does not govern legal tender.

Third, the UCC does not even purport to govern exhaustively all aspects of the transactions to which its provisions do apply. Many of its provisions obviously can come into play only by virtue of some key event, *e.g.*, "default," which may be defined by the terms of the agreement between the parties. *See, e.g.*, UCC 9-601. Furthermore, resort to supplemental principles of law outside the UCC will often be necessary. *See generally* UCC 1-103. Consider the following examples:

•   To apply the provisions on authorized and unauthorized signatures in Article 3 (UCC 3-402 and 3-403), local agency principles must be considered.

•   To determine what title a "transferor" has under UCC 2-403, it is essential to refer to non-UCC law.

•   The "grounds" of impossibility and frustration as a defense to the breach of a contract of sale are not exhaustively stated in the UCC. *See* UCC 2-613, 2-614, and 2-615. Presumably additional grounds recognized in "general contract law" can be invoked.

•   In addition, the UCC has its own "gaps"–situations arising within the framework of the UCC on specific aspects of which the UCC is altogether silent. We will return to this topic in the last section of this chapter.

Fourth, there are state statutes, most of which are regulatory in nature, which either supplement or supersede UCC provisions altogether. *See* UCC 2-102, 2-108, 9-201 for references to the possible existence of such statutes. Usury laws and so-called "Retail Installment Sales Acts" are outstanding examples. It is appropriate at this point to emphasize that the UCC does *not,* in terms, concern itself with the general problems of the *consumer* as consumer.

Fifth, the Uniform Commercial Code is *state* law. This means that any valid and conflicting federal commercial law supersedes it. Thus, for example, there are the Federal Consumer Protection Act (codified at 15 U.S.C. 1601 et seq.) and the Magnuson-Moss Warranty Act (codified at 15 U.S.C. 2301 et seq.). The Federal Bills of Lading Act (sometimes called the Pomerene Act) (codified at 49 U.S.C. 80101 et seq.) rather than Article 7 of the Code, applies to all interstate bills of lading transactions. In addition, one must consider the preemptive effect of the Convention on the International Sale of Goods (CISG), effective in the United States on January 1, 1988, and the Expedited Funds Availability Act, 12 U.S.C. 4001-4010 and its implementing Federal Regulation CC, 12 CFR Part 229.

Sixth, there is a growing body of federal regulatory law that supplements commercial law at many points. For example, the federal Food, Drug, and Cosmetic Act (codified at 21 U.S.C. 301 et seq.) imposes controls on the quality of goods sold and on the ways they are marketed. The Robinson-Patman Act (codified at 15 U.S.C. 13a, 13b and 21a) operates to regulate the price of some goods. Federal statutes govern the creation of security interests in some types of collateral. *See, e.g.*, the Ship Mortgage Act (codified at 46 U.S.C. 31321 et. seq.). *See* UCC 9-109(c)(1) and Comment 8.

Seventh, this survey of non-Code sources of commercial law would not be complete without some reference to procedural law. Generally, commercial claims are litigated in accordance with the procedures applicable in any ordinary case. There are, however, a few procedural doctrines that have a distinctively commercial flavor. Some of these are incorporated in the Code, although it generally does not purport to cover procedural law. *See, e.g.*, the "vouching in" provisions of UCC 2-607(5).

Finally, there are practices and attitudes of legal officials and of people involved in commerce which cannot really be captured in the language of any Code but which, nonetheless, have an inevitable impact on legal evolution. Professor Edwin W. Patterson has said of these that they seem "to be a part of the societal matrix, a kind of semantic and narrative substratum of law and other articulate forms of social control." 1 N.Y. LAW REVISION COMMISSION REPORT 56 (1955) (footnote omitted).

SECTION 4. INTERNATIONAL COMMERCIAL LAW

The United Nations Convention on Contracts for the International Sale of Goods (CISG) became effective in the United States on January 1, 1988. At present, 62 countries have ratified the Convention, including our NAFTA trading partners, Canada (1992) and Mexico (1989). England and Japan, however, have not ratified the CISG.*

In the United States, the CISG is a self-executing treaty with the preemptive force of federal law. Unless otherwise agreed, the CISG applies to "contracts of sale of goods between parties whose places of business are in different States * * * when the States are Contracting States." CISG Art. 1(a). Thus, the CISG, and not Article 2, would apply when an Illinois corporation buys goods from a Canadian seller or sells goods to a Mexican buyer. When applicable, the CISG preempts Article 2, Sales of the UCC. When inapplicable, however, the CISG does not displace Article 2. Both operate within their own sphere, creating horizontal bands of uniformity for the domestic and the international contract for the sale of goods.**

These materials will refer to and discuss the CISG where relevant. Remember, the scope of the CISG is narrower than Article 2 (for example, the CISG does not cover consumer contracts or claims for personal injury, CISG Art. 3) and the content of the Convention, in many places, differs from Article 2. For example, the CISG does not have a statute of frauds and makes no provision for the "battle of the forms."***

---

* The leading treatise on the CISG is JOHN HONNOLD, UNIFORM LAW FOR INTERNATIONAL SALES UNDER THE 1980 UNITED NATIONS CONVENTION (Kluwer, 3rd ed., 1999).

** *See* Franco Ferrari, *The Relationship Between the UCC and CISG and the Construction of Uniform Law*, 29 LOY. L.A. L. REV. 1021 (1996) (arguing that the two different schemes have different substantive principles and that the CISG should not be interpreted to have the same meaning as the Article 2 counterpart); Henry D. Gabriel, *The Inapplicability of the United Nations Convention on the International Sale of Goods as a Model for the Revision of Article Two of the Uniform Commercial Code*, 72 TUL. L. REV. 1995 (1998) (substantive and structural differences between Article 2 and the CISG leads to rejection of CISG principles in Article 2 revision). For an example of a court considering whether certain legal or equitable principles are preempted by the CISG, *see Geneva Pharmaceuticals Technology Corp. v. Barr Laboratories, Inc.*, 201 F. Supp. 2d 236 (S.D.N.Y. 2002) (promissory estoppel as alleged in case not preempted by the CISG even though the CISG was governing law).

*** *See* Richard E. Speidel, *The Revision of UCC Article 2, Sales in Light of the United*
(continued...)

The CISG has not been revised since 1980 and there is no mechanism in place to update or to keep the treaty current.[*] This explains, in part, the development and promulgation in 1994 of the UNIDROIT Principles of International Commercial Contracts.[**] The Principles, however, are not the law anywhere. They resemble a restatement of international contract law. Nevertheless, they present an attractive alternative to the CISG. For example, commercial parties in the United States and Mexico can exclude the operation of the CISG by agreement, *see* CISG Art. 6, and contract for the UNIDROIT Principles as the governing law. Similarly, commercial parties who agree to arbitrate may adopt the Principles as the law to govern the arbitration. UNIDROIT is working on a second phase of the project to cover topics not covered in the first statement of the Principles.[***]

Like the UCC, the CISG does not purport to be a complete statement of international law principles that govern an international sale of goods. Read CISG Article 7(2). How does this provision differ from UCC 1-103? What are the general principles on which the CISG is based? What are the "rules of private international law"?

Other international conventions may have an effect on commercial transactions. For example, the Convention on the Limitation Period in the International Sale of Goods (1974) as amended by the Protocol of April 11, 1980, has been ratified by 18 countries, including the United States. The Convention on International Financial Leasing has been ratified or acceded to by 9 countries and has been signed but not yet ratified by 9 more, including the United States. UNIDROIT has a

---

[***] (...continued)
Nations Convention on Contracts for the International Sale of Goods, 16 NW. J. INT'L L. & BUS. 165, 171-78 (1995) (comparing the CISG and UCC Article 2); Henry D. Gabriel, *A Primer on the United Nations Convention on the International Sale of Goods: From the Perspective of the Uniform Commercial Code,* 7 IND. INT'L & COMP. L. REV. 279 (1997).

[*] *See Symposium, Ten Years of the United Nations Sales Convention,* 17 J.L. & COM. 181-86 (1998) (discussing practice under the CISG).

[**] *See* Joseph M. Perillo, *UNIDROIT Principles of International Commercial Contracts: The Black Letter Text and a Review,* 63 FORDHAM L. REV. 281 (1994); Jorge Adame, *The UNIDROIT Principles and NAFTA,* 4 ANN. SURV. INT'L & COMP. L. 56 (1997); Klaus Peter Berger, *The Lex Mercatoria Doctrine and the UNIDROIT Principles Of International Commercial Contracts,* 28 LAW & POL'Y. INT'L BUS. 943 (1997).

[***] *See* UNIDROIT Work Programme for the 2002-2004 Triennium, at http://www.unidroit. org.

current project on developing a model law on leasing.[*] To view these international conventions and to determine what countries are bound by these conventions, *see* http://www.unidroit.org and http://www.uncitral.org.

SECTION 5.   AN EXERCISE IN UCC METHODOLOGY

It is now time to work with some cases and problems where UCC methodology is involved. Review the text in Section 2(D) *supra*, and keep the following points relevant to freedom to contract in mind.

First, it is possible that parties to a commercial transaction will try by agreement to opt out of the UCC when it applies. *See* UCC 1-301(c)(1) [former 1-105]. For example, a seller and a buyer subject to the version of Article 2 enacted in State A may agree (subject to some constraints) to be bound by the UCC of State B or some other specified non-UCC law. This power to opt out by agreement is consistent with CISG Article 6.

The question whether parties to a pure service contract or a mixed goods-services deal have power by agreement to opt into the UCC (which would not otherwise apply) is not answered by the UCC. UCITA 104 in the 2000 version of the act, enacted in Maryland and Virginia, confers controlled power on the parties to either opt out of or opt into UCITA. Thus, parties to a computer information transaction entered into in California could choose the law of Virginia, including UCITA, to govern their transaction and that agreement could be enforced in Virginia (at least).[**]

Second, parties subject to the UCC (and the CISG, *see* Article 6) have controlled power to vary the effect of some provisions of the UCC by agreement. UCC 1-302(1) [former 1-102(3)]. Unfortunately, there is no convenient list of those provisions the effect of which can be varied by agreement and those that cannot. *Compare* UCITA 106 and 115. Some help is given in UCC 1-302(b) and (c) and the Comments. Also the particular section itself may give some help. For example, sections fall into three categories:

(1) those which *explicitly* state they can be varied by agreement;

(2) those which *explicitly* state that they cannot be varied by agreement; and

---

[*] *See* UNIDROIT Work Programme for the 2002-2004 Triennium, at http://www.unidroit.org.

[**] Some states have enacted anti-UCITA provisions which purport to prevent opting into UCITA in transactions with their citizens. Iowa Stat. 554D.104 (2003).

(3) those which are not flagged one way or the other.

The first kind poses no problems for the drafter of a contract. The second kind, she must identify and keep in mind. *See, e.g.*, UCC 2-616(3), 2-718(1), 2-209(3), 2-318, 2-725(1). Provisions of the third type (unflagged either way) pose a real problem, for it is *clear* that some of these provisions cannot be varied by agreement, despite the general green light in UCC 1-302 [former 1-102(3)]. Examples are UCC 2-201 on the Statute of Frauds, UCC 2-719(3) protecting "underdogs," and such third party protection provisions as UCC 2-702, 2-502, and 2-403. Yet within this same broad category of unflagged provisions are some that clearly can be varied by agreement. See, for example, the Code provisions on recoverable damages for breach, UCC 2-713, 2-714 and 2-718. Article 2A has the same approach and consequently the same interpretive problem. The problem, then, is this: If, as is plainly the case, our third category of unflagged provisions includes some which can be varied by agreement and some which cannot, by what criteria are we to determine which is which?*

Third, even if applicable, the UCC may not cover all aspects of the transaction, UCC 1-103(b) provides:

> Unless displaced by the particular provisions of [the UCC], the principles of law and equity, including the law merchant and the law relative to capacity to contract, principal and agent, estoppel, fraud, misrepresentation, duress, coercion, mistake, bankruptcy, and other validating or invalidating cause supplement its provisions.

Thus, the UCC is built upon a foundation of contract, agency, property and other principles developed at common law. Sometimes the provisions of the UCC displace common law principles, or alternatively, common law principles are incorporated into the statutory language. In still other instances, common law principles are not stated but are implicitly relied upon in the statement of the UCC rule. In short, the UCC does not make a clean break from the common law.** Equitable principles (not displaced) generally remain intact under the foregoing provision, *even in the face of contrary contractual provisions*. Thus, the parties

---

* For an interesting discussion of the issue *see* Clark A. Remington, *Llewellyn, Anti-formalism and the Fear of Transcendental Nonsense: Codifying the Variability Rule in the Law of Sales*, 44 WAYNE L. REV. 29 (1998).

** *See* Grant Gilmore, *Article 9: What It Does for the Past*, 26 LA. L. REV. 285, 285-86 (1966); Richard Danzig, *A Comment on the Jurisprudence of the Uniform Commercial Code*, 27 STAN. L. REV. 621 (1975).

cannot contract out of the bearing of most equitable notions having to do with estoppel, fraud, misrepresentation, duress, coercion, mistake and the like.* UCITA adopts the same principle in UCITA 116.

Read the following cases and consider the types of arguments that you would make to determine whether the parties could alter the UCC rules by agreement and whether common law or equitable principles are displaced by the UCC rule.

B & W GLASS, INC. V. WEATHER SHIELD MFG., INC.
SUPREME COURT OF WYOMING, 1992
829 P. 2D 809

THOMAS, JUSTICE

The only question involved in this case is the one certified to this court by the United States Court of Appeals for the Tenth Circuit. In the Certification of Question of State Law, that court states the certified question to be:

> Under the law of the State of Wyoming, may an oral promise otherwise within the statute of frauds as pronounced [UCC § 2-201] and the Uniform Commercial Code, nevertheless be enforceable on the basis of promissory estoppel? *See* Restatement (Second) of Contracts § 90 (1981).

We hold that the doctrine of promissory estoppel can be applied under these circumstances to enforce an oral promise, and the certified question is answered in the affirmative. * * *

[B & W Glass prepared to bid (through the project's general manager) on a General Services Administration (GSA) contract for the replacement of all the windows in the federal courthouse in Casper, Wyoming. After extensive negotiations, B & W obtained an oral price quotation from Weather Shield to supply custom windows for the project. The oral bid of $101,725 was never confirmed in writing by Weather Shield. B & W made an oral bid to the project

---

* *See generally* Robert S. Summers, *General Equitable Principles Under Section 1-103 of the Uniform Commercial Code,* 72 NW. U. L. REV. 906 (1978). A marvelous source on the interrelationship of common law and the UCC is ROBERT A. HILLMAN, JULIAN B. MCDONNELL, AND STEVE H. NICKLES, COMMON LAW AND EQUITY UNDER THE UNIFORM COMMERCIAL CODE (1985). On whether the revision of UCC 1-103 has changed the type of analysis that a lawyer should engage in to determine whether common law or equitable principles supplement the principles in the UCC, *see* Sarah Howard Jenkins, *Preemption and Supplementation Under Revised 1-103: The Role of Common Law and Equity in the New UCC,* 54 SMU L. REV. 495 (2001).

manager who, after informing B & W that they were the low bid on the windows, used that bid in submitting an overall bid to the GSA. The overall bid was accepted by the GSA and in August, 1987, B & W signed a contract with the general manager to supply the windows.

After continued discussions between B & W and Weather Shield, Weather Shield declined to supply the custom windows pursuant to its prior oral bid. B & W then obtained the windows from another manufacturer for $226,579 and demanded the difference between the contract and the cover price from Weather Shield. When Weather Shield refused, B & W sued for breach of contract and added a promissory estoppel claim to the pleadings. Weather Shield moved for summary judgment on the ground that the alleged contract was subject to the statute of frauds, UCC 2-201, and that the promissory estoppel claim was not available on the facts. After some convoluted procedures, not described here, the district court entered a judgment for B & W.]

In an opinion order, * * * [t]he court ruled that the bid quotation was made "without any exceptions," which, under usage of the trade, meant the quote was for products meeting the plans and specifications that had been provided. The United States District Court concluded that promissory estoppel had been established and the oral contract between the parties existed and was enforceable despite the statute of frauds provision in Wyoming's version of the UCC. Judgment was entered against Weather Shield for breach of contract in the amount of $100,214.48, with interest. Weather Shield took an appeal to the United States Court of Appeals for the Tenth Circuit, which certified the promissory estoppel question to this court. * * *

The certified question presented by the United States Court of Appeals for the Tenth Circuit asks whether an equitable principle, promissory estoppel, will be applied to defeat the operation of a statute of frauds. The philosophical conflict embodied in this question implicates principles of statutory construction, fundamental fairness, and certainty in the law which have been the subject of legal debate in the English common law system since the Middle Ages. *See* HENRY L. MCCLINTOCK, HANDBOOK OF THE PRINCIPLES OF EQUITY § 22 (2nd ed. 1948). The policy choice required by this certified question is one that demands a detailed review. The analysis pursued considers the specific section or sections of the UCC that are applicable in this controversy; the effect of that application; the authorization under the UCC to invoke equitable principles generally; whether the UCC displaced equitable principles with its statute of frauds; the role of promissory estoppel in Wyoming's jurisprudence apart from statutes; and, finally, the application of promissory estoppel in the context of the UCC statute of frauds. *See* Robert S. Summers, *General Equitable Principles Under Section 1-103 of the Uniform Commercial Code*, 72 NW. U .L .REV. 906 (1978) [hereinafter *General Equitable Principles*].

Promissory estoppel is a doctrine incorporated in the law of contracts. RESTATEMENT (SECOND) CONTRACTS § 90 (1981). Judge Posner has provided a considered and succinct description of the doctrine: "If an unambiguous promise is made in circumstances calculated to induce reliance, and it does so, the promisee if hurt as a result can recover damages." *Goldstick v. ICM Realty*, 788 F.2d 456, 462 (7th Cir.1986). Promissory estoppel is recognized as both a sword and a shield-a cause of action and a defense. Equitable estoppel is a close relative, but it is a tort doctrine that requires proof of misrepresentation. *Goldstick.*

Neither party disputes the applicability of the UCC, as adopted in Wyoming, to the transaction that resulted in this litigation. At its most basic level, that transaction involved a sale of goods, windows, by a seller, Weather Shield, to a buyer, B & W. B & W contends an oral contract was formed between the parties upon which it relied, to its detriment. Weather Shield challenges the reliance upon an oral contract contending that, even if one existed, it was for goods priced at $500 or more and cannot be enforced under the UCC statute of frauds. * * *

In this case, there is no writing that satisfies the requirements of § 2-201(a) or (b). None of the three exceptions to the writing requirement, set forth in subsection (c) of the statute, apply to the facts as stated. Weather Shield contends that the exceptions found in subsections (b) and (c) are the exclusive exceptions to the statute of frauds recognized under the UCC. Weather Shield supports this argument by reference to the language: "Except as otherwise provided in this section...." UCC § 2-201(a). Weather Shield asserts that this language demonstrates the legislative intent to limit the exceptions. Acceptance of this restrictive view espoused by Weather Shield would result in a conclusion that the effect of § 2-201 is to prevent enforcement of the oral agreement between the parties.

B & W argues that the UCC, read as a whole, incorporates a provision that supplements the language of § 2-201 with the principles of equity, including promissory estoppel. It points to the provisions of UCC § 1-103. * * *

B & W's argument is that the language of § 2-201 does not specifically displace promissory estoppel as that doctrine supplements the provisions of the code pursuant to § 1-103. Acceptance of the liberal view espoused by B & W results in a conclusion that the effect of § 1-103 is to allow promissory estoppel to defeat the operation of the statutes of frauds.

Decisions of other courts offer persuasive support when questions of the interpretation of uniform laws arise. * * * The decisions on whether promissory estoppel will serve to avoid the UCC statute of frauds track a storm-battered course. *See* Vitauts M. Gulbis, *Annotation, Promissory Estoppel as Basis for Avoidance of UCC Statute of Frauds (UCC § 2-201)*, 29 A.L.R.4TH 1006 (1984 & Supp.1991). The majority position espouses the rule that principles of promissory estoppel under § 1-103 operate as an exception to the statute of frauds. The minority position is that estoppel does not constitute an exception to the requirements of § 2-201. Note, *Promissory Estoppel: Subcontractors' Liability in Construction Bidding Cases*, 63 N.C.L.REV. 387 (1985). B & W and Weather Shield vigorously urge the positions found in the authorities that support their respective views. We have identified appropriate points of departure for consideration in our review of this issue.

Two general themes can be identified in the authorities of those jurisdictions that approve a promissory estoppel exception to the UCC statute of frauds. If an estoppel exception has been generally recognized in that jurisdiction under other statutes of frauds, then the exception usually has been found in § 2-201. * * *

The *Allen M. Campbell* case [708 F.2d 930 (4th Cir. 1983)], arising under factually similar surroundings to this case, provides a useful example of the analysis and rationale used by those courts approving the use of promissory estoppel. Allen M. Campbell Co. had prepared a bid on a Department of the Navy contract to construct housing. Only one-half hour before the bids were due, Virginia Metal Industries telephoned Allen M. Campbell Co. and quoted a price for hollow metal doors and frames that would meet the plans and specifications. Allen M. Campbell Co. based its bid on the quoted price and was awarded the contract. Virginia Metal Industries then backed out of the contract and Allen M. Campbell Co. covered by purchasing doors from another supplier at a higher cost. The United States Court of Appeals for the Fourth Circuit ruled that North Carolina recognized and applied the doctrine of promissory estoppel. The court stated that, pursuant to § 1-103, equitable principles were available to supplement § 2-201 and, after surveying relevant case law, the court concluded that North Carolina's approval of promissory estoppel provisions in the RESTATEMENT (SECOND) OF CONTRACTS §§ 90, 139 (1981) signaled its acceptance of the view that promissory estoppel avoids the statute of frauds.

In those jurisdictions that have espoused the rule that promissory estoppel is not available to avoid the statute of frauds under the UCC, consistent themes also are discernable. The fundamental distinction begins with the refusal to consider § 1-103 as supplementing the UCC with principles of equity, including estoppel. * *

* Another reason those courts have chosen to deny the use of promissory estoppel as available to avoid § 2-201 is the refusal in those jurisdictions to permit the doctrines of estoppel to defeat general statutes of frauds. * * *

A leading decision that rejects the application of promissory estoppel to avoid the statute of frauds found in § 2-201 is *Lige Dickson*, 635 P.2d 103. The question presented in that case to the Supreme Court of Washington was whether an oral price protection agreement with a liquid asphalt supplier would be upheld. The buyer relied on the consistent selling price in submitting bids for construction contracts. The Washington court reviewed its previous position denying the invocation of promissory estoppel to overcome the general statute of frauds and noting the limiting language at the beginning of § 2-201, that court ruled promissory estoppel is not available to overcome the UCC's statute of frauds. The need for uniformity among different jurisdictions and decisions affecting commercial transactions was offered as another reason not to permit promissory estoppel to circumvent the statute of frauds in the UCC.

Conflicting decisions of state and federal courts in the same jurisdiction further magnify the divergence in precedent . * * *

In our view, the better-reasoned approach is articulated by those courts that have approved the majority view that promissory estoppel avoids § 2-201. We do not accept, however, the argument that this question can be resolved by simply adopting the logic of one line of decisions. The divergent authorities offer an opportunity for choice without specific policy concerns. That approach leads away from a primary duty of this court which is the charge that we implement legislative policy found in the enactment of the UCC. We conclude that the analysis of the certified question becomes primarily a matter of statutory interpretation for which Wyoming has established standards.

Questions that reach to statutory interpretation require the court to endeavor to perceive the legislative intent. * * * Legislative intent is to be ascertained, insofar as possible, from the language incorporated in the statute, which is viewed in light of its object and purpose. * * * Statutes that relate to the same subject matter should be harmonized whenever that is possible. * * * In pursuing this endeavor every subsection of a statute must be read in the context of all others to ascertain the meaning of the whole statute. * * *

In addition to these general rules of statutory construction, the UCC also has incorporated within it useful rules of construction and a statement of its purpose. The act is to be liberally construed and applied to promote its underlying purposes and policies. UCC § 1-102 [Revised UCC 1-103-Ed.]. * * * According to the legislative pronouncement, the purposes of the UCC are to simplify, clarify, and modernize the law governing commercial transactions; to permit continued expansion of commercial practices through custom, usage, and agreement of the parties; and to make uniform the law among the various jurisdictions. UCC § 1-102. Professors White and Summers suggest a further purpose of the UCC is "that the law of commercial transactions be, so far as reasonable, liberal and nontechnical." 1 JAMES J. WHITE & ROBERT S. SUMMERS, UNIFORM COMMERCIAL CODE § 4 (3d ed. 1988) [hereinafter WHITE & SUMMERS]. The authors apparently disagree, however, on the application of the doctrine of estoppel to avoid the statute of frauds. WHITE & SUMMERS §§ 2-6, 2-8. The official comments attached to the UCC, while not controlling an interpretation of the scope and intent of the Code, are persuasive. * * *

In Wyoming, rigid adherence to the UCC statute of frauds is contrary to the liberal construction philosophy surrounding the code. * * * Professor Corbin, in urging the adoption of the UCC by the several states, noted: "The purpose of the statute of frauds is to prevent the enforcement of alleged promises that never were made; it is not, and never has been, to justify contractors in repudiating promises that were in fact made." Arthur L. Corbin, *The Uniform Commercial Code-Sales; Should It Be Enacted?*, 59 YALE L.J. 821, 829 (1950). Another commentator asserts that the statute of frauds is the weapon of the written law to prevent fraud; estoppel is the equitable means invoked to achieve this end. 3 WALTER H.E. JAEGER, WILLISTON ON CONTRACTS § 533A (3rd ed. 1960).

In light of our approach to statutory construction, we are satisfied that, if promissory estoppel is to become an exception to § 2-201, it must be because of the provisions of § 1-103. Estoppel is specifically included in the listing of principles supplementing the UCC. UCC § 1-103. We previously have recognized the entry to general principles of law and equity found in § 1-103 to supplement the UCC. *Western Nat. Bank of Casper v. Harrison*, 577 P.2d 635 (Wyo.1978) (allowing the law of waiver to supplement UCC provisions). Unless it is displaced, § 1-103 imposes a duty to interpret and construe the UCC by taking into account the equities of a particular case. *General Equitable Principles*, 72 NW.U.L.REV. 906.

We adopt the suggestions of Professor Summers as a framework for our analysis of whether the equitable principle of promissory estoppel can apply despite the statute of frauds in the UCC. His proposition is that the supplementary principles of law and equity incorporated into the operation of the UCC by virtue of § 1-103 survive unless it can be established that: (1) the principle is explicitly displaced by name in the plain language of the statute; (2) the specific objectives of the section would be served only by displacement of the principles of law and equity; (3) the general objectives of the UCC are best furthered by displacement of those principles; and (4) the legislative history plainly indicates displacement. *General Equitable Principles*, 72 Nw.U.L.Rev. 906. We will apply these criteria in our consideration of the question of whether § 2-201 displaces promissory estoppel.

Certainly, the UCC does require that supplemental bodies of law be "explicitly displaced" to void the effect of § 1-103. Official Comment 1. Neither the text of § 2-201 nor the comments following it specifically refer to estoppel. WHITE & SUMMERS § 2-7. This silence on the part of the legislature in the language of the statute can not be construed to constitute a displacement of estoppel principles. *Potter*, 641 P.2d 628. For this reason, we disagree with the conclusions of the court in *Futch v. James River-Norwalk, Inc.*, 722 F.Supp. 1395 (S.D.Miss.), *aff'd*, 887 F.2d 1085 (5th Cir.1989), and *McDabco*, 548 F.Supp. 456, that the opening language of § 2-201 represents a displacement of the principles of promissory estoppel. As found in § 2-201, the phrase "[e]xcept as otherwise provided in this section" is simply a clause modifying the first subsection. UCC § 2-201. The intention of the Wyoming legislature in beginning Subsection (a) with that clause, is apparent from a reading of the entire section. Subsection (a) is the general statement of the statute of frauds applicable to the sale of goods. WHITE & SUMMERS § 2-3. The effect of the initial limiting language in subsection (a) is to alert the reader that the remaining subsections are disjunctive, and it serves to advise the reader of the proposition that the statutory exceptions to the statute of frauds are contained in subsections (b) and (c). Furthermore, the statutory exceptions listed in § 2-201(c) are not exhaustive. *Warder & Lee Elevator*, 274 N.W.2d 339; WHITE & SUMMERS § 2-7. Neither the language of the statute of frauds nor any legislative history indicates that § 2-201 displaces promissory estoppel.

Secondly, we conclude the specific objectives of § 2-201 would not be served by displacing promissory estoppel. The long-stated purpose of the statute of frauds is to prevent fraud from perjured testimony about nonexistent oral agreements. However, the concepts of equity and the passage of years resulted in the creation of exceptions to the writing requirement as a necessity to prevent substantive fraud. The part performance doctrine is one such exception that is specifically stated in the UCC. UCC § 2-201. Still, the UCC was not drafted to anticipate the equities of every possible transaction. The specific inclusion of § 1-103 permits the invocation of principles of both law and equity as necessary to the resolution of commercial disputes. An adherence to a strict policy of demanding a writing in all cases that are not specifically exempted by § 2-201(b) or (c) would allow unscrupulous contractors to perpetrate fraud after creating reliance. The courts should be vigilant to inhibit the defense of the statute of frauds when that defense becomes an instrument for perpetrating fraud. * * *

The third factor to be considered is whether the general objectives of the UCC would be served by displacement of promissory estoppel. We conclude they would not. The *Lige Dickson* court argued that uniformity among the several jurisdictions was the reason not to allow promissory estoppel to avoid the statute of frauds. That logic is not persuasive in view of the fact that the majority of jurisdictions allow promissory estoppel to avoid the provisions of § 2-201. *Drennan v. Star Paving Co.*, 51 Cal.2d 409, 333 P.2d 757 (1958), is a leading case allowing promissory estoppel to defeat a general statute of frauds. Writing for the Supreme Court of California, Justice Traynor clearly set forth the principle of fairness implicit in recognizing the doctrine of promissory estoppel:

> When [the general contractor] used [the subcontractor's] offer in computing his own bid, he bound himself to perform in reliance on [the subcontractor's] terms. Though [the subcontractor] did not bargain for this use of its bid neither did [the subcontractor] make it idly, indifferent to whether it would be used or not. On the contrary it is reasonable to suppose that [the subcontractor] submitted its bid to obtain the subcontract. It was bound to realize the substantial possibility that its bid would be the lowest, and that it would be included by [the general contractor] in his bid. It was to its own interest that the contractor be awarded the general contract; the lower the subcontract bid, the lower the general contractor's bid was likely to be and the greater its chance of acceptance and hence the greater [the subcontractor's] chance of getting the paving subcontract. [The subcontractor] had reason not only to expect [the general contractor] to rely on its bid but to want him to. Clearly [the subcontractor] had a stake in [the general contractor's] reliance on its bid. Given this interest and the fact that [the general contractor] is bound by his own bid, it is only fair that [the general contractor] should have at least an opportunity to accept [the subcontractor's bid] after the general contract has been awarded to him.

Drennan, 333 P.2d at 760.

The invocation of the doctrine of promissory estoppel to avoid § 2-201 is consistent with authority that permits promissory estoppel to avoid a general statute of frauds. *See* Robert A. Brazener, *Annotation, Comment Note-Promissory*

Estoppel As Basis For Avoidance Of Statute Of Frauds, 56 A.L.R.3RD 1037 (1974 & Supp.1991). The argument that application of promissory estoppel should change depending upon whether goods (UCC) or services (general statute) are involved simply begs the fundamental question of fairness. If the application of promissory estoppel is fair in one context, it must also be in the other. Reliance created by a subcontractor, who quotes a price for services, is the same as that which is created by another subcontractor, who quotes a price for goods. Therefore, in addition to the statutory exceptions found in § 2-201, the nonstatutory exception to the writing requirement, promissory estoppel, is also present through § 1-103.

* * *

A recognition that promissory estoppel avoids the UCC statute of frauds is consistent with our prior Wyoming cases. *See Inter-Mountain Threading, Inc. v. Baker Hughes Tubular Services, Inc.*, 812 P.2d 555 (Wyo.1991), and the cases cited in that opinion. While some courts have expressed a reservation to the effect that recognizing nonstatutory exceptions to the statute of frauds may render it a nullity, *McDabco*, 548 F.Supp. 456, Wyoming has accepted a role of leadership in invoking equitable principles to avoid injustice. The need to enforce an implied promise to mortgage some cattle resulted in the first approval in Wyoming of the doctrine of promissory estoppel as stated in the RESTATEMENT OF CONTRACTS, § 90 (1932). *Hanna State & Savings Bank v. Matson*, 53 Wyo. 1, 77 P.2d 621 (1938). In *Tremblay v. Reid*, 700 P.2d 391 (Wyo.1985), Wyoming adopted the principles of promissory estoppel as they are stated in the RESTATEMENT (SECOND) CONTRACTS § 90(1) (1981).

The drafters of the Restatement (Second) have taken an even more definite position on the availability of promissory estoppel to avoid the statute of frauds:

> (1) A promise which the promisor should reasonably expect to induce action or forbearance on the part of the promisee or a third person and which does induce the action or forbearance is enforceable notwithstanding the Statute of Frauds if injustice can be avoided only by enforcement of the promise. The remedy granted for breach is be limited as justice requires.

RESTATEMENT (SECOND) CONTRACTS § 139 (1981).

The drafters of the Restatement (Second) use *Vogel*, 294 P. 687, as an illustration of the section's application to avoid injustice. RESTATEMENT (SECOND) CONTRACTS § 139 (Reporter's Note 1981). In *Remilong v. Crolla*, 576 P.2d 461 (Wyo.1978), this court approved the use of promissory estoppel, as phrased in the RESTATEMENT (SECOND), to avoid the general statute of frauds in Wyoming. In that case, we ruled that buyers of land could enforce an oral promise from the seller that all trailers would be removed from adjacent lands.

Our most recent cases are demonstrative of the safeguards that are present in the application of the doctrine of promissory estoppel. The elements of promissory estoppel demand evidence that establishes: "(1) a clear and definite agreement; (2) proof that the party urging the doctrine acted to its detriment in reasonable reliance on the agreement; and (3) a finding that the equities support enforcement of the agreement." * * * The party who is asserting promissory estoppel is assigned the burden of establishing all of the elements of the doctrine with a standard of strict proof. * * *

We do not share the concern that was present in the English courts of the 17th Century to the effect that a writing is the sole method to avoid undetected perjured testimony. Our judicial system is capable of discerning perjury and reaching a determination in an instance in which a litigant establishes promissory estoppel by appropriately assuming his burden.

Consistently with the majority rule and the law in Wyoming relating to general statutes of frauds, we conclude that promissory estoppel can and does justify the enforcement of an oral promise otherwise within the statute of frauds in the UCC, as articulated in UCC § 2-201. Under the foregoing analysis, our answer to the certified question is "yes".

Notes

1.   Review the methodology discussion in Section 2(D), *supra*. Did the court consider all of the possible sources? How did the court do (in your opinion)?

2.   Does the court assume that the parties had reached an otherwise enforceable agreement but for the statute of frauds? Or does the court assume that Weather Shield simply made an offer which B & W had yet to accept after it learned that the project manager received a contract from GSA? What difference would it make?

The difference is this. If the court concluded than an oral contract was concluded, it was correct in deciding whether promissory estoppel was an exception to the statute of frauds. *See* RESTATEMENT (SECOND) CONTRACTS 139. If the court assumed that the price quote was only an offer then the question is whether B & W's reliance created an option contract, *see* RESTATEMENT (SECOND) CONTRACTS 87(2), to be accepted later. Under this assumption, the contract (if any) would be created after B & W's reliance and the promissory estoppel exception to the statute of frauds would not be available.

3. The court quotes from Justice Traynor's famous opinion in *Drennan v. Star Paving*. That case involved a price quote, not a completed agreement, and despite what the court said, the statute of frauds was not involved. The court held that because the price quote, treated as an offer, induced reliance an option contract was created and the offer could be accepted even though the offeror had attempted to revoke it.

4. Why should B & W's reliance trump the statute of fraud's effort to protect against perjured claims that a contract was made or certain terms were agreed to? To what extend did that reliance "corroborate evidence of the making and terms of the promise...?" *See* RESTATEMENT (SECOND) OF CONTRACTS 139(2)(c).

BLUE VALLEY COOPERATIVE V. NATIONAL FARMERS ORGANIZATION
SUPREME COURT OF NEBRASKA, 1999
257 NEB. 751, 600 N.W.2D 786

GERRARD, J.

I. NATURE OF CASE

Blue Valley Cooperative (BVC) sued National Farmers Organization (NFO) to recover contractual costs of storing and handling NFO's white corn. NFO counterclaimed that BVC's negligence had damaged NFO's white corn and that BVC had breached an oral contract to reimburse NFO for that damage. After a jury found in favor of BVC on the written contract cause of action and against NFO on NFO's counterclaims, the trial court awarded BVC prejudgment interest. NFO appeals the judgment entered pursuant to the jury's verdict and the court's award of prejudgment interest. For the reasons that follow, we affirm in part, and in part reverse and remand for a new trial on the negligence counterclaim. * * *

II. FACTUAL BACKGROUND

After a windstorm damaged grain bins that stored white corn belonging to certain NFO member-producers in 1993, NFO representatives contacted BVC to arrange for delivery and storage of the white corn at BVC's facility in Seward County. On July 9, 1993, BVC and NFO entered into a written agreement to facilitate such storage. The agreement stated that BVC was to receive and store NFO's white corn. The agreement recited that the white corn would be grade No. 2 with a moisture content of 15 percent. If any of the white corn received by BVC was offgrade or had a higher moisture content, the agreement called upon BVC to reject the load unless instructed otherwise by a representative of NFO.

The agreement also contained a waiver clause stating, "Quality liability will be waived if Blue Valley Cooperative is instructed to receive lesser than grade # 2 corn and moisture content higher than 15.0%." Under the agreement, NFO was to arrange for the white corn to be shipped out of BVC's facility by August 31, 1993. BVC was to load the grain onto railcars when the time came for the white corn to be shipped. The agreement placed the responsibility for railcar delay (demurrage) charges on NFO. Shortly after the parties entered into the agreement, NFO member-producers delivered approximately 115,000 bushels of their white corn to BVC.

Despite the agreement to remove the white corn from BVC by August 31, 1993, railcars were not dispatched to do so until January 21, 1994. On that day, a 54-car train arrived to haul the white corn to buyers in Mexico. NFO member- producers delivered more white corn from their farms to be commingled with the white corn stored at BVC and loaded onto the train. After BVC had loaded roughly 27 railcars with the NFO's commingled white corn, the Lincoln Inspection Service reported that the white corn was below grade No. 2 and had excessive damage. As such, BVC personnel unloaded the train and placed all the white corn back into BVC's storage facility.

BVC and NFO offered conflicting reasons at trial for the low grade of the corn. In particular, BVC presented testimony and exhibits suggesting that the white corn delivered by NFO had been infected with blue-eye mold. BVC witnesses testified that the blue-eye mold, as opposed to any negligent handling or storage, had caused the corn to deteriorate while warehoused at BVC and to ultimately rate below grade No. 2. Meanwhile, NFO witnesses asserted that heat had damaged the corn while stored at BVC's facility, which resulted from BVC's failure to keep the white corn cool and at a low moisture content.

After BVC unloaded the damaged white corn from the railcars, NFO member-producers delivered nearly 190,000 bushels of grade No. 2 white corn to fill the train on January 26, 1994. The railcars departed with the corn on February 9. BVC acknowledged that part of the reason for the railcar delay was having to load, unload, and reload the white corn. Burlington Northern Railroad billed BVC $15,120 for the demurrage on March 24, with a due date of April 8. BVC paid Burlington Northern Railroad, but remained confused about which of BVC's clients should be held accountable for the demurrage. For some reason, BVC agents thought the demurrage should be charged to Harvest States (a different BVC client) and did not realize that the demurrage was NFO's responsibility until sometime in

March 1995.

On March 1, 1994, representatives from NFO and BVC met to discuss how the remaining white corn would be disposed of and how costs and damages would be apportioned. At trial, the parties disputed what was orally agreed upon at that meeting. After the meeting, NFO paid BVC storage charges of $18,566.69 for storing the original 115,000 bushels of white corn from July 1993 to January 1994. NFO also paid BVC $19,058.59 for handling the 190,000 bushels of white corn delivered by NFO and loaded directly on railcars in January 1994. Finally, NFO paid BVC $2,566.82 for handling 25,668 bushels of the damaged white corn that NFO sold after January 1994. The remaining white corn was removed from BVC's facility by October 1994.

Thereafter, BVC initiated the instant suit claiming that NFO still owed BVC $8,843.03 in storage and handling costs (after discounting 2 cents per point on each bushel with damaged kernels) pursuant to the alleged oral agreement on March 1, 1994, and $15,120 in demurrage charges pursuant to the original written agreement. In response, NFO asserted counterclaims that BVC had negligently damaged NFO's white corn and breached an oral contract to reimburse NFO for that damage. NFO alleged damages in the amount of $77,398 by calculating the difference between the $3.05 per bushel the corn would have brought if it were grade No. 2 in January 1994 and the $2.60 per bushel for which it was actually sold.

On the morning of trial, NFO filed a motion in limine to exclude the waiver clause. NFO argued that the waiver clause was void and unenforceable under U.C.C. § 7-204 and, therefore, irrelevant. The trial court overruled NFO's motion. After the jurors were sworn but before any evidence was admitted, NFO objected to admission of the waiver clause. Again, the trial court overruled NFO's objection.

* * * *

The jury returned a verdict in favor of BVC on the written contract cause of action for demurrage charges (in the sum of $15,120) and against NFO on NFO's counterclaim for negligence. The jury found against each party's breach-of-an-oral-contract claim. The trial court entered judgment on the jury's verdict and, without explaining its rationale, awarded BVC prejudgment interest from May 8, 1994. NFO timely appealed.

* * * *

V. ANALYSIS
1. WAIVER CLAUSE IS UNENFORCEABLE

Although the question has not yet been addressed in Nebraska, we are persuaded that blanket waivers of liability in warehouse contracts-such as that in the written agreement between BVC and NFO-are unenforceable under § 7-204. There is no doubt that the contract containing the waiver clause at issue here is a warehouse contract. * * * Hence, § 7-204 controls whether the waiver clause is enforceable.

In pertinent part, § 7-204 states:

(1) A warehouseman is liable for damages for loss of or injury to the goods caused by his failure to exercise such care in regard to them as a reasonably careful man would exercise under like circumstances but unless otherwise agreed he is not liable for damages which could not have been avoided by the exercise of such care.

(2) *Damages may be limited by a term in the warehouse receipt or storage agreement limiting the amount of liability in case of loss or damage, and setting forth a specific liability per article or item, or value per unit of weight, beyond which the warehouseman shall not be liable.*

(Emphasis supplied.)

Statutory language is to be given its plain and ordinary meaning absent anything to the contrary; thus, an appellate court will not resort to interpretation to ascertain the meaning of statutory words which are plain, direct, and unambiguous. * * * Although official comments to the Uniform Commercial Code * * * are not binding, they are persuasive in matters of interpretation. * * * The stated purpose of § 7-204 in the official comment to that statute is to eliminate controversy surrounding contractual limitations on liability by setting forth conditions under which such could be done.

Moreover, the components of a series or collection of statutes pertaining to a certain subject matter may be conjunctively considered and construed to determine the intent of the Legislature so that different provisions of the act are consistent, harmonious, and sensible. * * * In setting out the purpose of the Uniform Commercial Code, § 1-102(3) [Revised 1-302–ed.] declares that the provisions of those statutes "may be varied by agreement, except as otherwise provided in the code and except that the obligations of good faith, diligence, reasonableness and care ... may not be disclaimed by agreement." Additionally, § 7-202(3) allows a warehouse keeper to insert in the receipt any terms that conform with "the provisions of the Uniform Commercial Code and do not impair [the warehouse keeper's] duty of care" as prescribed by § 7-204, and renders ineffective any contrary provisions. Taken together, these statutes reveal the legislative intent behind § 7-204, which was to provide the sole mechanism by which a warehouse keeper could contractually diminish exposure to liability or limit damages for negligence in an agreement to store a customer's goods.

We are also impressed that the consensus approach of other jurisdictions is to void waivers of liability that do not strictly conform to § 7-204. *See, Butler Mfg. Co. v. Americold Corp.*, 835 F.Supp. 1274 (D. Kan. 1993) (striking down warehouseman's blanket waiver for ordinary negligence); * * *

Nonetheless, other jurisdictions are quite willing to uphold damage- limiting clauses in warehouse contracts when such clauses conform to the terms of statutes very similar or identical to § 7-204. *See, International Nickel Co. v. Trammel Crow Distrib.*, 803 F.2d 150 (5th Cir.1986) (upholding clause that limited damages to 100 times base storage rate for nickel); *Sanfisket, Inc. v. Atlantic Cold Stor. Corp.*, 347 So.2d 647 (Fla.App.1977) (upholding clause that limited damages to 50 cents per pound of shrimp); *Keefe v. Bekins Van & Storage Co.*, 36 Colo.App. 382, 540 P.2d 1132 (1975) (upholding clause limiting damages to 10 cents per pound per article of household goods); *Dunfee v. Blue Rock Van & Storage, Inc.*, 266 A.2d 187 (Del.Super.1970) (upholding clause limiting damages to 60 cents per pound per article up to $1,000).

Because the above approach is sensible and consistent with Nebraska's legislative intent, we hold that a warehouse contract may reasonably limit a warehouse keeper's damages by setting forth a specific liability per article, item, or unit of weight, but may not disclaim or waive liability entirely under § 7-204. BVC maintains that the written agreement with NFO complied with § 7-204 in this manner insofar as it set forth "a specific liability per article or item." In other words, BVC claims that the phrase "lesser than grade # 2 corn and moisture content higher than 15.0%" represents an article or item. The flaw in this reasoning is that BVC's waiver clause did not *limit damages* for such an article or item; instead, it *eliminated liability* -which is exactly what the plain language of § 7-204 prohibits. Therefore, the waiver clause in BVC's contract was unenforceable.

* * * *

VI. CONCLUSION

To summarize, we hold that blanket waivers of liability-as opposed to reasonable limitations on damages per article, item, or unit of weight-in warehouse contracts are void under § 7-204. * * *

Affirmed in part, and in part reversed and remanded.

Problem 1-1

Consider the validity of the following clauses which purport to vary the effect of the sections cited. What method of analysis do you use in making your arguments about the validity of these clauses?

1. "Pursuant to the Basic Agreement, to which we have previously agreed, the parties shall make subsequent agreements for the purchase and sale of lumber, each such subsequent agreement to constitute a binding contract only when and if the parties have fully agreed to all material terms." *See* UCC 2-204(2), (3), and various gap-filler provisions in Part 3 of Article 2.

2. "In the event that buyer discovers a nonconformity upon delivery of said goods, buyer shall not be required to notify seller thereof, provided that buyer commences any legal proceedings therefor against seller within two years of discovery of said breach." *See* UCC 2-607(3)(a), 2-725.

3. "In the event buyer defaults hereunder, seller shall be entitled to recover the agreed price for said goods whether or not Article 2 of the Uniform Commercial Code so provides." *See* UCC 2-709.

4. Article 6 of the CISG provides that the "parties may exclude the application of the Convention or, subject to Article 12, derogate from or vary the effect of any of its provisions." Can Seller and Buyer exclude the application of UCC Article 2 to their contract for sale and, for example, choose the UNIDROIT Principles as applicable law? Can parties to a pure service contract choose UCC Article 2 as governing law?

5. Can parties to a sale of a factory machine run by software contract for UCITA to apply to the entire transaction?

Problem 1-2

In an action for damages for breach of warranty, a buyer contends that it suffered consequential damages recoverable under UCC 2-715(2)(a). Seller argues that the buyer has the burden of proof to demonstrate that the buyer properly mitigated its damages. Buyer argues that the seller has the burden of proof to demonstrate that the buyer failed to mitigate damages. How should this issue be resolved? How does UCC 1-103 play into the analysis of this issue? *See Federal Signal Corporation v. Safety Factors, Inc.*, 125 Wash. 2d 413, 886 P. 2d 172 (1994).

CHAPTER TWO

SCOPE: WHAT LAW APPLIES
TO THE TRANSACTION

SECTION 1.   A ROADMAP TO THE SALES AND LEASES ARTICLES OF THE UCC

As part of her essential background, the user of the UCC needs a basic roadmap to the provisions involved. The presentation here will be in terms of stages of the modern transaction for sale or lease of goods, which is typically for future delivery of goods on credit, and therefore a deal that progresses from initial agreement through performance to discharge. The discrete stages along the way are typically these: (i) agreement; (ii) post-agreement–pre-shipment; (iii) the stage of getting the goods (or documents therefor) to the buyer or lessee; (iv) receipt and inspection, and (v) payment. The overwhelming majority of deals progress all the way through to payment without incident. But a significant proportion do not, and these break down at different stages, in different ways, and for different reasons. Thus, what follows here will be "pathologically oriented" in the respect that, at each stage, the focus will be on the *kinds* of things that can go wrong in a sale or lease of goods.

The roadmap provides one way of organizing the material found in Articles 2 and 2A. Article 2 primarily deals with sales of goods whereas Article 2A primarily deals with leases of goods. Article 2A was modeled on the Article 2 transaction, with some changes to reflect the leasing transaction, and some provisions modeled on Article 9.* One caveat: because the discussion in this section is by way of prelude, it is necessarily general, to some extent oversimplified, and not comprehensive. In each of these respects, so, too, a roadmap.

A. The Agreement Stage

Contract formation. Perhaps the most drastic of all things that can go wrong is for the parties to assume that they have made a binding contract only to find that

---

* For a discussion of the background of Article 2A and the use of Article 2 as its template, *see* Amelia H. Boss, *The History of Article 2A: A Lesson for Practitioner and Scholar Alike*, 39 ALA. L. REV. 575 (1988).

in law they have not. This is much less of a risk, however, under Articles 2 and 2A than it is in general contract law. This is so for two reasons. First, these articles make contract formation easier than it is in the general law. Formalities are reduced. *See* UCC 2-201 and 2A-201 (relaxed statutes of frauds with several exceptions); UCC 2-203 and 2A-203 (abolishing the principles of sealed instruments for contracts covered by the articles). The consideration doctrine is modified with a bias toward contract formation. *See* UCC 2-205 and 2A-205 (no consideration needed to support a firm offer); UCC 2-209(1) and 2A-208(1) (no consideration needed to support an agreement to modify). The requirement that an acceptance must be precisely within the terms of an offer to constitute an acceptance is abolished. *See* UCC 2-206(1)(a), 2-206(3) [former 2-207(1)] and 2A-206(1).* In Article 2, a non-conforming shipment of goods in response to a unilateral offer is, under certain circumstances, nonetheless an acceptance. UCC 2-206(1)(b).** In addition, beginning of performance may be an acceptance if timely notice of acceptance is thereafter given. UCC 2-206(2) and 2A-206(2). Contracts can be formed by mere conduct alone, even though the precise moment of making is undetermined. UCC 2-204(1) and (2), 2A-204(1) and (2).

Second, a contract for sale or lease does not fail for indefiniteness if the parties have intended to make a contract and there is a reasonably certain basis for giving an appropriate remedy. UCC 2-204(3) and 2A-204(3). Further to this, Article 2 includes many "gap-filler" provisions which come into play to fill gaps in agreements that might otherwise fail under general contract law for indefiniteness. *See* UCC 2-204(3), 2-305, 2-306, 2-307, 2-308, 2-309, 2-310, 2-311, 2-503, 2-504, 2-507, and 2-511. Unlike Article 2, however, Article 2A does not have comparable "gap filler" provisions. The assumption is that a lease transaction is generally more structured and documented than a sales transaction leaving less room for "gap fillers" to fill in the deal of the parties.

Terms and meaning. In addition to failures of contract formation, disputes may arise over whether a term is or is not a part of the contract and whether a given term is to be interpreted in one way rather than another. These kinds of disputes can arise at any stage, but it is appropriate to allude to them here. On whether a term is or is not a part of the contract, the parol evidence rule governs in many situations. UCC 2-202 and 2A-202. Lawyers and judges will resolve problems of

---

* Article 2A does not have an analog to either UCC 2-207 or former 2-207.

** A comparable provision is omitted from Article 2A. *See* UCC 2A-206.

interpretation and construction in part by reference to UCC 1-103 [former 1-102(1)] on rules of construction, and to UCC 1-303 [former 1-205, 2-208, 2A-207] on course of performance, course of dealing and usage of trade. The alert, careful lawyer should, through careful drafting and advice, be able to reduce if not eliminate altogether any risks that the parties will fail to make a binding contract or even that significant disputes over interpretation will arise.

These issues of contract formation and inclusion and interpretation of terms in a contract are more fully explored in Chapters Three and Four, *infra*.

B. The Post-Agreement–Pre-Shipment Stage

A seller or lessor will either have the goods on hand, or have to manufacture them or acquire them elsewhere. In any of these events, there is often a time lapse between the date when the contract is made and the time when the goods are delivered to the buyer or the lessee. During this period, either party may repudiate, or it may become clear that one of the parties will not later be able to perform. The 2003 amendments to both Articles 2 and 2A adopt a definition of repudiation based on the RESTATEMENT (SECOND) OF CONTRACTS 250. UCC 2-610(2), 2A-402(2).

Breach by buyer or lessee. Assume it is the buyer or lessee who repudiates. The seller or lessor can call off the deal. *See* UCC 2-610(1)(b), 2-703(1)(f) [former 2-703(f)], 2A-402(1)(c), 2A-523(1)(f) [former 2A-523(1)(a)]. The seller or lessor may also seek damages for breach of the contract. UCC 2-706, 2-708, 2A-527, 2A-528. Can it choose to go forward with the transaction and force the goods on the buyer or the lessee? Yes, under limited circumstances. *See* UCC 2-704(1)(a), 2A-524(1)(a), 2-709(1)(b), 2A-529(1)(b). Sections 2-704(2) and 2A-524(2) gives the *manufacturing* seller or lessor flexibility in the event of repudiation.

Breach by seller or lessor. Now let us assume that the seller or the lessor repudiates at this stage. What are the buyer's or lessee's rights? The buyer or lessee may also call off the deal and obtain damages. *See* UCC 2-610(1)(b), 2A-402(1)(c), 2-711(2) [former 2-711(1)], 2A-508(1), 2-712, 2A-518, 2-713, and 2A-519. Can the buyer or lessee choose to go forward with the transaction and force the goods out of the seller or the lessor? *See* UCC 2-610(1)(b), 2A-402(1)(c), 2-711(2)(g) and (h) ([former 2-711(2)], 2A-508(1) [former 2A-508(2)]. As with most "goods oriented" remedies, this alternative may put the buyer or lessee in conflict with creditors of and purchasers from the seller or lessor. If the buyer or lessee has a prior perfected Article 9 security interest, it may prevail over those third parties under the rules of Article 9. Otherwise, the buyer or lessee must rely on its right under UCC 2-502 or 2A-522, if it is a pre-paying buyer or lessee, or on its right to specific performance or replevin as specified in UCC 2-716 or 2A-507A [former 2A-521]. These rights may be subject to third party interests. *See* UCC 2-402, 2A-307 and 2A-308.

Damage remedies. A closer look at the parties' damages remedy is in order. Can damage remedies be combined with other remedies? Yes. The UCC does not favor "election" doctrines, although the principle of UCC-based damages is stated in UCC 1-305 [former 1-106]. Cancellation does not extinguish a right to damages. *See* UCC 2-720, 2A-505(3). Are there any significant parallels between the seller's or lessor's damages remedy and that of the buyer or lessee? Yes. Both can go into the market and "fix" damages against the breaching party, so to speak. *See* UCC 2-706, 2A-527, 2-712, 2A-518. Yet neither is required to do this. Both can simply sue for damages for repudiation and get the full market-contract-price differential rather than the differential between contract and a substitute transaction consummated by the "reselling" seller or "releasing" lessor or "covering" buyer or lessee. *See* UCC 2-708(1), 2A-528(1), 2-713, 2A-518(1). Can the parties get consequential damages? Under both Articles 2 and 2A prior to the 2003 amendments it was clear that the buyer or lessee could. *See* UCC 2-715, 2A-520. Under the 2003 amendments to both Articles 2 and 2A, the seller or lessor may also recover consequential damages as long as the sale or lease is not a consumer contract. UCC 2-710, 2A-530.

The rights of a party to call off the deal, to get damages, or to go forward with the deal, are the basic remedial options.[*]

Inability to perform. After the agreement and prior to shipment, other things can go wrong besides repudiation. It may emerge that one of the parties will not, at the appointed time, be *able* to perform. In such circumstances, the aggrieved party may demand adequate assurances of performance. UCC 2-609, 2A-401. Failure to provide such assurances within a reasonable time is classed as a "repudiation." Prospective inability to perform will, when it exists, entitle the aggrieved party to pursue the same general remedial options as would be available

---

[*] The Article 2 scheme is carefully analyzed in detail in Ellen A. Peters, *Remedies for Breach of Contracts Relating to the Sale of Goods Under the Uniform Commercial Code: A Roadmap for Article Two*, 73 YALE L. J. 199 (1963). *See also* ROY RYDEN ANDERSON, DAMAGES UNDER THE UNIFORM COMMERCIAL CODE (2003). For a critique of the Article 2A provisions on lessor's remedies, *see* Donald J. Rapson, *Deficiencies and Ambiguities in Lessors' Remedies Under Article 2A: Using Official Comments to Cure Problems in the Statute*, 39 ALA. L. REV. 875 (1988).

upon repudiation.

Insolvency should be mentioned as a special form of prospective inability to perform which inherently introduces third parties. When opposing third party interests are in the picture, "going forward" with the deal becomes less desirable to the seller where the buyer is insolvent, and less freely available to the buyer where the seller is insolvent. *Compare* UCC 2-702(1), 2A-525(1) and 2-502(1), 2A-522(1).

Casualty to goods identified to the contract is another kind of event that can occur after contract and prior to shipment. In some circumstances, it will excuse the seller or lessor of the obligation to provide the goods. *See* UCC 2-613, 2A-221. The topic of casualty and attendant risk of loss problems will be considered in the next subsection.

Remedial issues for failure to perform are considered in Chapter Ten, *infra*. The parties' respective rights to the goods are considered in Chapter Nine, *infra*. Excuse of performance obligations is discussed in Chapter Seven, *infra*.

C. The Stage of Getting the Goods or Documents Therefor to the Buyer or Lessee

Duties of seller or lessor. Many Article 2 contracts call for the seller to deliver the goods to the buyer at the buyer's town or place of business. For the time, manner and place of delivery, *absent* such contractual stipulation, *see* UCC 2-309, 2-307, 2-308, 2-503 and 2-507. Article 2A does not contain any analogs to these sections. One explanation for such an omission is that the parties in a lease agreement generally have terms governing these items and therefore providing for gap fillers on these issues in Article 2A was unnecessary.

Here the primary focus is on the seller's performance. Several things can go wrong at this stage. The seller may deliver late, or at the wrong place, or in an improper manner. Also, the seller who is required or authorized to send the goods to the buyer must, unless otherwise agreed, make a "proper contract" of carriage and notify the buyer of shipment. *See* UCC 2-504.* The seller may simply fail to do this, thereby incurring liability to the buyer. Of course, the rights of the buyer upon default at this stage vary with the nature of the default. Can the buyer always call the deal off? No. *See, e.g.,* UCC 2-504, 2-612, 2-614. But it will generally be entitled to damages. *See* UCC 2-711.

---

* Article 2A has no comparable provision.

Article 2A does not spell out what the lessor has to do to perform its obligation of getting the goods to the lessee. However, Article 2A does in some circumstances prevent the lessee from calling off the deal due to the lessor's failure to perform its contractual obligation. UCC 2A-510, 2A-404. The lessee will generally be entitled to damages for the lessor's failure to perform. UCC 2A-508.

In some circumstances the seller or lessor may be excused from performing its contractual obligations, UCC 2-613, 2A-221 (casualty to identified goods required by the contract), 2-615, 2A-405 (excused performance), and in that case, the buyer or lessee has the option to accept the seller's or lessor's diminished performance or terminate the contract but without further right as against the seller or lessor. UCC 2-616, 2A-406.

Duties of carrier. The carrier may fail to perform *its* obligations. The duties of such a carrier will be specified in the contract of carriage (bill of lading) and in Article 7 of the UCC, where the deal is intrastate. If interstate, the Federal Bills of Lading Act governs. The carrier will be liable for damages caused by improper loading for which it is responsible. *See* UCC 7-301(d) [former 7-301(4)]. The carrier may negligently cause damage to the goods for which liability lies under UCC 7-309. Or the carrier may simply fail to follow instructions thereby causing loss. For example, the seller or lessor may have a right to stop the goods in transit, UCC 2-705, 2A-526, and the carrier may fail to honor stoppage instructions. *See* UCC 7-403. Here, though, the seller or lessor rather than the buyer or lessee would be the aggrieved party as against the carrier.

Risk of loss. The goods in transit may be lost or damaged (with or without the carrier's fault). The carrier's insurance will often cover most of the loss. But "risk of loss" problems can arise. Generally, risk passes to the buyer upon tender by the seller to the carrier under the normal type of contract, a shipment contract. UCC 2-509(1)(a), 2-503, cmt. 5. In that circumstance, the buyer bears the risk of something happening to the goods in transit. Sometimes, however, risk passes upon tender at destination when the contract calls for delivery at the buyer's city. *See* UCC 2-509(1)(b). Hence, as between seller and buyer, seller would be responsible for loss occurring during carriage in such a deal. It should be noted that UCC 2-510 says, among other things, that a seller cannot pass the risk of loss for nonconforming goods unless the buyer accepts the goods in spite of the nonconformity.

In a lease, the lessor retains the risk of loss in a lease that is not a finance lease. UCC 2A-219(1). If the risk is to pass to the lessee, the rules of UCC 2A-219(2) parallel the rules on shipment and destination contracts found in UCC 2-509(1). Again, if the risk is to pass to the lessee under the terms of the contract, the lessor cannot pass the risk of loss if the goods are nonconforming unless the lessee accepts the goods in spite of the nonconformity. UCC 2A-220.

Documents. The foregoing discussion has centered on deals for goods only. What if the sales contract calls for delivery of a document of title to the buyer in exchange for the buyer's cash payment on the spot or his signature to a time draft? *See* UCC 2-503(5). Because Article 2A has no comparable provision, the lessor's obligation to deliver a document of title would be governed by the parties' agreement. Most of the kinds of things that can go wrong in procuring and transmitting documents can be readily inventoried. As procured, the document may fail to describe the goods properly. *See* UCC 7-301. Or it may not be in correct form. *See* UCC 2-503(5)(a). The document may be lost or stolen. *See* UCC 7-601. Or it may get into the wrong hands, and, if negotiable, and the transferee takes by due negotiation, then the transferee will generally get title to the document and to the goods. *See* UCC 7-501 and UCC 7-502. *But see* UCC 7-503. Or the document may be altered. *See* UCC 7-306.

Issues of delivery, risk of loss, and insurance are covered in Chapters Six and Eight, *infra*.

D. The Receipt-Inspection Stage

In commercial deals, the receipt-inspection stage is the crucial stage. Here the seller or lessor will typically lose any control it has over the goods. Here the buyer or lessee will, usually for the first time, inspect and decide whether to accept or reject. The buyer or lessee will generally prefer to inspect before paying. Blind payment puts the buyer or lessee at a disadvantage: when the goods turn out not to be conforming, the buyer or lessee becomes a potential plaintiff, whereas, if there is to be litigation at all, it is generally better to be a potential defendant who has first inspected and then rejected the goods for nonconformity. The blindly paying buyer or lessee is also at a disadvantage because, as plaintiff, it must assume the risk of the seller's or lessor's insolvency to the satisfaction of any judgment. Further, the buyer or lessee who pays blindly may find that it has assumed control over and therefore responsibility for the goods.[*]

Inspection. Contracts often specifically provide for a right of the buyer or lessee to inspect before payment or acceptance. But what if the contract is silent? UCC 2-513 says that the buyer in an Article 2 transaction has a right to inspect

---

[*] *See generally*, John Honnold, *Buyer's Right of Rejection,* 97 U. PA. L. REV. 457 (1949).

before payment or acceptance unless the buyer has contracted it away. One way the buyer can give up this right is by agreeing to pay "against documents" covering the goods. UCC 2-513(3)(b), 2-512, 2-310. Although Article 2A does not contain comparable provisions, it too recognizes that the lessee has a right to inspect the goods before acceptance, UCC 2A-515, but does not address whether the lessee has a right to inspect the goods before payment. Presumably the timing of the payment obligation of the lessee in relation to the lessee's right to inspect the goods prior to acceptance is spelled out in the parties' agreement.

Duty to tender. What are the ways the seller or lessor can fail to perform at this stage (other than "failures of delivery" already considered)? In the main, the seller or lessor may fail to tender goods to which she has title, or fail to tender goods that are of the right quantity or of the right quality. These latter two kinds of breaches are not uncommon, as breaches go. And they both may take a variety of forms, depending on the nature of the goods. Similarly, the seller or lessor may tender non-conforming *documents* covering goods. What is the general standard of performance to which the seller or lessor is held? The contract is the first touchstone. But in general contract law, the doctrine of substantial performance permits some departure from the strict obligations of the contract, with the result that the non-performing party can still recover "on the contract." Is it the same under the UCC? Generally, no. UCC 2-601 and 2A-509 seemingly require "perfect tender." As to quality, the warranty provisions, UCC 2-312 through 2-315 and UCC 2A-210 through 2A-213, determine the relevant standard of performance as to quality of the goods to the extent the contract is silent. The perfect tender doctrine is, however, modified by the seller or lessor's ability to cure (UCC 2-508, 2A-513), the parties' agreement on modification of remedies (UCC 2-718, 2-719, 2A-503, 2A-504), and a substantial performance rule as it applies to nonconforming deliveries in an installment contract (UCC 2-612, 2A-510).

Rejection and revocation of acceptance. Assuming the seller or lessor has failed to make perfect tender, and that she cannot rely on the doctrine of substantial performance, what are the buyer's or lessee's rights? The basic damages remedies have already been outlined. *See* UCC 2-712 and 2A-518 (cover-based damages), 2-713 and 2A-519 (market-based damages). The emphasis here should be on the buyer's or lessee's "goods-oriented" options. If the buyer or lessee wishes, it may reject the goods. UCC 2-601, 2A-509. To do so, it has to jump through the right hoops, including timely notice to the seller or lessor and taking reasonable care of the rejected goods. *See* UCC 2-602, 2-605, 2A-509, 2A-512, and 2A-514. A merchant buyer or lessee may have additional duties in regard to care and disposition of the goods. *See* UCC 2-603, 2-604, 2A-511, 2A-512. The buyer or lessee may, however, want the seller or lessor to perform–to send goods that do conform. The buyer or lessee *may* be entitled to specific performance or replevin under UCC 2-716 or 2A-507A [former 2A-521].

What if the buyer or lessee has accepted the goods (UCC 2-606, 2A-515) and has later discovered a defect, or has accepted the goods with the seller's or lessor's assurances that non-conformities would be corrected, but such has not occurred? Has the buyer or lessee forever lost its right to throw the goods back at the seller or lessor? No. Revocation of acceptance is allowed in some circumstances. *See* UCC 2-608, 2A-517. But the buyer or lessee, again, must jump through the right hoops of timely notice and care of the goods. *See* UCC 2-608(2), 2-607(3)(a), 2A-517(4), 2A-516(3)(a). Such revocation of acceptance, along with rejection, leaves the buyer or lessee free, too, to pursue damages. *See* UCC 2-711, 2A-508.

Damages for accepted goods. Finally, the buyer or lessee may choose to retain non-conforming goods and recover damages. *See* UCC 2-714, 2A-519(3). But, if the buyer or lessee is to take this avenue, it must give timely notice of the breach. UCC 2-607, 2A-516. In commercial cases, this avenue is more common than in consumer cases, where the defect in the goods often makes them of no value at all, and the buyer's or lessee's main concern is to get damages for breach of warranty, often consisting of consequential damages based on personal injury or property damage. *See* UCC 2-715(2), 2A-520(2). Most of Article 2 litigation is warranty of quality litigation, consumer and non-consumer. The UCC's basic warranty provisions, to be treated intensively later, are UCC 2-313 through 2-318. Article 2A has comparable provisions in UCC 2A-210, 2A-212 through 2A-216.

Duties of buyer or lessee. We turn now to non-performance by the *buyer or lessee* at the receipt- inspection stage. The buyer may in an Article 2 transaction fail to provide proper facilities for presentation of the goods for inspection. *See* UCC 2-503(1). The buyer may make a wrongful demand for inspection. *See* UCC 2-513(3)(b). The buyer may fail to follow contractual or statutorily prescribed procedures for inspection. *See* UCC 2-513(1). Because the lessee's right to inspect the goods before acceptance is inferred from the requirements of UCC 2A-515 and not stated explicitly in Article 2A, whether the lessee has engaged in wrongful conduct in exercising its inspection right must be resolved by determining the agreement of the parties. A buyer or lessee may "impose" unagreed upon standards of conformity. The buyer or lessee may deny the seller's or lessor's right to cure. *See* UCC 2-508, 2A-513. The buyer or lessee may reject the goods in an installment contract when it does not have the right to reject the goods for some nonconformity.

See UCC 2-612, 2A-510. The buyer or lessee may mistakenly think the goods do not conform. The buyer or lessee may attempt to reject but fail to jump through prescribed rejection hoops. *See* UCC 2-602, 2A-509. The buyer or lessee may fail to take over the goods and care for or dispose of them as required. UCC 2-602 through 2-604, 2A-511 and 2A-512. Perhaps most significant in the usual run of cases, the buyer or lessee may refuse, for some reason, to pay at the required time. *See* UCC 2-507, 2A-523.

Remedies of seller or lessor. The appropriate maneuver for the seller or lessor will vary with the nature of the buyer's or lessee's breach and the course of action the buyer or lessee takes. Often the seller or lessor will want and will be entitled to damages, a general remedy already outlined at the post-agreement stage. *See* UCC 2-703, 2A-523. Here, the focus will be on the seller's or lessor's "goods-oriented" remedies assuming the buyer or lessee is retaining the goods and the seller's or lessor's right to the price or rent, whether or not the buyer or lessee retains the goods.

Generally, if the buyer or lessee is refusing payment, and payment is due at this stage, the seller or lessor will be entitled to reclaim the goods from the buyer or lessee. UCC 2-507(2), 2-511, 2A-525. As with most goods-oriented remedies, third parties may enter the picture and defeat the aggrieved party. As against creditors of the buyer, UCC 2-507(3) controls. As against creditors of the lessee, UCC 2A-307 controls. As against buyers from the buyer, UCC 2-507(3) and 2-403 must be consulted. As against buyers from the lessee, UCC 2A-305 provides the relevant rules. And, of course, as in all situations, any relevant cases must be considered. But the seller in an Article 2 transaction could retain a security interest in the goods with priority entitling it to defeat almost all third parties taking the goods from the buyer/debtor except "buyers in ordinary course of business" from the buyer/debtor. *See* UCC 9-103, 9-201, 9-320. A lessor's interest is better protected against third parties claiming through the lessee because of UCC 2A-305 and 2A-307.

And when is the seller or lessor entitled to the price or rent against a buyer or lessee in breach at this stage? If the buyer has accepted the goods (UCC 2-606, 2A-515) and has not properly rejected them or justifiably revoked acceptance of them, then the seller or lessor may have the price or rent. *See* UCC 2-709, 2A-529. The seller or lessor may also get the price or rent in two other, more restricted, situations under UCC 2-709 and 2A-529.

Warranty liability is considered in Chapter Five, *infra*, nonconforming tender and the right to reject or revoke acceptance are considered in Chapter Six, *infra*, and the remedies for nonconforming performance and accepted products are considered in Chapter Eleven, *infra.* Limitations on available remedies are considered in Chapter Twelve, *infra.*

E. The Payment Stage

Default rule. The overwhelming majority of transactions pass on through the payment stage without incident. But some hang up at this stage, too. Payment due on delivery has already been treated. But in the overwhelming majority of commercial deals, and in a substantial proportion of consumer deals, payment is strung out over some period *after* the buyer or lessee comes into possession of the goods. Credit is extended by the seller or lessor. Breakdowns in the payment process in deals of this nature will now be considered.

Credit sales. If the deal is silent on payment in a sale transaction, then payment is usually due when the buyer receives the goods. UCC 2-310(1). C.O.D. (collect on delivery) deals and transactions calling for payment of a draft upon presentation of documents may be thought of as similar to cash deals as payment is due when the buyer is to receive the documents. UCC 2-310(3). Article 2A does not contain any default rules on when payment is due, so this term must be governed by the parties' agreement.

Credit must be agreed upon. Terms vary. Extension of credit may be *secured* under Article 9. Also, a buyer or lessee may be required to sign a time draft, thus giving the seller or lessor the advantages of having a signed negotiable instrument to sue on. *See* UCC 3-301, 3-305(a). A buyer or lessee may fail to pay because of insolvency. In this situation, the seller or lessor will, again, be interested in goods-oriented remedies. The seller's right to recover the goods from the buyer is quite limited. UCC 2-702(2). The lessor's right is not as limited. UCC 2A-525. The seller's right is itself "subject to" the claims of certain parties under UCC 2-702(3) whereas the lessor's right is not generally subject to claims of the lessee's creditors. UCC 2A-307.

Payment by check. The buyer or lessee may undertake to pay by drawing a check to the order of the seller or lessor. A check is a negotiable instrument if in proper form (UCC 3-104). A check orders the drawer's bank to pay the payee or to the payee's order or to bearer. The drawer's bank may refuse to honor the check, for any one of a variety of reasons but most commonly because the check over-draws the buyer's or lessee's account.

Assume the check is dishonored. What action could the seller or lessor take? It could sue the buyer or lessee on the underlying obligation. *See* UCC 3-310(b).

But it could not recover from the bank, because a check is not an assignment (UCC 3-408) and a party is not liable on an instrument unless its signature appears thereon. *See* UCC 3-401. Nor is the seller or lessor recognized as a third party beneficiary of the contract of deposit between buyer's bank and buyer. It is possible, on the right facts, that the bank would be liable to the seller or lessor on a tort theory, such as conversion. *See* UCC 3-420.

If the buyer or lessee was not the drawer of the check, but simply was indorsing over to the seller or lessor a check made payable to the buyer or lessee, the seller or lessor might be a holder in due course under UCC 3-302 and, in an action against the drawer, immune from most ordinary defenses (*e.g.*, failure of consideration, fraud) that a drawer might have against someone suing him on the instrument. *See* UCC 3-414 and 3-305. Similarly, the seller or lessor might be a holder in due course against an indorser and immune from such defenses. *See* UCC 3-305. To hold such an indorser liable, though, the seller or lessor would have to give notice of dishonor as required by UCC 3-414(b), 3-415, and Part 5 of Article 3. There is the further possibility that the seller or lessor will be entitled to recover from a transferor of the instrument on a "warranty" theory. *See* UCC 3-416.

To recapitulate: Upon dishonor of a check given in payment for goods, the seller or lessor might have recovery against the buyer or lessee on the underlying obligation, or against the buyer or lessee and possibly other parties "on the instrument," or possibly against a transferor on a "warranty" theory.

So much for how things might go upon dishonor. What if the buyer's or lessee's bank does not dishonor the check, but rather, fails to pay the proper party, *i.e.*, the seller or lessor, or fails to pay the proper amount? Such events can occur in a variety of ways. We shall at this juncture consider only two situations. Assume the buyer or lessee draws a check to the seller or lessor, but is interrupted and does not sign the check as drawer. A thief steals the check, forges the buyer's or lessee's signature, and then takes the check to X who cashes it, giving thief the money. X presents the check to the buyer's or lessee's bank and the bank honors it. Later, the forgery is discovered. Buyer's or lessee's bank is not entitled to charge the drawer's account, because the item is not "properly payable." UCC 4-401(a). But the buyer or lessee is not, of course, discharged from liability to the seller or lessor and still must pay. Can the bank retrieve its loss from X? *See* UCC 3-418.

The seller or lessor may be a wrongdoer. What if the seller or lessor alters the amount of the check upward and the bank pays? Again, the drawer's account is not chargeable as to the excess unless he negligently contributed to the alteration. UCC

4-401, 3-406. The seller or lessor, if she can be found, can be prosecuted. And the bank can recover against seller or lessor.

So much for a *sample* of the kinds of things that can go wrong in the payment process where a check is used.

An intermediary bank or carrier may fail to perform its obligations in the payment process. The carrier in a C.O.D. deal may fail to pick up the cash. The bank in a documentary deal may (a) fail to secure proper payment from the buyer or lessee upon tender of the documents, or (b) fail to procure the buyer's or lessee's signature to a time draft as agreed. *See* UCC 4-501, 4-502, and 4-503. The moral for the seller or lessor is dual: utilize reliable intermediaries and deal with sound buyers or lessees.

What is the plight of a buyer or lessee who puts a check in the process of payment or signs a draft or pays cash on a sight draft and thereafter immediately discovers that the goods fail to conform? Is there anything that can be done, through prompt action, to "undo" what she has done? These questions will be treated in the context of specific cases in Chapter Six, *infra*.

F. Finance Leases

As can be seen by the above summary, many if not most of the Article 2A provisions are comparable to provisions from Article 2. Article 2A, however, provides for a type of transaction peculiar to leasing, a finance lease.[*] A finance lease is excruciatingly defined in UCC 2A-103(1)(l) [former 2A-103(1)(g)], but the basic concept is simple. A person who wishes to use goods picks out the goods from a supplier. Instead of buying the goods, the person who wants the goods convinces the finance lessor to purchase the goods from the supplier. The lessee supplies the specifications for the goods. The finance lessor then leases the goods to the lessee. There are two contracts involved: a supply contract between the supplier and the finance lessor and a lease contract between lessor and lessee.

Throughout Article 2A, the provisions distinguish between rules that apply to a finance lease and rules that apply to a non-finance lease. For example, UCC 2A-209 provides that the supplier's warranties pass through to the lessee, the intended beneficiary of these warranties. The lessor under a finance lease does not make a warranty of non-infringement, UCC 2A-211(2), an implied warranty of

---

[*] *See also* Steven R. Schoenfeld, *Commercial Law: The Finance Lease Under Article 2A of the Uniform Commercial Code*, 1989 ANN. SURV. AM. L. 565.

merchantability, UCC 2A-212, or an implied warranty of fitness for particular purpose, UCC 2A-213. The risk of loss provisions differ for a finance lease, UCC 2A-219 and 2A-220. The rules regulating excuse differ in the case of a finance lease. *See* UCC 2A-221(b), 2A-405(c), and 2A-406(1)(b). Once the lessee accepts the goods under a non-consumer finance lease, the lessee's obligations under the lease are irrevocable and independent of the supplier's obligations under the supply contract. *See* UCC 2A-407, 2A-209. Upon acceptance of the goods, the finance lessee's ability to revoke acceptance is limited. *See* UCC 2A-516(2), 2A-517.

G. Special Problems of Third Party Rights in a Lease Transaction

Given that the transfer of property rights from a lessor to a lessee is of a limited nature, *see* UCC 2A-103(1)(p) [former 2A-103(1)(j)], Article 2A has several provisions that deal explicitly with third party claims to the goods. These provisions are derived in part from comparable provisions in Article 9. Thus a lease contract is effective against third parties except as provided in Article 2A. *See* UCC 2A-301. *Compare* UCC 9-201. Article 2A adopts a policy that parties' rights under the lease contract are freely transferable. UCC 2A-303. *Compare* UCC 2-210, 9-407. Article 2A has several provisions that address priority of the rights of creditors of or purchasers from the lessor and lessee. UCC 2A-306, 2A-307, 2A-309, 2A-310. *Compare* UCC 9-333, 9-317, 9-320, 9-321, 9-323, 9-334 and 9-335. Article 2A also has provisions derived from UCC 2-403 on transfer of rights, UCC 2A-304 and 2A-305, and derived from UCC 2-402 on transactions treated as fraudulent as to creditors, UCC 2A-308.

H. Conclusion

This concludes what is intended only to be a *general outline* of the main stages of the unfolding sale or lease transaction, of the *kinds* of things that can go wrong at each stage, and of the relevant law bearing thereon. Every problem and principle considered in this chapter will be treated again, usually in depth. What the student should now have is: (1) a general overview of the modern commercial sales or lease transaction on credit as it progresses from the agreement stage through performance and payment; (2) some sense of the nature of the things that can go wrong at each stage; (3) a *functionally* useful roadmap through the structure of Article 2 and Article 2A; and (4) some idea of how Articles 3, 4, 7, and 9 may bear on a sale or lease transaction.

SECTION 2.   DETERMINING WHAT LAW APPLIES

In this section we consider more carefully the question of which articles of the UCC apply to what transactions. Some domestic transactions, such as a contract for professional services, are not covered by the UCC at all. Other transactions may be covered in whole or in part by one or more of the UCC articles. For example, a disputed claim arising under a contract for sale may be settled by a check drawn under Article 3 and paid under Article 4. And international sales are not covered by the UCC at all.

Remember, Article 1 applies "to a transaction to the extent that it is governed by another article of the [UCC.]" UCC 1-102. Thus, it is possible that the parties by agreement can determine which law applies, UCC 1-301 [former 1-105], or vary the effect of the provisions of the UCC that do apply. UCC 1-302 [former 1-102].

A. Analysis of the Scope of Article 2 and Article 2A

1.   Article 2: Sales

To what disputes does Article 2 apply, either directly or by analogy? Section 2-102 provides that "[u]nless the context otherwise requires, this Article applies to transactions in goods * * * ." Article 2, however, "does not apply to any transaction which although in the form of an unconditional contract to sell or present sale is intended to operate only as a security transaction * * *." *See* UCC 2-102. Section 2-102 raises more questions than its text answers.

Goods. What, for example, are goods? Read UCC 2-103(1)(k) and former 2-105(1). Identify the points of agreement and difference between these two definitions of "goods." Consider further the idea that "goods" also includes things attached to real estate. Read UCC 2-107. The 2003 amendments to Article 2 changed the definition of goods to exclude "information" and the "subject matter of foreign exchange transactions." UCC 2-103(1)(k) [former 2-105(1)]. *See also* UCC 2A-103(1)(n). Foreign exchange transactions is a defined term, UCC 2-103(1)(i), but "information" is not.

The information exclusion in amended Article 2. What is "information"? Based upon the comment about the definition of goods in UCC 2-103, you can glean that information includes software. Whether software should be a "good" for the purpose of falling within the scope of Article 2 was a very controversial issue during the Article 2 revision process. Prior to this amendment, many courts had held that software was a "good" and thus a sale or license of software was within the scope of Article 2.[*] Other courts have held that contracts to develop software are not contracts for the sale of goods but rather service contracts.[**] Does this distinction make sense in light of the inclusion of "specially manufactured goods" within the definition of "goods"?[***] Of course, the commentators have not been silent on the issue either.[****] For UCITA's take on what law should apply, *see* UCITA 103 and the relevant definitions. Licenses to provide software would be "computer information transactions." UCITA 102(a)(10), (11).

Identification and future sales of future goods. Notice that the Article 2 definition focuses on the "thing" being "movable at the time of identification to the contract for sale." When are goods identified to the contract? The question is answered in UCC 2-501. What difference does it make whether goods are identified? Goods must be "existing and identified before any interest in them" can pass to a buyer, UCC 2-105, whether that interest be title, UCC 2-401, or a "special" property interest, UCC 2-501(1). The importance of these property interests will be explored later. Note that a purported present sale of "future" goods, *i.e.*, goods that are neither existing nor identified, operates as a "contract to sell." *See* UCC 2-105(1) [former 2-105(2)]. Under the 2003 amendments, "future goods" are included within the meaning of "goods." What is the importance then of the designation of a purported present sale of future goods as a contract to sell? UCC 2-106. The intersection of four concepts, present sale, future sale, existing goods and future goods, creates at least four categories: a present sale of existing goods; a purported present sale of future goods, a future sale of existing goods, and

---

[*] *See e.g., Micro Data Base Systems Inc. v. Dharma Systems Inc.*, 148 F.3d 649 (7th Cir. 1998); *Advent Systems, Ltd. v. Unisys Corp.*, 925 F.2d 670 (3rd Cir. 1991).

[**] *See e.g., Pearl Investments LLC v. Standard I/O Inc.*, 257 F. Supp. 2d 326 (D. Me. 2003); *Multi-Tech Systems Inc. v. Floreat, Inc.*, 2002 WL 432016 (D. Minn. 2002).

[***] *See Birwelco-Monenary Inc. v. Infilco Degremont, Inc.*, 827 So. 2d 255 (Fla. Ct. App. 2001) (per curium) (held that definition of goods included specially manufactured goods so should not evaluate transaction under predominate purpose test used to distinguish services from goods transactions).

[****] Jean Braucher, *When Your Refrigerator Orders Groceries Online and Your Car Dials 911 After an Accident: Do We Really Need New Law for the World of Smart Goods*, 8 WASH. U.J. L. & POL'Y 241 (2002); Lorin Brennan, *Why Article 2 Cannot Apply to Software Transactions*, 38 DUQ. L. REV. 459 (2001).

a future sale of future goods. Are all of these transactions within the scope of Article 2?

Transactions in goods. There are a number of questions to answer here. What is a "transaction" in goods? Section 2-106(1) provides that "In this Article unless the context otherwise requires 'contract' and 'agreement' are limited to those relating to the present or future sale of goods." Thus, where those words are used in Article 2, the transaction is a sale or a contract to sell goods. But the word "transaction" is not clearly defined. Could it include a lease or a bailment? What about a gift?

In approaching this question, remember that there are two kinds of Code limitations on the seemingly unlimited scope of the word "transactions." First, there are other Articles, *e.g.*, Article 7 on bailments for storage or carriage and Article 2A on leases of goods which may supercede the specific provisions of Article 2. Second, many of the specific provisions of Article 2 are themselves cast in terms of "seller" and "buyer" or limited to "contracts for sale." *See* UCC 2-106(1). It would thus appear that some provisions of Article 2 might apply to a non-sales situation, *e.g.*, UCC 2-202, 2-206, 2-212, 2-213, while other provisions are, seemingly, limited to sales, *e.g.*, UCC 2-201, 2-205, 2-312, 2-313, 2-314 & 2-315.

What does UCC 2-102 mean when it states that it does not apply to a transaction "intended to operate only as a security transaction?" Read UCC 9-109 and the definition of goods in UCC 9-102(a)(44). See the comment to UCC 2-102. What happens when the transaction is potentially within the scope of both Article 2 and Article 9?

When does the context "otherwise" require? For example, if the "transaction" is other than a contract for sale, should the context be invoked to broaden or narrow the scope of Article 2? If the use of context broadens scope, should all or part of Article 2 be applied?

Other questions. Finally, if Article 2 does not directly apply, can it be extended by analogy to the dispute before the court? The comments if not the text of the UCC support this extension, *see* Comment 1, UCC 1-103 [former comment 1 to former 1-102], but the question remains when it is proper for a court to apply legislation to a dispute beyond the scope intended by the legislature.[*]

Even if Article 2 applies to a transaction, it may not contain the only rules that

---

[*] *See generally* Daniel E. Murray, *Under the Spreading Analogy of Article 2 of the Uniform Commercial Code,* 39 FORDHAM L. REV. 447 (1971).

apply to that transaction. Consumer law, other statutes dealing with specialized goods, or federal law may also apply. The 2003 amendments to Article 2 added UCC 2-108 which addresses the interrelationship between Article 2 and other law. Read that section. Article 2A has a comparable provision in UCC 2A-104.

2. Article 2A: Leases

Prior to the enactment of Article 2A, there was no body of statutory law dealing with the "true" lease. Frequently, courts struggled with whether they should apply Article 2 by analogy to the lease transaction.*

Leases of goods are now covered by Article 2A. Read UCC 2A-102 and the definition of "lease" in UCC 2A-103(1). Also read UCC 1-203 [former 1-201(37)]. How do you tell whether a transaction is a lease or a sale with a security interest? UCC 1-203 unfolds in several distinct steps.

First, the facts of each case rather than the form of the transaction control. UCC 1-203(a).

Second, UCC 1-203(b) states when a transaction in the form of a lease creates a security interest. A security interest is created "if the consideration that the lessee is to pay the lessor for the right to possession and use of the goods is an obligation for the term of the lease and is not subject to termination by the lessee" **and** any one of the four listed circumstances apply. For example, suppose that Lessor "leases" goods to Lessee for four years for $1,000 per year. Lessee had no right to terminate. At the end of the lease term, Lessee has an option to purchase the goods for $1. The transaction creates a security interest. UCC 1-203(b)(4), and (d).

The four listed circumstances identify cases where, at the end of the lease, the value of lessor's residual is nominal. The residual value should be significant in a lease. According to Edwin Huddleson:

At common law, the central feature of a true lease is the reservation of an economically meaningful interest to the lessor at the end of the lease term. Ordinarily this means two things: (1) at the outset of the lease the parties expect the goods to retain some significant residual value at the end of the lease terms; and (2) the lessor retains some entrepreneurial stake (either the possibility of gain or the risk of loss) in the value of the goods at the end of

---

* *See Barco Auto Leasing Corp. v. PSI Cosmetics, Inc.*, 478 N.Y.S.2d 505 (N.Y. Civ. Ct. 1984), where the court appeared to find a "true" lease, yet applied Article 2 to the dispute by analogy.

the lease term.

Edwin E. Huddleson, *Old Wine in New Bottles: UCC Article 2A–Leases*, 39 ALA. L. REV. 615, 625 (1988).

Third, assuming that the transaction is in the form of a lease and passes muster under UCC 1-203(b), UCC 1-203(c) states a number of factors that do not create a security interest "merely" because they are present. Review those factors please.[*]

Here are some problems. As you study them, ask "What difference does it make whether Article 2 or Article 2A applies?"

Problem 2-1

A. Farmer orally agreed to sell Buyer his wheat crop yet to be planted for $3 a bushel. Bad weather sharpened the demand for wheat. Before the crop was planted, Farmer repudiated the agreement with Buyer and sold the crop to Cecil for $4 a bushel. Buyer sued Farmer for damages. Farmer defended, invoking the statute of frauds. UCC 2-201. Buyer argued that UCC 2-201 does not apply to a contract for the future sale of future goods. What result? *See* UCC 2-102, 2-103, 2-105, 2-106, and 2-201.

B. Seller agreed to sell Buyer timber standing on Seller's land to be severed by Seller. Seller severed half of the timber but before Buyer could haul it away, all timber, standing or severed, that Buyer agreed to buy was destroyed by fire. Buyer argued that the UCC's risk of loss provisions applied. *See* UCC 2-102, 2-103, 2-107 and 2-509. Is Buyer correct?

C. Seller owned a building which he contracted to sell to Buyer who was to remove it from its concrete foundation, put it on skids, and drag it away. Before removal, Seller repudiated.

(1) Does Article 2 govern Buyer's remedial rights? *See* UCC 2-107, 2-711 and 2-713. In *Condon Bros., Inc. v. Simpson Timber Co.*, 966 P.2d 355 (Wash. App. 1998), the court held that the sale of a five mile section of railroad (rails and ties) affixed to the ground at the time of sale and to be severed by the buyer was a "structure" for purposes of UCC 2-107(1). Thus, Article 2 did not apply. Even though the railroad could be severed without materially harming the land, the court held that UCC 2-107(2) did not apply so long as the ties and rails were a "structure" as described in UCC 2-107(1) to be severed by the buyer.

---

[*] For a very comprehensive discussion of the history and various approaches to this issue, *see In re QDS Components, Inc.*, 292 B.R. 313 (Bankr. S.D. Ohio 2002).

(2) What if Seller was to remove the building and put it on skids for Buyer to drag away?

(3) Would it make any difference if Seller leased the building to Buyer? *See* UCC 2A-103(1)(n) [former subpara. (h)], 2A-217. Article 2A does not contain a provision comparable to UCC 2-107.

D. Structure Equipment, a manufacturer located in California, is negotiating a contract to sell or lease equipment to Bisko Industries, an Illinois company, on credit for a fixed return. If Bisko defaults in payment, Structure would like to be able to repossess the equipment, resell it and apply the proceeds to Bisko's obligation. Structure wants to be able to repossess the equipment and not have to worry about complying with the default provisions of Article 9, Part 6. You know that if the transaction is a lease covered by Article 2A, Structure will be able to do so under UCC 2A-525.

(1) Assume the contact with Bisko provides that Structure retained title to the goods until full payment of the price. Is this a lease or a sale with a security interest? *See* UCC 1-201(b)(35) [former 1-201(37)], 1-203, 2-102, 2-401, 2A-102, 2A-103 (definition of lease). Why won't this work?

(2) How would you structure the transaction to clearly provide that the transaction is a lease governed by Article 2A? Assume that the transaction did not create a security interest under UCC 1-203(b) and the document contained the following terms. Are you confident that a court would hold the transaction is a lease and not a disguised security transaction?

1. "Lessor and Lessee agree, and Lessee represents for the benefit of Lessor and its Assignee(s) that the Lease is intended to be a 'finance lease' and not a 'lease intended as security' as those terms are used in the Uniform Commercial Code and that the Lease is intended to be 'true lease' as the term is commonly used under the Internal Revenue Code of 1986, as amended." (Section 9(b) of the Master Lease)

2. "Lessee has no interest in the Equipment except as expressly set forth in the Lease, and that interest is a lease-hold interest." (Section 9(b) of the Master Lease)

3. "The parties agree that this lease is a 'Finance Lease' as defined by Section 2A-103(g) of the Uniform Commercial Code ('UCC'). Lessee acknowledges that either (a) that Lessee has reviewed and approved any written Supply Contract (as defined by UCC 2A-103(y)) covering the Equipment purchased from the 'Supplier' (as defined by UCC 2A-103(x)) thereof for lease to Lessee [sic] or (b) that Lessor has informed or advised

Lessee, in writing, either previously or by this Lease of the following (i) the identity of the Suppliers; (ii) that the Lessee may have rights under the Supply Contract; and (iii) that the Lessee may contact the supplier for a description of any such rights Lessee may have under the Supply Contract." (Section 6 of Master Lease).

4. "The Lease is a net lease, it being the intention of the parties that all costs, expenses, and liabilities associated with the Equipment or its lease shall be borne by Lessee." (Section 5 of the Master Lease)

5. "It is the express intention of the Lessor and Lessee that all rent and other sums payable to Lessee under the Lease shall be, and continue to be, payable in all events throughout the terms of the Lease. The Lease shall be binding upon the Lessee, its successors and permitted assigns * * *." (Section 5 of the Master Lease)

6. "Lessee's obligations under the Lease with respect to Assignee shall be absolute and unconditional and not be subject to any abatement, reduction, recoupment, defense, offset or counterclaim for any reason * * *." (Section 11 of the Master Lease)

7. "Lessee represents and warrants to Lessor and its Assignee(s)(i) that the execution, delivery and performance of this Master Agreement and Lease was duly authorized and that upon execution of this Master Agreement and the Lease by Lessee and Lessor, the Master Agreement and the Lease will be in full force and effect and constitute a valid legal and binding obligation of the Lessee, and enforceable against the Lessee in accordance with its respective terms." (Section 16 of the Master Lease)

8. "The foregoing representations and warranties shall survive the execution and delivery of the Lease and any amendments hereto and shall upon the written request of Lessor be made to Lessor's Assignee(s)." (Section 16 of the Master Lease)

9. "The Master Agreement and the Lease constitute the entire and only agreement between Lessee and Lessor with respect to the lease of the Equipment, and the parties have only those rights and have incurred only those obligations as specifically set forth herein." (Section 19 of the Master Lease)

10. "Lessee acknowledges that Lessor shall be entitled to claim for federal income tax purposes (i) deductions (hereinafter called 'Depreciation Deductions') on Lessor's cost of the Equipment for each of its tax years during the term of the Lease under any method of depreciation or other cost

recovery formula permitted by the Internal Revenue Code * * *. Lessee agrees to take no action inconsistent (including the voluntary substitution of Equipment) with the foregoing or which would result in the loss, disallowance, recapture or unavailability to Lessor of Depreciation, Deductions or Interest Deductions." (Section 18 of the Master Lease)

11. "The Lease constitutes the entire and final agreement between the Lessor and Lessee and may not be contradicted by evidence of prior, contemporaneous or subsequent oral discussions, negotiations or agreements of the parties." (Section 20 of the Master Lease)*

Could the parties, by their agreement, vary the effect of UCC 1-203 determining whether the transaction is a lease or a security interest? UCC 1-302 [former 1-102(3)].

E. Alice wants to buy the latest version of the Word Processing Suite software for use in her home computer. What law will govern the transaction if Alice:

(1) downloads a copy of the software from the Word Processing web site;

(2) purchases a copy of the software on CD from the local software store;

(3) agrees to license the software from an application provider available through her internet cable provider.

Does it matter what version of Article 2 is in effect in the jurisdiction? What if UCITA is in effect in the jurisdiction? *See Specht v. Netscape Communications*, 306 F.3d 17 (2nd Cir. 2002) (doubting whether Article 2 applied to downloaded software).

F. Craig speculates in the currency market, agreeing to buy and sell currencies through his brokerage account. He makes (or loses) money based upon fluctuations in the value of the currencies. Do either former or amended Article 2 apply to this transaction?

G. Craig also trades securities through his brokerage account. Does Article 2 apply to his transactions to buy or sell securities?

H. Craig is owed money under a contract with Able to whom Craig sold his car. Craig sold his rights under the contract to Baker. Does Article 2 apply to that transaction? *See also* UCC 9-109.

---

* The terms of lease printed above are taken from *In re Homeplace Stores, Inc.*, 228 B.R. 88, 90-91 (Bank. D. Del. 1998). For a discussion of the former 1-201(37) definition, *see* E. Carolyn Hochstadter Dicker and John P. Campo, *FF &E and the True Lease Question: Article 2A and Accompanying Amendments to UCC Section 1-201(37)*, 7 AM. BANKR. INST. L. REV. 517 (1999). The analysis should be the same under UCC 1-203.

B. Mixed Transactions

A contract for personal or professional services is not within the scope of Article 2. But suppose goods are supplied and services are provided in the same transaction? Does Article 2 apply to the entire transaction? Would the same problem arise in a lease contract where the lessor leases goods to the lessee and also provides services to the lessee? Would Article 2A apply to the entire transaction? Should the analysis from the Article 2 cases be used in deciding these questions under Article 2A?

COAKLEY & WILLIAMS, INC. V. SHATTERPROOF GLASS CORP.
UNITED STATES COURT OF APPEALS, FOURTH CIRCUIT, 1983
706 F.2D 456, APPEAL AFTER REMAND, 778 F.2D 196 (1985),
CERT. DENIED, 475 U.S. 1121 (1986)

MURNAGHAN, CIRCUIT JUDGE

The strategy of experienced trial lawyers is to avoid, in all but the clearest case, a defense on the basis of a Federal Rules of Civil Procedure 12(b)(6) motion contending that there has been a "failure to state a claim upon which relief can be granted." At so early a stage, all factual inferences must be made in favor of the plaintiff; the facts must be viewed as the plaintiff most strongly can plead them.

Hence, the issues presented to the district court, the foundation underlying much of the law which may govern at subsequent stages of the case, will be addressed in circumstances which may well prove unduly favorable to the plaintiff. With little or no chance of prevailing, the defendant, in filing a 12(b)(6) motion, risks educating the plaintiff to aspects of the case which might otherwise be overlooked or at least not arise in circumstances so predispositive to the plaintiff's side of things.

The present case illustrates the proposition. On an appeal from a dismissal under 12(b)(6) the accepted rule is "that a complaint should not be dismissed for failure to state a claim unless it appears beyond doubt that the plaintiff can prove no set of facts in support of his claim which would entitle him to relief." * * * Liberal construction in favor of the plaintiff is mandated. * * * We state as "facts" the allegations and inferences most favorable to the plaintiff.

Washington Plate Glass Company had a contract "to furnish and install aluminum and glass curtain wall and store front work"[1] on a building located in Lanham, Maryland being built by Coakley & Williams, Inc., the plaintiff. To accomplish its contractual undertaking, Washington purchased the glass spandrel required from the defendant, Shatterproof Glass Corp. Still other materials needed for the project, predominantly aluminum, it appears were acquired in part at least elsewhere.

The contract price under the Coakley and Washington agreement amounted to $262,500, subsequently increased by amendment to $271,350.[2] The glass purchased by Washington from Shatterproof cost $87,715.00,[3] with the proviso that units were "to be properly marked for field installation."

The work progressed and the contract for the aluminum and glass curtain wall and storefront work was completed in March of 1974. Discoloration of the glass ensued, and Coakley complained. To remedy the situation, Washington agreed to replace the glass at no cost to Coakley, and did in fact replace a substantial portion of the glass. Shatterproof supplied the replacement glass and reimbursed Washington for the cost of re-installation, accomplished in April of 1977.

By December of 1977, the glass had again discolored, and complaints began to flow from Coakley to Washington and Shatterproof in or about December 1978. Shatterproof declined to replace a second time. On January 14, 1981, Coakley filed suit against Shatterproof in the Circuit Court for Montgomery County, Maryland

---

[1] The contract referred to "Spandrel glass to be 1/4" gold reflective glass with 1" rigid insulation fastened to curtain wall members approximately 1-1/2" behind glass spandrel." In addition the agreement called on Washington to provide, *inter alia*: a Texas Aluminum 400 series wall system, vision glass, aluminum objects of several kinds, steel anchor clips, field fasteners, and porcelain enamel panels.

[2] Of that increase of $8,850, the bulk ($8,000) reflected specification of ASG Reflectoview Tru-Therm, 1 lite coated with 20 GI Gold and temperal monolithic spandrel 1/4" 20 GI Gold to match. The remaining $850 increase was due to a change in the corner configuration from aluminum panel to 1/4" Gold Reflectiveview glass.

[3] The complaint is silent as to dollar amounts assignable to the additional materials. Obviously, the more they cost, the less the amount of the contract price attributable to services. We are not inclined to rely on statements of counsel at the time of argument in lieu of well-pleaded allegations. Counsel for Coakley asserted that the evidence would show that the cost of materials was substantially in excess of the cost of installation, *i.e.* more than $130,000. Even without counsel's arguments as a basis, it is still appropriate to recognize that such a possibility is in no way foreclosed by the allegations in the complaint. The plaintiff, at the early 12(b)(6) stage, is entitled to the benefit of the doubt.

alleging breach of implied warranties of merchantability and fitness for a particular purpose. Reliance was placed on certain provisions of the Maryland Uniform Commercial Code, Annotated Code of Maryland, § 1-101 *et seq.* Removal to the United States District Court for the District of Maryland followed, and Shatterproof sought dismissal under Fed.R.Civ.P. 12(b)(6).

A hearing on the 12(b)(6) motion followed at which Shatterproof contended (1) that the U.C.C. was inapplicable, (2) that lack of privity was fatal to the claim, and (3) that the statute of limitations had run prior to commencement of the action. We now have the case before us on appeal from an order granting the 12(b)(6) motion and dismissing the case solely on the grounds that the U.C.C. was not applicable.

Whether the U.C.C. applies turns on a question as to whether the contract between Washington and Coakley involved principally a sale of goods, on the one hand, or a provision of services, on the other. U.C.C. § 2-314 creates an implied warranty "that the *goods* shall be merchantable" to be "implied in a contract for their sale." Section 2-315 establishes an implied warranty "that the *goods* shall be fit" for a particular purpose, "[w]here the seller at the time of contracting has reason to know [the] particular purpose." (Emphasis added.)

Consequently, unless there has been a buyer of goods, the U.C.C. warranties of merchantability and of fitness for a particular use do not apply. Furthermore, unless there has been a buyer of goods,[4] the elimination of a requirement of privity would not have been achieved.[5] Accordingly, both questions (1) as to the availability of the warranties and (2) as to the amenability of Shatterproof, who was not in privity with Coakley, to suit by Coakley, come down to whether the transactions between Washington and Coakley was a sale of goods or the provision of services.

To resolve that question, we must address ourselves to a welter of cases reaching varying results depending on the considerations deemed to predominate

---

[4] Under U.C.C. § 2-103(1)(a), the term "buyer" is defined, in unexceptional terms, as "a person who buys or contracts to buy goods."

[5] *See* U.C.C. § 2-314(1)(b): "Any previous requirement of privity is abolished as between the *buyer* and the seller in any action brought by the *buyer*." (Emphasis added.) Absent compliance with § 2-314(1)(b), the lack of privity would have been fatal to Coakley's maintenance of the cause of action. *E.g., Vaccarino v. Cozzubo,* 181 Md. 614, 31 A.2d 316 (1943). If the transaction was one for goods, Coakley was self-evidently the buyer. Shatterproof was the seller of goods in a transaction in which the intermediary, Washington, not Coakley, was the buyer. However, Washington's purpose in buying was to apply the items purchased to uses benefitting Coakley.

in each particular case.[6] It should not pass unnoticed that all were decided at summary judgment or beyond. No case involving the issue appears to have been disposed of at the Rule 12(b)(6) or demurrer stage. They emphasize, in particular, three aspects which may, or may not, constitute indicia of the nature of the contract: (1) the language of the contract, (2) the nature of the business of the supplier, and (3) the intrinsic worth of the materials involved.

A distillation of the cases * * * produces an inescapable conclusion that, on the facts in their present pro-plaintiff posture, a reasonable viewing of them would permit a factfinder to conclude that the contract between Washington and Coakley predominantly concerned a sale of goods, and consequently was governed by the U.C.C. A Rule 12(b)(6) motion simply cannot serve to dispose of the case.

As to the first of the emphasized aspects, the contract between Washington and Coakley speaks in terms of furnishing and installing a wall and performing storefront work. Clearly, at the very outset of performance Washington had the responsibility to bring to the affected premises the materials which ultimately would form the glass curtain wall and store front. The U.C.C. in § 2-105 defines "goods" as "*all* things (including specially manufactured goods) which are movable at the time of identification to the contract for sale other than the money in which the price is to be paid, investment securities (Title 8) and things in action." (Emphasis added.) That at least creates an uncertainty to be resolved only by a full factual presentation to determine whether the nature of the Washington business was predominantly the provision of goods or the furnishing of services. The fact that Coakley was a building contractor specializing in construction is not sufficient to provide a completely definitive answer. While often, and perhaps customarily, a contractor is engaged in the provision of services, the scope of a contractor's work is not necessarily monolithic and, in the present circumstances, it becomes a question of unresolved fact whether Coakley, for the purposes of the single

---

[6] *E.g., Bonebrake v. Cox,* 499 F.2d 951, 960 (8th Cir.1974) (The appeal was from an adjudication on the merits, following a full trial, and reached the conclusion that a contract to supply and install bowling equipment dealt predominantly with goods, even though the amount of services involved was substantial. "The test for inclusion or exclusion [in or from the provisions of the U.C.C.] is not whether they are mixed, but, granting that they are mixed, whether their predominant factor, their thrust, their purpose, reasonably stated, is the rendition of service, with goods incidentally involved (*e.g.,* contract with artist for painting) or is a transaction of sale, with labor incidentally involved (*e.g.,* installation of a water heater in a bathroom). The contract before us, construed in accordance with the applicable standards of the Code, is not excluded therefrom because it is 'mixed,' * * * ").

relationship to which we are restricted, was a buyer of goods.

In this connection, it is not irrelevant that Coakley has alleged that the purchases by Washington from Shatterproof included anchor clips and field fasteners. At the early stage at which we find ourselves, the allegation requires us to indulge the inference urged by counsel for Coakley that putting the glass in place was a simple snap-on process requiring little expenditure of time or labor. One can readily imagine, without the advantage of specificity deriving from a full trial on the merits, that the contract largely contemplated the provision of precast panels as goods, without the installation being nearly so extensive or significant as the supplying of the glass itself.

The fact that the contract does not follow a standard, routine or regularized form, coupled with the plaintiff's contention that standard form contracts are virtually universal for construction (*i.e.,* generally, service) contracts, operates to leave open the possibility of a finding that the contract is more one for goods than would be the customary construction contract.

Turning to the second point, the nature of Washington's business, the fact that Washington was a dealer and not a manufacturer does not have any particularly dispositive significance. Many retailers of goods function in the role of middleman. Shatterproof sold Washington materials in a transaction which unquestionably, on the sparse record before us at the preliminary stage at which we find ourselves, was a sale of goods, and the question comes down essentially to whether those materials or the services which Washington also provided under its contract with Coakley predominated. Without full consideration of as yet unascertained facts that question is simply not ripe for resolution. It is one of fact, not law; at least it is at this early stage.

Third, the complaint affords no realistic, and certainly no dispositive, information as to the value of the spandrels et al. in case of breakup into the component parts of the glass curtain wall and store front work. That can only be determined by further development of the record, and is, in all events, but one of several factors which must be evaluated in conjunction with all the others in resolving the ultimate factual issue: did Washington and Coakley deal primarily with goods or services?

Accordingly, Coakley has alleged enough to survive a motion to dismiss under Fed.R.Civ.P. 12(b)(6). Nor, at the other extreme, has it alleged too much, permitting sure ascertainment that services, not goods, were the gravamen of the transaction. Coakley should, therefore, be permitted to show, unless the statute of limitations bars recovery, that it was a buyer of goods and, therefore, entitled to proceed under the U.C.C. provisions.

* * *

[The court held that the claim was not barred under the statute of limitations, UCC 2-725.]

Accordingly, the judgment is reversed and the case remanded for further proceedings not inconsistent with this opinion.

[Some footnotes omitted. Those retained have been renumbered.]

Notes

1.   After trial, the trial court determined that services rather than goods predominated in the transaction and held that the plaintiff was not entitled to claim breach of the implied warranty of merchantability imposed by UCC 2-314. This result was affirmed on appeal, 778 F.2d 196 (4th Cir. 1985).

2.   The either-or effect of the "predominant purpose" test was rejected in *Anthony Pools v. Sheehan*, 455 A.2d 434, 441 (Md. 1983). Where services predominate, if the goods supplied (a diving board) were unmerchantable and caused loss (personal injuries), Article 2 could be applied both to impose an implied warranty of merchantability and to determine whether a clause purporting to disclaim the implied warranty of merchantability was enforceable. The court stressed that the goods had to be supplied under a commercial transaction, rather than a contract for professional services, and must "retain their character * * * after completion of the performance promised * * * ." Note, however, that the goods were supplied to a consumer who suffered personal injuries. Should that make a difference in the analysis? *See J.O. Hooker & Sons, Inc. v. Roberts Cabinet Co., Inc.*, 683 So.2d 396, 400 (Miss. 1996), where the court said that the test in a mixed transaction–a construction contract–turned on the nature of the contract and "upon whether the *dispute* in question primarily concerns the goods furnished or the services rendered under the contract."

3.   Cases applying the predominant purpose test have predictably come to conflicting results.[*] How can this conflict be reduced? Amended Article 2 ducked

---

[*] *See Brandt v. Boston Scientific Corp.*, 792 N.E.2d 296 (Ill. 2003) (transaction to implant a pubovaginal sling was a contract for the provision of services and not a sale of goods); *Mattoon v. City of Pittsfield*, 775 N.E.2d 770 (Mass. Ct. App. 2002) *rev. denied*, 782 N.E.2d 1084 (Mass. 2003) (provision of water by city was not a sale of goods but a provision of

(continued...)

the question. CISG Article 3(2) states that the Convention "does not apply to contracts in which the preponderant part of the party who furnishes goods consists in the supply of labour or other services." Is this a different test than the predominate purpose test?

4. The claim that software reduced to a disk is not goods because professional services predominate has rarely been accepted by the courts.[*]

5. Suppose the transaction is a license of software and a lease of hardware? What law applies?[**] Where the software is not classified as goods but the hardware is clearly goods, courts usually reject the argument that the transaction should be divided, with the movable goods covered by Article 2 and the software under other law.[***] How does UCITA 103 resolve this issue?

6. What law should apply when someone agrees to provide goods into which

---

[*] (...continued)
services, court noted it was not deciding whether the provision of bottled water was a sale of goods); *Princess Cruises, Inc. v. General Electric Co.*, 143 F.3d 828 (4th Cir. 1998), *cert. denied*, 525 U.S. 982 (1998) (contract for inspection and repair of a ship was a contract for services although goods would be provided as part of the service); *True North Composite Services LLC v. Trinity Industries*, 50 UCC Rep. Serv. 2d 683 (Fed. Cir. Ct. App. 2003) (contract for developing and manufacturing composite rail cars was a contract for the sale of goods); *Johnson Enterprises of Jacksonville, Inc. v. FPL Group, Inc.*, 162 F.3d 1290 (11th Cir. 1998) (contract for construction of cable TV systems was a contract for services); *Jackson Hole Traders, Inc. v. Joseph*, 931 P.2d 244 (Wyo. 1997) (Article 2 governed a contract for the manufacture and sale of clothing even though the agreement required labor on the part of the manufacturer); *AKA Distributing Co. v. Whirlpool Corp.*, 137 F.3d 1083 (8th Cir. 1998) (a contract for the distribution of floor care products where the distributor (seller) also provided engineering services to improve the products and made efforts to remedy product defects and resolve customer complaints was a sale of goods, with labor incidentally involved).

[*] *See e.g.*, *Olcott Intern. & Co. v. Micro Base Systems, Inc.*, 793 N.E.2d 1063 (Ind. Ct. App. 2003) (noncustomized software is goods); *Sagent Technology Inc. v. Micros Systems Inc.*, 276 F. Supp. 2d 464 (D. Md. 2003) (software embodied on a CD purchased for resale was a transaction in goods). *See also* Jeffrey B. Ritter, *Software Transactions and Uniformity: Accommodating Codes Under the Code*, 46 BUS. LAW. 1825 (1991); Ann Lousin, *Cases on the Scope of Article 2*, 46 BUS. LAW. 1855 (1991).

[**] *See Step-Saver Data Systems, Inc. v. Wyse Technology*, 939 F.2d 91 (3rd Cir. 1991) (applied Article 2 to a license of computer terminals and software).

[***] *See* Allen C. Schlinsog, Jr., *Advent Systems Ltd. v. Unisys Corp.: UCC Governs Software Transactions*, 4 SOFTWARE L.J. 611, 620-627 (1991).

software is integrated, so called "smart goods?" Consider a car with an on board computer to monitor and run various systems of the car. How about a hand-held data organizer, a cell phone, a digital camera, or a microwave with various programmable settings? Are the 2003 amendments to Article 2 any help on this issue? See the new comment 7 to UCC 2-103. Compare UCITA 103 for another approach. This issue was very controversial in the Article 2 revision process.[*]

7. No matter what state law applies, federal intellectual property law will also apply to licenses of software. *See* UCITA 105.[**]

Problem 2-2

A. Best Appliances Inc. agreed to sell and install a new gas stove and a new refrigerator in David's house. Best was required to run a gas line from the basement in David's house to the stove location and to run a water pipe from the basement to the refrigerator location in order to supply water for the automatic icemaker. Does Article 2 apply to this contract?

B. Rustic Furniture agreed to design and manufacture a new line of furniture for sale to Department Store for further sale to customers under the Department Store's label. Does Article 2 apply to this contract?

C. Stable Software Inc. agreed to design a computer controlled welding unit for use in Truecars Inc.'s assembly line. Stable Software was required to hire an equipment designer to design the unit and for which Stable would provide customized software to integrate the machine into Truecars' existing assembly line. Does Article 2 apply to the contract between Stable and Truecars?

---

[*] For a flavor of the debates, *see* Raymond T. Nimmer, *Images and Contract Law--What Law Applies to Transactions in Information*, 36 HOUS. L. REV. 1 (1999); Symposium, *Intellectual Property and Contract Law in the Information Age: The Impact of Article 2B of the Uniform Commercial Code on the Future of Transactions in Information and Electronic Commerce*, 13 BERKELEY TECH. L.J. 809-1287 (1998), as well as the Braucher and Brennan articles cited earlier in this Chapter.

[**] For an interesting discussion of contractual assent as it relates to licenses of software and intellectual property concepts, *see* J.H. Reichman and Jonathan A. Franklin, *Privately Legislated Intellectual Property Rights: Reconciling Freedom of Contract with Public Good Uses of Information*, 147 U. PA. L. REV. 875 (1999); David Nimmer, Elliot Brown, and Gary N. Frischling, *The Metamorphosis of Contract Into Expand*, 87 CALIF. L. REV. 17 (1999).

Although we have not yet plumbed the details of any of the substantive provisions of Article 2, Article 2A, or UCITA as of yet, the issue of scope provides the entry point into the substantive provisions of each act. Critical differences in principles regarding contract formation, warranties, and remedies for breach fuel debate over the proper scope of these three acts. As we explore these differences, keep in mind the overall policy issues the various approaches are attempting to solve.

C. United Nations Convention on Contracts for the International Sale of Goods (CISG)

To repeat, the CISG has been in force in the United States since January 1, 1988. It is now law in 62 countries, including our NAFTA trading partners, Canada since May 1, 1992, and Mexico since January 1, 1989. To the extent applicable, CISG is federal law which preempts Article 2, Sales. The CISG is supplemented by a Convention on the Limitation Period in the International Sale of Goods, which became effective in the United States on December 1, 1994. To what sales of goods does the CISG apply? Read Articles 1-6, 10 of the CISG and answer the following questions.

Problem 2-3

A. Buyer, located in California, made an oral contract over the telephone to buy 500 steel frames from a Canadian seller for $10,000. The goods were to be shipped by rail within 10 days. Four days later, Buyer called to cancel the deal, claiming that it did not need the frames and that, anyway, the oral contract was unenforceable under the statute of frauds. Buyer cited UCC 2-201. The seller countered with the argument that the CISG applied, citing Art. 1, and that under the CISG there is no requirement that a contract for sale be in writing. *See* Art. 11.

(1) Is this a "contract of sale of goods" within the scope of the CISG? *See* Art. 1(a). Note that the United States declared, as authorized by Art. 95, that it would not be bound by Art. 1(b).

(2) If so, are there any limitations or exclusions affecting this transaction in Art. 2 through 6?

(3) Can Buyer defend on the ground that the oral agreement was not in writing? *See* Art. 11. Note that the United States did not make the declaration authorized under Art. 96 that is implemented in Art. 12.

(4) Assume the contract was for the lease of 20 trucks from a Canadian lessor. What is the interaction between the CISG and Article 2A?

(5) Assume the contract was for the sale of 200 copies of the latest accounting software and UCITA was enacted in California. What is the interaction of UCITA and the CISG?

B. Ashley, a United States resident, ordered a new computer from a Canadian manufacturer. The order took place through the manufacturer's website. Alice designated her home address in Lansing, Michigan, as the shipping address. Is this transaction covered by the CISG?

C. Benson Machines, a United States company, agreed to manufacture and install new heating units for ABC Corp., a Canadian company, at the company's office in Detroit, Michigan. Is this transaction covered by the CISG?

D. Choice of Law and Choice of Forum Clauses

Choice of law and choice of forum clauses should be considered in the negotiation of any transaction. A choice of law clause provides that "the law of Jurisdiction X governs this contract." A choice of forum clause provides that "actions concerning this contract must be brought in X jurisdiction." As you read this section, consider whether these or similar clauses should be enforceable.

International transactions. Suppose Seller in Illinois and Buyer in Mexico are negotiating over a proposed five year contract for the supply of Buyer's requirements over a fixed annual minimum at a firm fixed price. If the parties' agreement does not otherwise specify, the CISG will govern the agreement. *See* CISG Art. 1, 10. The United States, as permitted by Article 95, has declared a reservation to CISG Art. 1(b). Thus, if the requirements of Article 1(a) are not satisfied, a citizen of the United States is not bound by the CISG even though the "rules of private international law lead to the application of the law of a Contracting State." If the parties do not want the CISG to govern the transaction, they may contract out or exclude the application of the Convention. *See* CISG Art. 6.

What law should be chosen if the parties exclude the application of the CISG? The parties may choose Illinois law, under which they get Article 2 of the UCC, or they may choose Mexican law. This is a matter of bargaining and care must be exercised to state clearly that Article 2 is chosen. If the contract merely selects Illinois law, the CISG, which is part of the law of Illinois, will preempt Article 2 and apply.* Other options include saying nothing about choice of law (a dubious choice) or choosing the new UNIDROIT Principles of International Commercial Contracts as the governing law. Although these principles are available for choice, they should be compared with the CISG and Article 2 before such a choice is made.

If disputes arise under the contract, what forum should resolve the matter, a court in the United States or a court in Mexico? Clearly, this matter should be resolved by a negotiated forum selection clause–a clause which U.S. courts, in any event, will readily enforce.**

Should the forum for dispute resolution be arbitration? If so, what law governs the arbitration process and from what sources do arbitration procedures derive? If the parties agree to arbitration (because it is thought to be quicker, less formal and less expensive than litigation), they will be governed by the U.N. Convention on International Arbitration (the so-called New York Convention) and applicable implementing law. Both countries have ratified the New York Convention and, in the United States, the Convention is implemented in 9 U.S.C. 201-209. Within this framework, they can, among other things, select applicable arbitration procedures, such as the A.A.A. (American Arbitration Association) international arbitration rules, and select applicable law to govern the arbitrators, such as the UNIDROIT Principles.

These questions and many more must be posed and answered in contracts for sale between NAFTA trading partners and any time that the transaction is between private persons with places of business in different countries.

Domestic transactions. How about purely United States domestic contracts? What considerations should go into picking the jurisdiction to provide the governing law and forum?

Article 2 does not have any provision governing choice of law or choice of forum. As to choice of law principles for UCC covered transactions, *see* UCC 1-301 [former 1-105]. To date, no state has yet enacted the new choice of law provision in new UCC 1-301 even if those states have otherwise enacted Revised Article 1. Those states enacting Revised Article 1 have enacted in essence old 1-

---

* *See Ajax Tool Works, Inc. v. Can-Eng. Mfg., Ltd.*, 2003 WL 223187 (N.D. Ill. 2003) (contract clause selecting law of Ontario incorporated the CISG as that was part of the governing law of Ontario).

** *See, e.g., Richards v. Lloyd's of London*, 135 F.3d 1289 (9th Cir. 1998), *cert. denied*, 119 S. Ct. 365 (1998) (enforcing a clause that chose both English securities law and England as the forum to resolve disputes).

105 in the place of new UCC 1-301. Article 2A contains a limitation on parties' choice of law and choice of forum in the case of a consumer lease. UCC 2A-106. UCITA contains provisions validating parties' choice of law, UCITA 109, and forum, UCITA 110.

What is at stake in validating parties' choice of law or forum clauses? Are choice of law and forum clauses just a specific application of the principle that the parties are free to vary the effect of UCC provisions by agreement? UCC 1-302 [former 1-102]. Should it make a difference in the analysis if the transaction was a fully negotiated transaction or a standard form transaction presented on a take it or leave it basis? Should choice of law and choice of forum clauses be treated differently than other clauses in standard form contracts?[*]

SECTION 3.   SOME BASIC CONCEPTS IN ARTICLE 2

A. Introduction

The present form of Article 2, Sales, emerged from a careful and critical review of the 1952 Official Text by the New York Law Revision Commission in 1953-55, and was promulgated in the 1958 Official Text of the Uniform Commercial Code. The principal draftsperson in the early drafts of Article 2 and its predecessor (the Revised Uniform Sales Act), and its most effective champion until his death in 1962, was Professor Karl N. Llewellyn.[**] Work under the joint auspices of the

---

[*] *See* Lee Goldman, *My Way and the Highway: The Law and Economics of Choice of Forum Clauses in Consumer Form Contracts*, 86 NW. U. L. REV. 700 (1992); William J. Woodward, Jr., *"Sale" of Law and Forum and the Widening Gulf Between "Consumer" and "Nonconsumer" Contracts in the UCC*, 75 WASH. U. L.Q. 243 (1997); Amelia H. Boss, *The Jurisdiction of Commercial Law: Party Autonomy in Choosing Applicable Law and Forum Under Proposed Revisions to the Uniform Commercial Code*, 32 INT'L LAW. 1067 (1998). For more on choice of law and choice of forum clauses, *see* Larry E. Ribstein, *From Efficiency to Politics in Contractual Choice of Law*, 37 GA. L. REV. 363 (2003); Erin Ann O'Hara, *The Jurisprudence and Politics of Forum-Selection Clauses*, 3 CHI. J. INT. L. 301 (2003). For an example of the factors that one court considered in enforcing a forum selection and choice of law clause, *see BAAN U.S.A. v. USA Truck, Inc.*, 105 S.W. 3d 784 (Ark. Ct. App. 2003) (analyzed reasonableness of clause in light of due process concerns).

[**] The drafts of Llewellyn's efforts from 1940-44 to revise the Uniform Sales Act are reproduced in ELIZABETH SLUSSER KELLY, UNIFORM COMMERCIAL CODE DRAFTS (1984), Vols. I and II.

National Conference of Commissioners on Uniform State Laws (NCCUSL) and the American Law Institute (ALI) began on January 1, 1945.* In a real sense, Article 2 is "Karl's Kode." His ideas and approach to commercial law, even though imperfectly achieved, tended to dominate the final product.**

According to Richard Danzig, Llewellyn did not regard law as a "body of deduced rules, or as an instrument chosen by social planners from among a universe of alternatives." Rather, he "saw law as an articulation and regularization * * * of a generally recognized and almost indisputably right rule * * * inherent in, but very possibly obscured by, existing patterns of relationships." For him, law was "immanent" or "imbedded" in any situation and it was the task of the law authority, usually a judge, to discover it. Under this view, the task of the legislature is to prescribe standards, such as commercial reasonableness, on how to find the law and leave the task of particularization, *i.e.*, finding the "situation sense," to the court.*** In the rejection of rules and the search for standards which responded to the behavior patterns of the disputants in context, Llewellyn was clearly in step with Arthur L. Corbin and other so-called "Realists."****

Article 2 was also influenced by the nature of the problems and actors with which it deals. According to Danzig:

> Commercial law is at the margin of public law. It deals with a sub-community ('merchants'), whose members occupy a status position distinct from society at large, whose disputes are often resolved by informal negotiation or in private forums, whose relationships tend to continue over time rather than ending with the culmination of single transactions, and whose primary rules derive from a sense of fairness wide-spread–if

---

* *See* William A. Schnader, *A Short History of the Preparation and Enactment of the Uniform Commercial Code*, 22 U. MIAMI L. REV. 1, 5 (1967).

** For useful discussion, *see* WILLIAM A. TWINING, KARL LLEWELLYN AND THE REALIST MOVEMENT (1973); Zipporah B. Wiseman, *The Limits of Vision: Karl Llewellyn and the Merchant Rules*, 100 HARV. L. REV. 465 (1987). *Compare* Kenneth M. Casebeer, *Escape from Liberalism: Fact and Value in Karl Llewellyn*, 1977 DUKE L.J. 671 *with* Richard Danzig, *A Comment on the Jurisprudence of the Uniform Commercial Code*, 27 STAN. L. REV. 621 (1975). *See also* Chris Williams, *Book Review*, 97 HARV. L. REV. 1495 (1984).

*** Danzig, *supra* note **, at 624-27.

**** *See* Richard E. Speidel, *Restatement Second: Omitted Terms and Contract Method*, 67 CORNELL L. REV. 785, 786-92 (1982).

imprecisely defined–within the commercial community.[*]
Some authors in more recent literature have debated this underlying premise of
Article 2, *i.e.*, that commercial law should reflect commercial norms of behavior.[**]

Given that Article 2A is modeled part on Article 2, the question is always how
much of Article 2's foundational concepts should carry over into Article 2A.
Should Article 2's foundational concepts carry over into UCITA as well? Disputes
about what counts as foundational concepts and what are peculiar issues for which
different rules are appropriate were the fuel for the failure of the hub and spoke
approach to the revision of Article 2.

B. Agreement, Not Promise, as the Foundation Stone

Students of commercial law have already learned a great deal about the concept
of promise in the first year course in contracts. The RESTATEMENT (SECOND) OF
CONTRACTS 1 even defines a contract as "a promise or a set of promises for the
breach of which the law provides a remedy, or the performance of which the law in
some way recognizes as a duty." It is true that the analysis of commercial
arrangements in terms of the concept of promise fits the facts of many contracts,
including many involving the sale of goods. But the analysis fails to fit many other
contracts, including some for the sale of goods, thus suggesting there must be a
more fundamental concept. That concept, as we will see, is the concept of
agreement, and this is the true foundation stone of Article 2.

Here we will offer some illustrative examples of features of consensual
arrangements for the sale of goods that are more felicitously analyzable in terms of
agreement rather than the exchange of promises as such. First, in the law of sales
many express warranties arise by virtue of the seller's "affirmations of fact," not

---

[*] Danzig, *supra* at 622-23.

[**] *See* Lisa Bernstein, *Merchant Law in a Merchant Court: Rethinking the Code's Search
for Immanent Business Norms*, 144 U. PA. L. REV. 1765 (1996); Kerry Lynn Macintosh,
*Liberty, Trade, and the Uniform Commercial Code: When Should Default Rules Be Based
on Business Practices?*, 38 WM. & MARY L. REV. 1465 (1997); *but see* David V. Snyder,
Language and Formalities in Commercial Contracts: A Defense of Custom and Conduct,
54 SMU L. REV. 617 (2001). For some perspective on whether changes in law are necessary
given changes in commercial practice and concerns, *see* John F. Dolan, *Changing
Commercial Practices and the Uniform Commercial Code*, 26 LOY. L.A. L. REV. 579 (1993);
Daniel Keating, *Measuring Sales Law Against Sales Practice: A Reality Check*, 17 J. L. &
COM. 99 (1997).

promises as such. UCC 2-313 expressly so states. Second, many other obligations in the law of sales arise in particular cases by virtue of tacit assumptions, custom, trade usage, course of dealing and course of performance. In such instances, there is rarely anything resembling an express promise, and the concept of an implied in fact promise seldom fits the facts more than fictionally. Third, many sale of goods transactions are not discrete, "one-shot" affairs but occur over time within longer term relationships. Many features of these relationships are not the subject of express promises (or even implied ones) yet they generate important obligations shored up by the code doctrine of good faith to which we will soon turn.[*] The broad structures of such relationships often pre-exist so that when the parties enter into a particular relation-general obligations attendant upon such a relation attach. Finally, countless discrete, "one-shot," exchanges take place each day in which no promises are made on either side yet the law imposes obligations on both parties. "Over the counter" sales and supermarket sales are only the most familiar of these. In all of the foregoing examples, the most fundamental concept at work is that of agreement, not promise (and even agreement does not account for everything). The Code itself recognizes the primacy of agreement. Read the definitions of "agreement" and "contract" in UCC 1-201. These definitions govern in both Article 2 and Article 2A transactions. Note that UCITA adopts similar definitions in UCITA 102. We will return to the concepts of agreement and contract when we consider contract formation and terms in Chapters Three and Four, *infra*.

C. The Article Two "Merchant" Concept

Article 2 includes several provisions in which the term "merchant" appears. Read the definition of merchant in UCC 2-104. The merchant concept is used in UCC 2-201 (statute of frauds); 2-205 (firm offer); 2-209 (modification, rescission and waiver); 2-312 (warranty of title); 2-314 (implied warranty of merchantability); 2-327 (sale on approval); 2-402 (rights of creditors of sellers); 2-403 (entrusting); 2-603 (care of goods rejected); 2-605 (waiver of buyer's objections); and 2-609 (adequate assurance of performance).

Article 2A also uses the merchant concept and relies on the Article 2 definition of merchant, UCC 2A-103(3). Article 2A uses the term merchant in UCC 2A-103(1) (merchant lessee); 2A-205 (firm offers); 2A-208 (modification, rescission

---

[*] *See* Richard E. Speidel, *The Characteristics and Challenges of Relational Contracts*, 94 NW. U. L. REV. 823 (2000).

and waiver); 2A-211(warranty of non-infringement); 2A-212 (warranty of merchantability); 2A-304 and 2A-305 (entrusting); and 2A-511 (merchant lessee's obligation regarding rejected goods).

UCITA uses the merchant concept in UCITA 102 (definition of merchant and consumer contract); 201 (statute of frauds); 204 (battle of the forms); 303 (modification and recession); 401 (warranty of non interference and noninfringment); 403 (merchantability); 404 (implied warranty of informational content); 613 (special rules regarding tri-party multilevel distribution contracts); 702 (waiver); and 708 (adequate assurance of performance).

Even though the merchant concept is important, do not be misled into thinking that Article 2, Article 2A, or UCITA requires a person to have merchant status for those acts to govern the transaction. Article 2 or Article 2A will apply to sales of goods or leases of goods, respectively, *even if no merchant is involved.*[*] Thus, if a consumer sells goods to another consumer, Article 2 will apply, although some particular provisions which focus on merchants may not apply. *See e.g.* UCC 2-314 (an implied warranty of merchantability only made by a merchant with respect to goods of that kind).

UCC 2-314, imposing an implied warranty of merchantability on one type of merchant, and UCC 2-201, the statute of frauds, seem to have generated the most litigation over who qualifies as a merchant. As you consider the following materials, ask yourself why do these statutes distinguish between merchants and non-merchants and, based upon the sections cited earlier, why would those rules not be appropriate to apply to a non-merchant as well.

Problem 2-4

A. Charlie is a cotton farmer who has engaged in the farming of cotton and other crops for over 25 years. Loeb is in the business of marketing raw cotton and has purchased cotton from Charlie for the last five years. On May 5, 2004, Loeb alleged that he and Charlie orally agreed that Charlie would sell and deliver 150 bales of cotton, October delivery, to him for $ 40 per bale. Loeb claims that he prepared a written confirmation of the sale that afternoon and mailed it to Charlie. Charlie concedes that the confirmation was received and was promptly consigned

---

[*] *See* Scott J. Burnham, *Why Do Law Students Insist That Article 2 of the Uniform Commercial Code Applies Only to Merchants and What Can We Do About It?*, 63 BROOK. L. REV. 1271 (1997).

to the trash heap. In October, Loeb asked for delivery and was informed by Charlie that there never was an oral agreement and that the cotton had been sold to Wilbur, another dealer, for $45 per bale. When Loeb sued for breach of contract, Charlie denied the existence of an agreement and, in the alternative, pleaded UCC 2-201(1) as a defense. Loeb responded that his confirmation was effective to take the case out of the rule of subsection (1). UCC 2-201(2). Charlie responded, however, that he was not a merchant and that the exception did not apply. How should the case be resolved?

B. Charlie runs a hardware store as a sole proprietor and has done so for over 25 years. Loeb is in the construction business and has purchased its tools from Charlie for the last five years. On May 5, 2004, Loeb alleged that it and Charlie agreed that Charlie would sell and deliver 150 cases of Stanley screw drivers for $40 per case. Loeb sent a written confirmation to Charlie that Charlie concedes was received. Charlie refused to deliver the tools and argued that the purported contract was unenforceable against him under UCC 2-201. Is he correct?

C. Is there a justifiable difference in result in these two cases? For an analysis of the Article 2 merchant rules, *see* Ingrid M. Hillinger, *The Article 2 Merchant Rules: Karl Llewellyn's Attempt to Achieve the Good, the True, the Beautiful in Commercial Law*, 73 GEO. L.J. 1141 (1985). Hillinger recounts early cases that held that farmers were not merchants based upon some of Llewellyn's comments which indicate that he did not consider farmers to be merchants. Nevertheless, Professor Llewellyn did not object to treating farmers as if they were merchants where practices were involved which are or ought to be typical and familiar to any person in business.[*] UCC 2-104, comment 2, appears to agree.

D. Zebra University decided to sell its excess office furniture. Zebra advertised the furniture for sale and sold it for a reasonable price to a startup business. Is Zebra a merchant? UCC 2-104. Did Zebra make the implied warranty of merchantability? UCC 2-314.

---

[*] For evidence that the issue of who is a "merchant" is still troublesome, *compare Ready Trucking, Inc. v. BP Exploration & Oil Co.*, 548 S.E.2d 420 (Ga. Ct. App. 2001) (interstate motor carrier purchasing fuel for use in its business was a merchant) *with Forms World of Illinois, Inc. v. Magna Bank N.A.*, 779 N.E.2d 917 (Ill. Ct. App. 2002), *appl. denied*, 787 N.E.2d 172 (Ill. 2003) (bank purchasing forms for use in its banking business was not a merchant).

D. Legal Controls on Contractual Behavior: Unconscionability and Good Faith

Below we discuss and consider UCC 2-302, providing that unconscionable contracts and clauses are invalid in Article 2 transactions, and UCC 1-304 [former 1-203], imposing a general obligation of good faith on the performance and enforcement of UCC-covered contracts. Please review UCC 2A-108 as well.

What definition of good faith is used in Articles 2 and 2A as amended by the 2003 amendments? Compare this definition to the definition in effect prior to the 2003 amendments. Former 1-201(19), 2-103(1)(b), 2A-103(4).

You have already met both of those concepts in your first year course in contracts. It is sometimes said that the unconscionability limitation on freedom of contract applies at the formation stage whereas the good faith limitation applies only to the performance or enforcement stage. Yet good faith may have some bearing on issues normally resolved at the formation stage, as with UCC 2-305(2). Indeed, good faith may even have a bearing on liability for acts or omissions of one party as early as the negotiation stage. Of course, this would have to be via UCC 1-103 on supplemental general principles, because UCC 1-304 [former 1-203] itself only imposes an obligation of good faith in the "performance" and "enforcement" of the contract. Similarly, the student will do well to entertain the possibility that unconscionability may have a bearing at *post* formation stages: *See, e.g.*, UCC 2-309.

As you read the following materials, focus on the test the court uses to determine if the clause or contract is unconscionable and the test the court uses to determine good faith.

ZAPATHA V. DAIRY MART, INC.
SUPREME JUDICIAL COURT OF MASSACHUSETTS, 1980
381 MASS. 284, 408 N.E.2D 1370

WILKINS, JUSTICE

We are concerned here with the question whether Dairy Mart, Inc. (Dairy Mart), lawfully undertook to terminate a franchise agreement under which the Zapathas operated a Dairy Mart store on Wilbraham Road in Springfield. The Zapathas brought this action seeking to enjoin the termination of the agreement, alleging that the contract provision purporting to authorize the termination of the franchise agreement without cause was unconscionable and that Dairy Mart's conduct was an unfair and deceptive act or practice in violation of G.L. c. 93A. The judge ruled that Dairy Mart did not act in good faith, that the termination provision was unconscionable, and that Dairy Mart's termination of the agreement without cause was an unfair and deceptive act. We granted Dairy Mart's application for direct appellate review of a judgment that stated that Dairy Mart could terminate the agreement only for good cause and that the attempted termination was null and void. We reverse the judgments.

Mr. Zapatha is a high school graduate who had attended college for one year and had also taken college evening courses in business administration and business law. From 1952 to May, 1973, he was employed by a company engaged in the business of electroplating. He rose through the ranks to foreman and then to the position of operations manager, at one time being in charge of all metal finishing in the plant with 150 people working under him. In May, 1973, he was discharged and began looking for other opportunities, in particular a business of his own. Several months later he met with a representative of Dairy Mart. Dairy Mart operates a chain of franchised "convenience" stores. The Dairy Mart representative told Mr. Zapatha that working for Dairy Mart was being in business for one's self and that such a business was very stable and secure. Mr. Zapatha signed an application to be considered for a franchise. In addition, he was presented with a brochure entitled "Here's a Chance," which made certain representations concerning the status of a franchise holder.[1]

Dairy Mart approved Mr. Zapatha's application and offered him a store in Agawam. On November 8, 1973, a representative of Dairy Mart showed him a form of franchise agreement, entitled Limited Franchise and License Agreement, asked him to read it, and explained that his wife would have to sign the agreement as well.

Under the terms of the agreement, Dairy Mart would license the Zapathas to operate a Dairy Mart store, using the Dairy Mart trademark and associated insignia, and utilizing Dairy Mart's "confidential" merchandising methods. Dairy Mart would furnish the store and the equipment and would pay rent and gas and electric bills as well as certain other costs of doing business. In return Dairy Mart would

---

[1] It included the following statements: " * * * you'll have the opportunity to own and run your own business * * * "; "We want to be sure we're hooking up with the right person. A person who sees the opportunity in owning his own business * * * who requires the security that a multi-million dollar parent company can offer him * * * who has the good judgment and business sense to take advantage of the unique independence that Dairy Mart offers its franchisees * * * We're looking for a partner * * * who can take the tools we offer and build a life of security and comfort * * *".

receive a franchise fee, computed as a percentage of the store's gross sales. The Zapathas would have to pay for the starting inventory, and maintain a minimum stock of saleable merchandise thereafter. They were also responsible for wages of employees, related taxes, and any sales taxes. The termination provision, which is set forth in full in the margin,[2] allowed either party, after twelve months, to terminate the agreement without cause on ninety days' written notice. In the event of termination initiated by it without cause, Dairy Mart agreed to repurchase the saleable merchandise inventory at retail prices, less 20%.

The Dairy Mart representative read and explained the termination provision to Mr. Zapatha. Mr. Zapatha later testified that, while he understood every word in the provision, he had interpreted it to mean that Dairy Mart could terminate the agreement only for cause. The Dairy Mart representative advised Mr. Zapatha to take the agreement to an attorney and said "I would prefer that you did." However, he also told Mr. Zapatha that the terms of the contract were not negotiable. The Zapathas signed the agreement without consulting an attorney. When the Zapathas took charge of the Agawam store, a representative of Dairy Mart worked with them to train them in Dairy Mart's methods of operation.

In 1974, another store became available on Wilbraham Road in Springfield, and the Zapathas elected to surrender the Agawam store. They executed a new franchise agreement, on an identical printed form, relating to the new location.

In November, 1977, Dairy Mart presented a new and more detailed form of "Independent Operator's Agreement" to the Zapathas for execution. Some of the terms were less favorable to the store operator than those of the earlier form of

---

[2] "(9) The term of this Limited Franchise and License Agreement shall be for a period of Twelve (12) months from date hereof, and shall continue uninterrupted thereafter. If DEALER desires to terminate after 12 months from date hereof, he shall do so by giving COMPANY a ninety (90) day written notice by Registered Mail of his intention to terminate. If COMPANY desires to terminate, it likewise shall give a ninety (90) day notice, except for the following reasons which shall not require any written notice and shall terminate the Franchise immediately:

"(a) Failure to pay bills to suppliers for inventory or other products when due.
"(b) Failure to pay Franchise Fees to COMPANY.
"(c) Failure to pay city, state or federal taxes as said taxes shall become due and payable.
"(d) Breach of any condition of this Agreement."

agreement.[3] Mr. Zapatha told representatives of Dairy Mart that he was content with the existing contract and had decided not to sign the new agreement. On January 20, 1978, Dairy Mart gave written notice to the Zapathas that their contract was being terminated effective in ninety days. The termination notice stated that Dairy Mart "remains available to enter into discussions with you with respect to entering into a new Independent Operator's Agreement; however, there is no assurance that Dairy Mart will enter into a new Agreement with you, or even if entered into, what terms such Agreement will contain." The notice also indicated that Dairy Mart was prepared to purchase the Zapathas' saleable inventory.

The judge found that Dairy Mart terminated the agreement solely because the Zapathas refused to sign the new agreement. He further found that, but for this one act, Dairy Mart did not behave in an unconscionable manner, in bad faith, or in disregard of its representations. There is no evidence that the Zapathas undertook to discuss a compromise of the differences that led to the notice of termination.

On these basic facts, the judge ruled that the franchise agreement was subject to the sales article of the Uniform Commercial Code (G.L. c. 106, art. 2) and, even if it were not, the principles of unconscionability and good faith expressed in that article applied to the franchise agreement by analogy. He further ruled that (1) the termination provision of the agreement was unconscionable because it authorized termination without cause, (2) the termination without cause violated Dairy Mart's obligation of good faith, and (3) the termination constituted "an unfair method of competition and unfair and deceptive act within the meaning of G.L. c. 93A, § 2."

1. We consider first the question whether the franchise agreement involves a "transaction in goods" within the meaning of those words in article two of the Uniform Commercial Code (G.L. c. 106, § 2-103, as appearing in St.1957, c. 765, § 1), and that consequently the provisions of the sales articles of the Uniform Commercial Code govern the relationship between the parties. The Zapathas point specifically to the authority of a court to refuse to enforce "any clause of the contract" that the court finds "to have been unconscionable at the time it was made." G.L. c. 106, § 2-302, as appearing in St.1957, c. 765, § 1. They point

---

[3] In his testimony, Mr. Zapatha said that he objected to a new provision under which Dairy Mart reserved the option to relocate an operator to a new location and to a requirement that the store be open from 7 A.M. to 11 P.M. every day. Previously the Zapathas' store had been open from 8 A.M. to 10 P.M.

There were other provisions, such as an obligation to pay future increases in the cost of heat and electricity, that were more burdensome to a franchisee. A few changes may have been to the advantage of the franchisee.

additionally to the obligation of good faith in the performance and enforcement of a contract imposed by G.L. c. 106, § 1-203, and to the specialized definition of "good faith" in the sales article as meaning "in the case of a merchant * * * honesty in fact and the observance of reasonable commercial standards of fair dealing in the trade." G.L. c. 106, § 2-103(1)(b), as appearing in St.1957, c. 765, § 1.[4]

We need not pause long over the question whether the franchise agreement and the relationship of the parties involved a transaction in goods. Certainly, the agreement required the plaintiffs to purchase goods from Dairy Mart. "Goods" for the purpose of the sales article means generally "all things * * * which are movable." G.L. c. 106, § 2-105(1), as appearing in St.1957, c. 765, § 1. However, the franchise agreement dealt with many subjects unrelated to the sale of goods by Dairy Mart. About 70% of the goods the plaintiffs sold were not purchased from Dairy Mart. Dairy Mart's profit was intended to come from the franchise fee and not from the sale of items to its franchisees. Thus, the sale of goods by Dairy Mart to the Zapathas was, in a commercial sense, a minor aspect of the entire relationship. We would be disinclined to import automatically all the provisions of the sales article into a relationship involving a variety of subjects other than the sale of goods, merely because the contract dealt in part with the sale of goods. Similarly, we would not be inclined to apply the sales article only to aspects of the agreement that concerned goods. Different principles of law might then govern separate portions of the same agreement with possibly inconsistent and unsatisfactory consequences.

We view the legislative statements of policy concerning good faith and unconscionability as fairly applicable to all aspects of the franchise agreement, not by subjecting the franchise relationship to the provisions of the sales article but rather by applying the stated principles by analogy. * * * This basic common law approach, applied to statutory statements of policy, permits a selective application of those principles expressed in a statute that reasonably should govern situations to which the statute does not apply explicitly. *See* Note, *Article Two of the Uniform Commercial Code and Franchise Distribution Agreements*, 1969 DUKE L.J. 959, 980-985.

---

[4] Generally throughout the Uniform Commercial Code, "good faith" is defined to mean "honesty in fact in the conduct or transaction concerned." G.L. c. 106, § 1-201(19). The definition of "good faith" in the sales article includes a higher standard of conduct by adding a requirement that "merchants" observe "reasonable commercial standards of fair dealing in the trade." G.L. c. 106, § 2-103(1)(b). There is no doubt that Dairy Mart is a "merchant" as defined under the sales article. *See* G.L. c. 106, § 2-104.

2. We consider first the plaintiffs' argument that the termination clause of the franchise agreement, authorizing Dairy Mart to terminate the agreement without cause, on ninety days' notice, was unconscionable by the standards expressed in G.L. c. 106, § 2-302.[5] The same standards are set forth in RESTATEMENT (SECOND) OF CONTRACTS § 234 (Tent. Drafts Nos. 1-7, 1973). The issue is one of law for the court, and the test is to be made as of the time the contract was made. G.L. c. 106, § 2-302(1), and comment 3 of the Official Comments. *See W.L. May, Co. v. Philco-Ford Corp.*, 273 Or. 701, 707, 543 P.2d 283 (1975). In measuring the unconscionability of the termination provision, the fact that the law imposes an obligation of good faith on Dairy Mart in its performance under the agreement should be weighed. *See W.L. May, Co. v. Philco-Ford Corp., supra* at 709, 543 P.2d 283.

The official comment to § 2-302 states that "[t]he basic test is whether, in the light of the general commercial background and the commercial needs of the particular trade or case, the clauses involved are so one-sided as to be unconscionable under the circumstances existing at the time of the making of the contract. * * * The principle is one of prevention of oppression and unfair surprise * * * and not of disturbance of allocation of risks because of superior bargaining power." Official Comment 1 to U.C.C. § 2-302.[6] Unconscionability is not defined in the Code, nor do the views expressed in the official comment provide a precise definition. The annotation prepared by the Massachusetts Advisory Committee on the Code states that "[t]he section appears to be intended to carry equity practice into the sales field." *See* 1 R. ANDERSON, UNIFORM COMMERCIAL CODE § 2-302:7 (1970) to the same effect. This court has not had occasion to consider in any detail the meaning of the word "unconscionable" in § 2-302. Because there is no clear, all-purpose definition of "unconscionable," nor could there be, unconscionability must be determined on a case by case basis. * * *

---

[5] The agreement permitted immediate termination on the occurrence of certain conditions which are not involved in this case.

[6] The comment has been criticized as useless and at best ambiguous (J. WHITE & R. SUMMERS, THE UNIFORM COMMERCIAL CODE, 116 [1972]), and § 2-302 has been characterized as devoid of any specific content. Leff, *Unconscionability and the Code—(The Emperor's New Clause*, 115 U. PA. L. REV. 485, 487-489 [1967]). On the other hand, it has been said that the strength of the unconscionability concept is its abstraction, permitting judicial creativity. *See* Ellinghaus, *In Defense of Unconscionability*, 78 YALE L.J. 757 (1969).

We start with a recognition that the Uniform Commercial Code itself implies that a contract provision allowing termination without cause is not per se unconscionable. * * * Section 2-309(3) provides that "[t]ermination of a contract by one party except on the happening of an agreed event requires that reasonable notification be received by the other party and an agreement dispensing with notification is invalid if its operation would be unconscionable." G.L. c. 106, § 2-309, as appearing in St.1957, c. 765, § 1. This language implies that termination of a sales contract without agreed "cause" is authorized by the Code, provided reasonable notice is given. * * * There is no suggestion that the ninety days' notice provided in the Dairy Mart franchise agreement was unreasonable.

We find no potential for unfair surprise to the Zapathas in the provision allowing termination without cause. We view the question of unfair surprise as focused on the circumstances under which the agreement was entered into.[7] The termination provision was neither obscurely worded, nor buried in fine print in the contract. *Contrast Williams v. Walker-Thomas Furniture Co.*, 350 F.2d 445, 449 (D.C. Cir. 1965). The provision was specifically pointed out to Mr. Zapatha before it was signed; Mr. Zapatha testified that he thought the provision was "straightforward," and he declined the opportunity to take the agreement to a lawyer for advice. The Zapathas had ample opportunity to consider the agreement before they signed it. Significantly, the subject of loss of employment was paramount in Mr. Zapatha's mind. He testified that he had held responsible jobs in one company from 1952 to 1973, that he had lost his employment, and that he "was looking for something that had a certain amount of security; something that was stable and something I could call my own." We conclude that a person of Mr. Zapatha's business experience and education should not have been surprised by the termination provision and, if in fact he was, there was no element of unfairness in the inclusion of that provision in the agreement. * * *

We further conclude that there was no oppression in the inclusion of a

---

[7] As we shall note subsequently, the concept of oppression deals with the substantive unfairness of the contract term. This two-part test for unconscionability involves determining whether there was "an absence of meaningful choice on the part of one of the parties, together with contract terms which are unreasonably favorable to the other party." *Williams v. Walker-Thomas Furniture Co.*, 350 F.2d 445, 449 (D.C. Cir. 1965). *See Corenswet, Inc. v. Amana Refrigeration, Inc.*, 594 F.2d 129, 139 (5th Cir. 1979). The inquiry involves a search for components of "procedural" and "substantive" unconscionability. *See generally* Leff, *Unconscionability and the Code–The Emperor's New Clause*, 115 PA. L. REV. 485 (1967). * * *

termination clause in the franchise agreement. We view the question of oppression as directed to the substantive fairness to the parties of permitting the termination provisions to operate as written. The Zapathas took over a going business on premises provided by Dairy Mart, using equipment furnished by Dairy Mart. As an investment, the Zapathas had only to purchase the inventory of goods to be sold but, as Dairy Mart concedes, on termination by it without cause Dairy Mart was obliged to repurchase all the Zapathas' saleable merchandise inventory, including items not purchased from Dairy Mart, at 80% of its retail value. There was no potential for forfeiture or loss of investment. There is no question here of a need for a reasonable time to recoup the franchisees' initial investment. *See* * * * Gellhorn, *Limitations on Contract Termination Rights–Franchise Cancellations*, 1967 DUKE L.J. 465, 479-481. The Zapathas were entitled to their net profits through the entire term of the agreement. They failed to sustain their burden of showing that the agreement allocated the risks and benefits connected with termination in an unreasonably disproportionate way and that the termination provision was not reasonably related to legitimate commercial needs of Dairy Mart.* * * To find the termination clause oppressive merely because it did not require cause for termination would be to establish an unwarranted barrier to the use of termination at will clauses in contracts in this Commonwealth, where each party received the anticipated and bargained for consideration during the full term of the agreement.

3. We see no basis on the record for concluding that Dairy Mart did not act in good faith, as that term is defined in the sales article ("honesty in fact and the observance of reasonable commercial standards of fair dealing in the trade"). G.L. c. 106, § 2-103(1)(b). There was no evidence that Dairy Mart failed to observe reasonable commercial standards of fair dealing in the trade in terminating the agreement. If there were such standards, there was no evidence of what they were.

The question then is whether there was evidence warranting a finding that Dairy Mart was not honest "in fact." The judge concluded that the absence of any commercial purpose for the termination other than the Zapathas' refusal to sign a new franchise agreement violated Dairy Mart's obligation of good faith. Dairy Mart's right to terminate was clear, and it exercised that right for a reason it openly disclosed. The sole test of "honesty in fact" is whether the person was honest. * * * We think that, whether or not termination according to the terms of the franchise agreement may have been arbitrary, it was not dishonest.[8]

---

[8] Under G.L. c. 106, § 1-203, "[e]very contract * * * imposes an obligation of good faith *in*
(continued...)

The judge concluded that bad faith was also manifested by Dairy Mart's introductory brochure, which made representations of "security, comfort, and independence." Although this brochure and Mr. Zapatha's mistaken understanding that Dairy Mart could terminate the agreement only for cause could not be relied on to vary the clear terms of the agreement, the introductory brochure is relevant to the question of good faith. However, although the brochure misstated a franchisee's status as the owner of his own business, it shows no lack of honesty in fact relating to the right of Dairy Mart to terminate the agreement. Furthermore, by the time the Zapathas executed the second agreement, and even the first agreement, they knew that they would operate the franchise, but that they would not own the assets used in the business (except the goods to be sold); that the franchise agreement could be terminated by them and, at least in some circumstances, by Dairy Mart; and that in fact the major investment of funds would be made by Dairy Mart. We conclude that the use of the brochure did not warrant a finding of an absence of "honesty in fact." *See Corenswet, Inc. v. Amana Refrigeration, Inc.,* 594 F.2d 129, 138 (5th Cir. 1979); *Mason v. Farmers Ins. Cos.,* 281 N.W.2d 344, 347 (Minn. 1979).[9] * * *

Judgments reversed.

[Some footnotes omitted. Those retained have been renumbered.]

---

[8] (...continued)
its performance or enforcement" (emphasis supplied). We shall assume that an act of termination falls within the "performance" of the agreement. *See Baker v. Ratzlaff,* 1 Kan. App. 2d 285, 288, 564 P.2d 153 (1977). *But see* Summers, *"Good Faith" in General Contract Law and the Sales Provisions of the Uniform Commercial Code,* 54 VA. L. REV. 195, 252 (1968).

[9] It has been suggested that, despite the limited definition of good faith in the Code, in some contexts the general obligation of good faith in § 1-203 can be used to import an objective standard of "decency, fairness or reasonableness in performance or enforcement" into a contract to which it applies. Farnsworth, *Good Faith Performance and Commercial Reasonableness Under the Uniform Commercial Code,* 30 U. CHI. L. REV. 666, 668 (1963). Good faith in this sense can be regarded as an "excluder," barring varied forms of unreasonable conduct in different circumstances. *See* Summers, *"Good Faith" in General Contract Law and the Sales Provisions of the Uniform Commercial Code,* 54 VA. L. REV. 195, 196 (1968). Rather than stretch the Code definition of good faith beyond the plain meaning of the words used to define good faith, we prefer, as we are about to do, to analyze the question of fairness and reasonableness independently of the Code.

Notes

1. What was the scope issue in *Zapatha*? If Article 2 does not apply to a franchise contract, how did the court justify applying the code provisions on good faith and unconscionability? *See* RESTATEMENT (SECOND) OF CONTRACTS 205, which provides that "[e]very contract imposes upon each party a duty of good faith and fair dealing in its performance and its enforcement," and 208, which gives a court power to refuse to enforce an unconscionable contract or term.

2. Courts typically classify contracts for the distribution of goods (as opposed to a franchise) as contracts for sale even though services are also involved. *See, e.g., Sally Beauty Products, Inc. v. Nexxus*, 801 F.2d 1001 (7th Cir. 1986).[*]

3. **Good faith.** UCC 1-304 [former 1-203] generally provides that "[e]very contract or duty within [the Uniform Commercial Code] imposes an obligation of good faith in its performance or enforcement." That section, however, does not create an independent cause of action. Rather, it must be tied to a specific obligation created by the contract, such as the duty to purchase requirements, UCC 2-306, or the discretion reserved to fix prices, UCC 2-305.[**]

UCC 1-201(b)(20) provides, unless the context otherwise requires, that good faith "means honesty in fact and the observance of reasonable commercial standards of fair dealing." Thus good faith has an objective and a subjective component. This definition applies to merchant and non-merchant alike and focuses on the "fairness of conduct" rather than the lack of ordinary care. Comment 4 to UCC 3-103. So what are "reasonable commercial standards of fair dealing?" The difficult questions are: (1) What is bad faith in any given situation; and (2) What are the remedies for bad faith? We will consider these questions throughout the materials.[***] For now,

---

[*] For an application of Article 2 to a franchise agreement, *see Belleville Toyota Inc. v. Toyota Motor Sales, U.S.A., Inc.*, 770 N.E.2d 177 (Ill. 2002). *But see Viva Vino Import Corp. v. Farnese Vini S.r.l.*, 2000 WL 1224903 (E.D. Pa. 2000) (held that the CISG did not apply to distributorship agreements).

[**] *See Northern Nat. Gas Co. v. Conoco, Inc.*, 986 S.W.2d 603, 606 (Tex. 1998) and PEB Commentary No. 10.

[***] *See* James J. White, *Good Faith and the Cooperative Antagonist*, 54 SMU L. REV. 679 (2001); Michael P. Van Alstine, *Of Textualism, Party Autonomy, and Good Faith*, 40 WM. & MARY L. REV. 1223 (1999); Christina L. Kunz, *Frontispiece on Good Faith: A Functional Approach Within the UCC*, 16 WM. MITCH. L. REV. 1105 (1990); Robert S. Summers,

(continued...)

consider this. In termination disputes, such as that in *Zapatha*, most courts have concluded that if the termination clause was conscionable at the time of contracting and the time period granted is reasonable, a party who follows the terms of the termination provision is in good faith regardless of its motives.*

4. **Unconscionability.** When is a contract or term unconscionable? Hear the words of the Washington Supreme Court in *Nelson v. McGoldrick*, 896 P.2d 1258, 1262 (Wash. 1995) (quotation marks omitted):

> The existence of an unconscionable bargain is a question of law for the courts * * * [It] is extremely difficult to articulate an operation definition of unconscionability. Two classifications of unconscionability have generally been recognized: (1) substantive unconscionability, involving those cases where a clause or term in the contract is alleged to be one-sided or overly harsh and (2) procedural unconscionability, relating to impropriety during the process of forming a contract * * * Substantive unconscionability involves those cases where a clause or term is alleged to be one-sided or overly harsh. * * * Shocking to the conscience, monstrously harsh, and exceedingly calloused are terms sometimes used to define substantive unconscionability. * * * Procedural unconscionability has been described as the lack of meaningful choice, considering all the circumstances surrounding the transaction including the manner in which the contract was entered, whether each party had a reasonable opportunity to understand the terms of the contract and whether the important terms were hidden in a maze of fine print. * * * It is important, however, that these three factors not be applied mechanically without regard to whether in truth a meaningful choice existed.

How does this description accord with that in *Zapatha*? Does this dichotomy between substantive and procedural unconscionability apply in the case of a consumer lease? *See* UCC 2A-108. How does the Article 2A provision differ from the Article 2 provision?** Is unconscionability a necessary or effective concept in

---

*** (...continued)
"Good Faith" in General Contract Law and the Sales Provisions of the Uniform Commercial Code, 54 VA. L. REV. 195 (1968).

* *See Sons of Thunder, Inc. v. Borden Inc.*, 690 A.2d 575 (N.J. 1997).

** Michael J. Herbert, *Unconscionability under Article 2A*, 21 U. TOL. L. REV. 715 (1990).

dealing with problems of contractual assent?*

5. For an interesting contrast in result if not in analysis, compare *Hutcherson v. Sears Roebuck & Co.*, 793 N.E.2d 886 (Ill. Ct. App. 2003) *appl. denied* 205 Ill. 2d 582 (Ill. 2003) (applying Arizona law, an amendment to a credit card agreement requiring that any disputes be taken to arbitration was not unconscionable) with *Ingle v. Circuit City Stores, Inc.*, 328 F.3d 1165 (9th Cir. 2003) (arbitration clause in employer-employee agreement was unconscionable). In *Brower v. Gateway 2000, Inc.*, 676 N.Y.S.2d 569 (N.Y.A.D. 1998) the court held that a clause requiring arbitration was substantively unconscionable when it required arbitration in the ICC forum where the up front fee was $4000, and the cost of the goods involved in the contract was considerably less. The court required arbitration but in a different forum.

6. UCITA adopted the Article 2 provision on unconscionability, UCITA 111, and subjective and objective definition of good faith, UCITA 102(a)(32). UCITA also provides a statement that the obligation of good faith applies to the performance or enforcement of contracts within the scope of UCITA. UCITA 116(b).

Problem 2-5

A. Seller, located in California, entered into a five year contract with Bruce, a dealer in Alberta, Canada, for the sale and distribution of specified machine tools. Seller agreed to help Bruce set up and administer the distribution system and to assist in the resolution of complaints about the goods. The contract contained a termination clause which gave Seller but not Bruce power to terminate the contract after the first six months "for any reason" upon giving 10 days notice. Bruce had objected to the clause, but was told by Seller that the clause was "non-negotiable. Take it or leave it." After the first year, Seller gave the 10 day notice and terminated the contract. The distributorship was then given to Trevor, a competitor of Bruce's and a distant relative of Seller's CEO. Bruce, claiming losses in excess

---

* *See* Robert A. Hillman, *Debunking Some Myths about Unconscionability: A New Framework for U.C.C. Section 2-302*, 67 CORNELL L. REV. 1 (1981); Harry G. Prince, *Unconscionability in California: A Need for Restraint and Consistency*, 46 HASTINGS L.J. 459 (1995); Michael Joachim Bonell, *Policing the International Commercial Contract Against Unfairness Under the Unidroit Principles*, 3 TUL. J. INT'L & COMP. L. 73 (1995); Carol B. Swanson, *Unconscionable Quandary: UCC Article 2 and the Unconscionability Doctrine*, 31 N.M. L. REV. 359 (2001).

of $500,000, argues that the termination clause was unconscionable or, if not, the termination was in bad faith. Seller argues that the CISG applies and that neither of Bruce's defenses are available in international contracts for sale.

(1) Does the CISG apply? *See* Art. 1(1)(a), Art. 3.

(2) Does the CISG impose a duty of good faith on Seller's exercise of the termination power? *See* Art. 7, Art. 29. What does good faith mean under the CISG? What arguments would you make about what it should mean?

(3) Is a claim of unconscionability available under the CISG? *See* Art. 4(a). If not, what law determines the "validity" of the termination clause?

B. In a contract for sale of a car, the document signed by the buyer provided that all disputes arising under the contract must be resolved in arbitration, with the arbitrator chosen by the seller. The clause also provided that the buyer would be responsible for half of the arbitrator's fee unless the seller won the dispute in which case, the buyer would be responsible for all fees. The buyer is college educated and read the document prior to signing it. The buyer did not like the clause and objected to it but the seller refused to sell the car to the buyer unless the buyer signed the document. The buyer really wanted the car and grudgingly signed the document. Predictably the car was a lemon and the buyer is consulting you regarding what it can do now. Is the buyer stuck with the arbitration clause?

PART TWO:
FORMATION AND TERMS
OF THE CONTRACT

CHAPTER THREE
CONTRACT FORMATION AND ENFORCEMENT

SECTION 1. INTRODUCTION; ELECTRONIC CONTRACTING

A classic function of courts and contract law is to determine when parties negotiating for an agreed exchange have concluded an enforceable bargain. At what point have they crossed the line beyond which neither party can withdraw without potential liability for breach?

The RESTATEMENT approach. Under the RESTATEMENT (SECOND) OF CONTRACTS, the answer depends upon concepts with which you should now be familiar. First, contract is defined as a "promise or a set of promises for the breach of which the law gives a remedy." Section 1. Not all promises, however, are contracts. In bargain transactions, defined in Section 3 of the RESTATEMENT as an agreed exchange of promises or performances, there must be a "bargain in which there is a manifestation of mutual assent to the exchange and a consideration." Section 17(1). According to Section 22(1), the manifestation of mutual assent to an exchange "ordinarily takes the form of an offer or proposal by one party followed by an acceptance by the other party or parties." An offer is defined as a "manifestation of willingness to enter into a bargain, so made as to justify another person in understanding that his assent to that bargain is invited and will conclude it." Section 24. An acceptance of an offer is defined as a "manifestation of assent to the terms thereof made by the offeree in a manner invited or required by the offer." Section 50(1).

To constitute consideration, "a performance or a return promise must be bargained for," Section 71(1), *i.e.*, "sought by the promisor in exchange for his promise and . . . given by the promisee in exchange for that promise." Section 71(2).

Article 2's approach. How does Article 2 conform to the Restatement formula, "Offer plus acceptance plus consideration = contract?"

First, contract "means the total legal obligation that results from the parties' agreement as determined by [the Uniform Commercial Code] as supplemented by any other laws." UCC 1-201(b)(12) [former 1-201(11)]. In contract formation disputes, the relevant provisions of the UCC are found in Article 2, Part 2, or in Article 2A, Part 2, as supplemented by UCC 1-103.

Second, agreement means the "bargain of the parties in fact as found in their language or inferred from other circumstances including, course of performance, course of dealing, or usage of trade as provided in Section 1-303." UCC 1-201(b)(3) [former 1-201(3), 1-205, 2-208]. Note that the definition of "bargain . . . in fact" does not include a requirement of a promise. Further, although the concept of bargain is consistent with an agreed exchange, there is no explicit requirement that the exchange be bargained for. In short, although the agreement may contain promises and the exchange may be bargained for, there is no explicit requirement of either a promise or consideration to satisfy the definition.[*]

Third, UCC 2-204 is the key formation section in Article 2, Part 2. Read it, please. Note that UCC 2-204(1) and (2) sweep away technical rules on how and when the contract is made: Important evidence will be "conduct by both parties which recognizes the existence of a contract." UCC 2-204(1). Further, UCC 2-204(3) provides a standard to deal with disputes where one party withdraws before all of the material terms have been agreed. Thus, there are no rules specifying the quantum of agreement that must be reached before a contract is formed. Rather, the issue turns on what the parties "intended" and whether the court can fill the "gaps" with reasonable certainty when giving an appropriate remedy. By "intended," UCC 2-204(3) presumably means an intention to conclude the bargain without further agreement, rather than an intention that the bargain be legally binding. *Compare* RESTATEMENT (SECOND) OF CONTRACTS 21 ("neither real nor apparent intention that a promise be legally binding is essential to the formation of a contract.").

Electronic contracting. The 2003 amendments to Articles 2 and 2A added new language and subsections that address contract formation using electronic means, including the use of electronic agents. Read UCC 2-204, 2A-204 and the relevant definitions in UCC 2-103 and 2A-103. The new language in UCC 2-204 and 2A-204 answers the argument that if there is no human involvement, the requisite intent to contract is missing. Even in states that have not yet enacted the 2003 amendments to Article 2 or Article 2A, support is found for forming contracts

---

[*] *See* John E. Murray, Jr., *The Article 2 Prism: The Underlying Philosophy of Article 2 of the Uniform Commercial Code,* 21 WASHBURN L. J. 1 (1981).

through the use of electronic agents in the Uniform Electronic Transactions Act (UETA) 14 and the federal Electronic Signatures in Global and National Commerce Act (E-Sign), 15 U.S.C. 7001(h).[*]

Consider the interaction of federal and state law in this area. Section 7001(a) of E-Sign states as a matter of federal law (for transactions affecting interstate or foreign commerce) that certain signatures, contracts, or other records shall not be denied validity "solely" because they are in electronic form or that an electronic record was used in contract formation. Subsection (b)(1) limits the statute to requirements that "contracts or other records be written, signed, or in non-electronic form" and subsection (b)(2) states that E-Sign does not require "any person to use or accept electronic records or electronic signatures."[**]   Section 7002(a) then exempts a state from E-Sign preemption if it has enacted UETA. But Section 7003(a)(3), while exempting most of the UCC from its coverage, does not exempt Articles 2 and 2A. Thus, transactions under those articles are subject to E-Sign unless they are covered by UETA, which of course is non-preempted state law. UETA applies to a transaction governed by Articles 2 and 2A. UETA 3(b)(2). Thus, UETA's validation principles would apply until the amendments to Articles 2 and 2A (which are consistent with UETA) are enacted into law. *See* UCC 2-108(4) and 2A-104(4) which take advantage of a provision in E-Sign allowing subsequent state law to opt out of E-Sign's rules to some extent. E-Sign, 15 U.S.C. 7002(a)(2).

An example of a common use of an electronic agent to demonstrate assent is a so-called "click wrap" agreement, where the person when using a computer to conduct a transaction clicks on the "I agree" button after a display of the terms of the agreement. This form of agreement is commonly used in the downloading or installation of software but it could just as easily be used in a sale of goods or a lease of goods.[***]

Another practice in the electronic environment is the use of so-called browse-

---

[*] UETA is in effect in 46 states and the District of Columbia. In order for UETA to govern an Article 2 or 2A transaction, however, the parties have to agree to conduct the transaction electronically. UETA 3 and 5(b).

[**] Section 7001(c) sets out some complicated disclosure rules where consumers are involved.

[***] *See* Christina L. Kunz, et al, *Click-Through Agreements: Strategies for Avoiding Disputes on Validity of Assent*, 57 BUS. LAW. 401 (2001); *I. Lan Systems, Inc. v. Netscout Service Level Corp.*, 183 F. Supp. 2d 328 (D. Mass. 2002) (enforcing click wrap agreement for software using Article 2 principles).

wrap agreements. In this type of transaction, the user of the electronic interface does not click on a button that indicates "I agree" but rather the website provides notice that the transaction is governed by a set of terms and that using the website or engaging in some defined conduct will bind the user to the terms. If the user engages in the designated conduct, is the user bound by those terms as a matter of contract law?*

The 2003 amendments also address issues, other than intent to contract, that might have proven troublesome in the electronic environment. Read UCC 2-211 through 2-213 and 2A-222 through 2A-224. *Compare* UETA 5, 7, and 9 and E-Sign, 15 U.S.C. 7001.** The theory of these various acts is that electronic communication is a medium that may require some additional rules but does not change the basic underlying legal principles of contract formation and determination of enforceable terms. Hence the provisions are minimal and encouraging of electronic commerce rather than more elaborate and directive.***

SECTION 2.   CONTRACT FORMATION: THE BASICS

Articles 2 and 2A provide relatively little in the way of positive law on contract formation and require reliance on common law principles, including the principles

---

* *See* Christina L. Kunz, et al, *Browse-Wrap Agreements: Validation of Implied Assent in Electronic Form Agreements*, 59 BUS. LAW. 279 (2003).

** For discussions of some of the issues concerning contract formation and enforcement that were thought to arise in the electronic context, *see* Raymond T. Nimmer, *Electronic Contracting: Legal Issues*, 14 J. MARSHALL J. COMPUTER & INFO. L. 211 (1996); Amelia H. Boss, *Searching for Security in the Law of Electronic Commerce*, 23 NOVA L. REV. 585 (1999); Walter A. Effross, *The Legal Architecture of Virtual Stores: World Wide Web Sites and the Uniform Commercial Code*, 34 SAN DIEGO L. REV. 1263 (1997); Maureen A. O'Rourke, *Progressing Towards a Uniform Commercial Code for Electronic Commerce or Racing Towards Nonuniformity*, 14 BERKELEY TECH. L.J. 635 (1999); Aristotle G. Mirzaian, *Y2K Who Cares? We Have Bigger Problems: Choice of Law in Electronic Contracts*, 6 RICH. J.L. & TECH. 20 (1999-2000); Amelia H. Boss, *Electronic Commerce and the Symbiotic Relationship Between International and Domestic Law Reform*, 72 TUL. L. REV. 1931 (1998). For current developments on the international front, *see* John D. Gregory, *The Proposed UNCITRAL Convention on Electronic Contracts*, 59 BUS. LAW. 313 (2003).

*** *See* Robert A. Hillman and Jeffrey J. Rachlinski, *Standard-Form Contracting in the Electronic Age*, 77 N.Y.U. L. REV. 429 (2002).

of offer and acceptance.[*] Consider the following case.

FLANAGAN V. CONSOLIDATED NUTRITION, L.C.
COURT OF APPEALS OF IOWA, 2001
627 N.W.2D 573

STREIT, P.J.

A feed company that wanted a long-term contract to sell pigs to a farmer was content to abide by certain stringent rules regarding contract formation as long as those rules worked to its advantage. Now that the farmer claims the parties did not have a contract under those rules, the company argues more flexible rules should apply. We affirm the trial court's finding that the parties did not have a contract.

I. Background Facts & Proceedings.

Kenneth Flanagan and Consolidated Nutrition dispute whether they have a contract to buy and sell pigs. Flanagan, an O'Brien County farmer, raises pigs at his wean-to-finish operation. Consolidated, an Iowa limited liability company with its principal place of business in Omaha, Nebraska, sells livestock feed products and pigs. Flanagan considered acquiring segregated early-weaned ("SEW") pigs[1] for his operation from Consolidated.

Sometime before June 5, 1998, Flanagan received an unsigned document from Consolidated titled "Weaned Pig Sales Agreement." The document set forth a purchase price of $33.25 per SEW pig and a term of three-and-one-half years. Flanagan returned the document to Bob Kneip, Consolidated's district manager in Le Mars, on June 10 after making various changes to it. The changes included the following: (1) inserting "+/- 20 head" into the phrase "Buyer agrees to purchase

---

[*] For evidence that the non-code law of offer and acceptance is alive and well, *see Echo, Inc. v. Whitson Co., Inc.*, 121 F.3d 1099 (7th Cir. 1997) (buyer's offer must be approved at seller's headquarters before acceptance); *Infocomp, Inc. v. Electra Products, Inc.*, 109 F.3d 902 (3rd Cir. 1997) (same); *Hyosung America, Inc. v. Sumagh Textile Co., Ltd.*, 137 F.3d 75 (2nd Cir. 1998) (acceptance of non-conforming goods acquiesces in future shipments of same non-conforming goods).

[1] SEW pigs are weaned earlier (ten to twenty-one days old) than conventionally-weaned pigs (twenty-eight to thirty-five days old) and are housed in nurseries segregated from the rest of the pig population. This process is intended to protect SEW pigs from endemic diseases. *See* Minnesota Impacts!: Performance of Segregated Early Weaned Pigs, at http://www.extension.umn.edu/mnimpacts/impact.asp?projectID=21 (last visited Feb. 16, 2001).

from Consolidated, and Consolidated agrees to sell to Buyer, approximately 1050 Segregated Early Weaned Pigs ("SEW Pigs") each 9 weeks during the term of this agreement;" (2) inserting a definition of "competitive" into a paragraph requiring Flanagan to purchase his feed requirements from Consolidated "[f]or so long as Consolidated's feed products and services are competitive with other suppliers;" (3) inserting a liquidated damages clause; and (4) changing the choice of law provision from Nebraska to Iowa. Flanagan did not sign the document.

On June 25 Flanagan went to Consolidated's Le Mars office to review the company's revised version of the "Weaned Pig Sales Agreement;" Kneip was not present. The document included Flanagan's definition of "competitive" and a damages clause acceptable to him. It did not include the phrase "+/- 20 head" or an Iowa choice of law provision. Flanagan again made these two changes to the document, initialed his changes, and signed and left one copy of the document at the office. This is the only document bearing Flanagan's actual signature.

Before June 29 Flanagan received a telephone call from Kneip regarding delivery of SEW pigs. Flanagan agreed to accept delivery of several hundred SEW pigs from Consolidated for $33.25 per pig beginning June 29-the same day as the contract commencement date set forth in the "Weaned Pig Sales Agreement" Flanagan had signed June 25. Both Flanagan and Kneip agreed the parties were not buying and selling the pigs pursuant to that document because Consolidated had not yet accepted it and returned it to Flanagan.[2]

On July 15 Flanagan received another version of the "Weaned Pig Sales Agreement." Terry Myers, one of Consolidated's vice-presidents, had signed the document. Once again, it did not include the phrase "+/- 20 head" or an Iowa choice of law provision. Flanagan did not sign the document or return it to Consolidated.

On August 12 Kneip called Flanagan asking whether he was ready for the next delivery of SEW pigs from Consolidated. Flanagan told Kneip he was not going to accept the pigs because the parties did not have a contract. The following day, Flanagan sent a letter to Consolidated reiterating the parties did not have a contract and stating he was withdrawing the offer he had made to Consolidated in Le Mars.

On August 20 Flanagan received yet another copy of a "Weaned Pig Sales Agreement" from Consolidated. The document appears to be a copy of the

---

[2] Kneip testified he did not recall saying Consolidated had not signed the "Weaned Pig Sales Agreement" as of June 29 and denied it was his opinion that, at that time, the parties did not have a contract. The trial court found Flanagan's testimony to the contrary more credible.

"Weaned Pig Sales Agreement" Flanagan changed and signed on June 25 except for the following: (1) someone made editing marks on the document that were consistent with the format and content of the "Weaned Pig Sales Agreement" Flanagan received on July 15; (2) the first paragraph of the document included the typewritten date June 25, 1998; and (3) Flanagan's copied signature and Terry Meyer's signature are at the end of the document.

Sometime after August 20 Flanagan and Consolidated agreed to disagree about whether they had a contract. Flanagan bought SEW pigs from Consolidated until August 1999, but generally paid only market price for them-not the higher price set forth in the parties' purported contract. During this period, Flanagan received another "Weaned Pig Sales Agreement" from Consolidated that the company claimed was the parties' contract. The document, sent December 16, appears to be a copy of the "Weaned Pig Sales Agreement" Flanagan signed on June 25, except it does not have an attachment defining "competitive." Nor does the document contain the editing marks or typewritten date found in the "Weaned Pig Sales Agreement" Flanagan received August 20. The document does bear Flanagan's copied signature and Terry Meyer's signature.

Flanagan filed a petition for declaratory judgment asking the district court to find the parties did not have a contract. Consolidated filed a counterclaim asking the court to find Flanagan owed the company over $90,000 for the SEW pigs for which he had not paid $33.25 per pig. After a bench trial, the court found the parties did not have a contract under either the common law or the Iowa Uniform Commercial Code (U.C.C.). Consolidated appeals. The company claims the parties had a binding long-term contract in which Flanagan was obligated to buy approximately 1050 SEW pigs every nine weeks for three-and-one-half years.

* * * *

III. The Merits.

Consolidated claims the U.C.C. applies to this case and, under the U.C.C., the parties had a contract. Specifically, Consolidated argues it presented Flanagan with an offer on June 25, 1998, in Le Mars and Flanagan accepted the offer that same day. Consolidated further argues the signed document Flanagan received on July 15 was a written confirmation of the parties' purported contract. *See* Iowa Code § 554.2207(1) (1997).

A. The U.C.C.

Consolidated's starting premise is correct: The U.C.C. undoubtedly applies to this case. Article 2 of the U.C.C. applies to "transactions in goods." *Id.* § 554.2102. Goods include "all things ... which are movable at the time of identification to the contract for sale other than the money which is to be paid, investment securities ... and things in action." *Id.* § 554.2105. Because this definition of "goods" encompasses livestock, article 2 governs the parties' purported contract to buy and sell SEW pigs. * * * *

The facts of this case warrant a brief discussion about the relationship between article 2 and the common law of contracts. Article 2 relaxes many of the legal formalisms and technicalities of contract formation associated with the common law of contracts. For example, at common law "an offer [has] to be accepted exactly 'as is' or the response amount[s] only to a counter-offer." * * * Similarly, when "an offer prescribes the place, time or manner of acceptance its terms in this respect must be complied with in order to create a contract." RESTATEMENT (SECOND) OF CONTRACTS § 60 (1981). In contrast, article 2 is less stringent: Section 554.2204(1) provides "[a] contract for sale of goods may be made in any manner sufficient to show agreement, including conduct by both parties which recognizes the existence of such a contract." Section 554.2206(1)(a) provides "an offer to make a contract shall be construed as inviting acceptance in any manner and by any medium reasonable in the circumstances." Finally, section 554.2207(1) provides "[a] definite and seasonable expression of acceptance or a written confirmation which is sent within a reasonable time operates as an acceptance even though it states terms additional to or different from those offered or agreed upon." [*See* UCC 2-206(3)–ed.]

Article 2 does not, of course, entirely eliminate the common law of contracts. *See* Iowa Code § 554.1103 ("Unless displaced by the particular provisions of this chapter, the principles of law and equity ... shall supplement its provisions."). Significantly, contracting parties like Flanagan and Consolidated must still reach an agreement in order to have an enforceable contract. * * * The relationship between this basic contract law principle and article 2's liberal rules regarding contract formation is as follows:

> [W]hen there is basic agreement, however manifested and whether or not the precise moment of agreement may be determined, failure to articulate that agreement in the precise language of a lawyer, with every difficulty and contingency considered and resolved, will not prevent formation of a contract [for the sale of goods]. But, of equal importance, if there be no basic agreement, the code will not imply one.

Kleinschmidt Div. of SCM Corp. v. Futuronics Corp., 41 N.Y.2d 972, 395 N.Y.S.2d 151, 363 N.E.2d 701, 702-03 (1977).

Nor does article 2 prevent parties involved in "transactions in goods" from adhering-by choice-to the common law rules of contract formation that have been replaced by the article's less stringent rules. For example, section 554.2206(1) relaxes common law rules concerning the means and medium of an acceptance to a particular offer-"unless otherwise unambiguously indicated by the language or circumstances." Iowa Code § 554.2206(1). Consequently, "where the circumstances indicate that a particular manner of contract formation is contemplated by the parties, a binding contract is not formed in the absence of compliance with the contemplated procedure." *Jim L. Shetakis Distrib. Co. v. Centel Communications Co.*, 104 Nev. 258, 756 P.2d 1186, 1188 (1988).

Equipped with this background information, we turn to the remainder of Consolidated's argument. As was stated previously, Consolidated argues it presented Flanagan with an offer on June 25, 1998, in Le Mars and Flanagan accepted the offer that same day. Consolidated further argues the July 15 document, with Flanagan's copied signature, was a written confirmation of the parties' purported contract.

B. Existence of a Contract.

The remainder of Consolidated's argument is misguided. Implicit in the company's argument that Flanagan accepted its offer on June 25 is the assumption the parties actually reached an agreement on that date. This assumption contradicts, of course, the trial court's finding that Consolidated and Flanagan had "no contract under the U.C.C." *See* Iowa Code § 554.1201(11) (stating a contract is the "total legal obligation which results from the parties' agreement").

We are bound by this finding of fact if it is supported by substantial evidence. * * * * Here, as will be discussed in greater detail below, the record shows Flanagan and Consolidated's concerted efforts to reach an agreement never culminated in a binding contract because they did not adhere to their self-imposed rules of contract formation. * * * * Accordingly, we must affirm the trial court.

Flanagan and Consolidated contemplated they would not have a binding contract until they both signed a "Weaned Pig Sales Agreement" that had been processed and approved by appropriate Consolidated personnel. Consolidated complains the facts tell a different story. The company's own conduct, however, belies its protestations. For example, after Flanagan signed the "Weaned Pig Sales Agreement" on June 25, Consolidated sent him a letter stating they would "get [his] contract back" after he gave them his financial statement-the implication being that some additional things had to happen before the parties had a binding contract. Moreover, when Consolidated returned the "Weaned Pig Sales Agreement" to Flanagan on July 15, it was a new version that did not incorporate all of Flanagan's June 25th alterations. Indeed, a Consolidated employee subsequently wrote a memo characterizing the document as a "new contract"-a fact at odds with the company's present claim the document merely confirmed the parties' purported June 25 contract. Rather, such conduct is consistent with the supposition the parties would not have a binding contract until they both signed a "Weaned Pig Sales Agreement" that had been processed and approved by appropriate Consolidated personnel.

Flanagan and Consolidated never timely complied with this manner of contract formation. The above-discussed conduct demonstrates that, as late as July 15, the parties were still engaged in efforts to reach an agreement. On August 12 Flanagan informed Consolidated he did not believe the parties had a contract and effectively revoked any offer he had made to the company. * * * On August 20 Flanagan received a "Weaned Pig Sales Agreement" from Consolidated bearing each party's signature. The inconsistencies between this document, the document Consolidated had delivered to Flanagan in July, and the document Consolidated later sent to Flanagan in December support the trial court's finding the August 20 document was part of Consolidated's belated attempt to establish the parties had a binding contract. These efforts by Consolidated to finally comply with the parties' self-imposed rules of contract formation were made after the company learned Flanagan was no longer interested in entering into a long-term contract-and, consequently, were made too late.

Thus, to reiterate, substantial evidence supports the trial court's finding that Flanagan and Consolidated had "no contract under the U.C.C." In reaching this conclusion, we have not overlooked the fact that on June 29, July 2, and July 6 of 1998 Flanagan accepted delivery of several hundred SEW pigs for $33.25 per pig-the price set forth in every "Weaned Pig Sales Agreement" exchanged between the parties. Consolidated argues this conduct demonstrates the existence of a binding long-term contract between the parties. *See* Iowa Code § 554.2204. Flanagan testified, however, the parties bought and sold these SEW pigs pursuant to a separate agreement because they did not have a binding long-term contract at that time. His explanation for his conduct is consistent with the theory of the case discussed above. Accordingly, we uphold the trial court's finding that Flanagan's testimony regarding this matter was more credible.

IV. Conclusion.

The facts and circumstances of this case show that Flanagan and Consolidated considered their interplay, their exchange of differing drafts, their proposals and counterproposals, as part of the dialogue of parties seeking to reach an agreement. They never met their goal. Consolidated cannot now ignore the parties' self-imposed rules of contract formation, wind back the clock, point to one of the earlier moments in the parties' contracting dialogue, and claim the parties had a binding contract as of that time. We affirm the trial court. Flanagan and Consolidated did not have a contract to buy and sell SEW pigs. Affirmed.

Problem 3-1

Read UCC 2-204 through 2-206 and 2A-204 through 2A-206. Identify the common law rule of contract formation that each section addresses and alters. Compare the rules from the UCC with the rules in the CISG Articles 14 through 24. What are the differences in scope and style between Article 2 and the CISG?

Problem 3-2

Abel visits Retailer's website and decides to order a new toaster advertised for sale on the website. Abel clicks on the picture of the toaster and adds the toaster to his electronic shopping cart.

A. A screen pops up with the various terms including the following: "Any disputes concerning any product provided through this website must be resolved in binding arbitration." Two buttons are under the pop up screen one of which states "I agree" and the other of which states "I disagree." To actually complete the purchase, Abel must click on the "I agree" button. Clicking on the "I disagree" button removes the item from the electronic shopping cart. Abel clicks on "I agree" and completes ordering of the toaster. When the toaster arrives, it is a miserable failure at toasting anything. Is Abel bound by the arbitration clause?

B. Assume instead of the pop up screen as described above, when Abel clicks on the picture of the toaster to place the toaster in his electronic shopping cart, the screen changes to provide a hyperlink which states, "click here for terms of sale." Abel does not click on the hyperlink but rather completes his purchase of the toaster. If Abel had clicked on the hyperlink, Abel would have seen the same arbitration clause as stated above. When the toaster arrives, it is a miserable failure at toasting anything. Is Abel bound by the arbitration clause?

Problem 3-3

Dealer is in the business of selling machine tools. After preliminary negotiations, Bosco Inc. mailed to Dealer a printed form prepared by Bosco inviting Dealer to make an offer to sell 10 described tools for $25,000. The form supplied by Bosco to Dealer contained five paragraphs of printed matter, inserted on a single page with blank lines to be filled in at the top as follows: "_____ offers to sell _____ [insert description] for a total price of _____". The form had a signature line at the bottom. The third paragraph above the signature line provided: THIS OFFER WILL BE HELD OPEN FOR 30 DAYS AFTER RECEIPT BY THE OFFEREE. Dealer filled in the blanks as requested by Bosco, signed the form on the signature line on the bottom, dating it May 30, and returned the form by mail to Bosco, who received it on June 3. On June 15, Dealer notified Bosco by fax that the offer was revoked: A better deal had been worked out with Crispy Inc. for the goods. On June 16, Bosco faxed to Dealer an acceptance of the offer, which was received the same day. Bosco insists there was a contract.

    A. Is Bosco correct? Start with UCC 2-205.

    B. What result under Article 2A?

    C. What result under the CISG? *See* Art. 16.

Note that UCC 2-205 states one method of creating an enforceable option without preempting other methods, such as a promise to hold the offer open that is supported by consideration or induces reliance. *See* RESTATEMENT (SECOND) OF CONTRACTS 87.

Problem 3-4

Seller, an equipment dealer, had a quantity of used equipment which it was willing to sell with a limited warranty for $50,000. On June 1, Retailer examined the equipment and discussed terms with Seller. An oral agreement was reached on all terms except price. On June 5, Retailer mailed Seller a signed offer to purchase the equipment for $40,000 and enclosed a $4,000 check as a down payment. Seller received the offer and check on June 7 and, on June 8, deposited the check in its business account. Seller did not communicate with Retailer. On June 10, Seller received an offer from Crispy, Inc. to purchase the equipment for $60,000 cash. Seller accepted the offer the same day. On June 11, Seller informed Retailer that its offer had been rejected and mailed to Retailer a cashier's check for $4,000.

Retailer claims that a contract was formed on June 8 when Seller deposited the check. Retailer supports its claim with the following arguments:

    (i) The offer should be construed as inviting an acceptance "in any manner and by any medium reasonable in the circumstances," and depositing the check was a reasonable manner of acceptance, UCC 2-206(1)(a);

    (ii) Depositing the check was the beginning of performance and a "reasonable mode of acceptance" under UCC 2-206(2); and

(iii) The sending by Retailer and the deposit by Seller of the check was "conduct by both parties which recognizes the existence of a contract," UCC 2-204(1), or demonstrated that the "parties have intended to make a contract" under UCC 2-204(3).

A. Which, if any, of these arguments should the court accept?

B. Would your analysis change if Seller was willing to lease the equipment and the parties agreed to an oral lease on all terms but price, followed by the written offer to lease for $40,000 with the $4,000 down payment?

C. Same analysis under the CISG? *See* Article 18.

Problem 3-5

Stable Earth, Inc., a manufacturer of fertilizer, and Brittany, a farmer, had done business for 5 years. When fertilizer was needed, Brittany would order through Stable Earth's website a specific quantity and quality of fertilizer. Stable Earth's computer system would send that order to the warehouse where the order would be filled at Stable Earth's current wholesale price, shipping the goods to Brittany by carrier FOB point of shipment. Frequently, Stable Earth would ship less or more than what Brittany ordered, depending upon what Stable Earth had on hand in the warehouse, but the deviation would never exceed 15%. Brittany invariably accepted and paid for what was actually shipped without objection. On July 10, during a time of price instability in the fertilizer market, Brittany used the website to order 500 bags of a specified fertilizer "for prompt shipment." The wholesale price on that date was $18 per bag. On July 12, Stable Earth shipped 400 bags of fertilizer to Brittany and mailed an invoice for the wholesale price on that date, $20.00 per bag. On July 15, while the goods were still in transit and the wholesale price was $25.00 per bag, Stable Earth notified Brittany that the order had been rejected and diverted the shipment to Carl, who agreed to pay $26 per bag.

A. Brittany claimed there was a contract for the sale of 500 bags of fertilizer on July 12 at $20.00. Brittany relied upon UCC 2-204, 2-206(1)(b) and 1-303 [former 1-205]. Is Brittany correct?

B. Why do you think UCC 2A-206 does not contain the provision from UCC 2-206(1)(b)?

C. How does the CISG deal with this issue? *See* Article 18.

Problem 3-6

In a transaction covered by the CISG, after negotiations where no agreement was reached, Buyer sends Seller a telex which states: "Send me some #1 grade Delaware Cobbler Potatoes." Seller promptly ships 1,000 bushels of #1 grade Delaware Cobbler potatoes which Buyer accepts and uses. Nothing is said about price. Buyer refuses to pay, citing CISG Article 14(1) and claiming that no contract was formed. Seller argues that a contract was validly concluded and that Buyer owes the market price for the goods "charged at the time of the conclusion of the contract." CISG Art. 55. Who is correct? How should a court interpret the language in Art. 55 that a contract must be "validly concluded" before a price term can be supplied? Can a contract be "validly made" through conduct of both parties under the CISG?*

Note: UCITA and Contract Formation Principles

While UCITA follows the basic concept of Article 2 regarding contract formation principles, UCITA 202(a) through (c) and UCITA 203, UCITA stands in sharp contrast to Article 2 when there is disagreement over a material term. Section 202(d) provides that a contract is not formed if there is "material disagreement about a material term," unless both parties have engaged in conduct that demonstrates an intent to contract. Does this provision add any more definition to the idea of "intent to contract" found in Articles 2 and 2A? In other words, if there is "material disagreement about a material term" in an Article 2 or 2A transaction, is there an "intent to contract"?

SECTION 3.   CONTRACT FORMATION: BATTLE OF THE FORMS

A. Under Former UCC 2-207

Every student knows of the "mirror-image" rule of general contract law: A purported "acceptance" which varies the terms of an offer is not an acceptance at all, but a counter-offer. *See* RESTATEMENT (SECOND) OF CONTRACTS 58 and 59.

---

* For an excellent analysis of the CISG contract formation provisions, *see* Michael P. Van Alstine, *Consensus, Dissensus, and Contractual Obligation Through the Prism of Uniform International Sales Law*, 37 VA. J. INT'L L. 1 (1996).

See also CISG Art. 19(1). And remember, a counteroffer can be accepted by conduct manifesting assent to the counteroffer.

Suppose, however, that the parties are dealing from a distance by the exchange of records. The records seem to agree on certain negotiated terms–price, quantity, time of delivery, method of payment–but the records contain standard terms prepared by each party which have not been read by the other party and over which neither party has negotiated. This is "boilerplate." The pressing question is whether any contract has been formed and, if so, what are the terms?

Under the common law rule, an attempt by an offeree (seller) to accept an offer from a buyer in a record that contained standard terms that added to or were different from the offer constituted a counteroffer. If the original offeree objectively assented to the counteroffer (by words or conduct) there was a contract on the counter-offeror's (seller's) terms–the infamous "last shot." Since it is widely believed that contracting parties rarely read the boiler plate, this gave the counter-offeror a strategic advantage and created a risk that the counter-offeree would be unfairly surprised to find that its blanket assent to the record included the standard terms.

Although not distinguishing between negotiated and standard terms, the former 2-207 was drafted to change the common law result in cases like that just noted. As one student aptly observed:

> At common law and under the Uniform Sales Act, a purported acceptance which modifies the terms of the offer is a rejection and a counter-offer. Although this rule is supposed to promote certainty in the terms of the agreement, businessmen frequently undertake performance in reliance on the mistaken assumption that such an "acceptance" has created a contract. Moreover, in the context of modern business practice of using standard forms to transmit and acknowledge orders, the rule encourages a "battle of the forms"–a constant effort by businessmen to gain an advantage in their transactions by qualifying their obligations by means of forms containing unilaterally beneficial conditions. In addition, the rule provides a loophole for parties wishing to extricate themselves from unfavorable deals which in commercial understanding have been closed. [Footnotes omitted.]

Note, 111 U. PA. L. REV. 132, 133 (1962).

Former 2-207, prior to the 2003 amendments, tried to deal with the battle of the forms situation. That section addressed two issues: (1) was a contract formed and if so, (2) what were the contract terms. The answer to the second question depended upon how the contract was formed, either by the exchange of records or by mutual conduct.

Former 2-207 was a much maligned section and generated a significant amount of litigation every year. Some of the flaws in former section 2-207 were: (i) the application of the section created arbitrary and uncertain outcomes; (ii) the terms the parties ended up with were not terms that they would have chosen if they had bargained about the terms; and (iii) the structure of the section created incentives for parties to draft completely one-sided forms in an effort to either get terms that were unduly favorable to the drafter or to preclude getting stuck with the other side's terms. Daniel Keating, *Exploring the Battle of the Forms in Action*, 98 MICH. L. REV. 2678 (2000).*

We will first analyze the battle of the forms analysis under section 2-207 prior to the 2003 amendments. Read former 2-207. List the questions you would have to ask and answer to determine whether a contract is formed and if so, the terms of the contract. Consider the analysis in the following case under former 2-207.

DAITOM, INC. V. PENNWALT CORP.
UNITED STATES COURT OF APPEALS, TENTH CIRCUIT, 1984
741 F.2D 1569

WILLIAM E. DOYLE, CIRCUIT JUDGE

[On September 7, 1976, the seller (Pennwalt), after negotiations with the buyer (Daitom), submitted a proposal for the sale of two rotary vacuum dryers with dust filters. The proposal was made in a typewritten writing to which pre-printed form conditions were attached and explicitly made part of the proposal. One term in the form conditions imposed a one year period after delivery within which Daitom could bring a law suit. On October 5, 1976, Daitom issued a purchase order, which consisted of a pre-printed form and 17 standard terms and conditions on the back. One of the terms of the "boilerplate" reserved to Daitom "all of its rights and remedies available at law." Pennwalt delivered the goods in May, 1977 but, because the plant in which they were to be installed was under construction, left the crates outside. On June 15, 1978, the goods were finally installed and operated. Serious defects were discovered, of which Pennwalt was notified on June 17, 1978.

---

* For a sample of recent cases, *see Standard Bent Glass Corp. v. Glassrobots Oy*, 333 F.3d 440 (3rd Cir. 2003); *Polytop Corp. v. Chipsco, Inc.*, 826 A. 2d 945 (R.I. 2003) (per curium); *Vulcan Automotive Equip. Ltd. v. Global Marine Engine & Parts, Inc.*, 240 F. Supp. 2d 156 (D.R.I. 2003); *Sibcoimtrex, Inc. v. American Foods Group, Inc.*, 241 F. Supp. 2d 104 (D. Mass. 2003); *Southern Illinois Riverboat Casino Cruises, Inc. v. Triangle Insulation and Sheet Metal Co.*, 302 F. 3d 667 (7th Cir. 2002).

When Pennwalt was unable to repair the defects, Daitom brought suit for breach of warranty on March 7, 1980. The trial court held, *inter alia*, that the one year limitation became part of the contract and, since the law suit was brought more than one year after delivery, granted a summary judgment against Daitom. On appeal, the judgment was reversed and the case remanded to the trial court.]

* * *

C. The Writings and the Contract

The trial court concluded that the parties' exchanged writings formed a contract. Thus, there was not a formal single document. Pennwalt's September 7, 1976 proposal constituted the offer and Daitom's October 5, 1976 purchase order constituted the acceptance.

It is essentially uncontested that Pennwalt's proposal constituted an offer. The proposal set forth in some detail the equipment to be sold to Daitom, the price, the terms of shipment, and specifically stated that the attached terms and conditions were an integral part of the proposal. One of those attached terms and conditions of sale limited the warranties to repair and replacement of defective parts and limited the period of one year from the date of delivery for any action for breach of warranty.[1]

---

[1] Paragraph 5 of the terms and conditions of sale stated in full (emphasis added):
   6. WARRANTIES:
   a. Seller warrants that at the time of delivery of the property to the carrier, it will be, unless otherwise specified, new, free and clear of all lawful liens and security interests or other encumbrances unknown to Buyer. If, within a period of one year from the date of *such delivery* any parts of the property (except property specified to be used property or normal wear parts) fail because of material or workmanship which was defective at the time of such delivery, Seller will repair such parts, or furnish parts to replace them f.o.b. Seller's or its supplier's plant, provided such failure is due solely to such defective material or workmanship and is not contributed to by any other cause, such as improper care or unreasonable use, and provided such defects are brought to Seller's attention for verification when first discovered, and the parts alleged to be so defective are returned, if requested, to Seller's or its supplier's plant. *No action for breach of warranty shall be brought more than one year after the cause of action has accrued*
      SELLER MAKES NO OTHER WARRANTY OF ANY KIND, EXPRESS OR IMPLIED, INCLUDING ANY WARRANTY OF FITNESS OF THE PROPERTY FOR ANY PARTICULAR PURPOSE EVEN IF THAT PURPOSE IS KNOWN TO SELLER.
      In no event shall Seller be liable for consequential damage.
   b. Because of varied interpretations of standards at the local level, Seller cannot

(continued...)

The proposal was sent to Kintech and forwarded to Daitom with a recommendation to accept the proposal. Daitom sent the October 5, 1976 purchase order to Pennwalt. This purchase order constituted an acceptance of Pennwalt's offer and formed a binding contract for the sale only pursuant to 2-207(1), despite the statement of terms additional to or different from those in the offer.[2] But these terms were not without meaning or consequence. However, the acceptance was not expressly conditioned on Pennwalt accepting these additional or different terms.

There is a provision which Daitom contends made the acceptance expressly conditional on Pennwalt's accepting the additional or different terms which appeared in the pre-printed, standard "boilerplate" provisions on the back of the purchase order. It stated:

> Acceptance. Immediate acceptance is required unless otherwise provided herein. It is understood and agreed that the written acceptance by Seller of this purchase order or the commencement of any work performance of any services hereunder by the Seller, (including the commencement of any work or the performance of any service with respect to samples), shall constitute acceptance by Seller of this purchase order and of all the terms and conditions of such acceptance is *expressly limited to such terms and conditions, unless each deviation is mutually recognized therefore in writing.* (Emphasis added.)

This language does not preclude the formation of a contract by the exchanged writings pursuant to § 2-207(1). Nor does it dictate the adoption of a conclusion holding that as a result the acceptance provided the applicable terms of the resulting contract. First, it is well established that a contract for the sale of goods may be

---

[1] (...continued)

warrant that the property meets the requirements of the Occupational Safety and Health Act.

[2] The principal additional or different terms referred to the reservation of warranties. Specifically:

(8) WARRANTY. The Seller warrants that the supplies covered by this purchase order will conform to the specifications, drawings, samples, or other descriptions furnished or specified by buyer, and will be fit and sufficient for the purpose intended, merchantable, of good material and workmanship, and free from defect. The warranties and remedies provided for in this paragraph * * * shall be in addition to those implied by or available at law and shall exist not withstanding [sic] the acceptance by Buyer of all or a part of this applies with respect to which such warranties and remedies are applicable.

made in any manner to show agreement, requiring merely that there be some objective manifestation of mutual assent, but that there must be. There is not a contract until it takes place. *See* U.C.C. § 2-204; * * * Here there is such an objective manifestation of agreement on essential terms of equipment specifications, price, and the terms of shipment and payment, all of which took place before the machinery was put to any test. The purchase order explicitly referred to and incorporated on its front Kintech's equipment specifications and Pennwalt's proposal. But we are unwilling to hold such a typewritten reference and incorporation by Daitom brings the matter to a close. The acceptance and warranty terms as provided for by the above excerpted acceptance clause, does manifest a willingness on all essential terms to accept the offer and form a contract. * * * This was, of course, before an attempt was made to use the equipment.

Second, the boilerplate provision does not directly address the instant case. The purchase order is drafted principally as an *offer* inviting acceptance. Although this court recognizes that the form may serve a dual condition depending on the circumstances, the imprecision of language that permits such service detracts from Daitom's argument of conditional acceptance.

Third, the courts are split on the application of § 2-207(1) and the meaning of "expressly made conditional on assent to the additional or different terms.". * * * *Roto-Lith Ltd. v. F.P. Bartlett & Co., Inc.*, 297 F.2d 497 (1st Cir. 1962) represents one extreme of the spectrum, that the offeree's response stating a term materially altering the contractual obligations solely to the disadvantage of the offeror constitutes a conditional acceptance. The other extreme of the spectrum is represented by *Dorton v. Collins & Aikman Corporation*, 453 F.2d 1161 (6th Cir. 1972), in which case the court held that the conditional nature of the acceptance should be so clearly expressed in a manner sufficient to notify the offeror that the offeree is unwilling to proceed with the transaction unless the additional or different terms are included in the contract. The middle of the spectrum providing that a response merely "predicating" acceptance on clarification, addition or modification is a conditional acceptance is represented by *Construction Aggregates Corp. v. Hewitt-Robins, Inc.*, 404 F.2d 505 (7th Cir. 1968), *cert. denied*, 395 U.S. 921, 89 S. Ct. 1774, 23 L. Ed. 2d 238 (1969).

The facts of this case, Daitom asserts, are not of a character that would suggest that there had been an unequivocal acceptance. The defendant-appellee was aware that the machinery had not even been tried. Once it was tried, it broke down in a very short time. It is hard to see a justifiable acceptance, Daitom asserts, when the buyer does not even know whether it works, and, in fact, learns after the fact, that it does not work. This fact alone renders the "contract" to be questionable.

The better view as to the meaning and application of "conditional acceptance," and the view most likely to be adopted by Pennsylvania, is the view in *Dorton* that the offeree must explicitly communicate his or her unwillingness to proceed with the transaction unless the additional or different terms in its response are accepted by the offeror. * * *

Having found an offer and an acceptance which was not made expressly conditional on assent to additional or different terms, we must now decide the effect of those additional or different terms on the resulting contract and what terms became part of it. The district court simply resolved this dispute by focusing solely on the period of limitations specified in Pennwalt's offer of September 7, 1976. Thus, the court held that while the offer explicitly specified a one-year period of limitations in accordance with § 2-725(1) allowing such a reduction, Daitom's acceptance of October 5, 1976 was silent as to the limitations period. Consequently, the court held that § 2-207(2) was inapplicable and the one-year limitations period controlled, effectively barring Daitom's action for breach of warranties.

While the district court's analysis undertook to resolve the issue without considering the question of the application of § 2-207(2) to additional or different terms, we cannot accept its approach or its conclusion. We are unable to ignore the plain implication of Daitom's reservation in its boilerplate warranties provision of all its rights and remedies available at law. Such an explicit reservation impliedly reserves the statutory period of limitations; without such a reservation, all other reservations of actions and remedies are without effect.

The statutory period of limitations under the U.C.C. is four years after the cause of action has accrued. UCC § 2-725(1). Were we to determine that this four-year period became a part of the contract rather than the shorter one-year period, Daitom's actions on breach of warranties were timely brought and summary judgment against Daitom was error.

We realize that our conclusion requires an inference to be drawn from a construction of Daitom's terms; however, such an inference and construction are consistent with the judicial reluctance to grant summary judgment where there is some reasonable doubt over the existence of a genuine material fact. * * * When taking into account the circumstances surrounding the application of the one-year limitations period, we have little hesitation in adopting the U.C.C.'s four-year limitations reservation, the application of which permits a trial on the merits. Thus, this court must recognize that certain terms in Daitom's acceptance differed from terms in Pennwalt's offer and decide which become part of the contract. The district court certainly erred in refusing to recognize such a conflict.

The difficulty in determining the effect of different terms in the acceptance is the imprecision of drafting evident in § 2-207. The language of the provision is silent on how different terms in the acceptance are to be treated once a contract is formed pursuant to § 2-207(1). That section provides that a contract may be formed by exchanged writings despite the existence of additional or different terms in the acceptance. Therefore, an offeree's response is treated as an acceptance while it may differ substantially from the offer. This section of the provision, then, reformed the mirror-image rule; that common law legal formality that prohibited the formation of a contract if the exchanged writings of offer and acceptance differed in any term.

Once a contract is recognized pursuant to § 2-207(1), § 2-207(2) provides the standard for determining if the additional terms stated in the acceptance become a part of the contract. Between merchants, such *additional* terms become part of the resulting contract *unless* 1) the offer expressly limited acceptance to its terms, 2) the additional terms materially alter the contract obligations, or 3) the offeror gives notice of his or her objection to the additional terms within a reasonable time. Should any one of these three possibilities occur, the *additional* terms are treated merely as proposals for incorporation in the contract and absent assent by the offeror the terms of the offer control. In any event, the existence of the additional terms does not prevent a contract from being formed.

Section 2-207(2) is silent on the treatment of terms stated in the acceptance that are *different,* rather than merely additional, from those stated in the offer. It is unclear whether "different" terms in the acceptance are intended to be included under the aegis of "additional" terms in § 2-207(2) and, therefore, fail to become part of the agreement if they materially alter the contract. Comment 3 suggests just such an inclusion.[3] However, Comment 6 suggests that different terms in exchanged writings must be assumed to constitute mutual objections by each party to the other's conflicting terms and result in a mutual "knockout" of both parties' conflicting terms; the missing terms to be supplied by the U.C.C.'s "gap-filler"

---

[3] Comment 3 states (emphasis added):

> Whether or not *additional or different* terms will become part of the agreement depends upon the provision of subsection (2).

It must be remembered that even official comments to enacted statutory text do not have the force of law and are only guidance in the interpretation of that text. *In re Bristol Associates, Inc.,* 505 F.2d 1056 (3d Cir. 1974) (while the comments to the Pennsylvania U.C.C. are not binding, the Pennsylvania Supreme Court gives substantial weight to the comments as evidencing application of the Code).

provisions.[4] At least one commentator, in support of this view, has suggested that the drafting history of the provision indicates that the word "different" was intentionally deleted from the final draft of § 2-207(2) to preclude its treatment under that subsection.[5] The plain language, comments, and drafting history of the provision, therefore, provide little helpful guidance in resolving the disagreement over the treatment of different terms pursuant to § 2-207.

Despite all this, the cases and commentators have suggested three possible approaches. The first of these is to treat "different" terms as included under the aegis of "additional" terms in § 2-207(2). Consequently, different terms in the acceptance would never become part of the contract, because, by definition, they would materially alter the contract (*i.e.*, the offeror's terms). Several courts have adopted this approach. * * *

The second approach, which leads to the same result as the first, is that the offeror's terms control because the offeree's different terms merely fall out; § 2-207(2) cannot rescue the different terms since that subsection applies only to *additional* terms. Under this approach, Comment 6 (apparently supporting a mutual rather than a single term knockout) is not applicable because it refers only to conflicting terms in confirmation forms following *oral* agreement, not conflicting terms in the *writings* that form the agreement. This approach is supported by Professor Summers. J.J. WHITE & R.S. SUMMERS, UNIFORM COMMERCIAL CODE, § 1-2, at 29 (2d ed. 1980).

The third, and preferable approach, which is commonly called the "knock-out" rule, is that the conflicting terms cancel one another. Under this view the offeree's form is treated only as an acceptance of the terms in the offeror's form which did not conflict. The ultimate contract, then, includes those non-conflicting terms and any other terms supplied by the U.C.C., including terms incorporated by course of performance (§ 2-208), course of dealing (§ 1-205), usage of trade (§ 1-205), and other "gap fillers" or "off-the-rack" terms (*e.g.*, implied warranty of fitness for

---

[4] Comment 6 states, in part:

> Where clauses on confirming forms sent by both parties conflict each party must be assumed to object to a clause of the other conflicting with one on the confirmation sent by himself * * *. The contract then consists of the terms expressly agreed to, terms on which the confirmations agree, and terms supplied by the Act, including subsection (2).

[5] *See* D.G. Baird & R. Weisberg, *Rules, Standards, and the Battle of the Forms: A Reassessment of § 2-207*, 68 VA. L. REV. 1217, 1240, n.61.

particular purpose, § 2-315). As stated previously, this approach finds some support in Comment 6. Professor White supports this approach as the most fair and consistent with the purposes of § 2-207. WHITE & SUMMERS, *supra*, at 29. Further, several courts have adopted or recognized the approach. * * *

We are of the opinion that this is the more reasonable approach, particularly when dealing with a case such as this where from the beginning the offeror's specified period of limitations would expire before the equipment was even installed. The approaches other than the "knock-out" approach would be inequitable and unjust because they invited the very kind of treatment which the defendant attempted to provide.

Thus, we are of the conclusion that if faced with this issue the Pennsylvania Supreme Court would adopt the "knock-out" rule and hold here that the conflicting terms in Pennwalt's offer and Daitom's acceptance regarding the period of limitations and applicable warranties cancel one another out. Consequently, the other provisions of the U.C.C. must be used to provide the missing terms.

This particular approach and result are supported persuasively by the underlying rationale and purpose behind the adoption of § 2-207. As stated previously, that provision was drafted to reform the infamous common law mirror-image rule and associated last-shot doctrine that enshrined the fortuitous positions of senders of forms and accorded undue advantages based on such fortuitous positions. WHITE & SUMMERS, *supra* at 25. To refuse to adopt the "knock-out" rule and instead adopt one of the remaining two approaches would serve to re-enshrine the undue advantages derived solely from the fortuitous positions of when a party sent a form. *Cf.*, 3 DUESENBERG & KING at 93 (1983 Supp.). This is because either approach other than the knock-out rule for different terms results in the offeror and his or her terms always prevailing solely because he or she sent the first form. Professor Summers argues that this advantage is not wholly unearned, because the offeree has an opportunity to review the offer, identify the conflicting terms and make his or her acceptance conditional. But this joinder misses the fundamental purpose of the U.C.C. in general and § 2-207 in particular, which is to preserve a contract and fill in any gaps if the parties intended to make a contract and there is a reasonable basis for giving an appropriate remedy. UCC 2-204(3); 2-207(1); 2-207(3). Thus, this approach gives the offeree some protection. While it is laudible [sic] for business persons to read the fine print and boilerplate provisions in exchanged forms, there is nothing in § 2-207 mandating such careful consideration. The provision seems drafted with a recognition of the reality that merchants seldom review exchanged forms with the scrutiny of lawyers. The "knock-out" rule is therefore the best approach. Even if a term eliminated by operation of the "knock-out" rule is reintroduced by operation of the U.C.C.'s gap-filler provisions, such a result does not indicate a weakness of the approach. On the contrary, at least the reintroduced term has the merit of being a term that the U.C.C. draftpersons regarded as fair.

We now address the question of reverse and remand regarding Counts I and II. The result of this court's holding is that the district court erred in granting summary judgment against Daitom on Counts I and II of its complaint. Operation of the "knock-out" rule to conflicting terms results in the instant case in the conflicting terms in the offer and acceptance regarding the period of limitations and applicable warranties cancelling. In the absence of any evidence of course of performance, course of dealing, or usage of trade providing the missing terms, §§ 2-725(1), 2-313, 2-314, 2-315 may operate to supply a four-year period of limitations, an express warranty, an implied warranty of merchantability, and an implied warranty of fitness for a particular purpose, respectively. The ruling of the district court on Counts I and II does not invite this kind of a broad inquiry, and thus, we must recognize the superiority in terms of justice of the "knock-out" rule. Consequently, the ruling of the district court on Counts I and II must be reversed and the matter remanded for trial consistent with this court's ruling.

* * *

[The court held that there was no Cause of Action in tort where an allegedly defective product caused only economic loss.]

Accordingly, the district court correctly concluded that Daitom's requested damages are not recoverable in tort. The court's summary judgment ruling against Daitom on Count III, therefore, should be affirmed. As explained above, we reverse the trial court with respect to Counts I and II. The cause is remanded for further proceedings consistent with this opinion.

BARRETT, CIRCUIT JUDGE, dissenting:

I respectfully dissent. Insofar as the issue of contract formation is concerned in this case, we are confronted with a "battle of the forms" case involving the interpretation and application of U.C.C. 2-207. I would affirm.

Pennwalt's proposal of September 7, 1976, was an "offer." It was submitted to Daitom in response to solicitations initiated by Daitom and it contained specific terms relating to price, delivery dates, etc., and its terms were held "open" for Daitom's acceptance within 30 days. In my view, Daitom accepted the offer with its purchase order. That order repeated the quantity, model number, and price for the items as those terms appeared in the Pennwalt proposal and, by reference, it incorporated four pages of specifications attached to Pennwalt's proposal or "offer." The purchase order did contain some different and additional language from that contained in Pennwalt's proposal. However, the Code has rejected the old mirror image rule. Thus, I agree with the district court's finding/ruling that a contract was formed in the circumstances described.

I also agree with the district court's conclusion that the terms of Pennwalt's proposal constituted the "terms of the contract." I do not agree, as Daitom argues, that its "acceptance" was made "conditional" upon Pennwalt's assent to the additional/different terms set forth in Daitom's purchase order. The court correctly found no such *express* condition in Daitom's acceptance.

The "knock-out" rule should not, in my view, be reached in this case. It can be applied only if, as Daitom argues and the majority agrees, the "conflicting terms" cancel each other out. The "knock-out" rule does have substantial support in the law, but I do not believe it is relevant in this case because the *only* conflicting terms relate to the *scope* of the warranty. In this case, it is not an important consideration because, pursuant to the express time limitations contained in Pennwalt's "offer," Daitom lost its right to assert any warranty claim. There was no term in Daitom's purchase order in conflict with the express one-year limitation within which to bring warranty actions. I agree with the district court's reasoning in rejecting Daitom's contentions that the one-year limitation period should not apply because (1) the term failed of "its essential purpose" of providing Daitom with a limited remedy under U.C.C. § 2-719(2) and (2) the time-limit was tolled due to Pennwalt's alleged fraudulent concealment of the defect. I concur with the trial court's finding that Daitom made no showing that the one-year limitation period was unreasonable because of some act of Pennwalt. As to the fraudulent concealment allegation, the court properly observed that Daitom did not plead this claim with the particularity required and, further, that the alleged fraudulent acts were not independent of the alleged breaches proper.

[Some footnotes omitted. Those retained are renumbered.]

Notes

1. The *Daitom* analysis was followed in *Superior Boiler Works, Inc. v. R.J. Sanders, Inc.*, 711 A.2d 628 (R.I. 1998). In that case, terms in the writings setting the time for shipment varied and canceled each other out. The court, in supplying a reasonable time for delivery, noted that the contract now contained a term that "neither party agreed to and, in fact, in regard to which each party expressed an entirely different preference." Nevertheless, the court stated that the parties could have protected themselves by expressly making acceptance conditional on assent

to a critical term and that, in any event, as merchants "both parties should have been well aware that their dealings were subject to the UCC and to its various gap-filling provisions."[*]

2. The following flow chart is one way to diagram the steps in the analysis under former 2-207. To start the flow chart, you must identify the communication that is an offer. Once you have identified the offer, then you ask:

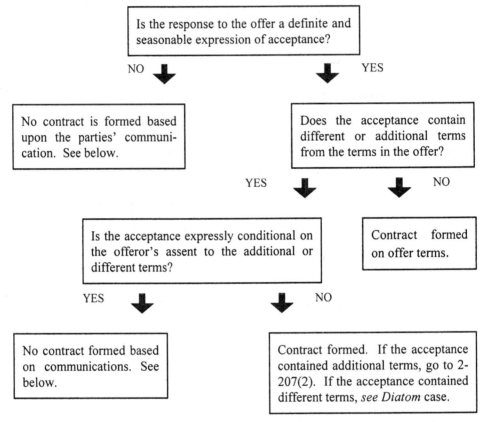

In any situation where the contract was not formed based upon the communications, a contract could be formed through the conduct of the parties. In that case, former 2-207(3) provided the applicable rule. Notice that former 2-207 also addressed "confirmations" that contained additional or different terms. Fit confirmations into the above flow chart.

---

[*] *Accord, Richardson v. Union Carbide Corp.*, 790 A.2d 962 (N.J. Supp. 2002); *contra, Steiner v. Mobil Oil Co.*, 569 P.2d 751 (Cal. 1977) (rejecting "knockout" rule where contract formed under former 2-207(1) despite "different" terms).

3.   The importance of clearly stating the term or terms to which agreement must be made before a contract is formed (the "my way or the highway" clause) cannot be overestimated. For example, the First Circuit has held that silence in an offer or acceptance does not incorporate Article 2's default rules as a basis for objection to terms contained in the other party's writing. *See Jom, Inc. v. Adell Plastics, Inc.*, 193 F.3d 47 (1st Cir. 1999). Moreover, once the terms are clearly stated, consistency and firmness in adherence to them is recommended. For example, if after the term is clearly stated both parties engage in conduct that concludes a contract, the terms of that contract were determined by former 2-207(3). How should the party insisting upon its own term deal with this risk?

Note: Arbitration and the Battle of the Forms

Arbitration clauses are frequently involved in "battle of the forms" disputes. When the underlying contract evidences a "transaction involving commerce" the Federal Arbitration Act, codified at 9 U.S.C. 1 through 16, applies. Although Section 2 of the FAA requires a "written provision" to arbitrate, the validity of the arbitration clause depends upon satisfying the "grounds as exist at law or in equity for the revocation of any contract." These grounds are found in state law in general and, when Article 2 applies, in UCC 2-207.*

The determination is tricky. The United States Supreme Court, in interpreting Section 2 of the Federal Arbitration Act, has held that state law on contract formation may not discriminate against, or single out for different treatment, a claimed federal right to arbitrate. Put differently, a state court, in interpreting former 2-207, must treat an arbitration clause in a standard form the same way that it would treat any other clause in a standard form. Thus, an interpretive rule that an arbitration clause was *per se* a material alteration or must be expressly assented to but which did not apply to, say, a disclaimer clause, would be highly suspect.**

Accepting that as a matter of federal law there must be consistency in treatment under former 2-207, there is still some disagreement over what the test for "material

---

* *See Dorton v. Collins & Aikman Corp.*, 453 F.2d 1161 (6th Cir. 1972) (remand case to determine whether Dorton had agreed to arbitration clause on the reverse side of Collin's acknowledgment form).

** *See Avedon Engineering, Inc. v. Seatex*, 126 F.3d 1279 (10th Cir. 1997), concluding that under New York any material, non-negotiated term, including arbitration, is presumed to be excluded from the contract unless expressly agreed to.

alteration" should be. Should it be a quantitative test, a question of unfair surprise, or some combination of both? Suppose, for example, that arbitration is regarded as a substantial deviation from the usual judicial remedies, but because of an extended course of dealing between the parties, one party knows or has reason to know that an arbitration clause will be included in the other's standard form. Is that party bound in the absence of express assent? One court has held "yes" on the grounds that there was implied assent to the clause and no unfair surprise.* But, again, a final solution was far from clear.**

The problem in international sales and arbitration is even more tricky. Assume that a buyer in California sends an offer in a record to a seller in Mexico City. The seller responds with a record that "accepts" the offer but, also, contains a clause requiring arbitration of "all disputes arising out of or relating to this contract" in Mexico City. The seller ships and the buyer accepts and uses the goods. A dispute over quality then arises. Under the CISG Article 19(1), the seller's reply is a counteroffer because it contains an additional term (the arbitration clause) that materially alters the offer. *See* CISG Art. 19(1), (2). Buyer's conduct in using the goods indicates assent to the counteroffer, including the arbitration clause. CISG Art. 18(1). But the arbitration clause is not necessarily enforceable. Unlike Section 2 of the FAA, which requires only that the arbitration clause be written, Article II(1) of the United Nations Convention on the Recognition and Enforcement of Foreign Arbitral Awards (The New York Convention) requires an "agreement in writing" to arbitrate and then defines "agreement in writing" to "include an arbitral clause in a contract or an arbitration agreement, signed by the parties, or contained in an exchange of letters or telegrams." Art. II(2). On the facts of this case, the arbitration clause in the seller's form was not signed by the buyer nor was it "contained in an exchange of letters or telegrams." Rather, the buyer seemingly assented to it by conduct but did not respond with a record in exchange. Thus, the clause is included in the contract by the provisions of the CISG but excluded (from

---

* *See Schulze & Burch Biscuit Co. v. Tree Top, Inc.*, 831 F.2d 709 (7th Cir. 1987).

** *See Stanley-Bostitch, Inc. v. Regenerative Environmental Equipment Co., Inc.*, 697 A.2d 323 (R.I. 1997) (an arbitration clause materially altered the offer and was not part of the contract); *Aceros Prefabricados, S.A. v. Tradearbed, Inc.*, 282 F. 3d 92 (2nd Cir. 2002) (arbitration clause did not materially alter the offer and was part of the contract). *See also Textile Unlimited v. AbmH & Co.*, 240 F.3d 781 (9th Cir. 2001) (where California UCC 2-207(3) applied, arbitration clause in writings of one party is out unless the other gives "specific and unequivocal" assent).

enforceability) by the New York Convention.

Problem 3-7

Based upon the formation sections of Article 2, including former 2-207, the *Diatom* case, *supra*, and the "flow chart" given above, how should the following problems be resolved? Is there a contract and, if so, what are its terms?

A. S and B conclude an oral agreement for the sale of goods. B sends a written, signed confirmation of the agreement. The written confirmation contains an arbitration clause which was not part of the parties' oral agreement. S ignores the confirmation and fails to deliver any goods. B claims that a contract was formed which contained an agreement to arbitrate.

B. B makes an offer to S to buy goods. The written offer contains a standard form arbitration clause. S accepts the offer by a separate signed writing. When S fails to deliver any goods, B claims breach and initiates arbitration.

C. B makes an offer to S to buy goods. S accepts the offer in a writing that contains a standard form arbitration clause. After B has received the acceptance, S ships the goods. Before the goods arrive the market price drops. B argues that no contract was formed and, in any event, the arbitration clause was not part of the agreement.

D. B makes an offer to S to buy goods. S sends an acknowledgment which purports to accept the offer but states clearly "there is no contract unless you agree to the arbitration clause on the back of this acknowledgment." B does not respond but when S ships the goods, B accepts and uses them. The goods do not conform to the contract. S denies that a contract was formed but, if so, contends the arbitration clause was part of the agreement.

E. B in New York makes an offer to buy goods from S in California. The offer states that all disputes will be resolved by arbitration under the rules of the International Chamber of Commerce in New York. S sends an acknowledgment purporting to accept the offer but also states that all disputes will be resolved by arbitration under the rules of End Dispute in Los Angeles. The goods are shipped and used. A dispute arises over the quality of the goods. B insists that there was a contract with arbitration in New York.

F. B, a small business, sees an advertisement for personal computers made by S. B writes to S stating the type of computer needed and the requisite components. S telephones B and they agree on the computer and the price. B gives S a credit card number and the computer is paid for. S then ships the computer. In the box are two pages of standard terms, one of which commits the parties to arbitrate all disputes under ICC Rules in New York. The terms state in bold type: "Use of the computer will constitute an acceptance of these terms." B uses the computer, which turns out to be unmerchantable. B concedes that a contract was formed but argues that the arbitration clause was not part of the agreement. What result? *See* text *infra* on the rolling contract concept.

B. The Reform (?) of UCC 2-207

Upon reading the endless cases and commentary on former 2-207, it seemed clear that some revision was in order. But what? Should Article 2 return to the common law "mirror image" rule? Or should a revision be drafted that more clearly achieved the objectives of former 2-207, which were to (1) preserve some contract where intended by the parties despite the presence of additional or different terms in the writings and (2) avoid unfair surprise when one party attempted to include additional or different terms to which the other had not expressly agreed in the contract. As a practical matter, in most cases the question ended up being what are the terms of the contract, not whether a contract was created.[*]

Read UCC 2-206(3) and 2-207 as amended by the 2003 amendments. Notice that Article 2A has no provision dealing with the battle of the forms situation either pre or post 2003 amendments. Thus, if the issue arose in the lease context, a court would use either the common law approach that the acceptance must be a mirror image of the offer to avoid being a counteroffer or alternatively, the court may decide to use the Article 2 approach by analogy. To date, no reported leasing cases seem to have confronted this issue.

Problem 3-8

A. Prepare a flow chart outlining the steps in the analysis under UCC 2-206 and 2-207 as amended by the 2003 amendments. Compare that flow chart to the flow chart presented earlier on former 2-207. Where is the analysis the same? Where is the analysis different?

B. Analyze Problem 3-7 under UCC 2-206(3) and 2-207 as amended by the 2003 amendments. What result?

C. Identify those issues that you think the courts will confront in the

---

[*] Symposium, *Ending the "Battle of the Forms": A Symposium on the Revision of Section 2-207 of the Uniform Commercial Code*, 49 BUS. LAW. 1019 (1994).

application of the revised sections. Will they continue to read the revision as if it applied only to standard form terms or will it be interpreted to "knock out" negotiated terms as well? How will the courts determine to what terms the parties have "agreed"?

D. Article 19 of the CISG rejects the approach of former 2-207 to the so-called "battle of the forms."[*] As a result, commercial parties under the CISG must read and object to terms in standard forms or risk agreeing to them.[**] Analyze Problem 3-7 as if the CISG applied to the issues.

Note: Battle of the Forms Under the UNIDROIT Principles

The UNIDROIT Principles of International Commercial Contracts directly confront the problem of surprising terms in standard terms in Articles 2.19 through 2.22.

First, Article 2.1 (unlike the CISG) explicitly states that a contract may be formed by "conduct of the parties that is sufficient to show agreement." Like CISG Art. 19, however, the Principles Article 2.11 treats a purported acceptance that contains "additions, limitations or other modifications" of an offer as a rejection and counteroffer unless the modifications do not materially alter the terms of the offer. Similarly, an offer or counteroffer can be accepted by conduct. Art. 2.6(1).

Second, Article 2.19(2) defines standard terms as "provisions which are prepared in advance for general and repeated use by one party and which are actually used without negotiation with the other party."

Third, Article 2.20(1) then excludes from the contract any standard term "that the other party could not reasonably have expected * * * unless it has been expressly accepted by that party." This principle would apply where both parties signed a writing containing standard terms or where an offer in a writing that contained standard terms was accepted by a writing or conduct that did not.

Fourth, Article 2.22 deals with the "battle of the forms." If both parties use

---

[*] *See* Henry D. Gabriel, *The Battle of the Forms: A Comparison of the United Nations Convention for the International Sale of Goods and the Uniform Commercial Code*, 49 BUS. LAW. 1053 (1994).

[**] *But see Chateau Des Charmes Wines Ltd. v. Sabate USA Inc.*, 328 F. 3d 528 (9th Cir. 2003) (party who did not object to forum selection clause in other side's invoice sent after agreement formed did not agree to clause as the CISG requires agreement to terms and does not enforce unilateral attempts to modify terms).

standard terms and reach agreement "except on those terms, a contract is concluded on the basis of the agreed terms and of any standard terms which are common in substance unless one party clearly indicates in advance, or later and without undue delay informs the other party, that it does not intend to be bound by such a contract." This, of course, is the "knockout" rule.

To review:

How would these principles apply when a purported acceptance contains standard terms that are additional to those in the offer and the counteroffer is accepted by conduct?

How would these principles apply when the offer contained a standard term and the purported acceptance contained a standard term that differed from that in the offer?*

Note: UCITA and Standard Form Contracting

UCITA appears to retain the approach that the method of formation has some bearing on determining the terms of the contract, taking an approach more akin to former 2-207 than to amended 2-207. *See* UCITA 204 through 210. One of the innovations of UCITA is the concept of a "mass-market" license, UCITA 102(a)(44) and (45), that attempts to deal with standard terms. *See* UCITA 209. This concept depends upon a defined concept of "manifest assent," UCITA 112, after "opportunity to review," UCITA 113. As further protection of the licensee, UCITA also provides for a "right of return" of the computer information for a refund if the licensee had to pay prior to having an opportunity to review the terms of the license.

One of the issues that made the mass market license provision controversial was the relationship between contract and copyright law. At issue is whether a contracting party, by manifesting assent to the license, may unknowingly give up rights the licensee may have under intellectual property law, such as the right to use the information in a way that constitutes "fair use" under copyright law but would not be permitted under the terms of the license.** UCITA's answer to the issue was

---

* For a survey of different countries' approaches to the battle of the forms issues concerning standard terms, *see* James R. Maxeiner, *Standard-Terms Contracting in the Global Electronic Age: European Alternatives*, 28 YALE J. INT'L L. 109 (2003).

** For discussion of that issue, *see* Mark A. Lemley, *Beyond Preemption: The Law and*
(continued...)

UCITA 105. Read that section. Are you satisfied with this answer?

C. The "Gateway" Problem

So far we have been contemplating a "battle of the forms" in which each party sends its own form and the question is what are the terms of the contract when the terms in the competing forms are not all the same. Notice that the amended UCC 2-207 is not limited to the battle of the forms situation. That section purports to determine what are the terms of the contract in all situations in which a contract is formed, not just when the parties send competing forms. Having said that, one of the other controversial issues in the revision of Article 2 was the issue of pre-sale disclosure of terms. In other words, should Article 2 be revised to require that the seller disclose the terms prior to purchase in order to have those terms be binding on the buyer? While that seems an odd question, the real issue is what is the effect of terms that come "in the box," so to speak, when the goods are shipped. Are those terms binding on the buyer if the buyer keeps the goods?

Prior to the 2003 amendments to Article 2, there was at least the following two approaches to that question under Article 2.[*] Judge Easterbrook, concluded that even though the buyer paid for and the seller shipped the goods before the terms were disclosed, there was a "rolling contract" that was not concluded until the buyer used the goods and UCC 2-207 did not apply where only one party used a standard form. *ProCD, Inc. v. Zeidenberg*, 86 F.3d 1447 (7th Cir. 1996); *Hill v. Gateway 2000, Inc.*, 105 F.3d 1147 (7th Cir. 1997), *cert. denied*, 118 S. Ct. 47 (1997); *accord, Westendorf v. Gateway 2000, Inc.*, 2000 W.L. 307369 (Del. Ch. 2000), *aff'd*, 763 A.2d 92 (Del. Supr. 2000) (table). This analysis was rejected in *Klocek v. Gateway, Inc.*, 104 F. Supp. 2d 1332 (D. Kan. 2000) where the court held that the terms that came with the product were proposals for addition to the contract under former 2-

---

[**] (...continued)
Policy of Intellectual Property Licensing, 87 CALIF. L. REV. 111 (1999); Michael J. Madison, *Legal-Ware: Contract and Copyright in the Digital Age*, 67 FORDHAM L. REV. 1025 (1998); Raymond T. Nimmer, *Breaking Barriers: The Relation Between Contract and Intellectual Property Law*, 13 BERKELEY TECH. L.J. 827 (1998); Maureen A. O'Rourke, *Drawing the Boundary Between Copyright and Contract: Copyright Preemption of Software License Terms*, 45 DUKE L.J. 479 (1995).

[*] For some commentators views, *see* Robert A. Hillman, *Rolling Contracts*, 71 FORDHAM L. REV. 743 (2002); James J. White, *Default Rules in Sales and the Myth of Contracting Out*, 48 LOY. L. REV. 53 (2002).

207 and that the buyer did not expressly agree to that proposal. *But see Brower v. Gateway 2000, Inc.*, 676 N.Y.S.2d 569 (N.Y.A.D. 1998), where the court refused to apply former 2-207 to a transaction where the contract was not formed until the 30-day period had expired but held that the arbitration clause, because of the prohibitive cost involved in the arbitration, was substantively unconscionable. How does amended UCC 2-207 deal with the issue?

Problem 3-9

B operates a business over the Internet from his own home. He comes to you with the following problem. B, responding to advertising, ordered a fancy laptop computer from Dellway Computer by mail. B's letter specified the model by number. Dellway responded by fax confirming the order and specifying the price, to be paid by credit card. B faxed a reply with his credit card number, the credit card charge was approved and Dellway shipped the computer. Upon arrival, B unpacked the computer and found attached to the keyboard a paper containing "standard terms and conditions." B did not read the form. Rather, B booted up the computer and, after several days of use, discovered what he thought was a major defect. Dellway disagreed and refused B's request to return the computer for a refund. When B persisted, Dellway pointed out that there was an arbitration clause in the form and that B, by not objecting to the term, had agreed in writing to arbitrate. B argued that the term was not part of the contract because it was not disclosed at the time B paid for or took delivery of the computer and that his keeping the computer was not agreement to any attempted modification.

Dellway argued that no contract was formed before B opened the box and that the standard terms along with the tendered computer constituted an offer that B had an option to accept by using the computer or reject by returning the computer for a refund. Since B did the former, a contract was formed and included the terms in the box.

How should this case be resolved under UCC 2-204 through 2-207 after the 2003 amendments? *See also* UCC 2-209(1) regarding modifications.

SECTION 4. THE STATUTE OF FRAUDS

A. History and Purposes

A statute of frauds imposes additional conditions upon the enforceability of agreements which otherwise qualify as contracts. In general, there must be a writing consistent with the existence of a contract, specifying some if not all of the terms, and signed or authenticated by the party to be charged. Read UCC 2-201 and 2A-201.

At least three justifications for the statute of frauds have been asserted. First, the statute avoids fraudulent or perjured claims that a contract was made. Second, the statute avoids fraudulent or perjured claims regarding the terms of a contract admittedly made. Third, the statute encourages the useful business habit of making a writing. *See* Lawrence Vold, *The Application of the Statute of Frauds Under the Uniform Sales Act,* 15 MINN. L. REV. 391, 393-94 (1931).

The first two justifications have long been criticized as anachronistic. The conditions existing in 17th Century England—uncontrolled jury discretion, restrictions upon the competency of witnesses and immature contract doctrine—no longer obtain.* Attacks of this sort, plus the opportunity provided by the statute for "technical unmeritorious defenses" induced Parliament, in 1954, to repeal the statute of frauds provision in the British Sale of Goods Act.**

The third justification is more difficult to undercut. According to Professor Vold, the "cases that justify the statute are * * * the thousands of uncontested current transactions where misunderstanding and controversy are avoided by the presence of a writing which the statute at least indirectly aided to procure. * * *" Vold, *supra.**** Karl Llewellyn agreed with Vold's assessment and his views were influential in the drafting of UCC 2-201.****

Should there be a statute of frauds for contracts for sale of goods? England repealed their statute in 1955 and there is no statute of frauds in the CISG. *See* Article 11, which is subject to a possible reservation under Article 12.

Early drafts of Article 2 in the recent revision process did not contain a statute

---

* *See* Hugh E. Willis, *The Statute of Frauds–A Legal Anachronism,* 3 IND. L.J. 427, 429-31 (1928).

** *See* C. Grunfeld, *Law Reform (Enforcement of Contracts) Act, 1954,* 17 MOD. L. REV. 451 (1954).

*** *But see* Comment, *The Statute of Frauds and the Business Community: A Re-Appraisal in Light of Prevailing Practices,* 66 YALE L.J. 1038 (1957) (reliance on an oral order rather than the practice of employing writings is prevalent practice).

**** *See* Karl N. Llewellyn, *What Price Contract? An Essay in Perspective,* 40 YALE L.J. 704, 746-48 (1931). *See also* Jason S. Johnson, *The Statute of Frauds and Business Norms: A Testable Game-Theoretic Model,* 144 U. PA. L. REV. 1859 (1996) (favoring retention).

of frauds. The reasons were twofold. First, the primary purpose of any statute of frauds is to prevent fraud in the assertion by one party that some contract was made or fraud regarding terms of that contract. The modern fact finding process is more than able to detect fraud without the aid of a statute from the 17th Century. Second, the current statute as interpreted by courts tends to promote fraud when it is used by defendants to avoid liability on oral agreements or agreements based upon conduct that clearly were made and could be proved.

A slightly modified version of the statute of frauds was subsequently returned to Article 2 drafts. Many observers concluded the statute served other purposes, such as creating incentives to reduce agreements to writing and reducing uncertainty in proof, and that use of the statute of frauds as a surrogate for a summary judgment motion was beneficial. The arguments on both sides were somewhat impressionistic.

The amendments to UCC 2-201 were as follows. First, the threshold dollar amount is $5,000 rather than $500. Second, the defined word "record" was substituted for "writing" to conform with the requirements for electronic contracting. Third, subsection (3)(b) clarifies that the so-called admission exception where the admission is "in the party's testimony or otherwise under oath" rather than "in court." Fourth, a new subsection (4) provides that a "contract that is enforceable under this section is not unenforceable merely because it is not capable of being performed within one year or any other period after its making." Finally, it should be noted that former 1-106, the residual statute of frauds in Article 1, has been deleted from Revised Article 1.

UCITA 201 follows the lead of amended UCC 2-201 and 2A-201.

B. Satisfying the Statute of Frauds

The following problems and cases illustrate some of the issues that have arisen over the scope and application of UCC 2-201. To what extent will the same issues arise under UCC 2A-201? Does UCC 2A-201 raise any additional issues?

CASAZZA V. KISER
UNITED STATES COURT OF APPEALS, EIGHTH CIRCUIT, 2002
313 F.3D 414

BOWMAN, CIRCUIT JUDGE

This appeal arises from James Casazza's ill-fated effort to purchase a fifty-two-foot sailboat named the *"Andante"* from Joseph C. Kiser. Casazza sued

Kiser seeking damages under the legal theories of breach of contract and promissory estoppel for Kiser's failure to sell him this boat. The District Court granted Kiser's motion to dismiss. We affirm.

I. *Background*

In late May 2001, Casazza read Kiser's listing of the *Andante* on an internet sales site. Shortly thereafter, Casazza contacted Kiser and expressed an interest in purchasing the boat. They agreed to meet during the weekend of June 2, 2001, in Ft. Lauderdale, Florida, where the *Andante* was located. Casazza first viewed the boat on June 2 and looked at it again with Kiser the following day. Casazza and Kiser met again on June 4, 2001, and, according to Casazza, negotiated an agreement for Casazza's purchase of the *Andante*. The details of this agreement were handwritten by each party on separate sheets of paper and at some point converted, presumably by Casazza, into a typewritten agreement (collectively, the "purchase terms"). That agreement provided for a sales price of $200,000 for the boat. The agreement further stated the sale was contingent on a marine survey, including a sea trial, satisfactory to Casazza. Among other provisions, the agreement also required payment by wire transfer and replacement of the mast step, and it detailed the logistics of transferring the boat from Florida to Virginia. Kiser never signed the agreement and the marine survey and sea trial did not take place.

During their meeting on June 4, Kiser gave Casazza a blank Coast Guard bill of sale to complete. The next day, Kiser and Casazza executed a software license transfer agreement for the boat's navigational software. This license agreement is the only document in the dispute signed by both parties and it does not refer to the *Andante*. Following these events, Casazza arranged for a marine survey, obtained an estimate for repair of the mast step, visited marinas, and tentatively reserved slip space for the *Andante* at a marina in Virginia. Things apparently went awry a week later, however, when Kiser informed Casazza that he would not sell him the boat. In response, Casazza initiated this suit and sought a temporary restraining order (TRO) to prevent Kiser from selling the *Andante* to someone else. While the application for the TRO was pending, but before Kiser had notice of it, Kiser sold the boat. Casazza amended his complaint and Kiser moved to dismiss the case on the basis of the statute of frauds. Casazza responded to Kiser's motion to dismiss and filed a Federal Rule of Civil Procedure 56(f) motion and affidavit requesting that the District Court's consideration of the motion to dismiss be delayed pending additional discovery.

On January 15, 2002, the District Court dismissed the action, concluding that additional discovery would not assist the court in the resolution of whether the statute of frauds applies to the dispute and that the defense barred Casazza's breach of contract and promissory estoppel claims. The District Court denied Casazza's motion for reconsideration. On appeal, Casazza argues the District Court erred in dismissing his claims.

II. *Discussion*
* * * *

We review de novo a district court's order granting a motion to dismiss, viewing the allegations in the complaint in the light most favorable to the plaintiff. * * * * Like the District Court, we must accept the allegations of the complaint as true and dismiss the case only when "it appears beyond doubt that the plaintiff can prove no set of facts in support of his claim which would entitle him to relief." *Conley v. Gibson,* 355 U.S. 41, 45-46, 78 S.Ct. 99, 2 L.Ed.2d 80 (1957).

A. *The Statute of Frauds Defense*

Casazza contends the District Court erred when it dismissed his breach of contract claim, holding it was barred by the statute of frauds. Subject to certain limited exceptions, the statute of frauds renders unenforceable any unwritten contract for the sale of goods with a value over $500. * * * * [Court applied Minnesota law–Ed.] Because Kiser raised the statute of frauds defense in his motion to dismiss, Casazza was required to affirmatively show the existence of an appropriate writing or an exception to this defense in order to avoid dismissal by the District Court. In this appeal, Casazza argues that the alleged contract was taken out of the statute of frauds by (1) the doctrine of part performance, (2) the existence of a sufficient writing, and (3) the possibility that Kiser may have a sufficient writing or that Kiser might admit a contract was formed between the parties had the District Court granted Casazza's request for additional time for discovery. All these arguments are without merit.

(1) *Part Performance*

Under the part-performance exception to the statute of frauds, a writing is not required "with respect to goods for which payment has been made and accepted or which have been received and accepted." [Minn Stat.]§ 336.2- 201(3)(c). Here, Casazza contends that his acceptance of the navigational software constitutes part performance of the parties' alleged agreement concerning the sale of the *Andante*. In support of this claim, Casazza relies on section 336.2-606(2) (2000), which provides that "[a]cceptance of a part of any commercial unit is acceptance of that entire unit." According to Casazza, the navigational software is part of the *Andante*.

Thus, Casazza argues, when he accepted this software, he accepted the *Andante.*

First, we question the applicability of section 336.2-606(2) to the present dispute. The drafters of the commercial code designed this provision to limit a buyer's right of revocation of acceptance to whole units. *See* Minn.Stat. Ann. § 336.2-606(2) (West 2002) Prof. Robert C. McClure, Minnesota Code Comment (1966) (noting that "a buyer, when making a partial rejection, cannot unnecessarily destroy the value of a commercial unit"). As the Ninth Circuit observed of the uniform provision at issue here, "The commercial unit provision is included to protect *a seller* from having a buyer return *less* than a commercial unit. Return of less than a commercial unit would leave the seller with only components of a commercial unit, which would have severely reduced market value." *S & R Metals, Inc. v. C. Itoh & Co. (America),* 859 F.2d 814, 817 (9th Cir.1988) (first emphasis added) (citing *Abbett v. Thompson,* 148 Ind.App. 25, 263 N.E.2d 733, 735-36 (1970) (holding buyer could not keep some parts of a car wash machine and revoke acceptance of the rest because the entire machine was a commercial unit and would have little value to the seller if incomplete)).

Second, even assuming section 336.2-606(2) applies to the instant dispute, we conclude that under no circumstances could the software and the *Andante* be considered a single "commercial unit." Minnesota's Uniform Commercial Code states that:

> "Commercial unit" means such a unit of goods as by commercial usage is a single whole for purposes of sale and division of which materially impairs its character or value on the market or in use. A commercial unit may be a single article (as a machine) or a set of articles (as a suite of furniture or an assortment of sizes) or a quantity (as a bale, gross, or carload) or any other unit treated in use or in the relevant market as a single whole.

Minn.Stat. § 336.2-105(6) (2000). Viewing Casazza's allegations in the light most favorable to him, we are hard-pressed to see how the navigational software and the *Andante* are a "single whole." Notably, Casazza concedes that the navigational software was purchased years after the *Andante* was built and that Kiser sold the boat to another party without it. Though Casazza distinguishes some cases cited in Kiser's brief, Casazza fails to cite a single case in support of his position that this Court should treat the *Andante* and the navigational software as a commercial unit, and our own research has not revealed any authority supporting this position. In short, we agree with the District Court that the doctrine of part performance cannot transmute Kiser's gift of the navigational software into a contract for the sale of the *Andante.*

(2) *Sufficient Writing*

Casazza also argues that the statute of frauds is inapplicable to this dispute because there is a sufficient writing showing the existence of a contract between the parties. The primary purpose of the writing requirement in the statute of frauds is to demonstrate that a contract for sale has indeed been made. *See* 1, JAMES J. WHITE & ROBERT S. SUMMERS, UNIFORM COMMERCIAL CODE § 2-4, at 63 (4th ed.1995). But the statute does not require one writing containing all the terms. *See Simplex Supplies, Inc. v. Abhe & Svoboda, Inc.,* 586 N.W.2d 797, 801 (Minn.Ct.App.1998). Rather, "[s]everal papers may be taken together to make up the memorandum, providing they refer to one another, or are so connected together, by reference or by internal evidence, that parol testimony is not necessary to establish their connection with the contract." *Id.* (quoting *Olson v. Sharpless,* 53 Minn. 91, 55 N.W. 125, 126 (1893)). In addition, "[t]he signature can be found on any document and may consist of 'any symbol executed or adopted by a party with present intention to authenticate a writing.'" *Id.* (quoting Minn.Stat. § 336.1-201 (39) (1996)). Casazza argues that the purchase terms, in particular the notes allegedly made by Kiser, and the executed software license transfer agreement constitute a sufficient writing. We disagree.

Casazza admits that he does not have a copy of a document that satisfies the statute of frauds. Casazza attempts to overcome this obstacle by arguing his pleadings reference the existence of a handwritten document allegedly prepared by Kiser, which--along with the executed software transfer agreement-- constitute a sufficient writing. The typewritten agreement attached to Casazza's amended complaint is not signed by Kiser and there is no allegation that Kiser participated in its preparation. While Kiser did sign the software license transfer agreement, that document does not refer to any contemplated, proposed, or agreed contract for the sale of the *Andante.* We refuse to allow Casazza to proceed with his breach of contract claim on this basis because to do so would eviscerate the statute of frauds. Casazza has failed to produce any document, or combination of documents, that satisfy the statute of frauds' writing requirement. Casazza's statements that a writing sufficient to satisfy the statute of frauds *may* exist is not enough to defeat Kiser's motion to dismiss.

(3) *Admissions Exception*

In a related argument, Casazza argues that the admissions exception to the statute of frauds applies to this dispute. *See* Minn.Stat. § 336.2- 201(3)(b) (2000). That subsection provides that even when there is no signed writing sufficient to satisfy the writing requirement, the proponent of the exception can escape the requirements of the statute of frauds "if the party against whom enforcement is sought admits in pleading, testimony or otherwise in court that a contract for sale was made." *Id.* Here, Kiser has made no such admission. Nonetheless, Casazza argues that had the District Court granted his request for additional time for discovery pursuant to Fed.R.Civ.P. 56(f), Kiser might have made such an admission. Specifically, Casazza claims that Kiser may have a sufficient writing or that Kiser might admit a contract was formed between the parties if he were deposed. The District Court denied the request and found that resolution of whether the statute of frauds applies to the dispute did not require further factual development.

In light of our decision affirming the District Court's decision to dismiss Casazza's breach of contract claim, we need not reach the discovery issues raised in Casazza's Rule 56(f) petition. * * * The District Court held a hearing on the motion to dismiss on January 14, 2002. By that time--six months after the suit was filed--Casazza still had not produced any writing sufficient to satisfy the statute of frauds nor had he obtained an admission from Kiser that a contract existed. Given the period of time that elapsed and the conclusory nature of Casazza's request for a continuance, we find the District Court did not abuse its discretion by denying further discovery and ruling on the motion to dismiss. * * *

B. *Promissory Estoppel*

Casazza alternatively argues that even if the alleged contract fails to satisfy the statute of frauds, his case should be permitted to proceed because a statute of frauds defense is inapplicable to his promissory estoppel claim. The District Court rejected this argument, holding that Casazza's promissory estoppel claim rests on the same purported promise that forms the basis of his breach of contract claim and that to allow Casazza to pursue the promissory estoppel claim, despite the lack of a sufficient writing, "would negate the purpose of the statute of frauds." Memorandum and Order, January 15, 2002, at 5 n. 1.

Promissory estoppel implies "a contract in law where none exists in fact." *Grouse v. Group Health Plan, Inc.,* 306 N.W.2d 114, 116 (Minn.1981). "Under promissory estoppel, a promise which is expected to induce definite action by the promisee, and does induce the action, is binding if injustice can be avoided only by enforcing the promise." *Cohen v. Cowles Media Co.,* 479 N.W.2d 387, 391 (Minn.1992) (citations omitted); *see also Grouse,* 306 N.W.2d at 116.

In *Del Hayes & Sons, Inc. v. Mitchell,* 304 Minn. 275, 230 N.W.2d 588, 593-94 (1975), the Minnesota Supreme Court identified three approaches courts have taken concerning the applicability of the statute of frauds defense to promissory estoppel claims. Under the first (or "RESTATEMENT") approach, "promissory estoppel will defeat the statute of frauds only when the promise relied upon is a promise to reduce the contract to writing." *Id.* The second approach described by the court, and adopted in numerous jurisdictions, rejects "the view that promissory estoppel can remove an oral contract from the statute of frauds." *Id.* at 594; *see also Lige Dickson Co. v. Union Oil Co.,* 96 Wash.2d 291, 635 P.2d 103, 107 (1981) (holding "promissory estoppel cannot be used to overcome the statute of frauds in a case which involves the sale of goods"). According to the court, jurisdictions that have adopted this approach "do so because a promissory estoppel exception would likely render the statute of frauds nugatory." *Del Hayes,* 230 N.W.2d at 594; *see also McDabco, Inc. v. Chet Adams Co.,* 548 F.Supp. 456, 461 (D.S.C.1982) ("The [South Carolina] legislature has provided that the only exceptions to the requirements of a written contract of sale are provided in Sections 36-2-201(2) and (3). Promissory estoppel is not included within these subsections."). The third and least restrictive approach described by the court states that an oral promise can satisfy the statute of frauds only "where the detrimental reliance is of such a character and magnitude that refusal to enforce the contract would permit one party to perpetrate a fraud." *Del Hayes,* 230 N.W.2d at 594. The court went on to note that "[a] mere refusal to perform an oral agreement, unaccompanied by unconscionable conduct, however, is not such a fraud as will justify disregarding the statute." *Id.; see also Resolution Trust Corp. v. Flanagan,* 821 F.Supp. 572, 574 (D.Minn.1993) ("under the doctrine of promissory estoppel, a party seeking to take an agreement out of the 'statute of frauds must demonstrate that application of the statute of frauds would protect, rather than prevent, the perpetration of a fraud'" (citations omitted)). The *Del Hayes* court did not endorse any particular view and held that, under any approach, promissory estoppel was not available so as to remove the oral contract at issue in that case from the statute of frauds. *Del Hayes,* 230 N.W.2d at 594.

In this case, the District Court apparently adopted the second or "restrictive" approach, which prohibits Casazza from doing an end-run around the statute of frauds because his promissory estoppel claim is based on the very promise that the statute otherwise bars. We might be inclined to agree with Casazza that Minnesota does not endorse such a hard-nosed view. * * * Nonetheless, we affirm the District Court's dismissal of Casazza's promissory estoppel claim. Even if we assume Casazza is correct that Minnesota does not endorse the view that promissory estoppel can never overcome the statute of frauds defense in a case such as this, he fails to convince us that his claim could proceed under either of the remaining approaches discussed by the Minnesota Supreme Court in *Del Hayes.*

Casazza's promissory estoppel claim fails under the RESTATEMENT approach because he did not sufficiently allege that Kiser promised to reduce their oral agreement to writing. Casazza argues he made a sufficient allegation in his amended complaint, where he alleged that Kiser asked him to complete a blank Coast Guard bill of sale. In ruling on Casazza's motion for reconsideration, the District Court rejected this argument and held that "[e]ven a liberal reading of the Complaint ... does not support the inclusion of such a claim." Order, February 7, 2002, at 2. Based on our own review of the amended complaint, we agree. The bill of sale is mentioned in only one line of Casazza's five-page amended complaint. Nowhere in this complaint does Casazza specifically allege that Kiser promised to reduce their oral agreement to writing. * * *

Casazza's promissory estoppel claim also fails under the so-called least restrictive approach. Under this approach, Casazza's promissory estoppel claim can only proceed "where the detrimental reliance is of such a character and magnitude that refusal to enforce the contract would permit one party to perpetrate a fraud." *Del Hayes,* 230 N.W.2d at 594; * * * Here, Casazza alleges that he and Kiser reached an agreement on the sale of the *Andante* and that he subsequently arranged for a survey, obtained an estimate for some repairs, visited marinas, and tentatively arranged slip space for the boat. Casazza also alleges that a week later, Kiser told him he was not going to sell him the boat. Nowhere in Casazza's amended complaint does he allege that Kiser did anything that would constitute a fraud. At most, Casazza alleges that Kiser broke their oral agreement after Casazza had expended some money and time in anticipation of buying the boat.

Casazza's allegations simply do not amount to detrimental reliance of the sort required to take this agreement out of the statute of frauds. *See Del Hayes,* 230 N.W.2d at 594 n. 11 ("The fraud most commonly treated as taking an agreement out of the Statute of Frauds" occurs where "the other party has been induced to make expenditures or a change of situation * *, *so that the refusal to complete the execution of the agreement is not merely a denial of rights which it was intended to confer, but the infliction of an unjust and unconscionable injury and loss.*" (quoting 3 WILLISTON, CONTRACTS (3d ed.) § 533A, p. 798) (emphasis added) (alteration in *Del Hayes*)). Whatever we might think of Kiser's behavior, we find nothing in the pleadings to suggest that judicial refusal to enforce the oral agreement "would permit one party to perpetrate a fraud." *Id.* "[A] mere refusal to perform an oral agreement unaccompanied by unconscionable conduct ... is not such a fraud as will justify disregarding the statute." *Id.; see also Pako Corp.,* 109 B.R. at 382. Casazza's promissory estoppel claim therefore must fail.

III. *Conclusion*

For the reasons stated, we affirm the order of the District Court dismissing Casazza's suit.

[Footnotes omitted]

GENERAL TRADING INTERNATIONAL, INC. V. WAL-MART STORES, INC.
UNITED STATES COURT OF APPEALS, EIGHTH CIRCUIT, 2003
320 F.3D 831

BOWMAN, CIRCUIT JUDGE

General Trading International, Inc. (GTI), sued Wal-Mart Stores, Inc., for breach of contract, action for goods sold, and action on account in a dispute arising out of Wal-Mart's alleged failure to pay for large numbers of decorative "vine reindeer" sold to Wal-Mart for resale to the public during the 1999 Christmas season. Wal-Mart counterclaimed for breach of contract and for fraud. According to Wal-Mart, most of the reindeer, manufactured in Haiti, were "scary-looking" and unsuitable for sale as Christmas merchandise. Wal-Mart claims that GTI orally agreed to absorb $200,000 of the purchase price because of Wal-Mart's dissatisfaction with the quality of the product. GTI, denying the existence of the alleged oral agreement, filed a motion for partial summary judgment, seeking an award of $200,000 of the unpaid balance, by arguing that the alleged oral agreement was unenforceable and violated the statute of frauds. The District Court granted partial summary judgment in favor of GTI and submitted the remaining claims to a jury, which returned a verdict in GTI's favor. Subsequently, the District Court denied Wal-Mart's motion for judgment as a matter of law or for a new trial and GTI's request for attorney fees. Wal-Mart appeals the grant of partial summary judgment and the denial of its motion for a new trial. GTI cross appeals the denial of attorney fees. We affirm.

I. *Background*

* * * In February 1999, Beth Gitlin, a seasonal buyer for Wal-Mart, began negotiating with Patrick Francis, the president of GTI (a company that sells seasonal craft items to large retailers) for the purchase of 250,000 vine reindeer for resale to Wal-Mart customers during the 1999 Christmas season. In March 1999, GTI executed Wal-Mart's standard vendor agreement. The vendor agreement provided that any changes in the agreement must be in writing and executed by both parties. Wal-Mart issued separate purchase orders, covering price and quantity terms, to

GTI for the purchase of the reindeer.

In mid-August 1999, Wal-Mart noticed serious defects with the reindeer when the first shipments began arriving at its stores and warehouses. Gitlin estimated that, at that time, at least seventy percent of the reindeer were of poor quality. A Wal-Mart employee described the reindeer as "[m]oldy, broken grapevines, shapes that no more resembled a deer than they did a rabbit ... scary-looking." *Id.* at 3 (quoting Estes Dep. at 19). During the next few weeks, Gitlin communicated with Francis about quality problems with the product. On September 13, 1999, Wal-Mart directed GTI to cancel all further shipments of the reindeer.

On September 23, 1999, Gitlin met with Francis and Jeff Kuhn, a GTI representative, to discuss the slow sales and quality problems. During that meeting, Wal-Mart agreed to accept delivery of any reindeer GTI had already manufactured (approximately 25,000), but at a lower price than the prior purchase orders. In addition, Gitlin requested that GTI agree to Wal-Mart's withholding of $400,000 owed to GTI for potential claims for defective merchandise. Finally, according to Wal-Mart, GTI orally agreed, at some point before September 30, to reduce the total amount due from Wal-Mart by $200,000 because of Wal-Mart's price markdown of the reindeer at its stores in view of their poor quality. On September 30, 1999, Gitlin sent Francis and Kuhn an e- mail stating that sales of the reindeer were "too low" and that Wal-Mart would take a price markdown on the product within the next two weeks. E-mail from Gitlin to Francis and Kuhn (Sept. 30, 1999) (Gitlin's Sept. 30 e-mail). In that e-mail, Gitlin also stated that she was "also concerned about the defective percentage and claims at the end of the season. You say they normally run less than 10%. I'm going to be conservative and estimate 20%. I'm going to change the reserve on the account to $600,000 and will release the rest of the payments." *Id.* Gitlin did not receive a response to this e- mail from Francis or Kuhn.

On November 12, 1999, Kuhn sent Gitlin an e-mail stating GTI's frustration in obtaining payment from Wal-Mart on past-due invoices for the reindeer. In that e-mail, Kuhn noted that Gitlin said Wal-Mart was "going to hold $400,000 against future defective claims." E-Mail from Kuhn to Gitlin (Nov. 12, 1999). Gitlin replied three days later asking Kuhn to call her to discuss the matter. Gitlin and Kuhn spoke on November 19, 1999, and Gitlin sent Kuhn an e-mail that same day in which she stated, "As we both agree, we have $600,000 on hold now. $200,000 was to go to Markdowns and $400,000 was to cover claims. If you are willing to do this, then I will be able to consider reducing the amount on hold from $600,000 to $500,000." E-mail from Gitlin to Kuhn (Nov. 19, 1999) (Gitlin's Nov. 19 e-mail). Counsel for GTI sent Gitlin a facsimile letter that day demanding payment of the entire balance owed to GTI. Kuhn replied to Gitlin on November 22 and stated that "GTI would accept Wal-Mart withholding the amount of $400,000.00 for present and future charge backs." E-mail from Kuhn to Gitlin (Nov. 22, 1999). Kuhn sent Gitlin another e-mail on November 24 and stated that "[t]he principals [sic] of GTI's position is unwavering and non-negotiable. We want a check for $521,429 next week and on 1/15-2/1/2000 the $400,000 reserve will be revisited and adjusted accordingly." E-mail from Kuhn to Gitlin (Nov. 24, 1999). Thereafter, during the next several weeks, Gitlin and Kuhn continued to exchange e-mails, which can be characterized primarily as GTI continuing to demand immediate payment of outstanding invoices, or some settlement thereof, and Wal-Mart reiterating its position that GTI agreed to Wal-Mart's retention of funds for defective merchandise claims and $200,000 for price markdowns. GTI never acknowledged the $200,000 for price markdowns in any of its correspondence with Wal-Mart.

In December 2000, GTI sued Wal-Mart for breach of contract, action for goods sold, and action on account, alleging that GTI had shipped Wal-Mart 176,217 vine reindeer at an agreed price of $1,839,777.96, of which Wal-Mart had only paid $1,444,093.79. Wal-Mart counterclaimed for fraud and breach of contract. On October 1, 2001, GTI filed a motion for partial summary judgment, seeking an award of $200,000 of the unpaid balance, by arguing that the vendor agreement precluded any oral modifications and that the statute of frauds barred the alleged oral agreement to deduct $200,000 for price markdowns. The District Court granted GTI's motion on January 15, 2002, concluding that both the terms of the vendor agreement and the provisions of the statute of frauds barred the oral agreement to reduce $200,000 from the amount owed to GTI. The jury heard the remaining claims the next month and returned a verdict in favor of GTI on its breach of contract claim, awarding GTI $63,280, and in favor of GTI on Wal-Mart's counterclaim for breach of contract. Subsequently, the District Court denied Wal-Mart's motion for judgment as a matter of law or new trial and GTI's request for an award of attorney fees. On appeal, Wal-Mart contends the District Court erred in granting partial summary judgment to GTI on the $200,000 claim and abused its discretion in denying Wal-Mart's motion for a new trial on the ground that the erroneous grant of partial summary judgment prejudiced Wal-Mart in the trial of the remainder of the case. GTI cross appeals, arguing the denial of its request for attorney fees was an abuse of discretion.

II. *Discussion*

* * * *

A. *Wal-Mart's Appeal*

Wal-Mart first argues the District Court erred when it granted partial summary judgment in favor of GTI by holding that the oral agreement to reduce $200,000 from the amount owed to GTI for price markdowns was barred by the statute of frauds. Subject to certain limited exceptions, the statute-of-frauds provision of the Arkansas version of the Uniform Commercial Code (U.C.C.) renders unenforceable any unwritten contract for the sale of goods with a value of more than $500 "unless there is some writing sufficient to indicate that a contract for sale has been made between the parties and signed by the party against whom enforcement is sought." Ark.Code Ann. § 4-2-201(1) (Michie 2001).[1] Both parties agree the case is governed by the so-called "merchants' exception" to the statute of frauds. Under the merchants' exception, a confirmatory writing setting forth the terms of the agreement is sufficient if the recipient of the writing knows its contents and fails to object in writing within ten days. *See* § 4-2-201(2) (Michie 2001). Here, Wal-Mart claims GTI did not object within ten days of Wal-Mart's sending GTI a confirmatory writing of the oral agreement for the $200,000 allowance. Specifically, Wal-Mart argues Gitlin's September 30 e-mail as well as her other e-mails to Kuhn and Francis are confirmatory memoranda to which GTI did not object in writing.

The question of whether a writing constitutes a confirmation of an oral agreement sufficient to satisfy the statute of frauds is a question of law for the court. * * * In this case, the District Court concluded that as a matter of law none of Wal-Mart's e-mails were sufficient. We agree.

We turn first to Gitlin's September 30 e-mail to Francis and Kuhn. In that e-mail, Gitlin stated that she was "going to change the reserve on the account to $600,000." Gitlin's Sept. 30 e-mail. According to Wal-Mart, this e-mail clearly indicates that Wal-Mart believed the original contract had been changed. Moreover, Wal-Mart argues that "although the breakdown of the $600,000 into a $400,000 reserve allowance for defective merchandise claims and a $200,000 for a markdown allowance is not explicit, it is strongly implied by the text of the e-mail." Br. of

---

[1] Because the contract, both as written and as allegedly modified, is for the sale of goods in excess of $500, the oral modification itself must satisfy the requirements of the statute of frauds. Ark.Code Ann. § 4-2-209(3) (Michie 2001) ("The requirements of the statute of frauds section of this chapter (§ 4-2-201) must be satisfied if the contract as modified is within its provisions.").

Appellant at 34. GTI does not dispute that it never responded to this e-mail. Instead, GTI argues that Gitlin's September 30 e-mail is not a confirmatory writing under § 4-2-201(1).

While the merchants' exception does not require a confirmatory writing to be signed by the party to be charged, *see* § 4-2-201(2), the writing still must satisfy the dictates of § 2-201(1). *See St. Ansgar Mills, Inc. v. Streit*, 613 N.W.2d 289, 294 (Iowa 2000) ("[A] writing is still required [under § 2-201(2)], but it does not need to be signed by the party against whom the contract is sought to be enforced."); *Howard Constr. Co. v. Jeff-Cole Quarries, Inc.*, 669 S.W.2d 221, 227 (Mo.Ct.App.1983) ("[C]ourts have found that the § 2-201(2) confirmatory memorandum must satisfy the 'sufficient to indicate' requirement of § 2-201(1)"). Under the U.C.C., "[a]ll that is required [for a writing to indicate a contract for sale has been made under § 2-201(1)] is that the writing afford a basis for believing that the offered oral evidence rests on a real transaction." U.C.C. § 2-201, cmt. 1. Most courts that have interpreted the "sufficient to indicate" requirement "have required that the writing indicate the consummation of a contract, not mere negotiations." *Howard Constr. Co.*, 669 S.W.2d at 227. Thus, writings that contain language evincing a tentative agreement or writings that lack language indicating a binding or complete agreement have been found insufficient. *Id.; cf. M.K. Metals, Inc. v. Container Recovery Corp.*, 645 F.2d 583, 591 (8th Cir.1981) (concluding that the terms of the agreement were so specifically geared to the desires of the party to be charged that the agreement reflected a complete contract) (applying Missouri U.C.C.).

Based upon our review of Gitlin's September 30 e-mail, we agree with GTI that this e-mail fails sufficiently to indicate the formation or existence of any agreement between the parties through inference or otherwise. This e-mail is simply devoid of any language concerning an agreement on the issue of $200,000 for markdowns. While the e-mail references a $600,000 reserve, it does not state what, if any, portion of that amount was agreed to be set aside for markdowns. At most, the e-mail shows Wal-Mart's unilateral effort at taking a markdown on the reindeer and changing the reserve, e.g., "I will be taking a MD on this either next week or the following ... I'm going to change the reserve on the account to $600,000." Gitlin's Sept. 30 e-mail. In summary, the language in the e-mail does not constitute a sufficient writing for purposes of the statute of frauds because it does not evince any agreement between the parties on price markdowns. *See R.S. Bennett & Co. v. Econ. Mech. Indus.*, 606 F.2d 182, 186 (7th Cir.1979) (a § 2-201(2) writing must "indicate [ ] that the parties have already made a deal or reached an agreement") (applying Illinois U.C.C.).

Wal-Mart next argues that even if the September 30 e-mail is not a sufficient writing, Gitlin's subsequent e-mails to Kuhn and Francis constitute confirmatory memoranda. In particular, Wal-Mart points to Gitlin's e-mail to Kuhn on November 19 in which she stated, "As we both agree, we have $600,000 on hold now. $200,000 was to go to Markdowns and $400,000 was to cover claims. If you are willing to do this, then I will be able to consider reducing the amount on hold from $600,000 to $500,000." Gitlin's Nov. 19 e-mail. GTI does not directly refute that this or subsequent e-mails from Gitlin could constitute confirmatory memorandums. Instead, GTI argues that it filed timely objections to these writings. Specifically, Kuhn replied on November 22 and 24 and offered to sign a letter authorizing Wal-Mart to retain $400,000 for defective merchandise claims, but he also demanded immediate payment on all outstanding invoices, noting that GTI's position was not negotiable.

Section 4-2-201(2) does not prescribe any particular form for an objection to a confirmatory writing. Nonetheless, both parties agree that courts require an unequivocal objection to a confirmatory writing alleging an oral agreement. *See, e.g., M.K. Metals, Inc.,* 645 F.2d at 592 (holding response to a purchase order was not an adequate objection under § 2-201(2) because it did not challenge the price term in the purchase order, but rather stated that "there was someone who was willing to pay more than the amount stated in the purchase order") (applying Missouri U.C.C.). Here, Wal-Mart argues that GTI did not unequivocally object to its confirmatory writing because GTI failed specifically to object to the $200,000 for price markdowns in its November 22 and 24 e-mail responses to Gitlin's e-mails. In analyzing these e-mails, the District Court concluded that GTI's "reply e-mails including different terms and containing demands for payment of the amount due on the invoices, less a reserve, constitute objections under § 2-201(2)." Mem. Op. at 26. Though GTI failed to mention the $200,000 in its responses, it is clear when viewing the responses as a whole that GTI never agreed to Gitlin's assertion that they had reached an agreement on markdowns. Instead, GTI's responses, with a demand for full payment, less a reserve for defective merchandise claims, can only be characterized as unequivocal objections to any agreement on markdowns.

On the facts of this case, the merchants' exception to the statute of frauds has not been satisfied. Accordingly, we find the District Court did not err in granting partial summary judgment in favor of GTI on its claim for $200,000 of the unpaid balance of the reindeers' purchase price.

* * * *

III. *Conclusion*

For the reasons stated, we affirm the orders of the District Court granting partial summary judgment in favor of GTI and denying GTI's request for attorney fees.

[Some footnotes omitted, those retained have been renumbered.]

Notes

1.   Review *B& W Glass* from Chapter One on the issue of promissory estoppel and the statute of frauds.   The court in *Casazza* seems to understate the RESTATEMENT rule found in Section 139, which is premised on the proposition that the very oral promise otherwise barred by the statute of frauds may indue sufficient reliance to justify enforcement of that promise. Do the 2003 amendments to UCC 2-201 change the analysis? Would that carry over to UCC 2A-201 as well?

2.   Would the analysis in the previous two cases change in any other respect if the cases were to be decided under amended UCC 2-201?

3.   Note that modifications may come within the statute of frauds as well. Read UCC 2-209 and 2A-209. We will consider modifications further in Chapter Seven, *infra*. For now, ask yourself this question, if a party is contending that an agreement has been modified, does there need to be a record indicating that a modification took place?

4.   What is the effect of a finding that a record meets the statute of frauds requirement? Does that mean that a contract exists?

Problem 3-10

On February 1, S, a farmer, entered into an oral contract with B, a grain dealer, to plant his fields in corn and to harvest and deliver the output for $2.30 per bushel by October 1. B immediately resold the corn to C, a cereal producer, for $2.60 per bushel. On April 1, before the fields had been planted, S informed B that he had entered into a written contract with D, another dealer, to sell his output of corn for $3.00 per bushel. B claimed a breach of contract, but S's lawyer stated that the alleged contract was not enforceable because of the statute of frauds. As B's lawyer, identify and assess all arguments that the transaction was not within the scope of UCC 2-201(1).

Problem 3-11

On February 1, S, a farmer, entered into an oral contract with B, a grain dealer, to plant his fields in corn and to harvest and deliver the output for $2.30 per bushel by October 1. B immediately resold the corn to C, a cereal producer, for $2.60 per bushel. On April 1, S wrote and signed the following note to B: "The rising corn futures prices makes it necessary for me to cancel our deal. Sorry. Perhaps we can do business again next year." B's lawyer argues that if the oral transaction was within the scope of UCC 2-201(1), that statute was satisfied by the note. B is also prepared to prove that the parties had done business for 10 years and that S had always sold B the output from his land. As S's lawyer, identify and assess all of the arguments to the contrary.

Problem 3-12

On February 1, B wrote S a signed letter asking whether S would be willing to sell his output of corn "again this year." In response, S had hand written but not signed the following note, which was delivered by a family member: "George. Output is fine, but no deal until we agree on a fair price." On February 5, B (George) visited S on the farm and an oral agreement was reached to sell the output of corn at $2.30 per bushel. On February 7, B mailed the following letter to S, which was received by S on February 9: "Dear Silas. This is to confirm our agreement for the sale of corn at $2.30 per bushel, delivery by October 1. George." S did not respond to the letter. On April 1, S wrote the following signed note to B: "Dear George: We never had a deal. I have sold my output to D. (s) Silas." B's lawyer makes two arguments: (1) The statute of frauds was satisfied by application of UCC 2-201(2); (2) When all of the writings are considered, the statute of frauds has been satisfied. How would you rule?

Problem 3-13

IBM and Epprecht entered an oral agreement allegedly for the production by Epprecht of 50,000 print-head assemblies for computers. The assemblies were to conform to particular specifications prepared and furnished by IBM. IBM issued purchase orders for 7,000 assemblies, 4,000 of which were accepted and 3,000 of which were rejected by IBM. IBM paid the price of the assemblies accepted but, claiming quality problems, refused to pay anything for the rejected assemblies and canceled the agreement. Epprecht, alleging the facts stated above, sued for damages caused by IBM's "wrongful" rejection of 3,000 units. IBM moved for a summary judgment on the basis of UCC 2-201. Epprecht argued that the summary judgment should be denied: The statute of frauds was satisfied under UCC 2-201(3)(a) & (c). (What is the effect of IBM's purchase orders on the statute of frauds analysis?) Epprecht cited *Impossible Electronic Techniques, Inc. v. Wackenhut Protective Systems, Inc.*, 669 F.2d 1026, 1036-37 (5th Cir. 1982), where the court stated that the "statute exempts contracts involving 'specially manufactured' goods from the writing requirement because in these cases the very nature of the goods serves as a reliable indication that a contract was indeed formed." Further:

> Where the seller has commenced or completed the manufacture of goods that conform to the special needs of a particular buyer and thereby are not suitable for sale to others, not only is the likelihood of a perjured claim of a contract diminished, but denying enforcement to such a contract would impose substantial hardship on the aggrieved party. * * * The unfairness is especially acute where * * * the seller has incurred substantial, unrecoverable expense in reliance on the oral promise of the buyer. * * * The crucial inquiry is whether the manufacturer could sell the goods in the ordinary course of his business to someone other than the original buyer. If with slight alterations the goods could be so sold, then they are not specially manufactured; if, however, essential changes are necessary to render the goods marketable by the seller to others, then the exception does apply.

How should the court rule?

CHAPTER FOUR

TERMS OF THE AGREEMENT: SOURCES AND MEANING

SECTION 1.   "GAP FILLERS" AS TERMS OF THE CONTRACT

A.   The Scope of Agreement in Fact: A Reprise

In the bargain envisioned by the drafters of the FIRST RESTATEMENT OF CONTRACTS, promulgated in 1931, the transaction was a relatively discrete exchange and the parties were expected to agree on all of the material terms before a contract was formed. Thus, if material terms, such as quantity or price, were left open or to be agreed, the odds were strong that a court would hold that no enforceable contract was created until there was agreement.[*]

In the bargain envisioned by the drafters of Article 2 and Article 2A, the transaction is not limited to a discrete exchange where promises are made. As we have seen, the definition of agreement, UCC 1-201(b)(3), employs a broader theory of relevant behavior. In addition to any language used, the bargain can be derived from the particular parties' past, present and future conduct, as well as the practices and usages of others engaging in exchange in the same trade or market. Read UCC 1-303 [former 1-205, 2-208, 2A-207]. Course of performance, course of dealing and usage of trade are the concepts used to encompass both the parties' behavior and the practices in a trade or market.

In short, Articles 2 and 2A allows for relational[**] as well as discrete exchange. Thus, the parties may, by choice or because of complexity, intend to conclude a bargain without agreeing on every material term. Even in a discrete exchange, they may leave an important term, such as the price, open, or to be agreed, or to be fixed

---

[*] Examples of this approach include *Transamerica Equip. Leasing Corp. v. Union Bank*, 426 F.2d 273 (9th Cir. 1970); *Walker v. Keith*, 382 S.W.2d 198 (Ky. 1964); *Wilhelm Lubrication Co. v. Brattrud,* 268 N.W. 634 (Minn. 1936).

[**] *See* Ian R. Macneil, *Relational Contract: What We Do and Do Not Know,* 1985 WIS. L. REV. 483, 485-91. *See generally*, Symposium, *Relational Contract Theory: Unanswered Questions*, 94 NW. U. L. REV. 737 (2000); Melvin Aron Eisenberg, *The Emergence of Dynamic Contract Law*, 88 CAL. L. REV. 1743 (2000).

by one of the parties. In exchanges of longer duration or where circumstances are expected to change in unanticipated ways, this technique is especially salutary. It obviates the need for complete risk allocation at the time of contracting and puts a premium on negotiation and adjustment in the light of change.

What is the effect of open or incomplete terms on contract formation? As we learned in the last chapter, UCC 2-204(3) and 2A-204(3) do not require complete agreement on material terms. Rather, these sections incorporate standards that permit the parties to conclude a contract "even though one or more terms are left open" if they have "intended to make a contract" and there is a "reasonably certain basis for giving an appropriate remedy." Thus, the court must decide whether the parties intended to conclude the bargain and, thus, to "make" a contract, when a material term is left open or to be agreed. In line with basic contract principles, the parties' intent to contract must be manifested objectively in some manner. What factors are relevant to this determination of intent? This intent may be found with the help of course of performance, course of dealing, and usage of trade given that those items are part of the bargain of the parties. The best evidence of this intention is "conduct by both parties which recognizes the existence of such a contract." UCC 2-204(1), 2A-204(1). Experience suggests that the more important and complex the term, the less likely it is that the requisite intention is present.

B. "Gap Fillers" as Terms of the Contract

1. "Gap Fillers" Supplied by the UCC

If the parties did so intend to contract, the next question is whether there is a "reasonably certain basis for giving an appropriate remedy?" Article 2, Part 3, itself, provides many terms to fill "gaps" in the agreement, which will then become part of the contract. UCC 1-201(b)(12) [former 1-201(11)]. Study these "off the rack" gap fillers now, for in many cases they will furnish the basis for certainty of remedy:

- UCC 2-304(1) (price payable in money or otherwise);
- UCC 2-305 (open price term);
- UCC 2-306(1) (no unreasonably disproportionate quantity can be supplied or ordered);
- UCC 2-306(2) (best efforts in an exclusive dealing arrangement);
- UCC 2-307 (all goods must be tendered in a single delivery);
- UCC 2-308 (place where delivery to be made);

- UCC 2-309 (time for delivery and duration of contract are a "reasonable" time);
- UCC 2-310 (when and where payment is due);
- UCC 2-312 through 2-318 (warranties);
- UCC 2A-209 (relationship between supplier and finance lessor or lessee);
- UCC 2A-210 through 2A-216 (warranties).

Notice the lack of comparable Article 2A gap fillers covering price, quantity, delivery, and payment. How should the absence of gap fillers in Article 2A impact the resolution of these questions in a leasing transaction?

Article 2, prior to the 2003 amendments, contained several sections concerning the meaning of shipping terms that parties would use in shipping goods from the seller to the buyer. Former 2-319 through 2-324. These terms have been deleted by the 2003 amendments to Article 2 as out of date in commercial practice. Thus, parties will have to submit evidence on the meaning of the shipping term. That evidence could come from course of performance, course of dealing, or usage of trade. A source of possible terms and their meanings could be the Incoterms promulgated by the International Chamber of Commerce.[*]

These "gap fillers" permit parties who intend to contract to leave terms open or indefinite with the security that some standard of reasonableness will be available to complete the contract.[**] Another permitted technique is to leave discretion for fixing or defining the terms of performance to one of the parties. Thus, the agreement may provide that the price is to be the price fixed by the seller at the time of delivery, or that the quantity ordered is to be the buyer's requirements. Similarly, the buyer may agree to use "best efforts" to market a product or to purchase described goods "if satisfied" or both parties may agree to negotiate over an open term in the future. The parties may agree that one of the parties has discretion to decide how the contract will be performed. *See* UCC 2-311. What effect will reserved discretion by one party have on the enforceability of the agreement? Will the illusory character of the deal mean that there was not consideration? If not, what controls should be imposed upon the exercise of that discretion? *See* UCC 1-304 [former 1-203] (good faith duty in performance and enforcement of the

---

[*] *See* http://www.iccwbo.org.

[**] These provisions are based upon an underlying philosophy of commercial reasonableness. *See generally* Richard E. Speidel, *Restatement Second: Omitted Terms and Contract Method,* 67 CORNELL L. REV. 785 (1982) (concluding that the UCC provides inadequate guidance on how to establish reasonableness). *See also* Robert E. Scott, *A Theory of Self-Enforcing Indefinite Agreements*, 103 COLUM. L. REV. 1641 (2003).

contract).

To the extent that the parties have agreed to a term that would be contrary to the "gap filler", the parties' agreement would control. There would be no "gap" to fill in the parties' agreement. UCC 1-302 [former 1-102(3) and (4)]. For example, trade usage may be introduced to supplement terms of the agreement, but it is not a "gap" filler. It is part of the parties' agreement. Many commentators have described the "gap" fillers in computer terminology. They are "default" rules that operate in the absence of contrary agreement. The question is what should these default rules be?

2. The Content of "Gap Fillers"

In a broad sense, "default rules" include both the terms supplied by the UCC to fill gaps in the agreement and certain "rules" of sales law where the parties have power to vary the effect of those rules by agreement but have not done so. UCC 2-305(1) is an example of the first type and UCC 2-715(2)(a) is an example of the second. UCC 2-719(3). Read those sections. Do you see why?

Although we are concerned with the first type in this section, it is useful to note the broader academic debate (primarily among economists) over whether default rules are efficient. What default rules have the best chance to reduce the transaction costs involved in bargaining for, performing, and enforcing the contract? This is a matter of some dispute. Should it be a rule that most parties would have probably agreed to if able to engage in costless bargaining or should it be a rule, somewhat arbitrary, that is the easiest for the parties to bargain around? The former is a more complex, reasonable rule that lowers transaction costs when the parties accept it without bargaining, but increases them if the parties bargain in fact. The latter minimizes transaction costs if the parties in fact bargain around it, but increases them if the parties are forced to live with a rule that neither probably would have wanted. According to David Charny, this requires one set of default rules when it is probable that the parties will bargain and another set for cases where it is probable that they will not.[*]

To further complicate analysis, other commentators have urged rules that

---

[*] *See* David Charny, *Hypothetical Bargains: The Normative Structure of Contract Interpretation,* 89 MICH. L. REV. 1815 (1991). *See also* Charles J. Goetz & Robert E. Scott, *The Limits of Expanded Choice: An Analysis of the Interactions Between Express and Implied Terms,* 73 CAL. L. REV. 261 (1985); Mark P. Gergen, *The Use of Open Terms in Contract,* 92 COLUM. L. REV. 997 (1992).

deviate from what most parties would have wanted by requiring one party with a strategic advantage in bargaining to reveal critical information to the other. These so-called "penalty" default rules decrease transaction costs if the relevant information is disclosed *ex ante* contracting and penalize the non-disclosing party if it is not.* Still further, other commentators have begun to debate the appropriate default rules for relational contracts.** Another argument is that the rules should be based on business practices in order to respect individual autonomy reflected in the exercise of free choice in the market.***

In light of this debate, here are some questions to answer:

(1) How would you characterize the "gap filling" default rules in Article 2, Part 3 or Article 2A, Part 2? Are they responsive to what reasonable parties would probably have agreed or are they designed to facilitate ease in bargaining around?

(2) Does this debate help explain why Article 2A has fewer default rules than Article 2? What terms must be present in an Article 2A transaction? (*see* UCC 2A-201.)

(3) Can you identify a "penalty" default rule in Article 2, Part 3? [Hint. What is the effect of omitting a quantity term?] Look at UCC 2-315. What is the penalty for the buyer's failure to communicate particular purposes to the seller?

Problem 4-1

A. Seller, a dealer in Delaware Cobbler Potatoes, sells existing goods from cold storage. On February 1, Seller agreed, in a writing signed by both parties, to sell Buyer "1,000 sacks of Delaware Cobbler Potatoes." The writing contained no other terms except the following clause: "The parties to this agreement intend to make a contract and consider themselves bound to this writing." On March 15,

---

* *See, e.g.*, Ian Ayres & Robert H. Gertner, *Filling Gaps in Incomplete Contracts: An Economic Theory of Default Rules,* 99 YALE L.J. 87 (1989).

** *See, e.g.*, the articles by Clayton P. Gillette, Douglas G. Baird, and Robert E. Scott in 19 J. LEGAL STUD. 535-616 (1990). For an interesting essay positing that economic analysis has not succeeded in either explaining or reforming existing contract doctrine, *see* Eric A. Posner, *Economic Analysis of Contract Law After Three Decades: Success or Failure?*, 112 YALE L. J. 829 (2003). *But see, Festschrift to Charles J. Geotz and Robert E. Scott*, 6 VA. J. 6-121 (2003) (celebrating success of economic analysis of default rules).

*** Kerry Lynn Macintosh, *Liberty, Trade, and the Uniform Commercial Code: When Should Default Rules Be Based on Business Practices?*, 38 WM. & MARY L. REV. 1465 (1997).

Seller notified Buyer to come and pick up the potatoes. Buyer responded that Seller must deliver the potatoes to Buyer's plant. Seller refused. On March 15, the market price of that type of potatoes was $10 per sack.

    1.   What terms are missing? Is there an enforceable contract? UCC 2-204 and 2-201. Is there a reasonable basis for providing an appropriate remedy? UCC 2-708(1), 2-713

    2.   Is either party liable for breach of contract? UCC 2-204, 2-305, 2-308, 2-309, 2-703, 2-711.

    3.   Assume that in the previous 5 times that Buyer and Seller engaged in similar conduct, Seller had always delivered the potatoes to Buyer at Buyer's plant. Does that change your analysis? UCC 1-201(b)(3), (12) and 1-303 [former 1-201(3), 1-205, 2-208].

    B. Seller, a dealer in Delaware Cobbler Potatoes, sells existing goods from cold storage. On February 1, Seller agreed, in a writing signed by both parties, to sell to Buyer "Delaware Cobbler Potatoes for $7 per sack with delivery no later than March 15." The writing contained no other terms except the following clause: "The parties to this agreement intend to make a contract and consider themselves bound to this writing." When Buyer arrived to pick up the potatoes, Seller refused to deliver. On March 15, the market price for Delaware Cobblers was $10 per sack.

    1.   What terms are missing? Is there an enforceable contract? UCC 2-204 and 2-201. Is there a reasonable basis for providing an appropriate remedy? UCC 2-708(1), 2-713.

    2.   Is Seller liable for breach of contract? UCC 2-204, 2-711.

    3.   Assume that in the previous 5 times that Buyer and Seller engaged in similar conduct, the Buyer had taken 1,000 sacks of the potatoes. Does that change your analysis? UCC 1-201(b)(3), (12) and 1-303 [former 1-201(3), 1-205, 2-208].

Problem 4-2

    Lessor agreed in a record signed by both parties to lease one skid loader to Lessee for $500 per month for a stated one year period. Nothing was stated in the record concerning delivery of the skid loader. Lessee insisted the Lessor deliver the skid loader to Lessee's place of business and Lessor insisted that Lessee come pick it up. Lessee refused to pick up the skid loader or to pay the monthly rental fee until Lessor delivered the skid loader. Lessor sued Lessee for breach of contract.

    A. Is this an enforceable lease contract? UCC 2A-204, 2A-201.

    B. If so, has anyone breached the contract? UCC 2A-501, 2A-508, 2A-523.

C. If you were representing either party in this lawsuit, what type of evidence would you be looking for to determine whether Lessor had an obligation to deliver the goods to Lessee's location? Does Article 2 have any relevance to your analysis? UCC 2-308.

Note: UCITA and Default Rules

UCITA occupies a middle ground between the thorough provision of gap fillers in Article 2 and the skimpy provision of gap fillers in Article 2A. UCITA 202 is the analog to UCC 2-204 and 2A-204, allowing a license to be enforceable if the parties intend to contract and there is a reasonably certain basis for a remedy. UCITA then supplies gap fillers that control a party's discretion if that party is to specify the "particulars of performance" (UCITA 305), that require performance in a reasonable manner if a term is left open (UCITA 306), that fill in implied terms concerning the scope of the license (UCITA 307), that provide a standard for performance to a party's satisfaction (UCITA 308), and that provide certain warranties to a licensee (UCITA 401 through 410). UCITA demonstrates the fine line between contract interpretation and supplementation as many of the provisions cited above speak to both issues, providing both guidance on how to interpret terms in the license and gap fillers to supply terms not in the license.

Note: The CISG and Default Rules

The CISG contains several provisions detailing the obligations of the seller and the buyer in a contract for a sale of goods. As with Article 2 and 2A, these rules are subject to contrary agreement of the parties. Article 6. In terms of the seller's delivery obligation, Article 31 states where the seller must deliver, Article 33 provides when the seller must deliver, and Article 35 addresses the quality of the goods the seller must deliver. In terms of the buyer's obligation to take the goods and pay the price, Article 55 addresses open price contracts, Article 57 states the place of payment, Articles 58 and 59 addresses when the buyer must pay, and Article 60 addresses the obligation to take delivery of the goods.

SECTION 2.   OPEN TERMS

In this section, we address more specifically some of the issues that have arisen in applying Article 2 gap fillers on quantity, price, delivery, and payment.

Remember, in each case in which the gap filler provision is applied, there has to have already been a determination that the parties intended to conclude a bargain and that their agreement does not otherwise address the issue that the gap filler addresses.

A problem for the attorney asked to plan a long-term contract for the sale of goods is to draft an agreement which is legally enforceable and preserves flexibility in the areas thought by the client to be the most troublesome or uncertain during performance. The seasoned practitioner may say that the real challenge is to achieve realistic flexibility and risk allocation rather than legal enforceability.[*]

The lawyer must understand the client's business needs and risks, assess the probability of changed circumstances, draft appropriate clauses and, in negotiating with the other side, be capable of achieving a mutually satisfactory agreement. This challenge is strikingly posed when problems of quantity and price are involved.[**] So it is to issues concerning quantity and price that we first turn.

A. Quantity

Our primary concern in this subsection is with "output" and "requirements" contracts. Remember, the statute of frauds, UCC 2-201(1), states that a "contract is not enforceable . . . beyond the quantity of goods shown " in the record "signed by the party against which enforcement is sought." A commitment to supply output or to buy requirements, however, is a quantity term which, because it can be interpreted and limited under UCC 2-306, satisfies the statute of frauds.[***] Article 2A requires that the leased goods be described in the record and the lease term be specified. UCC 2A-201(1)(b). UCITA 201 requires the record to specify the copy or subject matter to which the contract refers.

---

[*] *See* Ian R. Macneil, *Contracts: Adjustment of Long-term Economic Relations Under Classical, Neoclassical and Relational Contract Law,* 72 Nw. U. L. REV. 854 (1978) (difficulties in planning long-term supply contract).

[**] Victor P. Goldberg, *Price Adjustments in Long-Term Contracts,* 1985 WIS. L. REV. 527; Note, *Requirements Contracts: Problems of Drafting and Construction,* 78 HARV. L. REV. 1212 (1965).

[***] *See PMC Corp. v. Houston Wire & Cable Co.,* 797 A.2d 125, 128-31(N.H. 2002). For effective criticism of the statute of fraud's quantity policy, *see* Caroline N. Bruckel, *The Weed and the Web: Section 2-201's Corruption of the Code's Substantive Provisions–The Quantity Problem,* 1983 U. ILL. L.F. 811.

Notice that Article 2A does not have a provision comparable to UCC 2-306. While UCITA has a provision regarding interpretation of the scope of the license, UCITA 307, it too has no analog to UCC 2-306. Why the difference between the three approaches? Couldn't the parties agree to lease or license their outputs or requirements?

Once past the issue of the statute of frauds, other issues remain in interpreting UCC 2-306. To have an enforceable requirements contract, must the buyer agree to get all of its requirements exclusively from the seller? To have an enforceable output contract, must the seller agree to provide all of its output exclusively to the buyer? What is the relationship between the good faith requirement and the "unreasonably disproportionate" test? What if the buyer, in good faith, has no requirements or the seller, in good faith, has no output? Has the buyer or seller in those situations required or provided amounts "unreasonably disproportionate" to any stated estimates or prior provided amounts? What does good faith mean in this context? How does one determine whether the amounts provided are "unreasonably" disproportionate? We offer one case (with no apologies for its length) which deals successfully with some of these questions.

ORANGE & ROCKLAND, ETC. V. AMERADA HESS CORP.
SUPREME COURT OF NEW YORK, APPELLATE DIVISION, 1977
59 A.D.2D 110, 397 N.Y.S.2D 814

MARGETT, JUSTICE

* * * In a fuel oil supply contract executed in early December, 1969, defendant Amerada Hess Corporation (Hess) agreed to supply the requirements of plaintiff Orange and Rockland Utilities, Inc. (O & R) at plaintiff's Lovett generating plant in Tompkins Cove, New York. A fixed price of $2.14 per barrel for No. 6 fuel oil, with a sulphur content of 1% or less, was to continue at least through September 30, 1974, with the price subject to renegotiation at that time. Estimates of the amounts required by plaintiff were included in the contract clause entitled "Quantity". Insofar as those estimates are relevant to the instant controversy, they were as follows:

    1970–1,750,000 barrels
    1971–1,380,000 barrels
    1972–1,500,000 barrels
    1973–1,500,000 barrels

The estimates had been prepared by plaintiff on December 30, 1968, as part of a five-year budget projection. The estimates anticipated that gas would be the primary fuel used for generation during the period in question. This was a result of the lower cost of gas and of the fact that gas became readily available for power generation during the warmer months of the year as a result of decreased use by gas customers. Plaintiff expressly reserved its right to burn as much gas as it chose by the inclusion, in the "Quantity" provision of the requirements contract, of a clause to the effect that "[n]othing herein shall preclude the use by Buyer of * * * natural gas in such quantities as may be or become available."

Within five months of the execution of the requirements contract, the price of fuel oil began to ascend rapidly. On April 24, 1970 the market price of the oil supplied to plaintiff stood at between $2.65 and $2.73 per barrel. On May 1, 1970 the price was in excess of $3 per barrel. The rise continued and was in excess of $3.50 per barrel by mid-August, and more than $4 per barrel by the end of October, 1970. By March, 1971 the lowest market price was $4.30 per barrel–more than double the price set forth in the subject contract.

Coincident with the earliest of these increases in the cost of oil, O & R proceeded to notify Hess, on four separate dates, of increases in the fuel oil requirements estimates for the year. By letter dated April 16, 1970, O & R notified Hess that it was expected that over 1,460,000 barrels of oil would be consumed over the period April-December, 1970. Since well over 600,000 barrels of oil had been consumed during the first three months of the year, the total increase anticipated at that time was well in excess of 300,000 barrels over the estimate given in the contract.

Eight days later, by letter dated April 24, 1970, O & R furnished Hess with a revised estimate for the period May through December, 1970. The figure given was nearly 1,580,000 barrels which, when combined with quantities which had already been delivered or were in the process of delivery during the month of April, exceeded the contract estimate by over 700,000 barrels–a 40% increase.

The following month the estimates were again increased–this time to nearly one million barrels above the contract estimate. Hess was so notified by letter dated May 22, 1970. Finally, a letter dated June 19, 1970 indicates a revised estimate of more than one million barrels in excess of the 1,750,000 barrels mentioned in the contract; an increase of about 63%.

On May 22, 1970, the date of the third of the revised estimates, representatives of the two companies met to discuss the increased demands. At that meeting O & R's president allegedly attributed the increased need for oil to the fact that O & R could make more money *selling* gas than burning it for power generation. Hess

refused to meet the revised requirements, but offered to supply the amount of the contract estimate for the year 1970, plus an additional 10 percent.

The June 19, 1970, letter referred to above recited that the Hess position was "wholly unacceptable" to O & R. It attributed the vastly increased estimates to (a) an inability to burn as much natural gas as had been planned and (b) the fact that O & R had been "required" to meet higher electrical demands on its "own system" and to furnish "more electricity to interconnected systems" than had been anticipated.

Thereafter, for the remainder of 1970, Hess continued to supply the amount of the contract estimates plus 10 percent. A proposal by Hess, in October, 1970, to modify the existing contract by setting minimum and maximum quantities, and by setting a price keyed to market prices, was ignored by O & R. Although the proposed modification set a price 65 cents lower than the market price, it was more advantageous for O & R to insist on delivery of the estimated amounts in the December, 1969 contract (at $2.14 per barrel) and to purchase additional amounts required at the full market price.

During the remainder of the contract period Hess continued to deliver quantities approximately equal to the estimates stated in the subject contract. O & R purchased additional oil for its Lovett plant from other suppliers. The contract between Hess and O & R terminated one year prematurely by reason of an environmental regulation which took effect on October 1, 1973 and which necessarily curtailed the use of No. 6 fuel oil with a sulphur content as high as 1%. During the period 1971 through September, 1973 O & R consistently used more than double its contract estimates of oil at Lovett. * * *

[In mid-1972, O&R sued Hess for damages measured by the difference between the actual cost of fuel during the period in question and the contract price. In March, 1976, the trial court held that O&R acted in bad faith, specifically because the "plaintiff's greatly increased oil consumption was due primarily to (a) increases in sales of electricity to other utilities and (b) a net shift from other fuels, primarily gas, to oil." Because of its finding of bad faith the trial court did not decide whether O&R's demands were unreasonably disproportionate to the estimates in the contract. On appeal, the appellate division decided that the New Jersey version of UCC 2-306(1) applied and, after deciding both the good and the unreasonably disproportionate issues, affirmed the trial court.]

There is, as Trial Term observed, a good deal of pre-Code case law on the requirement of "good faith". It is well settled that a buyer in a rising market cannot use a fixed price in a requirements contract for speculation. * * * Nor can a buyer arbitrarily and unilaterally change certain conditions prevailing at the time of the contract so as to take advantage of market conditions at the seller's expense. * * *

There is no judicial precedent with respect to the meaning of the term "unreasonably disproportionate" which appears in subdivision (1) of section 2-306 of the UCC. Obviously this language is not the equivalent of "lack of good faith"–it is an elementary rule of construction that effect must be given, if possible, to every word, clause and sentence of a statute. * * * The phrase is keyed to stated estimates or, if there be none, to "normal or otherwise comparable prior" requirements. While "reasonable elasticity" is contemplated by the section (*see* Official Comment, par. 2 to UCC § 2-306), an agreed estimate shows a clear limit on the intended elasticity, similar to that found in a contract containing minimum and maximum requirements (*see* Official Comment, par. 2 to UCC § 2-306). The estimate "is to be regarded as a center around which the parties intend the variation to occur" (*supra*).

The limitation imposed by the term "unreasonably disproportionate" represents a departure from prior case law, wherein estimates were generally treated as having been made simply for the convenience of the parties and of no operative significance. * * * It is salutary in that it insures that the expectations of the parties will be more fully realized in spite of unexpected and fortuitous market conditions. * * * Thus, even where one party acts with complete good faith, the section limits the other party's risk in accordance with the reasonable expectations of the parties.

It would be unwise to attempt to define the phrase "unreasonably disproportionate" in terms of rigid quantities. In order that the limitation contemplated by the section take effect, it is not enough that a demand for requirements be disproportionate to the stated estimate; it must be *unreasonably* so in view of the expectation of the parties. A number of factors should be taken into account in the event a buyer's requirements greatly exceed the contract estimate. These include the following: (1) the amount by which the requirements exceed the contract estimate; (2) whether the seller had any reasonable basis on which to forecast or anticipate the requested increase * * * ; (3) the amount, if any, by which the market price of the goods in question exceeded the contract price; (4) whether such an increase in market price was itself fortuitous; and (5) the reason for the increase in requirements.

Turning once again to the facts of the instant case, we conclude that, at least as to the year in which this controversy first arose, there was ample evidence to justify a finding of lack of good faith on plaintiff's part. Even through the thicket of divergent and contrasting figures entered into exhibit at trial, the following picture emerges: non-firm sales from plaintiff's Lovett plant, presumably in large part to the New York Power Pool, increased nearly sixfold from 67,867 megawatt hours in 1969 to 390,017 megawatt hours in 1970. The significance of that increase in *non-firm* sales lies in the fact that such sales did not enter into the budget calculations which formed the basis of the estimates included in the contract. Even assuming that a prudent seller of oil could anticipate some additional requirements generated by non-firm sales, an increase of the magnitude which occurred in 1970 is unforeseeable. That increase, of 322,150 megawatt hours, translates into the equivalent of over 500,000 barrels of oil. The conclusion is inescapable that this dramatic change in plaintiff's relationship with the New York Power Pool came about as a result of the subject requirements contract, which insured it a steady flow of cheap oil despite swiftly rising prices. O & R's use of the subject contract to suddenly and dramatically propel itself into the position of a large seller of power to other utilities evidences a lack of good faith dealing.

In addition to this massive increase in sales of power to other utilities, the evidence indicates that at about the time O & R was demanding roughly one million barrels of oil in excess of the 1970 contract estimate, there was an internal O & R proposal to release gas to a supplier which represented the equivalent of 542,000 barrels of oil. An internal O & R memorandum dated May 26, 1970 (four days after the meeting at which Hess refused to supply the one million additional barrels demanded) recommended that in view of the Hess position, the proposed release be canceled. Significantly, O & R never did burn as much oil as had been demanded in May and June, 1970. Its total usage for the year was 2,294,845 barrels–471,155 barrels less than its maximum demand. This was explained, by O & R officials, in part, on the ground that their "gas department" had made a "pessimistic estimate" which did not turn out to be quite true.

Thus it appears that in May, 1970 Hess refused an O & R demand of roughly one million barrels in excess of the contract estimate, which demand was occasioned by greatly increased sales to other utilities and a proposed release of gas which might otherwise normally have been burned for power generation. The former factor is tantamount to making the other utilities in the State silent partners to the contract * * *, while the latter factor amounts to a unilateral and arbitrary change in the conditions prevailing at the time of the contract so as to take advantage of market conditions at the seller's expense. Hess was therefore justified in 1970 in refusing to meet plaintiff's demands, by reason of the fact that plaintiff's "requirements" were not incurred in good faith.

With respect to subsequent years however, the record is ambiguous as to the cause of plaintiff's drastically increased requirements. Non-firm sales from Lovett actually declined slightly in 1971 and 1972 although they were still greatly in excess of 1969 sales. If one takes 1969 as a base year, increased non-firm sales from Lovett in 1971 amounted to the equivalent of about one-half million barrels of oil, while in 1972 they amounted to the equivalent of just over 300,000 barrels. Comparable figures for 1973 are impossible to arrive at with any degree of confidence because sales figures in the record are for the full year, while defendant's obligation to supply oil extended through only three-quarters of the year. In any event, it is apparent that O & R's tremendously expanded use of oil during the period subsequent to 1970 cannot be explained solely by reference to increased sales to other utilities. In 1971 oil use exceeded the contract estimate by over 1,750,000 barrels; the 1972 figure was in excess of 1,825,000 barrels; and for the first nine months of 1973 the increase was more than 1,275,000 barrels.

It appears that a large portion of the difference between actual use and contract estimates during this period can be attributed to a rather large decline in plaintiff's "actual take" of gas as opposed to the estimates of gas availability which were made in 1968 (and which were used in the computation of the December 30, 1968 budget). This decline, with the equivalent figure in barrels of oil, was as follows:

	Estimate (Mcf)	Actual Take (Mcf)	Decrease	Equiv. Barrels of Oil
1971–	40,615,000	34,518,000	6,097,000	1,016,167
1972–	43,661,000	36,274,000	7,387,000	1,231,167
1973 (9 mos.)	34,034,700	25,783,000	8,251,700	1,275,283

Even allowing for the fact that O & R's actual system requirements were slightly lower during this period than the estimated system requirements (thus theoretically leaving more gas available for electric generation), it is clear that the decline from the estimates in gas received by O & R was a very major factor in plaintiff's increased use of oil during this period.

The record is unclear as to why this decline came about. Plaintiff introduced into evidence a Public Service Commission memorandum which indicates that gas supplies available to interstate transmission companies had become extremely tight. However plaintiff failed to call one witness who was expert in its gas operations and who could testify as to the link, if any, between this general shortage and plaintiff's operations. While an unfavorable inference may be drawn when a party fails to produce evidence which is within his control and which he is naturally expected to produce, we decline to speculate as to causes of the decline in gas received by plaintiff. In any event, such speculation is not necessary for resolution of this appeal.

We hold that under the circumstances of this case, any demand by plaintiff for more than double its contract estimates, was, as a matter of law, "unreasonably disproportionate" (UCC, § 2-306, subd. [1]) to those estimates. We do not adopt the factor of more than double the contract estimates as any sort of an inflexible yardstick. Rather, we apply those standards set forth earlier in this opinion, which are calculated to limit a party's risk in accordance with the reasonable expectations of the parties.

Here, as noted, plaintiff's requirements during the period 1971 through September, 1973, were more than double the contract estimates. Defendant had no reasonable basis on which to forecast or anticipate an increase of this magnitude. Indeed the contract suggests the parties contemplated that any variations from the estimate would be on the downside—else why did plaintiff expressly reserve for itself the right to burn as much as it chose? The market price of the grade of oil supplied had more than doubled by March, 1971. It stayed at or above $4.00 per barrel for the rest of the applicable period and had reached nearly $5.00 per barrel by the end of September, 1973. The record is silent as to whether defendant had any reason to anticipate this enormous increase in oil prices. Finally, the increase in requirements was due in part to plaintiff's increased sales to other utilities and also due to a significant decline in anticipated deliveries of gas, the cause of which was inadequately explained by plaintiff. The quantities of oil utilized by plaintiff during the period subsequent to 1970 were not within the reasonable expectations of the parties when the contract was executed, and accordingly we hold that those "requirements" were unreasonably disproportionate to the contract estimates (*see* UCC, § 2-306, subd. [1]).

Judgment of the Supreme Court, Rockland County, entered June 4, 1976, affirmed, with costs.

Notes

1. How should a party disadvantaged by a market shift (here the seller) bargain over a possible agreed price adjustment? What was Amerada Hess's strategy? *See* UCC 1-308 [former 1-207].

2. When is a buyer in a requirements contract in bad faith for having too many requirements? Assuming good faith, when are a buyer's actual requirements disproportionate? What is the proper test? The court in *Orange & Rockland* used factors existing and events foreseeable at the time of contracting to determine whether the buyer's orders were "unreasonably disproportionate" to the stated estimates. Where the estimates did not apply, however, the court used motives and factors existing at the time the requirements were ordered to determine whether the buyer's conduct was in bad faith. The buyer lost on both counts. Suppose, however, that the amounts ordered were unreasonably disproportionate to the stated estimates but the buyer's actual requirements were in good faith. Which limitation upon the exercise of discretion should prevail under UCC 2-306(1)?[*]

3. Suppose a seller or a buyer has no output or requirements or suspends a product line in good faith. Is that decision subject to the "unreasonably disproportionate" limitation in UCC 2-306(1)? Despite some linguistic uncertainty in the statute, the courts have held that the answer is no.[**]

4. What is good faith in the situation where the buyer's requirements are drastically reduced or the buyer goes out of business? As one court put it, the "seller assumes the risk of all good faith variations in the buyer's requirements even to the extent of a determination to liquidate or discontinue the business." It might be said that the buyer's duty to buy is conditioned upon the existence of actual requirements. Further:

> The rule is based on a reliance on the self-interest of the buyer, who ordinarily will seek to have the largest possible requirements. Protection against abuse is afforded by penetrating through any device by which the requirement is siphoned off in some other form to the detriment of the

---

[*] *See* Stacy A. Silkworth, *Quantity Variation in Open Quantity Cases*, 51 U. PITT. L. REV. 235 (1991).

[**] *See Empire Gas Corp. v. American Bakeries Co.*, 840 F.2d 1333 (7th Cir. 1988); *Brewster of Lynchburg, Inc. v. Dial Corp.*, 33 F.3d 355 (4th Cir. 1994); *Schwak, Inc. v. Donruss Trading Cards Inc.*, 746 N.E.2d 18 (Ill. Ct. App. 2001); *Dienes Corp. v. Long Island Railroad Co.*, 2002 WL 603043 (E.D.N.Y. 2002). *But see Simcala, Inc. v. American Coal Trade, Inc.*, 821 So. 2d 197 (Ala. 2001) (holding both tests apply so buyer may be in breach even if requirements decreased in good faith if the requirements are unreasonably disproportionate to the stated estimates). For an example of a court holding that a decrease in seller's output is only governed by the good faith test and not the unreasonably disproportionate test, *see Waste Stream Environmental, Inc. v. Lynn Water and Sewer Commission*, 2003 WL 917086 (Super. Ct. Mass. 2003).

seller. The requirement of good faith is the means by which this is enforced and self-interest in its undistorted form is maintained as the standard.

HML Corporation v. General Foods Corporation, 365 F.2d 77 (3rd Cir. 1966) (burden on seller to prove bad faith).[*]

What, then, is bad faith in this setting? What if the decision is not to curtail losses but simply to make more profits on an alternative line of production? Inferences of bad faith abound when the seller has some demand for its output or the buyer still has some requirements and the decision is "merely to curtail losses." UCC 2-306, cmt. 2. A leading case is *Feld v. Henry S. Levy & Sons, Inc.*, 335 N.E.2d 320, 323 (N.Y. 1975), where the court concluded that an "output" seller was justified in a good faith cessation of a single operation rather than entire business "only if its losses from continuance would be more than trivial." A cessation "merely to curtail losses" would be improper. Should the amount of loss from continued performance be the major issue? How much is too much? Are the comments to UCC 2-306 any guidance on this issue?

5. What precautions should be taken in the contract to avoid disputes of this sort? Since 1977, there has been little litigation of significance on the issues decided in *Orange & Rockland*.[**]

Problem 4-3

Seller, a wholesale dealer in plywood, and Buyer, a producer of pine veneer, entered into a five year contract under which Buyer agreed to purchase 50,000

---

[*] *See* Comment, *And Then There Were None: Requirements Contracts and the Buyer Who Does Not Buy*, 64 WASH. L. REV. 871 (1989).

[**] *See Canusa Corp. v. A & R Lobosco, Inc.*, 986 F. Supp. 723 (E.D.N.Y. 1997) (seller's reduced output under "output" contract in bad faith); *Homestake Mining Co. v. Washington Public Power Supply System*, 476 F.Supp. 1162, 1167-69 (N.D.Cal.1979) (bad faith for buyer under requirements contract to insist on goods not needed for the particular business activity referred to in contract). For commentary, *see* WHITE & SUMMERS, § 3-8; Note, *Requirements Contracts, "More or Less," Under the Uniform Commercial Code*, 33 RUTGERS L. REV. 105 (1980). For discussions of the good faith issue in flexible quantity contracts, *see* Steven J. Burton, *Breach of Contract and the Common Law Duty to Perform in Good Faith*, 94 HARV. L. REV. 369 (1980); Timothy J. Muris, *Opportunistic Behavior and the Law of Contracts*, 65 MINN. L. REV. 521(1981); Victor P. Goldberg, *Discretion in Long-Term Quantity Contracts: Reining in Good Faith*, 35 U.C. DAVIS L. REV. 319 (2002).

square feet of plywood per year at $1.00 per square foot. Terms on the time and method of shipment and payment were also agreed. The written contract was dated July 1, 1999.

A. On July 1, 2002, the market price of plywood had climbed to $4.00 per square foot. The increase was due, primarily, to sharpened demand for forest products. Buyer was operating at full capacity and Seller could resell all of the plywood obtained from the manufacturers. Seller, however, was unhappy with its arrangement with Buyer. Buyer, no softy, said: "Tough. You assumed the risk!" Is Buyer correct?

B. Assume the same facts except that Buyer agreed to purchase its annual "requirements" of plywood from Seller at $1.00 per square foot. The contract did not explicitly say "all of our requirements exclusively from Seller." Furthermore, the contract did not provide for estimates of quantity or maximum-minimum quantities which Buyer could not exceed. Buyer's annual requirements for the first three years were 25,000, 32,500 and 35,000 square feet. During the fourth year, with the market price at $4.50 per square foot, Buyer requested a total of 60,000 square feet, the capacity of its production facility. Seller objected and Buyer, still no softy, said: "Tough. You assumed the risk!"

Seller's lawyer responded by quoting to buyer's lawyer during negotiations from *Billings Cottonseed, Inc. v. Albany Oil Mill, Inc.*, 328 S.E.2d 426, 429-30 (Ga. Ct. App. 1985):

> Appellant's argument that a valid requirements contract was established by partial performance on its part is also without merit. Ordinarily, partial performance renders enforceable a contract unenforceable for lack of consideration and mutuality by supplying the lack of mutuality * * * There can be no partial performance in the context of a requirements contract, however, for it is the promise of exclusivity that provides the consideration to the seller. * * * The promise to buy alone is not sufficient performance, for without exclusivity the purchaser's promise is merely to buy when he wants and the promise of the seller becomes merely an invitation for orders.
>
> * * * Thus, the requisite mutuality is not supplied." (Citations omitted.)

What arguments should Buyer make at this point? Should they prevail?[*]

---

[*] *See*, particularly, Caroline N. Bruckel, *Consideration in Exclusive and Nonexclusive Open Quantity Contracts Under the U.C.C.: A Proposal for a New System of Validation*, 68 MINN. L. REV. 117 (1983), who rejects the exclusivity requirement. Most courts, however, disagree and search for exclusive dealing as to all or part of the buyer's requirements. *See, e.g., PMC*

(continued...)

C. Assume the same facts as B above except that in the fourth year, Buyer requested a total of 5,000 square feet of plywood due to an economic depression in the local building market, which dropped the demand for pine veneer. Seller objected and once again Buyer responded: "Tough. You assumed the risk." What arguments do you make on behalf of Seller?

D. In light of hindsight, what is the best contractual arrangement for an enterprise selling plywood to a producer with a finite capacity, in a period where there is uncertainty regarding future prices and demand:

(1) Fixed-price plus "requirements," with an upper limit on quantity;

(2) Fixed-price plus an agreement to sell all or a specified part of the seller's "output" of plywood exclusively to the buyer;

(3) An "open" or market price plus either a requirements or an output agreement;

(4) Either separate contracts or short term, i.e., one year, arrangements with fixed prices and fixed quantities;

(5) Other? For example, in *Lenape Resources Corp. v. Tennessee Gas Pipeline Co.*, 925 S.W.2d 565 (Tex. 1996), the parties entered a long-term "take or pay" contract at a relatively fixed price. Seller, a natural gas producer, agreed to supply "85% of delivery capacity" over the course of the contract. Natural gas prices plunged and Buyer sought to get out of the contract. Seller, under pressure from other buyers, substantially increased its capacity to produce by drilling new wells and entering into so-called "farm-out" agreements. Buyer claimed that Seller's increased output was in bad faith and was "unreasonably disproportionate" under UCC 2-306(1). The court, in a long opinion with even longer dissents, held that no output contract was created and that UCC 2-306(1) did not apply. Buyer, therefore, assumed the risk of Seller's increased capacity.

Note: Best Efforts in Exclusive Dealing Relationships

UCC 2-306(2) provides that a "lawful agreement by either the seller or the buyer for exclusive dealing in the kind of goods concerned imposes unless otherwise agreed an obligation by the seller to use best efforts to supply the goods

---

* (...continued)

Corp. v. Houston Wire & Cable Co., 797 A.2d 125 (N.H. 2002); *In re Anchor Glass Container Corp.*, 297 B.R. 887 (Bankr. M.D. Fla. 2003); *Roger Edwards LLC v. Fiddes & Sons Ltd.*, 245 F. Supp. 2d 251 (D. Me. 2003); *Essco Geometric v. Harvard Industries*, 46 F.3d 718 (8th Cir. 1995); *United Services Auto Ass'n. v. Schlang*, 894 P.2d 967 (Nev. 1995).

and by the buyer to use best efforts to promote their sale."

An exclusive dealing relationship is a continuing, highly interdependent agency, franchise or contract for distribution. It facilitates the manufacturer's effort to market the goods. It is common for the distributor to agree to order requirements as generated by "best efforts" from and to deal exclusively in some defined territory with the manufacturer. When the agreement to use "best efforts" is coupled with exclusive dealing, there is consideration.[*] There is some risk, however, that the arrangement, because of its restriction upon competition, will run afoul of the antitrust laws.[**] In any event, the arrangement must be lawful under state and federal law and an agreement by the distributor to make best efforts must exist.[***] UCC 2-306(2) presumes that the "best efforts" agreement exists unless the parties have otherwise agreed.[****]

What are "best efforts" when the duty is part of the agreement? Beyond the requirement that the distributor make an honest effort in the particular setting, there is disagreement among the courts. For a leading case and some helpful analysis, *see Bloor v. Falstaff Brewing Corp.*, 601 F.2d 609 (2nd Cir. 1979) and Charles J. Goetz & Robert E. Scott, *Principles of Relational Contracts,* 67 VA. L. REV. 1089 (1981).

B. Price

In a market directed economy, the sale price is the result of seller costs, buyer demand, information available to and negotiations between the parties, and the quality of competition in the relevant market area. Since price is a material term in any sale, the determination of what price was agreed, as well as the method for ascertainment, is important when disputes arise.

Under Article 2, the parties, if they so intend, can conclude a contract with an open or indefinite price "if there is a reasonably certain basis for giving an appropriate remedy." UCC 2-204(3), 2-305(1). In such cases, "the price is a

---

[*] *Hunt Foods, Inc. v. Phillips*, 248 F.2d 23 (9th Cir. 1957).

[**] *See* L. SULLIVAN, ANTI-TRUST 163-66 (1977).

[***] *See Gerard v. Almouli*, 746 F.2d 936 (2nd Cir. 1984) (no best efforts agreement where condition precedent fails).

[****] *See Tigg Corp. v. Dow Corning Corp.*, 962 F.2d 1119 (3rd Cir. 1992) (requirements contract with exclusive dealing clause imposes best efforts duty on buyer).

reasonable price at the time for delivery" if any of the three circumstances stated in UCC 2-305(1) have occurred. Read that subsection, please. If, on the other hand, there was no intention to be bound "unless the price be fixed or agreed and it is not fixed or agreed," the remedies of the parties are limited to restitution. UCC 2-305(4).* In *Flowers Baking Co. of Lynchburg, Inc. v. R-P Packaging, Inc.*, 329 S.E.2d 462, 465 (Va. 1985), the court, in concluding that there was no intention to contract, stated:

> While it is true that the UCC has greatly modified the rigors of the common-law rules governing the formation of contracts, it remains a prerequisite that the parties' words and conduct must manifest an intention to be bound. Although they may make a contract which deliberately leaves material terms open for future determination, no contract results where their words and conduct demonstrate a lack of intention to contract. * * * Such a lack is not remedied by evidence of custom and usage in the trade * * * or by a written memorandum purporting to confirm oral discussion which did not in themselves amount to an agreement * * *.

The parties may also agree that one of the parties is to fix the price. Prior to the 1952 Official Text, UCC 2-305(2) provided: "A price to be fixed by the seller or by the buyer means a reasonable price for him to fix and he has the burden of establishing its reasonableness." *See* PROPOSED FINAL DRAFT, SPRING 1950. Comment 3 provided: "Subsection (2) * * * grants a reasonable leeway within which the party chosen by the contract may fix the price, but it also limits him to a 'reasonable price.' The uncommercial idea that an agreement that the seller may fix the price means that he may fix any price he may wish is rejected not only by the express qualification of subsection (2) that the price so fixed must be reasonable, but also by the obligation of good faith and of commercial standards imposed by this Act."

Section 2-305(2) now uses the good faith concept to cabin the price fixer's discretion. How much discretion does a party have to fix a price that is not a reasonable market price?** In *Au Rustproofing Center, Inc. v. Gulf Oil Corp.*, 755

---

* The pre-Code law is reviewed in William L. Prosser, *Open Price in Contracts For the Sale of Goods,* 16 MINN. L. REV. 733 (1932); Comment, *UCC Section 2-305(1)(c): Open Price Terms and the Intention of the Parties in Sales Contracts,* 1 VALPO. L. REV. 381 (1967).

** *See TCP Industries, Inc. v. Uniroyal, Inc.*, 661 F. 2d 542 (6ᵗʰ Cir. 1981) (setting prices for a chemical within a range of market prices on both the spot and long term market was good
(continued...)

F.2d 1231 (6th Cir. 1985), Au contracted with Gulf to be a Gulf dealer for a period of ten years. Gulf agreed to pay Au a special allowance of two cents per gallon on all gasoline purchased at a "tankwagon" price to be set without contractual restriction by Gulf. After the 1973 oil crisis ruptured the market, Gulf suspended the special discount and charged Au a "tankwagon" price that was not competitive with other suppliers in the relevant market area. As a result, Au's gross margins substantially declined. In the ensuing litigation, the court held, *inter alia*, that Gulf had no duty to fix competitive gasoline prices for its dealers:

> [A]lthough Gulf assumed the implied duty of a party controlling the price to set a reasonable price * * * the record does not establish that the high price Gulf charged to Au was so unreasonable that it negated Gulf's substantial performance of the implied duty. * * * Gulf is required to fix a price in good faith. * * * Good faith includes observance of reasonable commercial standards of fair dealing in the trade or the general range of market prices. * * * Au contends that because its competitors sold gasoline for less than Au could buy it from Gulf, Gulf's prices were unreasonable. * * * In our view, this contention is insufficient to establish that prices set by Gulf contravened reasonable commercial standards in the gasoline market or otherwise constituted bad faith or commercially unreasonable behavior.

Id. at 1235-36. Fixing the "tankwagon" price continues to generate litigation. Consider the following case.

MATHIS V. EXXON CORPORATION
UNITED STATES COURT OF APPEALS, FIFTH CIRCUIT, 2002
302 F.3D 448

JERRY E. SMITH, CIRCUIT JUDGE

This is a breach of contract suit brought by fifty-four gasoline station franchisees against Exxon Corporation ("Exxon") for violating the Texas analogue

---

** (...continued)
faith); *Wayman v. Amoco Oil Co.*, 923 F. Supp. 1322 (D. Kan. 1996) (suggesting that the price must be fixed in a "normal" or "usual" non-discriminatory process); *Havird Oil Co. v. Marathon Oil Co.*, 149 F.3d 283 (4th Cir. 1998) (good faith price fixed where seller charged all its customers a non-discriminatory wholesale price which was competitive with other wholesalers and conduct followed "reasonable commercial standards of fair dealing in the trade").

of the Uniform Commercial Code's open price provision. We affirm.

I.

Exxon markets its commercial gas bound for retailers primarily through three arrangements: franchisee contracts, jobber contracts, and company operated retail stores ("CORS"). A franchisee rents Exxon-branded gas stations and enters into a sales contract for the purchase of Exxon-brand gas. The contract sets the monthly quantity of gas the franchisee must purchase and allows Exxon to set the price he must pay. The franchisee pays the dealer tank wagon price ("DTW") and takes delivery of the gas at his station.

A jobber contract requires the purchaser to pay the "rack price," which usually is lower than the price charged to franchisees. There is no sale of gas to CORS by Exxon, because the stores are owned by Exxon and staffed by its employees. Instead, an intra-company accounting is recorded that is equivalent to the price charged franchisees in the same price zone.

All the plaintiff franchisees operate stations in the greater Houston, Texas, and Corpus Christi, Texas, areas. The genesis of the dispute is the allegation that Exxon has violated the law and its contracts with these franchisees for the purpose of converting their stores to CORS by driving the franchisees out of business.

Since 1994, franchisees have been barred from purchasing their gas from jobbers, so all their purchases have been governed by the terms of the Retail Motor Fuel Store Sales Agreement, under which the "DEALER agrees to buy and receive directly from EXXON all of the EXXON-branded gasoline bought by DEALER, and at least seventy-five percent (75%) of the volume shown in [a specified schedule].... DEALER will pay EXXON for delivered products at EXXON's price in effect at the time of the loading of the delivery vehicle."

This "price in effect," also known as the dealer tank wagon price ("DTW"), forms the heart of the present dispute. Exxon claims this arrangement is the industry standard and that almost all franchisor-franchisee sales of gasoline are governed by a similar price term. Plaintiffs respond that the DTW price charged under this clause is "consistently higher" than the rack price paid by jobbers plus transportation costs.

The franchisees originally filed Sherman Act, Clayton, Act, and Petroleum Marketing Practices Act ("PMPA") claims against Exxon in addition to the breach of contract claim. The antitrust claims were abandoned, and the district court granted Exxon a judgment as a matter of law ("j.m.l.") on the PMPA claims. The court retained jurisdiction over the purely state law causes of action that had been supplemental to the federal claims.

Trial proceeded solely on the Texas breach of contract action, with only six plaintiffs testifying. The thrust of their testimony was that Exxon had set the DTW price at an uncompetitive level to drive them out of business (so as to replace their stores with CORS). Some of the plaintiffs testified that their franchises were unprofitable; they presented documents and witnesses to show that Exxon intended that result to drive them out of business.

The franchisees also submitted a market study showing that 62% of the franchisees in Corpus Christi were selling gas below the DTW price. The franchisees supported their theory of the case by calling Barry Pulliam as an expert witness on the economics of the gasoline market in Houston and Corpus Christi. Pulliam concluded that Exxon's DTW price was not commercially reasonable from an economic perspective because it was a price that, over time, put the purchaser at a competitive disadvantage. Pulliam noted that "commercial reasonableness" is a legal term, and he was not there to define it for the jury.

Pulliam's conclusion rested on two main facts. First, he showed that 75% of the franchisee's competitors were able to purchase gasoline at a lower price. Second, he calculated a commercially reasonable DTW price by adding normal distribution charges to the average rack price of gasoline charged by Exxon and its competitors. He concluded that Exxon's DTW price exceeded the sum of these other prices by four or more cents per gallon.

Exxon countered with Michael Keeley, who testified that Exxon's DTW price was commercially reasonable because it reflected the company's investment in land, the store, transportation, and managers. Keeley explained that Exxon recovers these costs through rent and the sale of gas.

The jury awarded $5,723,657--exactly 60% of the overcharge calculated by Pulliam. * * * [Exxon appealed on three grounds, only one of which is reproduced here.]

II.

Exxon contends that because it charged its franchisees a DTW price comparable to that charged by its competitors, the breach of contract claim is precluded as a matter of law. * * * The question is whether there was evidence permitting the jury to conclude that Exxon breached a term of the franchise agreement.

III.

Texas law, which tracks the Uniform Commercial Code, implies a good faith component in any contract with an open price term. Specifically,

[t]he parties if they so intend can conclude a contract for sale even though the price is not settled. In such a case the price is a reasonable price at the

time of delivery ... A price to be fixed by the seller or by the buyer means
a price for him to fix in good faith.

Tex. Com. & Bus. Code Ann. § 2.305 (Vernon 2002). The parties agree that the
franchise agreement term governing the purchase of gasoline is an open price term.

The meaning of "good faith" is further defined in several other sections of the
code. The definitions section explains good faith as "honesty in fact in the conduct
or transaction concerned." Tex. Com. & Bus. Code Ann. § 1.201(19) (Vernon
2002). Wherever the term "good faith" is used throughout the code, it means "as
least what is here stated." Tex. Com. & Bus. Code Ann. § 1.201(19) cmt. 19
(Vernon 2002).

Additional meaning to the term may be added within a given article. *Id.*
Section 2.103, regarding merchants, further explains the term: " 'Good faith' in the
case of a merchant means honesty in fact and the observance of reasonable
commercial standards of fair dealing in the trade." Tex. Com. & Bus. Code Ann. §
2.103 (Vernon 2002). Finally, "[g]ood faith includes the observance of reasonable
commercial standards of fair dealing in the trade if the party is a merchant. (Section
2.103). But, in the normal case a 'posted price,' 'price in effect,' 'market price,' or
the like satisfies the good faith requirement." Tex. Com. & Bus. Code Ann. § 2.305
cmt. 3 (Vernon 2002).

The key disagreement is over what constitutes a breach of the duty of good
faith. Exxon contends it has satisfied that duty because it has charged the plaintiffs
a DTW price within the range of its competitors' DTW prices, thereby satisfying
the "commercial reasonableness" meaning of good faith. Plaintiffs respond that
good faith encompasses both objective and subjective duties. Even if Exxon is
right, and its prices are within the range of its competitors', the argument runs, a
subjective intent to drive the franchisees out of business would abridge the good
faith duty of the open price term.

The pivotal provision is comment 3 to § 2.305. Some of the language of
comment 3 and § 2.103 leaves the meaning of good faith for open price terms in
doubt. Comment 3 mentions that good faith "includes" commercial reasonableness,
but notes that certain established prices satisfy the good faith requirement. Section
2.103 defines good faith with the subjective "honesty in fact" test. Thus, plaintiffs
argue that an open price set according to a fixed schedule is set in good faith only
if there is no improper motive animating the price-setter. Exxon replies that
comment 3 speaks directly to prices set by a fixed schedule and consecrates them
as in good faith per se.

In the absence of comment 3, there is no doubt Exxon would be subject to both the subjective "honesty in fact" good faith of § 1.201(19) and the objective "commercial reasonableness" good faith of § 2.103. The difficult question is whether comment 3 creates an exception to the normal principles of good faith governing the sale of goods.

No court in this circuit, and no Texas state court, has squarely addressed this question. Fortunately, because the Texas open price provision replicates that of the UCC, we can seek guidance from other courts.

To decide whether comment 3 creates an exception, we turn first to the text of the comment and the related sections of the Texas version of the UCC. In full, comment 3 reads,

> Subsection (2), dealing with the situation where the price is to be fixed by one party rejects the uncommercial idea that an agreement that the seller may fix the price means that he may fix any price he may wish by the express qualification that the price so fixed must be fixed in good faith. Good faith includes observance of reasonable commercial standards of fair dealing in the trade if the party is a merchant. (Section 2-103). But in the normal case a "posted price" or a future seller's or buyer's "given price," "price in effect," "market price," or the like satisfies the good faith requirement.

Tex. Com. & Bus. Code Ann. § 2.305 cmt. 3 (Vernon 2002).

The bare text offers little to resolve the question. First, the comment notes that good faith "includes" reasonable commercial standards. This implies that the good faith required of a merchant setting an open price term encompasses both objective and subjective elements. The comment also creates a good faith safe harbor for such merchants when they use various sorts of fixed prices. But this safe harbor is applicable only in the "normal case." This suggests the safe harbor is not absolute, but it does nothing to define what takes a case out of the safe harbor.

As we will explain, we conclude that the "normal case" of comment 3 is coextensive with a merchant's residual "honesty in fact" duty embodied in §§ 1.201(19) and 2.103. Thus, the comment embraces both the objective (commercial reasonableness) and subjective (honesty in fact) senses of good faith; objective good faith is satisfied by a "price in effect" as long as there is honesty in fact (a "normal case"). This conclusion finds support in three sources: the structure of the UCC, its legislative history, and the caselaw.

Reading comment 3 to embody two different meanings of "good faith" tracks the general structure of the UCC. Courts and commentators have recognized that the meaning of "good faith" is not uniform throughout the code. The cases and commentary treat the "good faith" found in article 1 as subjective and the good faith found only in article 2 as objective. Thus, there is nothing inconsistent in comment 3's using "good faith" in both the objective and the subjective senses.

The history of comment 3 bolsters this conclusion. Some drafters of the UCC worried that for the "great many industries where sales are not made at fixed prices," such as the steel industry, where "practically every contract" is made at "the seller's price in effect," if § 2-305 "is to apply ... it means that in every case the seller is going to be in a lawsuit ... or he could be, because there isn't any outside standard at all." *Proceedings of Enlarged Editorial Bd. Of Am. Law Inst.* (Sunday Morning Session, Jan. 28, 1951) (statement of Bernard Broeker). The drafters considered wholly exempting such contracts from § 2-305, or stating that for a price in effect, the only test is whether the merchant engaged in price discrimination. One drafter explained that the steel industry wanted to make "clear that we do not have to establish that we are fixing reasonable prices, because that gets you into the rate of return of profit, whether you are using borrowed money, and all those questions." *Id.*

The committee responded to these worries with the current comment 3: "[I]n the normal case a 'posted price' or a future seller's or buyer's 'given price,' 'price in effect,' 'market price,' or the like satisfies the good faith requirement." The drafter's solution was to avoid objective good faith challenges to prices set by reference to some "price in effect," while preserving challenges to discriminatory pricing. *See Hearing Before the Enlarged Editorial Board January* 27-29, 1951, VI BUSINESS LAWYER 164, 186 (1951) (explaining this intent). Nothing in the proceedings leading to the addition of comment 3 suggests that the overall subjective good faith duty of §§ 1-201 and 2-103 was to be supplanted; the evidence is quite to the contrary.

The drafters ultimately rejected two suggested addendums to § 2-305:

An agreement to the effect that the price shall be or be adjusted to, or be based upon, or determined by reference to the seller's going price, price in effect, regular price, market price, established price, or the like, at the time of the agreement or at any earlier or later time, is not an agreement to which this subsection is applicable. ... An agreement such as this is an agreement under which the seller or the buyer does not have any burden of showing anything other than that he has not singled out the particular other party for discrimination.

Proceedings of Enlarged Editorial Bd. (statement of Bernard Broeker). Both of these recommendations are more sweeping than is the language ultimately adopted.

The first would have omitted any mention of the good faith duty for open price provisions; the second would have limited the duty of the price- setter to that of avoiding discrimination.

The existing comment, however, avoids challenges to prices set according to an open price term unless that challenge is outside the normal type of case. Although price discrimination was the type of aberrant case on the minds of the drafters, price discrimination is merely a subset of what constitutes such an aberrant case. Any lack of subjective, honesty-in-fact good faith is abnormal; price discrimination is only the most obvious way a price-setter acts in bad faith--by treating similarly-situated buyers differently.

The caselaw supports this interpretation of comment 3. Courts that have addressed the normalcy question have consistently held that a lack of subjective good faith takes a challenge outside the bounds of what is normal.[1]

Like the plaintiffs in *Nanakuli, Allapattah,* and *Wayman,* the franchisees here are alleging a breach of good faith grounded not in Exxon's failure to price in accord with an established schedule, but in its failure to set the price in good faith. Suits recognizing such a cause of action are rare, and with good reason: We would be ill-advised to consider a case to be outside the norm based only on an allegation of improper motive by the party setting the price.

Plaintiffs produced enough evidence to escape comment 3's "normal case" limitation. They showed, for example, that Exxon planned to replace a number of its franchises with CORS, that the DTW price was higher than the sum of the rack price and transportation, that Exxon prevented the franchisees from purchasing gas from jobbers after 1994, and that a number of franchisees were unprofitable or

---

[1] *See, e.g., Nanakuli Paving & Rock Co. v. Shell Oil Co.*, 664 F.2d 772, 806 (9th Cir.1981) (stating that "the dispute here was not over the amount of the increase--that is, the price that the seller fixed--but over the manner in which that increase was put into effect"); *Allapattah v. Exxon Corp.*, 61 F.Supp.2d 1308, 1322 (S.D.Fla.1999) ("Because the parties' dispute is not over the actual amount of the purchase price Exxon charged for its wholesale gasoline to its dealers, but rather over the manner in which the wholesale price was calculated without considering the double charge for credit card processing, the instant action is not the 'normal' case."); *cf. Wayman v. Amoco Oil Co.*, 923 F.Supp. 1322, 1349 (D.Kan.1996), *aff'd*, 145 F.3d 1347 (10th Cir.1998) ("[T]his court believes the present case is a normal case. If there was evidence that Amoco had, for example, engaged in discriminatory pricing or tried to run plaintiffs out of business, then the court's decision might be different.").

non-competitive.[2]

For example, one Exxon document stated that the company's "Marketing Strategy for 1992-1997 is to reduce Dealer stores (est. 30%)." Another document set forth Exxon's plans to reduce dealer stations in Houston from 95 to 45, and to increase CORS from 83 to 150, between 1997 and 2003. James Carter, the Regional Director of the Exxon/Mobil Fuels Marketing Company, testified that Exxon made more of a profit from a CORS than from an independent lessee store. These plans and observations were validated by the fact that the number of dealer stations steadily declined.

An exhibit called the "Houston Screening Study" evaluated the strategy of "surplusing" (i.e., eliminating) 21 of 37 locations inside the Highway 610 loop. Of the 93 lessee-dealer stations, 69 would be done away with, but 73 of the 91 CORS would be kept.

Further indication of plans to shift from dealer-lessees to CORS is shown by Exxon's dissatisfaction with outlets featuring service bays. Exxon documents showed that service bays--generally associated with lessee-dealer locations-- were becoming less profitable, while stations with convenience stores-- generally associated with CORS--were the wave of the future. A document entitled "Retail Store Chain Outlook" revealed Exxon's plan to reduce stations with service bays from 2,506 to 190 from 1991 to 2005. That document included a plan to "[e]xpand CORS to improve profitability and to compete efficiently with private brands/distributors" and "[e]mphasize CORS operations in markets with high level of rack to retail competition."

Exxon's answer on appeal is that these documents "say nothing about using pricing to accomplish a 'plan' to eliminate dealers." Although that is so, there was sufficient evidence on this issue to go to the jury, which was free to, and apparently did, draw the inference connecting pricing to the elimination of dealer-lessees. The consequence of the jury's decision is that this case exceeds the "normal case" limit of § 2.305 comment 3.

We still, however, must examine the content of the duty of subjective good faith. Although no Texas or Fifth Circuit case has squarely addressed the meaning of the good faith clause of § 2.305, Texas courts repeatedly have held that the

---

[2] This case is distinguishable from *Meyer v. Amerada Hess*, 541 F.Supp. 321 (D.N.J.1982), in which the court found "no evidence" of dishonesty in the setting of a DTW price. In Meyer, though, the only evidence tending to show bad faith was the retailer's unprofitability. *Id.* at 331. Significantly, other retailers were profiting, and the plaintiff retailer was being charged rent below the economic value of the property. *Id.* at 332.

"honesty in fact" definition of good faith found in § 1.201(19) is tied to the actual belief of the participant in the transaction. Thus, the same version of the facts accepted by the jury--that Exxon intended to drive the franchisees out of business--that takes this case out of the "normal" set of cases for purposes of comment 3 also satisfies the criteria for bad faith.[3]

Exxon's bad faith, in this regard, is shown by the record. Facing the competition of self-service stations that were either selling food and other goods or had bare pumps with no overhead costs incurred in servicing vehicles, Exxon decided years ago that retail marketing through franchise dealers was becoming economically unsound. Although Exxon decided to move to CORS in Houston and jobbers in Corpus Christi, this decision was not communicated to its franchisees. Because of profit from their other sales, CORS could, and did, sell gas for less than the franchise dealers paid to Exxon for their gas. And the jobbers delivered Exxon gas to their dealers for less than Exxon franchisees were required to pay for their delivered gas, but Exxon prohibited its franchisees from buying at this lower price from the jobbers.

The loss of competitive position and profit to plaintiff franchisees was inevitable and foreseeable to Exxon. Although Exxon witnesses denied receiving complaints, its dealers testified that they had complained often and for years, without success, until the very eve of trial.

Accordingly, the jury's finding that Exxon breached its duty of good faith in setting the DTW price it charged the plaintiffs is not without foundation in the law or the evidence. As we have recounted, plaintiffs offered ample evidence tending to prove their version of price-setting. Accordingly, there is no error in the refusal to grant Exxon j.m.l. on the breach of contract claim. * * * * Affirmed. [Some footnotes omitted. Those retained have been renumbered.]

Notes

1. The *Mathis* reasoning was followed in a remarkably similar case in Texas

---

[3] *See also Allapattah*, 61 F.Supp.2d at 1322 (explaining that "a merchant [who] acts in a manner intended to drive a franchisee out of business" violates the duty of good faith found in the UCC). Similarly, one court has recognized that a "predatory intent" to "set the prices with the intent to drive [franchisees] out of business and take over the stations" is a claim cognizable under the good faith provisions of the UCC. *E.S. Bills, Inc. v. Tzucanow*, 38 Cal.3d 824, 215 Cal.Rptr. 278, 700 P.2d 1280, 1283-84 (1985).

state court. *HRN, Inc. v. Shell Oil Co.*, 102 S.W. 3d 205 (Tex. Ct. App. 2003) (same plaintiff's lawyers). The *Mathis* reasoning regarding the meaning of good faith was rejected in *Tom-Lin Enterprises, Inc. v. Sunoco, Inc.*, 349 F.3d 277 (6th Cir. 2003). The *Tom-Lin* court stated that under Ohio law, as opposed to Texas law, "honesty in fact" has an objective meaning. An action was not honest in fact if "commercially unjustifiable." *Id.* at 281. If that were true in Texas, would the *Mathis* court have come to a different conclusion?

2. What is the relationship between UCC 2-305(2) and (3)? In other words, if the price is not fixed in good faith, does UCC 2-305(3) come into play or is it aimed at a different fact scenario? Review the new definition of "good faith" in UCC 1-201(b)(20). Does that help?

3. Why would parties not just agree to a price instead of leaving the price open? How would you structure a deal to buy or sell goods in a volatile market?*

4. Neither Article 2A or UCITA contain a gap filler directed at an open price term. UCITA 305, concerning terms to be specified by one party, could be used regarding price. Such specification must be made in good faith and be commercially reasonable. UCITA 305(1). *Compare* CISG Art. 55.

Problem 4-4

Seller agreed in a writing signed by both Seller and Buyer to sell 1,000 sacks of Delaware Cobbler potatoes to Buyer, delivery at Buyer's plant by March 15, at a price "to be fixed by the seller." The market price on February 1 was $7 per sack. On March 15, Seller tendered delivery of the goods and fixed a price of $20 per sack. The current market price was $12 and rising. Buyer rejected the tender and "covered" under UCC 2-712 for $13 per sack. Both parties claim that the other breached the contract. Who should prevail?

Problem 4-5

In 1973, S, a producer of iron ore, and B, a manufacturer of steel, entered a 25 year contract for the supply of iron ore. S was obligated to deliver between 1,000 and 1,500 tons per month by rail. B agreed to pay the regular net contract rate for a ton of iron ore as published every three months in a trade Journal entitled "Iron and Steel World." The contract provided that in the event "Iron and Steel World"

---

* *See* Victor P. Goldberg, *Price Adjustment in Long-Term Contracts*, 1985 WIS. L. REV. 527.

ceased publication, "the parties shall mutually agree upon a rate for such iron ore, taking into consideration the contract rate being charged for one ton of iron ore by similarly situated parties." No provision for arbitration or mediation was made in the contract.

The relationship prospered. For a time, a representative of S served on B's board of directors and the parties frequently met to discuss economic developments and how the profits of both could be improved. In 1998, the contract was renewed for another 20 years, and S agreed to pay a 5% surcharge for each ton accepted to help B pay for new equipment purchased to deal exclusively with iron ore from S's mines.

In 2003, with the steel industry picking up steam because of the increasing demand in China, "Iron and Steel World" ceased publication. At the same time, S was approached by another steel manufacturer with a much more attractive proposal for a long-term contract. S and B negotiated a price for the first six months of 2003, but S refused to negotiate thereafter and terminated the contract. S argued either that the parties did not intend to contract if "Iron and Steel World" failed to publish a net price for iron ore or that if they did so intend the contract failed for indefiniteness. Either way, the contract was at an end. B argued that the requisite intention to contract was present in the parties course of performance and that other objective evidence existed in the market from which a price could be determined. Moreover, B urged the court to order S to comply with the contract by negotiating over a price and if no agreement was reached to either fill the gap with a "reasonable price" or appoint a mediator.

What result? Please support your conclusions by references to Article 2.*

Problem 4-6

B manufactures precious metal products and provides refining services. On July 1, S delivered 1,600 ounces of sterling silver to B under a contract for sale. B was to process the metal to determine its silver content and fix the price by multiplying the amount of silver by the market price on that day. S understood that B's normal processing time was four to six weeks. Due to B's negligence, however,

---

* The problem is taken from the case of *Oglebay Norton Co. v. Armco, Inc.*, 556 N.E.2d 515 (Ohio 1990), where the court adopted B's arguments. The *Oglebay* case is analyzed in Richard E. Speidel, *The Characteristics and Challenges of Relational Contracts,* 94 Nw. U. L. Rev. 823, 831-37 (2000).

the silver was misplaced and not found and processed until November 1. During this period, the per ounce price of silver was on the rise: July 1, it was $17.25; August 1, it was $18.50; August 15, it was $20; and November 1 it was $28. S, citing UCC 2-305(3), claims that it can cancel the contract and recover the silver and sell it on the open market (which continues to rise). B argues that the case is governed by UCC 2-305(2): thus, there was an enforceable contract even if B acted in bad faith and the price should be a reasonable price at the time when B should have completed the processing and fixed the price. How should the court rule?

C. Delivery Terms and Payment of the Price

If the parties' agreement does not otherwise provide, all goods called for by the contract will be tendered in a single delivery, UCC 2-307, at the seller's place of business or residence, UCC 2-308. The time for shipment or delivery is a reasonable time and the duration of the contact is also a reasonable time. UCC 2-309.* Specifications regarding assortment of the goods are generally the buyer's option and specifications regarding shipment are generally the seller's option. UCC 2-311(2). The buyer is generally obligated to pay at the time the buyer receives the goods, UCC 2-310(1) and (2), unless the buyer has agreed to pay against documents of title, in which case, payment must be made when the documents are received. UCC 2-310(3). Other particulars of performance may be specified by the parties after the making of the contract as long as they do so in good faith and within the limits of commercial reasonableness. UCC 2-311(1). We will come back to delivery and payment obligations of the parties in Chapter Six, *infra.*

SECTION 3. PRE-CONTRACT FACTS WHICH VARY, SUPPLEMENT, OR GIVE MEANING TO THE AGREEMENT

A. Introduction

Suppose the parties have concluded a bargain which is enforceable as a contract under Article 2 or Article 2A. Some or all of the terms of the bargain are contained

---

* *See Marjam Supply Co. v. BCT Walls & Ceilings, Inc.*, 2003 WL 21497515 (E.D. Pa. 2003) (factors that determine reasonable time for delivery include the nature of the goods, the purpose that the goods will be used for, the extent of the seller's knowledge of the buyer's intentions, transportation conditions, and the nature of the market).

in a record and authenticated by both parties. After performance commences, a dispute erupts over the obligations under the contract. The dispute may involve either the scope of the terms or the meaning of the terms embodied in the record. In either case, there is an honest disagreement. A party, to support an argument about the scope or meaning of the terms in the record, will undoubtedly seek to introduce evidence beyond the "four corners" of the record. Can the other party exclude this evidence and, if so, under what circumstances?

Reread the definition of agreement in UCC 1-201(b)(3). Under this expansive definition, agreement may include terms in the record and terms derived from "other circumstances including" trade usage, a prior course of dealing between the parties or the negotiations leading up to the particular bargain at stake. *See* UCC 1-303 [former 1-205, 2-208, 2A-207]. The question is when will terms that are extrinsic to the record be excluded from the evidence used to prove the parties' agreement.

The answer, found in the so-called parol evidence rule as set forth in UCC 2-202 and 2A-202 is when the parties expressly or impliedly have agreed to exclude those extrinsic terms. Put differently, the parties may evidence their intent to exclude the terms not in a record by adopting a record that is a final statement of all or some of the terms. If the parties have that intent as to a record, the parol evidence rule operates as a gate keeper that determines what evidence the finder of fact may consider in deciding terms that have actually been agreed to by the parties.

The first question to ask is whether the parol evidence rule applies at all. Read UCC 2-202 and 2A-202. For the rule to apply at all, the parties must have a record "intended by the parties as a final expression of their agreement with respect to such terms as are included therein." In the RESTATEMENT parlance, the parties have intended to at least partially "integrate" their agreement into a record. RESTATEMENT (SECOND) OF CONTRACTS 210.

Assuming that there is a record into which the agreement is at least partially integrated, the next question to ask is what evidence is barred and what evidence is admissible. The answer depends, in part, on the purpose for which the evidence is proffered. For example, if the evidence is offered to aid in the interpretation of terms already in the record, the parol evidence rule (strictly speaking) does not apply at all. On the other hand, if the evidence is offered to show terms that were agreed to prior or contemporaneously with the record but are not contained in the record, the parol evidence rule (depending on the intention of the parties) may apply.

If there is a partial integration, evidence that is barred is evidence of prior or contemporaneous agreements which contradict terms in the record. Evidence that is not barred is evidence of usage of trade, course of dealing, course of performance, and consistent additional terms to supplement terms in the record. However, if the agreement is totally integrated into the record (i.e. "complete and exclusive"), evidence of consistent additional terms to supplement the terms in the record is not allowed. In either a partially or totally integrated agreement, evidence of usage of trade, course of dealing, and course of performance are admissible to explain the terms in the record.

What should the test be to determine whether the agreement is totally or partially integrated into the record? What should be the test to determine whether the additional terms are consistent or contradictory? Can usage of trade, course of performance, and course of dealing be admitted to supplement the terms in the record if that evidence "contradicts" a term in the record? UCC 1-303 [former 1-205, 2-208, 2A-207]. Can the parties by agreement exclude evidence of usage of trade, course of performance, and course of dealing to either supplement or explain the terms in the record? What evidence other than usage of trade, course of dealing, and course of performance can be used to explain or interpret terms in the record? Does the term in the record have to be ambiguous in order for that explanatory evidence to be admitted? Is evidence drawn from the parties' discussions subsequent to the execution of the record admissible to supplement or explain a term in the record? Does the parol evidence rule bar evidence of fraud or mistake even if that evidence comes from the time period prior to execution of the record? These questions will occupy us in this section.

The following two cases address former 2-202 prior to its amendment in 2003. Compare former 2-202 to UCC 2-202 as amended in 2003. Would the result in these cases be altered if the amended version of UCC 2-202 applied?

B. Effect of Usage of Trade and Course of Dealing

COLUMBIA NITROGEN CORP. V. ROYSTER CO.
UNITED STATES COURT OF APPEALS, FOURTH CIRCUIT, 1971
451 F.2D 3

BUTZNER, CIRCUIT JUDGE

Columbia Nitrogen Corp. appeals a judgment in the amount of $750,000 in favor of F.S. Royster Guano Co. for breach of a contract for the sale of phosphate to Columbia by Royster. Columbia defended on the grounds that the contract, construed in light of the usage of the trade and course of dealing, imposed no duty to accept at the quoted prices the minimum quantities stated in the contract. It also asserted an antitrust defense and counterclaim based on Royster's alleged reciprocal trade practices. The district court excluded the evidence about course of dealing and usage of the trade. It submitted the antitrust issues based on coercive reciprocity to the jury, but refused to submit the alternative theory of non-coercive reciprocity. The jury found for Royster on both the contract claim and the antitrust counterclaim. We hold that Columbia's proffered evidence was improperly excluded and Columbia is entitled to a new trial on the contractual issues. With respect to the antitrust issues, we affirm.

I.

Royster manufactures and markets mixed fertilizers, the principal components of which are nitrogen, phosphate and potash. Columbia is primarily a producer of nitrogen, although it manufactures some mixed fertilizer. For several years Royster had been a major purchaser of Columbia's products, but Columbia had never been a significant customer of Royster. In the fall of 1966, Royster constructed a facility which enabled it to produce more phosphate than it needed in its own operations. After extensive negotiations, the companies executed a contract for Royster's sale of a minimum of 31,000 tons of phosphate each year for three years to Columbia, with an option to extend the term. The contract stated the price per ton, subject to an escalation clause dependent on production costs.

Phosphate prices soon plunged precipitously. Unable to resell the phosphate at a competitive price, Columbia ordered only part of the scheduled tonnage. At Columbia's request, Royster lowered its price for diammonium phosphate on shipments for three months in 1967, but specified that subsequent shipments would be at the original contract price. Even with this concession, Royster's price was still substantially above the market. As a result, Columbia ordered less than a tenth of the phosphate Royster was to ship in the first contract year. When pressed by Royster, Columbia offered to take the phosphate at the current market price and resell it without brokerage fee. Royster, however, insisted on the contract price. When Columbia refused delivery, Royster sold the unaccepted phosphate for Columbia's account at a price substantially below the contract price.

II.

Columbia assigns error to the pretrial ruling of the district court excluding all evidence on usage of the trade and course of dealing between the parties. It offered the testimony of witnesses with long experience in the trade that because of uncertain crop and weather conditions, farming practices, and government agricultural programs, express price and quantity terms in contracts for materials in the mixed fertilizer industry are mere projections to be adjusted according to market forces.[1]

Columbia also offered proof of its business dealings with Royster over the six-year period preceding the phosphate contract. Since Columbia had not been a significant purchaser of Royster's products, these dealings were almost exclusively nitrogen sales to Royster or exchanges of stock carried in inventory. The pattern which emerges, Columbia claimed, is one of repeated and substantial deviation from the stated amount or price, including four instances where Royster took none of the goods for which it had contracted. Columbia offered proof that the total variance amounted to more than $500,000 in reduced sales. This experience, a Columbia officer offered to testify, formed the basis of an understanding on which he

---

[1] Typical of the proffered testimony are the following excerpts:

"The contracts generally entered into between buyer and seller of materials has always been, in my opinion, construed to be the buyer's best estimate of his anticipated requirements for a given period of time. It is well known in our industry that weather conditions, farming practices, government farm control programs, change requirements from time to time. And therefore allowances were always made to meet these circumstances as they arose."

"Tonnage requirements fluctuate greatly, and that is one reason that the contracts are not considered as binding as most contracts are, because the buyer normally would buy on historical basis, but his normal average use would be per annum of any given material. Now that can be affected very decidedly by adverse weather conditions such as a drought, or a flood, or maybe governmental programs which we have been faced with for many, many years, seed grain programs. They pay the farmer not to plant. If he doesn't plant, he doesn't use the fertilizer. When the contracts are made, we do not know of all these contingencies and what they are going to be. So the contract is made for what is considered a fair estimate of his requirements. And, the contract is considered binding to the extent, on him morally, that if he uses the tonnage that he will execute the contract in good faith as the buyer. * * *"

"I have never heard of a contract of this type being enforced legally. * * * Well, it undoubtedly sounds ridiculous to people from other industries, but there is a very definite, several very definite reasons why the fertilizer business is always operated under what we call gentlemen's agreements. * * *"

"The custom in the fertilizer industry is that the seller either meets the competitive situation or releases the buyer from it upon proof that he can buy it at that price * * *. [T]hey will either have the option of meeting it or releasing him from taking additional tonnage or holding him to that price. * * *" And this custom exists "regardless of the contractual provisions."

"[T]he custom was that [these contracts] were not worth the cost of the paper they were printed on."

depended in conducting negotiations with Royster.

The district court held that the evidence should be excluded. It ruled that "custom and usage or course of dealing are not admissible to contradict the express, plain, unambiguous language of a valid written contract, which by virtue of its detail negates the proposition that the contract is open to variances in its terms."

* * *A number of Virginia cases have held that extrinsic evidence may not be received to explain or supplement a written contract unless the court finds the writing is ambiguous. * * * This rule, however, has been changed by the Uniform Commercial Code which Virginia has adopted. The Code expressly states that it "shall be liberally construed and applied to promote its underlying purposes and policies," which include "the expansion of commercial practices through custom, usage and agreement of the parties. * * *" Va. Code Ann. § 8.1-102 (1965). The importance of usage of trade and course of dealing between the parties is shown by § 8.2-202, which authorizes their use to explain or supplement a contract. The official comment states this section rejects the old rule that evidence of course of dealing or usage of trade can be introduced only when the contract is ambiguous. And the Virginia commentators, noting that "[t]his section reflects a more liberal approach to the introduction of parol evidence * * * than has been followed in Virginia," express the opinion that * * * similar Virginia cases no longer should be followed. Va. Code Ann. § 8.2-202, Va. Comment. * * * We hold, therefore, that a finding of ambiguity is not necessary for the admission of extrinsic evidence about the usage of the trade and the parties' course of dealing.

We turn next to Royster's claim that Columbia's evidence was properly excluded because it was inconsistent with the express terms of their agreement. There can be no doubt that the Uniform Commercial Code restates the well established rule that evidence of usage of trade and course of dealing should be excluded whenever it cannot be reasonably construed as consistent with the terms of the contract. *Division of Triple T Service, Inc. v. Mobil Oil Corp.*, 60 Misc. 2d 720, 304 N.Y.S.2d 191, 203 (1969), *aff'd mem.*, 311 N.Y.S.2d 961 (1970). Royster argues that the evidence should be excluded as inconsistent because the contract contains detailed provisions regarding the base price, escalation, minimum tonnage, and delivery schedules. The argument is based on the premise that because a contract appears on its face to be complete, evidence of course of dealing and usage of trade should be excluded. We believe, however, that neither the language nor the policy of the Code supports such a broad exclusionary rule. Section 8.2-202 expressly allows evidence of course of dealing or usage of trade to explain or supplement terms intended by the parties as a final expression of their agreement.

When this section is read in light of Va. Code Ann. § 8.1-205(4), it is clear that the test of admissibility is not whether the contract appears on its face to be complete in every detail, but whether the proffered evidence of course of dealing and trade usage reasonably can be construed as consistent with the express terms of the agreement.

The proffered testimony sought to establish that because of changing weather conditions, farming practices, and government agricultural programs, dealers adjusted prices, quantities, and delivery schedules to reflect declining market conditions. For the following reasons it is reasonable to construe this evidence as consistent with the express terms of the contract:

The contract does not expressly state that course of dealing and usage of trade cannot be used to explain or supplement the written contract.

The contract is silent about adjusting prices and quantities to reflect a declining market. It neither permits nor prohibits adjustment, and this neutrality provides a fitting occasion for recourse to usage of trade and prior dealing to supplement the contract and explain its terms.

Minimum tonnages and additional quantities are expressed in terms of "Products Supplied Under Contract." Significantly, they are not expressed as just "Products" or as "Products Purchased Under Contract." The description used by the parties is consistent with the proffered testimony.

Finally, the default clause of the contract refers only to the failure of the buyer to pay for delivered phosphate. During the contract negotiations, Columbia rejected a Royster proposal for liquidated damages of $10 for each ton Columbia declined to accept. On the other hand, Royster rejected a Columbia proposal for a clause that tied the price to the market by obligating Royster to conform its price to offers Columbia received from other phosphate producers. The parties, having rejected both proposals, failed to state any consequences of Columbia's refusal to take delivery–the kind of default Royster alleges in this case. Royster insists that we span this hiatus by applying the general law of contracts permitting recovery of damages upon the buyer's refusal to take delivery according to the written provisions of the contract. This solution is not what the Uniform Commercial Code prescribes. Before allowing damages, a court must first determine whether the buyer has in fact defaulted. It must do this by supplementing and explaining the agreement with evidence of trade usage and course of dealing that is consistent with the contract's express terms. Va. Code Ann. §§ 8.1-205(4), 8.2-202. Faithful adherence to this mandate reflects the reality of the marketplace and avoids the overly legalistic interpretations which the Code seeks to abolish.

Royster also contends that Columbia's proffered testimony was properly rejected because it dealt with mutual willingness of buyer and seller to adjust contract terms to the market. Columbia, Royster protests, seeks unilateral adjustment. This argument misses the point. What Columbia seeks to show is a practice of mutual adjustments so prevalent in the industry and in prior dealings between the parties that it formed a part of the agreement governing this transaction. It is not insisting on a unilateral right to modify the contract.

Nor can we accept Royster's contention that the testimony should be excluded under the contract clause:

> "No verbal understanding will be recognized by either party hereto; this contract expresses all the terms and conditions of the agreement, shall be signed in duplicate, and shall not become operative until approved in writing by the Seller."

Course of dealing and trade usage are not synonymous with verbal understandings, terms and conditions. Section 8.2-202 draws a distinction between supplementing a written contract by consistent additional terms and supplementing it by course of dealing or usage of trade. Evidence of additional terms must be excluded when "the court finds the writing to have been intended also as a complete and exclusive statement of the terms of the agreement." Significantly, no similar limitation is placed on the introduction of evidence of course of dealing or usage of trade. Indeed the official comment notes that course of dealing and usage of trade, unless carefully negated, are admissible to supplement the terms of any writing, and that contracts are to be read on the assumption that these elements were taken for granted when the document was phrased. Since the Code assigns course of dealing and trade usage unique and important roles, they should not be conclusively rejected by reading them into stereotyped language that makes no specific reference to them. *Cf. Provident Tradesmen' Bank & Trust Co. v. Pemberton*, 196 Pa. Super. 180, 173 A.2d 780. Indeed, the Code's official commentators urge that overly simplistic and overly legalistic interpretation of a contract should be shunned.

We conclude therefore that Columbia's evidence about course of dealing and usage of trade should have been admitted. Its exclusion requires that the judgment against Columbia must be set aside and the case retried. * * *

[After affirming the district court's charges to the jury on modification and damage issues and judgment on the antitrust issue, the court remanded the case for a new trial.] [Some footnotes omitted. Those retained are renumbered.]

Notes

1. To achieve the outcome in *Columbia Nitrogen*, the moving party was required: (1) to prove the existence and scope of the trade usage "as facts," UCC 1-303(c) [former 1-205(2)]; (2) to prove that both parties were in the trade or, if not, that they were or "should be" aware of the usage, UCC 1-303 (d) [former 1-205(3)]; (3) to persuade the court to admit the usage for a proper purpose, *i.e.*, to "give particular meaning to and supplement or qualify" the terms of the agreement, UCC 1-303(d) [former 1-205(3)]; (4) to survive a possible claim that the established usage was unreasonable, UCC 1-303, cmt. 5 [former 1-205, cmt. 6]; and (5) to persuade the court that the usage can be "construed wherever reasonable as consistent" with any express terms purporting to "contract out" of the usage. UCC 1-303(e) [former 1-205(4)]. The outcome in the *Columbia Nitrogen* case has been criticized:

> The court's attempt to demonstrate a possible consistent interpretation is a strained exercise in semantic quibbling that * * * boggles the reasonable mind. The opinion reads so poorly because the court did not address the correct issue. * * * The inquiry should have examined the relationship of the usage of trade to the facts of the case. That 'contracts' have been treated as 'fair estimates' is not enough: additional facts must be known about the types of contracts so regarded. * * * The * * * opinion, however, did not discuss relevance and only stated some of the facts about the usage of trade. The facts that are detailed in the opinion require further inquiry because they indicate that the disputed contract was unlike the contracts treated as estimates in the trade.

Roger W. Kirst, *Usage of Trade and Course of Dealing: Subversion of the UCC Theory,* 1977 U. ILL. L. F. 811, 844-45 (footnotes omitted). Do you agree?

2. Shell Oil entered long-term contracts for the supply of Nanakuli's asphalt requirements on the Island of Oahu, Hawaii. Under the 1969 contract, the price was to be Shell's posted price at the time of delivery. In January, 1974, Shell raised the price from $44 to $76 per ton. Nanakuli, however, had previously committed 7,200 tons of asphalt to paving contractors at prices calculated at the $44 per ton price. When Shell charged $76 per ton for the asphalt, Nanakuli refused to pay this price and claimed that it was entitled to "price protection" under a usage of the asphalt paving trade in Hawaii and that this usage was incorporated into the contract. Price protection required that Shell hold the price on all tonnage committed in reliance upon the $44 per ton price prior to the price increase. The jury returned a verdict

of $220,000 for Nanakuli on the ground that Shell had breached the contract by failing to protect the $44 price. The federal district judge set aside the verdict and granted Shell's motion for judgment n.o.v. The Ninth Circuit Court of Appeals vacated the district court's decision and reinstated the jury verdict.

In a long, complex opinion, which was clearly sympathetic to the UCC's emphasis on context, the Court held, *inter alia*, that: (1) the trial judge did not abuse his discretion in defining the applicable trade as the asphalt paving trade, rather than the purchase and sale of asphalt alone; (2) the "price protection" usage in that trade was established and Shell was or should have been aware of it; (3) the usage was reinforced by the conduct of Shell in the performance of the contract with Nanakuli; and (4) the jury could have reasonably construed the price protection usage as consistent with the express price term in the contract and a clause purporting to exclude all prior "oral" agreements from the writing.

The court stated that the agreement must be examined in "light of the close, symbiotic relations between Shell and Nanakuli on the island of Oahu, whereby the expansion of Shell on the island was intimately connected with the business growth of Nanakuli." In addition, the UCC "looks to the actual performance of a contract as the best indication of what the parties intended those terms to mean." Finally, the court concluded that "price protection" was consistent with the express price term "as long as it does not totally negate it." The usage "only came into play at times of price increases and only for work committed prior to those increases on non-escalation contracts." It was, therefore an "exception to, rather than a total negation of, the express price term" which was known to Shell and constituted an "intended part of the agreement, as that term is broadly defined by the Code. * * *" *Nanakuli Paving & Rock Co. v. Shell Oil Co., Inc.*, 664 F.2d 772 (9th Cir. 1981). The *Nanakuli* court cited and discussed *Columbia Nitrogen* as a "leading case" in a group of federal decisions that "usually have been lenient in not ruling out consistent additional terms or trade usage for apparent inconsistency with express terms." The court, however, noted Professor Kirst's criticism of *Columbia Nitrogen* for failing to examine the relationship of the trade usage to the facts of the case, but concluded that this objection had been met in *Nanakuli*.*

3. It is clear that particular parties can "contract out" of a general usage of trade which otherwise would be part of the agreement. UCC 1-303(e) [former 1-

---

* *See generally* Amy H. Kastley, *Stock Equipment for the Bargain in Fact: Trade Usage, "Express Terms," and Consistency Under Section 1-205 of the Uniform Commercial Code*, 64 N. Car. L. Rev. 777, 788-791 (1986).

205(4)]. Draft a one sentence clause which, in your judgment, would be effective to exclude the usages involved in the *Columbia Nitrogen* and *Shell Oil* cases.

4.   A number of questions have been raised about the UCC's link between agreement in particular deals and trade usage. Is usage of trade an appropriate type of evidence to supplement or interpret terms in the writing? Does usage of trade actually exist in a given industry?[*] Does usage of trade, to the extent it can be proven, reflect principles that the parties would want in their agreement?[**] If such usage is not allowed as evidence on these types of issues, is there a superior mechanism for interpreting or supplementing the written terms given the limits of drafting and of the human ability to think of all the possibilities?[***]

C. The Parol Evidence Rule

ALASKA NORTHERN DEVELOPMENT, INC. V. ALYESKA PIPELINE SERVICE CO.
SUPREME COURT OF ALASKA, 1983
666 P.2D 33, *CERT. DENIED*, 464 U.S. 1041 (1984)

COMPTON, JUSTICE

Alaska Northern Development, Inc. ("AND") appeals a judgment in favor of

---

[*]   *See* Lisa Bernstein, *The Questionable Empirical Basis of Article 2's Incorporation Strategy: A Preliminary Study*, 66 U. CHI. L. REV. 710 (1999).

[**]   *See* Lisa Bernstein, *Merchant Law in a Merchant Court: Rethinking the Code's Search for Immanent Business Norms*, 144 U. PA. L. REV. 1765 (1996); Richard A. Epstein, *Confusion About Custom: Disentangling Informal Customs from Standard Contractual Provisions*, 66 U. CHI. L. REV. 821 (1999). *But see* Deborah A. Schmedemann, *Beyond Words: An Empirical Study of Context in Contract Creation*, 55 S.C. L. REV. 145 (2003); David V. Snyder, *Language and Formalities in Commercial Contracts: A Defense of Custom and Conduct*, 54 SMU L. REV. 617 (2001).

[***]   *See* Clayton P. Gillette, *Harmony and Stasis in Trade Usages For International Sales*, 39 VA. J. INT'L L. 707 (1999). *See also* Robert E. Scott, *The Case for Formalism in Relational Contract*, 94 NW. U. L. REV. 847 (2000) (arguing that the Code's "grand experiment in functional interpretation" has failed because the parties are competent to resolve disputes in context and the courts are incompetent to search for and apply trade usage). *But see* William J. Woodward, Jr., *Neoformalism in a Real World of Forms*, 2001 WIS. L. REV. 971 (2001) (arguing that move to increased formalism in interpretation of contracts is based upon a false premise of the negotiated deal rather than the usual situation of standard form contracts).

Alyeska Pipeline Service Co. ("Alyeska") in a dispute involving contract formation and interpretation. For the reasons stated below, we affirm.

I. Factual and Procedural Background

In late October or early November 1976, David Reed, a shareholder and corporate president of AND, initiated discussion with Alyeska personnel in Fairbanks regarding the purchase of surplus parts. The Alyeska employees with whom Reed dealt were Juel Tyson, Clarence Terwilleger and Donald Bruce.

After a series of discussions, Terwilleger indicated that Reed's proposal should be put in writing so it could be submitted to management. With the assistance of AND's legal counsel, Reed prepared a letter of intent dated December 10, 1976. In this letter, AND proposed to purchase "the entire Alyeska inventory of Caterpillar parts." The place for the purchase price was left blank.

Alyeska responded with its own letter of intent dated December 11, 1976. The letter was drafted by Bruce and Tyson in consultation with William Rickett, Alyeska's manager of Contracts and Material Management. Again, the price term was absent. The letter contained the following language, which is the focus of this lawsuit: "Please consider this as said letter of intent, *subject to the final approval of the owner committee.*" (Emphasis added.)

Reed was given an unsigned draft of the December 11 letter, which was reviewed by AND's legal counsel. Reed then met with Rickett, and they agreed on sixty-five percent of Alyeska's price as the price term to be filled in the blank on the December 11 letter. Rickett filled in the blank as agreed and signed the letter. In March 1977, the owner committee rejected the proposal embodied in the December 11 letter of intent.

AND contends that the parties understood the subject to approval language to mean that the Alyeska owner committee[1] would review the proposed agreement only to determine whether the price was fair and reasonable. Alyeska contends that Reed was never advised of any such limitation on the authority of the owner committee. In April 1977, AND filed a complaint alleging that there was a contract between AND and Alyeska, which Alyeska breached. The complaint was later amended to include counts for reformation and punitive damages. * * *

[Alyeska moved for summary judgment on the punitive damages and breach of contract counts. The superior court granted summary judgment in favor of Alyeska on both counts. The court doubted whether any contract was formed and stated that

---

[1] The owner committee is composed of the owner oil companies of Alyeska, a joint venture.

the "only way in which AND might prevail was on the [theory that] the letters could be construed as an offer followed by a counter-offer limiting the authority of the owner committee to review only the contract price." The court ruled that AND could not establish a breach of contract claim under [that] construction of the letters because the parol evidence rule barred the admission of extrinsic evidence that might limit the scope of the owner committee's approval power.[2] The only recourse for AND, therefore, was to seek reformation of the December 11 letter that limited the owner committee approval clause. After a six week trial, the court denied reformation, granted Alyeska's motion and awarded attorney fees.]

On appeal, AND does not challenge the superior court's denial of reformation. Instead, it contends that the superior court erred in granting summary judgment on the breach of contract and punitive damages counts, erred in denying a trial by jury on the reformation count, erred in not permitting cross-examination for purposes of impeachment, and erred in awarding attorney's fees to Alyeska.

II. Application of the Parol Evidence Rule

The superior court held that the parol evidence rule of the Uniform Commercial Code, section 2-202, codified as AS 45.02.202, applied to the December 11 letter and therefore no extrinsic evidence could be presented to a jury which limited the owner committee's right of approval. AND contends that the court erred in applying the parol evidence rule. We disagree.

In order to exclude parol evidence concerning the inclusion of additional terms to a writing, a court must make the following determinations. First, the court must determine whether the writing under scrutiny was integrated, *i.e.*, intended by the parties as a final expression of their agreement with respect to some or all of the terms included in the writing. Second, the court must determine whether evidence of a prior or contemporaneous agreement contradicts or is inconsistent with the integrated portion. If the evidence is contradictory or inconsistent, it is inadmissible. If it is consistent, it may nevertheless be excluded if the court concludes that the consistent term would necessarily have been included in the writing by the parties if they had intended it to be part of their agreement. AS 45.02.202; *Braund, Inc. v. White*, 486 P.2d 50, 56 (Alaska 1971); U.C.C. § 2-202 comment 3 (1977).

---

[2] AND also predicated its breach of contract claim on the existence of a prior oral agreement. The superior court implicitly rejected this theory in its analysis of the parol evidence rule.

A. Was the December 11 Letter a Partial Integration?

An integrated writing exists where the parties intend that the writing be a final expression of one or more terms of their agreement. *Kupka v. Morey,* 541 P.2d 740, 747 n.8 (Alaska 1975); RESTATEMENT (SECOND) OF CONTRACTS § 209(a) (1979). Whether a writing is integrated is a question of fact to be determined by the court in accordance with all relevant evidence. RESTATEMENT (SECOND) OF CONTRACTS § 209 comment c (1979).

In granting summary judgment on the breach of contract claim, the superior court stated that it had carefully considered all relevant evidence, including oral and written records of all facets of the business deal in question, to arrive at its finding that the agreement was partially integrated.[3]   After the six-week trial on the reformation issue, the superior court reaffirmed this finding:

35. The plaintiff initially contends that the letter of December 11, 1976 (the letter) was not integrated or partially integrated and therefore the court was in error in granting summary judgment in favor of defendant on the contract counts of the plaintiff's complaint on September 26, 1980.

36. After considering the evidence submitted at trial, the court reaffirms its prior conclusion that the letter was integrated as to the Owners Committee's approval clause.

37. The parties intended to write down their discussions in a comprehensive form which allowed Reed to seek financing and allow the primary actors (Tyson, Bruce, Terwilleger, Rickett) to submit the concept embodied by the letter to higher management. * * *

38. There are three subjects upon which plaintiff seeks reformation. * * * As to the first, [limiting the Owner Committee to a consideration of price] which has been plaintiff's primary focus, the court finds that such reference was integrated such that the parole [sic] evidence rule would bar

---

[3] At the hearing on AND's Motion for Clarification, the superior court stated: [I]t seems to me absolutely conclusive on this evidence, and I'm making this as a finding of fact, that this agreement is partially integrated, and I'm not making it by reference only to the four corners of the—of the writings but reference to all the extrinsic evidence that has been proffered to me, read everybody's deposition, considered in detail all the processes of negotiations, everything that was said and done by everybody as related by them up till the time that Rickett included the language in the letter and turned it over to Reed. So we're not here talking about the for [sic] corners or ambiguity or anything like that. We're talking about all the extrinsic evidence, meaning on balance to a conclusion more probable than not that this is a partially integrated agreement.

any inconsistent testimony. Testimony that the owners were limited to "price" in their review is inconsistent. * * *

41. With respect to the Owners Committee's approval clause, according to the plaintiff's contention the owners were entitled to review the transaction, on whatever basis, only one time. This was testified to by both Mr. Reed and argued by plaintiff in closing. * * * It was also conceded in closing that the review by the owners, on whatever standard, would occur prior to any formal contract being negotiated and executed. * * * This is also consistent with the testimony of each of the participants.

42. In addition, Mr. Reed, in consultation with Ed Merdes and Henry Camarot, his attorneys, tendered the letter of March 4, 1977, as a document which could serve as "the contract". * * * The March 4 letter contains no further reference to the Owners Committee's approval function * * * . Therefore, I find that as to the Owners Committee's approval * * * the letter of December 11 constitutes an integration or partial integration * * * . This having been established, the analysis outlined by the court on September 26, 1980, when granting defendant's motion for summary judgment on the contract claims is applicable. [Citations omitted.]

After reviewing the record, we cannot say that this finding of a partial integration was clearly erroneous. * * *

B. Does the Excluded Evidence Contradict the Integrated Terms?

Having found a partial integration, the next determination is whether the excluded evidence contradicts the integrated portion of the writing. Comment b to section 215 of the RESTATEMENT (SECOND) OF CONTRACTS is helpful in resolving this issue.[4] Comment b states:

> An earlier agreement may help the interpretation of a later one, but it may not contradict a binding later integrated agreement. Whether there is a contradiction depends * * * on whether the two are consistent or inconsistent. This is a question which often cannot be determined from the face of the writing; the writing must first be applied to its subject matter

---

[4] RESTATEMENT (SECOND) OF CONTRACTS § 215, which parallels the rule stated in U.C.C. § 2-202, reads:

"Except as stated in the preceding Section, where there is a binding agreement, either completely or partially integrated, evidence of prior or contemporaneous agreements or negotiations is not admissible in evidence to contradict a term of the writing."

and placed in context. The question is then decided by the court as part of a question of interpretation. Where reasonable people could differ as to the credibility of the evidence offered and the evidence if believed could lead a reasonable person to interpret the writing as claimed by the proponent of the evidence, the question of credibility and the choice among reasonable inferences should be treated as questions of fact. But the asserted meaning must be one to which the language of the writing, read in context, is reasonably susceptible. If no other meaning is reasonable, the court should rule as a matter of law that the meaning is established.

According to comment b, therefore, a question of interpretation may arise before the contradiction issue can be resolved. If the evidence conflicts, the choice between competing inferences is for the trier of fact to resolve. *Alyeska Pipeline Service Co. v. O'Kelley,* 645 P.2d 767, 771 n.2 (Alaska 1982). The meaning is determined as a matter of law, however, if "the asserted meaning [is not] one to which the language of the writing, read in context, is reasonably susceptible." RESTATEMENT (SECOND) OF CONTRACTS § 215 comment b (1979). *See also* J. CALAMARI & J. PERILLO, THE LAW OF CONTRACTS §§ 3-12, 3-13 (2d ed. 1977).

AND contends that the superior court erred in granting summary judgment because the evidence conflicted as to the meaning of the owner committee approval clause. It concludes that under *Alyeska* it was entitled to a jury trial on the interpretation issue. Alyeska contends, and the superior court ruled, that a jury trial was inappropriate because, as a matter of law, AND's asserted meaning of the clause at issue was not reasonably susceptible to the language of the writing. The superior court stated:

> The Court is making the * * * ruling that the offer of evidence to show that Rickett's letter really meant to limit owner committee approval to the price term alone * * * is not reasonably susceptible–or the writing is not reasonably susceptible to that purpose. And therefore, that extrinsic evidence operates to contradict the writing, not specific words in the writing, but the words in the context of the totality of the writing and the totality of the extrinsic evidence.

We agree that the words used in the December 11 letter are not reasonably susceptible to the interpretation advanced by AND. Therefore, we find no merit to AND's contention that it was entitled to a jury trial on the interpretation issue.

After rejecting the extrinsic evidence for purposes of interpretation, the superior court found AND's offered testimony, that the owner committee's approval power was limited to approval of the price, to be inconsistent with and contradictory to the language used by the negotiators in the December 11 letter. AND contends that the offered testimony did not contradict, but rather explained or supplemented the writing with consistent additional terms. For this contention, AND relies on the standard articulated in *Hunt Foods & Industries, Inc. v. Doliner*, 26 A.D.2d 41, 270 N.Y.S.2d 937 (N.Y. App. 1966). In *Hunt Foods*, the defendant signed an option agreement under which he agreed to sell stock to Hunt Foods at a given price per share. When Hunt Foods attempted to exercise the option, the defendant contended that the option could only be exercised if the defendant had received offers from a third party. The court held that section 2-202 did not bar this evidence from being admitted because it held that the proposed oral condition to the option agreement was not "inconsistent" within the meaning of section 2-202; to be inconsistent, "the term must contradict or negate a term of the writing. A term or condition which has a lesser effect is provable." *Id.* 270 N.Y.S.2d at 940.

The narrow view of consistency expressed in *Hunt Foods* has been criticized. In *Snyder v. Herbert Greenbaum & Associates, Inc.*, 38 Md. App. 144, 380 A.2d 618 (Md. App. 1977), the court held that the parol evidence of a contractual right to unilateral rescission was inconsistent with a written agreement for the sale and installation of carpeting. The court defined "inconsistency" as used in section 2-202(b) as "the absence of reasonable harmony in terms of the language *and* respective obligations of the parties." *Id.* 380 A.2d at 623 (emphasis in original). * * * We agree with this view of inconsistency and reject the view expressed in *Hunt Foods*.[5] Under this definition of inconsistency, it is clear that the proffered parol evidence limiting the owner committee's right of final approval to price is inconsistent with the integrated term that unconditionally gives the committee the right to approval. Therefore, the superior court was correct in refusing to admit parol evidence on this issue.[6] * * *

---

[5] *Hunt Foods* was implicitly rejected in *Johnson v. Curran*, 633 P.2d 994, 996-97 (Alaska 1981) (parol evidence concerning an early termination right based on nightclub owner's dissatisfaction with the band's performance was inconsistent with parties' written contract specifying definite time without mention of any right of early termination and thus inadmissible).

[6] Our affirmance of the superior court's holding that the proposed version is inconsistent with the integrated clause obviates discussion of whether the addition, if consistent, would have been included in the December 11 letter. Furthermore, we decline to reach AND's contentions regarding the applicability of U.C.C. § 2-207 because AND never raised the § 2-207 argument at the superior court level. *See, e.g., Jeffries v. Glacier State Telephone Co.*,

(continued...)

[The court also held that the trial court was correct to deny a jury trial on the reformation issue and to grant a summary judgment against AND on the punitive damage issue.] [Some footnotes omitted. Those retained have been renumbered.]

Notes

1.   In the absence of a "merger" clause, how does the court determine whether the writing was "intended by the parties as a final expression of their agreement" as to some or all of the terms? UCC 2-202, 2A-202. Put differently, how does one evaluate the decision in the *Alaska Northern* case that the writing was intended to be a partial integration with regard to the "approval" clauses? The question is important because in the absence of any integration, the term limiting the power to reject would be part of the agreement, whether included in the writing or not.

UCC 2-202 and the comments are silent on this question. It may be useful to indulge a presumption, *see* UCC 1-206 [former 1-201(31)], that a writing which "reasonably appears to be a complete agreement" is "an integrated agreement unless it is established by other evidence that the writing did not constitute a final expression." RESTATEMENT, (SECOND) OF CONTRACTS 209(3).* Since there was no "other" persuasive evidence in the *Alaska Northern* case, the determination that the parties intended a partial integration at least seems sound. What constitutes "other" evidence? According to Comment (c) to RESTATEMENT 210, incompleteness of the writing may be shown by "any relevant evidence, oral or written, that an apparently complete writing never became fully effective, or that it was modified after initial adoption."

2.   If the writing is integrated in whole or in part, terms in that writing "may not be contradicted by evidence of any prior agreement or of a contemporaneous oral agreement." UCC 2-202, 2A-202; RESTATEMENT (SECOND) OF CONTRACTS 215.** But if there is a partial integration, as in *Alaska Northern,* the writing may

---

[6] (...continued)
604 P.2d 4, 11 (Alaska 1979).

* *See Intershoe, Inc. v. Bankers Trust Co.*, 571 N.E.2d 641 (N.Y. 1991) (form and content of currency trade confirmation support integration in the absence of other evidence).

** *See Phelps v. Spivey*, 486 S.E.2d 226 (N.C. App. 1997) (oral agreement contradicts term
(continued...)

be supplemented "by evidence of consistent additional terms." UCC 2-202(b), 2A-202(b). RESTATEMENT (SECOND) OF CONTRACTS 216(2) puts the matter more affirmatively: "An agreement is not completely integrated if the writing omits a consistent additional term." We now return to a question that has dominated the trade usage cases: What is a consistent additional term? Is the "absence of reasonable harmony" test*** applied in *Alaska Northern* the same as the test expressed in Comment 3 to UCC 2-202, *i.e.*, that the term, if agreed upon, "would certainly have been included in the document * * *?" Or, must the "consistent additional agreed term" be one "as in the circumstances might naturally be omitted from the writing?" RESTATEMENT (SECOND) OF CONTRACTS 216(2)(b).

3. What is the effect of a "merger" clause providing that the writing is the "final and complete agreement of the parties" and that there are "no understandings, agreements, or obligations unless specifically set forth in the writing?" The clause is regarded as persuasive but not necessarily conclusive evidence of an intention to integrate the writing. Many courts have permitted the trial court to hold a preliminary hearing on whether, despite the merger clause, both parties intended a total integration.**** Assuming the requisite intention and assuming that the clause is not unconscionable***** and that the clause or the contract was not induced by fraud,****** and that there was no other evidence establishing a contrary intention, the UCC answer seems clear: the writing may neither be contradicted by evidence of "any prior agreement or of a contemporaneous agreement" nor "supplemented * * * by evidence of consistent additional terms." UCC 2-202. May, however, the total integration be explained or supplemented by course of dealing or usage of

---

** (...continued)
in writing).

*** For still another application of the "absence of reasonable harmony" test, *see ARB, Inc. v. E-Systems, Inc.*, 663 F.2d 189 (D.C. Cir. 1980) (after review of extrinsic evidence, "merger" clause held to express genuine intention of parties).

**** *See Betaco, Inc. v. Cessna Aircraft Co.*, 103 F.3d 1281 (7th Cir. 1996) (intention to integrate found); *Sierra Diesel Injection Service, Inc. v. Burroughs Corp., Inc.*, 890 F.2d 108 (9th Cir. 1989) (no intent to integrate found).

***** *Seibel v. Layne & Bowler, Inc.*, 641 P.2d 668 (Or. Ct. App. 1982) (ordinary consumer unfairly surprised by fine-print merger clause in standard form contract).

****** *See* UCC 1-103 and *Franklin v. Lovitt Equipment Co.*, 420 So.2d 1370 (Miss. 1982).

trade or by course of performance? Despite some ambiguity in former 2-202, the answer appears to be yes, subject to the limitations imposed by UCC 1-303(e) [former 1-205(4)]. Thus, evidence of a prior course of dealing has been admitted to explain or supplement the terms of an integrated writing and evidence of trade usage and a prior course of dealing that was thought to "contradict" terms in the writing has been excluded.[*] We return, then, full circle to the test of consistency raised in the trade usage cases.[**]

    4. Given the similar construction of UCITA 301 and 302, the same sets of issues will likely arise in a licensing transaction.

    5. **CISG.** There is no provision comparable to UCC 2-202 in the CISG. Rather, Article 11 provides: "A contract of sale need not be concluded in or evidenced by writing and is not subject to any other requirements as to form. It may be proved by any means, including witnesses." This Article and Articles 8 and 9 persuaded the Eleventh Circuit that the parol evidence rule did not apply in actions involving CISG and that so-called "subjective intent" evidence was admissible to show that certain terms in the writing were not part of the contract. In *MCC-Marble Ceramic Center, Inc. v. Ceramica Nuova D'Agostino, S.P.A.*, 144 F.3d 1384 (11th Cir. 1998), *cert. denied*, 526 U.S. 1687 (1999), the court admitted evidence from affidavits that both parties (agents of seller and buyer) intended, subjectively it would appear, that standard terms on the back of a written purchase order were not part of the contract even though both signed the purchase order under a clear term (in Italian) incorporating standard terms (favoring the seller) on the back. The court relied upon CISG Art. 8(1), which provides:

> For the purpose of this Convention statements made by and other conduct
> of the party are to be interpreted according to his intent where the other
> party knew or could not have been unaware what that intent was.

The court then relied on CISG Art. 11 to reject the argument that the parol evidence rule excluded the prior oral agreement because it conflicted with the written term of incorporation.

    Suppose there had been a merger clause in the contract. Would the CISG

---

[*] *See, e.g., Ralph's Distributing Co. v. AMF, Inc.*, 667 F.2d 670 (8th Cir. 1981) (evidence admitted). *See, e.g., General Aviation, Inc. v. Cessna Aircraft Co.*, 915 F.2d 1038 (6th Cir. 1990) (evidence excluded); *General Plumbing & Heating, Inc. v. American Air Filter Co.*, 696 F.2d 375 (5th Cir. 1983) (same).

[**] *See* Eyal Zamir, *The Inverted Hierarchy of Contract Interpretation and Supplementation*, 97 COLUM. L. REV. 1710 (1997) (discussing hierarchy of terms in contract interpretation.

permit evidence of terms that add to or contradict the agreement?

Problem 4-7

Fiber Industries sold fiber to carpet manufacturers for use in the making of carpets. Salem Carpet bought trademark fiber from Fiber Industries on an order-by-order basis. There was no written agreement other than the individual purchase orders. Both Salem's purchase order form and Fiber Industries acknowledgment form contained "merger" clauses, which provided that the form "contains all the terms and conditions of the purchase agreement and shall constitute the complete and exclusive agreement between Seller and Purchaser." In August, 2003 Fiber Industries announced that it was withdrawing from the carpet industry, but that it would supply all customers in an "orderly fashion" until the phase-out was complete. Salem accepted a final order of fiber at a contract price of $407,128.40, but refused to pay the full amount because of losses suffered as a result of Fiber Industries' withdrawal from the market. Salem claimed that there was a "customary practice" in the carpet industry obligating Fiber Industries to fill all orders made by Salem during the projected market life of any carpet style which utilized fiber manufactured by Fiber Industries. Salem was prepared to establish a usage that the "carpet manufacturer will continue to make its branded fiber available for the useful life of the carpet style or for sufficient time to allow the carpet manufacturer to produce and sell sufficient carpet to recoup the large start-up expenses incurred in introducing and marketing a new line of branded carpet."

A. Assume that both contract forms were silent on the issue. Assume, further, that the usage could be established. Should the court admit evidence of the usage?

B. Assume that instead of establishing that evidence under the rubric of "usage of trade," Salem wanted to introduce evidence to the same effect based upon the discussions of the parties that occurred before Salem ordered the fiber. Again assume that both contract forms were silent on the issue. Should that evidence be admitted?

Note: Contract Interpretation Under the UCC

Under UCC 2-202 or 2A-202, the parol evidence rule has little to do with issues of contract interpretation. Rather, extrinsic evidence is admissible to assist the trier of fact in determining the meaning of a term which is part of the agreement. At least where the source of relevant evidence is course of dealing or usage of trade or course of performance, there is no requirement that the language be ambiguous before the evidence is admissible. *See* UCC 2-202(2) [former 2-202, cmt. 1(c)].[*] This is consistent with the belief of the so-called "realists" that words do not have a "plain meaning" that can be determined from the four corners of a writing. As Chief Justice Traynor put it, the "test of admissibility of extrinsic evidence to explain the meaning of a written instrument is not whether it appears to the court to be plain and unambiguous on its face, but whether the offered evidence is relevant to prove a meaning to which the language of the instrument is reasonably susceptible." *Pacific Gas and Elec. Co. v. G.W. Thomas Drayage & Rigging Co.,* 442 P.2d 641, 644 (Cal. 1968).[**]

In interpreting a contract, a wide range of facts, including trade usage, may be relevant. Thus, the "meaning of the agreement of the parties is to be determined by the language used by them and by their action, read and interpreted in the light of commercial practices and other surrounding circumstances." UCC 1-303, cmt. 1 [former 1-205, cmt. 1]. Even so, the plaintiff must still establish that its understanding of the terms should prevail over the understanding of the other party. The UCC does not provide a standard to resolve disputes of this sort. According to the RESTATEMENT (SECOND), however, in order for the plaintiff to prevail, he would have to establish that either (a) he did not know the different meaning attached by the defendant to the term and the defendant knew the meaning attached by the plaintiff, or (b) the plaintiff had no reason to know of the different meaning attached by the defendant and the defendant had reason to know the meaning attached by the plaintiff. *See* RESTATEMENT (SECOND) OF CONTRACTS 201. *See also* RESTATEMENT (SECOND) OF CONTRACTS 202-203, 219-223.

How is extrinsic evidence proved? Trade usage and other context evidence are facts to be established by the moving party, *i.e.,* the party seeking to persuade the court that her interpretation of the scope or meaning of the agreement should prevail. UCC 1-303 [former 1-205]. Since these facts are normally not presumed

---

[*] *See Campbell Farms v. Wald,* 578 N.W.2d 96 (N.D. 1998).

[**] *See* E. Allan Farnsworth, *"Meaning" in the Law of Contracts,* 76 YALE L.J. 939 (1967); Arthur L. Corbin, *The Interpretation of Words and the Parol Evidence Rule,* 50 CORNELL L.Q. 161 (1965); Margaret H. Kniffen, *A New Trend in Contract Interpretation: The Search for Reality as Opposed to Virtual Reality,* 74 OR. L. REV. 643 (1995); Eric A. Posner, *The Parol Evidence Rule, the Plain Meaning Rule, and the Principles of Contract Interpretation,* 146 U. PENN. L. REV. 533 (1998); Peter Linzer, *The Comfort of Certainty: Plain Meaning and the Parol Evidence Rule,* 71 FORDHAM L. REV. 799 (2002).

to exist, the plaintiff has the "burden of establishing" them, *i.e.*, she must persuade the "triers of fact that the existence of the fact is more probable than its non-existence." UCC 1-201(b)(8). The moving party, therefore, has both the burden of production and the burden of persuasion. These burdens are normally satisfied, if at all, through expert witnesses and documents in an atmosphere where objections to the expert's qualifications, the authenticity of documents and hearsay and relevance are routine.[*]

Problem 4-8

Return to Problem 4-7. Assume that Salem's purchase order provided that the seller of goods supplied pursuant to the purchase order promises to "support the integration of all materials supplied to the buyer into the carpet manufactured by the buyer." Assume that under the analysis pursuant to UCC 2-207, that term in the purchase order was part of the parties' agreement.

A. Salem argues that the usage of trade evidence will demonstrate what was meant by that term. Assuming the usage of trade is established, should evidence of that usage be admitted?

B. Assume that instead of establishing that evidence under the rubric of "usage of trade," Salem wanted to introduce evidence to the same effect based upon the discussions of the parties that occurred before Salem ordered the fiber. Should that evidence be admitted?

Note: *Effect of "Usage" and "Practice" Under the CISG*

Article 9(1) of the CISG provides that the "parties are bound by any usage to which they have agreed and by any practices which they have established between themselves." Unless otherwise agreed, the parties "are considered * * * to have impliedly made applicable to their contract or its formation a usage of which the parties knew or ought to have known and which in international trade is widely

---

[*] *See, e.g.*, C. MCCORMICK, EVIDENCE § 13 (5th ed. 1999 & Supp. 2003); James W. McElhaney, *Expert Witnesses and the Federal Rules of Evidence*, 28 MERCER L. REV. 463 (1977). The pitfalls in this process are illustrated by the "Chicken" case, *Frigaliment Importing Co. v. B.N.S. Int'l Sales Corp.*, 190 F. Supp. 116 (S.D.N.Y. 1960); Ronald J. Allen & Robert A. Hillman, *Evidentiary Problems In–And Solutions For–the Uniform Commercial Code*, 1984 DUKE L.J. 92, 98 (arguing that the UCC should have a comprehensive approach to burdens of production and persuasion).

known to, and regularly observed by, parties to contracts of the type involved in the particular trade concerned." CISG Art. 9(2). Although Article 8(3) states that usages and practices are relevant to determining the intention of the parties, the CISG does not clearly say that they may supplement or qualify terms in the contract. *See* UCC 1-303 [former 1-205]. But is such clarity needed?

Unlike UCC 1-304 [former 1-203], the CISG does not directly impose a duty of good faith in the performance or enforcement of the contract. Rather, Article 7(1) provides that in "the interpretation of this Convention, regard is to be had to its international character and to the need to promote uniformity in its application and the observance of good faith in international trade." Does this mean that the parties never have a duty to act in good faith? Suppose there is a good faith usage in the particular trade? What about CISG Art. 7(2)? How would you use this subsection to include a duty of good faith?

CHAPTER FIVE

BREACH OF WARRANTY AS TO THE QUALITY OF THE PRODUCT SOLD

SECTION 1.   INTRODUCTION

A. Warranty Theory: Some History

The contract may provide language or terms relevant to the quality of the goods the seller has agreed to deliver. For example, the goods will be described and the agreement may contain detailed performance specifications or promises about what the goods will do after delivery. Thus, whether the goods conformed to the contract at the time of delivery may be answered by the express terms of the contract.

Suppose, however, that express terms do not answer the question. In these cases, disputes over the quality of a good sold frequently end up in court. The buyer's claim is that the goods, because of a condition existing at the time of tender, failed to conform to expectations regarding basic attributes or suitability. The seller's response may be that the buyer assumed the risk. More particularly, the argument is that since neither party knew of the condition at the time of delivery, *i.e.*, both were equally ignorant, and the buyer could have discovered the condition by inspection or otherwise, there is no sound reason, absent fraud, deceit or mutual mistake, why the seller should bear the risk. Thus, the stage is set, the seller will contend, for application of the doctrine of caveat emptor, the "universal structural characteristic of the law of sales."[*]

One "sound" reason for protecting the buyer's expectations is found in the law of warranty. Warranty is a representational theory of liability. It depends upon the answers to two key questions: (1) What did the seller affirm, represent or promise, expressly or impliedly, about the quality of the product sold to the buyer; and (2) Was the buyer justified in incorporating the representations into its expectations of quality? The first question poses primarily a question of fact. The second question is primarily a question of law. Clearly, not everything a seller says about the product will become part of the contract. To the extent that representations of

---

[*] Ernst Rabel, *The Nature of Warranty of Quality,* 24 TUL. L. REV. 273, 274 n.5 (1950). *See* Walton H. Hamilton, *The Ancient Maxim Caveat Emptor,* 40 YALE L.J. 1133 (1931).

quality become part of the agreement (even though not contained in a writing that documents terms of the deal), however, they constitute a standard of quality–a warranty–to which the product must conform at the time of delivery.

The Anglo-American history of warranty reveals, in commercial transactions at least,[*] a slow but steady erosion of the doctrine of caveat emptor. The following account, taken from the sources cited below, touches the doctrinal tip of a much larger social iceberg.[**]

Warranty disputes involving claims for economic loss first arose between sellers and buyers who were in privity of contract. In the early 17th Century, however, these claims were asserted in tort as an action on the case. The buyer had to establish the elements of deceit, *i.e.*, that the seller made an express

---

[*] There are, in fact, three legal worlds of product liability. The first, with which this Chapter is concerned, concerns disputes over quality between commercial parties where only economic loss is involved. These disputes are governed, in the main, by Article 2. The second involves disputes between individuals and commercial sellers over "defective" products which have caused personal injuries. These disputes are governed primarily by the law of torts, *i.e.*, the law of strict products liability, *see* RESTATEMENT (THIRD) OF TORTS: PRODUCTS LIABILITY (1998), but also may involve claims under Article 2, *see* UCC 2-715(2)(b). The third involves disputes between individual consumers and commercial sellers over quality where economic loss and, perhaps, property damage has occurred. These are governed in part by Article 2 and tort law and in part by a patchwork of federal and supplemental state consumer protection laws. *See* David A. Rice, *Product Quality Laws and the Economics of Federalism*, 65 B.U. L. REV. 1 (1985); William K. Jones, *Product Defects Causing Commercial Loss: The Ascendancy of Contract over Tort*, 44 U. MIAMI L. REV. 731 (1990).

[**] Linda J. Rusch, *Products Liability Trapped By History: Our Choice of Rules Rules Our Choices*, 76 TEMPLE L. REV. 739 (2003); Marshall S. Shapo, *Products at the Millennium: Traversing a Transverse Section*, 53 S.C. L. REV. 1031 (2002); James J. White, *Reverberations from the Collision of Tort and Warranty*, 53 S.C.L. REV. 1067 (2002); Frances E. Zollers, et al, *Looking Backward, Looking Forward: Reflections on Twenty Years of Product Liability Reform*, 50 SYRACUSE L. REV. 1019 (2000); Richard E. Speidel, *Warranty Theory, Economic Loss, and the Privity Requirement: Once More Into the Void*, 67 B.U. L. REV. 9 (1987); Ingrid M. Hillinger, *The Merchant of Section 2-314: Who Needs Him?*, 34 HASTINGS L. REV. 747 (1983); Herbert D. Titus, *Restatement (Second) of Torts Section 402A and the Uniform Commercial Code*, 22 STAN. L. REV. 713 (1970); William L. Prosser, *The Implied Warranty of Merchantable Quality*, 27 MINN. L. REV. 117 (1943); Karl N. Llewellyn, *On Warranty of Quality and Society*, 36 COLUM. L. REV. 699 (1936); Walton H. Hamilton, *The Ancient Maxim Caveat Emptor*, 40 YALE L.J. 1133 (1931); Samuel Williston, *Representation and Warranty in Sales–Heilbut v. Buckleton*, 27 HARV. L. REV. 1 (1913); Emlin McClain, *Implied Warranties in Sales*, 7 HARV. L. REV. 213 (1903).

representation about the nature of the goods knowing it to be false.

By 1790, the action of deceit, with its requirements of scienter by the representor and reliance by the representee, had developed into a separate writ or action. At about the same time, the English courts first permitted an express warranty claim to be brought in assumpsit, the action in which most contract claims were pursued.

By 1802, scienter was no longer a requirement in assumpsit for breach of an express warranty, but other limiting formalities, *i.e.*, that the representation must be an express term of the contract and intended by the seller to be a warranty, still remained. This early interaction between representations of quality made in exchange transactions and the tort forms of action led Dean Prosser to conclude that warranty was a "freak hybrid born of the illicit intercourse of tort and contract."[*]
The New York Court of Appeals, in a personal injury case, concluded:

> Accordingly, for some 400 years the action rested not on an enforcible (sic) promise but on a wrong or tort. In the historical development of the law of warranty, however, as so often happens in law and life in general, accident was evidently confused with essence: from the fact that the cases which arose involved contractual relationships and represented enforcible (sic) promises, the courts seem to have concluded that the contract was the essence of the action* * *. The occasion for the warranty was constituted a necessary condition of it.

Randy Knitwear, Inc. v. American Cyanamid Co., 181 N.E.2d 399, 401 n.2 (N.Y. 1962).

During the 19th Century, warranty theory developed into the tripartite form which we know today: an express warranty, an implied warranty of fitness for particular purpose, and an implied warranty of merchantability (fitness for "ordinary" purposes). The implied warranties emerged, inferentially, at the point where the seller's express representations about or description of the goods failed to cover the exact issue in dispute. All three were captured, in the late 19th Century, by the British Sale of Goods Act and, later, in the American Uniform Sales Act. They appear as UCC 2-313, 2-314 and 2-315 in Article 2 and were carried into Article 2A in UCC 2A-210, 2A-212 and 2A-213. In the 2003 amendments to Article 2, two new sections were added, UCC 2-313A and 2-313B, that address express warranty-like obligations in a non-privity context. The 2003 amendments

---

[*] William L. Prosser, *The Assault Upon the Citadel (Strict Liability to the Consumer)*, 69 YALE L.J. 1099, 1126 (1960).

also restricted UCC 2-313 to the privity context. We will return to examine each of these warranties and obligations in more detail. Before looking at warranty theory under the UCC, a few general questions should be kept in mind.

First, warranties, arising as they do from contracts for sale, have been treated as terms of the contract. Two consequences flow from this treatment: (1) a breach of warranty is a breach of contract, entitling the seller to recover direct and consequential economic loss measured by the expectation interest; and (2) privity of contract has usually been required between the seller and buyer, especially where the buyer claims only economic loss. Are these consequences inevitable? For example, should a plaintiff injured in person by a defective product be permitted to recover under a warranty theory? Should a buyer who suffers only economic loss caused by an unmerchantable product manufactured by a remote seller be permitted to recover on a warranty theory without privity of contract?

Second, the tort of misrepresentation has developed apart from warranty theory. In general, the misrepresentation of fact must be material and at least negligently made. In addition, the plaintiff must justifiably rely upon it and is limited, in many cases, to the recovery of out-of-pocket economic loss. But when the misrepresentation concerns goods sold, there is an obvious overlap with the theory of express warranty. Which should prevail in these cases, express warranties under the UCC or tort theory? Should it make any difference if the misrepresentation is made fraudulently as opposed to negligently?

Third, in the last 25 years a special body of law has developed to protect individual consumers who purchase goods for personal, family or household purposes and suffer economic loss. Uneven though this development has been, it reflects a conclusion that there is usually an imbalance of capacity between the individual and the enterprise and that this imbalance creates a risk of exploitation in bargaining or unprovable fraud by the enterprise. The legal response includes the federal Magnuson-Moss Warranty Act and state legislation, such as the "lemon" laws. Is this development justified? If so, how much government regulation is necessary to correct the imbalance, whether it be in bargaining power, information or capacity for choice, and should that regulation be included in the UCC?

Fourth, defective and dangerous products manufactured by sellers frequently cause damage to the person or property of purchasers and other foreseeable users or consumers. Since the great case of *McPherson v. Buick Motor Company,* 111 N.E. 1050 (N.Y. 1916), decided in 1916, injured parties have been able, privity or not, to sue the manufacturer in negligence. Since the 1960s, with the promulgation of Section 402A of the RESTATEMENT (SECOND) OF TORTS, and now with the new

RESTATEMENT (THIRD) OF TORTS: PRODUCTS LIABILITY (1998), injured parties have been permitted to sue under the theory of strict products liability.* Although negligence theory has not been preempted, it has been eclipsed by strict liability.

Given these developments in the law of products liability, to what extent does Article 2 preempt tort law where the seller has breached a warranty and the buyer has suffered personal injuries or property loss? Should the buyer with both a claim in warranty and a claim in strict tort be able to choose which to pursue? And what about products that cause only economic loss or cause damage only to the product sold? Should these claims be limited to warranty theory under the UCC or may they also be pursued under negligence or strict liability in tort theory? What difference does it make? (Think about what must be proved to establish liability, statute of limitations differences, measurement of damages, and ability to limit remedies.) In the materials in this Chapter and Chapter Eleven, *infra*, we will try to provide some answers to these questions.

To the extent that Article 2A and UCITA follow the Article 2 model, should the warranties provided in those types of commercial transactions be influenced by the struggle between warranty and tort liability that has taken place under Article 2?**

B. Warranties Under the Code: An Introduction

In Article 2, according to Comment 6 to UCC 2-313 [former comment 4 to former 2-313], the basic purpose of warranty law is to determine "what it is that the seller has in essence agreed to sell." As you are now fully aware, agreement means the "bargain of the parties in fact as found in their language or inferred from other circumstances." UCC 1-201(b)(3) [former 1-201(3)]. Thus, whether the buyer's or lessee's understanding of quality is consistent with the agreement may depend, among other things, upon the description, what the seller or lessor has said, common uses in the trade, the price paid, and the extent to which the buyer or lessee has

---

* For a brief historical view by the co-reporters of the development of the new RESTATEMENT, *see* James Henderson & Aaron Twerski, *What Europe, Japan and Other Countries Can Learn from the New American Restatement of Products Liability*, 34 TEX. INT'L L.J. 1 (1999). The new RESTATEMENT generated much controversy. For a collection of the literature about the controversy, *see* Linda J. Rusch, *Products Liability Trapped by History: Our Choice of Rules Rules Our Choices*, 76 TEMPLE L. REV. 739, 749 fn. 37 (2003).

** *See* Stephen T. Whelan, et al, *Leases*, 50 BUS. LAW. 1481, 1487-88 (1995) (discussing products liability in tort in lease transactions).

communicated particular needs to the seller or lessor. Indeed, the more detailed the agreement on quality and the allocation of risks, the less room there is for legitimate dispute over conformity of the goods to the contract.

The UCC drafters have selected an approach which yields warranties of different kinds, including express warranties, UCC 2-313, 2A-210, implied warranties of merchantability, UCC 2-314, 2A-212, and implied warranties of fitness for particular purpose, UCC 2-315, 2A-213, –a tripartite approach. (The implied warranty of title and against infringement, UCC 2-312, 2A-211 will be treated later.) In so doing, the drafters rejected the unitary approach suggested by the theory of contract and, at the same time, preserved the close tie between warranty and the contract.

The initial question, therefore, asks whether the UCC's tripartite approach to the problem supports any breach of warranty claim at all. That is, was a warranty even made? The answer to this question will be determined by whether the elements necessary to create a warranty are met as well as by the possible application of exclusionary rules, *i.e.*, disclaimers or rules of interpretation, which neutralize facts that otherwise would support a warranty claim. *See* UCC 2-316, 2A-214, 2-317, 2A-215 & 2-202, 2A-202. These rules proceed on the assumption that what is rooted in contract can, under controlled circumstances, be taken away or altered by contract. The second question is whether a warranty made by the seller has in fact been breached and caused harm to the plaintiff and whether the plaintiff is entitled to bring an action for breach of the warranty against the seller. We will consider these issues in this Chapter.

After answering these initial questions, one then needs to consider the remedial issues. When did the buyer or lessee discover the alleged breach of warranty? This has immense practical importance. If the defect is discovered before acceptance, the remedy of rejection may be available (UCC 2-601, 2-612, 2A-509, 2A-510) in addition to damage remedies (UCC 2-711, 2A-508). The remedial problems become more complicated after acceptance, and the degree of complication is closely related to how soon thereafter the defect was discovered.* As a general rule, the earlier the breach is discovered and the quicker remedial options are exercised, the better off the buyer or lessee will be. Issues regarding rejection and revocation

---

* The risks of delay stem from the UCC's notice requirements (UCC 2-605, 2-607, 2A-514, 2A-516), statute of limitations (UCC 2-725, 2A-506), limitations on the ability to revoke acceptance (UCC 2-608, 2A-517), allocations of the burden of proof (UCC 2-607, 2A-516), and the difficulties in proving damages, including consequential damages (UCC 2-714, 2-715, 2A-519, 2A-520).

of acceptance will be considered in Chapter Six, *infra*. Issues regarding measurement of damages will be considered in Chapters Ten and Eleven, *infra*. Finally, did the seller or lessor validly alter by contract the normal remedies available to the plaintiff upon breach of warranty? Relevant Code sections include UCC 2-718, 2A-504, 2-719, 2A-503, 2-302, 2A-108. We will consider remedy limitations in Chapter Twelve, *infra*.

Notice how closely the Article 2A provisions cited above follow the Article 2 model. Following the Article 2 approach arose out of case law that had long applied Article 2 to leasing transactions. Can you identify any major differences between the Article 2 and 2A provisions cited above? For example, notice that neither of the implied warranties in Article 2A arise in a finance lease. Can you identify the reason why the baseline expectation is that a finance lessor should not make implied warranties of merchantability or fitness for a particular purpose? Warranties under an Article 2A finance lease are also considered in this Chapter.

C. Warranties under the CISG and UCITA

As we explore express and implied warranties below, we will also consider the warranty schemes under other law such as the CISG and UCITA. As you think about how these other bodies of law deal with warranty issues, consider the extent to which the issues raised above concerning Article 2 and 2A warranties are relevant to warranties under another regime.

SECTION 2.   EXPRESS WARRANTIES

Our task in this section is to determine when the elements necessary to create an express warranty are satisfied. Read UCC 2-313 and 2A-210. To help develop an understanding of what is in play in those sections, let's start with some history.

In the famous case of *Seixas v. Woods*, 2 Cai. R. 48, 2 Am. Dec. 215 (N.Y. Sup. Ct. 1804), the seller described the goods as "brazilletto" wood. What was delivered to the buyer was peachum wood, an inferior quality wood. Neither the seller or the buyer knew that the wood was not brazilletto wood (it is not clear whether both parties assumed that it was brazilletto wood) until it was delivered to the buyer. The court in deciding for the seller on the buyer's claim for return of the purchase price stated:

> The mentioning the wood as brazilletto wood in the bill of parcels and
> in the advertisement some days previous to the sale, did not amount to a

warranty to the plaintiffs. To make an affirmation at the time of the sale a warranty, it must appear by evidence to be so intended; * * * and not to have been a mere matter of judgment and opinion, and of which the defendant had no particular knowledge. Here it is admitted the defendant was equally ignorant with the plaintiffs, and could have had no such intention.

Id. The intention requirement was part of the pre-Code American law of warranty:

Though to constitute a warranty requires no particular form of words, the naked averment of a fact is neither a warranty itself nor evidence of it. In connection with other circumstances, it certainly may be taken into consideration; but the jury must be satisfied from the whole, that the vendor actually, and not constructively, consented to be bound for the truth of his representation.

Gibson, C.J. in *McFarland v. Newman*, 9 Watts 55, 60, 34 Am. Dec. 497 (Pa. 1839).* Both Articles 2 and 2A reject this pre-UCC law by stating that the seller or lessor need not have a specific intention to make a warranty before there is an express warranty. Both Articles also reject the idea that the representation be in writing or use the word "warrant" or "guarantee" in order to constitute an express warranty. UCC 2-313, 2A-210.

So what is now required to make an express warranty? Consider the following questions. What is an affirmation of fact? How is this different than the seller or lessor's "opinion or commendation of the goods"? What is a promise relating to the goods? How is this different than a remedial promise? The concept of a remedial promise was added in the 2003 amendments to UCC 2-313 and defined in UCC 2-103. (Notice "remedial promise" was not added to UCC 2A-210 or 2A-103). What is a description of the goods? How is a description different than an affirmation of fact regarding the goods? What is a sample or a model?

Notice that an affirmation of fact, a promise relating to the goods (other than a remedial promise), a description of the goods, a sample, or a model must be part of the "basis of the bargain" in order for an express warranty to be created. What does "basis of the bargain" mean? Does the concept incorporate a reliance requirement, that is, must the plaintiff seeking to recover for breach of an express

---

* *See also McNeir v. Greer-Hale Chinchilla Ranch*, 74 S.E.2d 165 (Va. 1953) (representations constituted warranty if seller intended that they should be relied upon and they were in fact relied upon by buyer as an inducement to purchase); Samuel J. Stoljar, *Conditions, Warranties and Descriptions of Quality in Sale of Goods, Part I*, 15 MOD. L. REV. 425, 428-29 (1952).

warranty have to prove that it relied on the seller's representations in order to show that the seller made an express warranty? Under pre-UCC law, reliance played a critical component in creating an express warranty. The affirmation must have led a reasonable buyer to believe that such statements had been made to induce the bargain and to make the purchase in reliance on those statements. *See* Section 12, Uniform Sales Act.[*] The reliance test, however, has been replaced by a "basis of the bargain" test in UCC 2-313 and 2A-210. To what extent is reliance still a part of the "basis of the bargain"? Should it matter that the buyer might know that what the seller is representing might not be true? What about representations that take place after the contract is initially formed? Can those representations be part of the "basis of the bargain?" Why should there be a special test for representations of the seller? Does the "basis of the bargain" test make sense if the seller's representation is part of a document which memorializes the parties' agreement?[**] Why are such representations subject to the "basis of the bargain" test, unlike other contract promises?

As you read the following cases applying UCC 2-313, consider whether the following list of factors, could or should help determine whether a seller's representation meets the "basis of the bargain" requirement: (a) the seller's statement was plain and unambiguous; (b) the seller's statement concerned a matter of objective importance to the buyer; (c) the attribute or quality involved was not something the buyer could easily ascertain on his own; (d) the seller was more of an expert in the matter than the buyer; (e) the buyer based her decision to buy in part on the seller's statements; (f) nothing indicated that the seller should not be taken seriously; (g) the seller did not say things that should have put the buyer "on his guard" so to speak; (h) the remedy the buyer sought was especially appropriate and would not be unduly harsh on the seller; and (i) the price tends to support the buyer's claim.

---

[*] *See also Hansen v. Firestone Tire & Rubber Co.*, 276 F.2d 254, 257 (6th Cir. 1960); SAMUEL WILLISTON, SALES § 15-6 (5th ed. 1994).

[**] *See* Sidney Kwestel, *Express Warranty as Contractual–The Need for a Clear Approach*, 53 MERCER L. REV. 557 (2002); *James River Equipment Co. v. Beadle County Equipment, Inc.*, 646 N.W.2d 265 (S.D. 2002).

SESSA V. RIEGLE
UNITED STATES DISTRICT COURT, EASTERN DISTRICT OF PENNSYLVANIA, 1977
427 F. SUPP. 760, *AFF'D WITHOUT OPINION*, 568 F.2D 770 (3D CIR. 1978)

[Sessa purchased from Riegle a standard bred race horse named Tarport Conaway for $25,000. Before the sale, Sessa's friend Maloney examined the horse and reported that he "liked him." Also, Riegle, in a telephone conversation with Sessa, stated among other things that Sessa would like the horse and that he was a "good one" and "sound." The sale was then completed and, after problems in transportation were resolved, the horse was delivered some days later. Shortly thereafter the horse went lame in his hind legs due to a thrombosis which stopped the flow of blood through the arteries. The experts were unable to identify the cause of the thrombosis and the testimony did not establish that the condition was present before Riegle shipped the horse by carrier. Although the condition improved and Tarport Conaway was able to race, Sessa sued for damages under UCC 2-714(2) to be measured in part by the costs incurred in treating the condition. The case was tried without a jury and the court, after making findings of fact, issued the following opinion.]

HANNUM, DISTRICT JUDGE

* * *

II. Express Warranties

On March 10, 1973, the day of the sale of Tarport Conaway, Sessa and Riegle had a telephone conversation during which the horse was discussed in general terms. Arrangements were made for transportation, and Riegle gave Sessa some instructions for driving Tarport Conaway based on Riegle's experience with him. Sessa contends that certain statements made by Riegle during that conversation constitute express warranties on which Riegle is liable in this action. The most important of these is Riegle's alleged statement that, "the horse is sound," or words to that effect.

In deciding whether statements by a seller constitute express warranties, the court must look to UCC § 2-313 which presents three fundamental issues. First, the court must determine whether the seller's statement constitutes an "affirmation of fact or promise" or "description of the goods" under § 2-313(1)(a) or (b) or whether it is rather "merely the seller's opinion or commendation of the goods" under § 2-313(2). Second, assuming the court finds the language used susceptible to creation of a warranty, it must then be determined whether the statement was "part of the basis of the bargain." If it was, an express warranty exists and, as the third issue, the court must determine whether the warranty was breached.

With respect to the first issue, the court finds that in the circumstances of this case, words to the effect that "The horse is sound" spoken during the telephone conversation between Sessa and Riegle constitute an opinion or commendation rather than express warranty. This determination is a question for the trier of fact. * * * There is nothing talismanic or thaumaturgic about the use of the word "sound." Whether use of that language constitutes warranty, or mere opinion or commendation depends on the circumstances of the sale and the type of goods sold. While § 2-313 makes it clear that no specific words need be used and no specific intent need be present, not every statement by a seller is an express warranty.

Several older Pennsylvania cases dealing with horse sales show that similar statements as to soundness are not always similarly treated under warranty law. In *Wilkinson v. Stettler*, 46 Pa. Super. 407 (1911), the statement that a horse "was solid and sound and would work any place" was held not to constitute an express warranty. This result was followed in *Walker v. Kirk*, 72 Pa. Super. 534 (1919) which considered the statement, "This mare is sound and all right and a good worker double." *Walker* was decided after the passage of § 12 of the Uniform Sales Act, the precursor of U.C.C. § 2-313 and thus presumably rests on the standard there established. The Official Comments to U.C.C. § 2-313 indicate that no changes in the law of warranties under Uniform Sales Act § 12 were intended.

However, in *Flood v. Yeager*, 52 Pa. Super. 637 (1912) an express warranty was found where the plaintiff informed the defendant that, "he did not know anything at all about a horse and that he did not want * * * the defendant to make a mean deal with him; whereupon the defendant said that the horse was solid and sound; that he would guarantee him to be solid and sound" 52 Pa. Super. at 638. While all three of these cases are premised partly on the now displaced rule that specific intent to warrant is a necessary concomitant of an express warranty, they do show that statements of the same tenor receive varying treatment depending on the surrounding circumstances.

The results in these cases are all consistent with custom among horse traders as alluded to by Gene Riegle. He testified that it is "not a common thing" to guarantee a horse, that he has never guaranteed a horse unless he had an "understanding" with the buyer and that he did not guarantee Tarport Conaway. In other words, because horses are fragile creatures, susceptible to myriad maladies, detectable and undetectable, only where there is an "understanding" that an ignorant buyer, is relying totally on a knowledgeable seller not "to make a mean deal," are statements as to soundness taken to be anything more than the seller's opinion or commendation.

The facts suggest no special "understanding" between Sessa and Riegle. Sessa was a knowledgeable buyer, having been involved with standardbreds for some years. Also, Sessa sent Maloney, an even more knowledgeable horseman, as his agent to inspect the horse.

Also mitigating against the finding of express warranty is the nature of the conversation between Sessa and Riegle. It seemed largely collateral to the sale rather than an essential part of it. Although Sessa testified that Riegle's "personal guarantee" given during the conversation was the quintessence of the sale, the credible evidence suggests otherwise. While on the telephone, Riegle made statements to the effect that "the horse is a good one" and "you will like him." These bland statements are obviously opinion or commendation, and the statement, "The horse is sound," falling within their penumbra takes on their character as such.

Under all the facts and circumstances of this case, it is clear to the Court that Riegle's statements were not of such a character as to give rise to express warranties under § 2-313(1) but were opinion or commendation under § 2-313(2).

Even assuming that Riegle's statements could be express warranties, it is not clear that they were "part of the basis of the bargain," the second requisite of § 2-313. This is essentially a reliance requirement and is inextricably intertwined with the initial determination as to whether given language may constitute an express warranty since affirmations, promises and descriptions tend to become part of the basis of the bargain. It was the intention of the drafters of the U.C.C. not to require a strong showing of reliance. In fact, they envisioned that all statements of the seller became part of the basis of the bargain unless clear affirmative proof is shown to the contrary. *See* Official Comments 3 and 8 to U.C.C. § 2-313, 12A P.S. § 2-313.

It is Sessa's contention that his conversation with Riegle was the principal factor inducing him to enter the bargain. He would have the court believe that Maloney was merely a messenger to deliver the check. The evidence shows, however, that Sessa was relying primarily on Maloney to advise him in connection with the sale. Maloney testified that he had talked to Sessa about the horse on several occasions and expressed the opinion that he was convinced "beyond the shadow of a doubt" that he was a good buy. With respect to his authority to buy the horse he testified

"Well, Mr. Sessa said he had enough confidence and faith in me and my integrity and honesty that I, what I did say about the horse, I was representing the horse as he is or as he was, and that if the horse, in my estimation, was that type of a horse and at that given price, the fixed price of $25,000 he would buy the horse."

When, at the airport, Maloney protested that he did not want to accept full responsibility to go to Ohio alone, Sessa told him * * * "I take your word. I–I trust your judgment and I trust your–your honesty, that if this horse is right, everything will be all right." In Ohio, Maloney examined the horse, jogged him and reported to Sessa over the telephone that he "liked him."

The court believes that Maloney's opinion was the principal, if not the only, factor which motivated Sessa to purchase the horse. The conversation with Riegle played a negligible role in his decision. * * *

[The court concluded that even if an express warranty had been made, Sessa had accepted the horse and had failed to prove by a preponderance of the evidence that the horse was not sound at the time of tender.]   [Footnotes omitted.]

Notes

1.   Does "soundness" have a meaning in the horse trade?   Consider the following from *Simpson v. Widger*, 709 A.2d 1366, 1371 (N.J. Super. A.D. 1998):

> The concept of soundness in a horse is somewhat complex. . . .Soundness in a horse has been described in these words:
>
> > A *sound* horse is free from any abnormality in the form or function of any part. A s*erviceably sound* horse is one capable of doing his job although he may have some minor unsoundness or blemish not serious enough to incapacitate him. No other quality is more important than soundness in determining a horse's value. [JOHN M. KAYS, THE HORSE, A COMPLETE GUIDE TO ITS CARE AND HANDLING 3 (3rd ed., Arco Publishing, Inc.1982)]

Is usage of trade, course of performance, or course of dealing relevant to the question of what is an affirmation of fact?

2.   Note that the court first concludes that the seller's statement that the horse was "sound" was "puffing" rather than an affirmation of fact but then decides, in the alternative, even if it was an affirmation of fact, it did not become part of the basis of the bargain.   How does the court draw these important lines?   What evidence did the court look at in *Sessa* to determine if what the seller said was the "basis of the bargain"?   Is the court talking about reliance?

KEITH V. BUCHANAN
COURT OF APPEALS OF CALIFORNIA, SECOND DISTRICT, 1985
173 CAL. APP. 3D 13, 220 CAL. RPTR. 392

OCHOA, ASSOCIATE JUSTICE

This breach of warranty case is before this court after the trial court granted defendants' motion for judgment at the close of plaintiff's case during the trial proceedings. We hold that an express warranty under section 2313 of the California Uniform Commercial Code was created in this matter, and that actual reliance on the seller's factual representation need not be shown by the buyer. The representation is presumed to be part of the basis of the bargain, and the burden is on the seller to prove that the representation was not a consideration inducing the bargain. We affirm all other aspects of the trial court's judgment but reverse in regard to its finding that no express warranty was created and remand for further proceedings consistent with this opinion.

Statement of Facts

Plaintiff, Brian Keith, purchased a sailboat from defendants in November 1978 for a total purchase price of $75,610. Even though plaintiff belonged to the Waikiki Yacht Club, had attended a sailing school, had joined the Coast Guard Auxiliary, and had sailed on many yachts in order to ascertain his preferences, he had not previously owned a yacht. He attended a boat show in Long Beach during October 1978 and looked at a number of boats, speaking to sales representatives and obtaining advertising literature. In the literature, the sailboat which is the subject of this action, called an "Island Trader 41," was described as a seaworthy vessel. In one sales brochure, this vessel is described as "a picture of sure-footed seaworthiness." In another, it is called "a carefully well-equipped, and very seaworthy live-aboard vessel." Plaintiff testified he relied on representations in the sales brochures in regard to the purchase. Plaintiff and a sales representative also discussed plaintiff's desire for a boat which was ocean-going and would cruise long distances.

Plaintiff asked his friend, Buddy Ebsen, who was involved in a boat building enterprise, to inspect the boat. Mr. Ebsen and one of his associates, both of whom had extensive experience with sailboats, observed the boat and advised plaintiff that the vessel would suit his stated needs. A deposit was paid on the boat, a purchase contract was entered into, and optional accessories for the boat were ordered. After delivery of the vessel, a dispute arose in regard to its seaworthiness.

Plaintiff filed the instant lawsuit alleging causes of action in breach of express warranty and breach of implied warranty. The trial court granted defendants' Code of Civil Procedure section 631.8 motion for judgment at the close of plaintiff's case. The court found that no express warranty was established by the evidence because none of the defendants had undertaken in writing to preserve or maintain the utility or performance of the vessel, nor to provide compensation for any failure in utility or performance. It found that the written statements produced at trial were opinions or commendations of the vessel. The court further found that no implied warranty of fitness was created because the plaintiff did not rely on the skill and judgment of defendants to select and furnish a suitable vessel, but had rather relied on his own experts in selecting the vessel.

Discussion

I. Express Warranty

California Uniform Commercial Code section 2313 provides, inter alia, that express warranties are created by (1) any affirmation of fact or promise made by the seller to the buyer which relates to the goods and becomes part of the basis of the bargain, and (2) any description of the goods which is made part of the basis of the bargain. Formal words such as "warranty" or "guarantee" are not required to make a warranty, but the seller's affirmation of the value of the goods or an expression of opinion or commendation of the goods does not create an express warranty. * * *

California Uniform Commercial Code section 2313, regarding express warranties, was enacted in 1963 and consists of the official text of Uniform Commercial Code section 2-313 without change. In deciding whether a statement made by a seller constitutes an express warranty under this provision, the court must deal with three fundamental issues. First, the court must determine whether the seller's statement constitutes an "affirmation of fact or promise" or "description of the goods" under California Uniform Commercial Code section 2313, subdivision (1)(a) or (b) or whether it is rather "merely the seller's opinion or commendation of the goods" under section 2313, subdivision (2). Second, assuming the court finds the language used susceptible to creation of a warranty, it must then be determined whether the statement was "part of the basis of the bargain." Third, the court must determine whether the warranty was breached. (*See Sessa v. Riegle* (E.D. Pa. 1977) 427 F. Supp. 760, 765.)

A warranty relates to the title, character, quality, identity, or condition of the goods. The purpose of the law of warranty is to determine what it is that the seller has in essence agreed to sell. * * * "Express warranties are chisels in the hands of buyers and sellers. With these tools, the parties to a sale sculpt a monument representing the goods. Having selected a stone, the buyer and seller may leave it almost bare, allowing considerable play in the qualities that fit its contours. Or the parties may chisel away inexactitudes until a well-defined shape emerges. The seller is bound to deliver, and the buyer to accept, goods that match the sculpted form. [Fn. omitted.]" (*Special Project: Article Two Warranties in Commercial Transactions, Express Warranties–Section 2-313* (1978-79) 64 CORNELL L. REV. 30 (hereafter cited as *Warranties in Commercial Transactions*) at pp. 43-44.)

A. Affirmation of fact, promise or description versus statement of opinion, commendation or value

"The determination as to whether a particular statement is an expression of opinion or an affirmation of fact is often difficult, and frequently is dependent upon the facts and circumstances existing at the time the statement is made." (*Willson v. Municipal Bond Co.* (1936) 7 Cal. 2d 144, 150, 59 P.2d 974.) Recent decisions have evidenced a trend toward narrowing the scope of representations which are considered opinion, sometimes referred to as "puffing" or "sales talk," resulting in an expansion of the liability that flows from broad statements of manufacturers or retailers as to the quality of their products. Courts have liberally construed affirmations of quality made by sellers in favor of injured consumers. * * * It has even been suggested "that in an age of consumerism all seller's statements, except the most blatant sales pitch, may give rise to an express warranty." (1 ALDERMAN AND DOLE, A TRANSACTIONAL GUIDE TO THE UNIFORM COMMERCIAL CODE (2d ed. 1983) p. 89.)

Courts in other states have struggled in efforts to create a formula for distinguishing between affirmations of fact, promises, or descriptions of goods on the one hand, and value, opinion, or commendation statements on the other. The code comment indicates that the basic question is: "What statements of the seller have in the circumstances and in objective judgment become part of the basis of the bargain?" The commentators indicated that the language of subsection (2) of the code section was included because "common experience discloses that some statements or predictions cannot fairly be viewed as entering into the bargain." (*See* U. Com. Code com. 8 to Cal. U. Com. Code, § 2313, West's Ann. Com. Code (1964) p. 250.)

Statements made by a seller during the course of negotiation over a contract are presumptively affirmations of fact unless it can be demonstrated that the buyer could only have reasonably considered the statement as a statement of the seller's opinion. Commentators have noted several factors which tend to indicate an opinion statement. These are (1) a lack of specificity in the statement made, (2) a statement that is made in an equivocal manner, or (3) a statement which reveals that the goods are experimental in nature. (*See Warranties in Commercial Transactions, supra,* at pp. 61-65.)

It is clear that statements made by a manufacturer or retailer in an advertising brochure which is disseminated to the consuming public in order to induce sales can create express warranties. * * * In the instant case, the vessel purchased was described in sales brochures as "a picture of sure-footed seaworthiness" and "a carefully well-equipped and very seaworthy vessel." The seller's representative was aware that appellant was looking for a vessel sufficient for long distance ocean-going cruises. The statements in the brochure are specific and unequivocal in asserting that the vessel is seaworthy. Nothing in the negotiation indicates that the vessel is experimental in nature. In fact, one sales brochure assures prospective buyers that production of the vessel was commenced "after years of careful testing." The representations regarding seaworthiness made in sales brochures regarding the Island Trader 41 were affirmations of fact relating to the quality or condition of the vessel.

B. "Part of the basis of the bargain" Test

Under former provisions of law, a purchaser was required to prove that he or she acted in reliance upon representations made by the seller. * * * California Uniform Commercial Code section 2313 indicates only that the seller's statements must become "part of the basis of the bargain." According to official comment 3 to this Uniform Commercial Code provision, "no particular reliance * * * need be shown in order to weave [the seller's affirmations of fact] into the fabric of the agreement. Rather, any fact which is to take such affirmations, once made, out of the agreement requires clear affirmative proof." (*See* U. Com. Code com. 3 to Cal. U. Com. Code, § 2313, West's Ann. Com. Code (1964) p. 249.)

The California Supreme Court, in discussing the continued viability of the reliance factor, noted that commentators have disagreed in regard to the impact of this development. Some have indicated that it shifts the burden of proving non-reliance to the seller, and others have indicated that the code eliminates the concept of reliance altogether. * * * The court did not resolve this issue, but noted that decisions of other states prior to that time had "ignored the significance of the new standard and have held that consumer reliance still is a vital ingredient for recovery based on express warranty." [*Hauter v. Zogarts*, 534 P.2d 377 (Cal. 1975)]

The shift in language clearly changes the degree to which it must be shown that the seller's representation affected the buyer's decision to enter into the agreement. A buyer need not show that he would not have entered into the agreement absent the warranty or even that it was a dominant factor inducing the agreement. A warranty statement is deemed to be part of the basis of the bargain and to have been relied upon as one of the inducements for the purchase of the product. In other words, the buyer's demonstration of reliance on an express warranty is "not a prerequisite for breach of warranty, as long as the express warranty involved became part of the bargain. *See* WHITE & SUMMERS, UNIFORM COMMERCIAL CODE (2d ed. 1980) § 9-4. If, however, the resulting bargain does not rest at all on the representations of the seller, those representations cannot be considered as becoming any part of the 'basis of the bargain.' * * * " (*Allied Fidelity Ins. Co. v. Pico* (Nev. S. Ct.1983) 656 P.2d 849, 850.)

The official Uniform Commercial Code comment in regard to section 2-313 "indicates that in actual practice affirmations of fact made by the seller about the goods during a bargain are regarded as part of the description of those goods; hence no particular reliance on such statements need be shown in order to weave them into the fabric of the agreement."* * * It is clear from the new language of this code section that the concept of reliance has been purposefully abandoned. * * *

The change of the language in section 2313 of the California Uniform Commercial Code modifies both the degree of reliance and the burden of proof in express warranties under the code. The representation need only be part of the basis of the bargain, or merely a factor or consideration inducing the buyer to enter into the bargain. A warranty statement made by a seller is presumptively part of the basis of the bargain, and the burden is on the seller to prove that the resulting bargain does not rest at all on the representation.

The buyer's actual knowledge of the true condition of the goods prior to the making of the contract may make it plain that the seller's statement was not relied upon as one of the inducements for the purchase, but the burden is on the seller to demonstrate such knowledge on the part of the buyer. Where the buyer inspects the goods before purchase, he may be deemed to have waived the seller's express warranties. But, an examination or inspection by the buyer of the goods does not necessarily discharge the seller from an express warranty if the defect was not actually discovered and waived. * * * Appellant's inspection of the boat by his own experts does not constitute a waiver of the express warranty of seaworthiness. Prior to the making of the contract, appellant had experienced boat builders observe the boat, but there was no testing of the vessel in the water.[1] Such a warranty (seaworthiness) necessarily relates to the time when the vessel has been put to sea * * * and has been shown to be reasonably fit and adequate in materials, construction, and equipment for its intended purposes. * * *

In this case, appellant was aware of the representations regarding seaworthiness by the seller prior to contracting. He also had expressed to the seller's representative his desire for a long distance ocean-going vessel. Although he had other experts inspect the vessel, the inspection was limited and would not have indicated whether or not the vessel was seaworthy. It is clear that the seller has not overcome the presumption that the representations regarding seaworthiness were part of the basis of this bargain. * * *

[The court upheld the trial court's conclusion that the seller did not make and breach an implied warranty of fitness for particular purpose under UCC 2-315: The buyer did not rely on the seller's skill and judgment in selecting a suitable boat.]

[Some footnotes omitted. Those retained have been renumbered.]

Notes

1.　The court in *Keith* cites with approval the three step "basis of the bargain" test employed in *Sessa* but then reaches the opposite result. Can the cases be reconciled? Should Buddy Ebsen be fired as an expert on seaworthiness?

2.　How do we know initially whether a statement is an affirmation of fact or an opinion? In *Royal Business Machines, Inc. v. Lorraine Corp.*, 633 F.2d 34, 41 (7th Cir. 1980), the court stated: "The decisive test for whether a given representation is a warranty or merely an expression of the seller's opinion is whether the seller asserts a fact of which the buyer is ignorant or merely states an

---

[1] Evidence was presented of examination or inspection of the boat after the making of the contract of sale and prior to delivery and acceptance of the vessel. Such an inspection would be irrelevant to any issue of express warranty. Although it deals with implied warranties as opposed to express warranties, the Uniform Commercial Code comment 8 to section 2-316 (Cal. U. Com. Code, § 2316) is instructive: "Under paragraph (b) of subdivision (3) warranties may be excluded or modified by the circumstances where the buyer examines the goods or a sample or model of them *before entering into the contract. 'Examination' as used in this paragraph is not synonymous with inspection before acceptance or at any other time after the contract has been made. It goes rather to the nature of the responsibility assumed by the seller at the time of the making of the contract.*" (*See* U. Com. Code com. 8 to Cal. U. Com. Code, § 2316, West's Ann. Com. Code (1964) p. 308, emphasis added.)

opinion or judgment on a matter of which the seller has no special knowledge and on which the buyer may be expected also to have an opinion and to exercise his judgment."* *See also* the new comment 10 to amended UCC 2-313.

Problem 5-1

Saldo is a dealer in dry chemicals, selling at wholesale to a variety of buyers. Saldo purchased 2,000 pounds of a copper sulphate described as "blue vitriol" from the Copco Mfgr. Co. The goods arrived in 20 sealed barrels. The barrels were unmarked but the invoice described the goods as "vitriol." The barrels were offered for sale at a quarterly wholesale auction. One of the barrels was opened for prospective buyers to examine. It contained a bluish crystalline substance which one of the prospective buyers thought "looked strange." The purchasing agent of Barston Chemicals, Inc., a dealer which frequently sold at retail, also inspected the barrel. He stated to the auctioneer that while the substance looked like blue vitriol, it could be "green" vitriol, a less valuable chemical. Upon consultation with Saldo, the auctioneer announced that "the next sale will be a 20-barrel lot of blue vitriol in sound order."

After spirited bidding, Barston Chemicals was high bidder at $.15 per pound. The price was paid and the goods were removed to the Barston warehouse, where they were immediately resold to a third party at $.18 per pound. The next day, however, it was discovered that the substance in the open barrel had turned green. Chemical analysis revealed that the substance was in fact "green" vitriol in sound order, worth about $.10 per pound at wholesale and $.13 per pound at retail. All of the other barrels contained "green" vitriol. In order to distinguish "green" from "blue" vitriol, either a chemical analysis must be done or the "green" vitriol allowed to stand in the open air for 10 or more hours.

Barston promptly notified Saldo of the situation, revoked its acceptance, and demanded the return of the purchase price paid and damages for breach of warranty. The Barston purchasing agent stated that he was "not sure" what was in the barrel when he first examined it but after the auctioneer announced the sale, bid on the

---

* *Accord, Royal Typewriter Co. v. Xerographic Supplies Corp.*, 719 F.2d 1092 (11th Cir. 1983); *see also Ruffin v. Shaw Industries, Inc.*, 149 F.3d 294, 302 (4th Cir. 1998) (statement of store manager that certain carpet "was a higher quality carpet than what [plaintiff] brought in[to the store]" was puffing); *Boud v. SDNCO, Inc.*, 54 P. 3d 1131 (Utah 2002) ("best performance" and "suburb handling" in brochure were not specific enough to be express warranties).

assumption that it was blue vitriol. Saldo claims that its officers honestly believed that the barrels contained blue vitriol, but that no warranty was intended and that Barston, as a professional chemical dealer, assumed the risk that the substance was green vitriol.

A. Did the seller (speaking through the auctioneer) make an express warranty in this case? If so, was it by affirmation or promise, description or sample? *See* UCC 2-313. In general, auctioneers, as agents for the seller, do not make warranties unless they fail to disclose that they are selling for a principal.

B. Suppose that the seller had stated that the goods were "vitriol" yet the buyer had assumed they were "blue" vitriol. What result? *Compare* UCC 2-313 *with* UCC 2-314. Does the description "vitriol" simply identify the goods or does it reveal basic attributes or quality?*

C. Suppose the sale was for a 20 barrel lot and one barrel was opened, tested and found to be blue vitriol. After the sale, it was discovered that 10 barrels in the lot contained green vitriol. What is the buyer's best argument on these facts?

Note: The "Basis of the Bargain" Test

There is some disagreement over whether the "basis of the bargain" requirement in UCC 2-313 requires reliance by the buyer and, if so, who has the burden of proof. Following *Keith v. Buchanan, supra*, many courts and commentators have concluded that an affirmation of fact made by the seller to the buyer becomes part of the basis of the bargain unless the seller proves that the buyer was unaware of the representation or did not rely on or believe it.** This view is clearly supported by the comments to UCC 2-313.

The legislative history is interesting. As we have indicated above, the "basis

---

* *See* Jacob S. Ziegel, *The Seller's Liability for Defective Goods at Common Law*, 12 MCGILL L.J. 183, 186-87 (1966).

** *See, e.g., Buettner v. R. W. Martin & Sons, Inc.*, 47 F.3d 116 (4th Cir. 1995) (Virginia law); *Tolmie Farms, Inc. v. J.R. Simplot, Inc.*, 862 P.2d 299 (Idaho 1993); *Torres v. Northwest Engineering Co.*, 949 P.2d 1004 (Haw. Ct. App. 1998); *Weng v. Allison*, 678 N.E.2d 1254 (Ill. Ct. App. 1997): *Cipollone v. Liggett Group, Inc.*, 893 F.2d 541, 563 (3rd Cir. 1990) (seller must have opportunity to prove by "clear and convincing" evidence that the buyer knew the affirmation was untrue) *reversed on other grounds*, 505 U.S. 504 (1992). *See also* Thomas J. Holdych & Bruce D. Mann, *The Basis of the Bargain Requirement: A Market and Economic Based Analysis of Express Warranties–Getting What You Pay For and Paying For What You Get*, 45 DE PAUL L. REV. 781 (1996).

of the bargain" language came from the reliance requirement in section 12 of the Uniform Sales Act that required the buyer to purchase goods "relying thereon." That language first turned into the "basis of the bargain" language in section 37 in the Final Draft No. 1 of 1944 draft of the Uniform Revised Sales Act. What is now UCC 2-313(2)(a) [former subsection (1)] read as follows in the 1944 act:

> Express warranties by the seller are created as follows:
>
> (a) Any affirmation of fact or promise which relates to the goods and is made by the seller to the buyer as a part of the bargain creates an express warranty that the goods shall conform to the affirmation or promise.

The quoted language was later changed to its current form apparently to make UCC 2-313(2)(a) correspond with (2)(b) and (2)(c).

In the 1943 meeting of the National Commissioners in Chicago, Professor Mentschikoff, the associate reporter, described the relevant changes as follows: "Major changes in this section over the old act [Uniform Sales Act] are simply verbal." It is possible, therefore, that all the commentators and courts who have read so much into the omission of any form of the verb "rely" and into its replacement with the "basis of the bargain" language have been barking up the wrong tree. Conceivably Llewellyn, Mentschikoff and the Commissioners did not mean to dilute the reliance requirement at all, but only to expand—ever so slightly—the acts that might be regarded as reliance.

In fact, the comment published in 1944 with section 37, almost certainly written by Professor Llewellyn, suggests that he would not have intended to include events remote from the deal to be part of the basis of the bargain.

> Unified contract basis of warranty: Under this Act warranties are an essential part of the contract for sale. Fundamentally, all warranties are summed up in "description" under the present section; it requires the whole net effect of the bargain to effectively describe what kind and quality of thing the seller has assumed obligation to sell and deliver. It does serve convenience to particularize rules on warranty which deal with some familiar and recurrent sets of fact, but the object remains single: it is to arrive at the net description which defines the seller's obligation. The present section therefore deals with affirmations of fact by the seller exactly as it deals with any other part of a negotiation which ends in a contract. No specific intention to make a warranty is needed, to make the affirmation a part of the net description of the goods. No agreement that the affirmation shall constitute a warranty is needed. In life, affirmations of fact which relate to the goods and which are made by a seller in

connection with a bargain about goods are taken as part of the description
of the goods contracted about; in life, no particular reliance needs to be
shown in order to weave such affirmations into the fabric of the agreement.
Instead, what needs an affirmative showing is that there has been any fact
which gives clear objective justification for the unusual result of taking
such affirmations out of what has been agreed upon.   Under some
circumstances, an examination by a buyer before he closes the bargain may
go very far in this direction; see Section 41(2)(b) and Comment thereon.
Under some circumstances, words may do the same, either in regard to an
"affirmation" or in regard to the content of what looks on the surface as a
"description"; see Comment to Section 53 on sale by auction.

2 ELIZABETH S. KELLY, UNIFORM COMMERCIAL CODE DRAFTS at 155-56 (1984)
(emphasis added).

The quoted comment suggests that Llewellyn was not abandoning the idea of
reliance and that mostly he had in mind face-to-face dealings where the affirmations
might be made orally or in writing by the seller to the buyer.   The comment
discusses disclosures as a "part of negotiation." The comment also recognizes the
possibility that some affirmations, even those made in face-to-face settings, might
not constitute warranties because there was no reliance.   The comment also
contemplates cases where the buyer's examination or the fact that there was an
auction sale might exclude reliance.[*]

If one chooses to expand the "bargain" beyond things actually seen and
perceived, the buyer is on a slippery slope. For example, can the purchaser of
packaged products such as an electric razor claim that assertions contained on the
document inside the package–unseen at the time of purchase–constituted express
warranties? It is hard to deny that such statements could and should give rise to
liability; indeed, cases hold that assertions in operating manuals for automobiles and
the like that are never read by the buyer prior to the purchase may constitute express
warranties. Yet if one acknowledges that such terms can become the basis of the
bargain, where does one stop on the slope that leads to advertisements published by
the defendants but never seen by the plaintiff. Perhaps never seen by any resident
of the particular plaintiff's state?   For example, would an assertion by a
manufacturer about product quality made in the interior of China, only in Chinese,

---

[*] For an argument that Llewellyn meant to reject the reliance standard, *see* Charles A.
Heckman, *'Reliance' or 'Common Honesty of Speech': The History and Interpretation of
Section 2-313 of the Uniform Commercial Code*, 38 CASE W. RES. L. REV. 1 (1987-88).

and seen only by Chinese citizens constitute an express warranty that is part of the basis the bargain for a buyer in New Jersey? If reliance means anything, that case is hard to swallow, but where then does one draw the line between the case of the electric razor and the case of the advertising published in a distant land and never seen? Of course, one can say that the purchaser of an electric razor expects to get some instructions and statements within the box and that the buyer of a GM pickup truck expects the same. In that sense there might possibly be "reliance." Is that a satisfactory distinction? *Compare* UCC 2-313B (added by the 2003 amendments) requiring that a remote purchaser have "knowledge of" and an "expectation that" the goods will conform to an affirmation of fact made by the remote seller to the public.

Now consider the following case. What does it add to your understanding of the requirements for an express warranty, more specifically, the requirement that the seller's representation be part of the basis of the bargain?

ROGATH V. SIEBENMANN
UNITED STATES COURT OF APPEALS, SECOND CIRCUIT, 1997
129 F.3D 261

MCLAUGHLIN, CIRCUIT JUDGE

BACKGROUND

This case revolves around a painting, entitled "Self Portrait," supposedly painted in 1972 by a well-known English artist, Francis Bacon.

In July 1993, defendant Werner Siebenmann sold the Painting to plaintiff David Rogath for $570,000. In the Bill of Sale, Siebenmann described the provenance of the Painting and warranted that he was the sole owner of the Painting, that it was authentic, and that he was not aware of any challenge to its authenticity.

Problems arose three months later when Rogath sold the Painting to Acquavella Contemporary Art, Inc., in New York, for $950,000. Acquavella learned of a challenge to the Painting's authenticity and, on November 1, 1993, requested that Rogath refund the $950,000 and take back the Painting. Rogath did so, and then sued Siebenmann in the Southern District of New York (Batts, J.) for breach of contract, breach of warranty and fraud.

Rogath moved for partial summary judgment on the breach of warranty claims, and the district court granted his motion. *See Rogath v. Siebenmann*, 941 F. Supp. 416, 422-24 (S.D.N.Y. 1996). The court concluded that (1) Siebenmann was unsure of the provenance of the Painting when he sold it to Rogath; (2) he was not the sole owner of the Painting; and (3) when he sold the Painting to Rogath he already knew of a challenge to the Painting's authenticity by the Marlborough Fine Art Gallery in London. *See id.* The court awarded Rogath $950,000 in damages, the price at which he had sold it to Acquavella. *See id.* at 424-25. The court dismissed, *sua sponte*, Rogath's remaining claims for fraud and breach of contract "in light of the full recovery on the warranties granted herein." *Id.* at 425. Finally, a few days later, the court denied Rogath's motion to attach the money that Siebenmann had remaining from the proceeds of the initial sale to Rogath.

Siebenmann appeals the grant of partial summary judgment. Rogath cross-appeals the denial of his motion for attachment and the dismissal of his fraud and breach of contract claims.

DISCUSSION

Siebenmann concedes that his promises and representations set forth in the Bill of Sale constitute warranties under New York law. He claims, however, that Rogath was fully aware when he bought the Painting that questions of authenticity and provenance had already been raised regarding the Painting. He maintains that, under New York law, Rogath therefore cannot rest claims for breach of warranty on the representations made in the Bill of Sale.

We review *de novo* the district court's disposition of Rogath's motion for partial summary judgment. * * * The parties agree that New York law applies.

A. Breach of Warranty under New York Law

The Bill of Sale provides:

> In order to induce David Rogath to make the purchase, Seller * * * make[s] the following warranties, representations and covenants to and with the Buyer.
>
> 1. That the Seller is the sole and absolute owner of the painting and has full right and authority to sell and transfer same; having acquired title as described in a copy of the Statement of Provenance signed by Seller annexed hereto and incorporated herein; [and] that the Seller has no knowledge of any challenge to Seller's title and authenticity of the Painting. * * *

Because the Bill of Sale was a contract for the sale of goods, Rogath's breach of warranty claims are governed by Article Two of the Uniform Commercial Code ("UCC"). * * * Section 2-313 of the UCC provides that "[a]ny description of the goods which is made part of the basis of the bargain creates an express warranty that the goods shall conform to the description." N.Y.U.C.C. § 2-313(1)(b) (McKinney 1993).

Whether the "basis of the bargain" requirement implies that the buyer must rely on the seller's statements to recover and what the nature of that reliance requirement is are unsettled questions. * * * Not surprisingly, this same confusion haunted the New York courts for a time. * * *

Some courts reasoned that the buyer must have relied upon the accuracy of the seller's affirmations or promises in order to recover . * * *

Other courts paid lip service to a "reliance" requirement, but found that the requirement was met if the buyer relied on the seller's promise as part of "the basis of the bargain" in entering into the contract; the buyer need not show that he relied on the truthfulness of the warranties. * * *

Finally, some courts reasoned that there is a "reliance" requirement only when there is a dispute as to whether a warranty was in fact given by the seller. These courts concluded that no reliance of any kind is required "where the existence of an express warranty in a contract is conceded by both parties." * * * In these cases, the buyer need establish only a breach of the warranty.

In 1990 New York's Court of Appeals dispelled much of the confusion when it squarely adopted the "basis of the bargain" description of the reliance required to recover for breach of an express warranty. In *CBS Inc. v. Ziff-Davis Publishing Co.*, 75 N.Y.2d 496, 554 N.Y.S.2d 449, 553 N.E.2d 997 (1990), the court concluded that "[t]his view of 'reliance'-i.e., as requiring no more than reliance on the express warranty as being a part of the bargain between the parties-reflects the prevailing perception of an action for breach of express warranty as one that is no longer grounded in tort, but essentially in contract." *Id.* at 452, 553 N.E.2d at 1001. The court reasoned that "[t]he critical question is not whether the buyer believed in the truth of the warranted information * * * but whether [he] believed [he] was purchasing the [seller's] promise [as to its truth]." *Id.* at 452-53, 553 N.E.2d at 1000- 001 (quotations omitted and some insertions altered).

CBS was not decided on the basis of the UCC, probably because the sale of the magazine business at issue did not constitute the sale of goods. * * * Nevertheless, the court relied heavily on UCC authorities, *see CBS*, 554 N.Y.S.2d 449, 553 N.E.2d at 1000-001, expressly noting that "analogy to the Uniform Commercial Code is 'instructive'." *Id.* at 454 n.4, 553 N.E.2d at 1002 n.4.

In 1992, in a case also involving the sale of a business, we followed the New York Court of Appeals and delineated fine factual distinctions in the law of warranties: a court must evaluate both the extent and the source of the buyer's knowledge about the truth of what the seller is warranting. "Where a buyer closes on a contract in the full knowledge and acceptance of facts *disclosed by the seller* which would constitute a breach of warranty under the terms of the contract, the buyer should be foreclosed from later asserting the breach. In that situation, unless the buyer expressly preserves his rights under the warranties * * *, we think the buyer has waived the breach." *Galli v. Metz*, 973 F.2d 145, 151 (2d Cir. 1992) (emphasis added); * * * The buyer may preserve his rights by expressly stating that disputes regarding the accuracy of the seller's warranties are unresolved, and that by signing the agreement the buyer does not waive any rights to enforce the terms of the agreement. *See Galli*, 973 F.2d at 150.

On the other hand, if the seller is not the source of the buyer's knowledge, *e.g.*, if it is merely "common knowledge" that the facts warranted are false, or the buyer has been informed of the falsity of the facts by some third party, the buyer may prevail in his claim for breach of warranty. In these cases, it is not unrealistic to assume that the buyer purchased the seller's warranty "as insurance against any future claims," and that is why he insisted on the inclusion of the warranties in the bill of sale. *Galli*, 973 F.2d at 151; * * *

In short, where the seller discloses up front the inaccuracy of certain of his warranties, it cannot be said that the buyer-absent the express preservation of his rights-believed he was purchasing the seller's promise as to the truth of the warranties. Accordingly, what the buyer knew and, most importantly, whether he got that knowledge from the seller are the critical questions. *See Galli*, 973 F.2d at 151; *Chateaugay*, 155 B.R. at 650-51.

1. What Siebenmann Knew

Here, as the district court pointed out, Siebenmann, the seller, produced no evidence to contradict Rogath's evidence that Siebenmann knew of the cloud that hung over the Painting's authenticity before he sold it to Rogath. Siebenmann admits that he was told that the Marlborough Gallery was troubled by certain peculiarities of the Painting-including shiny black paint (as opposed to the matte black that Bacon apparently preferred) and the use of pink paint (which Bacon evidently did not use)-that suggested that Bacon was not the painter.

Siebenmann also admits that Julian Barran, a London art dealer, had earlier refused to buy the Painting because of doubts harbored by the Marlborough Gallery. Moreover, there was uncontroverted evidence that, on a prior occasion, Siebenmann's attempted sale of the Painting to a client of Robert Peter Miller, the owner of an art gallery in New York, was aborted when (1) Miller learned that the Marlborough had concerns about the Painting's authenticity, and (2) David Sylvester, a British art critic, advised Miller not to proceed with the purchase because of the Marlborough objection and because Sylvester himself was not sure of the authenticity of the Painting.

Finally, Siebenmann does not deny that in June 1993 he received a fax from Anita Goldstein, an art dealer in Zurich, Switzerland, stating that "everybody is afraid of the authenticity" of the Painting.

2. What Siebenmann Told Rogath: Reasonable Inferences

In an affidavit in opposition to Rogath's motion for partial summary judgment, Siebenmann stated that "I spoke directly with David Rogath about the controversy created by the Marlborough Gallery towards this painting." He also said that, in a phone conversation with Rogath on July 13, 1993, "I specifically mentioned Marlborough Gallery and the 'problems' or the 'controversy' that it had produced for this painting. * * * Mr. Rogath brushed aside the Marlborough Gallery controversy. He told me he had experienced difficulties with this particular gallery in the past and did not consider them to be especially reputable." In his deposition, Siebenmann added that he told Rogath on the phone "that I had problems with the Marlborough Gallery."

Siebenmann also filed an affidavit from Ronald Alley, the curator of the Tate Gallery in London, England, and the author of a survey of Bacon's work as well as several other writings about Bacon. Alley stated:

> I was phoned by Mr David Rogath, hitherto unknown to me, who said that he was thinking of buying the painting and asked whether it was correct that I had seen it and thought it to be authentic. My reply, to the best of my recollection, can be summarized as follows: "It is a picture which did not pass through Marlborough Fine Art and is said to have a provenance which sounds quite plausible but is more or less impossible to check. Both Ms Beston of Marlborough Fine Art and David Sylvester say they don't think it is by Bacon, but Sylvester knows it only from a photograph. I flew to Geneva for the day to look at it in a warehouse and felt convinced it was genuine."

For his part, Rogath denied that he was aware of any challenges to the authenticity or provenance of the Painting before entering into the Bill of Sale. He stated in his affidavit:

> During our telephone conversation, Mr. Siebenmann did not tell me

that the Marlborough Gallery had "questioned" or "reserved judgment" about the Painting, or had caused any "problems" or "controversy" concerning the Painting. He said nothing at all like that during the conversation. Neither did Mr. Alley, in our subsequent conversation, refer to any such matters. He certainly did not tell me that Ms. Beston and Mr. Sylvester "don't think it is by Bacon." In fact, I spoke with Mr. Alley after the inauthenticity of the Painting had become known to me.* * * Had either Mr. Siebenmann or Mr. Alley hinted to me that the Painting was of questioned authenticity, it would have been a "red flag" for me, as I had no desire to spend some $600,000 dollars to purchase a painting the authenticity of which was in dispute.* * *

Here, the Bill of Sale states that the warranties induced Rogath to buy the Painting, but Rogath did not "expressly preserve his rights" under the Bill of Sale, as required by *Galli.** * *Accordingly, exactly what Siebenmann told Rogath is clearly crucial. * * * On the other hand, what Alley may have told Rogath about the authenticity and provenance of the Painting is immaterial.* * *Only if the seller, Siebenmann himself, informed Rogath of doubts about the provenance or challenges to authenticity will Rogath be deemed to have waived any claims for breach of warranty arising from the written representations appearing in the Bill of Sale.

* * * As Rogath emphasizes, Siebenmann nowhere specifically alleges that he informed Rogath of his doubts about the authenticity and provenance of the Painting. He merely alluded to the "controversy" or "problems" with the Marlborough Gallery. Still, Siebenmann's testimony, however ambiguous, may justify the inference that Rogath knew more than he now claims to have known when he entered into the Bill of Sale.

At the very least, there is indisputable ambiguity in the affidavits about the pivotal exchange between Rogath and Siebenmann. We are satisfied that genuine issues of fact persist. In this posture, we must draw all reasonable inferences in Siebenmann's favor. * * * Accordingly, as regards the Marlborough challenge, summary judgment on Rogath's claims for breach of the warranties of provenance and no challenges to authenticity is inappropriate. * * *

3. What Sylvester Said

Sylvester's doubts about the Painting also cannot justify summary judgment for Rogath, but for different reasons. Siebenmann was aware that "Sylvester advised Miller not to proceed with the purchase of the Painting because of the 'Marlborough objection and that he wasn't sure himself of the authenticity of the painting.'"

Siebenmann did not claim to have disclosed to Rogath Sylvester's statement. Indeed, in his affidavit opposing Rogath's summary judgment motion, Siebenmann stated that he did not consider Sylvester's doubts to be a challenge. Siebenmann's nondisclosure could constitute a breach of warranty-but only if Sylvester's statement was a "challenge" to authenticity. We conclude that the question of whether Sylvester's statement constituted a challenge poses factual issues for trial.

A contractual term is ambiguous where it may be ascribed "conflicting reasonable interpretations." *Mellon Bank, N.A. v. United Bank Corp. of N.Y.*, 31 F.3d 113, 116 (2d Cir. 1994). "As a general matter, we have held that when a contract is ambiguous, its interpretation becomes a question of fact and summary judgment is inappropriate." *Id.*

Although the parties apparently agree as to what Sylvester said, reasonable minds could differ as to whether what he said constituted a challenge apart from the Marlborough challenge. Sylvester's recommendation that the buyer not proceed "because of the Marlborough objection" could reasonably be interpreted as merely advice to heed the Marlborough challenge. Further, a rational juror could interpret the statement that "[Sylvester] wasn't sure" as evincing an ambivalence on the part of Sylvester that did not rise to the level of a challenge, especially given that Sylvester himself had not seen the Painting, but only photographs of it.

In this context, moreover, the term may well be a specialized one. It is hardly clear as a matter of law that "challenge" includes every mention by one person of the fact that a challenge has been made by another person (or, for example, that it would include Anita Goldstein's statement that "everybody is afraid of the authenticity" of the Painting). Nor is it clear as a matter of law whether the term "challenge" would include an expression of uncertainty by someone who had never seen the painting in question. If Siebenmann proffers art-industry or other evidence as to the meaning of this ambiguous contract term, its meaning will be a question for the jury at trial. * * *

CONCLUSION

The order granting Rogath's motion for partial summary judgment is vacated, and the case is remanded to the district court for disposition not inconsistent with this opinion.

―――――――

The following case considers a seller's representation after the contract is formed. Can those representations be part of the "basis of the bargain"?

DOWNIE V. ABEX CORP.
UNITED STATES COURT OF APPEALS, TENTH CIRCUIT, 1984
741 F.2D 1235

[Plaintiffs, the Downies, sued for personal injuries suffered when an airplane passenger loading bridge (Jetway) manufactured by defendant, Abex, collapsed. The defendant filed a third-party complaint against General Motors, the manufacturer of ball-screw assembly which, allegedly, caused the Jetway to fail. The jury found that GM had made and breached a post-sale express warranty that the ball-screw assembly would not fail. The trial court, however, granted GM's motion for judgment n.o.v. on the express warranty claim. Upon appeal, the ruling of the trial court was reversed and the case remanded.]

* * *

II

A

Abex contends that the trial court erred in granting GM's motion for judgment n.o.v. on the express warranty issue. A trial judge may grant a motion for judgment notwithstanding the verdict only if "the facts and inferences point so strongly and overwhelmingly in favor of one party that the Court believes that reasonable men could not arrive at a contrary verdict." * * * Further, in considering a motion for judgment n.o.v. the trial judge must consider all the evidence and reasonable inferences therefrom in the light most favorable to the party against whom the motion is directed. * * * Section 2-313 of the Uniform Commercial Code governs express warranties. * * * Thus, we must determine whether a rational jury could have concluded that GM made an affirmation of fact or promise concerning the failed ball-screw assembly, and, if so, whether it could find that affirmation of fact or promise became part of the basis of the bargain.

B

The original GM warranty was limited to defects in materials and workmanship and specifically excluded all other express or implied warranties. However, the evidence would permit a reasonable jury to find that on at least three occasions GM represented to Abex that its ball-screw assembly was fail-safe and would prevent a free-fall of the Jetway even if the bearings fell out of the assembly.

First, there was the following testimony concerning an exchange that took place on March 30, 1977, when GM employees John Martuch and Lowell Smith made a sales maintenance call on the Jetway manufacturing facilities in Ogden, Utah:

"Q. (by Abex's counsel) And at that time did either you or Mr. Smith state to Russ Williams and Bob Saunders that if the balls were lost and the deflectors were in place, that there would be interference and there would be no free-fall?

A. (by Mr. Martuch) That is correct.

Q. And there was discussion about that being a fail-safe feature; isn't that correct?

A. That is correct.

Q. And in that discussion neither you nor Mr. Smith limited that statement to the 3-inch ball screw?

A. We were talking about specifically a 3-inch ball screw.

Q. But no one said 3-inch, did they?

A. They didn't have to. There was a print on the table that we were using as a reference that was a 3-inch ball screw.

Q. But no one said, 'We want to make perfectly certain that we're only talking about that drawing'?

A. We were talking about that assembly.

Q. But you never pointed that out, did you?

The Court: Gentlemen, Let's not talk two at one time. She's got to take everything here.

Q. (by Abex's counsel): You never specifically said that, though, did you?

A. Not that I remember."

R. X, 106-07.

Second, Martuch sent a letter to Abex dated April 7, 1977, which referred specifically to life/load charts for "the 3 inch and 4 inch BCD units you use." Pl. Ex. 8. The letter included ten copies of a document describing the design and operation of the patented yolk deflector system. The document stated, "If all balls should be lost from a ball nut equipped with deflectors, these yolk-type units will then cause the ball not to function as a threaded nut. This is a true fail safe feature." Pl. Ex. 7.

Third, GM invited Kenneth Noall and Russell Williams of Abex's Jetway division to Saginaw, Michigan, in May 1977 to observe a test of the fail-safe features of the ball-screw assembly. The test impressed Williams and he asked for and received the test sample. Noall remarked that the fail-safe feature was "worth its weight in gold to our customers." R. IX, 109.

GM argues that all discussions and representations regarding the safety of the ball-screw assemblies were limited to the three-inch assembly, and that the evidence unequivocally establishes that no one from Abex specifically recalled the use of the words "fail-safe" either during the conversations in Ogden or the testing in Saginaw. However, regardless of whether anyone specifically used the words "fail-safe," the literature on the ball-screw assemblies described the yolk deflector mechanism as a "fail safe feature" and did not distinguish between three- and four-inch assemblies. Pl. Ex. 7. In 1977 the three- and four-inch ball-screw assemblies were the only assemblies with yolk deflectors that Abex used in its passenger loading bridges. GM knew that Abex used three- and four-inch assemblies to elevate the bridge. More important, GM, in an internal memorandum, acknowledged Abex's keen interest in the safety features of both the three- and four-inch assemblies. Lowell Smith, in a consumer contact report, stated, "I was requested by Bob Saunders of Jetway to supply a written communication to verify the deflectors in the 3" or 4" BCD ball screws will support the 10' 6" load rating with the balls removed from the ball nut." Pl.Ex. 13. Kenneth Noall testified that he understood that the load compression test in Saginaw applied to all ball-screw assemblies equipped with yolk deflectors, R. IX, 105-06, and Russell Williams declared that GM never stated that its tests or representations were limited only to the three-inch assemblies. *Id.* at 230-31.

GM contends that even if GM salesmen and Abex engineers used the word "fail-safe," the use constituted mere puffing rather than any affirmation of fact or promise giving rise to an express warranty. The line between puffing and warranting is often difficult to draw, but the more specific the statement the more likely it constitutes a warranty. J. WHITE & R. SUMMERS, UNIFORM COMMERCIAL CODE 329 (1980). On the basis of the evidence in the record and resolving all facts and inferences in the light most favorable to Abex, we conclude that a rational jury could have found that GM made affirmations of fact or promises that both the three- and four-inch ball-screw assemblies equipped with yolk deflectors were fail-safe.

C

We next must determine whether a rational jury could have found that GM's affirmations of fact or promises became part of the basis of the bargain for the sale of the ball-screw assemblies. UCC § 2-313 clearly contemplates that warranties made after the sale may become a basis of the bargain. Official Comment 7 to § 2-313 provides:

> "The precise time when words of description or affirmation are made
> * * * is not material. The sole question is whether the language * * * [is]
> fairly to be regarded as a part of the contract. If language is used after the

closing of the deal (as when the buyer when taking delivery asks and receives an additional assurance), the warranty becomes a modification, and need not be supported by consideration if it is otherwise reasonable and in order."

In *Bigelow v. Agway, Inc.*, 506 F.2d 551 (2d Cir. 1974), the court considered whether a salesman's oral statements constituted a valid post-sale warranty modification. In *Bigelow* a farmer sued the manufacturer and distributor of a chemical used to treat hay before baling. Although most farmers will not bale hay with a moisture level higher than twenty to twenty-five percent, apparently the plaintiff was told that the chemical would safely permit the baling of hay with a higher moisture level. Two months after the sale and use of the chemical, defendant's salesman guaranteed that hay treated with the chemical was safe to bale even though it contained a moisture level of thirty-two to thirty-four percent. The farmer baled the hay, and the level of moisture resulted in a fire that destroyed his entire crop. Rejecting defendant's argument that the salesman's representation was not a basis of the bargain, the Second Circuit noted,

> "Although defendants might conceivably contend that since [the salesman's] representations postdated the delivery of the [treatment] * * * and therefore could not be the 'basis of the bargain' as required for recovery * * *, it is undisputed that the [salesman's] visit * * * was to promote the sale of the product. Thus, they might constitute an actionable modification of the warranty."

Id. at 555 n.6. Similarly, in the case at bar a rational jury could have found that GM's post-sale representations about the safety of ball-screw assemblies with yolk deflectors were designed to promote future sales. This is especially true since GM sent Abex brochures discussing the safety features for distribution to Abex's customers.

GM argues* * * that Abex must prove reliance on the express warranty in order to establish that the warranty was part of the basis of the bargain. Official Comment 3 to UCC § 2-313 states, "in actual practice affirmations of fact made by the seller * * * are regarded as part of the description of those goods; hence no particular reliance on such statements need be shown in order to weave them into the fabric of the agreement .* * *" We need not decide whether an express warranty may exist without reliance, *see* J. WHITE & R. SUMMERS, UNIFORM COMMERCIAL CODE 333 (1980) ("Possibly for lack of any other meaningful standard, courts must employ the test of whether buyer relied on the affirmation of fact or promise * * *"), because Abex presented sufficient evidence for a rational jury to find that Abex did rely on GM's express warranty. Robert Saunders, Director of Research and Development and Technical Marketing for Abex, testified that he was not concerned about making safety modifications on Abex's existing stock of ball-screw assemblies because of GM's representations:

> "Q. (by Abex's counsel) Did you feel it was necessary to either alter your existing stock or the ball screws out in the field with runout threads?
>
> A. (by Mr. Saunders) No.
>
> Q. Why not?
>
> A. Because the design that we had, either the thread runout or–the washer was somewhat less critical because of the existence of the deflector yokes.
>
> Q. All right. In other words, you weren't so concerned about the safety features because of the representations about the yoke deflectors?
>
> A. That's correct."

R. IX, 42.

GM contends that Abex cannot recover for breach of express warranty because there was no mutual agreement to modify the limited written warranty as required by § 2-313. In *Cargill, Inc. v. Stafford*, 553 F.2d 1222, 1225 (10th Cir. 1977), we noted that the UCC contains an objective test of mutuality of assent as "manifested by the conduct of the parties." On the basis of the evidence presented in this case, we hold that after resolving all factual inferences in favor of Abex, a rational jury could have found that both parties recognized and assented to a warranty on the absolute safety of ball-screw assemblies equipped with yolk deflectors.

III

GM contends that its breach of the express warranty did not proximately cause Abex damage because the collapse of the Jetway had nothing to do with the failure of the yolk deflectors. However, since Abex presented evidence that the screw free-fell through the nut and that GM warranted that the yolk deflectors would engage the nut, we must resolve any doubts in favor of Abex.

Reversed and remanded for further proceedings consistent with this opinion.

[Footnotes omitted.]

Notes

In *Controlled Environments Construction, Inc. v. Key Industrial Refrigeration Co.*, 670 N.W.2d 771 (Neb. 2003), the court first held that the four year statute of limitations in UCC 2-725(1) had run on an "extended warranty" on compressors sold by Hill-Phoenix to CEC:

Alternatively, CEC argues that Hill-Phoenix issued a new 4-year extended warranty on the compressors in 1995. If a new warranty was given, CEC asserts, its 1998 claim for breach of warranty would be timely. The court found the alleged warranty extension by Hill-Phoenix did not "implicate" the statute of limitations. Prior to deciding if the 1995 memorandum did in fact give CEC a new warranty, we need to determine whether a warranty can be given postsale and, if so, whether it starts the statute of limitations running anew.

[UCC 2-725(1] prohibits the parties, at least by original agreement, from extending the statute of limitations. Some courts, however, relying on [UCC 2-313], allow a seller to extend a new express warranty or modify a contract of sale after the sale has been completed. * * * Other courts have concluded that once a legally binding contract exists, subsequent affirmations and/or statements are not part of the basis of the bargain because the buyer could not have relied on them in making the deal.* * *

Courts that are willing to find a valid postsale modification or new warranty make two key inquiries prior to such a finding. First, obviously, the court must find that the statement or affirmation by the seller is a warranty. Clearly, the 1995 memorandum by Vana is an explicit obligation which satisfies this first step. Second, and more importantly, to the extent a seller can create a postsale warranty or modification of the contract for sale, this ability appears to be limited in time. Comment 7 to [UCC 2-313] states:

> The precise time when words of description or affirmation are made or samples are shown is not material. The sole question is whether the language or samples or models are *fairly to be regarded as part of the contract.* If language is used after the closing of the deal (as when the buyer when taking delivery asks and receives an additional assurance), the warranty becomes a modification, and need not be supported by consideration if it is otherwise reasonable and in order (Section 2-209).

(Emphasis supplied.) * * *

In interpreting this comment, respected commentators have concluded that comment 7 "contemplate[s] only the cases of face-to-face dealings that occur while the deal is still warm," and "urge a different rule for seller's statements made more than a short period beyond the conclusion of the agreement." 1 JAMES J. WHITE & ROBERT S. SUMMERS, UNIFORM COMMERCIAL CODE § 9-5 at 498 (4th ed.1995). Thus, it is unlikely that Hill-Phoenix effectuated a modification of the old warranty, or created a new warranty, as the memorandum was written 2 years after delivery of the good. * * *

Note: Express Warranties and Privity

Prior to the 2003 amendments to UCC 2-313, many courts held that a lack of privity was not a bar to recovery on an express warranty.[*] In other words, if a remote seller makes a representation that otherwise meets the test of UCC 2-313, the fact that the buyer suing on the express warranty was not in privity with (did not buy the goods from) the seller did not preclude the suit. The rationale for this is very simple as stated by one court:

> To hold otherwise could allow unscrupulous manufacturers who make public representations about their product's performance to remain insulated from express-warranty liability if consumers did not purchase the product directly from them.

U.S. Tire-Tech, Inc. v. Boeran, B.V., 110 S.W.3d 194, 198 (Tex. Ct. App. 2003). The 2003 amendments modify that analysis. Section 2-313 now apparently requires privity of contract and two new sections, UCC 2-313A and 2-313B, impose some liability on a seller for express warranty-like representations made to a remote purchaser. (Notice that the restriction to privity contexts was not carried over into Article 2A, UCC 2A-210.) Both of the new sections are modeled on UCC 2-313.

Problem 5-2

Best Towing, Inc. purchased a new tow truck, model E100, from Dealer. In discussions with Dealer's sales representative, Best received assurances that the new tow truck could tow vehicles weighing up to three tons and that Best would be very happy with the tow truck. Best also picked up the sales brochure for the model E100 which was provided by the manufacturer. In the brochure it stated that the

---

[*] *See e.g., Tex Enterprises, Inc. v. Brockway Standard, Inc.*, 66 P.3d 625 (Wash. 2003) (distinguishing express warranty from implied warranty regarding relaxation of privity requirement).

E100 was the "best tow truck made for passenger vehicle towing." Maximum towing capacity was listed as two tons. When Best took delivery of the new tow truck, Dealer gave to Best an owner's manual which contained the following language: "Manufacturer warrants that the vehicle shall be free of defects in material and workmanship for 1 year from date of delivery. Manufacturer makes no other warranties, express or implied." After using the truck for about one month in its towing business, the frame of the truck broke while pulling a vehicle weighing two and a half tons from a ditch.

A. What must Best prove to be entitled to recover from Dealer and the manufacturer for breach of an express warranty or the obligations under UCC 2-313A or 2-313B?

B. Assume the transaction between Dealer and Best was a lease covered by Article 2A. Does that change what Best must prove to recover for breach of an express warranty from either Dealer or the manufacturer?

Note: Express Warranties Under the CISG

Article 30 of the CISG states that the seller "must deliver the goods * * * as required by the contract and this Convention." Article 35(1) then provides that the seller "must deliver goods which are the * * * quality and description required by the contract and which are contained or packaged in the manner required by the contract." Unless the parties have agreed otherwise, the goods do not conform to the contract unless they "possess the qualities of goods which the seller has held out to the buyer as a sample or model" and "are contained or packaged in the manner usual for such goods or, where there is not such manner, in a manner adequate to preserve and protect the goods." Art. 35(2)(c)-(d). Note that neither the phrase "express warranty" nor "basis of the bargain" is used and the "sample or model" issue is treated as a "gap filler."

The key question is what does the contract require. The answer is easy when the description of the goods and representations and promises dealing with the quality of the goods are contained in a writing assented to by both parties. But suppose that the core description or that representations about the goods made to the buyer during negotiations or after the contract is formed do not appear in the written contract. Presumably, the buyer must prove that the description or affirmations are part of the contract and that the goods failed to conform. In this process, there is considerable latitude for extrinsic evidence to be admitted. *See* CISG Art. 8, 9, 11, 12; Andrew J. Kennedy, *Recent Developments: Nonconforming*

Goods Under the CISG–What's A Buyer to Do?, 16 DICK. J. INT'L L. 319 (1998).

Problem 5-3

Would your analysis of Problem 5-2 change if the transaction between Best and Dealer were covered by the CISG? If both Best and Dealer were U.S. companies and the manufacturer was a Canadian company, would the CISG govern the obligation of the manufacturer to Best?

Note: Express Warranties Under UCITA

UCITA 402 is modeled on UCC 2-313, providing for express warranties regarding information. Does this mean all "information," even though the scope of UCITA is computer information transactions? Section 402 deals with affirmations of fact, descriptions, models, samples or demonstrations. Notice it does not provide for "promises relating to" the information. Each of the representations must be part of the basis of the bargain. Subsection (b) provides that "puffing" does not create an express warranty and excludes aesthetics or the like of informational content from being an express warranty. Subsection (c) provides that warranties as to published informational content arise, if at all, under common law principles. UCITA 102(a)(52) (definition of "published informational content").

SECTION 3.   IMPLIED WARRANTIES

A. Introduction

The line between an express warranty and the implied warranties of merchantability, UCC 2-314, 2A-212, and fitness for particular purpose, UCC 2-315, 2A-213, can be very fine. The common ground, of course, is the contract description of the goods. Depending on the facts, the description can create an express warranty, UCC 2-313, 2A-210, provide a standard to measure merchantability, UCC 2-314, 2A-212, and describe goods which meet the buyer's particular purposes, UCC 2-315, 2A-213. In fact, the "sale by description" is thought to be the transaction from which implied warranty theory evolved.[*]

---

[*] *See, e.g., Gardiner v. Gray*, 4 Camb. 144, 171 Eng. Rep. 46 (1815); William L. Prosser,
(continued...)

But if neither the description of the goods nor the seller's other affirmations or promises cover the buyer's particular expectations of quality, how, if at all, is the gap in the agreement to be filled? Implied warranties are clearly terms of the agreement. Are they implied in fact or imposed by law? If the latter, what justifications support the imposition? We will consider these questions in this Section.

Problem 5-4

Read UCC 2-314, 2A-212, and 2-315, 2A-213. Make up an abstract list of the types of facts a plaintiff would not have to prove to show breach of an implied warranty of merchantability but would have to prove to show breach of an implied warranty of fitness for a particular purpose.

B. Merchantability

UCC 2-314(1) provides that "a warranty that the goods shall be merchantable is implied in a contract for their sale if the seller is a merchant with respect to goods of that kind." Compare this statement to the definition of merchant in UCC 2-104. Is a seller who "deals in goods of the kind" a merchant that makes the warranty of merchantability? How about a seller who holds itself out having knowledge or skill "peculiar" to the goods involved?

UCC 2-314(2) provides standards to measure merchantability. After reading the text and the comments, do you have a sense of what the merchant seller is responsible for when it sells the goods? What is the rationale for imposing this obligation on a merchant seller? UCC 2-314(3) provides that "other implied warranties may arise from course of dealing or usage of trade."

UCC 2A-212 follows the same structure for lease transactions that are not finance leases. The implied warranty of merchantability may be "excluded or modified" by agreement. UCC 2-316(2) and (3). *Compare* UCC 2A-214(2) and (3).

---

* (...continued)

The Implied Warranty of Merchantable Quality, 27 MINN. L. REV. 117, 139-45 (1943); Samuel Williston, *Representation and Warranty in Sales–Heilbut v. Buckleton*, 27 HARV. L. REV. 1, 13 (1913).

AGOOS KID CO., INC. V. BLUMENTHAL IMPORT CORP.
SUPREME JUDICIAL COURT OF MASSACHUSETTS, 1932
282 MASS. 1, 184 N.E. 279

[Blumenthal Import Corporation contracted to sell to Agoos Kid Company four thousand dozen "Bagdad goat skins dry salted." Payment was to be "Net cash or domestic letter of credit against documents." Agoos paid without inspecting the skins. Serious defects in the skins showed up for which Agoos sued Blumenthal. Judgment was entered in favor of Agoos and Blumenthal appealed.]
CROSBY, J

* * * Upon the question whether there was an implied warranty of merchantable quality under [Uniform Sales Act 15(2)] the following facts were found: The goods described in the contracts known in the trade as "Bagdad goat skins dry salted" are a well known article of commerce. The defendant maintains an organization in various places in Asia Minor and India for the purpose of collecting dry salted skins for shipment to the United States and at the time of the collection of the skins in question it had a representative in Bagdad. At times such representatives buy from local collectors and butchers skins which have been cured by the dry salting process. This process is efficient in preserving the texture of the skins only when an attempt is not made to dry them too quickly by the hot rays of the sun, which is likely to result in a rotting of the inside of the skin, where it cannot be detected by ocular or manual inspection or in any other practicable way until the skins are put into the process of being made into leather. With reasonable precaution in the care and selection of the skins in the Orient, a certain number of improperly cured and rotted skins is likely to be found in a large lot. Both parties were aware of this fact. In the trade it is considered that a lot is normal if it does not appear that more than one and one half per cent, or at the most three per cent, are improperly cured and therefore worthless. "Certainly a lot containing more than three per cent of rotted skins is abnormal." It was found that so far as defects appeared the defendant was ignorant of their condition, and the same was true of the plaintiff until the defects were shown in the plaintiff's tannery. Beginning with the first pack of skins of the first shipment the plaintiff, on January 14, 1931, began the process of manufacturing them into leather, and at different times thereafter all the other packs were put through the process, and many of them showed that more than three per cent were rotten. The entire first shipment was finally put through the process, and it was found that "the defects in the first shipment were very material and important and extended to nearly half the skins contained in it." Upon the

foregoing findings which were warranted by the evidence, the further finding was warranted that the goods delivered by the first shipment were not of merchantable quality.

The contracts in question were for a sale of goods by description and there was an implied warranty that they would correspond with the description. G.L. c. 106, § 16. "The goods are merchantable when they are of the general kind which they are described or supposed to be when bought." WILLISTON ON SALES (2d Ed.) § 243. "Where goods of a character commonly known in trade are ordered by description, and there is no inspection, there is an implied warranty that those furnished will be such as are merchantable under the descriptive term used by the parties. The purchaser is entitled to get what he ordered." *Leavitt v. Fiberloid Co.*, 196 Mass. 440, 451, 82 N.E. 682, 687, 15 L.R.A., N.S., 855,. * * * The plaintiff did not contract to buy seven thousand dozen goat skins, one half of which were to be rotten and worthless. It agreed to buy that number of skins dry salted, and there was an implied warranty that, with the exception of not more than three per cent thereof, they should be of merchantable quality.* * * Although it was found that a lot of dry salted goat skins is deemed of merchantable quality and reasonably fit for the purpose of making it into leather if the defect here existing is limited to not more than three per cent of the lot, it was found that the first shipment was not merchantable throughout "within this definition, and was not reasonably fit throughout within this definition for the purpose of being made into leather." * * *

[The court reversed because the trial court had excluded defendant's evidence of a custom in the trade to notify the seller of defective skins before starting to process them.]

Notes

In an influential article, written in 1943, William L. Prosser, later a principal architect of strict tort liability, suggested three overlapping justifications for the implied warranty of merchantability. The first was that the seller had made a "misrepresentation of fact" upon which the buyer had relied. For Prosser, this was "obviously" a tort theory. The second was that the warranty "has in fact been agreed upon by the parties as an unexpressed term of the contract for sale." The warranty was inferred from language, conduct, circumstances and was "pure" contract. The third was that the warranty was "imposed by law" as a matter of policy. The loss from "defective" goods should be placed upon the seller "because he is best able to bear it and distribute it to the public, and because it is considered that the buyer is entitled to protection at the seller's expense." For the third justification, Prosser had in mind cases where defective food caused personal injuries to buyers and consumers. *See* William L. Prosser, *The Implied Warranty of Merchantable Quality*, 27 MINN. L. REV. 117, 122 (1943). Do you agree with Prosser's classifications? Where would you place the *Agoos Kid* case?

VALLEY IRON & STEEL CO. V. THORIN
SUPREME COURT OF OREGON, 1977
278 OR. 103, 562 P.2D 1212

LENT, J

Plaintiff brought an action in assumpsit for the reasonable value of goods sold and delivered to the defendant. Defendant pleaded affirmative defenses, alleging breaches of the implied warranties of merchantability and fitness for particular purpose. ORS 72.3140; 72.3150. Following a trial to the court, judgment was entered in favor of plaintiff. Defendant appeals, claiming that the court erred in failing to find breaches of the implied warranties and improperly fixed the amount of damages.

Because of the trial court's general finding in favor of plaintiff, we review the evidence in the light most favorable to its contentions.

Plaintiff is a corporation engaged in the manufacture of cast iron products. In 1974 defendant was establishing a retail store to sell equipment and supplies for tree-planting contractors and workers. In September of that year, defendant's agent, Steven Gibbs, met with Roger Herring, Manager of Valley Iron & Steel. Mr. Gibbs inquired if plaintiff could manufacture castings of hoedad collars. A hoedad is a forestry tool used for planting seedling trees. The collar of a hoedad secures the metal blade to a wooden handle.

Mr. Gibbs showed plaintiff a sample collar casting made by Western Fire Equipment and asked if plaintiff could duplicate the casting. The sample collar was shown with a handle, and Mr. Gibbs explained that the tool was an impact tool used for planting trees and that occasionally rocks are struck during the planting process. Plaintiff's witness, Mr. Herring, testified:

> * * * Mr. Gibbs came in, spoke to me, told me that he needed this particular type of casting, briefly described its intended use, asked me if we could make them.
>
> I indicated we could. It was a very brief discussion in regards to the

type of material we were going to use, and I indicated that because there was potential chance of hitting rock in this * * * operation * * * that it would have to be made out of somewhat of a durable material.

Mr. Herring suggested that the castings be made of durable iron. The parties agreed upon a price, and after defendant obtained a core box and pattern from the model collar, manufacturing commenced. The collars were delivered to defendant in early October, 1974.

Problems developed with the finished product. Defendant's customers complained that the castings were breaking. Eventually defendant returned up to 80% of the castings to the plaintiff. Another foundry later made satisfactory castings from the same core box and pattern but from mild steel instead of cast iron.

At the conclusion of the trial, the court made the following findings:

"I am not going to make any specific findings–just some general findings–but I will say that my general findings are based upon two findings, I suppose. One is that Mr. Gibbs' directions to Mr. Herring in this case were not sufficient in the sense that the Court believes that he knew enough about what he was doing when he went out there to give directions, and the Court does not feel that Mr. Herring did anything that was legally wrong and then didn't comply with what he said he was going to do.

"In other words, the Court believes that the one at fault was Mr. Gibbs in this particular case. 'Fault' may not be exactly the correct word, but that it was the legal duty of Mr. Gibbs to do more than he did, rather than Mr. Herring doing more than he did.

"So, the Court–then, the general finding is that I am finding for the plaintiff."

Defendant contends on appeal that the court erred in failing to find the existence of an implied warranty of merchantability under ORS 72.3140 and an implied warranty of fitness for a particular purpose under ORS 72.3150. * * *

In denying defendant any recovery under [the implied warranty of merchantability], the trial court must have concluded either that plaintiff was not a "merchant with respect to goods of that kind" or that the goods were "fit for the ordinary purposes for which such goods are used." It is undisputed that the products were "goods" and that there was a "contract for their sale." Any implied warranty which existed was not excluded or modified under ORS 72.3160.

"Merchant" is defined by ORS 72.1040 as "a person who deals in goods of the kind or otherwise by his occupation holds himself out as having knowledge or skill peculiar to the practices or goods involved in the transaction . * * *" While the evidence shows that plaintiff was unfamiliar with hoedads and had not previously manufactured hoedad collars, plaintiff did hold itself out, by operating a foundry, as having skill in the "practice" of casting iron and presumably in the selection of materials to be used in manufacturing castings. Inasmuch as this transaction involved the selection of the type of metal appropriate for hoedad collars, plaintiff was a merchant.

Likewise, plaintiff, for purposes of ORS 72.3140, was a merchant "with respect to goods of that kind"; *i.e.*, castings. Whether this provision is interpreted broadly (in this case to mean castings) or narrowly (to mean hoedad collars) would depend upon the facts of the case. Only merchants, under the Code, warrant merchantability; and this is so because of their expertise or familiarity with the processes or products involved in the transaction. This skill or knowledge is presumed from previous similar transactions. Plaintiff has in the past assisted buyers in choosing particular types of metals to fulfill various tasks in its manufacture of castings. Where the alleged unfitness under ORS 72.3140 arises from this type of choice, plaintiff should be held to the stricter standard imposed on merchants.

The remaining issue is whether the collars were "fit for the ordinary purposes for which such goods are used." The ordinary purpose of custom-made castings depends upon their designated use. Without such a tag the uses would vary so much that any function could be isolated as "ordinary."

The trial court felt that plaintiff was unaware of the intended use. However, the testimony of Mr. Herring shows the contrary. Plaintiff knew that the castings were to join the handle and blade in tree-planting impact tools which occasionally would strike rock. Since the castings were not fit for this purpose, the warranty was breached.

Similarly, plaintiff breached the warranty of fitness for a particular purpose. ORS 72.3150 provides:

> "Implied warranty: fitness for particular purpose. Where the seller at the time of contracting has reason to know any particular purpose for which the goods are required and that the buyer is relying on the seller's skill or judgment to select or furnish suitable goods, there is unless excluded or modified under ORS 72.3160 an implied warranty that the goods shall be fit for such purpose."

Official Comment 1 to this section states that:

> "Under this section the buyer need not bring home to the seller actual knowledge of the particular purpose for which the goods are intended or of

his reliance on the seller's skill and judgment, if the circumstances are such that the seller has reason to realize the purpose intended or that the reliance exists. The buyer, of course, must actually be relying on the seller."

In this case, the undisputed evidence shows that the buyer made known the intended purpose and that the choice of metal to be used was left to the discretion of the seller. From this the seller had "reason to know" that buyer was relying on its judgment. It is also plain that the buyer did so rely. It follows that the warranty existed and evidence existed that it was breached.

The trial court rested its decision upon the "fault" of the defendant in failing to provide additional information on the intended use of the castings. "Fault," as such, is irrelevant when dealing with implied warranties. * * * It is true that the existence of a warranty of fitness for a particular purpose depends in part upon the comparative knowledge and skill of the parties. * * * Here, however, defendant made known his general requirements and the purpose for which the goods were to be used. We fail to see what more the defendant could have disclosed. Where, as here, the needs of a buyer are disclosed and the seller has reason to know of the buyer's reliance, it is incumbent upon the seller to further inquire as to the buyer's wants before representing that the goods can be provided. * * *

In this case the trial court found that the reasonable value of each casting was $3.75. She estimated the value of the goods returned to be $27.42. Implicit in this finding is the conclusion that 457 of the 571 pieces were returned to the seller. Because we conclude that defendant rightfully revoked acceptance under ORS 72.6080(1)(b), inasmuch as the goods were unfit, defendant has no further obligation as to the returned goods. ORS 72.6020(2)(c). The defendant, however, is obligated to pay for the remaining 114 castings which it accepted. Accordingly, under our powers as enumerated in the Oregon Constitution, Am Art VII § 3, plaintiff's judgment is reduced to $427.50 (the value of 114 pieces at $3.75 per unit). Affirmed as modified. [Footnotes omitted.]

Notes

1.   Why should the implied warranty of merchantability be limited to sellers or lessors who are merchants "with respect to goods of that kind?" UCC 2-314(1), 2A-212(1). As the court in *Thorin* recognizes, the merchant requirement for UCC 2-314(1), 2A-212(1) is narrower than the definition of "merchant" in UCC 2-104(1) and 2A-103(3). *Compare* UCC 2-201(2) & former 2-207(2). How can a seller or

lessor who had never made, sold, or leased a hoedad collar be a merchant "with respect to goods of that kind?" Isn't this an isolated sale?*

2. Who is a merchant for purposes of UCC 2-314(1), and presumably UCC 2A-212(1), is a mixed question of law and fact that depends upon the circumstances of each case.** The question whether a farmer who sells livestock or raises crops grown on his own land is a merchant is frequently litigated with diverse results.*** In *Dotts v. Bennett*, 382 N.W.2d 85 (Iowa 1986), however, the court rejected the argument that a farmer who sells only a crop grown annually (hay) was not, as a matter of law, a merchant. The jury verdict that the farmer was a merchant with respect to hay was supported by the following factors:

> He had been a lifetime farmer; he had 100 to 150 acres in hay in 1981; he has sold about twenty percent of his hay for fifteen years; he has advertised hay for sale; at one time he sold a large quantity of hay to parties in southern Missouri; he has done some custom hay farming; he considers himself a knowledgeable hay farmer; and he has had continuing education in farming. * * *

382 N.W.2d at 89.

3. Cattle and other livestock are frequently sold at auction. Suppose the farmer-owner is not a merchant under UCC 2-314(1) but the auctioneer clearly is: he regularly deals in goods of that kind. Does the auctioneer make an implied warranty of merchantability? In *Powers v. Coffeyville Livestock Sales Co., Inc.*, 665 F.2d 311 (10th Cir. 1981), the answer was no if the auctioneer had revealed the identity of its principal. Disclosure prevented the auctioneer from being a seller at common law and the court incorporated the common law rule through former 1-103 to supplement the definition of seller in former 2-103(1)(d), which was ambiguous on the point.

4. How did the buyer in *Valley Iron* demonstrate that the collars were unmerchantable? What was the ordinary purpose of the collars? Was that different

---

* *See Fred J. Moore, Inc. v. Schinmann*, 700 P.2d 754 (Wash. Ct. App. 1985) (farmer who made "isolated" sale not a dealer in goods of that kind); *Smith v. Stewart*, 667 P.2d 358 (Kan. 1983) (seller of used yacht does not make an implied warranty of merchantability).

** *Ferragamo v. Massachusetts Bay Transportation Authority*, 481 N.E.2d 477 (Mass. 1985) (upheld jury verdict that MBTA is merchant with respect to sporadic sale of old trolley cars).

*** *See Vince v. Broome*, 443 So. 2d 23 (Miss. 1983) (farmer held to be merchant with regard to cattle sold, four judges dissenting).

from the particular purpose of the collars?

DELANO GROWERS' COOPERATIVE WINERY V. SUPREME WINE CO., INC.
SUPREME JUDICIAL COURT OF MASSACHUSETTS, 1985
393 MASS. 666, 473 N.E.2D 1066

NOLAN, JUSTICE

The plaintiff, Delano Growers' Cooperative Winery (Delano), appeals from a final judgment dismissing its complaint and awarding $160,634, with interest, to the defendant, Supreme Wine Co., Inc. (Supreme), on its counterclaim. Supreme appeals from that portion of the judgment which granted Delano an "offset" of $25,823.25 to Supreme's damages under the counterclaim. For the reasons stated below, we affirm the judgment.

Delano filed a complaint in Suffolk County Superior Court seeking $25,823.25 for wine sold and delivered. Supreme admitted receipt of the wine and filed a counterclaim for breach of contract alleging that earlier shipments of wine for which payment had been made and all of the wine for which no payment had been made had spoiled due to the presence of lactobacillus trichodes (Fresno mold). As a defense, Supreme asserted that it did not owe Delano $25,823.25 because the wine was not merchantable. Supreme also sought incidental and consequential damages alleging that the "sick wine" destroyed its reputation and market thereby forcing the company into liquidation.[1] * * *

---

[1] Supreme purchased all of its sweet wine and some of its nonsweet wine from Delano. Fresno mold only damaged the sweet wine. Supreme's customers began returning defective Delano wine prior to the shipment for which Delano claims in its complaint that it is owed $25,823.25 (the unpaid shipment). Supreme paid for all prior shipments. Supreme's customers continued to return defective Delano wine after Supreme received and bottled the wine in the unpaid shipment. One-half of the unpaid shipment consisted of sweet wine. The record does not indicate what portion of the unpaid shipment or total shipments consisted of damaged wine. However, we need not resolve this question to affirm the judgment in this case. Supreme proved that 8,000 cases of wine were defective. Supreme normally sold this wine to its retail customers for $13 per case. This per case price included the amount Supreme paid Delano for the wine, Supreme's other costs, and its profits. The judge calculated damages by multiplying the number of cases proved as damaged (8,000) by the per case price ($13). The resultant amount includes all of Supreme's cost for wine including the amount remaining unpaid on the last shipment. The judge then deducted the amount that Supreme had not paid for wine ($25,823.25) and made other adjustments as discussed below. This prevents overcompensating Supreme because the per case price ($13) included

(continued...)

The facts as found by the master and accepted by the judge may be summarized as follows. Supreme operated a wine bottling plant in Boston from 1935 to November, 1978. It purchased finished wine, ready for bottling and consumption, from California, selling it to retailers after bottling under Supreme's label.

In 1968, Supreme began buying sweet wine from Delano, a California winery. By the spring of 1973, Supreme was purchasing all its sweet wine from Delano. Delano shipped this wine to Supreme's bottling plant in Boston in tank cars. When the wine arrived, Supreme took samples from each compartment of the tank cars. The samples were labeled, dated, sealed, and kept in Supreme's safe. Supreme then pumped the wine into redwood vats in its building. The wine was pumped through a filter into storage tanks from which it was later filtered into bottles for delivery.

Until April or May, 1973, Supreme did not experience any difficulty with Delano wine. Supreme then began receiving widespread returns of certain sweet wine from its customers. The wine was producing sediment, was cloudy, and contained a cottony or hairy substance. Supreme could identify the defective sweet wine as Delano wine because it purchased all its sweet wine from Delano. Supreme also matched the returned defective wine with the samples taken from the Delano wine on delivery. This identification was corroborated somewhat by shipment records, the dates of bottling and the color to which the Delano wine was blended.

Supreme made oral reports and complaints about the problem to Delano. It also sent Delano samples from the Delano shipment. When the help promised by Harold Roland, Delano's manager, did not materialize, Supreme purchased wine from another California grower in June, July, and August, 1973. Supreme bottled and sold that wine and received no complaints or returns on it. Roland, with renewed promises of assistance, induced Supreme to recommence purchasing from Delano in September, 1973.

Delano made four shipments of sweet wine to Supreme between September 28 and December 20, 1973. Each shipment invoice stated that payment was due forty-five days from the invoice date. Supreme paid all but the last invoice, which was in the amount of $25,823.25. It withheld payment for that amount as customers continued to return defective wine which was identified as Delano wine. When oral reports and complaints evoked no tangible help, Vito Bracciale, assistant to

---

[1] (...continued)
Supreme's cost for the wine as if it were actually paid. The $25,823.25 represents a portion of this cost that was not paid. This calculation also factors out any need to determine the amount of undamaged wine Supreme received as damages are based solely on the actual amount of defective wine.

Supreme's president, wrote to Roland on April 9, 1974. This letter requested assistance and explained Supreme's crisis caused by the defective wine. The letter also indicated the high number of returns caused by this defective wine.

In response to this letter, Delano sent James Lunt, an assistant winemaker, to Supreme's bottling plant. His microscopic examination of the defective wine and a microscopic examination by Delano's chemist in California showed that the wine contained Fresno mold. Lunt had earlier observed the mold in the samples returned to Delano by Supreme. These were samples from the tank cars taken on arrival at Supreme and samples from wine returned by Supreme's customers.

While Lunt was at Supreme, customers returned a number of cases of Delano wine containing Fresno mold. After examining these returns, Lunt told Supreme to pasteurize, refilter, rebottle, and resell the defective wine. Supreme followed Lunt's directions and reprocessed 8,000 cases of spoiled wine (5,000 cases returned from customers and 3,000 cases still on hand). During this process, 1,000 cases were lost through breakage, spillage, and shrinkage. Supreme sold the remaining cases of reprocessed wine at a reduced rate. * * *

2. Delano's breach of the implied warranty of merchantability. This sale of wine by Delano is governed by the Uniform Commercial Code, G.L. c. 106. Delano impliedly warranted that the goods were of merchantable quality. G.L. c. 106, § 2-314. *See Regina Grape Prods. Co. v. Supreme Wine Co.*, 357 Mass. 631, 635, 260 N.E.2d 219 (1970). This warranty required the wine to "pass without objection in the trade under the contract description" and be reasonably suited for ordinary uses for which goods of that kind are sold. * * *

The contract in this case required Delano to deliver "finished wine" to Supreme. Delano contends that, when it delivered wine that appeared good and which could be bottled, its obligation was satisfied. In support, Delano argues that all California sweet wine contained Fresno mold. Therefore, the presence of Fresno mold could not cause a wine to be unmerchantable. Furthermore, Delano states that an alleged trade usage required Supreme to add sulfur dioxide to the wine to inhibit further growth of these bacteria. Delano's arguments fail to persuade us.

Delano argues that uncontroverted testimony indicated that all California sweet wine contained Fresno mold. The judge acknowledged this testimony. However, the judge found that Supreme never experienced any trouble with bacteria until the 1973 problem with Delano wine. The sweet wine which Supreme bought from other California growers in 1973 did not present any bacterial problems. None of this wine was returned with Fresno mold. Furthermore, the judge found that the bacterial problem could have been prevented and controlled by Delano. Although

Fresno mold may have been present in all California sweet wine, there is no indication that it was allowed to go unchecked and thereby destroy the merchantability of finished wine. Supreme's prior experience with Delano and its experience with other California sweet wine in 1973 indicate that the mold could be controlled. The presence of Fresno mold, as it was in the Delano wines, caused those wines to be unmarketable.

Delano argues that Supreme's failure to follow minimum industry standards prevents it from recovering for the unmerchantable wine. The judge specifically ruled that Delano had failed to meet its burden of establishing such standards as a usage of trade applicable to Supreme. Even if Delano had met its burden, its argument would fail. A course of dealing between parties controls the interpretation of usage of trade. G.L. c. 106, § 1-205(4). In this case, Supreme consistently followed the same procedure in processing Delano wine since 1968. This clearly established a course of dealing between Delano and Supreme. Any usage of trade followed in areas outside of Massachusetts cannot control this long-standing course of dealing between the parties.

Course of dealing [handwritten margin note]

Once Supreme initially accepted Delano wine it had the burden of establishing that there was a breach of the warranty of merchantability. * * * Supreme has met that burden. Supreme identified all the returned wine as Delano wine. Delano's chemist also found traces of Fresno mold in the samples "from the compartments of the tank cars in which Delano wine arrived in Boston and wine from the bottles returned by customers." The wine in its returned state was neither merchantable nor fit for bottling or consumption. Only through extensive reprocessing could Supreme mitigate the loss from this wine. The course of dealing between the parties supports the conclusion that the finished wine shipped by Delano normally was ready for bottling and drinking. Although the Delano sweet wine could be bottled shortly thereafter, it could not be drunk.

Delano was required to anticipate the environment in which it was reasonable for its product to be used.* * * It was reasonably foreseeable that the unchecked presence of Fresno mold would substantially impair the value of the wine. That result occurred. The Delano wine could not pass in the trade as finished wine without objection, was not fit for the ordinary purposes for which finished wine was used, and therefore, was unmerchantable. *See* G.L. c. 106, § 2-314. * * *

[Some footnotes omitted. Those retained have been renumbered.]

———

Notes

1.   To prevail, the buyer must establish that the goods were unmerchantable at the time the seller tendered delivery. *See* UCC 2-725, *compare* UCC 2A-506 which does not adopt the same rule for lease transactions. Does that change the time for determining when the implied warranty was breached in a lease transaction? In *Delano Growers*, to which standards of merchantability in UCC 2-314(2) did the wine fail to conform? How did the buyer avoid the possible conclusion that there was a normal amount of Fresno mold in the wine at delivery but that it got "out of hand" while the wine was being processed by the buyer?

2.   In most disputes over merchantability, the key factual question is whether goods sold or leased under a contract description were "fit for the ordinary purposes for which such goods are used." UCC 2-314(2)(c). *See also* UCC 2A-212(2)(c). The trier of fact must know whether the product "conformed to the standard performance of like products used in the trade * * * (and this determination) may depend on testimony of persons familiar with industry standards and local practices and is a question of fact." *Pisano v. American Leasing*, 146 Cal. App. 3d 194, 194 Cal. Rptr. 77, 80 (1983). Without any evidence of relevant trade standards or uses, the merchantability claim may fail.* Similarly, if, because of the newness or complexity of the product, no average or usual standards for determining performance or quality can be determined, the "ordinary purposes" standard will not help the buyer.**

3.   **Food.** The *Delano Growers'* case involved wine sold by the producer to a dealer for resale to individuals for consumption. Although Fresno mold was arguably a natural ingredient in the wine, the course of dealing between the parties and the seller's failure to treat the wine before delivery persuaded the court that the particular wine was unmerchantable. The buyer suffered only economic loss. No personal injuries were involved.

Suppose, however, that a restaurant serves an oyster stew containing ground glass, causing personal injury to a customer. This is an easy case, right? Under UCC 2-314(1), the seller is a "merchant with respect to goods of that kind" and the

---

* *See Royal Business Machines, Inc. v. Lorraine Corp.*, 633 F.2d 34 (7th Cir. 1980).

** *See, e.g., Price Brothers Co. v. Philadelphia Gear Corp.*, 649 F.2d 416 (6th Cir. 1981). *See also Comark Merchandising, Inc. v. Highland Group, Inc.*, 932 F.2d 1196 (7th Cir. 1991) (no warranty liability where ordinary use not established and buyer refused to inform seller of its particular intended use).

"serving for value of food or drink to be consumed either on the premises or elsewhere is a sale." Moreover, the glass, a "foreign" ingredient, makes the stew unmerchantable under UCC 2-314(2)(a) and (c). Thus, in most states Customer can sue Restaurant for breach of the implied warranty and recover for "injury to person * * * proximately resulting from any breach of warranty." UCC 2-715(2)(b).

The issue is more complicated if personal injury results from, say, an oyster shell in the stew or from a virus contained in the tissue of the oyster. Is this stew, like cigarettes made from good tobacco and not contaminated by pesticides, "fit for the ordinary purposes for which such goods are used?" Traditionally, the answer turned on whether the ingredient was classified as foreign or natural to the goods. If the former, the seller is liable. If the latter, the responsibility to take precautions is on the buyer.*

More recently, many states have adopted some variation of a "reasonable expectations" test. Under this test, the seller will not prevail simply because the ingredient is "natural" to the product. Thus, in Illinois the question is whether a "reasonable consumer" would expect that the product might contain the substance which caused the injury.** On the other hand, Massachusetts has rejected a test based on what a hypothetical reasonable consumer would expect in favor of a more particularized inquiry. The question is what a consumer of the buyer's age and experience might reasonably expect.***

What about a virus or bacteria in a raw oyster under the reasonable expectation test? What about that highly toxic fugu fish served at a very high price in some Japanese restaurants? If properly prepared, the customer is left with minor numbness in the extremities. If improperly prepared, the customer, so to speak, "joins the fishes."

What about cigarettes made from "good" tobacco that still cause cancer?

---

* See Mix v. Ingersoll Candy Co., 59 P.2d 144 (Cal. 1936) (chicken bone in chicken pie is a substance "natural" to that type of food).

** See Jackson v. Nestle-Beich, Inc., 589 N.E.2d 547 (Ill. 1992) (presence of pecan shell in chocolate covered pecan caramel candy a "factor" in analysis); accord, Mitchell v. BBB Services Co., 582 S.E.2d 470 (Ga. Ct. App. 2003). See also Mexicali Rose v. Superior Court, 822 P.2d 1292 (Cal. 1992), where the court stated that if the ingredient (a chicken bone) was natural to the preparation of the food served (a chicken enchilada) it is reasonably expected by its very nature and the food is not unfit for human consumption.

*** See Phillips v. Town of West Springfield, 540 N.E.2d 1331 (Mass. 1989) (turkey bone in processed turkey served in a school cafeteria).

Consider the opinion of the Supreme Court of Texas in *American Tobacco Co., Inc. v. Grinnell*, 951 S.W.2d 420, 435 (Tex. 1997):

> An implied warranty contrary to the community's common knowledge cannot exist. * * * Because the general health dangers of cigarettes are commonly known by the community, no expectation of safety arises with respect to cigarettes when they are purchased. As American [Tobacco Co.] established the common-knowledge defense for the general health risks associated with cigarettes as a matter of law, it also conclusively negated the claims asserting that it implied warranted that its cigarettes were safe for consumption. To the extent this claim relates to the general health risks of cigarettes, summary judgment was proper. However * * * American did not conclusively establish that the danger of nicotine addiction was common knowledge in 1952. The common-knowledge defense does not preclude the * * * implied warranty claims to the extent they relate to the addictive quality of cigarettes.

4. **Blood and other body parts**. Suppose a hospital supplies defective blood or other body parts, such as kidneys, hearts, or semen and personal injuries result to the user. If the transaction was a sale, the strict liability principle underlying the implied warranty of merchantability or modern products liability law could be invoked against the hospital or other supplier. To counter this, almost every state has some type of "blood shield" statute. For example, the Minnesota statute provides:

> The provision or use of any part of a human body, including blood, blood components, bone marrow, or solid organs from living donors, for the purpose of injection, transfusion, or transplantation in the human body is the rendition of a health care service by each person participating in the provision or use and is not a sale of goods, as that term is defined in section 336.2-105, paragraph (1), or a sale of a product.

Minn. Stat. 525.9221(e). At a minimum, the legislature attempts to immunize suppliers of blood and other body parts from implied warranty liability under Article 2 and, in some cases, from strict liability in tort.* In general, liability for

---

* *See, e.g., Doe v. Travenol Laboratories, Inc.*, 698 F. Supp. 780 (D. Minn. 1988) (interpreting Minnesota statutes); *Gibson v. Methodist Hospital*, 822 S.W.2d 95 (Tex. App. 1991) (since blood not a "product" under statute, no liability in warranty or strict tort).

negligence in testing or failing to test the blood is preserved.[*] Obviously, the "blood shield" legislation is far from uniform, so care must be taken to determine the scope of immunity in each state.

Note: Merchantability and Used Goods

Used or "pre-owned" goods are frequently sold at auctions or directly by their owners. These goods include such "big ticket" items as automobiles, trucks, farm and construction equipment and computers. In the absence of an express warranty, to what standard of merchantability must a merchant seller or lessor conform under UCC 2-314 or 2A-212 when selling or leasing used goods?

Some help is provided by a leading case, *International Petroleum Services, Inc. v. S & N Well Service, Inc.*, 639 P.2d 29 (Kan. 1982). First, assuming the seller is a merchant, most courts and commentators recognize that an implied warranty of merchantability arises, unless disclaimed, in contracts for the sale of new and used goods. Second, UCC 2-314(2) and 2A-212(2) provide a minimum standard of merchantability. This standard can be augmented by agreement, including course of dealing and relevant trade usages. UCC 2-314(3), 2A-212(3). Otherwise, the goods must conform to "normal commercial expectations." As the court stated:

> [The] ordinary buyer in a normal commercial transaction has a right to expect that the goods * * * will not turn out to be completely worthless. The purchaser cannot be expected to purchase goods offered by a merchant for sale and use and then find the goods are suitable only for the junk pile. On the other hand, a buyer who has purchased goods without obtaining an express warranty as to their quality and condition cannot reasonably expect that those goods will be the finest of all possible goods of that kind. Protection of the buyer under the uniform commercial code lies between these two extremes. If an item is used or is second hand, surely less can be expected in the way of quality than if the item is purchased new.

International Petroleum Services, 639 P.2d at 32.

Third, what standard is appropriate to determine the merchantability of used goods of a particular description? This depends upon the circumstances of the transaction. The type and complexity of the goods is one factor. In addition: "The buyer's knowledge that the goods are used, the extent of their prior use, and

---

[*] *See* Dana J. Finberg, Note, *Blood Bank and Blood Products Manufacturer Liability in Transfusion-Related AIDS Cases*, 26 U. RICH. L. REV. 519 (1992).

whether the goods are significantly discounted may help determine what standards of quality should apply to the transaction." *Id.*, 639 P.2d at 34. For example, if there is a functioning market for goods of that type and description and a competitive price can be determined, the price paid in the particular sale may be an excellent index of the nature and scope of the seller's obligation. *See* UCC 2-314, cmt. 9 [former cmt. 7]. Although a "sound price" does not always warrant a "sound product," the price charged can provide some assistance in determining the level of quality the buyer can reasonably expect.

Problem 5-5

B, a farmer, purchased a used 1995 Ford 150 pickup truck from S, a dealer, for $5,000. The four-wheel drive vehicle had been driven 80,000 "tough" miles without any serious mechanical problems. Although refusing to make any express warranties, the seller made no attempt to disclaim or exclude warranties at the time of sale.

Thirty days and 10,000 miles later, the engine failed due to a condition existing at the time of sale. B had the engine replaced for $2,500 and sued S for breach of the implied warranty of merchantability. At the trial, B established that the $5,000 purchase price was at the low end of the "blue book" range for a 1995 Ford 150 pickup truck. B's expert testified that a 1995 Ford 150 pickup truck with the particular condition of B's would have a fair market value of $750. On cross-examination, the expert conceded that the particular vehicle would "pass without objection in the trade under the contract description." B introduced no additional evidence. S moved for a directed verdict. What result? Any difference if this is a lease transaction?

C. Overlap Between Merchantability and Strict Tort Liability

Castro v. QVC Network, Inc.
UNITED STATES COURT OF APPEALS, SECOND CIRCUIT, 1998
139 F.3D 114

CALABRESI, CIRCUIT JUDGE

In this diversity products liability action, plaintiffs-appellants alleged, in separate causes of action for strict liability and for breach of warranty, that defendants-appellees manufactured and sold a defective roasting pan that injured one of the appellants. The United States District Court for the Eastern District of New York (Leonard D. Wexler, *Judge*) rejected appellants' request to charge the jury separately on each cause of action and, instead, instructed the jury only on the strict liability charge. The jury found for appellees and the court denied appellants' motion for a new trial. This appeal followed. We hold that, under New York law, the jury should have been instructed separately on each charge, and, accordingly, reverse and remand for a new trial on the breach of warranty claim.

I. BACKGROUND

In early November 1993, appellee QVC Network, Inc. ("QVC"), operator of a cable television home-shopping channel, advertised, as part of a one-day Thanksgiving promotion, the "T-Fal Jumbo Resistal Roaster." The roaster, manufactured by U.S.A. T-Fal Corp. ("T-Fal"), was described as suitable for, among other things, cooking a twenty-five pound turkey.[1] Appellant Loyda Castro bought the roasting pan by mail and used it to prepare a twenty- pound turkey on Thanksgiving Day, 1993.

Mrs. Castro was injured when she attempted to remove the turkey and roasting pan from the oven. Using insulated mittens, she gripped the pan's handles with the first two fingers on each hand (the maximum grip allowed by the small size of the handles) and took the pan out of the oven. As the turkey tipped toward her, she lost control of the pan, spilling the hot drippings and fat that had accumulated in it during the cooking and basting process. As a result, she suffered second and third degree burns to her foot and ankle, which, over time, has led to scarring, intermittent paresthesia, and ankle swelling.

It is uncontested that in their complaint appellants alleged that the pan was defective and that its defects gave rise to separate causes of action for strict liability and for breach of warranty. Moreover, in the pre-charge conference, appellants' counsel repeatedly requested separate jury charges on strict liability and for breach of warranty. The district court, nevertheless, denied the request for a separate charge on breach of warranty. Judge Wexler stated that "you can't collect twice for the same thing," and deemed the warranty charge unnecessary and "duplicative."

---

[1] At the time that QVC and T-Fal agreed to conduct the Thanksgiving promotion, T-Fal did not have in its product line a pan large enough to roast a turkey. T-Fal therefore asked its parent company, located in France, to provide a suitable roasting pan as soon as possible. The parent provided a pan (designed originally without handles and for other purposes). To this pan two small handles were added so that it could be used to roast a turkey. T-Fal shipped the pan to QVC in time for the early November campaign.

The court, therefore, only gave the jury the New York pattern strict products liability charge.

The jury returned a verdict for appellees QVC and T-Fal. * * * Appellants subsequently moved, pursuant to Federal Rule of Civil Procedure 59, that the jury verdict be set aside and a new trial be ordered for various reasons including that the court had failed to charge the jury on appellants' claim for breach of warranty. * * * [T]he district court denied appellants' Rule 59 motion, reasoning that the breach of warranty and strict products liability claims were "virtually the same." This appeal followed.

II. DISCUSSION
* * *

A. Two Definitions of "Defective" Product Design

Products liability law has long been bedeviled by the search for an appropriate definition of "defective" product design.[2] Over the years, both in the cases and in the literature, two approaches have come to predominate. The first is the risk/utility theory, which focuses on whether the benefits of a product outweigh the dangers of its design.[3] The second is the consumer expectations theory, which focuses on what a buyer/user of a product would properly expect that the product would be suited for.[4]

---

[2] *See generally* W. Page Keeton, *The Meaning of Defect in Products Liability Law,* 45 Mo. L.REV. 579 (1980); W. Page Keeton, *Product Liability and the Meaning of Defect,* 5 ST. MARY'S L.J. 30 (1973); Guido Calabresi & Jon T. Hirschoff, *Toward a Test for Strict Liability in Torts,* 81 YALE L.J. 1055 (1972).

[3] According to the New York Court of Appeals, the risk/utility calculus, which requires "a weighing of the product's benefits against its risks," *Denny v. Ford Motor Co.,* 87 N.Y.2d 248, 257, 639 N.Y.S.2d 250, 662 N.E.2d 730, 735 (1995), is " 'functionally synonymous'" with traditional negligence analysis, *id.* at 258, 639 N.Y.S.2d 250, 662 N.E.2d 730 (citation omitted). Despite the fact that there are some significant differences, the risk/utility calculus is in many ways similar to the Learned Hand negligence test. *See Liriano v. Hobart Corp.,* 132 F.3d 124, 131 n. 12 (2d Cir.1998) (explaining that the most important difference between the two tests is that traditional negligence strikes its cost/benefit balance on the basis of what is known or ought to be known at the time the defendant acted, while the risk/utility test takes into account all relevant information that has become available subsequent to the defendant's actions).

[4] The New York Court of Appeals explains that "the UCC's concept of a 'defective' product
(continued...)

Not all states accept both of these approaches. Some define design defect only according to the risk/utility approach. * * * Others define design defect solely in terms of the consumer expectations theory. * * *[5]

One of the first states to accept both approaches was California, which in *Barker v. Lull Engineering Co.,* 20 Cal.3d 413, 143 Cal.Rptr. 225, 573 P.2d 443 (1978), held that "a product may be found defective in design, so as to subject a manufacturer to strict liability for resulting injuries, under either of two alternative tests"--consumer expectations and risk/utility. *Id.* at 430-32, 143 Cal.Rptr. at 237, 573 P.2d at 455.[6] Several states have followed suit and have adopted both theories.

* * * Prior to the recent case of *Denny v. Ford Motor Co.,* 87 N.Y.2d 248, 639 N.Y.S.2d 250, 662 N.E.2d 730 (1995), it was not clear whether New York recognized both tests. In *Denny,* the plaintiff was injured when her Ford Bronco II sports utility vehicle rolled over when she slammed on the brakes to avoid hitting a deer in the vehicle's path. *See Denny v. Ford Motor Co.,* 42 F.3d 106, 108 (2d Cir.1994), certifying questions to *Denny,* 87 N.Y.2d 248, 639 N.Y.S.2d 250, 662 N.E.2d 730. The plaintiff asserted claims for strict products liability and for breach

---

[4] (...continued)
requires an inquiry only into whether the product in question was 'fit for the ordinary purposes for which such goods are used.'" *Denny,* 87 N.Y.2d at 258, 639 N.Y.S.2d 250, 662 N.E.2d at 736 (quoting U.C.C. § 2-314(2)(c)). Thus, the breach of warranty cause of action "is one involving true 'strict' liability, since recovery may be had upon a showing that the product was not minimally safe for its expected purpose." *Id.* at 259, 639 N.Y.S.2d 250, 662 N.E.2d 730. Some scholars have characterized this inquiry as centering on whether the manufacturer or the user is in a better position to decide about safety. *See* Calabresi & Hirschoff, *supra* note 2, at 1060.

[5] Still others apply a "modified consumer expectations test" that incorporates risk/utility factors into the consumer expectations analysis. * * *

[6] The court stated:
First, a product may be found defective in design if the plaintiff establishes that the product failed to perform as safely as an ordinary customer would expect when used in an intended or reasonably foreseeable manner. Second, a product may alternatively be found defective in design if the plaintiff demonstrates that the product's design proximately caused his injury and the defendant fails to establish, in light of the relevant factors, that, on balance, the benefits of the challenged design outweigh the risk of danger inherent in such design.
Barker, 143 Cal.Rptr. 225, 573 P.2d at 455-56. Placement of the burden of proving the product's risks and utility on the manufacturer is not, however, a necessary part of the risk/utility test. * * *

of implied warranty, and the district judge--over the objection of defendant Ford--submitted both causes of action to the jury. *See id.* The jury ruled in favor of Ford on the strict liability claim, but found for the plaintiff on the implied warranty claim. *See id.* at 109-10. On appeal, Ford argued that the jury's verdicts on the strict products liability claim and the breach of warranty claim were inconsistent because the causes of action were identical. *See id.* at 107.

This court certified the *Denny* case to the New York Court of Appeals to answer the following questions: (1) "whether, under New York law, the strict products liability and implied warranty claims are identical"; and (2) "whether, if the claims are different, the strict products liability claim is broader than the implied warranty claim and encompasses the latter." *Id.* at 111-12.

In response to the certified questions, the Court of Appeals held that in a products liability case a cause of action for strict liability is not identical to a claim for breach of warranty. * * * Moreover, the court held that a strict liability claim is not per se broader than a breach of warranty claim such that the former encompasses the latter. * * * Thus, while claims of strict products liability and breach of warranty are often used interchangeably, under New York law the two causes of action are definitively different. The imposition of strict liability for an alleged design "defect" is determined by a risk-utility standard, * * *. The notion of "defect" in a U.C.C.-based breach of warranty claim focuses, instead, on consumer expectations. * * *

B. When Should a Jury be Charged on Both Strict Liability and Warranty Causes of Action?

Since *Denny*, then, it has been settled that the risk/utility and consumer expectations theories of design defect can, in New York, be the bases of distinct causes of action: one for strict products liability and one for breach of warranty. This fact, however, does not settle the question of when a jury must be charged separately on each cause of action and when, instead, the two causes are, on the facts of the specific case, sufficiently similar to each other so that one charge to the jury is enough.

While eminent jurists have at times been troubled by this issue,[7] the New York

---

[7] Thus Justice Traynor in the early and seminal California strict products liability case, *Greenman v. Yuba Power Products,* 59 Cal.2d 57, 27 Cal.Rptr. 697, 377 P.2d 897 (1963), did not make a clear distinction between them. *See id.* at 64, 27 Cal.Rptr. at 701, 377 P.2d at 901 ("[I]t should not be controlling [for purposes of establishing a manufacturer's liability]

(continued...)

Court of Appeals in *Denny* was quite clear on when the two causes of action might meld and when, instead, they are to be treated as separate. It did this by adding its own twist to the distinction--namely, what can aptly be called the "dual purpose" requirement. * * * Thus in *Denny,* the Court of Appeals pointed out that the fact that a product's overall benefits might outweigh its overall risks does not preclude the possibility that consumers may have been misled into using the product in a context in which it was dangerously unsafe. * * * And this, the New York court emphasized, could be so even though the benefits in other uses might make the product sufficiently reasonable so that it passed the risk/utility test.

In *Denny,* the Ford Bronco II was not designed as a conventional passenger automobile. Instead, it was designed as an off-road, dual purpose vehicle.[8] But in its marketing of the Bronco II, Ford stressed its suitability for commuting and for suburban and city driving. * * * Under the circumstances, the Court of Appeals explained that a rational factfinder could conclude that the Bronco's utility as an off-road vehicle outweighed the risk of injury resulting from roll-over accidents (thus passing the risk/utility test), but at the same time find that the vehicle was not safe for the "ordinary purpose" of daily driving for which it was also marketed and sold (thus flunking the consumer expectations test). * * *

That is precisely the situation before us. The jury had before it evidence that the product was designed, marketed, and sold as a multiple-use product. The pan was originally manufactured and sold in France as an all-purpose cooking dish without handles. And at trial, the jury saw a videotape of a QVC representative

---

[7] (...continued)
whether plaintiff selected the [product] because of the statements in the brochure, or because of the [product's] own appearance of excellence that belied the defect lurking beneath the surface, or because he merely assumed that it would safely do the jobs it was built to do."). And likewise, Judge Eschbach in *Sills v. Massey- Ferguson, Inc.,* 296 F.Supp. 776 (N.D.Ind.1969), stated that although they represented different causes of action, in the case before him, he could not distinguish between them, and then added that "[w]hile this court is unwilling to hold that there is *never* a significant difference between the two theories, it is plain that the outcome of the vast majority of cases is not affected by this fine legal distinction." *Id.* at 779.

[8] Indeed, as Ford argued, the design features that appellant complained of--high center of gravity, narrow track width, short wheel base, and a specially tailored suspension system--were important to preserve the vehicle's utility for off-road use. * * * But, it was these same design features that made the vehicle susceptible to rollover accidents during evasive maneuvers on paved roads. * * *

demonstrating to the television audience that the pan, in addition to serving as a suitable roaster for a twenty-five pound turkey, could also be used to cook casseroles, cutlets, cookies, and other low-volume foods.[9] The court charged the jury that "[a] product is defective if it is not reasonably safe[,] [t]hat is, if the product is so likely to be harmful to persons that a reasonable person who had actual knowledge of its potential for producing injury would conclude that it should not have been marketed in that condition." And, so instructed, the jury presumably found that the pan, because it had many advantages in a variety of uses, did not fail the risk/utility test.

But it was also the case that the pan was advertised as suitable for a particular use--cooking a twenty-five pound turkey. Indeed, T-Fal added handles to the pan in order to fill QVC's request for a roasting pan that it could use in its Thanksgiving promotion. The product was, therefore, sold as appropriately used for roasting a twenty-five pound turkey. And it was in that use that allegedly the product failed and injured the appellant.

In such circumstances, New York law is clear that a general charge on strict products liability based on the risk/utility approach does not suffice. The jury could have found that the roasting pan's overall utility for cooking low-volume foods outweighed the risk of injury when cooking heavier foods, but that the product was nonetheless unsafe for the purpose for which it was marketed and sold--roasting a twenty-five pound turkey--and, as such, was defective under the consumer expectations test. That being so, the appellants were entitled to a separate breach of warranty charge.[10]

---

[9] Appellants also introduced into evidence a "sell sheet" prepared by T-Fal, which described for the QVC salespersons the uses and characteristics of the product, including not only cooking a twenty-five pound turkey, but also an extensive list of several low-volume foods, such as cake, lasagna, and stuffed potatoes. While the "sell-sheet" was an internal document, and therefore, could not have influenced consumer expectations, it does shed light on the meaning of the videotaped commercial.

[10] Appellees argue that "[t]he roaster had only a single purpose which was to be a vessel for cooking." But that misses the point of the dual purpose test. Indeed, the same argument could have been made in the *Denny* case: that the Ford Bronco II had a single purpose, namely driving. What characterizes both of these cases, however, is that there was evidence before the jury of the "dual purposes" to which the products could be put. As the Court of Appeals stated in *Denny,* it is "the nature of the proof and the way in which the fact issues [are] litigated [that] demonstrate[ ] how the two causes of action can diverge." * * * In the

(continued...)

III. CONCLUSION

In light of the evidence presented by appellants of the multi-purpose nature of the product at issue, the district court, applying New York law, should have granted appellants' request for a separate jury charge on the breach of warranty claim in addition to the charge on the strict liability claim. Accordingly, we reverse the order of the district court denying the motion for a new trial, and remand the case for a new trial on the breach of warranty claim, consistent with this opinion.

[Some footnotes omitted. Those retained have been renumbered.]

Notes

1. One of the tensions between strict product liability in tort and warranty liability under the UCC is whether the concept of product defect in tort is coextensive with the concept of unmerchantable under the UCC where the alleged defect results in injury to person or damage to property. This issue was quite controversial, particularly in the concept of design defects, in the drafting of the RESTATEMENT (THIRD) OF TORTS: PRODUCT LIABILITY.[*] The RESTATEMENT (THIRD) approach in comment n to § 2 provides:

> This Restatement contemplates that a well coordinated body of law governing liability for harm to persons or property arising out of the sale of defective products requires a consistent definition of defect, and that the definition properly should come from tort law, whether the claim carries a tort label or one of implied warranty of merchantability.

2. Read Comment 7 to amended UCC 2-314. What is the import of that comment? Whether the courts will follow that direction is still uncertain.[**] Would

---

[10] (...continued)
instant case, given the evidence before the jury of the pan's dual purposes, the failure to charge the jury on breach of warranty could not be harmless error.

[*] *See e.g.,* Marshall S. Shapo, *In Search of the Law of Products Liability: The ALI Restatement Project,* 48 VAND. L. REV. 631 (1995); John F. Vargo, *The Emperor's New Clothes: The American Law Institute Adorns a "New Cloth" for Section 402A Products Liability Design Defects - A Survey of the States Reveals a Different Weave,* 26 U. MEM. L. REV. 493 (1996).

[**] *Compare Potter v. Chicago Pneumatic Tool Co.,* 694 A.2d 1319 (Conn. 1997) (rejecting
(continued...)

the result in *Castro* been different if the amended UCC 2-314 and its comment had been the governing law? If so, is that a wise result? We will return to this issue in Chapter Eleven, *infra*, after you have fully explored the UCC approach to liability and remedies for breach of warranty.

D. Fitness for Particular Purpose

Read UCC 2-315 and 2A-213. How does the implied warranty of "fitness" differ from the implied warranty of "merchantability" in UCC 2-314 and 2A-212? Is it easier or harder to prove? To what extent do they overlap? For example, suppose buyer's or lessee's particular purpose is the same as the ordinary purpose for which the described goods are used. If the seller or lessor is a merchant, should you plead and prove both implied warranties or just one? Which one?

LEWIS V. MOBIL OIL CORP.
UNITED STATES COURT OF APPEALS, EIGHTH CIRCUIT, 1971
438 F.2D 500

GIBSON, CIRCUIT JUDGE

In this diversity case the defendant appeals from a judgment entered on a jury verdict in favor of the plaintiff in the amount of $89,250 for damages alleged to be caused by use of defendant's oil.

Plaintiff Lewis has been doing business as a sawmill operator in Cove, Arkansas, since 1956. In 1963, in order to meet competition, Lewis decided to convert his power equipment to hydraulic equipment. He purchased a hydraulic system in May 1963, from a competitor who was installing a new system. The used system was in good operating condition at the time Lewis purchased it. It was stored at his plant until November 1964, while a new mill building was being built, at which time it was installed. Following the installation, Lewis requested from Frank Rowe, a local Mobil oil dealer, the proper hydraulic fluid to operate his machinery. The prior owner of the hydraulic system had used Pacemaker oil supplied by Cities Service, but plaintiff had been a customer of Mobil's for many

---

** (...continued)
the RESTATEMENT (THIRD): PRODUCT LIABILITY test for defective design) *with Hyundai Motor Co. v. Rodriguez*, 995 S.W.2d 661 (Tex. 1999) (equating merchantability and design defect tests).

years and desired to continue with Mobil. Rowe said he didn't know what the proper lubricant for Lewis' machinery was, but would find out. The only information given to Rowe by Lewis was that the machinery was operated by a gear-type pump; Rowe did not request any further information. He apparently contacted a Mobil representative for a recommendation, though this is not entirely clear, and sold plaintiff a product known as Ambrex 810. This is a straight mineral oil with no chemical additives.

Within a few days after operation of the new equipment commenced, plaintiff began experiencing difficulty with its operation. The oil changed color, foamed over, and got hot. The oil was changed a number of times, with no improvement. By late April 1965, approximately six months after operations with the equipment had begun, the system broke down, and a complete new system was installed. The cause of the breakdown was undetermined, but apparently by this time there was some suspicion of the oil being used. Plaintiff Lewis requested Rowe to be sure he was supplying the right kind of oil. Ambrex 810 continued to be supplied.

From April 1965 until April 1967, plaintiff continued to have trouble with the system, principally with the pumps which supplied the pressure. Six new pumps were required during this period, as they continually broke down. During this period, the kind of pump used was a Commercial pump which was specified by the designer of the hydraulic system. The filtration of oil for this pump was by means of a metal strainer, which was cleaned daily by the plaintiff in accordance with the instruction given with the equipment.

In April 1967, the plaintiff changed the brand of pump from a Commercial to a Tyrone pump. The Tyrone pump, instead of using the metal strainer filtration alone, used a disposable filter element in addition. Ambrex 810 oil was also recommended by Mobil and used with this pump, which completely broke down three weeks later. At this point, plaintiff was visited for the first time by a representative of Mobil Oil Corporation, as well as a representative of the Tyrone pump manufacturer.

On the occasion of this visit, May 9, 1967, plaintiff's system was completely flushed and cleaned, a new Tyrone pump installed, and on the pump manufacturer's and Mobil's representative's recommendation, a new oil was used which contained certain chemical additives, principally a "defoamant." Following these changes, plaintiff's system worked satisfactorily up until the time of trial, some two and one-half years later.

Briefly stated, plaintiff's theory of his case is that Mobil supplied him with an oil which was warranted fit for use in his hydraulic system, that the oil was not suitable for such use because it did not contain certain additives, and that it was the improper oil which caused the mechanical breakdowns, with consequent loss to his business. The defendant contends that there was no warranty of fitness, that the breakdowns were caused not by the oil but by improper filtration, and that in any event there can be no recovery of loss of profits in this case.

I. The Existence of Warranties

Defendant maintains that there was no warranty of fitness in this case, that at most there was only a warranty of merchantability and that there was no proof of breach of this warranty, since there was no proof that Ambrex 810 is unfit for use in hydraulic systems generally. We find it unnecessary to consider whether the warranty of merchantability was breached, although there is some proof in the record to that effect, since we conclude that there was a warranty of fitness.

Plaintiff Lewis testified that he had been a longtime customer of Mobil Oil, and that his only source of contact with the company was through Frank Rowe, Mobil's local dealer, with whom he did almost all his business. It was common knowledge in the community that Lewis was converting his sawmill operation into a hydraulic system. Rowe knew this, and in fact had visited his mill on business matters several times during the course of the changeover. When operations with the new machinery were about to commence, Lewis asked Rowe to get him the proper hydraulic fluid. Rowe asked him what kind of a system he had, and Lewis replied it was a Commercial-pump type. This was all the information asked or given. Neither Lewis nor Rowe knew what the oil requirements for the system were, and Rowe, knew that Lewis knew nothing more specific about his requirements. Lewis also testified that after he began having trouble with his operations, while there were several possible sources of the difficulty the oil was one suspected source, and he several times asked Rowe to be sure he was furnishing him with the right kind.

Rowe's testimony for the most part confirmed Lewis'. It may be noted here that Mobil does not contest Rowe's authority to represent it in this transaction, and therefore whatever warranties may be implied because of the dealings between Rowe and Lewis are attributable to Mobil. Rowe admitted knowing Lewis was converting to a hydraulic system and that Lewis asked him to supply the fluid. He testified that he did not know what should be used and relayed the request to a superior in the Mobil organization, who recommended Ambrex 810. This is what was supplied.

When the first Tyrone pump was installed in April 1967, Rowe referred the request for a proper oil recommendation to Ted Klock, a Mobil engineer. Klock recommended Ambrex 810. When this pump failed a few weeks later, Klock visited the Lewis plant to inspect the equipment. The system was flushed out completely and the oil was changed to DTE-23 and Del Vac Special containing several additives. After this, no further trouble was experienced.

This evidence adequately establishes an implied warranty of fitness. Arkansas has adopted the Uniform Commercial Code's provision for an implied warranty of fitness:

> "Where the seller at the time of contracting has reason to know any particular purpose for which the goods are required and that the buyer is relying on the seller's skill or judgment to select or furnish suitable goods, there is unless excluded or modified under the next section an implied warranty that the goods shall be fit for such purpose." 7C Ark. Stat. Ann. § 85-2-315 (1961).

Under this provision of the Code, there are two requirements for an implied warranty of fitness: (1) that the seller have "reason to know" of the use for which the goods are purchased, and (2) that the buyer relies on the seller's expertise in supplying the proper product. Both of these requirements are amply met by the proof in this case. Lewis' testimony, as confirmed by that of Rowe and Klock, shows that the oil was purchased specifically for his hydraulic system, not for just a hydraulic system in general, and that Mobil certainly knew of this specific purpose. It is also clear that Lewis was relying on Mobil to supply him with the proper oil for the system, since at the time of his purchases, he made clear that he didn't know what kind was necessary.

Mobil contends that there was no warranty of fitness for use in his particular system because he didn't specify that he needed an oil with additives, and alternatively that he didn't give them enough information for them to determine that an additive oil was required. However, it seems that the circumstances of this case come directly within that situation described in the first comment to this provision of the Uniform Commercial Code:

> "1. Whether or not this warranty arises in any individual case is basically a question of fact to be determined by the circumstances of the contracting. Under this section the buyer need not bring home to the seller *actual knowledge of the particular purpose* for which the goods are intended or of his reliance on the seller's skill and judgment, if the circumstances are such that the seller has reason to realize the purpose intended or that the reliance exists." 7C Ark. Stat. Ann. § 85-2-315, Comment 1 (1961) (emphasis added).

Here Lewis made it clear that the oil was purchased for his system, that he didn't know what oil should be used, and that he was relying on Mobil to supply the proper product. If any further information was needed, it was incumbent upon Mobil to get it before making its recommendation. That it could have easily gotten the necessary information is evidenced by the fact that after plaintiff's continuing complaints, Mobil's engineer visited the plant, and, upon inspection, changed the recommendation that had previously been made.

Additionally, Mobil contends that even if there were an implied warranty of fitness, it does not cover the circumstances of this case because of the abnormal features which the plaintiff's system contained, namely an inadequate filtration system and a capacity to entrain excessive air. There are several answers to this contention. First of all, the contention goes essentially to the question of causation–*i.e.*, whether the damage was caused by a breach of warranty or by some other cause–and not to the existence of a warranty of fitness in the first place. Secondly, assuming that certain peculiarities in the plaintiff's system did exist, the whole point of an implied warranty of fitness is that a product be suitable for a specific purpose, and that a seller should not supply a product which is not so suited. Thirdly, there is no evidence in the record that the plaintiff's system was unique or abnormal in these respects. It operated satisfactorily under the prior owner, and the new system has operated satisfactorily after it was adequately cleaned and an additive type oil used.

* * * Thus, Mobil's defense that there was no warranty of fitness because of an "abnormal use" of the oil is not appropriate here. * * *

[The court next held that there was adequate evidence to sustain the jury's verdict that the plaintiff's damage was caused by the breach of warranty and not by variations in the plaintiff's system or inadequate maintenance.]

Notes

1. Was UCC 2-315 the proper warranty provision for application in *Lewis*? Put another way, could the court have reached the same result under an express warranty or an implied warranty of merchantability?

2. Suppose Mr. Lewis had asked Mr. Rowe to provide him with literature describing "oil that I might use in my new commercial hydraulic equipment." If Rowe had furnished literature describing oil with and oil without chemical additives and Mr. Rowe had thereafter ordered Ambrex 810, would the subsequent sale be

with an implied warranty of fitness for particular purpose? To test your judgment, *see Axion Corp. v. G.D.C. Leasing Corp.*, 269 N.E.2d 664 (Mass. 1971).

3. Assuming that Mr. Lewis relied upon Mobil's skill and judgment, suppose Mobil had established that Ambrex 810 would work satisfactorily in some "commercial pump" hydraulic systems but not work in the particular system owned by Mr. Lewis. Assume further that Mr. Lewis was using his system for ordinary purposes. Should this affect the result in the case? Consider this explication of the difference between ordinary and particular purpose in *Ingram River Equipment, Inc. v. Pott Industries, Inc.*, 816 F.2d 1231, 1233-35 (8ᵗʰ Cir. 1987). After quoting comment 2 to 2-315, the court continues:

> Ingram's purpose for the goods it purchased from Pott was to use them to carry heavy petroleum products on the Mississippi and its tributaries and to heat those products to facilitate their discharge in cold climates. Pott characterizes the goods at issue as heating-coil-equipped tank barges, and argues that carrying and heating heavy petroleum products is the customary use of such products. Pott maintains that Ingram's use of the barges and the heating coils is not unique or peculiar to Ingram's business, since others use heating-coil-equipped tank barges in precisely the same manner; Pott itself had constructed over thirty such barges for use in the same manner before it built these four for Ingram.

> Ingram, however, rejoins that Pott errs in suggesting that its use of the goods must be unique to fall within the fitness-for-a-particular-purpose warranty, arguing instead that the question is one of degree. According to Ingram, the proper characterization of the goods here is tank barges, rather than heating-coil-equipped tank barges. Tank barges, Ingram continues, are used to carry a multitude of cargoes, including a variety of chemicals, molasses, and oils and fuel oils of many kinds. The barges here were equipped with steam coils to enable Ingram to carry a particular kind of cargo--cargo that sometimes requires heating to aid discharge. Further, neither Pott nor Ingram deals solely or predominantly in barges that have steam coils; Pott builds and Ingram operates all sorts of barges. In these circumstances, Ingram concludes, the particular-purpose requirement is met.

> We agree with Ingram that its use of the goods need not be one-of-a-kind to meet the requirements of § 400.2-315. It is doubtful that even the Comment's example of using a shoe to climb mountains would qualify as a unique use of the shoe. Instead, as we read Comment 2, the

key inquiry is not whether anyone else can be found who puts the goods to the same use, but whether the buyer's use is sufficiently different from the customary use of the goods to make it not an ordinary use of the goods; that a buyer's use is not entirely idiosyncratic does not mean that it is ordinary. * * * Therefore, that others put tank barges to the same use as Ingram does not preclude finding that a warranty of fitness exists.

Whether Ingram's purpose diverges sufficiently from the customary purposes of other buyers to be considered particular turns to a great extent on whether one accepts Pott's characterization of the goods as heating-coil-equipped tank barges, or instead accepts Ingram's portrayal of them as tank barges, which have been equipped with heating coils to serve a particular purpose. And this in turn hinges upon how the factual context in which Ingram and Pott struck their bargain is interpreted. To return to the Comment's shoe illustration, is this case more like one in which a buyer goes to a general shoe store and buys a pair of shoes for mountain climbing, or one in which a buyer goes to a mountain-climbing gear store to buy shoes for this purpose? This is, ultimately, a question of fact. * * * Here, since Ingram operates and Pott builds barges for a variety of uses, we are unable to conclude that the District Court was clearly erroneous in finding that an implied warranty of fitness for a particular purpose arose.

Pott argues that the District Court's opinion made no such finding, that it found only that the pipe supplied to Ingram was intended to be used in a steam coil heating system, and that the pipe did not serve its intended purpose. * * * Any pipe furnished for use in a steam coil heating system, Pott argues, would be used to heat product in order to discharge it more easily, so such a use cannot be called a particular purpose. If the District Court opinion contained only the paragraph relied on by Pott in advancing this argument, it might have merit, but we think it would be a mistake to parse the opinion as if it were a regulation or a section of the Internal Revenue Code. When the entire opinion is read in context, it is apparent to us that the District Court regarded the product being sold not as pipe, but rather as barges, * * * that it believed the barges to be intended for a particular purpose, that is, the transportation of heavy oil, and that it found the barges inadequate for this particular purpose because they were equipped with defective pipe. It is arguable, and Pott has argued, that such a view of the transaction is inconsistent with the construction placed on § 2-315 by some courts, but this contention also misses the mark. The

Uniform Commercial Code has no force of law on its own. Its binding legal effect is derived from enactment by the legislatures of particular states. Although uniformity of interpretation is of course desirable, complete uniformity is not possible, and the Code is, in terms of the present case, simply a Missouri statute to be interpreted in the usual fashion. One problem that arises in interpretation is where to put the uncertain line between ordinary and particular purposes of goods sold. The placement of this line is a case-by-case process that reflects, over time, the public policy of the enacting state. Here, there is no opinion of the Supreme Court or Court of Appeals of Missouri in point, and the District Court, presided over by an experienced Missouri lawyer, has held in favor of Ingram's claim of warranty of fitness for a particular purpose. We do not find the District Court's opinion deficient in analysis or unreasoned.

Note: Implied Warranties Under the CISG

Article 35 of the CISG, without using the word "warranty," captures the essence of the UCC's implied warranties of merchantability and fitness. For the counterpart to UCC 2-314, *see* CISG Art. 35(2)(a), and for the counterpart to UCC 2-315, *see* CISG Art. 35(2)(b). What are the differences? As previously noted, Art. 35(2) is available if the conformity issue is not resolved "by the contract." Art. 35(1). Review Art. 7 & Art. 8. Do you think that buyers under the CISG get more or less protection than under the UCC?

Note: Implied Warranties Under UCITA

UCITA 403 provides for an implied warranty of merchantability for computer programs. The merchantability implied warranty is divided between the expectations of the end user and the expectations of the distributor. Notice that the list of criteria that determine the content of the implied warranty of merchantability is much abbreviated from the list found in UCC 2-314.

UCITA 404 provides for an implied warranty that the merchant exercised reasonable care as to accuracy of informational content. See UCITA 102(a)(37).

UCITA 405 provides an implied warranty of fitness for computer information. Notice the bifurcation of the implied warranty in subsection (a) to provide a different standard for the implied warranty if the licensor is providing services as opposed to a product. Subsection (c) provides an implied warranty of system integration in some circumstances.

E. Finance Leases

The tripartite structure of Article 2 regarding express and implied warranties and the so-called disclaimer provision have been carried wholesale into Article 2A with very few differences. The major exception is that a finance lessor may be accountable for express warranties made under UCC 2A-210 but not for an implied warranty of merchantability under UCC 2A-212 or an implied warranty of fitness for a particular purpose under UCC 2A-213. The rationale for that approach is that a finance lease is merely a financing arrangement and the finance lessor is usually not a merchant in goods of the kind or equipped with the skill or judgment in selecting the goods for the lessee to make it fair for the finance lessor to be liable for those warranties. Reread UCC 2A-103 (definition of finance lease). Do you see how that assumption is embedded into the definition?

The finance lessee should look to the supplier of the goods for warranties about the quality of the goods. Read UCC 2A-209. In addition, UCC 2A-407 provides that in a finance lease, the lessee's obligations under the lease are irrevocable and independent upon the lessee's acceptance of the goods. Read UCC 2A-407. Do you see how that provision may benefit a finance lessor who has made and breached an express warranty?[*]

What legal rules govern the warranties the supplier makes to the finance lessor that are passed through to the finance lessee pursuant to UCC 2A-209?

Problem 5-6

Global Electronics manufactures telephone equipment. Vacation Villa and Global Electronics execute a contract in which Vacation Villa will purchase telephone equipment. That contract to purchase is assigned to Great Finance Co. Great Finance Co. purchases the telephone equipment from Global Electronics and then leases the equipment to Vacation Villa. The telephone equipment malfunctions after installation. Vacation Villa stops making payments on the lease to Great Finance and sues Global Electronics and Great Finance for breach of the warranty of merchantability. Great Finance counter sues Vacation Villa for the

---

[*] *See* Steven R. Schoenfeld, *Commercial Law: The Finance Lease under Article 2A of the Uniform Commercial Code*, 1989 ANN. SURV. AM. L. 565.

lease payments.

A. Apply the appropriate provisions of Articles 2 and 2A to this situation.

B. Assume that Global Electronics requires anyone who wants to lease equipment to lease the equipment from Great Finance Co. Does that give Vacation Villa an argument that it might successfully assert in its lawsuit with Great Finance? Consider the following case, decided before Article 2A was in effect. Does Article 2A preclude applying the reasoning of the case to this situation?

MERCEDES-BENZ CREDIT CORP. V. LOTITO
SUPERIOR COURT OF NEW JERSEY, APPELLATE DIVISION, 1997
306 N.J. SUPER. 25, 703 A.2D 288

PAUL G. LEVY, J.A.D.

This issue presented for decision in this case is whether a leasing company which is closely affiliated with an automobile manufacturer, a distributor and a dealer, yet still a separate entity, is subject to a customer's defense of breach of warranty. The specific question here is whether the leasing company may enforce a vehicle lease over a defense that the vehicle suffers from manufacturing defects in breach of the new car warranty. We hold that enforcement must await determination of the breach of warranty issues.

Defendant selected a luxury car offered for sale by Ray Catena Motor Car Corp. (Catena) and chose to lease the vehicle. Using a form of lease provided by plaintiff, Mercedes-Benz Credit Corporation (MBCC), Catena as lessor and defendant as lessee executed a lease on July 10, 1993, for a new Mercedes Benz model 500SL, at the monthly rate of $1,419 for forty-eight months. The total monthly payments would be $68,112 with a stated residual value of $53,585. The lease provided for simultaneous assignment by Catena to MBCC, "pursuant to the terms of the Dealer Automobile Purchase and Lease Assignment by and between Lessor and [MBCC]," and the certificate of title was issued to MBCC.

The terms of the lease purported to insulate MBCC from liability for breach of any warranty or any claim by defendant with respect to the car. The pertinent parts of the relevant paragraphs state:

6. VEHICLE WARRANTIES AND DISCLAIMERS.

To the extent they are assignable, you [lessor] agree to assign to me [defendant] all your rights and remedies under the manufacturer's standard written warranties applicable to the vehicle. I acknowledge that you make no express warranties regarding the vehicle as to its condition, merchantability, or fitness for use, that you disclaim any implied warranties and that I am leasing it from you "as is".

19. ABATEMENT

The monthly rent shall be paid for the full term of the lease * * * without setoff, counterclaim, reduction, abatement, suspension, deferment, or any other defense because of * * * unsatisfactory performance of the vehicle or for any other reason whatever including, but not limited to, mechanical or warranty problems. * * *

Paragraph nineteen also provided that defendant agreed to use the manufacturer's dispute resolution system before taking any action against MBCC if there was a dispute regarding the manufacturer's warranty.

When defendant leased the car, he received warranties on the vehicle from both the manufacturer and the dealer. The warranty from the manufacturer provided that Mercedes-Benz of North America (MBNA) would "make any repairs or replacements necessary, to correct defects in material or workmanship." Catena, as the authorized Mercedes dealer, was a "co-warrantor." Both the express warranties and any warranties implied by law were to last for either forty-eight months or 50,000 miles, whichever came first.

Defendant paid the monthly rent on the lease for twenty-five months, but he was continually dissatisfied with the car's performance. He experienced repeated problems with it and frequently returned to Catena for repairs during that period of time. Aside from scheduled maintenance, forty-eight days were used to perform $22,269 of warranty work at Catena. Defendant admits he never informed MBCC of problems with the car, but rather, dealt with personnel at the Catena dealership, because it was his belief that the two entities were the same.

Frustrated at the fact that the car repeatedly manifested problems and could not seem to be repaired properly, defendant stopped paying on the lease in July 1995. In November 1995, MBCC filed an action against defendant in the Law Division, alleging that defendant was in default of payments due on the lease. It therefore requested a writ of replevin ordering defendant to turn over the vehicle, as well as damages for monies due and unpaid under the lease. Defendant filed an answer with separate defenses and a counterclaim against MBCC; one of the separate defenses asserted that MBCC breached the applicable warranties "in conspiracy with the third-party defendants" and thereby breached the lease. Also included was a third-party action against MBCC, Catena, MBNA, and Mercedes-Benz A.G. (MBAG), a German company that manufactured the automobile in question. MBNA, MBCC and MBAG are each subsidiaries of Daimler-Benz A.G., a German corporation.

Defendant surrendered the car in January 1996, and MBCC eventually sold it at auction. When the final credits and charges were totaled, MBCC claimed defendant owed it $34,443.13 including attorneys' fees and costs of $5,506.06.[1] MBCC was granted summary judgment in that amount and defendant's counterclaim was dismissed with prejudice. The order granting that relief was certified as a final judgment, pursuant to R. 4:42-2, leaving the third-party action to be prosecuted. * * *

Regardless of the legal analyses expressed by the parties, we believe the starting point must be *Unico v. Owen*, 50 N.J. 101, 232 A.2d 405 (1967).

In *Unico*, a consumer responded to an advertisement to purchase 140 record albums and a stereo from Universal Stereo Corporation. The purchase price was financed through a retail installment contract and note providing for a down payment and thirty-six monthly payments. Universal was to deliver the records over a six-year period. Universal and the buyer entered into an installment contract, which consisted of "11 fine print paragraphs."[2] The contract was directly assigned to a lender, Unico, as patently contemplated. The "reasonable and normal expectation" of the buyer was that "performance of the delivery obligation was a condition precedent to his undertaking to make installment payments." * * * However, there was a clause stating that if the contract was assigned, the buyer's liability to the assignee would be "immediate and absolute and not affected by any default whatsoever of the Seller signing this contract." The buyer also agreed not to set up any defense viable against the seller if sued by the note's assignee for nonpayment. * * *

Unico was a "partnership formed expressly for the purpose of financing Universal Stereo Corporation" which had "a substantial degree of control of [the] entire business" of Universal. * * * Specifically, Unico set forth the credit qualifications of buyers, the requirements for making the notes and the endorsements, and the maximum length of term for the consumer contracts involved. * * * The Court summarized this control as one in which Unico "had a thorough knowledge of the nature and method of operation of Universal's business [and] also exercised control over it." * * * "To say the relationship between Unico and the business operations of Universal was close, and that Unico was involved

---

[1] The figures were not contested.

[2] The Court's opinion makes no mention of a disclaimer of warranty clause in the contract.

therein, is to put it mildly." * * *

The buyer received the stereo and the first delivery of twelve albums and he paid the next succeeding twelve monthly installments, but he never received another record album. When Unico sought payment several months later, the buyer advised that payments would be resumed if the albums were delivered. None were delivered because Universal was insolvent, and Unico sued for the balance due on the note plus attorneys fees. The trial court found Unico was not a holder in due course of the note and Universal's breach of the contract barred recovery.

On appeal, our Supreme Court noted the disparity of more than two years between the payment obligation and the delivery obligation. Calling this "hyper-executory," the Court expressed concern over this disparity in rights between buyer and seller or transferee. Together with the provisions governing the defenses against the assignee, the Court described the arrangement as "designed to put the buyer-consumer in an unfair and burdensome legal strait jacket" from which there was no "escape no matter what the default of the seller, while permitting the note-holder, contract-assignee to force payment from [the buyer] while enveloping itself in the formal status of holder in due course." * * *

The Supreme Court upheld the buyer's right to defend against the suit for payment on the note based on the seller's alleged default. Holder in due course status was neither necessary nor desirable when the transferee knew a great deal about, or controlled or participated in, the underlying transaction. * * * Consistent with other decisions protecting the consumer in transactions involving a consumer and a commercial entity, such as *Henningsen v. Bloomfield Motors*, 32 N.J. 358, 161 A.2d 69 (1960), the Court explained that courts should give special scrutiny to such contracts to ensure that they were consistent with "principles of equity and public policy." * * * Underlying these decisions was the inequality in bargaining power between the typical consumer and lender; the lender had not only more economic and bargaining power, but greater expertise, along with the ability to write adhesion contracts that unduly favored the lender. * * *

Accordingly, the Court declared that in "consumer good sales cases," holder in due course status would be denied to finance companies whose "involvement with the seller's business is * * * close, and whose knowledge of * * * the terms of the underlying sale agreement is * * * pervasive." *Id.* at 116, 232 A.2d 405.[3] The

---

[3] The protection was extended to the plaintiff not in his capacity as "buyer" but rather as "consumer." Thus, the policy of consumer protection supporting this holding applies equally

(continued...)

Court relied on decisions from other states which also denied holder in due course status in cases involving not only individual buyers, but commercial ones as well. * * *

The Court explained its holding succinctly:

For purposes of consumer goods transactions, we hold that where the seller's performance is executory in character and when it appears from the totality of the arrangements between dealer and financer that the financer has had a substantial voice in setting standards for the underlying transaction, or has approved the standards established by the dealer, and has agreed to take all or a predetermined or substantial quantity of the negotiable paper which is backed by such standards, the financer should be considered a participant in the original transaction and therefore not entitled to holder in due course status.

[*Id.* at 122-23, 232 A.2d 405.]

The Court, however, reserved decision on the very issue presented in this case: "whether, when the buyer's claim is breach of warranty as distinguished from failure of consideration, the seller's default as to the former may be raised as defenses against the financer." * * * The Court also struck as unconscionable the clause in which the buyer promised that in the event the lender sued, the buyer would waive any defenses otherwise good against the seller. * * * The legalistic waiver provision, buried in a small-print contract, was "fraught with opportunities for misuse" and therefore would be stricken as unconscionable. * * * Citing N.J.S.A. 12A:2-302 and 12A:9-206, the Court observed "in the enactment of these two sections of the Code an intention to leave in the hands of the courts the continued application of common law principles in deciding in consumer goods cases whether such waiver clauses as the one imposed on Owen in this case are so one-sided as to be contrary to public policy." * * * We now take the next step and hold that a consumer lessee may raise a breach of warranty against the lessor when there is a sufficiently close relationship between the seller, the manufacturer and the lessor, and that an attempt to disclaim such obligations by contract is unenforceable.

In *Unico* and here, there is a tripartite contract involving a consumer, a buyer, and a financer. The difference, however, is that *Unico* involved a loan with an

---

[3] (...continued)
to buyers as well as lessees. *See A-Leet Leasing Corp. v. Kingshead Corp.*, 150 N.J. Super. 384, 392, 375 A.2d 1208 (App. Div.) (" 'in this day of expanding rental and leasing enterprises,' the consumer who leases a product should be given protection equivalent to the consumer who purchases."), *cert. denied*, 75 N.J. 528, 384 A.2d 508 (1977).

affiliated company, while this case involves a lease with an affiliated company. However, that makes no difference. These two types of arrangements are truly similar, especially from the individual consumer's perspective. In each case, a financing company supplies capital to an individual buyer in order to acquire a product, here an automobile.

As in *Unico*, the relationship between the lessor (MBCC) and the dealer (Catena) and the manufacturer (MBNA and Daimler-Benz) is very close. MBCC created the lease form and authorized personnel at dealerships to execute the leases essentially on its behalf. Although MBCC was not literally dominating the sales component of Mercedes-Benz's business, the fact remains that MBCC had a close involvement with Catena and MBCC's knowledge of "the terms of the underlying sale agreement" was extensive. * * * Thus, there is sufficient closeness between the financer and the seller here to justify treating this case similarly to *Unico*.

The disparity in bargaining power evident in *Unico*, which cannot be denied as a reason for the decision, is also sufficiently similar in this case. Decisions like *Unico* are plainly based, in part, on economic disparity or knowledge disparity between buyer and seller/lender. And, although the buyer here was able to afford a luxury car with high monthly payments and was a successful businessman, more able than most consumers to evaluate lease and finance options, he is still an individual consumer subject to the pressures attendant to an adhesion contract.

In addition, study of Article 2A of the Uniform Commercial Code is required as a source of public policy because it will govern all leasing transactions after January 10, 1995. L. 1994, c. 114, s 12. Although not applicable to this transaction which was made a year before the legislation was enacted, the Code imposes on certain lessors both implied and express warranties with respect to the goods. *See* N.J.S.A. 12A:2A-212, -213. Nothing in the adoption of Article 2A, as a source of public policy governing lease law, bars extending the rule of *Unico* (dealing with failure of consideration as a defense to a loan contract) to this case (dealing with breach of warranty as a defense to a lease contract). To the contrary, the comments to Article 2A make it clear that the courts will determine, case-by-case, whether finance lessors that are "affiliate[s] of the supplier of goods" should answer for a seller's warranty. Official Comment to U.C.C. § 2A-101, "Finance Leases"; Official Comment to U.C.C. § 2A-103(h).

Expanding the defenses which may be asserted against a lessor in a consumer goods transaction involving close ties between seller, manufacturer and lessor requires a balancing of the rights of the consumer and these entities. A major consideration of *Unico* is protection of consumer expectations and rights, such as the notion that if a consumer buys a product and that product is defective, the consumer does not have to pay for it unless its warranties were validly disclaimed; rather, it will be repaired or the purchase price will be returned. This is a sound and reasonable expectation to protect. Thus, if a consumer bought a new car and received warranties on it, absent unusual circumstances it would be expected that the seller will answer for any defects and fix them. Similarly, where a truly independent lender finances a consumer's acquisition of a car, it is ordinarily expected that the lender will not be responsible if the car is a "lemon." But the financing agency here is not truly independent, and is instead an affiliated company with relations so close to the actual seller that they are equivalent to the relationship the court scrutinized in *Unico*.

Of course in *Unico*, the seller was insolvent and the consumer could only look to the lender as a source of recovery. Here, plaintiff's reasonable expectations as a consumer can be satisfied by Catena or MBNA if the warranties were breached. Other jurisdictions have subjected an affiliated financer to warranty liability when the seller cannot answer for a breach of warranty. *See U.S. Roofing v. Credit Alliance Corp.*, 228 Cal. App. 3d 1431, 279 Cal. Rptr. 533 (1991) (a lessor may disclaim warranties in equipment selected solely by the lessee provided that the lessee "has an adequate remedy against the manufacturer or supplier for any defect in the equipment.")

We hold, however, that the financial stability of the expected warrantor is not the qualifier to assertion of a breach of warranty as a defense to a suit for breach of the lease or the loan on which the original sale was based. * * *

Thus, if defendant proves the car to be defective and that he was damaged thereby, the case becomes a question of which component in the chain of distribution of Mercedes-Benz products will bear the loss caused by a manufacturing defect: the manufacturer, its financing company, or its franchisee. Of course, that loss could be more than, less than or the same as the damages proved by MBCC for defendant's failure to maintain the lease. * * *

[I]f defendant fails to show the car is defective, MBCC will have an award against defendant. On the other hand, if defendant succeeds in showing the car is defective, his liability to MBCC may be erased or reduced. In addition, MBCC or defendant or both may have awards against the third-party defendants. * * *

This disposition recognizes the disparity in economic power between a consumer like defendant and companies like the third-party defendants. The latter are clearly more able than an individual consumer to "absorb the impact of a single imprudent or unfair exchange." *Unico, supra*, 50 N.J. at 110, 232 A.2d 405. * * *

[Some footnotes omitted. Those retained have been renumbered.]

Notes

1. This case was remanded for trial on the breach of warranty claim. *See Mercedes-Benz Credit Corp. v. Lotito*, 328 N.J. Super. 491, 746 A.2d 480 (N.J. App. Div. 2000) for the appeal after remand.

2. The finance lease is a credit transaction in that the lessee takes possession of the goods and promises to pay the agreed price in installments with interest. This works to the financial benefit of the seller, who gets immediate value for the goods from the finance lessor, and the finance lessor, who probably pays a discounted value for the goods and can enforce the stream of installment payments against the lessee without bearing any risk that the goods are unmerchantable. In these cases, the lessee must obtain financing for its obligations from other sources and runs the risk that the seller has made no warranties or is bankrupt.

UCC 2A-407(1), however, does not apply to a consumer lease. Thus, the "hell or high water" effect of the finance lease depends upon the enforceability of an appropriate clause in the consumer lease. Moreover, UCC 2A-407(3) subjects the validity of such a clause to other applicable law.

Consider the following situations where the seller delivers goods to a consumer buyer on credit and the goods are unmerchantable:

A. Buyer issues a negotiable promissory note for the price plus interest to the order of Seller. Seller then negotiates the note to C who becomes a holder in due course and, in theory, free from any defenses that arise in the contract between S and B.

B. Buyer promises to pay in installments and agrees (in the contract for sale) not to assert any defenses arising in the contract with S against any third party to whom the contract rights have been assigned. In theory, this agreement not to assert defenses is enforceable by the third party against B.

Now study the FTC Holder-in-Due-Course Regulations, 16 CFR Part 433. What is their effect on the two transactions above? Suppose the contract contained a "hell-or-high-water" clause?

Note: Finance Licenses Under UCITA

UCITA contains provisions that parallel Article 2A's provisions on finance leases. First review the following definitions, UCITA 102(a)(29) (financial accommodation contract) and 102(a)(31) (financier). Now read UCITA 508. This section contemplates that the financier will become the licensee and then re-license the information to the ultimate licensee. Notice that the financier does not make implied warranties to the accommodated licensee but may be liable to the licensee for express warranties. UCITA 508(b)(2). The UCITA analog to UCC 2A-407 is UCITA 509.

UCITA also contains provisions that contemplate the financier will not be a licensee of the information. UCITA 507. Notice that a financier is someone who is not an Article 9 secured party. A person who takes a security interest in information will be governed by Article 9 of the UCC. UCITA 509 also applies to the situation where the financier is not a licensee.

UCITA 510 and 511 govern remedies for the financiers in both situations.

F. Proof of Breach: Effect of Lack of Causation and Plaintiff's Contributory Behavior

So far the primary issue addressed has been whether the seller or lessor made a warranty, express or implied, to the buyer or lessee. Here we are concerned about what the buyer or lessee must prove to establish a breach of that warranty and that the breach caused the loss complained of. The answers turn, in part, upon the type of warranty made and the quantum and quality of proof required to get the case to the jury. In addition, the seller or lessor must be alert to possible misuse of the goods by the buyer or lessee and other conduct suggesting contributory "fault" or assumption of risk. These issues frequently arise in commercial litigation after the buyer has accepted the goods and is unable to revoke acceptance. *See* UCC 2-607.

According to Mr. Phelan, an experienced Chicago trial attorney, the plaintiff maximizes the chances of proving both breach and causation when the facts and inferences from the following sources are cumulated: (1) the allegedly non-conforming product; (2) the circumstances surrounding the "accident;" (3) the life history of the product; (4) relevant trade usages and practices with regard to products of the same description; and (5) conduct by the buyer in inspecting, maintaining and using the product, both before and after the "accident." *See* Richard J. Phelan and Bradley B. Falkof, *Proving a Defect in a Commercial Products Liability Case*, 24 TRIAL LAW. GUIDE 10 (1980).

CHATFIELD V. SHERWIN-WILLIAMS CO.
SUPREME COURT OF MINNESOTA, 1978
266 N.W.2D 171

PER CURIAM

In this action to recover damages allegedly resulting from breaches of warranty in the sale of red barn paint, the jury found by a special verdict that defendant paint manufacturer breached an express warranty that the paint was "good barn paint" and the implied warranties of merchantability and fitness for a particular purpose. It also found that the breaches were a direct cause of plaintiff's damages; that plaintiff was negligent and his negligence was a direct cause of his consequential damages; that 85 percent of the fault causing such consequential damages was attributable to defendant and 15 percent to plaintiff; and that plaintiff sustained general damages of $1,116 and consequential damages of $13,357. The court ordered judgment for plaintiff for $14,473, the total amount assessed by the jury. Defendant appeals, challenging the sufficiency of the evidence to establish breaches of the warranties and that such breaches were a proximate cause of plaintiff's damages. Defendant also contends that plaintiff is precluded from recovery of damages because he did not follow defendant's directions in using its product. Our review satisfies us that the issues raised were properly submitted to the jury and that the judgment appealed from should be affirmed.

In the winter of 1974, plaintiff, an experienced professional painter of farm buildings, purchased 330 gallons of "Commonwealth Ranch Red" paint from defendant for $4.65 per gallon. Before making the purchase plaintiff asked Wendell Swenson, manager of defendant's Wilmar store, if it would be good paint and if he would have any trouble with it. Swenson told plaintiff that people had used this paint on barns for many years and that it was "tried and true." He added, "Besides, this is Sherwin-Williams, you know. It couldn't have a bad name and be that big." Plaintiff then purchased the paint, used 240 gallons on barns and other buildings at 11 farms, and sold the rest to his father who is also a professional painter.

The label on the paint cans plaintiff purchased contained the following directions:

"New Wood and Extremely Weathered Surfaces:

Add 1 to 2 quarts of raw linseed oil per gallon to the first coat. Brush it well into surface. When spraying follow immediately with thorough brushing to work paint into pores. Second coat should be brushed on at package consistency or thinned with up to a pint of S-W exolvent or

turpentine per gallon for spraying."
Plaintiff admitted that he never added as much as 1 to 2 quarts of linseed oil and said that when he used that much the paint wrinkled. He said that when painting dry areas, he added as much linseed oil as he thought necessary, depending on the condition of the wood. He thought a ratio of 20 percent was usually correct. He said that under the eaves and along the upper two-thirds of the buildings the wood is often in better condition than the wood below, the lower 5 or 6 feet of a barn usually requiring linseed oil. Plaintiff did not apply the paint with a brush, claiming that his spraying equipment made the paint penetrate into the surfaces far more thoroughly than brushing could.

Several customers testified that plaintiff spray-painted their buildings with Commonwealth Ranch Red during the summer of 1975. The buildings varied in age (from a barn built in 1906 to one built in 1965) and in their need for paint. The customers said they were well satisfied with plaintiff's work in preparing the surfaces and painting the buildings. Within 1 to 4 months after the jobs were completed, however, the owners noticed that the color was fading on their buildings. Witnesses said the surfaces looked chalky, the color continued to bleach, and the paint was chipping and could be rubbed off. Plaintiff testified that the buildings which his father had painted with the 90 gallons he had obtained from plaintiff also faded. After receiving complaints from his customers, plaintiff in turn made complaints to defendant which were ignored for several months. Finally, in April 1975, defendant sent George Linmark, a chemist employed by defendant, to investigate the matter. Linmark looked at the buildings plaintiff had painted on two farms and told him, plaintiff testified, that the wood had been well prepared and the paint well applied. Plaintiff testified that Linmark could not explain why the fading had occurred. Subsequently, plaintiff received a letter saying that defendant had decided to do nothing about the paint because the fading "was to be expected with that quality of paint."

Plaintiff admitted on cross-examination that he had read the instructions on the paint cans and had not added as much linseed oil as they directed. When plaintiff rested, defendant moved for a directed verdict on the ground that plaintiff's evidence showed no negligence on its part and showed that plaintiff had been negligent in using his judgment instead of the manufacturer's. The court denied the motion.

Defendant then called Linmark, a chemist with experience in formulating Sherwin-Williams paint, as an expert witness. He said that the 330 gallons of paint which plaintiff had bought was from a 3,000-gallon batch and that defendant had received no complaints about the rest of the batch. Although defendant stores a sample from each batch it manufactures, it did not test any sample from the batch which was the source of plaintiff's paint to see if it would fade, apparently because it was not clear at first which batch had been the source of plaintiff's purchase.

Linmark testified that paint has two essential ingredients, pigments and vehicles or binders. In Commonwealth Ranch Red, the pigment which gives the color is iron oxide, comprising 14 percent of the pigment, and most of the rest of the pigment is calcium carbonate, which by itself is a white powder but is colorless when added to the paint. The vehicle or binder holds the pigment and causes the paint to adhere to the surface of a building. The binder in defendant's paint consisted of tall oil alkyd resin, blown fish oil, mineral spirits, and raw linseed oil. In Linmark's opinion the fading was caused by insufficient reinforcement of the paint with more linseed oil. He said that on weathered surfaces some of the binder in the paint soaks into the wood or old paint if the new paint being applied is not reinforced with linseed oil, and that when the remaining binder is eroded by the ultraviolet rays of the sun, the pigment stands loose. Thus, he said, the calcium carbonate in Commonwealth Ranch Red became visible, giving the paint the appearance of fading.

Linmark also testified that paint wrinkles if applied too thickly and that linseed oil in any quantity does not cause wrinkling. He admitted telling plaintiff in April 1975 that he had done a good job and that in Linmark's opinion there was "a fade problem." He looked at only two of the sets of buildings plaintiff had painted and admitted that he did not know whether plaintiff had added enough linseed oil in the various jobs. He also said that the paint plaintiff purchased was "the bottom of the line."

In rebuttal, plaintiff's father, Robert Chatfield, testified that he used some of the 90 gallons he had acquired from plaintiff and that he too received complaints of fading. He added 1 quart of linseed oil to 5 gallons of paint while painting a barn for a customer and found that the paint became too thin and would run. He said he applied some of the paint to part of his own buildings without using any linseed oil and they also faded. He purchased other Commonwealth Ranch Red from defendant's Wilmar store himself and applied it to his buildings without adding linseed oil. He said the areas to which he had applied this paint did not fade.

In submitting the case to the jury, the trial court refused to charge that defendant was not liable if plaintiff's use of the product was abnormal or not in accordance with adequate instructions. He instructed the jury that in determining whether plaintiff was negligent they could consider whether he used the paint in accordance with defendant's directions and submitted questions in response to which, as stated, the jury found plaintiff negligent and attributed 15 percent of the fault causing his consequential damage to that negligence.

1. Although apparently not contesting the existence of the warranties on which plaintiff brought suit, defendant argues that its motions for a directed verdict and for judgment notwithstanding the verdict should have been granted because plaintiff did not adduce sufficient proof that the paint faded prematurely because of an inherent defect and thus did not establish any breach of the warranties. It also argues that plaintiff did not prove that any breach of warranty proximately caused his damages, as is essential to recovery. * * * Defendant's contentions require an examination of plaintiff's evidence in the light most favorable to the verdict.

At the time defendant moved for a directed verdict, plaintiff had presented testimony that he had done a good workmanlike job, testimony which permitted the jury to infer that poor workmanship did not cause the fading. Plaintiff's proof also showed that some areas he had painted did not need linseed oil and that the paint had faded quite uniformly within 1 to 4 months after application, both in areas where he had used linseed oil and in areas where he had not. He admitted that he never added as much linseed oil as defendant's directions advised he should use with "extremely weathered" surfaces but said he added it in a ratio of 20 percent when he thought it was needed. He further testified that defendant informed him that fading was to be expected with a paint of the quality of Commonwealth Ranch Red. This evidence, although it does not directly establish the cause of the fading, furnishes substantial support for the inference that the paint faded because of an inherent defect.

Defendant urges, however, that plaintiff was required to have the paint analyzed and to present expert testimony about the existence and nature of any alleged defect. Although the importance of expert testimony in products liability actions has been emphasized in several cases, this court has said that there is no hard-and-fast rule requiring plaintiff to introduce such testimony. * * * In several earlier breach-of-warranty cases, chemical analysis of the product was not required to establish the breach of warranty. * * *

In *Nelson v. Wilkins Dodge, Inc.*, Minn., 256 N.W.2d 472, 476 (1977), an action for breach of implied warranties in the sale of a pickup, the court held that a defective condition can be proved by circumstantial evidence, saying:

"Plaintiffs assert that there can be no question that proximate cause has been demonstrated with respect to the paint bubbles, the inverted taillight covers, and the loosened windshield-wiper blade and arm and shift lever.

Defendant suggests that the paint bubbles and the loosened windshield wiper, horn bracket, and shift lever just as probably resulted from the continuous and hard use to which plaintiffs put the pickup as from any defect inherent in the vehicle when plaintiffs purchased it. Although liability for breach of warranty attaches only when a defect existing in the goods causes a breakdown in quality, * * * generally no specific defect need be alleged, and a defective condition can be proved by circumstantial evidence. * * * No direct evidence was introduced as to the causes of the conditions in question. It is reasonable to suppose, however, that vehicles that are fit for ordinary purposes probably do not display these defects this early, even if they are driven a great deal within a short period of time. Thus, the causes of the faulty paint, windshield wiper, horn bracket, and shift lever were questions that should have been decided by the jury. A fortiori, the cause of the inverted taillight covers was a jury question."

Other courts have also held that circumstantial evidence may be sufficient to show the causal relation between the use of a warranted product and the injury which followed its use. * * *

We conclude that although plaintiff's proof of causation was not direct, if his evidence is viewed in the light most favorable to the verdict, the jury could infer from the fact that the fading was quite uniform that the presence or absence of linseed oil had no effect on the fading. Defendant admitted that there was a "fade problem" and fading within so short a time was to be expected with Commonwealth Ranch Red. From this it could be inferred that it was not "good barn paint," not of merchantable quality, and not suitable for the purpose for which plaintiff bought it. Thus, defendant's motions for a directed verdict and for judgment notwithstanding the verdict were properly denied.

2. Defendant also argues that, assuming the warranties involved here were breached, plaintiff is precluded from recovery of damages because he used the paint contrary to the directions and such "misuse" was beyond the scope of the warranties. Although defendant cites several cases in support of this claim–*Chisholm v. J.R. Simplot Co.*, 94 Idaho 682, 495 P.2d 1113 (1972); *Elanco Products Co. v. Akin-Tunnell*, 516 S.W.2d 726 (Tex. Civ. App. 1974); *Iverson Paints, Inc. v. Wirth Corp.*, 94 Idaho 43, 480 P.2d 889 (1971); *Brown v. General Motors Corp.*, 355 F.2d 814 (4th Cir. 1966)–all are distinguishable from this case. In the *Chisholm* case, watering the fields within a specified time was essential to activate the weed killer which was alleged to have been defective, and the importance of following that direction should have been obvious to plaintiffs. In

Iverson also, the directions for using the machine were very precise, and they were almost completely ignored–neither of which is the fact here. In the *Elanco* case the manufacturer had stressed the necessity of following directions and had disclaimed any affirmations made about the product unless the directions were followed. The court accordingly treated compliance with the directions as a condition precedent to the existence of the express warranty sued on. Here no comparable stress was laid on the importance of the directions, and they certainly were not specific and precise as to quantity. In *Brown*, plaintiff did not establish that there had been a breach of warranty, and that his use of a tractor by starting it when it was in gear was abnormal and unpredictable. Plaintiff used the paint here for its intended purpose.

We conclude that the trial court correctly instructed the jury that it could consider whether plaintiff complied with defendant's directions in determining whether he was negligent and whether his negligence was a cause of his consequential damages.

We also find little merit in defendant's argument that, if there was a defect in the paint, plaintiff failed to mitigate his damages by continuing to use the paint after he found it wrinkled when combined with the prescribed amount of linseed oil. Plaintiff did not know the paint would fade because, as he thought, defendant's directions called for too much linseed oil. Defendant's argument also assumes that plaintiff was at all times required to add linseed oil, a conclusion not compelled by the evidence. In any event, the court properly instructed the jury on plaintiff's duty to mitigate damages after learning of the breaches of warranty.

Defendant urges, finally, that the trial court improperly awarded plaintiff all of the consequential damages assessed by the jury and argues that these damages should have been reduced by 15 percent to reflect the proportion of fault which the jury attributed to plaintiff's negligence. Whether a comparative-fault principle should be applied in breach-of-warranty actions has not been determined in this state. * * * Although reducing a party's consequential damages by an amount reflecting the extent to which his own conduct caused them appears to be equitable, appropriate under Minn. St. 336.2-715(2)(b), and compatible with our approach in a recent products liability action based on strict liability, * * * we decline to consider this issue since it was not presented to the trial court and has been raised for the first time on appeal. * * *

Affirmed. [Footnotes omitted.]

———————

Notes

1. No sample was offered from the batch of paint purchased and applied to the barns. How did the buyer survive the seller's motion for directed verdict? In *American Fertilizer Specialists, Inc. v. Wood*, 635 P.2d 592, 595-96 (Okla. 1981), the court, in affirming the trial court's decision for the buyer, stated: "Facts may be proved by circumstantial, as well as by positive or direct evidence, and it is not necessary that the proof rise to that degree of certainty which will exclude every other reasonable conclusion than the one arrived at by the trier of the facts. It is only required that it appears more probable that the defendant's poor grass crop was the result of the failure of the fertilizer sold by plaintiff to defendant to nourish and enrich defendant's grass lands than any other possible cause."[*] As one court put it, the buyer must present circumstantial proof "which, if believed by the trier of fact, makes the plaintiff's theory of the case more probable than the theory of the defendant." *Hollingsworth v. Queen Carpet, Inc.*, 827 S.W.2d 306, 309 (Tenn. Ct. App. 1991).

2. The buyer in *Chatfield* failed to follow the seller's printed directions for use. Why didn't the buyer's failure constitute either a use of the product that was not ordinary, thereby undercutting the claim that an implied warranty of merchantability was breached, or a misuse of a product otherwise fit for ordinary purposes, thereby establishing that breach of warranty did not cause the loss? In *Hutchinson Utilities Commission v. Curtiss-Wright Corp.*, 775 F.2d 231 (8th Cir. 1985), the Eighth Circuit, relying on *Chatfield*, held that an agreed inspection schedule was not a condition precedent to the buyer's claim and that a defect in the goods rather than the failure to inspect was the "proximate" cause of the loss.

3. Assuming that the plaintiff in *Chatfield* was, to some degree, at "fault" in mixing the paint, what effect should that have on the issues of liability and remedy?

---

[*] For cases in accord, *see Davidson Oil Country Supply Co. v. Klockner, Inc.*, 908 F.2d 1238 (5th Cir. 1990) (court erred in excluding evidence that similar goods had failed under similar circumstances); *Plas-Tex, Inc. v. U.S. Steel Corp.*, 772 S.W.2d 442 (Tex. 1989) (proof of defect in product and proper use by plaintiff gets case to jury); *McLaughlin v. Michelin Tire Corp.*, 778 P.2d 59 (Wyo. 1989) (test for circumstantial evidence differs for merchantability and fitness warranties); *Nevada Contract Services, Inc. v. Squirrel Companies, Inc.*, 68 P.3d 896 (Nev. 2003) (per curium) (plaintiff need not prove precise technical cause of malfunction as long as show that product malfunction likely to result from breach of warranty). *But see Ford Motor Co. v. General Accident Insurance Co.*, 779 A.2d 362 (Md. Ct. App. 2001) (plaintiff must prove specific defect to recover for breach of implied warranty of merchantability).

Consider these possibilities:

(a) The warranty, although made, was not breached;

(b) Although the warranty was made and breached, the plaintiff's "fault" barred it from recovery;

(c) The plaintiff's "fault," whether misuse or failure to discover, is no per se bar, but it may be considered in determining whether the breach caused the loss complained of; and

(d) The plaintiff's "fault" may be used to reduce damages otherwise proximately caused by the breach.

Which, if any, of these possibilities did *Chatfield* employ?

4. The Minnesota Comparative Negligence Statute, Minn. Stat. Ann. 604.01(1) (2004), provides that contributory fault is no bar in an action to "recover damages for fault resulting in death, in injury to person or property, or in economic loss, if the contributory fault was not greater than the fault of the person against whom recovery is sought, but any damages allowed shall be diminished in proportion to the amount of fault attributable to the person recovering." The statute defines "fault" to include "breach of warranty, unreasonable assumption of risk not constituting an express consent or primary assumption of risk, misuse of a product and unreasonable failure to avoid an injury or to mitigate damages." 604.01 subd. (1a). The Supreme Court of Minnesota has since held that, in an action to recover for personal injuries and economic loss allegedly caused by a breach of warranty, it was proper to use the plaintiff's "fault" to reduce consequential damages but not direct damages caused by the breach. *See Peterson v. Bendix Home Systems, Inc.*, 318 N.W.2d 50 (Minn. 1982). Should these later developments change the outcome in *Chatfield*?

5. The courts and legislatures, in applying concepts of comparative fault to product liability suits, have stopped short of cases where only economic loss is involved: The plaintiff, when suing on a warranty theory, must claim damages to person or property before any "fault" comparison will be made. An example is *Fiske v. MacGregor, Div. of Brunswick*, 464 A.2d 719 (R.I. 1983).[*]

As we shall see in Chapter Eleven, *infra*, Article 2 of the UCC is the exclusive source of law in warranty disputes where only economic loss is involved. How does

---

[*] *See also* the *Cipollone* "cigarette" litigation, *supra*. The issues are discussed in Todd Leff & Joseph V. Pinto, *Comparative Negligence in Strict Products Liability: The Courts Render the Final Judgment*, 89 DICK. L. REV. 915 (1985); David C. Sobelsohn, *Comparing Fault*, 60 IND. L.J. 413 (1985); Jacqueline S. Bollas, Note, *Use of the Comparative Negligence Doctrine in Warranty Actions*, 45 OHIO ST. U. L. J. 763 (1984).

Article 2 deal with problems of the buyer's fault? With this question in mind, re-read Article 2, Parts Six and Seven. Make a list of the "penalties," if any, that the buyer must pay for failure to take reasonable steps to discover the non-conformity or otherwise to avoid the loss. Look for the comparable sections in Article 2A.

SECTION 4.　DISCLAIMERS AND LIMITATIONS OF WARRANTIES

If the seller or lessor makes an express or implied warranty that is a term of the contract can it, with the buyer's or lessee's consent, then disclaim or modify the warranty? If an express warranty is made, the answer is no. *See* UCC 2-316(1) and 2A-214(1). If implied warranties are made, the answer is yes if the requirements of UCC 2-316(2) and (3) or 2A-214(2) and (3) are met. The 2003 amendments to UCC 2-316 and 2A-214 created new language for use in disclaiming implied warranties in consumer contracts. Review UCC 2-316 and 2A-214 and work through the following cases and problem.

Remember to distinguish clauses that disclaim or limit warranties from those that liquidate damages or limit or exclude damages resulting from a breach. *See* UCC 2-316(4). The latter issues are governed by UCC 2-718, 2A-504 and 2-719, 2A-503.

MARTIN V. JOSEPH HARRIS CO., INC.
UNITED STATES COURT OF APPEALS, SIXTH CIRCUIT, 1985
767 F.2D 296

MILBURN, CIRCUIT JUDGE

The defendant, Joseph Harris Co., Inc., brings this appeal following the district court's granting the plaintiffs' motion for a judgment not withstanding the verdict and a second trial in plaintiffs' action for damages as a result of defective seeds. Because we hold that the district court was correct in holding that, under the facts of this case, the disclaimer of warranty and limitation of remedy clause used by the defendant was unconscionable under Michigan law, and because we further hold that the district court properly held that the implied warranty of merchantability was breached as a matter of law, we affirm.

I.

Plaintiffs Duane Martin and Robert Rick ("Martin and Rick") were commercial farmers in Michigan. In August of 1972, Martin and Rick placed independent orders for cabbage seed with the defendant, Joseph Harris Co., Inc. ("Harris Seed"), a national producer and distributor of seed. Plaintiffs had been customers of Harris Seed for several years and, as in earlier transactions, the order form supplied by Harris Seed included a clause disclaiming the implied warranty of merchantability and limiting buyers' remedies to the purchase price of the seed.[1] A similar clause was also used by Harris Seed's competitors for the same purpose. Neither of the plaintiffs read the clause nor did the salesman make any attempt either to point it out or to explain its purpose.

Three to four months after placing their orders, plaintiffs received Harris Seed's 1973 Commercial Vegetable Growers Catalog. Included in the lower right-hand corner of one page of the catalog was a notification that Harris Seed would no longer "hot water" treat cabbage seed. Hot water treatment had successfully been used since 1947 to eradicate a fungus known as phoma lingam or "black leg," a seed borne disease that causes affected plants to rot before maturing.[2]

Plaintiffs planted their cabbage crop in April and May of 1973, using, among other seed, that supplied by Harris Seed. In mid-July, Harris Seed notified plaintiffs that the seed lot used to fill plaintiffs' order was infected with black leg. Although plaintiffs attempted to minimize the effect of the disease, large portions of their cabbage crops were destroyed. However, in marketing their smaller than usual crop, both plaintiffs made a profit equal to or higher than previous years. This unusual profit margin was due to the rise in market price for cabbage in 1973, which in turn was affected in part by the fact that the 1973 black leg epidemic reduced the

---

[1] The disclaimer of warranties and exclusion of remedies clause, which was printed in the order form, seed catalogs and on the seed packages, appeared as follows:

NOTICE TO BUYER: Joseph Harris Company, Inc. warrants that seeds and plants it sells conform to the label descriptions as required by Federal and State seed laws. IT MAKES NO OTHER WARRANTIES, EXPRESS OR IMPLIED, OF MERCHANTABILITY, FITNESS FOR PURPOSE, OR OTHERWISE, AND IN ANY EVENT ITS LIABILITY FOR BREACH OF ANY WARRANTY OR CONTRACT WITH RESPECT TO SUCH SEEDS OR PLANTS IS LIMITED TO THE PURCHASE PRICE OF SUCH SEEDS OR PLANTS.

No question has been raised as to whether this clause complies with the requirements of Mich. Comp. Laws Ann. § 440.2316 (U.C.C. § 2-316).

[2] According to testimony at trial, the only black leg epidemic between 1947 and 1973 was in 1966, and was traced to cabbage seed imported from Australia. The 1947 and the 1973 black leg was traced to State of Washington produced cabbage seed.

amount of available cabbage.

On August 5, 1975, plaintiffs brought this action. After a hearing on the enforceability of the disclaimer of warranty and limitation of liability clause, the district court ruled that the clause was unconscionable and, therefore, unenforceable. A jury was impaneled to try plaintiffs' legal liability theories of negligence and breach of implied warranty. Following a six-day trial the jury returned a verdict against plaintiffs on both theories; however, the district court granted the plaintiffs' motion for a j.n.o.v. on the implied warranty issue. A second jury impaneled to hear the issue of damages returned verdicts in favor of Martin in the amount of Thirty-six Thousand ($36,000.00) Dollars and in favor of Rick in the amount of Sixteen Thousand ($16,000.00) Dollars.

II.

Our review of the district court's rulings in this diversity case is controlled by the State of Michigan's version of the Uniform Commercial Code, Mich. Comp. Laws Ann. § 440.1101 *et seq.* As we have often stated, "[w]hen this court is reviewing a district judge's interpretation of state law, we give 'considerable weight' to the interpretation of the judge." *Bagwell v. Canal Insurance Co.*, 663 F.2d 710, 712 (6th Cir. 1981). Accordingly, "if a federal district judge has reached a permissible conclusion upon a question of local law, the Court of Appeals should not reverse even though it may think the law should be otherwise."* * *

A.

The first issue raised by Harris Seed is whether the district court erred in holding the disclaimer and limitation clause unconscionable under U.C.C. § 2-302. The question of the unconscionability of a contract clause is one of law for the court to decide in light of "its commercial setting, purpose and effect." U.C.C. § 2-302. Since the Code does not define unconscionability, the district court reviewed case law to aid it in its resolution of this question.

A threshold problem in this context is whether under Michigan law warranty disclaimers which comply with U.C.C. § 2-316 are limited by U.C.C. § 2-302. In holding Harris Seed's disclaimer clause unconscionable under the facts of this case, the district court implicitly held that U.C.C. § 2-302 is a limitation on U.C.C. § 2-316. Harris Seed argues that by enacting § 2-316 the Michigan Legislature "unequivocally [authorized the] exclusion or modification of the implied warranty of merchantability by disclaimer." We have been presented with no Michigan cases resolving this issue; however, a number of arguments support the district court's conclusion that § 2-316 is not insulated from review under § 2-302. First, § 2-302 provides that "any clause" of a contract may be found unconscionable. Similarly, "section 2-316 does not state expressly that all disclaimers meeting its requirements are immune from general policing provisions like section 2-302. * * * " J. WHITE & R. SUMMERS, HANDBOOK OF THE LAW UNDER THE UNIFORM COMMERCIAL CODE, § 12-11, at 476 (2d ed. 1980). Had the drafters of the Uniform Commercial Code or the Michigan Legislature chosen to limit the application of § 2-302, language expressly so stating could easily have been included. Furthermore, as pointed out by Professors White and Summers:

> Comment 1 [to § 2-302] lists and describes ten cases which are presumably intended to illustrate the underlying basis of the section: In seven of those cases disclaimers of warranty were denied full effect. It is difficult to reconcile the intent on the part of the draftsman to immunize disclaimers from the effect of 2-302 with the fact that they used cases in which courts struck down disclaimers to illustrate the concept of unconscionability.

Id. (footnotes omitted). Therefore, because this issue is unsettled under Michigan law and according the district court's conclusion "considerable weight," we hold that the district court correctly relied upon § 2-302 as a limitation on § 2-316.

We next turn to a more troublesome subissue; viz., whether within the special facts of this case the disclaimer and exclusionary clause was unconscionable under Michigan law. As has often been stated, commercial contracts will rarely be found unconscionable,* * * because in the commercial setting the relationship is between business parties and is not so one-sided as to give one party the bargaining power to impose unconscionable terms on the other party.

In making its determination of unconscionability, the district court relied upon *Allen v. Michigan Bell Telephone*, 18 Mich. App. 632, 171 N.W.2d 689 (1969).[3] In *Allen* an insurance agent contracted with Michigan Bell Telephone Company to place advertisements in the classified telephone directory. When the advertisements

---

[3] Although it may be, as Harris Seed argues, that the criticisms of *Allen* by courts, *see, e.g.*, *Robinson Insurance & Real Estate, Inc. v. Southwestern Bell*, 366 F.Supp. 307 (W.D.Ark.1973), and commentators, *see* J. WHITE & R. SUMMERS, HANDBOOK OF THE LAW UNDER THE UNIFORM COMMERCIAL CODE, § 4-9, at 172 (2d Ed.1980) are well founded, the Michigan Appellate Court's holding is nevertheless an appropriate guide to our inquiry in the present case. *Cf. Simpson v. Jefferson Standard Life Insurance Co.*, 465 F.2d 1320, 1323 (6th Cir. 1972) ("[d]ecisions of intermediate state courts must be followed by the federal courts unless there is reason to believe they would not be followed by the state's highest court.").

were not included, he brought an action for damages. To defend the action, Michigan Bell Telephone Company relied on a limitation of remedies clause which, if upheld, would have limited the plaintiff's recovery to the contract price. In refusing to uphold the limitation, the Michigan court stated "the principle of freedom to contract does not carry a license to insert any provision in an agreement which a party deems advantageous." *Id.* at 691-92. Rather, the court stated that:

> [i]mplicit in the principle of freedom of contract is the concept that at the time of contracting each party has a realistic alternative to acceptance of the terms offered. Where goods and services can only be obtained from one source (or several sources on non-competitive terms) the choices of one who desires to purchase are limited to acceptance of the terms offered or doing without. Depending on the nature of the goods or services and the purchaser's needs, doing without may or may not be a realistic alternative. Where it is not, one who successfully exacts agreement to an unreasonable term cannot insist on the court's enforcing it on the ground that it was "freely" entered into, when it was not. * * *
>
> There are then two inquiries in a case such as this: (1) what is the relative bargaining power of the parties, their relative economic strength, the alternative sources of supply, in a word, what are their options?; (2) is the challenged term substantively reasonable?

Id. at 692.

With reference to the test announced in *Allen*, Harris Seed argues that the relative bargaining power of the parties is not a proper consideration under § 2-302. This is an issue on which courts and commentators have taken varying approaches.* * * We agree with the district court that relative bargaining power is an appropriate consideration in determining unconscionability under the Michigan Uniform Commercial Code.

Other closely related factors suggested by the Michigan court in *Allen* for determining the presence of procedural unconscionability are the relative economic strength of the parties and the alternative sources of supply. With reference to the relative economic strength of the parties, we note that Harris Seed is a large national producer and distributor of seed, dealing here with independent, relatively small farmers. As to alternative sources of supply, the farmers were faced with a situation where all seed distributors placed disclaimers and exclusionary clauses in their contracts. Thus, this presents a situation where "goods [could] only be obtained from * * * several sources on non-competitive terms * * * and doing without [was] not a realistic alternative."

Another pertinent factor considered by the district court in its unconscionability finding was that Harris Seed's salesman did not make Martin and Rick, who were uncounseled laymen, aware of the fact that the clauses in question altered significant statutory rights. Such a disclosure is an important consideration under Michigan law. * * *

Furthermore, although the terms of the 1972 sale appeared to be the same as in previous years (unknown to Martin and Rick), Harris Seed decided to discontinue the hot water treatment of its cabbage seed, a standard practice for the previous twenty-six years. This decision by Harris Seed was one which had far-reaching consequences to the purchasers of its cabbage seed. As noted above, hot water treatment had been successful in preventing black leg in Washington State produced cabbage seed since 1947, and although Martin and Rick were unaware of the potential effects of black leg, or indeed even what black leg was, Harris Seed had considerable expertise in such matters.

Another important consideration is the fact that the presence of black leg in cabbage seed creates a latent defect. Although in many cases the fact that a latent defect is present seems to be dispositive, * * * we note only that it is important to the disposition of this case.

Significantly, in the present case not only was the defect latent, but it was also one which was within the control of Harris Seed to prevent. Even if Martin and Rick had been apprised of and understood the significance of Harris Seed's decision to discontinue hot water treatment, they would have been unable to detect the presence of the disease in the seed until their crop had developed into young plants. If Harris Seed were permitted to rely on the disclaimer and limitation clause to avoid liability under the facts of this case, the farmers who had no notice of, ability to detect, or control over the presence of the black leg could lose their livelihood. On the other hand, Harris Seed which had the knowledge, expertise and means to prevent the disease would only lose a few hundred dollars. Given the unique facts of this case, and giving "considerable weight" to the district court's decision that Michigan law would not permit the disclaimer and limitation clause to be enforced under such circumstances, we affirm the district court's finding of unconscionability.

* * *

[Some footnotes omitted. Those retained are renumbered.]

Notes

1. Did the seller's disclaimer satisfy the requirements of former 2-316(2)? How would you describe those requirements?[*]

2. How could the seller have avoided the result in this case?

3. Note that the disclaimer was printed on the order form supplied by the seller. In seed cases, the courts have been even more hostile to disclaimers printed on the package or bag of seeds and not seen by the buyer until after the contract is formed, if at all.[**]

4. The United States and many states have enacted laws to protect the purchasers of seeds from falsely labeled products. The laws are backed by criminal sanctions. *See* 7 U.S.C. 1551. These seed statutes, however, do not preempt Article 2 of the UCC. Thus, even if the seller complies with the statutory labeling requirements, it may still be liable for breach of warranty under the UCC.[***]

5. In *Herrick v. Monsanto Co.*, 874 F.2d 594 (8th Cir. 1989), the plaintiff's crop failed due to an allegedly defective herbicide. The court, relying upon UCC 2-719(3) and UCC 2-302, held that a clause excluding seller's liability for consequential damages was unconscionable because it left the buyer without an adequate remedy. In *Lindemann v. Eli Lilly & Co.*, 816 F.2d 199 (5th Cir. 1987), however, the court upheld a clause excluding consequential damages resulting from an allegedly defective weed control chemical. The clause was present during a 20 year course of dealing, and the parties dealt at arms length and intended to allocate unknown or undeterminable risks. The *Martin* case was distinguished by the court in *Lindemann* but was not discussed in *Herrick*.

6. Read UCC 2-316. Prior to the 2003 amendments, the requirements for an effective disclaimer were the same for commercial and consumer contracts. Amended UCC 2-316 now provides different requirements for consumer contracts.

---

[*] For a highly critical analysis of former 2-316(2), *see Cate v. Dover Corp.*, 790 S.W.2d 559 (Tex. 1990).

[**] *See, e.g., Walker v. American Cyanamid Co.*, 948 P.2d 1123 (Idaho 1997) (language on product label ambiguous); *Gold Kist, Inc. v. Citizens & Southern National Bank of South Carolina*, 333 S.E.2d 67 (S.C. 1985) (disclaimer not part of agreement). *See also Step-Saver Data Systems, Inc. v. Wyse Technology*, 939 F.2d 91 (3rd Cir. 1991) (disclaimer on box containing computer software not conspicuous).

[***] *See, e.g., Hanson v. Funk Seeds International*, 373 N.W.2d 30 (S.D. 1985).

What are they? Do the requirements adequately inform a consumer buyer that he or she bears the risk if the goods are not merchantable or fail to meet particular purposes? Can you think of better language. Various non-UCC statutes may restrict or preclude the ability to disclaim warranties.[*]

Problem 5-7

B, an experienced commercial fisherman, purchased a new diesel engine for his fishing boat from S. In the discussions prior to the sale, S and B discussed the power that B needed for the fishing boat. S recommended the Powertrane 1000 which B purchased. The engine was installed by S. Over the next 4 months, a number of mechanical problems arose, including the emission of excessive quantities of heavy black smoke. S was unable to correct the problems and the engine was removed from the boat. B thinks that the engine did not function properly due to it not having enough power to propel the fishing boat. B's expert will testify that the engine was unmerchantable due to the recurring mechanical problems.

At the time of contracting, B had signed a purchase order prepared by S. The face of the purchase order contained a number of terms and conditions. In the center of the face, this statement appeared: BOTH THIS ORDER AND ITS ACCEPTANCE ARE SUBJECT TO TERMS AND CONDITIONS STATED IN THIS ORDER. On the reverse side of the order at the top of the page, the following words appeared: TERMS AND CONDITIONS. Under that caption were eleven numbered paragraphs, one of which contained a disclaimer in the following form: THE SELLER HEREBY DISCLAIMS AND EXCLUDES ALL IMPLIED WARRANTIES, INCLUDING THE IMPLIED WARRANTY OF MERCHANTABILITY. B did not nor was he asked to read anything on the back of the purchase order. B received a fully executed copy of the order by mail before the engine was installed.

A. B sued S for damages resulting from breach of an implied warranty of merchantability. S defended on the ground that the warranty had been effectively disclaimed under UCC 2-316(2). What result?

B. If B was not a commercial fisherman but buying the engine for use on his pleasure boat, would you get the same result under amended UCC 2-316(2)?

---

[*] *See* Donald F. Clifford, *Non-UCC Statutory Provisions Affecting Warranty Disclaimers and Remedies in Sales of Goods*, 71 N.C. L. REV. 1011 (1993).

C. Assume the manufacturer of the engine had advertised the engine in a boating magazine, stating that the Powertrane 1000 had sufficient power for boats up to 50 feet long. B's boat is 40 feet long. The advertisement stated also stated: "Nothing in this advertisement is a warranty." Does B have a good cause of action against the manufacturer for breach of the UCC 2-313B obligation?

Problem 5-8

L, a boat dealer, advertised a 42 foot Pearson sailing sloop for sale. The boat was manufactured in 1960 and had a wooden hull. R, an experienced sailor, had never purchased a sloop with a wooden hull. Without the assistance of a third party, R examined the boat carefully and could find nothing wrong. She questioned L who, at various times stated: "This beauty was her owner's pride and joy. It's in great shape;" "The boat is sound. It rides the waves like a dream;" "The wood is solid throughout. We will replace any dry rot free of charge."

R agreed to buy the sloop for $50,000. R purchased the boat for her own personal use. At the time of contracting, R signed a writing prepared by L which on the front provided, in part, as follows: "WARRANTIES. Buyer is buying the goods AS IS WHERE IS and no representations or statements have been made by seller except as herein stated, so that no warranty, express or implied, arises apart from this writing."

R took delivery of the boat, paid the purchase price and went for a long, wet sail. The boat appeared to leak at the stern. An expert was hired to inspect the area and found extensive dry rot, which had clearly been there at the time of the sale. The estimated cost to repair the boat was $15,000.

A. R claimed damages for breach of warranty. L argued that all warranties, express or implied, had been disclaimed. Is L correct?

B. Should it matter when the disclaimers were delivered to R? Suppose the record with the disclaimers were delivered to R after R signed a purchase agreement to buy the boat? *See Terrell v. R & A Manufacturing Partners, Ltd.*, 835 So. 2d 216 (Ala. Ct. App. 2002) (holding that disclaimers delivered after the contract was formed were not binding on buyer).

Note: Disclaimers of Warranty Under the CISG

The CISG does not have a comparable section on disclaimers of warranties. Rather, Article 35(3) limits the seller's liability under that Article if the buyer "knew or could not have been unaware" of the nonconformity at the time of contract formation.

Note: Disclaimers of Warranty Under UCITA

Disclaimers and modifications of warranty are governed by UCITA 406 and 407. These sections are modeled on the concepts found in former 2-316 and distinguish between disclaimers of express and implied warranties. These sections incorporate by reference the disclaimers allowed under UCC 2-316 and 2A-214.

SECTION 5. EXTENSION OF WARRANTY OBLIGATIONS

In this section, we consider who beside the buyer may be a proper plaintiff in a case for breach of warranty. We have already briefly considered the new sections which address express warranty-like obligations of remote sellers to purchasers not in privity with the seller. UCC 2-313A and 2-313B.[*] Notice that these sections define a remote purchaser to include a lessee who is leasing from a buyer who purchased the goods from the manufacturer. Parallel sections were not added to Article 2A.

UCC 2-318 allows the express and implied warranties considered above, the remote obligations under UCC 2-313A and 2-313B, and remedial promises to be extended to certain persons designated in each alternative. *Compare* UCC 2A-216. The theory of UCC 2-318 is one of derivative liability. The persons designated are deemed third party beneficiaries of the obligation that the seller has made to a buyer. If the seller has not incurred an obligation, there is nothing to extend to the designated class of persons. If the seller incurred an obligation and has also limited remedies or otherwise restricted the ability to recover on the warranty or obligation, that limitation binds the remote party as well. Each of the three alternatives prohibits the seller from preventing the extension of the obligation to a person who has suffered personal injury because of the breach of the warranty or obligation.

The statutory language of UCC 2-318 is only the starting point for your

---

[*] Courts enforced express warranties against remote sellers prior to the 2003 amendments. *See* Harry M. Flechtner, *Enforcing Manufacturers' Warranties, "Pass Through" Warranties, and the Like: Can the Buyer Get a Refund?* 50 RUTGERS L. REV. 397 (1998); Curtis R. Reitz, *Manufacturers' Warranties of Consumer Goods*, 75 WASH. U. L.Q. 357 (1997); Donald F. Clifford, *Express Warranty Liability of Remote Sellers: One Purchase, Two Relationships*, 75 WASH. U. L.Q. 413 (1997).

analysis of who is a proper plaintiff to bring a breach of warranty claim. The courts have taken to heart the former comment to former 2-318 which stated that the section was not in any way to restrict the category of persons who could recover for breach of warranty.* That sentiment is repeated in Comment 2 to amended UCC 2-318. The steps in the analysis are:

1.   Has an express warranty, implied warranty, a warranty-like obligation, or a remedial promise been made to the buyer or lessee?

2.   If yes, does UCC 2-318 or UCC 2A-216 extend that obligation to the plaintiff who is alleging injury by virtue of breach of that obligation? As part of this analysis special attention should also be focused on whether the seller has attempted to limit the extension and whether that limitation will be respected.

3.   If either UCC 2-318 or UCC 2A-216 does not operate to extend the obligation to the plaintiff, does the case law in the state do so?

Apply this analysis to the following problem.

Problem 5-9

BF, a camera manufacturer, developed a plan to establish a three-dimensional photography business. 3M agreed to supply BF with a three-dimensional film development process, consisting of a new emulsion to be combined with an existing backcoat sauce. 3M impliedly warranted to BF that the process was merchantable but the contract contained a term excluding liability for any and all consequential damages. In anticipation of this process, BF contracted with F, another camera manufacturer, and G, the manufacturer of film processors, to supply a stipulated quantity of the 3M process over a five year period. 3M then delivered a quantity of process to BF who resold part of the process to F but not yet to G. Shortly thereafter and before any process was delivered to G, it became clear that the new process would not work (the photos faded and lost their three-dimensional effect) and that 3M could do nothing about it. In short BF went out of business and F and

---

* *See* Alex Devience, Jr., *The Developing Line Between Warranty and Tort Liability Under the Uniform Commercial Code: Does 2-318 Make a Difference?*, 2 DEPAUL BUS. L.J. 295 (1990); William L. Stallworth, *An Analysis of Warranty Claims Instituted by Non-Privity Plaintiffs in Jurisdictions that Have Adopted Uniform Commercial Code Section 2-318 (Alternative A)*, 20 PEPP. L. REV. 1215 (1993); William L. Stallworth, *An Analysis of Warranty Claims Instituted by Non-Privity Plaintiffs in Jurisdictions That Have Adopted Uniform Commercial Code Section 2-318 (Alternatives B & C)*, 27 AKRON L. REV. 197 (1993).

G lost the profits that would have been theirs if the process had worked. BF, F and G now sue 3M for breach of warranty and to recover lost profits.

A. How should BF's claim against 3M be resolved?

B. How should F and G's claim against 3M be resolved under UCC 2-318? *See Minnesota Mining & Mfg. Co. v. Nishika Ltd*, 565 N.W.2d 16 (Minn. 1997).

Under UCITA, extension of warranty is governed by section 409. Notice that unlike UCC 2-318 or 2A-216, the extension does not depend upon what harm is suffered and the warrantor may limit the class of person to whom the warranty extends even if personal injury results.[*] The CISG does not address rights of persons not in privity with the seller.

To test your understanding of the material covered in this chapter, consider the following problem.

Problem 5-10

Greg purchased a new Sudzer dishwasher from Quality Appliances. The sales person, Shelley, told Greg that the Sudzer was the best dishwasher made and would not rust even if installed in a location that had very hard water due to special materials in the tub and racks of the washer. After deciding to buy the Sudzer, Greg signed a document which provided the following:

QUALITY APPLIANCES MAKES NO WARRANTIES, EXPRESS OR IMPLIED, INCLUDING BUT NOT LIMITED TO THE IMPLIED WARRANTY OF MERCHANTABILITY OR FITNESS FOR A PARTICULAR PURPOSE. IN NO CIRCUMSTANCES SHALL QUALITY APPLIANCES BE LIABLE FOR CONSEQUENTIAL OR INCIDENTAL DAMAGES. Buyer agrees that Quality Appliances has made no representations about any product purchased from Quality Appliances.

Greg also received the owner's manual for the Sudzer dishwasher provided by the Sudzer manufacturer. The owner's manual provided the following:

ONE YEAR LIMITED WARRANTY

---

[*] The comment to the section states that tort liability is not a concern as personal injury will rarely result from breach of warranty regarding computer information. Given that software controls the functioning of many types of goods, is that a realistic assessment of the risk of tort liability? *See* Peter A. Alces, *W(h)ither Warranty: The B(l)oom of Products Liability Theory in the Case of Deficient Software Design*, 87 CALIF. L. REV. 269 (1999).

Seller agrees to repair or replace any defective part free of charge for one year from date of purchase. SELLER MAKES NO OTHER WARRANTIES, EXPRESS OR IMPLIED. IN NO CIRCUMSTANCES SHALL SELLER BE LIABLE FOR CONSEQUENTIAL OR INCIDENTAL DAMAGES.

The owner's manual stated that the machine could be connected to city water lines as well as rural areas serviced by wells. No special instructions for rural areas was provided.

Greg had purchased the dishwasher on behalf of his son and new daughter-in-law. They lived in a rural area where they used well water which was extremely hard water. The water was treated with a water softener in an attempt to ameliorate the hardness of the water. Greg had the dishwasher properly installed in his son and daughter-in-law's house. Greg's son repaid his father the amount for the dishwasher. Having a dishwasher was extremely important to the couple as they ran a catering business out of their home and many times spent long hours doing dishes. Having a quality dishwasher would enable them to increase the amount of time they could spend preparing food and doing more catering jobs.

Within a month after installation, the racks and tub started to show signs of rust. The dishwasher was also not very effective in cleaning dishes, resulting in having to hand wash the dishes about half of the time. Greg's son complained to Quality Appliances who told him to take it up with the manufacturer. The manufacturer maintained there was nothing wrong with the dishwasher, that the difficulty in cleaning was due to the hard water. It recommended a different water treatment system which the son and daughter-in-law could not afford.

Who has a cause of action for breach of a warranty or other obligation against Quality Appliances and the manufacturer?

PART THREE:
PERFORMANCE OF THE CONTRACT

CHAPTER SIX

DELIVERY AND PAYMENT

SECTION 1.   TENDER, INSPECTION, AND PAYMENT

At some point in the transaction, the seller, lessor or licensor will be obligated to tender to the buyer, lessee or licensee products that conform to the contract. A failure to deliver on time or the tender of products that do not conform to the contract requirements is a breach of contract, for which the buyer, lessee or licensee has appropriate remedies.

Let us first consider the Article 2 regime as it relates to the seller's and buyer's obligations in performance of the contract.   Read UCC 2-301.   The seller's obligation is to deliver goods that conform to the contract requirements and the buyer's obligation is to accept and pay for those goods. But this section does not tell us who is to tender first. Read UCC 2-507(1) and 2-511(1). These sections set as the default rule, concurrent conditions. The seller's tender of the goods is a condition to the buyer's obligation to accept and pay for the goods and the buyer's tender of payment is a condition to the seller's obligation to tender the goods. If the parties have not agreed that either the seller or buyer should tender first and neither party tenders performance, there is no breach of contract. This situation rarely arises as usually the parties agree that one of the parties will tender their performance first.

A. The Basic Scenario

Seller's tender of delivery. Let us assume, that the parties have agreed that the seller will tender the goods first. What are the seller's obligations in making that tender of goods? Read UCC 2-503(1) which sets forth the basic obligation. If the parties have not otherwise agreed, where will the seller be obligated to tender the goods? Read UCC 2-308. What quantity of goods must the seller tender? Read UCC 2-307 and 2-612(1). Now try your hand at this simple problem.

Problem 6-1

Seller agreed to tender 100 bushels of wheat to Buyer on April 3 for $4 per bushel.

A. On April 3, Seller called Buyer and told her the wheat was ready to be picked up. When Buyer arrived that afternoon, Seller only had 95 bushels available and the auger usually used to load the wheat into trucks was broken down. Has Seller complied with its tender obligation?

B. On April 3, Seller called Buyer and told her the wheat was ready to be picked up. When Buyer arrived that afternoon, Buyer tested the wheat Seller had available and it was clearly moldy. Has Seller complied with its tender obligation? What do you need to know to answer that question?

C. On April 3, Seller called Buyer and told her the wheat was ready to be picked up. When Seller called Buyer to come and get the wheat, Seller told Buyer that she better get there in 2 hours or Seller was going to sell the wheat to someone else. Has Seller complied with its tender obligation?

D. On April 3, Seller called Buyer and told her the wheat was ready to be picked up. When Buyer arrived that afternoon, Buyer did not have a truck capable of holding 100 bushels of wheat. Has Seller complied with its tender obligation?

E. Buyer and Seller had agreed that Seller would deliver the wheat to Buyer's farm on April 3. On April 3, Seller drove onto Buyer's farm with the truckload of wheat in one of Seller's own trucks. Buyer did not have her storage facility cleaned out and asked Seller to come back the next day. Has Seller complied with its tender obligation? Has Buyer breached the contract?

Buyer's right to inspect. Now add another layer of analysis. Once the seller tenders delivery of the goods, the buyer will want to inspect the goods. Read UCC 2-513(1) and (4). The buyer's right of inspection fits nicely with the buyer's obligation to accept and pay for conforming goods. The ability to inspect the goods prior to payment or acceptance protects the buyer from accepting or paying for nonconforming goods. UCC 2-513(1). *See also* UCC 2-310(a). As to the meaning of acceptance, read UCC 2-606. Do not equate the buyer's taking physical possession of the goods as being "acceptance" of the goods. In fact, one of the ways a buyer may inspect goods is to take possession and test the goods for a reasonable period of time. The buyer's inspection right is to allow the buyer to determine if the goods conform to the contract requirements. Of course a buyer may agree to waive its right to inspect before payment or acceptance but that agreement is not presumed. The buyer's inspection opportunity is not limitless, rather it is a "reasonable opportunity" to inspect. So in Problem 6-1, in all circumstances set forth in that problem, upon Seller's tender of the wheat, buyer would have had a right to inspect the wheat before the buyer was obligated to pay for or accept the wheat. Notice that the buyer's right to inspect also arises upon "identification" of the goods to the contract. "Identification," defined in UCC 2-501, occurs prior to seller's tender of delivery. Thus in Problem 6-1, if Seller had identified the wheat to the contract, Buyer could have exercised her right to inspect the wheat before the Seller's tender if that was reasonable under the circumstances.

For non-conformity discovered at the receipt-inspection stage, the buyer *may,* depending upon the circumstances, have a choice between (1) "goods-oriented" remedies such as rejection (UCC 2-601) and revocation of acceptance (UCC 2-608), and (2) "damages-oriented" remedies (UCC 2-713 and 2-714). And the buyer may be able, in the circumstances, to combine these remedies, *i.e.*, throw the goods back at the seller and also seek damages. *See* UCC 2-711.

Why might it be important for the buyer to discover non-conformity and reject the goods prior to accepting or paying for them? In addition to not paying for non-conforming goods, the buyer may wish to avoid costly unloading and storage of bulky goods. Even if not obligated to pay at the time of delivery, i.e. where the seller has agreed to credit terms, the buyer should be concerned to identify any non-conformity at least in advance of "acceptance" (UCC 2-606). Acceptance of the goods imposes a duty on the buyer to pay, UCC 2-607(1), and buyers do not want to pay for significantly non-conforming goods. Moreover, acceptance precludes *rejection* of the goods. UCC 2-607(2) and 2-601. But this does not necessarily mean the buyer will be unable to throw the goods back at the seller. If the non-conformity is discovered after acceptance, the buyer may be able to revoke her acceptance under UCC 2-608. But we will see that it is harder to throw goods back at a seller under UCC 2-608 than it is under UCC 2-601. Finally, the burden of establishing breach with regard to accepted goods is on the buyer. UCC 2-607(4).

Thus it remains true that so far as goods-oriented remedies are concerned the buyer will be best off if she discovers non-conformity prior to acceptance and rejects. But if the buyer discovers a non-conformity and either rejects or later revokes acceptance, the buyer will escape the bargain (which may in itself be highly advantageous), and also shift any resulting loss due to depreciation back on the seller.

Although the right to inspect has important practical consequences, there are few cases interpreting UCC 2-513.[*] Analytically, one should ask and answer at least four questions under UCC 2-513: (1) does the buyer have a right to inspect at all (in most cases the answer is yes) and, if so, is the right exercisable before or after payment and acceptance (in most cases the answer is before); (2) where is the place and time of inspection, *see* UCC 2-513(1); (3) what is the proper method of inspection; and (4) how are the expenses of inspection allocated between the parties?

Problem 6-2

Student A, who was on the law review and actually attended class, agreed to sell his notes from the course on Commercial Transactions to student B for $100. The agreement was made on January 20 and A was to deliver the notes on February 1 at the law school. On February 1, A and B met to complete the exchange. A had placed the notes in a green canvas bag. Displaying the bag, A said to B: "Here are the notes. May I please have the $100." B refused to pay until he had a chance to inspect the contents of the bag. A refused either to untie the string around or relinquish possession of the bag. When the impasse could not be broken, A stated to B that the "deal was off." Later that afternoon A sold the notes to student C for $150. What is the legal position of A and B under the UCC? More specifically, has A complied with his tender obligation? *See* UCC 2-503, comment 2.

How must the buyer pay the seller for the goods? Agreements to sell on credit are not presumed. Read UCC 2-511(2). Presumably cash, checks or a funds transfer would all be acceptable means of payment unless the parties have agreed to a particular payment mechanism.

B.   The Seller's Shipment of Goods to the Buyer

Seller's tender of delivery. Now consider the situation where the seller has agreed to tender first and also agreed to ship the goods to the buyer. A seller who is going to ship goods to the buyer using a carrier (not the seller's own trucks) will

---

[*] For rare examples, *see* HCI Chemicals (USA), Inc. v. Henkel KGaA, 966 F.2d 1018 (5th Cir. 1992) (holding that the place for inspection specified in UCC 2-513(1) was not displaced by agreement); *D.C. Leathers, Inc. v. Gelmart Indus., Inc.*, 125 A.D.2d 738, 509 N.Y.S.2d 161 (1986) (trade usage and prior course of dealing help determine reasonable place for inspection).

ship the goods either under a "shipment" contract or a "destination" contract. Read UCC 2-503, comment 5. In a "shipment" contract, the seller's tender obligation is governed by UCC 2-503(2) and 2-504. If the contract is a destination contract, the seller's tender obligation is determined by UCC 2-503(3). In order for the seller to avoid breaching the contract, the goods must conform to the contract at the time the seller tenders delivery. In a shipment contract, that time is when the goods are put in the hands of the carrier. In a destination contract, that time is when the goods are tendered to the buyer by the carrier.

All shipments have a destination listed. Listing a destination for the shipment of goods does not mean the seller has agreed to a destination contract. The key inquiry is in the agreement between the buyer and the seller; has the seller agreed to take responsibility for the goods during shipment. If not, then the contract is a shipment contract. If so, then the contract is a destination contract. One of the primary mechanisms for deciding whether the parties have agreed to a shipment or a destination contract is the use of "shipping terms" like FOB (free on board) or CIF (cost, insurance and freight). Prior to the 2003 amendments, Article 2 contained several statutorily defined shipping terms in sections 2-319 through 2-324. Those sections have been deleted as out of step with modern practice. The meaning of the shipping terms the parties use will have to be determined in another way, most likely by usage of trade, course of dealing and course of performance. Another source of the meaning of shipping terms used is the Incoterms, promulgated by the International Chamber of Commerce (ICC). The ICC periodically revises those terms in light of current practice. The current terms can be accessed at http://www.iccwbo.org. Because the default rule is that of a "shipment" contract, in order for the buyer and seller to have agreed to a "destination" contract, that agreement must be clearly shown.

Buyer's right to inspect. How does shipment of the goods affect the buyer's right to inspect? Reread UCC 2-513. Unless the buyer and seller have agreed that the buyer's right to inspect is altered, the buyer still has the right to inspect goods in either a shipment or a destination contract before the buyer is obligated to pay for the goods or accept them. The buyer may inspect the goods at any reasonable time or place and may do so when the goods arrive at the destination even if tender of delivery has taken place early (as in a shipment contract). The buyer may hire a third party to accomplish that inspection.[*] Because conformity of the goods in a shipment contract is determined at the time the goods are placed in the hands of

---

[*] *See e.g., Bartlett & Co., Grain v. Merchants Co.*, 323 F.2d 501 (5th Cir. 1963).

carrier, the buyer has an incentive to inspect the goods at that point to determine if the goods conform to the contract as the conformity issue will have an effect on risk of loss during transit.* We will consider risk of loss issues in Chapter Eight *infra*.

Payment against documents. One of the ways that the buyer and seller may have altered the buyer's right to inspect is for the buyer to agree to "pay against documents." UCC 2-513(3). When goods are shipped on a carrier, the carrier will usually issue a form of a document of title known as a bill of lading. Read the definition of document of title and bill of lading in UCC 1-201. The carrier is a type of bailee, someone who takes possession, but not ownership, of the goods, in order to do something with the goods that the bailor wants done with them. Rights and obligations arising out of a document of title and the bailment relationship are governed, in part, by UCC Article 7.

Documents of title come in two flavors, negotiable and non-negotiable. UCC 7-104. A party with a negotiable document of title may have the ability to convey more rights than it might have in respect to the goods the documents covers. UCC 7-502. A bill of lading functions as a receipt for the goods and as the contract for carriage of the goods. If the bill of lading is negotiable, it also serves as evidence of good title to the goods. *Id.* The carrier will want that document of title presented to it at the destination of the goods in order to make sure that the carrier is releasing the goods to the right person. The carrier's responsibility during transit is governed by Article 7, *see* UCC 7-309 prescribing the duty of care, and applicable federal law.**

So when a seller of goods delivers the goods to a carrier in either a shipment or a destination contract, the carrier will issue a bill of lading. That bill of lading may be either negotiable or non-negotiable. The form in which the bill of lading is issued may be prescribed in the contract for sale between the buyer and seller. Notice that in a shipment contract, part of the seller's tender obligation is to obtain the documents necessary for the buyer to obtain the goods. UCC 2-504(b). If the buyer has not agreed with the seller to pay against presentation of the documents to the buyer, the seller may simply send the bill of lading to the buyer or if an electronic bill of lading is used, enable the buyer to obtain control of the bill of lading. UCC 7-106. The buyer will then be able to use the bill of lading to obtain

---

* *See S-Creek Ranch, Inc. v. Monier & Co.*, 509 P.2d 777 (Wyo. 1973) (buyer must prove goods defective at time risk of loss was to pass).

** For an example, *see Paper Magic Group, Inc. v. J.B. Hunt Transport, Inc.*, 318 F.3d 458 (3rd Cir. 2003)

the goods from the carrier.

The contract for sale may also require that the buyer pay for the goods in order to obtain the bill of lading which the carrier previously issued. If the buyer has agreed to do so, then the buyer has waived its right to inspect the goods prior to payment for the goods, unless one of two exceptions apply. The first exception is found in the except clause of UCC 2-513(3)(b) and the other exception is found in UCC 2-512. However, if the buyer has waived its right to inspect the goods prior to payment in this manner, the buyer still retains its right to inspect the goods prior to acceptance, UCC 2-513(1), and payment for the goods is not acceptance of the goods. UCC 2-512(2). Payment by the buyer against the documents does not waive any argument that the goods do not conform to the contract requirements although the buyer will no longer have a right to assert defects in the documents that are apparent on the face of the documents. UCC 2-605(2). The buyer's payment obligation becomes due when it receives the documents of title. UCC 2-310(c).

An agreement to pay against documents may be found in either a shipment contract or a destination contract. Merely issuance of documents in the course of transporting the goods does not mean that the buyer has agreed to pay against the documents issued. One way to determine if the buyer has agreed to pay against documents is by the interpretation of the shipping terms. For example, under former 2-320, a "CIF" term was presumed to encompass the agreement of the buyer to pay against documents. An agreement to pay against documents may involve either negotiable or non-negotiable documents.

In any case in which the seller is required to deliver documents, whether the buyer has agreed to pay against the documents or not, the seller has the obligation stated in UCC 2-503(5).

Shipment under reservation. One more piece needs to be considered before trying your hand at some problems. When the seller is either required or authorized to ship goods to the buyer, the seller may ship the goods under reservation. UCC 2-310(b). Shipment under reservation is a method for the seller to reserve a security interest in the goods in order to make sure the goods are not finally released to the buyer until the buyer has paid for the goods. UCC 2-505(1) tells us what constitutes a shipment under reservation. If the seller has agreed to sell the goods on credit to the buyer, the seller who ships under reservation would have breached the contract for sale with the buyer. Even if the seller breaches the contract for sale with the buyer by shipping under reservation when it had no right to do so, the buyer's rights in regard to the goods or the rights under a negotiable document of title are not impaired. UCC 2-505(2). Mere shipment under reservation is not a waiver of the buyer's right to inspect the goods before payment. UCC 2-310(b).

Problem 6-3

Seller contracted with Buyer to ship a carload of factory equipment from Chicago to Phoenix, F.O.B. point of shipment. The contract price was $10,000, to be paid by a cashier's check. Nothing was said about when payment was to be made. Seller shipped the goods on October 1, with delivery expected on October 5. Carrier issued a negotiable bill of lading "to the order of Seller" and delivered it to Seller. That afternoon Seller sent the bill of lading to an agent in Phoenix. The bill of lading arrived on October 2 and on October 3, while the goods where still en-route from Chicago, the agent tendered the bill of lading to Buyer and demanded payment. Buyer refused to pay, arguing there was no duty to pay until the goods were tendered.

A. Is this argument correct? What additional facts do you need to know in order to answer this question? *See* UCC 2-505, 2-513, 2-310.

B. Assume that this is a shipment contract. Seller contracted with B & O railroad to ship the equipment to Buyer. Seller neglected to inform B & O that the equipment needed to be very securely tied down in order to avoid any shifting en route. Any shifting had the potential to damage sensitive components installed inside each piece of equipment. B & O secured the equipment in the usual manner which allowed some shifting of contents during shipment. When the equipment arrived and after Buyer inspected the equipment, Buyer determined that some of the equipment was not functioning properly. Assuming that Buyer could prove the failure to function properly was caused by the load shifts during transit, does Buyer have a good argument that Seller breached its tender obligation?

Problem 6-4

Seller, an equipment manufacturer, agreed to sell 10 standard lathes to Buyer, a retail business located in Topeka.

A. If the contract said nothing about mode of payment or inspection, but Seller, worried about Buyer's credit, shipped the goods "under reservation" by procuring a non-negotiable bill of lading naming itself as consignee, UCC 2-505(1)(b), would this be a breach of contract? Would it "alter" Buyer's right to inspect? UCC 2-310(b) and 2-513(1) and (3).

B. If the contract called for Buyer to pay against a sight draft with bill of lading (negotiable) attached, would Buyer be entitled to inspect before payment? Would it make any difference that the goods happened to arrive in Topeka ahead of the documents? UCC 2-513 and Comment 5. A sight draft is a draft (UCC 3-104) drawn by the seller to the order of the seller which orders the buyer to pay the contract price in cash "at sight" to the party presenting the draft.

C. If the contract called for Buyer to pay against a sight draft with bill of lading (negotiable) attached and the documents were in due form but the goods had been destroyed by fire while in the carrier's possession and Buyer knew this, could Buyer dishonor the sight draft without breaching the contract? UCC 2-512.

D. If the contract called for Buyer to pay against a sight draft with bill of lading (negotiable) attached and the bill was stamped "inspection allowed" would Buyer be entitled to inspect the goods prior to payment?

We will return to the documentary draft transaction (using drafts and documents of title as a mechanism for obtaining payment) after we consider one more method of tender of delivery.

C. Goods in the Hands of a Bailee and Delivery Without Moving the Goods

Let us assume that the goods that are the subject of the contract for sale are stored in a warehouse. The seller and buyer agree that the seller will tender the goods which will remain in the warehouse until the buyer needs them. Read UCC 2-503(4) which governs the seller's tender of delivery obligation. A warehouse is a type of a bailee. A warehouse, when it takes goods for storage, may issue a warehouse receipt for the goods. A warehouse receipt is a type of a document of title. Read the definition of warehouse receipt in UCC 1-201. Just as we saw with bills of lading, a warehouse receipt may be either negotiable or non-negotiable.

Under UCC 2-503(4), what are the four ways in which the seller could fulfill its tender obligation if the parties have not otherwise agreed? Notice that the buyer may object to the seller fulfilling its tender obligation by tendering a non-negotiable document of title or by tendering a direction in a record addressed to a bailee to deliver the goods to the buyer. Notice that if the bailee does not honor the non-negotiable document of title or the direction to deliver, the seller's tender is defeated.

As with contracts involving shipment of the goods, the buyer may have agreed in this situation to pay against documents with the same effect as we learned previously on its right to inspect prior to payment. UCC 2-513(3) and comment 5, 2-310(c). Merely because a warehouse receipt is issued does not mean that the buyer has agreed to pay against tender of that document. In any case in which the seller is required to deliver documents, whether the buyer has agreed to pay against the documents or not, the seller has the obligation stated in UCC 2-503(5).

Problem 6-5

Seller, an appliance manufacturer, contracted to sell 200 ovens to Buyer, an appliance retailer. Buyer did not have sufficient capacity to store the ovens at Buyer's premises, so Seller and Buyer agreed that the ovens would remain in the warehouse run by Bonded Storage, Inc. Delivery was due on April 5 and on that day Seller offered to indorse a negotiable warehouse receipt covering 200 ovens to Buyer if Buyer would pay the purchase price in full. Buyer refused because it wanted to pay for the ovens as it took each one out of storage after it was sold to a customer. Has Seller complied with its tender obligations? Does Buyer have a right to pay as it has asserted?

D. The Documentary Draft Transaction

In any transaction in which the seller has procured documents of title from the carrier or warehouse, the seller must somehow get the documents to the buyer to enable the buyer to retrieve the goods from the carrier or the warehouse. The seller may simply send the documents to the buyer. Of course if the buyer has agreed to pay against the documents, the seller will not want to release the documents to the buyer without getting the payment.

The seller may use the banking system as a method of getting the documents of title to the buyer. When using the banking system to present the documents to the buyer, the seller will often use a draft payable to the order of the seller, drawn on the buyer, and signed by the seller. UCC 3-104. The seller will give that draft and accompanying documents of title to the seller's bank. The seller's bank will forward the draft and documents through the banking system to the buyer's bank. UCC 4-501. When the draft and the documents arrive at the buyer's bank, the buyer's bank will present the draft and the documents to the buyer. UCC 4-503. If the draft is payable more than three days after presentment to the buyer, the bank will insist on the buyer's "acceptance" of the draft in order to release the documents to the buyer. UCC 4-503, 2-514. Acceptance of a draft is the drawee's (in this case the buyer) signed engagement to pay written on the draft. UCC 3-409. The buyer's "acceptance" of the draft obligates the buyer to pay according to the terms of the draft as accepted. UCC 3-413. If the draft is payable within the three days after presentment, the bank will release the documents to the buyer only upon payment. UCC 4-503, 2-514. Upon release of the documents to the buyer, the buyer may obtain the goods from the bailee. If the buyer fails to pay or accept the draft as required, the buyer's bank (known as the 'presenting bank') has some ability to deal with the goods. UCC 4-503 and 4-504. The presenting bank will seek instructions from its transferor, which will be communicated back to the seller. UCC 4-501.

Obviously, the documentary draft mechanism is used most often when the buyer and the seller are separated by distance and the buyer has agreed to pay against the documents. If the seller uses the documentary draft mechanism and the buyer has not agreed to pay against documents, the seller has breached its contract with the buyer by impairing the buyer's right to inspect the goods prior to payment.

A variation on this basic transaction is the seller's sale of the draft and the documents to a bank for a discounted amount. The bank would have a security interest in the draft and the documents. UCC 4-210. In addition, the bank is an Article 2 financing agency, UCC 2-104(2), and has rights as to the goods as specified in UCC 2-506 and 2-707.[*]

E. The Letter of Credit Transaction

A common method of payment in international and some domestic transactions is by a letter of credit. In international sales the parties may incorporate the letter of credit rules in ICP 500, prepared by the International Chamber of Commerce. In domestic sales, Article 5 of the UCC, which closely follows ICP 500, is likely to apply. The buyer's agreement to pay by letter of credit is a term in the contract for sale and a failure to provide the letter of credit is a breach of contract. *See* UCC 2-325. But the relationship between the buyer and the issuing bank and the issuing bank with the beneficiary of the letter of credit (the seller) and other banks is not treated in either the CISG or Article 2.

The objective in a letter of credit is for the seller to obtain payment contemporaneously with shipment of the goods rather than upon tender of the goods

---

[*] For an excellent discussion of the documentary draft transaction in greater detail, *see* E. Allan Farnsworth, *Documentary Drafts Under the Uniform Commercial Code*, 22 BUS. LAW. 479 (1967).

or the documents to the buyer. Suppose that Seller and Buyer have concluded a contract for sale of a carload of factory equipment for the price of $500,000 to be paid by letter of credit. Seller is to ship the goods from California to New York. Under UCC Article 5, the following steps are likely.

First, Buyer (Applicant) will go to a New York commercial bank (Issuer) and request Issuer to issue a letter of credit for the benefit of Seller (Beneficiary) for $500,000, the contract price. Applicant will undoubtedly be a customer of Issuer and already have a commercial account with the bank.

Second, Issuer will issue an irrevocable letter of credit for the benefit of Seller (Beneficiary). *See* UCC 5-106(a). In essence, the letter of credit is an authenticated record undertaking to pay the amount designated in the letter of credit (usually the contract price) to the beneficiary if a documentary presentation is made to the Issuer or a designated bank. *See* UCC 5-102(a)(10), 5-104. For example, the letter of credit might state that if Beneficiary presents a sight draft, a negotiable bill of lading for the goods, an invoice, and an insurance certificate to Issuer or a designated confirming bank (Confirmer), the Issuer or Confirmer will pay the draft. Review the definitions in UCC 5-102. Thus, Issuer will send the letter of Credit to Beneficiary and probably arrange for the documentary presentation to be made to a Confirmer in California. The rights and duties of a Confirmer are the same as Issuer. *See* UCC 5-107(a).

Third, Seller (Beneficiary) will ship the goods to Buyer (Applicant), obtain the required documents from the carrier and others and draw a draft on Issuer or Confirmer for the letter of credit amount. Beneficiary will then make a documentary presentation to Confirmer who will inspect the documents and honor the presentation if it "appears on its face strictly to comply with the terms and conditions of the letter of credit." UCC 5-108(a). This is the so-called "strict compliance" rule. If the honor was proper, Issuer is discharged from its obligations under the letter of credit and is entitled to reimbursement from Buyer (Applicant) "in immediately available funds not later than the date of its payment of funds." UCC 5-108(i)(1). More to the point, Buyer has paid Seller for the goods and is now entitled (Issuer will send the bill of lading to Buyer) to take them from the carrier on arrival in New York.

Fourth, if the documentary presentation strictly complies with the letter of credit, Issuer cannot dishonor because of defenses between Seller and Buyer in the contract for sale. For example, suppose Confirmer knows that the goods shipped do not conform to the contract or that they have been destroyed by fire after shipment. Unless a required document is forged or materially fraudulent, Confirmer must honor the letter of credit. *See* UCC 5-109, dealing with fraud and forgery in required documents. In these cases, Buyer has paid the price and must reimburse Issuer. Any defenses must be asserted independently against Seller. UCC 2-605(2) and the accompanying comments after the 2003 amendments makes clear that the Issuer's honor of the letter of credit does not waive any claims by Buyer against Seller that there are defects in the documents.

Finally, suppose Confirmer wrongfully dishonors or improperly honors a presentation. Both actions are breaches by Confirmer. In the former, Beneficiary is deprived of money to which it is entitled and in the latter Beneficiary obtains a payment to which it is not entitled under the letter of credit. How does Article 5 deal with these situations? *See* UCC 5-111. Is an improper dishonor by Confirmer a breach of contract by Buyer?

Note: Delivery, Inspection, and Payment Under Article 2A

Unlike the voluminous attention to tender, delivery, and payment in Article 2, Article 2A does not contain any counterparts to the Article 2 sections reviewed above. The default rules regarding tendering the goods to the lessee and the lessee's payment obligation will be determined by the lease contract as interpreted in light of course of dealing, course of performance and usage of trade. What explains this lack of attention to the tender and payment process in Article 2A?

In fact, the performance based default rules in Article 2A are focused on insecurity, repudiation and excuse. *See* UCC Article 2A, Part 4. We will address those provisions in Chapters Seven and Ten, *infra*.

Article 2A does not explicitly provide for the lessee's right to inspect the goods. Article 2A has no counterpart to UCC 2-512 or 2-513. The right to inspect under Article 2A is recognized, however, in UCC 2A-515, which provides that acceptance occurs after the lessee has a reasonable time to inspect. Having an opportunity to inspect in order to reject the goods before acceptance is as important to a lessee as it is to a buyer, and is perhaps more important to finance lessees given UCC 2A-407's provision regarding hell or high water clauses. Can you think of a reason why counterparts to UCC 2-513(1) and (4) were not included in Article 2A?

Note: Delivery, Inspection, and Payment Under the CISG

The seller's general duty to delivery the goods and hand over the documents in Article 30 is particularized in Articles 31-34. Article 31 deals with the place of delivery in cases where the seller is not "bound to deliver the goods at any other particular place." If the contract does not involve carriage of the goods, the place of delivery is determined by Article 31(b) & (c). If carriage of goods is involved, the place for delivery (absent contrary agreement) is stated in Article 31(a) and the seller's duties with regard to shipment are stated in Article 32. Article 33 determines the time for delivery and Article 34 deals with cases where the seller is bound to hand over documents relating to the goods.

If the contract involves carriage of the goods, the seller must hand over the goods "to the first carrier for transmission to the buyer." Art. 31(a). For example, if a seller in Chicago has agreed to transport the goods to a buyer in Paris (and there is no other delivery term), the first (and only) carrier may be a flight from Chicago to Paris or it might be a train from Chicago to New York even though the goods will then be delivered to a vessel for shipment. Article 32 states what the seller's obligations are when goods are handed over to the first carrier. Note that the seller has a limited duty to notify the buyer, Art. 32(1), and has no duty to arrange for the carriage of the goods or to obtain insurance on their carriage unless required by the contract. Art.32(2)-(3). Please read these sections and compare UCC 2-504.

In other cases, the place of delivery is stated in Art. 31(b) or (c). *Compare* UCC 2-508. Suppose the goods are in the hands of a bailee? Where is the place of delivery? In either case, the time or date for delivery is either determined by the contract, Art. 33(a), or stated in Art. 33(b)-(c).

Under Article 53, the "buyer must pay the price for the goods and take delivery of them as required by the contract and this Convention." In the absence of contrary agreement, the place for payment is stated in Article 57 and the time for payment is stated in Article 58. Assuming a timely tender of goods or documents at the proper place, the buyer's right to examine the goods is stated in Articles 38-40. The buyer's general duty to pay the price and take delivery is stated in Article 53. The buyer, however, is not bound to pay until he has had an opportunity to examine the goods, unless the procedures for payment or the agreement is inconsistent with the right to examine. Art. 58(3).

But Article 58(2) states that if the contract involves "carriage of the goods, the seller may dispatch the goods on terms whereby the goods, or documents controlling their disposition, will not be handed over to the buyer except against payment of the price." No agreement by the buyer is required. The usual practice, reflected in the cases and the Revised American Foreign Trade Definitions of 1941, is that unless otherwise agreed the buyer must pay against documents of title even though the goods are still in the middle of the ocean. *See E. Clemens Horst Co. v.*

Biddell Bros., (1912) App. Cas. 18. While the buyer must wait until the goods arrive to inspect, he can discount the documents of title or use them as collateral to obtain a loan if the delay puts him under a financial strain. These and other issues are well treated in JOHN HONNOLD, UNIFORM LAW FOR INTERNATIONAL SALES, Pt. 3, Chapter III, § 1 (Kluwer, 3d ed. 1999).

Note: Delivery, Inspection, and Payment Under UCITA

UCITA 601 sets forth the general performance obligation of the parties. The performance obligation under UCITA depends upon what performance the contract requires; access to information, delivery of a copy of information or development of information. For performance consisting of delivery of a copy, the reader should find the rules from UCITA very similar to the rules from Article 2.

UCITA 602 provides the default obligation of a licensor to enable use of the information. As can be seen from reading the section and comments, enabling use of the information may be as simple as granting permission to use the information. Sometimes enabling use may require providing software that allows the licensee to access the information or providing a copy of the information. Section 604 states that when the licensee is being provided with the entire benefit and that benefit cannot be returned, inspection rights are limited to inspecting media, labels or packaging prior to tender but not the information itself.

If the performance consists of supplying a copy of information to the licensee, UCITA 606-610 apply. Section 606 is the analog to UCC 2-308 and 2-503. It addresses the default rule for place for delivery of that copy as well as the appropriate manner for tender of the copy. Section 606(b)(1) addresses the situation where a copy is held by a third person (similar to when goods are held by a bailee). UCITA 606(b)(2) and (3) address the "shipment" and "destination" contracts with changes to reflect that delivery of a copy may be by electronic means.

UCITA 607 adopts the concurrent conditions model of UCC 2-507 and 2-511 and the presumption that if payment is required upon delivery of a copy, all copies must be tendered in a single delivery as in UCC 2-307.

When a copy is tendered, UCITA 608, which parallels UCC 2-513, the licensee has the right to inspect the copy before payment or acceptance. In a further parallel to UCC 2-512, UCITA 608 also provides that if the agreement so provides the licensee can waive its right to inspect before payment. As we shall see, UCITA also contains the same acceptance, rejection, revocation of acceptance paradigm as Articles 2 and 2A when the subject matter is a copy of computer information.

UCITA 609, 704, 707. The inspection right under UCITA 608 thus functions in a similar manner as to copies of information, limited by UCITA 604, as the inspection right under UCC 2-512 and 2-513 functions as to goods.

If performance consists of granting access to information over a period of time as opposed to delivering a copy, UCITA 611 provides default rules that govern both the scope of the right of access and the availability of access. If the contract is to provide support services for computer information, UCITA 612 provides a standard for judging whether the obligation has been performed. Notice that an express agreement is required to have an obligation to actually correct problems. The default standard for support services is a reasonable efforts standard.

SECTION 2. REJECTION, ACCEPTANCE, AND REVOCATION OF ACCEPTANCE

A. Rejection or Acceptance

1. The Rightfulness of the Rejection

Once the seller or lessor tenders the goods, the buyer or lessee must decide whether to accept or reject the goods. This represents an important choice for the buyer or lessee as it will affect the remedies the buyer or lessee may obtain. Once goods are accepted, they can no longer be rejected, UCC 2-607(2), 2A-516(2), although in some circumstances the acceptance may be revoked. UCC 2-608, 2A-517. The ability to revoke acceptance of the goods is more limited than the ability to reject the goods. The buyer or lessee who accepts the goods must pay for the goods at the contract rate, subject to any adjustment for the nonconformity. UCC 2-607(1), 2A-516(1), 2-714, 2A-519, 2-717. If the buyer or lessee wrongfully rejects the goods, the seller or lessor may pursue appropriate remedies for breach of contract under UCC 2-703 or 2A-523.

When does the buyer or lessee have a right to reject the goods the seller or lessor has tendered? Read UCC 2-601 and 2-612(2), 2A-509 and 2A-510(1). Notice that the standard for a rightful rejection differs depending upon whether the parties have entered into an installment contract. UCC 2-612(1) defines an installment sales contract and UCC 2A-103(1) defines an installment lease contract.

UCC 2-601 and 2A-509 provide that in a non-installment contract the standard for rejection is "if the goods or the tender of delivery fail in any respect to conform to the contract." This rule is known as the "perfect tender" rule regardless of the nature of the defect or its impact upon the buyer or the lessee. Compare the standard in non-installment contracts with the "substantial impairment" standard for installment contracts. UCC 2-612 and 2A-510.*

Why the different standard for rejection in the two types of contracts? The Permanent Editorial Board of the UCC declined to follow a recommendation that the buyer's right to reject in a non-installment contract be limited to cases of material breach. The Board's reasons were that the buyer should not be required to guess at his peril whether a breach is material and that proof of materiality would sometimes require disclosure of the buyer's private affairs, such as trade secrets and processes.**

So are there any limits on the buyer's or lessee's right to reject in a non-installment contract? The most important limit is to determine whether the goods or the tender of delivery do in fact fail to conform to the requirements of the contract. UCC 2-106. In this respect, all we have studied up to this point comes into play to determine what are the requirements of tender of delivery and conformity to the requirements of the contract. Consider the other limitation stated in the statute itself. The parties may agree that the buyer or lessee does not have a right to reject the goods based upon their agreement to limit remedies or liquidate damages. UCC 2-718, 2-719, 2A-503, 2A-504.

Another limitation is possibly the obligation of good faith. Reread UCC 1-304 [former 1-203]. If the buyer assigns as a reason for rejection an insubstantial breach

---

* *See Moulton Cavity & Mold, Inc. v. Lyn-Flex Indus., Inc.*, 396 A.2d 1024 (Me. 1979) (trial court erred in charge that UCC 2-601 was satisfied by "substantial performance").

** The "perfect tender" rule in UCC 2-601 has been criticized in the courts, *see D.P. Technology Corp. v. Sherwood Tool, Inc.*, 751 F. Supp. 1038 (D. Conn. 1990) (unfair where breach is delay in delivery with no serious harm to buyer) and by the commentators, *see, e.g.*, Jody S. Kraus, *Decoupling Sales Law from the Acceptance-Rejection Fulcrum*, 104 YALE L.J. 129 (1994); John A. Sebert, *Rejection, Revocation and Cure Under Article 2 of the Uniform Commercial Code: Some Modest Proposals*, 84 NW. U. L. REV. 375 (1990). A study group appointed to consider the possible revision of Article 2, however, concluded that the "perfect tender" rule should be retained, with an effort made to collect citations to the various limitations on its exercise all in one place. Since the strict performance rule does not apply in installment contracts and, in *de facto* operation, results in a substantial impairment test, no revision is required. *See* Preliminary Report, Uniform Commercial Code Article 2 Study Group, reprinted under the title *An Appraisal of the March 1, 1990, Preliminary Report of the Uniform Commercial Code Article 2 Study Group*, 16 DEL. J. OF CORP. L. 981, 1157-1162 (1991). *See also PEB Study Group: Uniform Commercial Code, Article 2 Executive Summary*, 46 BUS. LAW. 1869, 1881 (1991).

by the seller, has he violated the obligation of good faith imposed on the "performance or enforcement" of "every contract or duty within the UCC?" It has been suggested that a buyer will "often try to escape from a performance quite within the business understanding of the contract, though not the legal, if he finds either that he can purchase the very same goods at a cheaper price on the open market or that his resale market has all but disappeared." The desire to avoid losses or to make greater profits "overcomes the possible desire to be a 'square shooter' and to shoulder his part of that risk of price fluctuation which any present contract for future delivery carries, both for the seller and for the buyer." Lawrence R. Eno, *Price Movement and Unstated Objections to the Defective Performance of Sales Contracts,* 44 YALE L.J. 782, 801 (1935). According to Judge Learned Hand, in this setting "such words as * * * 'good faith' * * * appear to us to obscure the issue. The promisor may in fact be satisfied with the performance, but not with the bargain, in which case, of course, he must pay." *Thompson-Starrett Co. v. La Belle Iron Works,* 17 F.2d 536, 541 (2nd Cir. 1927). But is the conclusion one which a court should reach under the UCC? If so, does this cut down the UCC's "perfect tender" rule in UCC 2-601 and 2A-509?

Try your hand at determining whether the buyer is entitled to reject the goods in the following problem.

Problem 6-6

Sodfill, Inc. is a grower of vegetables and Blurtaste Co. is a manufacturer of catsup. On April 1, the parties entered into a written contract for the sale of 1,000 bushels of Lady Dove tomatoes at $4.50 per bushel, to be shipped F.O.B. point of shipment on or before July 15 and delivered to Blurtaste in "green" condition, a term having definite meaning in the trade. The goods were to be delivered in a single lot and payment was to be made 30 days after the goods were received. Nothing was said in the agreement about rejection.

A. Assuming there is no evidence regarding the impact upon the value of the bargain, could Blurtaste properly reject all of the goods in the following circumstances:

    1. a timely tender of 990 bushels of "green" Lady Doves;

    2. a timely tender of 1,000 bushels of tomatoes, 10 of which did not contain "green" Lady Doves;

    3. a tender of 1,000 bushels of "green" Lady Doves which were shipped on July 16;

4. a tender of 1,000 bushels of "green" Lady Doves which were shipped on July 14 but, because of an erroneous delivery instruction by Sodfill, did not arrive until 3 days after the normal time for shipment had expired. *See* UCC 2-504, 2-601, & 2-614.

B. Could Blurtaste accept 500 bushels of good tomatoes and reject 500 bushels of bad without incurring liability for the whole? *See* UCC 2-601, 2-105(5) [former subsection (6)].

C. If you represented Sodfill, what sort of clause would you draft to limit or eliminate the buyer's rejection right under UCC 2-601? How could you insure that it became part of the contract?

Now consider the standard for rejection of an installment in an installment contract. What is an installment contract? UCC 2-612(1). *See also* UCC 2-307. A rightful rejection of an installment can be accomplished if a non-conforming installment "substantially impairs the value of that installment to the buyer." UCC 2-612(2). Why do installment contracts have a different standard for rejection?

When is the value of the installment substantially impaired? Many courts have equated the substantial impairment standard with the material breach standard, which was the test under Section 45 of the Uniform Sales Act. The 2003 amendments deleted the requirement that the non-conformity in the installment could not be cured as part of the standard for rejection of the installment. Compare former 2-612(2) to UCC 2-612(2). The provision on cure in both installment and non-installment contracts will be considered *infra*.

UCC 2-612(3) provides that if the value of the whole contract is substantially impaired, there is a breach of the whole contract. Read UCC 2-711. Is the buyer entitled to exercise remedies in an installment contract if there is not a breach of the whole contract? Assume that a seller has tendered a nonconforming installment that does not substantially impair the value of the installment nor result in a breach of the whole contract under UCC 2-612(3). What is the buyer's recourse?

Article 2A adopted the same scheme for installment leases as Article 2 has for installment contracts for sale. UCC 2A-510, 2A-508.

Consider the following case as it explores the standard for rejection in an installment contract and the ability of the buyer to exercise remedies under former 2-612 and 2-711. Would the analysis be the same under amended UCC 2-612 and 2-711?

MIDWEST MOBILE DIAGNOSTIC IMAGING V. DYNAMICS CORP. OF AMERICA
UNITED STATES DISTRICT COURT, WESTERN DISTRICT OF MICHIGAN, 1997
965 F. SUPP. 1003, *AFF'D*, 165 F.3D 27 (6TH CIR. 1998)

[Plaintiff, MMDI, contracted with Dynamics to manufacture and supply four trailers designed to contain mobile MRI systems. In the purchase agreement, dated August 10, 1995, there was a firm commitment by Dynamics to deliver the first trailer on December 1, 1995. This was important to MMDI because of a high demand for the system in South West Michigan. MMDI, relying on the commitment, booked the system for use in December. The other three trailers were to be delivered separately at times to be agreed. In November, 1995, it appeared that the first trailer would conform to the contract and MMDI advanced Dynamics $384,5000 of the price. The trailer when delivered, however, did not conform to the contract. Dynamics attempted to cure the non-conformity and missed the December 1, 1995 deadline. Subsequently, Phillips, a third party retained by MMDI to certify the MRI system, refused to certify the repaired unit. A bracing structure installed to correct the original problem now impaired the operation of the scanner magnet. Dynamics disagreed with Phillips but MMDI, nevertheless, canceled the contract, rented a substitute trailer and contracted with another manufacturer for two new trailers. MMDI then sued Dynamics to recover the advance payment and for expenses of $185,250 in renting the substitute trailer.]

* * *

V. ANALYSIS

A. Breach of contract

The primary issue for resolution by the Court is whether MMDI rightfully rejected E&W's tender of the first trailer and then subsequently canceled the contract, or if its actions in mid-December constituted anticipatory repudiation of the contract. Having previously determined that Michigan law controls in the instant case, the Court simply notes that the Michigan version of the Uniform Commercial Code [hereinafter the "UCC"] applies to this sales contract* * *.

1. Installment Contract

Before turning to the specific questions of rejection and cancellation, the Court must first resolve a threshold issue. Under the UCC, the parties' rights to reject, cure, and cancel under an installment contract differ substantially from those defined under a single delivery contract. Consequently, resolution of whether the contract is an installment contract is of primary concern. Section 2-612(1) defines an "installment contract" as "one which requires or authorizes the delivery of goods in separate lots to be separately accepted. * * *" The commentary following this section emphasizes that the "definition of an installment contract is phrased more broadly in this Article [than in its previous incarnation as the Uniform Sales Act] so as to cover installment deliveries tacitly authorized by the circumstances or by the option of either party." § 2-612, cmt. 1.

Plaintiff argues that the contract between itself and E&W does not constitute an installment contract because it authorizes delivery in commercial units, and not lots, as required by subsection (1). However, upon review of the Code section defining those terms, it becomes clear that those terms are not mutually exclusive. Section 2-105 defines a "lot" as a "parcel or single article which is the subject matter of a separate sale or delivery, whether or not it is sufficient to perform the contract." The same section defines a commercial unit as "such a unit of goods as by commercial usage is a single whole for purposes of sale and division of which materially impairs its character or value on the market or in use. A commercial unit may be a single article (as a machine) or a set of articles (as a suite of furniture or an assortment of sizes) or a quantity (as a bale, gross, or carload) or any other unit treated in use or in the relevant market as a single whole." Thus, a lot, which is the measure of goods that the contract states will be delivered together in one installment, can be a single commercial unit. Consequently, § 2-612 applies wherever a contract for multiple items authorizes the delivery of the items in separate groups at different times, whether or not the installment constitutes a commercial unit.

The contract between MMDI and E&W for the sale of four trailers authorizes the delivery of each trailer separately. While the written contract does not explicitly state this delivery schedule, it does authorize separate delivery. Paragraph 2 of the contract assumes separate delivery dates by setting out a payment schedule wherein the balance for *each* unit is due at the time of shipment. Furthermore, based on the parties' testimony it is clear that both parties understood the trailers would be delivered in separate installments. Indeed, neither party disputes that they agreed to have the trailers delivered at four separate times. Therefore, the Court finds that the contract in dispute is an installment contract.

2. Right of Rejection

Section 2-612, therefore, is the starting point for the Court's analysis of MMDI's actions on December 13, 1995. * * * Under § 2-612, the buyer's right to reject is far more limited than the corresponding fight [sic] to reject under a single delivery contract defined under § 2-601. Under § 2-601, a buyer has the right to reject, "if the goods or tender of delivery fail in any respect to conform to the contract.* * *" Known as the "perfect tender" rule, this standard requires a very high level of conformity. Under this rule, the buyer may reject a seller's tender for any trivial defect, whether it be in the quality of the goods, the timing of performance, or the manner of delivery.[1] To avoid injustice, the Code limits the buyer's correlative right to cancel the contract upon such rejection by providing a right to cure under § 2-508. § 2- 508, cmt. 2. Under § 2-508, the seller has a right to cure if s/he seasonably notifies the buyer of the intent to do so, and either 1) the time for performance has not yet passed, or 2) the seller had reason to believe that the goods were in conformity with the contract. Thus, § 2-508's right to cure serves to temper the buyer's expansive right to reject under a single delivery contract.

* * * Section 2-612 creates an exception to the perfect tender rule * * *. Under subsection (2), a buyer may not reject nonconforming tender unless the defect substantially impairs the value of the installment. In addition, "if the nonconformity is curable and the seller gives adequate assurances of cure," the buyer must accept the installment. § 2-612, cmt. 5. But even if rejection is proper under subsection 2, cancellation of the contract is not appropriate unless the defect substantially impairs the value of the whole contract. § 2-612(3), cmt. 6. Because this section significantly restricts the buyer's right to cancel under an installment contract, there is no corresponding necessity for reference to § 2-508; * * *.[2]

---

[1] There is some conflicting case law and commentary concerning the efficacy of the "perfect tender" rule even in the context of a single delivery contract. For discussion of this controversy, see William H. Lawrence, *Appropriate Standards for a Buyer's Refusal to Keep Goods Tendered by a Seller*, 35 WM. & MARY L. REV. 1635 (1994). Given that the "perfect tender" rule does not apply in this case, this controversy does not effect the Court's determination in any way.

[2] Courts of other jurisdictions have reached differing conclusions with regard to the interaction between §§ 2-612 and 2-508. *See, e.g., Arkla Energy Resources v. Roye Realty & Dev., Inc.*, 9 F.3d 855 (10th Cir.1993); *Bodine*, 97 Ill. Dec. at 906, 493 N.E.2d at 713; *Bevel-Fold, Inc. v. Bose Corp.*, 9 Mass.App.Ct. 576, 402 N.E.2d 1104, 1108 (1980); *Continental Forest Prods., Inc. v. White Lumber Sales Inc.*, 256 Or. 466, 474 P.2d 1, 4 (1970). This Court does not find the arguments of these other courts persuasive, however, and notes that their decisions are not binding on this Court. Nevertheless, the Court also notes that, since the time for delivery of the first installment had already passed on December 1, 1995 (*see infra* § 2(a)) and defendant could not have reasonably believed and, in fact, did not believe that the trailer was in conformity with the contract on that date, defendant had no

(continued...)

a. Delivery Date

Before proceeding with the analysis of MMDI's December 13 rejection, the Court initially notes that E&W's tender on December 13 constituted a cure attempt for the wall-flexing defect which delayed the delivery of the first trailer beyond the agreed upon delivery date. Although under § 2-612 the delivery date does not cut off the seller's right to cure, it does have an effect on the rights of the parties. * * *

In the instant case, the original, written contract included no definite delivery date. Instead, the contract left the delivery term to be agreed upon at a later date. At the time of execution, the parties both expected delivery of the first trailer to take place in October. During the months after the execution of the contract, however, the parties modified the deadline for the first installment of the contract on several occasions. As noted above, upon review of the testimony and documentary evidence, the Court finds that, whatever delivery date the parties had agreed upon prior to November 1995, by early November they had renegotiated their agreement to establish a December 1, 1995 delivery date. *See* § 2-209 (sales contract may be modified by oral or written agreement without consideration, so long as agreement does not state otherwise).

Defendant argues, however, that, even if the parties had at one point agreed upon a December 1, 1995 deadline, when the first trailer failed the Philips road test on November 28, 1995, the parties renegotiated the delivery term to allow E&W a reasonable time to cure the defect. While E&W is correct that, as of December 1, it had a reasonable time in which to cure the wall-flexing problem, the Court disagrees that MMDI's willingness to wait for a cure constitutes an agreement to extend the delivery deadline. Because the parties believed that the defect was curable and E&W, without solicitation, unequivocally promised to cure it, under § 2-612, MMDI had no choice but to accept an offer of cure. To reject the installment on November 28 would have constituted a violation of § 2-612. The Court, therefore, finds that any negotiations the parties engaged in regarding delivery after discovery of the wall-flexing problem, did not constitute a modification of the delivery date for the first installment, but rather involved negotiation regarding cure. Since no specific date for delivery of a cure was agreed upon during those negotiations, under section 2-309(1), E&W had a reasonable time to effectuate a cure. Although there is some question as to whether further delay would have been

---

[2] (...continued)
right to cure under § 2- 508.

reasonable, the Court finds that, as of December 13, 1995, a reasonable time had not yet passed. Therefore, defendant's tender of a cure was timely.

b. Substantial Impairment of the Installment

The Court's conclusion that E&W's December 13 tender was an attempt to cure the November 28 breach raises another question: which standard of conformity applies to cure under an installment contract, perfect tender or substantial impairment? Looking to the rationale behind § 2-612, the Court notes that the very purpose of allowing the seller time to cure under this section is to permit it additional time to meet the obligations of the contract. The assumption is that, because the parties have an ongoing relationship, the seller should be given an opportunity to make up the deficiency. This section was not designed to allow the seller to have a never-ending series of chances to bring the item into conformity with the contract. Nor was it enacted to force the buyer to accept a nonconforming product as satisfaction of the contract. Consequently, it is logical that a tender of cure should be required to meet the higher "perfect tender" standard. On its face, however, § 2-612, which generally defines a buyer's right to reject goods under an installment contract, requires only substantial impairment in this context as well. Thus, there is some question as to which is the appropriate standard. The answer is not crucial however, since the trailer in this case fails under both standards. Because a decision on this point will not effect the ultimate outcome in this case, the Court declines to address the issue. Instead, the Court proceeds with the substantial impairment analysis provided by § 2-612.

To establish substantial impairment of the value of an installment, the buyer "'must present objective evidence that with respect to its own needs, the value of the goods was substantially impaired.'" *Arkla Energy Resources v. Roye Realty & Dev., Inc.*, 9 F.3d 855, 862 (10th Cir. 1993) (quoting *Bodine Sewer, Inc. v. Eastern Illinois Precast, Inc.*, 143 Ill. App. 3d 920, 97 Ill. Dec. 898, 906, 493 N.E.2d 705, 713 (1986)). *See also* § 2-612, cmt 4. The existence of such nonconformity depends on the facts and circumstances of each case, and "can turn not only on the quality of the goods but also on such factors as time * * *, and the like." § 2-612, cmt. 4. *See, eg., Colonial Dodge, Inc. v. Miller*, 420 Mich. 452, 457- 58, 362 N.W.2d 704 (1984) (holding missing spare tire in new car had special devaluing effect for the buyer and thus could constitute substantial impairment). Finally, whether nonconformity rises to the level of substantial impairment may be judged by reference to the concept of material breach under traditional contract law. * * *

In the instant case, plaintiff alleges several aspects in which defendant's

December 13 tender failed to conform to contract obligations. Plaintiff contends that the trailer tendered on December 13 with the bracing structure did not conform to the parties' agreement because: 1) it was not and could not be certified by Philips without conditions for use with the 1.5T scanner and 2) its interior design did not conform with the parties' agreements. Because of these defects, MMDI argues that the value of trailer was reduced substantially. Defendant, on the other hand, contends that the contract required only that the trailer meet the technical specifications provided by Philips, and that, therefore, the December 13 trailer was in complete compliance with its terms.

The written contract signed by the parties in this case is relatively skeletal and thus, requires interpretation. The Court's fundamental purpose in interpreting the terms of the contract is to give effect to the intent of the parties as it existed at the time the agreement was made. * * * Furthermore, the Code explicitly authorizes courts to look to the parties' course of dealings and performance and to the usage of terms in trade in interpreting the terms of the contract. §§ 1-205, 2-202, and 2-208.

As instructed by the commentary to § 2-612, the Court begins the substantial impairment analysis by looking to the "normal and specifically known purposes of the contract." § 2-612, cmt. 4. Reviewing the evidence presented, the Court finds that the primary purpose of the contract was to provide the plaintiff with four trailers for use with the Philips 1.5T scanner. With that in mind, the parties agreed that the trailers would be constructed in accordance with the specifications provided by Philips and that the trailer would be not be ready for delivery until Philips certification had been received. Philips did not, however, ever certify the trailer for unconditional use with the bracing structure. Because the bracing structure prevented normal service of the scanner magnet, it was only approved as a temporary fix. * * *

[The court held that Phillips, in exercising its discretion to disapprove the unit, acted reasonably and in good faith. In addition, the court concluded that Dynamics breached an agreement that the interior of the trailer be aesthetically pleasing.]

Such a condition of satisfaction by one of the parties to the contract will only be excused if approval is withheld unreasonably. * * * In the instant case, upon review of photographs of the bracing structure and testimony of those experienced in this industry, and in light of the fact that the interior of the trailer should match that of a hospital and not a construction site, the Court finds that plaintiff's refusal to approve the aesthetics of the design was commercially reasonable. Given that an integral aspect of the trailer's function is to serve as a clinic for patients undergoing medical procedures, and given MMDI's clients' expectations after having viewed the trailer at the open house, such a defect in the trailer's interior also reduced the value of the trailer substantially.

Upon review of the evidence, the Court finds that the bracing structure substantially impaired the value of the first trailer. Although the trailer met the express technical Philips' specifications for wall-flexing, it was never certified by the manufacturer. The failure of this condition does not relieve defendant of liability because it was defendant's failure to properly construct the trailer that prevented certification. In light of the specific facts and circumstances of this case, the Court finds that this deficiency substantially impaired the value of the installment. When coupled with the trailer's failure to conform with the aesthetic requirements of the contract and the delay caused by the cure attempt, the Court holds that the cure attempt clearly constitutes a substantial breach within the meaning of § 2-612(2).

Substantial impairment, however, does not in itself justify rejection of the installment. As noted above, the buyer must still accept tender if the defect can be cured and the seller gives adequate assurances. Under § 2-612, as opposed to § 2-609, it is incumbent upon the seller to assure the buyer that cure would be forthcoming. * * * Defendant has failed in this regard. The Court notes that neither E&W's statements during the December 13 conference call nor the letter sent the following day constituted adequate assurances. On the contrary, during the December 13 conference call, Andrew Pike, the President of E&W denied the existence of a defect, disclaimed any continuing obligation to cure under the contract, and stated that he did not believe a better design could be made which would remedy the wall-flexing problem. Furthermore, on December 14, Mr. Pike again ignored the servicing problems that the bracing structure had caused, ignored the fact that the bracing structure had not been approved for permanent use by Philips, and reiterated his doubt that the design could be constructed in a more aesthetically pleasing manner. Under these circumstances, the Court finds that MMDI's rejection of E&W's cure on December 13 constituted a rightful rejection under § 2-612(2).[3]

---

[3] Defendant argues that, as of December 13, it still had a right to cure under § 2-508 and that it was not required to give assurances unless plaintiff requested them in writing under § 2-609. The Court reiterates that, under § 2-508, defendant's right to cure was cut off on December 1. Furthermore, § 2-612, unlike § 2-609, does not require the aggrieved party to request assurances. In an installment contract, where the seller's right to cure is more

(continued...)

3. Cancellation

a. Substantial Impairment of Contract as a Whole

The fact that rejection of one installment is proper does not necessarily justify cancellation of the entire contract. Under § 2-612(3) the right to cancel does not arise unless the nonconforming goods substantially impair the value of the *entire* contract. Indeed, as noted above, the very purpose of the substantial impairment requirement of § 2-612(3) is to preclude parties from canceling an installment contract for trivial defects. * * *

Whether a breach constitutes "substantial impairment" of the entire contract is a question of fact. * * * To make such a determination, the Court should consider "the cumulative effect of [the breaching party's] performance under the contract, based on the totality of the circumstances * * *." Ultimately, "[w]hether the non-conformity in any given installment justifies cancellation as to the future depends, not on whether such non-conformity indicates an intent or likelihood that future deliveries will also be defective, but whether the non-conformity substantially impairs the value of the whole contract." § 2-612, cmt. 6. Thus, the question is one of present breach which focuses on the importance of the nonconforming installment relative to the contract as a whole. If the nonconformity only impairs the aggrieved party's security with regard to future installments, s/he "has the right to demand adequate assurances but [ ] not an immediate right to cancel the entire contract." § 2-612, cmt. 6. The right to cancel will be triggered only if "material inconvenience or injustice will result if the aggrieved party is forced to wait and receive an ultimate tender minus the part or aspect repudiated." § 2-610, cmt. 3 (noting the test for anticipatory repudiation under § 2-610 is the same as the test for cancellation under § 2-612(3)).

In the instant case, there is substantial evidence that one of the primary purposes of this contract was to provide MMDI with a fourth mobile MRI trailer so that it could meet the growing demand for its services. Thus, impairment of one of the four installments would have a substantial negative impact on MMDI. Moreover, an early delivery time was of primary importance to MMDI, as E&W was well

---

[3] (...continued)
expansive it stands to reason that the burden would fall on the seller to show that it had the present ability and the intent to cure any remaining defect. * * * In the instant case, defendant gave no indication that it either had the capability to satisfy the contract or the will to do so. On the contrary, E&W's President, gave MMDI the impression that cure was not possible and indicated clearly that he was not required to do anything more under the contract. Under such circumstances, MMDI's rejection was rightful.

aware. By failing to cure the November 28 breach on the first installment, E&W substantially delayed completion of the remainder of the contract which delayed MMDI's ability to begin use of the 1.5T MRI trailer it had promised to its customers at the open house on November 3. Having found that substantial injustice would be done to plaintiff if it were required to accept the remaining three trailers after substantial delay as satisfaction of the contract, the Court finds that plaintiff rightfully canceled the contract on December 18, 1995.

4. Damages

[The court held that MMDI could recover the full amount of the price advanced to Dynamics, $384,500, and incidental damages measured by the cost to obtain a replacement unit, some $185,250. UCC 2-711, 2-715(1).] * * *

VI. CONCLUSION

For the foregoing reasons, plaintiff is awarded expectation and incidental damages in the amount of $569,250. * * *

[Some footnotes omitted. Those retained have been renumbered.]

Notes

1. The court identifies and then struggles with several questions in the interpretation and application of former 2-612. What were those questions and how did the court resolve them?

2. Under what circumstances can the seller "cure" the non-conformity in a rightfully rejected installment? Amended UCC 2-612(2) and 2-508 tried to clarify the matter. Did it succeed?

Problem 6-7

Return to Problem 6-6 with the following change. Suppose Sodfill agreed to ship 500 bushels by July 15 and the balance by August 1, payment to be made by September 1. Could the buyer reject if the first tender was: 10 bushels short; 1% off on quality; shipped 1 day late? *See* UCC 2-612.

2.   Procedural Requirements of Effective Rejection

Suppose, upon inspection, the buyer finds a non-conformity which would support a rightful rejection of the goods under UCC 2-601. How does the buyer make an effective rejection? Read UCC 2-602. *Compare* UCC 2-607(3)(a). If the buyer fails to make an effective rejection, he has accepted the goods. UCC 2-606(1)(b). To test the interplay between these sections, suppose that S delivers non-conforming goods on June 1 and because of their complexity a "reasonable opportunity to inspect" will take two weeks. B has not discovered a non-conformity by June 14, but by June 21 it is clear that the goods do not conform. B then notifies S of the specific problem on July 1 and attempts to reject the goods. Is this rejection effective? The answer is yes if B has had a reasonable opportunity to inspect and rejects (by "seasonable" notice) "within a reasonable time after their delivery or tender." The reasonable time is measured from the time of delivery not from the time where B discovered or should have discovered the non-conformity. *Compare* UCC 2-608(2), 2-607(3)(a).

A second set of problems concerns the content of the notice the buyer is to give the seller. Need it state all, part, or none of the defects ascertainable by reasonable inspection as a condition to relying upon them to justify rejection? The Article 2 answer is provided in UCC 2-605.[*]

Article 2A also requires the rejection to take place within a reasonable time and upon seasonable notice. UCC 2A-509(2). A lessee who fails to make an effective rejection has accepted the goods. UCC 2A-515(1)(b). The content of the notice of rejection in a lease is governed by UCC 2A-514.

In *Bead Chain Manufacturing Co. v. Saxton Products, Inc.*, 439 A.2d 314 (Conn. 1981) the Supreme Court of Connecticut, (Ellen Peters, J.), remarked that the "consequence of an ineffective rejection is that the buyer is held to have accepted the goods, * * * and thereafter becomes liable for their purchase price. * * *" 439 A.2d at 318, n.2. On the other hand, in *Integrated Circuits Unlimited v. E.F. Johnson Co.*, 875 F.2d 1040 (2ⁿᵈ Cir. 1989), the court held that a rejection which was "wrongful" under UCC 2-601 but effective under UCC 2-602(1) and 2-605 was not an acceptance under UCC 2-606. The seller could recover damages for wrongful rejection but not the price.

---

[*] The pre-UCC cases are collected and analyzed in Lawrence R. Eno, *Price Movement and Unstated Objections to the Defective Performance of Sales Contracts,* 44 YALE L.J. 782 (1935).

The combination of the concepts of a "rightful or wrongful" rejection and an "effective or ineffective" rejection provides for four possible outcomes:

1. the buyer's rejection is rightful and effective,
2. the buyer's rejection is rightful but ineffective,
3. the buyer's rejection is wrongful but effective, or
4. the buyer's rejection is wrongful and ineffective.

Determine the consequences of each circumstance on the following two questions: (i) has the buyer accepted the goods and (ii) who has breached the contract.

Problem 6-8

Suppose the seller tenders goods at the time specified in the contract. Upon inspection, the buyer finds what she considers to be two defects. Accordingly, she promptly notifies the seller of rejection, thus satisfying UCC 2-602(1). However, the notice of rejection specified only one defect and this later turns out to be an insufficient ground for rejection. The unstated objection, while present in fact, could have been cured by the seller under UCC 2-508(2). Seller takes the goods back and sues the buyer for breach. Who wins?

3. What Constitutes Acceptance of the Goods

So far, we have focused on the right to inspect and the remedy of rejection when defects in the tender of delivery are actually discovered. Through both inspection and rejection the buyer or lessee seeks to avoid accepting products that do not conform to the contract requirements. Now we will be concerned with two additional but related questions. First, exactly when does a buyer or lessee accept the goods? UCC 2-606, 2A-515. Second, what is the legal effect of an acceptance? This is particularly important when the goods as accepted are actually non-conforming. *See* UCC 2-510(1), 2-607, 2A-516. In a later section, we will discuss when the buyer or lessee may "revoke" his acceptance and what is the effect of a proper revocation of acceptance. UCC 2-608, 2A-517. Regardless of how the acceptance occurs, a buyer or lessee with non-conforming goods on his hands will be in a different and, perhaps, more difficult remedial posture than if the remedy of rejection had properly been invoked. Because the complexity of many products and the casualness of most inspections naturally contribute to a high incidence of acceptance, a thorough appreciation of this "posture" by the commercial lawyer is required.

PLATEQ CORP. OF NORTH HAVEN V. MACHLETT LABORATORIES, INC.
SUPREME COURT OF CONNECTICUT, 1983
189 CONN. 433, 456 A.2D 786

PETERS, JUDGE

In this action by a seller of specially manufactured goods to recover their purchase price from a commercial buyer, the principal issue is whether the buyer accepted the goods before it attempted to cancel the contract of sale. The plaintiff, Plateq Corporation of North Haven, sued the defendant, The Machlett Laboratories, Inc., to recover damages, measured by the contract price and incidental damages, arising out of the defendant's allegedly wrongful cancellation of a written contract for the manufacture and sale of two leadcovered steel tanks and appurtenant stands. The defendant denied liability and counterclaimed for damages. After a full hearing, the trial court found for the plaintiff both on its complaint and on the defendant's counterclaim. The defendant has appealed.

The trial court, in its memorandum of decision, found the following facts. On July 9, 1976, the defendant ordered from the plaintiff two leadcovered steel tanks to be constructed by the plaintiff according to specifications supplied by the defendant. The parties understood that the tanks were designed for the special purpose of testing x-ray tubes and were required to be radiation-proof within certain federal standards. Accordingly, the contract provided that the tanks would be tested for radiation leaks after their installation on the defendant's premises. The plaintiff undertook to correct, at its own cost, any deficiencies that this post-installation test might uncover.[1] The plaintiff had not previously constructed such tanks, nor had the defendant previously designed tanks for this purpose. The contract was amended on August 9, 1976, to add construction of two metal stands to hold the tanks. All the goods were to be delivered to the defendant at the plaintiff's place of business.[2]

Although the plaintiff encountered difficulties both in performing according to the contract specifications and in completing performance within the time required,

---

[1] The contract incorporated precise specifications in the form of detailed drawings. The drawings for the tank and the tank cover contained specific manufacturing instructions as well as provision 6: "Tank with cover will be tested for radiation leaks after installation. Any deficiencies must be corrected by the vendor."

[2] The purchase order sent by the defendant to the plaintiff stipulated that the goods were to be shipped "F.O.B. Origin."

the defendant did no more than call these deficiencies to the plaintiff's attention during various inspections in September and early October, 1976. By October 11, 1976, performance was belatedly but substantially completed. On that date, Albert Yannello, the defendant's engineer, noted some remaining deficiencies which the plaintiff promised to remedy by the next day, so that the goods would then be ready for delivery. Yannello gave no indication to the plaintiff that this arrangement was in any way unsatisfactory to the defendant. Not only did Yannello communicate general acquiescence in the plaintiff's proposed tender but he specifically led the plaintiff to believe that the defendant's truck would pick up the tanks and the stands within a day or two. Instead of sending its truck, the defendant sent a notice of total cancellation which the plaintiff received on October 14, 1976. That notice failed to particularize the grounds upon which cancellation was based.[3]

On this factual basis, the trial court, having concluded that the transaction was a contract for the sale of goods falling within the Uniform Commercial Code, General Statutes §§ 42a-2-101 *et seq.*, considered whether the defendant had accepted the goods. The court determined that the defendant had accepted the tanks, primarily by signifying its willingness to take them despite their nonconformities, in accordance with General Statutes § 42a-2-606(1)(a), and secondarily by failing to make an effective rejection, in accordance with General Statutes § 42a-2-606(1)(b). Once the tanks had been accepted, the defendant could rightfully revoke its acceptance under General Statutes § 42a-2-608 only by showing substantial impairment of their value to the defendant. In part because the defendant's conduct had foreclosed any post-installation inspection, the court concluded that such impairment had not been proved. Since the tanks were not readily resaleable on the open market, the plaintiff was entitled, upon the defendant's wrongful revocation of acceptance, to recover their contract price, minus salvage value, plus interest. General Statutes §§ 42a-2-703; 42a-2-709(1)(b). Accordingly, the trial court awarded the plaintiff damages in the amount of $14,837.92.

In its appeal, the defendant raises four principal claims of error. It maintains that the trial court erred: (1) in invoking the "cure" section, General Statutes § 42a-2-508, when there had been no tender by the plaintiff seller; (2) in concluding, in

---

[3] The defendant sent the plaintiff a telegram stating: "This order is hereby terminated for your breach, in that you have continuously failed to perform according to your commitment in spite of additional time given you to cure your delinquency. We will hold you liable for all damages incured [sic] by Machlett including excess cost of reprocurement."

accordance with the acceptance section, General Statutes § 42a-2-606(1), that the defendant had "signified" to the plaintiff its willingness to take the contract goods; (3) in misconstruing the defendant's statutory and contractual rights of inspection; and (4) in refusing to find that the defendant's letter of cancellation was occasioned by the plaintiff's breach. We find no error.

Upon analysis, all of the defendant's claims of error are variations upon one central theme. The defendant claims that on October 11, when its engineer Yannello conducted the last examination on the plaintiff's premises, the tanks were so incomplete and unsatisfactory that the defendant was rightfully entitled to conclude that the plaintiff would never make a conforming tender. From this scenario, the defendant argues that it was justified in cancelling the contract of sale. It denies that the seller's conduct was sufficient to warrant a finding of tender, or its own conduct sufficient to warrant a finding of acceptance. The difficulty with this argument is that it is inconsistent with the underlying facts found by the trial court. Although the testimony was in dispute, there was evidence of record to support the trial court's findings to the contrary. The defendant cannot sustain its burden of establishing that a trial court's findings of fact are clearly erroneous; * * * by the mere recitation in its brief of conflicting testimony entirely unsupported by reference to pages of the transcript. * * * There is simply no fit between the defendant's claims and the trial court's finding that, by October 11, 1976, performance was in substantial compliance with the terms of the contract. The trial court further found that on that day the defendant was notified that the goods would be ready for tender the following day and that the defendant responded to this notification by promising to send its truck to pick up the tanks in accordance with the contract.

On the trial court's finding of facts, it was warranted in concluding, on two independent grounds, that the defendant had accepted the goods it had ordered from the plaintiff. Under the provisions of the Uniform Commercial Code, General Statutes § 42a-2-606(1) "[a]cceptance of goods occurs when the buyer (a) after a reasonable opportunity to inspect the goods signifies to the seller * * * that he will take * * * them in spite of their nonconformity; or (b) fails to make an effective rejection."[4]

In concluding that the defendant had "signified" to the plaintiff its willingness

---

[4] General Statutes § 42a-2-606(1)(c) provides a third ground, the exercise of dominion, for finding acceptance but that ground was not considered by the trial court, presumably because it has no apparent factual relevance to the circumstances of this case. * * *

to "take" the tanks despite possible remaining minor defects, the trial court necessarily found that the defendant had had a reasonable opportunity to inspect the goods. The defendant does not maintain that its engineer, or the other inspectors on previous visits, had inadequate access to the tanks, or inadequate experience to conduct a reasonable examination. It recognizes that inspection of goods when the buyer undertakes to pick up the goods is ordinarily at the seller's place of tender. *See* General Statutes §§ 42a-2-503, 42a-2-507, 42a-2-513; *see also* WHITE & SUMMERS, UNIFORM COMMERCIAL CODE § 3-5 (2d ed. 1980). The defendant argues, however, that its contract, in providing for inspection for radiation leaks after installation of the tanks at its premises, necessarily postponed its inspection rights to that time. The trial court considered this argument and rejected it, and so do we. It was reasonable, in the context of this contract for the special manufacture of goods with which neither party had had prior experience, to limit this clause to adjustments to take place after tender and acceptance. After acceptance, a buyer may still, in appropriate cases, revoke its acceptance, General Statutes § 42a-2-608, or recover damages for breach of warranty, General Statutes § 42a-2-714. The trial court reasonably concluded that a post-installation test was intended to safeguard these rights of the defendant as well as to afford the plaintiff a final opportunity to make needed adjustments. The court was therefore justified in concluding that there had been an acceptance within § 42a-2-606(1)(a). A buyer may be found to have accepted goods despite their known nonconformity * * * and despite the absence of actual delivery to the buyer. * * *

The trial court's alternate ground for concluding that the tanks had been accepted was the defendant's failure to make an effective rejection. Pursuant to General Statutes § 42a-2-606(1)(b), an acceptance occurs when, after a reasonable opportunity to inspect, a buyer has failed to make "an effective rejection as provided by subsection (1) of section 42a-2-602." The latter subsection, in turn, makes a rejection "ineffective unless the buyer seasonably notifies the seller." General Statutes § 42a-2-605(1)(a) goes on to provide that a buyer is precluded from relying, as a basis for rejection, upon unparticularized defects in his notice of rejection, if the defects were such that, with seasonable notice, the seller could have cured by making a substituted, conforming tender. The defendant does not question the trial court's determination that its telegram of cancellation failed to comply with the requirement of particularization contained in § 42a-2-605(1). Instead, the defendant argues that the plaintiff was not entitled to an opportunity to cure, under General Statutes § 42a-2-508, because the plaintiff had never made a tender of the tanks. That argument founders, however, on the trial court's finding that the seller was ready to make a tender on the day following the last inspection by the defendant's engineer and would have done so but for its receipt of the defendant's telegram of cancellation. The trial court furthermore found that the defendant's unparticularized telegram of cancellation wrongfully interfered with the plaintiff's contractual right to cure any remaining post-installation defects. In these circumstances, the telegram of cancellation constituted both a wrongful and an ineffective rejection on the part of the defendant.* * *

Once the conclusion is reached that the defendant accepted the tanks, its further rights of cancellation under the contract are limited by the governing provisions of the Uniform Commercial Code. "The buyer's acceptance of goods, despite their alleged nonconformity, is a watershed. After acceptance, the buyer must pay for the goods at the contract rate; General Statutes § 42a-2-607(1); and bears the burden of establishing their nonconformity. General Statutes § 42a-2-607(4)." *Stelco Industries, Inc. v. Cohen*, 182 Conn. 561, 563-64, 438 A.2d 759 (1980). After acceptance, the buyer may only avoid liability for the contract price by invoking the provision which permits revocation of acceptance. That provision, General Statutes § 42a-2-608(1), requires proof that the "nonconformity [of the goods] substantially impairs [their] value to him." * * * On this question, which is an issue of fact; * * * the trial court again found against the defendant. Since the defendant has provided no basis for any argument that the trial court was clearly erroneous in finding that the defendant had not met its burden of proof to show that the goods were substantially nonconforming, we can find no error in the conclusion that the defendant's cancellation constituted an unauthorized and hence wrongful revocation of acceptance.

Finally, the defendant in its brief, although not in its statement of the issues presented, challenges the trial court's conclusion about the remedial consequences of its earlier determinations. Although the trial court might have found the plaintiff entitled to recover the contract price because of the defendant's acceptance of the goods; General Statutes §§ 42a-2-703(e) and 42a-2-709(1)(a); the court chose instead to rely on General Statutes § 42a-2-709(1)(b), which permits a price action for contract goods that cannot, after reasonable effort, be resold at a reasonable price.[5] Since the contract goods in this case were concededly specially

---

[5] * * * It should be noted that § 42a-2-709(1)(b) is not premised on a buyer's acceptance. Instead, it requires a showing that the goods were, before the buyer's cancellation, "identified to the contract." In the circumstances of this case, that precondition was presumably met by their special manufacture and by the defendant's acquiescence in their imminent tender. *See*

(continued...)

manufactured for the defendant, the defendant cannot and does not contest the trial court's finding that any effort to resell them on the open market would have been unavailing. In the light of this finding, the defendant can only reiterate its argument, which we have already rejected, that the primary default was that of the plaintiff rather than that of the defendant. The trial court's conclusion to the contrary supports both its award to the plaintiff and its denial of the defendant's counterclaim. There is no error. In this opinion the other Judges concurred.

[Some footnotes omitted. Those retained have been renumbered.]

Notes

1. In *Zabriskie Chevrolet, Inc. v. Smith*, 240 A.2d 195, 201-02 (N.J. Super. 1968), the court had this to say about whether the defendant accepted a new car with a defective transmission:

> It is clear that a buyer does not accept goods until he has had a "reasonable opportunity to inspect." Defendant sought to purchase a new car. He assumed what every new car buyer has a right to assume and, indeed, has been led to assume by the high powered advertising techniques of the auto industry–that his new car, with the exception of very minor adjustments, would be mechanically new and factory-furnished, operate perfectly, and be free of substantial defects. The vehicle delivered to defendant did not measure up to these representations. Plaintiff contends that defendant had "reasonable opportunity to inspect" by the privilege to take the car for a typical "spin around the block" before signing the purchase order. If by this contention plaintiff equates a spin around the block with "reasonable opportunity to inspect," the contention is illusory and unrealistic. To the layman, the complicated mechanisms of today's automobiles are a complete mystery. To have the automobile inspected by someone with sufficient

---

[5] (...continued)

WHITE & SUMMERS, UNIFORM COMMERCIAL CODE, § 7-5 (2d ed. 1980). The defendant has not, on this appeal, argued the absence of identification.

It should further be noted that § 42a-2-709(1)(b), because it is not premised on acceptance, would have afforded the seller the right to recover the contract price even if the trial court had found the conduct of the buyer to be a wrongful rejection (because of the failure to give the seller an opportunity to cure) rather than a wrongful revocation of acceptance.

expertise to disassemble the vehicle in order to discover latent defects before the contract is signed, is assuredly impossible and highly impractical. *Cf. Massari v. Accurate Bushing Co.*, 8 N.J. 299, 313, 85 A.2d 260. Consequently, the first few miles of driving become even more significant to the excited new car buyer. This is the buyer's first reasonable opportunity to enjoy his new vehicle to see if it conforms to what it was represented to be and whether he is getting what he bargained for. How long the buyer may drive the new car under the guise of inspection of new goods is not an issue in the present case. It is clear that defendant discovered the nonconformity within 7/10 of a mile and minutes after leaving plaintiff's showroom. Certainly this was well within the ambit of "reasonable opportunity to inspect." That the vehicle was grievously defective when it left plaintiff's possession is a compelling conclusion, as is the conclusion that in a legal sense defendant never accepted the vehicle. Nor could the dealer under such circumstances require acceptance. *Cf.* Code Comment 2 (subsection 2) to N.J.S. 12A:2-106, N.J.S.A.: "It is in general intended to continue the policy of requiring exact performance by the seller of his obligations as a condition to his right to require acceptance. * * * "

2.   It is not unusual for the buyer to use tendered goods to determine whether they conform to the contract. In short, use is necessary to have a "reasonable opportunity" to inspect them. UCC 2-606(1)(b). The buyer, however, must avoid doing "any act inconsistent with the seller's ownership." UCC 2-606(1)(c). Suppose, for example, that the seller tenders coiled steel and the buyer processes it before discovering the nonconformity. The use and fabrication may both accept the goods, UCC 2-606(1)(c), and preclude revocation because of "substantial change in the condition of the goods." UCC 2-608(2).*

3.   Of the many cases involving UCC 2-606, the bulk involve the question whether the buyer, after having a reasonable opportunity to inspect the goods, has failed to "make an effective rejection," UCC 2-606(1)(b), that is, has failed to reject the goods within "a reasonable time after their delivery of tender." UCC 2-602(1). Like words or conduct indicating that the buyer will take the goods, silence for an

---

* *See Intervale Steel Corp. v. Borg & Beck Div., Borg-Warner Corp.*, 578 F. Supp. 1081 (E.D. Mich. 1984). *But see Alimenta (U.S.A.), Inc. v. Anheuser-Busch Companies, Inc.*, 803 F.2d 1160 (11th Cir. 1986), finding that a use (blanching peanuts) that constituted acceptance did not preclude revocation of acceptance because the value of the goods was not diminished.

unreasonable time induces the seller to believe that there is no problem with the tender of delivery. Whether an acceptance by failing to reject has occurred may turn on several factors, e.g., the nature of the defect (latent or patent), agreement on the time in which notice must be given, express warranties or assurances that problems will be corrected by the buyer, effort or lack of it by the buyer to test or inspect the goods, use of the goods by the buyer after the defect was or should have been discovered, special conditions indicating that prompt action is required, and so forth.* In most cases, the difficulty will be in applying the legal principles to complicated or controverted facts. More may be at stake than simply losing the right to reject. At some point an unreasonable delay in rejecting may foreclose either a subsequent revocation of acceptance, UCC 2-608(2), or any remedy for the non-conformity, UCC 2-607(3)(a).

4. Under UCC 2-607(2), as well as its predecessor, Uniform Sales Act 49, the fact of acceptance does not automatically preclude further remedies even though the buyer had a reasonable opportunity to inspect and the defect was "patent." This is an apparent concession to the assumption that the normal buyer's inspection will be less than adequate to deal with the complexities of defective tenders or products. In short, the buyer will not be deprived of any remedy simply because he should have discovered the particular defect complained of. But if acceptance "precludes rejection of the goods accepted," UCC 2-607(2), and the "buyer must pay at the contract rate for any goods accepted," UCC 2-607(1), what remedies remain for the buyer? The choice is between "revoking" the acceptance under UCC 2-608 or seeking damages "for breach in regard to accepted goods" under UCC 2-714. If revocation of acceptance is available and pursued, the buyer "has the same rights and duties with regard to the goods involved as if he had rejected them." UCC 2-608(3). He may recover so much of the price as has been paid and "cover" under UCC 2-712 or recover damages under UCC 2-713. UCC 2-711. If UCC 2-608 is not invoked or unavailable, the buyer must pay the contract price reduced by the amount of damages caused by the breach, UCC 2-717, and measured under UCC 2-714 and UCC 2-715.

The distinction between "latent" and "patent" defects, however, does appear in the UCC. UCC 2-607(3)(a) provides that where a tender has been accepted "the buyer must within a reasonable time after he discovers or should have discovered any breach notify the seller of breach." As we shall see, this provision has

---

* For an excellent example, *see Intervale Steel Corp. v. Borg & Beck Div., Borg-Warner Corp.*, 578 F. Supp. 1081 (E.D. Mich. 1984).

generated controversy where defects in accepted goods cause damage to person or property. In commercial cases, however, the purpose of notification would seem to be to inform the seller "that the transaction is claimed to involve a breach, and thus [open] the way for normal settlement through negotiation." UCC 2-607, comment 4. Unlike the detail required by UCC 2-605 when goods are rejected, the content of notification under UCC 2-607(3) "need merely be sufficient to let the seller know that the transaction is still troublesome and must be watched." Comment 4. Three main issues arise in the cases: (1) What is a reasonable time for the notice to be given?; (2) What is the required content of the notice?;* and (3) What is the required notice in the non privity situation?** We will return to the question of notice under UCC 2-607 in Chapter Eleven, *infra*.

Problem 6-9

On October 19, Dr. Miron, a physician who owned some race horses, attended an auction without his trainer. He observed a race horse named "Red Carpet" as he was led into the ring for sale. During a lull in the bidding, the auctioneer recited Red Carpet's "track record" and warranted him to be "sound." Thereafter, bidding picked up and Dr. Miron was the high bidder at $32,000. He took immediate possession and transported Red Carpet by van to his barn at a racetrack some 50 miles away. The next morning, Dr. Miron's trainer inspected Red Carpet and found him to be lame. The left hind leg was swollen and sensitive. X-rays later revealed a broken splint bone. Before noon on October 20, Dr. Miron notified the seller that the horse was not sound as warranted and demanded that the horse be taken back. Seller refused and insisted that the full price be paid. You have been retained to represent Dr. Miron. The Seller has agreed to take the horse back if Dr. Miron will pay $20,000. Otherwise, he will sue for the full price under UCC 2-709(1). What would you advise the good doctor to do? After some probing, you have accumulated the following evidence:

(a) X-rays showing a broken splint bone in the left hind leg;

---

* *Compare Cliffstar Corp. v. Elmar Industries Inc.*, 678 N.Y.S.2d 222 (Sup. Ct. App. Div. 1998) (repeated complaints sufficient notice) *with Thomas G. Faria Corp. v. Dama Jewelry Technology Inc.*, 31 UCC Rep. Serv. 2d 115 (D.R.I. 1996) (merchant buyer must inform merchant seller there was a breach, complaints insufficient).

** *See* Harry G. Prince, *Overprotecting the Consumer? Section 2-607(3)(a) Notice of Breach in NonPrivity Contexts*, 66 N.C. L. REV. 107 (1987).

(b) Expert testimony that a broken splint bone renders a race horse unsound and, because the symptoms appear quickly, can be discovered by an inspection;

(c) Dr. Miron's affidavit that he was an inexperienced horse buyer, that he attended the auction without a trainer, that he did not examine the horse before the sale and that he did not inspect the horse's legs before transporting him to the barn;

(d) The testimony of other persons who attended the sale that they had examined Red Carpet before the auction and found no symptoms of a broken splint bone;

(e) Testimony of Dr. Miron's trainer that the problem was found and notice given within 24 hours of the sale. However, no blood tests were taken to determine whether the horse had been drugged at the time of sale.[*]

4. Duties Regarding Rejected Goods

When a buyer or lessee has effectively rejected goods, what duties does she have as to those goods? Read UCC 2-602, 2-603, 2-604, 2A-509, 2A-511, 2A-512. What is the risk the buyer or lessee runs if she takes actions in using, altering, or disposing of the goods?[**] Consider the addition of UCC 2-608(4) in the 2003 amendments. Does that change the analysis? How does the buyer's or lessee's obligations change if she has paid part of the purchase price or rent in advance? *See* UCC 2-711(3), 2A-508(4) [former subs. (5)]. If the buyer or lessee is a merchant, does it change her duties in regard to the goods? Does it make any difference in the buyer's or lessee's obligations regarding the goods if the buyer has wrongfully but effectively rejected the goods? Here is just one illustration of the trouble these sections can give.

BORGES V. MAGIC VALLEY FOODS, INC.
SUPREME COURT OF IDAHO, 1980
101 IDAHO 494, 616 P.2D 273

SHEPARD, J.

This is an appeal from a judgment following a jury verdict which awarded

---

[*] This problem is based on *Miron v. Yonkers Raceway, Inc.*, 400 F.2d 112 (2nd Cir. 1968).

[**] *See* John R. Bates, *Continued Use of Goods After Rejection or Revocation of Acceptance: The UCC Rule Revealed, Reviewed, and Revised*, 25 RUTGERS L.J. 1 (1993).

plaintiffs-respondents Borges and G & B Land and Cattle Company $12,832.00 for potatoes received by defendant-appellant Magic West pursuant to a contract with respondents. We affirm.

In 1975, respondents grew and harvested approximately 45,000 c.w.t. of potatoes, which were stored in a cellar near Buhl, Idaho. Magic West inspected those potatoes and, although their inspection indicated that some contained a "hollow heart" defect, Magic West agreed to purchase them for $3.80 per c.w.t. "Hollow heart" indicates a vacant space in the middle of the potato. The purchase contract provided that "if internal problems develop making these potatoes unfit for fresh pack shipping, this contract becomes null and void." It was agreed that the cost of transporting the potatoes from the storage cellar to the processing plant would be borne by Magic West. Examination of the potatoes by State inspectors would occur at the plant to determine that the number of potatoes affected by the hollow heart defect did not exceed the limit prescribed for shipping under the fresh pack grade.

The potatoes were transported to the processing plant, where more than 30,000 c.w.t. were processed and shipped under the fresh pack grade. In March, 1976, State inspectors declared the remaining 4,838.77 c.w.t. of potatoes unfit for the fresh pack grade because of the increased incidence of hollow heart condition.[1] On March 31, 1976, the parties met to discuss the problem of the remaining potatoes and it was apparently agreed that Magic West should attempt to blend them with other potatoes of a higher grade in the hope that such a blend would meet fresh pack grade standards. That experiment failed and Magic West, without notifying the respondents, processed the remaining 4,838.77 c.w.t. of potatoes into flakes and sold them for $1.25 per c.w.t. The evidence in the record disclosed that the remaining potatoes could not be removed from the processing plant without destroying at least one-third of the potatoes.

Respondents demanded the contract price of $3.80 per c.w.t. for the potatoes sold as flakes. Magic West refused, and instead offered to pay $1.25 per c.w.t. This action resulted. The jury returned a general verdict to the respondents of $12,832.00 and the trial court also awarded $6,975.00 as and for attorney fees and

---

[1] There were also potatoes still in storage which Magic West never paid for due to the hollow heart problems. There is no dispute with regard to those potatoes. Respondents eventually sold them for $3.00 per c.w.t. to be used as french fries. There were also 702 c.w.t. of defective potatoes in transit to the plant on March 31, 1977. The respondents agreed to accept $1.25 per c.w.t. for those potatoes from Magic West.

costs to the respondents.[2]

Magic West's basic contention is that the 4,838.77 c.w.t. of potatoes were clearly defective and that they were never accepted. It is claimed that when Magic West processed the potatoes into flakes and sold them for $1.25 per c.w.t., they were only following respondents' instructions.

The potatoes in the instant case were clearly movable at the time they were identified in the contract, I.C. § 28-2-105, and, hence, were "goods" within the purview of the Idaho Uniform Commercial Code, I.C. §§ 28-2-101 to -2-725, and the dispute is governed by the provisions of the Uniform Commercial Code.

It is clear and undisputed that Magic West had the responsibility of transporting the potatoes from the storage cellar to the processing plant and that State inspection would occur at the plant. It is also clear that the 4,838.77 c.w.t. of potatoes, unable to make the fresh pack grade, did not conform to the contract and gave Magic West the right of rejection. IC § 28-2-601(a). Also, it is not disputed that when Magic West determined that the potatoes would not meet fresh pack grade, Magic West so notified the respondents and met with them to determine what disposition should be made of the potatoes. The record is unclear as to precisely what was decided at that March 31, 1976 meeting, but respondents apparently approved of Magic West's proposal to blend the defective potatoes with those with higher quality in an attempt to meet the fresh pack grade. However, it is clear that no agreement on price was reached at that meeting.

A buyer must pay the contract rate for any goods accepted. I.C. § 28-2-607(1). Generally, a buyer is deemed to have accepted defective goods when, knowing of the defect, he resells the goods without notifying the seller. *See* WHITE & SUMMERS, UNIFORM COMMERCIAL CODE, § 8-2 (2d ed. 1980); 67 Am Jur2d Sales (1973). A buyer accepts goods whenever he does any act inconsistent with the seller's ownership. I.C. § 28-2-606(1)(c). Respondents assert that Magic West's processing of the remaining potatoes into flakes and the subsequent sale constituted acts inconsistent with the respondents' ownership.

Magic West argues, however, that their processing of the potatoes into flakes and their subsequent sale did not constitute an acceptance, but rather was a

---

[2] Both parties agreed that the jury had apparently awarded respondents the full contract price of $3.80 per c.w.t. for the potatoes in dispute. If no deductions were made, a jury award of $3.80 per c.w.t. would have resulted in a jury verdict of $18,387.32 [$3.80 × 4838.77]. Obviously, some deductions were made although they are not apparent from the record and were not explained or challenged by counsel. For purposes of this appeal, we assume, as counsel do, that the jury awarded $3.80 per c.w.t. for the potatoes in dispute.

permissible resale under the provisions of either I.C. § 28-2-603(1) or I.C. § 28-2-604. I.C. § 28-2-603(1) provides:

"Subject to any security interest in the buyer * * *, when the seller has no agent or place of business at the market of rejection a merchant buyer is under a duty after rejection of goods in his possession or control to follow any reasonable instructions received from the seller with respect to the goods and in the absence of such instructions to make reasonable efforts to sell them for the seller's account if they are perishable or threaten to decline in value speedily."

I.C. § 28-2-604 provides:

"Subject to the provisions of the immediately preceding section on perishables if the seller gives no instructions within a reasonable time after notification of rejection the buyer may store the rejected goods for the seller's account or reship them to him or resell them for the seller's account with reimbursement as provided in the preceding section. Such action is not acceptance or conversion."

We note that both I.C. § 28-2-603(1) and I.C. § 28-2-604 were given in their entirety as instructions to the jury. We find it unclear from the record whether the respondents had agents or a place of business at the "market of rejection." Also, the duty to resell under I.C. § 28-2-603(1) is triggered by an absence of instructions from a seller. Here, given the state of the record and its lack of clarity and the conflicting evidence, the jury could have reasonably found that the respondents did instruct Magic West to attempt to blend the potatoes, but did not instruct them to process the potatoes into flakes. While I.C. § 28-2-604 allows a buyer an option to resell rejected goods if the seller gives no instructions within a reasonable time after the notification of rejection, the jury could have reasonably found that respondents' instructions were only to blend the potatoes in hope of accomplishing fresh pack grade and that Magic West's processing of the potatoes into flakes and subsequent resale thereof was a precipitate action taken before the lapse of a reasonable time within which respondents could give further instructions.

In addition, even if a reasonable time had elapsed, thus permitting Magic West to resell the potatoes, the jury properly could have concluded that processing of the potatoes by Magic West was an acceptance rather than a resale. There was no evidence presented either of an attempt to resell the potatoes in the bins to an independent third party, or of the value of the potatoes in the bins, less damage caused by removal, should it have been effected. Absent any evidence that the $1.25 per c.w.t. offered by Magic West was the highest value obtainable for the potatoes, Magic West's use of the potatoes in the ordinary course of its own business (presumably for profit) was an act inconsistent with the seller's ownership, and constituted an acceptance of the goods. I.C. § 28-2-606(1)(c).

The jury was adequately and correctly instructed regarding the provisions of I.C. § 28-2-603(1) and I.C. § 28-2-604, which constituted Magic West's theory of its duty or option of resale because of an absence of instructions from respondents. The jury was at liberty to reject Magic West's theory of defense based on substantial, albeit conflicting, evidence that Magic West's resale of the potatoes after processing them into flakes constituted an acceptance and Magic West was hence liable for the full contract price.

We have examined appellants' remaining assignments of error and find them to be without merit. Affirmed. Costs to respondents.

[Footnotes have been renumbered.]

B. Revocation of Acceptance

Scope and effect. One of the consequences of accepting goods is that the buyer loses the rejection remedy provided in UCC 2-601 or 2-612(2). UCC 2-607(2). He is not necessarily "stuck" with the goods, however, since UCC 2-608 provides a controlled opportunity to "revoke" the acceptance. This is not, however, the same thing as canceling the contract for breach or rescinding the contract. An effective revocation of acceptance neutralizes the effect of acceptance and enables the buyer to cancel the contract and pursue other available remedies under UCC 2-711. *See Welken v. Conley*, 252 N.W.2d 311 (N.D.1977). UCC 2-608(3) provides that a buyer who revokes acceptance "has the same rights and duties with regard to the goods involved as if the buyer had rejected them." These duties include the duties of the bailee imposed by UCC 2-602(2) and the rights and obligations set forth in UCC 2-603 and 2-604.

The buyer who revokes acceptance of the goods under UCC 2-608 could cancel the contract if the seller chooses not to exercise its right to cure. UCC 2-711. A possible strategy, however, is for the buyer to keep the contract intact and negotiate for the repair or replacement of the goods involved. In any event, the buyer who attempts a revocation is required to work with the "weasel" words in UCC 2-608 which must be particularized in each case. Nonetheless, the commercial lawyer should spend some time with this section since the frustrated buyer who is unable to get satisfaction from the seller will be likely to seek advice about what to do with non-conforming goods which have been accepted, are still in his possession and may have been paid for in whole or in part.

Requirements to revoke. There are several questions which must be answered under UCC 2-608.

First, what is the effect of the buyer's discovery or failure to discover the non-conformity at the time of acceptance? In the former case, revocation is possible if the goods were accepted on the "reasonable assumption that its non-conformity would be cured and it has not been seasonably cured." UCC 2-608(1)(a). In the latter case, revocation is possible if acceptance was "reasonably induced either by the difficulty of discovery before acceptance or the seller's assurances." UCC 2-608(1)(b). Revised UCC 2-508 clarifies that the seller has a right to cure under the latter case but not the former. Do you see why?[*]

Second, the non-conformity, to justify revocation, must "substantially impair" the value "to the buyer" of the goods accepted. UCC 2-608(1). What does this mean? An emerging view is that the court must make an objective determination that the value of the goods has been substantially impaired but that the determination must be made from the perspective of the particular buyer. Thus, even though leaks and dry rot in a sloop could have been repaired, the defect occurred in a vital part of the boat and "severely undermined" the buyer's confidence in its integrity as a sailing vessel. Its value was "substantially impaired."[**]

Third, revocation of acceptance "must occur within a reasonable time after the buyer discovers or should have discovered the ground for it. * * * " UCC 2-608(2). What is prompt action and what is an unreasonable delay are questions of fact.

Fourth, the revocation of acceptance, even if otherwise proper, must occur "before any substantial change in condition of the goods which is not caused by their own defects."[***] This puts a premium on quick action where perishable

---

[*] The courts were divided on the issue prior to the revision. Howard Foss, *The Seller's Right to Cure When the Buyer Revokes Acceptance: Erase the Line in the Sand*, 16 S. ILL. U. L.J. 1 (1991).

[**] Former 2-612(2) utilized an objective substantial impairment standard. The 2003 amendments change the standard under UCC 2-612(2) to be in accord with the substantial impairment standard utilized under UCC 2-608.

[***] *Basselen v. General Motors Corp.*, 792 N.E.2d 498 (Ill. Ct. App. 2003) (driving van for an additional 23,000 miles prior to revocation meant car not in substantially same condition
(continued...)

commodities are involved. It also limits the scope of revocation where the goods were components or other items to be used or consumed in a manufacturing process.

Fifth, the revocation is "not effective until the buyer notifies the seller of it." UCC 2-608(2). Is it enough for the buyer to pick up the telephone and say to the seller: "That last delivery was a disaster. We're getting out of this deal?" Apparently not. In *Solar Kinetics Corp. v. Joseph T. Ryerson & Son, Inc.*, 488 F. Supp. 1237 (D. Conn. 1980), the court held that the notice, to be adequate, must inform the seller that the buyer has revoked, which goods are involved and the nature of the defect. *Cf.* UCC 2-607(3). This position is supported by the 2003 amendments to UCC 2-605 which apply the rule of that section to revocations of acceptance when the defect was ascertainable by reasonable inspection.

Finally, the buyer has to take care of the goods as to which the buyer has revoked acceptance. UCC 2-608(3).

What is the effect of a justified and effective revocation of acceptance? What is the effect of a justified but ineffective revocation of acceptance? What is the effect of a purportedly timely but unjustified revocation of acceptance? Does the buyer have to pay for the goods in any of those situations? UCC 2-709.

Effect of use by the buyer of the goods after a rightful and effective rejection or a justified and effective revocation of acceptance. What is the effect of use by the buyer of the goods after a justifiable revocation? Prior to the 2003 amendments, former 2-608 did not provide an answer. Based upon former 2-602(2)(a), it appeared that "any exercise of ownership by the buyer" was "wrongful against the seller" and could be treated as a re-acceptance of the goods under former 2-606(1)(c) or the tort of conversion. A few courts, however, managed to extract a principle of reasonable use from these sections.[*] As a result, a reasonable use is

---

*** (...continued)
and revocation of acceptance barred).

* *Johannsen v. Minnesota Valley Ford Tractor Co.*, 304 N.W.2d 654 (Minn. 1981) (use of tractor for several months was reasonable); *Romy v. Picker International, Inc.*, 1992 WL 70403 (E.D. Pa. 1992), *aff'd*, 986 F.2d 1409 (3rd Cir. 1993) (use of MRI machine by doctor after revocation was reasonable and part of the duty to mitigate damages); *North River Homes, Inc. v. Bosarge*, 594 So. 2d 1153 (Miss. 1992) (use of mobile home for 12 months after revocation justified by seller's assurances of cure and buyer's financial inability to move); *Braden v. Stem*, 571 So. 2d 1116 (Ala. 1990) (buyer's use of used car for seven months after revocation justified because buyer needed the car to transport a child); *Cuesta v. Classic Wheels, Inc.*, 818 A.2d 448 (N.J. App. Div. 2003) (use of the car for two years
(continued...)

not a re-acceptance but the buyer must pay the seller for the value of that use.

This principle is endorsed by the 2003 amendments which added subsection (4) to UCC 2-608. Read that subsection, please. *See also* UCC 2-606. How does a court determine whether a use is reasonable? As indicated in the new comment 8 to the section, the reason that the buyer had to use the goods is critical to determining reasonable use.[*] Another factor that might be important is if the buyer has attempted to reject or revoke acceptance but the seller would not accept a return of the goods. As one pre-revision court put it:

> The reasonableness of the buyer's use of a defective good is a question of fact for the jury that is to be based on the facts and circumstances of each case. Several factors that the jury may consider include the seller's instructions to the buyer after revocation of acceptance; the degree of economic and other hardship that the buyer would suffer if he discontinued using the defective good; the reasonableness of the buyer's use after revocation as a method of mitigating damages; the degree of prejudice to the seller; and whether the seller acted in bad faith.

Johannsen v. Minnesota Valley Ford Tractor Co., 304 N.W.2d 654, 658 (Minn. 1981).

Problem 6-10

Return to the facts of Problem 6-9. Suppose that Dr. Miron could establish that Red Carpet was not sound when the hammer fell.[**] The seller, however, argued that Dr. Miron had accepted the horse and that revocation of acceptance was barred under UCC 2-608(2).

A. How would you respond? Is it easier or harder to satisfy the notice requirements under UCC 2-608(2) than under UCC 2-602(1)?

B. What does Dr. Miron have to say in his revocation attempt in order to have

---

[*] (...continued)
after attempted revocation could be reasonable, remanded for determination).

[*] *See also Wilk Paving, Inc. v. Southworth-Milton, Inc.*, 649 A.2d 778 (Vt. 1994).

[**] Who has the burden of proof in this situation? *Compare* UCC 2-607(4). *See also Keck v. Wacker*, 413 F.Supp. 1377 (E.D. Ky. 1976), another horse case, holding that where an acceptance was revoked the burden was on the seller to show that the horse conformed to the contract. Does this make sense? *See* UCC 2-515.

an effective revocation of acceptance? UCC 2-605.

C. What are Dr. Miron's obligations regarding the horse if he has revoked acceptance of the horse? UCC 2-608(3), 2-602, 2-603, 2-604.

D. What are Dr. Miron's obligations to the seller if the court holds that his attempted revocation notice was timely but not justified?

Privity. Another issue that has arisen in the cases with mixed results is the ability of a buyer to revoke acceptance of the goods due to a manufacturer's breach of warranty. This arises when the dealer who is in privity with the buyer has not made or breached any warranties and the manufacturer who is not in privity with the buyer has breached the warranties resulting in a substantial impairment of the value of the goods to the buyer.* How do the new UCC 2-313A and 2-313B handle this issue?

Article 2A. Under Article 2A, revocation of acceptance parallels the Article 2 provision as to substantial impairment, notice, and rights after revocation. *Compare* UCC 2-608 *with* 2A-517. One notable difference, however, concerns the right to revoke acceptance in a finance lease. Remember that in a non-consumer finance lease, upon acceptance of the goods, the lessee is obligated to pay regardless of conformity of the goods to the lease contract. UCC 2A-407. If the nonconformity of the goods substantially impairs the value to a finance lessee who has accepted the goods, the finance lessee may revoke acceptance only if the acceptance was reasonably induced by the lessor's assurances. In addition a lessee, including a consumer lessee under a finance lease, may revoke acceptance if the lessor defaults and such default substantially impairs the value to the lessee. Of course if the contract so provides, a lessee may have additional rights to revoke acceptance.

C. The Right to Cure

Scope of right. UCC 2-508 and 2A-513 permit the seller or lessor to cure a defective tender and thus avoid the buyer's or lessee's rightful rejection remedy.

---

* For an analysis of the issue, *see* Gary L. Monserud, *Judgment Against a Non-Breaching Seller: The Cost of Outrunning the Law to do Justice Under Section 2-608 of the Uniform Commerical Code*, 70 N.D. L. REV. 809 (1994); *Fode v. Capital RV Center, Inc.*, 575 N.W.2d 682 (N.D. 1998) (allowing revocation in non-privity situation); and *Neal v. SMC Corp.*, 99 S.W.3d 813 (Tex. Ct. App. 2003) (not allowing revocation in non-privity situation).

The 2003 amendments completely revised this section. Under the pre-amended and amended UCC 2-508 and 2A-513, consider the following questions. First, when does the seller or lessor have a right to cure? Why doesn't a seller or lessor in a consumer contract have a right to cure after revocation of acceptance? Second, how does the seller or lessor effect a "good" cure? Third, what is the effect of a "good" cure on the question whether the buyer or lessee has an action for a breach of contract? Fourth, what is the effect of a buyer's or lessee's refusal to allow the seller or lessor to cure when the seller or lessor has a right to do so?

Under the amended UCC 2-508 and 2A-513 (as well as the former provisions), the seller or lessor's right to cure is provided in two circumstances. The first is when the time for performance has not yet expired. UCC 2-508(1) and 2A-513(1). Note that in this situation the seller or lessor has the right to cure whether the buyer or lessee likes it or not. The second circumstance is when the time for performance has expired. UCC 2-508(2) and 2A-513(3). In this circumstance, the right to cure now depends upon whether the cure is "appropriate and timely under the circumstances." The section previously asked whether the seller or lessor "had reasonable grounds to believe" the tender that was in fact non-conforming was acceptable to the buyer. This created issues regarding whether the seller had to know that the tender was non-conforming at the time of tender. The leading case held no. *T. W. Oil, Inc. v. Consolidated Edison Co. of New York, Inc.*, 443 N.E.2d 932 (N.Y. Ct. App. 1982). The new standard focuses on the buyer's or lessee's circumstances to determine whether the seller's or lessor's proffered cure must be accepted.

However, the buyer or lessee may not compel the seller or lessor to cure under any circumstances unless the parties have so agreed. If the buyer or lessee wants a defect corrected by the seller or lessor, the recourse is a negotiated agreement. Otherwise, she must reject and cover under UCC 2-712 or 2A-518.

Of course, the parties may agree to lessor or greater cure obligations than what is provided in the statute. Many manufacturers of complex, expensive goods seek, with the help of retailers, to make a single warranty that the goods are "free from defects in material and workmanship" and to limit the remedy for breach of that warranty to "repair or replacement" of defective parts. If these efforts are successful, the buyer must permit the seller to cure and may not reject the goods under UCC 2-601 or revoke acceptance under UCC 2-608. *See* UCC 2-719.[*] Article 2A would allow the same result. UCC 2A-503. The legal effect of an

---

[*] *Mercury Marine v. Clear River Construction Co.*, 839 So.2d 508 (Miss. 2003).

agreed method of cure is treated in Chapter Twelve, *infra*.

Ability to cancel. Read UCC 2-711 carefully. In a non-installment contract, a buyer who "rightfully rejects" or "justifiably revokes acceptance" may cancel the contract. There is no requirement that the breach "substantially impair" the value of the contract before the buyer may cancel the contract. *Compare* UCC 2-612(3). Nevertheless, if buyer has rightfully rejected or justifiably revoked acceptance and seller has "seasonably" notified buyer of its intention to make a cure permitted by UCC 2-508, buyer's power to cancel should be suspended until seller has a reasonable time to cure.[*] If, however, the proffered cure exceeds the scope of UCC 2-508, then buyer is free to pursue the remedial option granted in UCC 2-711.[**] A lessee has similar rights to cancel, UCC 2A-508.

Cure of nonconforming consumer goods. Assuming a rightful rejection and a "seasonable" notice by seller of an intention to cure, the question remains: What is a "conforming" delivery, UCC 2-508(1), or tender, UCC 2-508(2)? Is it a tender of repaired goods, or new conforming goods or a money allowance? Put differently, should buyer be permitted to cancel and cover if seller tenders repaired rather than new goods? The question has arisen with some frequency in cases involving consumer goods and, in any event, turns on whether the offer to repair will result in goods that conform to the contract. An offer to repair goods which if perfect would still not conform to the contract is not a proper cure.[***]

Two early consumer cases staked out the territory. In *Wilson v. Scampoli*, 228 A.2d 848 (D.C. Ct. App. 1967), the goods were a new color T.V. with a defective picture tube. Seller offered to replace the tube and buyer, insisting on a new T.V., refused. The court held that the right to cure under UCC 2-508 included the making of "minor repairs or reasonable adjustments" and that buyer had deprived seller of an adequate opportunity to determine whether repair or replacement was proper. In *Zabriskie Chevrolet, Inc. v. Smith*, 240 A.2d 195 (N.J. Super. 1968), the goods were a new car with a defective transmission. The court, conceding that UCC 2-508 was unclear and influenced by recent consumer law developments in New Jersey, concluded that seller's offer to cure by replacing the transmission was inadequate.

---

[*] *See Leitchfield Development Corp. v. Clark*, 757 S.W.2d 207 (Ky. Ct. App. 1988).

[**] *See Travelers Indemnity Co. v. Maho Machine Tool Corp.*, 952 F.2d 26 (2nd Cir. 1991) (seller improperly conditioned cure offer on buyer's payment of cost to return rejected goods).

[***] *See Bowen v. Foust*, 925 S.W.2d 211 (Mo. Ct. App. 1996).

The court stated that it "was not the intention of the Legislature that the right to 'cure' is a limitless one to be controlled only by the will of the seller." Rather, the limits of "cure" are defined by the "agreement or contemplation of the parties" and for a "majority of people the purchase of a new car is a major investment, rationalized by the peace of mind that flows from its dependability and safety."

Cure after justifiable revocation of acceptance. The previous version of UCC 2-508 limited cure to cases where the buyer rejected a non-conforming tender of delivery. There was a disagreement over whether the seller had a right to cure after a justifiable revocation of acceptance, especially where the buyer accepted the goods without discovering the non-conformity. UCC 2-608(1)(b). If the buyer discovered the non-conformity at the time of acceptance, however, the revocation was not justified unless the goods were "accepted on the reasonable assumption that its non-conformity would be cured and it has not been seasonably cured." UCC 2-608(1)(a). So the seller had a chance to cure in that latter situation.

Amended UCC 2-508 now explicitly permits the seller to cure a justifiable revocation of acceptance made under UCC 2-608(1)(b) in a non-consumer contract. The buyer's notice of revocation, required under UCC 2-608(2), must now comply with amended UCC 2-605(1): The failure to state a particular defect "in connection with" a justifiable revocation of acceptance may preclude the buyer from relying on that defect "where the seller had a right to cure the defect and could have cured it if stated seasonably." UCC 2-605(1)(a).

Cure after a rightful rejection in an installment contract. The previous version of UCC 2-612(2) permitted rejection of an installment if the "non-conformity substantially impairs the value of that installment and cannot be cured." Comment 5 tried to explain the phrase "cannot be cured" and, in the process, provided guidance that was not found in UCC 2-508 (or anywhere else in Article 2). There was also confusion in the courts. Some thought that UCC 2-508 limited rejections under UCC 2-612(2) and others concluded that it did not, primarily because cure was not needed to temper the rejection right where rejection required substantial impairment of the value of the installment. *See Midwest Mobile Diagnostic Imaging v. Dynamics Corp. of America, supra.*

Amended UCC 2-612(2) deletes the phrase "and cannot be cured." But amended UCC 2-508 expands the scope of cure to include rejections under UCC 2-612 and, presumably, the particularization expected in UCC 2-605(1) also applies to rejections under UCC 2-612.

Problem 6-11

Buyer purchases bolts for its assembly process from Seller. Due to limited storage space at Buyer's plant, Seller has agreed to deliver the bolts "just in time" for use in the Buyer's process. Buyer stores at its plant only 2 to 3 day's worth of bolts. Due to a mix up at the Seller's shipping department, the bolts due to Buyer's plant on Wednesday were not delivered on Wednesday. Buyer called Seller and Seller promised that the bolts would be there no later than the following Monday. Buyer protests because under current production rates, Buyer will not have enough bolts to get through the entire day on Monday. Seller says it will try and get the bolts there more quickly but can not promise that the bolts will be there before the end of the day on Monday. What are Buyer's options at this point? What are the risks of each course of action? What should Buyer do to preserve the most flexibility in making arguments later on if Buyer sues Seller for breach of contract?

Note: "Fundamental Breach" and "Avoidance" of the Contract in International Sales

Professor John Honnold has observed that one of the "thorniest problems" in the law of sales is "when will the breach by one party free the other party of his obligation to perform?" JOHN HONNOLD, UNIFORM LAW FOR INTERNATIONAL SALES, pt. I, Chapter 2, § 27 (Kluwer, 3d ed. 1999). This problem has special significance in international sales "because of the cost of transporting goods to a distant buyer and the difficulty of disposing of rejected goods." *Ibid.*

The CISG deals with problems created by the seller's delay in performance or delivery of non-conforming goods in the following manner. Let us consider only the case of non-conforming goods. Suppose the seller has tendered goods which fail to conform to the contract. The buyer discovers the non-conformity after "examination" of the goods, Article 38, and preserves his rights by giving "notice to the seller specifying the nature of the lack of conformity within a reasonable time after he has discovered it or ought to have discovered it." Article 39(1). What are these "rights"? *See* Art. 45, where a remedial road map is set forth.

First, there is no right to reject the tender. The buyer owes the price but may have several remedial options, including damages for breach of contract, Article 74, and reduction of the price "in the same proportion as the value that the goods actually delivered had at the time of the delivery bears to the value that conforming goods would have had at that time." Art. 50.

Second, under Article 46, the buyer has three remedial options in the nature of specific performance other than trying to avoid or cancel the contract for "fundamental" breach: See Art. 25 on "fundamental breach" and Article 26 on notice.

1. The buyer may "require performance by the seller of his obligations unless the buyer has resorted to a remedy which is inconsistent with this requirement." Art. 46(1).

2. The buyer may "require the delivery of substitute goods * * * if the lack of conformity constitutes a fundamental breach." Art. 46(2). Fundamental breach is defined in Article 25 as a breach that "results in such detriment to the other party as substantially to deprive him of what he is entitled to expect under the contract, unless the party in breach did not foresee and a reasonable person of the same kind in the same circumstances would not have foreseen such a result."

3. The buyer may "require the seller to remedy the lack of conformity by repair, unless this is unreasonable having regard to all the circumstances." Art. 46(3).

Third, the buyer may still try to avoid the contract for fundamental breach. There are two routes to avoidance, direct and indirect. The indirect route is through Article 47(1), which permits the buyer to "fix an additional period of time of reasonable length for performance by the seller of his obligations." [This is called the Nachfrist rule.] In the case of non-delivery of the goods, the buyer may avoid the contract if the seller does not deliver the goods within the additional time period fixed. Art. 49(1)(b). The direct route is through Article 49(1)(a), which permits avoidance "if the failure by the seller to perform any of his obligations under the contract or this Convention amounts to a fundamental breach of contract." *See* Art. 49(2), setting forth further conditions of time and notice.

Fourth, if the contract has not been avoided for fundamental breach under Article 49, the seller has a broad right to cure as stated in Article 37 (cure before delivery) and Article 48 (cure after delivery). *Compare* Article 48 *with* UCC 2-508. Thus, if the buyer discovered a breach after delivery and the contract has not been avoided under Article 49(1), the seller could cure by remedying "at his own expense any failure to perform his obligations, if he can do so without unreasonable delay and without causing the buyer unreasonable inconvenience * * *." Article 48(1).

Finally, if the contract is properly avoided for fundamental breach (but not otherwise), the buyer may recover damages under either Article 75 (cover) or Article 76 (contract price/market price). The effects of avoidance are spelled out in Articles 81-85 and duties to preserve the goods are imposed in Articles 85-88.

Enough has been said to indicate that the CISG has rejected "perfect tender" for rules that tend to preserve the contract for less than a "fundamental" breach and maximize the seller's opportunity to cure. In short, the CISG preserves the contract and fosters adjustments, while protecting the buyer's right to damages for losses caused during the "cure" period. At the same time, one can see that the Convention's solution will not be simple to understand and administer and this problem is complicated by a sometimes murky drafting history. Nevertheless, we believe Professor Honnold's book sheds considerable light on the 1980 Convention and recommend it as the perfect place to start.[*]

Note: Rejection, Acceptance, Revocation of Acceptance, and Cure Under UCITA

For most transactions UCITA 601 adopts the rule that a party is entitled to the other party's performance as long as the performing party has not committed a material breach. For definition of material breach, *see* UCITA 701(c). Thus in most cases, a copy of information may be rejected only upon a material breach. UCITA 704(a). For mass-market transactions that call for tender of a single copy of the information, UCITA adopts the "perfect tender" rule. UCITA 704(b). The rejection of the copy must be made within a reasonable time, upon seasonable notice to the tendering party. UCITA 704(c).

Acceptance of a copy is governed by UCITA 609. Acceptance of the copy does not preclude revocation of acceptance of the copy under UCITA 707. Acceptance of a copy obligates the accepting party for the price and precludes rejection of the copy. UCITA 610. Notice of the breach must be given to preserve remedies. UCITA 610(c), 702(c).

UCITA 703 addresses the right of either party in breach to cure. Subsection (a) follows former 2-508 in allowing for the breaching party to have a right to cure. It is not limited to rejection or revocation of acceptance of a copy of the information. Subsection (b) states an obligation to provide a cure of a non-material breach in delivery of a single copy.

UCITA also addresses performance obligations that do not depend upon the

---

[*] For a comparative view, *see* Catherine Piché, *The Convention on Contracts for the International Sale of Goods and the Uniform Commercial Code Remedies in Light of Remedial Principles Recognized under U.S. Law: Are the Remedies of Granting Additional Time to the Defaulting Parties and of Reduction of Price Fair and Efficient Ones?*, 28 N.C. J. OF INT'L LAW & COMM. REG. 519 (2003).

acceptance/rejection dichotomy. UCITA 603 addresses information provided subject to the satisfaction of a recipient. UCITA 604 addresses information delivery that results in the recipient obtaining the benefit of the performance that cannot be returned. UCITA 613 applies when a dealer is providing a copy of computer information from a publisher to an end user. This section allows the end user to return the copy to the dealer in the event the end user does not manifest assent to the terms of the publisher's license. This is separate from the acceptance and rejection fulcrum discussed above as this right to return is not conditioned on a breach of the contract requirements but is based upon a theory of assent to contract terms in a non-privity situation.

SECTION 3.   TERMINATION

Termination and cancellation of a contract are two terms that are frequently confused. Under Article 2, termination refers to ending a contract for a reason other than breach of a contract. Cancellation, however, is a party putting an end to a contract as a remedy for the other party's breach. UCC 2-106(3) and (4). Article 2A and UCITA use the same terminology. UCC 2A-103(1), UCITA 102(a)(8) and (64). You have already briefly read about cancellation and it will be addressed again in the chapters on remedies for breach.

Three questions must be answered when addressing termination of a contract: (i) When does a party have a right to terminate the contract; (ii) How is termination effected; and (iii) What is the effect of termination?

The starting point for analysis is UCC 2-106(3). That section addresses the first and third questions. UCC 2-309 addresses the first and second questions. *Compare* UCC 2A-505, which provides minimal guidance, *with* UCITA 616 through 618, which provide extensive guidance particularly on the effect and enforcement of a termination. Is there a commercial reason why that degree of specificity is more important in a license of computer information than in a lease or sale of goods?

The CISG has no provision dealing with an agreed termination.

Review *Zapatha v. Dairy Mart, Inc.*, 408 N.E.2d 1370 (Mass. 1980), *supra*, Chapter One. To what extent is the power to terminate a contract under an agreed termination provision limited by the duty of good faith?

SECTION 4.   PUTTING IT ALL TOGETHER

Here are a couple of problems designed to foster a review of the materials we have covered so far in the course.

Problem 6-12

On February 1, 2003, B contracted with S to manufacture a new machine for its plant. The price was $500,000, 25% to be paid at the time of contracting and the balance to be paid 30 days after delivery. B supplied the performance specifications, which required the machine to have the capacity to produce 50 units per hour. S was to deliver, install, and test the machine on or about June 1, 2003.

On June 1, S delivered and installed the machine and gave it a two hour test run. B's purchasing officer, who was present, was impressed (there were no apparent problems) but said she would like "a little more time to see how it works." The 25% down payment was made. By June 14, however, a problem in production per hour was noticed and by June 21 it was clear that the machine, even though operating smoothly, was producing only 40 units per hour. B's engineers searched for the problem, but finally gave up because they could not find it. B continued to use the machine throughout this period, but the purchasing officer was already looking for a different manufacturer.

On July 1, S telephoned to inquire how things were going and to request payment of the balance of the price. B, for the first time, informed S that the machine was not producing 50 units per hour. The same day, B faxed a notice to S stating, in essence, that (1) the machine's production of 40 units per hour did not conform to the contract, (2) B was rejecting the machine and would not pay the price, and (3) S should pick it up immediately.

On July 5, S's engineers appeared at B's plant and asked to inspect the machine. By July 7, S's engineers conceded that there was a problem with the machine that existed at the time it was installed. S offered to repair the machine at its cost and stated that when repaired the machine would be "good as new." B declined the offer, stating that S had no right to "cure" the defect and that B would not pay the balance of the price unless S delivered a new machine. S refused, stating that repair was the best it could do.

On July 10, B contracted with Epoch Manufacturing for a similar machine. The price was $750,000 and delivery was promised for September 1. B continued to use S's machine until September 1, when Epoch's machine was delivered and installed. Epoch's machine works perfectly. S refused to pick up its machine or to give directions to B for disposition. The machine was stored in a separate building on B's property.

On September 20, S sued B and claimed the balance of the price due for goods sold, *see* UCC 2-709(1), plus various incidental damages, UCC 2-710. After a bench trial, the court ruled in favor of S. In a brief opinion, the court stated that, in its opinion, B had no remedy even though the machine admittedly did not conform to the contract at the time of delivery. The court said:

> I'm not a UCC expert (who is?), but it appears to me that B neither rejected the goods nor revoked acceptance in a proper manner. Thus, B accepted the goods and owes the price. Furthermore, any notices that B tried to give S were too little and too late.

A. You represent B and have been asked to develop the best argument(s) to reverse the judgment on appeal. Your client wants a careful analysis of the relevant law that shows the strengths and weaknesses of the case. Please cite and discuss the applicable UCC sections.

B. Your client wants to know whether the analysis or result would change under the 2003 amendments to UCC Article 2. Be specific.

Problem 6-13

You are a district court judge. The following case has just been tried in a bench trial. The following are the facts you have heard.

S, a lumber wholesaler located in Billings, Montana, and B, a lumber yard located in Minneapolis Minnesota, signed a written document that provided as follows:

> S will deliver to B, FOB Billings, 50 pallets of plywood sheets 50"
> by 65" on November 1, 2001. Price is $100 per pallet. Shipment
> will be by rail or truck at discretion of S.

On October 30, 2001, S delivered to Burlington Northern Railyard in Billings, 45 pallets of plywood sheets measuring 50" by 65" for shipment to B in Minneapolis. S obtained a non-negotiable bill of lading from Burlington Northern naming itself as consignee and sent the document to B by Federal Express on November 1, 2001. B received the non-negotiable bill of lading on November 2, 2001.

On November 5, 2001, Burlington Northern notified B that 45 pallets were available for pickup. B went to the railyard and wanted to inspect the plywood before loading it on its trucks. Burlington Northern called S to see if inspection should be allowed. S said no as B had not paid for the goods yet. B argued with S but to no avail. B then loaded the 45 pallets unopened and transported them to its place of business.

Upon opening the pallets on November 6, B discovered the pallets contained 90 sheets of plywood per pallet. B telephoned S to complain that S had not delivered 50 pallets and that each of the 45 pallets delivered were short 10 sheets. S replied that as far as S knows, that in the wholesale trade each pallet always has 90 sheets, not 100. B maintained at trial that B has never heard of such a thing, each pallet it has purchased from other wholesalers always contained 100 sheets.

On November 30, 2001, B sent S a fax stating that B rejected the plywood "due to the shortage in delivery" and requested that S send instructions as to what to do with the plywood. S faxed a reply stating that B had no right to reject, that S would not take the plywood back, and demanded the price for 45 pallets of plywood. B stored the plywood from the 45 pallets in its warehouse for a month and then sold the plywood for $80 per pallet in December. S sued B for the price of the plywood. B denied liability for the price and counterclaimed for damages for breach of contract.

Write the opinion deciding the case.

CHAPTER SEVEN

EXCUSE FROM OR ADJUSTMENT
OF THE CONTRACT
FOR CHANGED CIRCUMSTANCES

SECTION 1.   RELIEF FROM CHANGED CIRCUMSTANCES

The question, "Who bears what risks of changed circumstances in a contract?" is intriguing and eternal. If the "risk events" have been identified in the bargaining process and explicitly allocated in the agreement and if the agreement is otherwise enforceable, *i.e.* not unconscionable or avoidable for fraud, the answer is clear: the particular risk allocation in the contract should prevail. Thus, an agreed fixed price in a contract for sale is said to allocate the risk that, during performance, the market price for similar goods will go up or down.

But suppose there is neither an agreed nor a "tacit" risk allocation, yet the person seeking relief has made an unconditional promise. The seller agrees to deliver the goods by December 1 and the agreement says nothing about the risk that a strike may close the seller's major source of supply. When, if ever, should a court grant some relief from changed circumstances? What form should that relief take?

The UCC provides a starting point for answers in Sections 2-613 through 2-616. *See also* UCC 2A-221 and 2A-404 through 2A-407 in the event the transaction is a lease. Suppose the parties, in response to changed circumstances, agree to modify or adjust the contract. When should a court enforce an agreed adjustment? The starting point here is UCC 2-209. *See also* UCC 2A-208.

These problems have arisen with distressing frequency in the topsy-turvy economy of the last 40 years. We will take a brief look at some of them here.*

---

* For background, *see* John Elofson, *The Dilemma of Changed Circumstances in Contract Law: An Economic Analysis of the Foreseeability and Risk Bearer Tests*, 30 COLUM. J. OF L. & SOC. PROB. 1 (1996); Steven Walt, *Expectations, Loss Distribution and Commercial Impracticability*, 24 IND. L. REV. 65 (1990); John D. Wladis, *Impracticability as Risk Allocation: The Effect of Changed Circumstances Upon Contract Obligations for the Sale of Goods*, 22 GA. L. REV. 503 (1988). For an analysis of the law's treatment of frustration of contractual purpose as opposed to impracticability *see* Nicholas R. Weiskop, *Frustration of Contractual Purpose--Doctrine or Myth?*, 70 ST. JOHN'S L. REV. 239 (1996).

A. Loss of Identified Goods

Read UCC 2-613 and 2A-221. When do these sections excuse the seller's or lessor's performance obligation? What are the buyer's or lessee's options when the seller or lessor asserts excuse under these sections?

Problem 7-1

S, an art dealer, owned an etching by Picasso. B, a collector, examined it at S's gallery and, after negotiations, S agreed to sell it to B for $75,000. Under the written contract for sale, B was to return with a cashier's check the next day and pick up the etching. B returned check in hand but, alas, the Picasso was destroyed by fire during the night.

A. What are the rights and duties of the parties? *See* UCC 2-613 and 2-509. Would it matter what caused the fire? Suppose the fire was caused by a neglected coffee pot, a short in the wiring, or a lightening strike? *See* UCC 2-613, cmt. 1.

B. Suppose, instead, that the Picasso, unknown to S, had been stolen and was replevied from S by the true owner prior to B's return rather than destroyed by fire? Any difference in analysis?

C. Would it make any difference if this was a lease transaction? *See* UCC 2A-221 and 2A-219. An international sale? *See* CISG Art. 79(1).

D. Assume that S had agreed to sell to B print #10 from a series. After the agreement was made, print #10 was damaged by water. S has in its possession print #12, undamaged, from the same series. Is S excused from delivery?

E. In any case in which S would be able to be excused under UCC 2-613 or 2A-221, what are B's options?

B. Failure of Delivery or Payment Mechanisms

Read UCC 2-614 and 2A-404. These provisions operate as both an excuse from exact performance of the contract and as a requirement to accept substituted performance in some circumstances.

Problem 7-2

A. On March 1, Seller agreed to sell a specialized MRI machine to Buyer, a private hospital. Seller agreed to ship the MRI by UPX, a carrier, by October 1, and Buyer agreed to pay the $25,000 price by a letter of credit issued by Pristine Bank. On September 15, Buyer learned that it could purchase a better MRI from another person for $20,000. Shortly thereafter, UPX went on strike and could not deliver Seller's MRI and Pristine Bank declared bankruptcy and could not issue the letter of credit.

    1. Buyer claims that it is excused from the contract. Do you agree? What happens next?

    2. Assume this was a lease transaction. Any difference in analysis?

B. Suppose that in 1990, S and B entered into a twenty year supply contract under which S was to deliver an agreed quantity of goods each year to B in Germany and B was to pay an agreed price in Marks. Subsequently, the European Union decided to displace the currency of its members with one currency, the Euro. The effective date of the total displacement was January 1, 2002. B is unhappy with the contract and wonders whether the displacement will provide grounds for excuse.

    1. B argues that an act of government has made performance as agreed impracticable, if not impossible. Do you agree? *See* UCC 2-614(2), 2-615(a). *Compare* Article 79 of the CISG.

    2. Any difference in analysis if this was a lease transaction? UCC 2A-404, 2A-405(a).

C. The Basic Assumption Test: Force Majeure Events

Read UCC 2-615 and 2A-405. Identify what a seller or lessor must demonstrate to be excused from its performance obligation under these sections. How do the principles embodied in these sections differ from the principles we have looked at in UCC 2-613, 2-614, 2A-221 and 2A-404? If the seller or lessor is excused, what must it do to take advantage of the excuse? What are the options of the buyer or lessee when the seller or lessor claims excuse under these sections? Read UCC 2-616 and 2A-406.

WICKLIFFE FARMS, INC. V. OWENSBORO GRAIN CO.
COURT OF APPEALS OF KENTUCKY, 1984
684 S.W.2D 17

DUNN, JUDGE

This is an appeal from a summary judgment in favor of appellee, Owensboro Grain Company, entered in the Daviess Circuit Court September 9, 1982, as amended September 29, 1982. The action arises out of a contract to sell No. 2 white corn and the defense of impossibility of performance resulting from a drought.

The appellant, Wickliffe Farms, Inc., in business since 1971, farms several contiguous farms in Muhlenberg County. Of the approximate 1980 acres it farms, the corporation owns about 250 acres, Reynolds Wickliffe, its president and principal shareholder, owns about 1000 acres, and Reynolds' father's estate, the J.W. Wickliffe Estate, owns 730 acres.

The Corporation had done business with the appellee, Owensboro Grain, since 1975, primarily thru Reynolds Wickliffe, representing the corporation, and Julian G. "Sonny" Hayden, employed by Owensboro Grain as a grain merchandiser.

In February, 1980, Wickliffe contacted Hayden by telephone and they orally agreed that the corporation would deliver 35,000 bushels of No. 2 white corn at $3.70 per bushel to Owensboro Grain between December 15, 1980, and January 31, 1981. The agreement was confirmed in a writing executed by Owensboro Grain and signed by Wickliffe on behalf of the corporation. The agreement, prepared by Owensboro Grain, was on its standard "fill in the blanks" form as to quantity, the grain commodity, the price, the routing, and shipment date. It was dated February 29, 1980, and identified the corporation as the accepting party. It contained no additional language of any significance other than the following part of a small print "force majeure" clause unilaterally favoring Owensboro Grain:

> All agreements, undertakings, obligations or liabilities hereunder, made or to be kept and performed by Owensboro Grain Company, are made and shall be kept and performed subject to and contingent upon strikes, embargoes, fires, accidents, war restrictions, acts of God, or other conditions over which Owensboro Grain Company has no control and any inability on its part to keep, perform or satisfy the agreements, undertakings, obligations or liabilities hereunder caused or brought about by reason of any of the foregoing conditions shall, at the option of Owensboro Grain Company, render this contract null and void and the parties hereto shall have no further rights or obligations hereunder * * *.

Owensboro Grain's principal business is dealing in the Chicago Board of Trade market area by purchasing grain for future delivery and by arranging an immediate sale of it to consumers or exporters at a margin of profit the market will competitively allow. In reference to his employer's business generally and to the instant transaction specifically, Hayden testified: " * * * my orders from the stockholders are to buy it, sell it, or hedge it. In this case you have to sell it because you can't hedge it."

In keeping with this practice, immediately after the contract was executed for Wickliffe to deliver the No. 2 white corn in the future, Owensboro Grain sold the 35,000 bushels, along with white corn similarly purchased from other farmers, to C.B. Fox, an exporter, at a price that guaranteed a 20 to 25 cent profit.

Unfortunately, in the summer of 1980, Muhlenburg County, together with the rest of western Kentucky, suffered a severe drought. Wickliffe's No. 2 white corn crop was severely damaged as were the crops of the other farmers in the area. Consequently, Wickliffe was unable to produce sufficient No. 2 white corn to fulfill its contract. In January, 1981, it delivered its entire crop, 18,718.57 bushels, to Owensboro Grain and was paid the agreed amount of $3.70 per bushel.

As a result of the short delivery, Owensboro Grain was required to purchase the amount of the shortage at $5.54 per bushel, the then market price, to satisfy its obligation to C.B. Fox entered into as a result of its futures contract with Wickliffe. The total amount spent to make up the bushels' deficit was $29,306.57. This amount was not withheld as a "set off" when it paid Wickliffe for the corn it managed to deliver, but $19,157.07 was withheld from amounts owed Wickliffe for purchase of corn and soybeans in January and February, 1982, by Owensboro Grain.

Wickliffe sued Owensboro Grain in the Daviess Circuit Court for the amount of the sale of the corn and soybeans. Owensboro Grain counterclaimed for its loss resulting from the partial non-delivery of No. 2 white corn in 1981. The trial court entered summary judgment in favor of Owensboro Grain on its counterclaim, later amended to include interest.

On appeal, as well as in the trial court, Wickliffe primarily relies on the defense of impossibility of performance caused by the severe drought, a "force majeure." We agree with the trial court that this defense is not applicable since the contract did not specify the land on which the corn was to be grown. Hence, we affirm.

There is no disagreement that the provisions of § 2-615 of the Uniform Commercial Code (U.C.C.) (1978), adopted as KRS 355.2-615, address the issue before us; also, there is no disagreement that there is no Kentucky law interpreting KRS 355.2-615, particularly with reference to U.C.C. § 2-615 comment 9 (1978), which in pertinent part is as follows:

> The case of a farmer who has contracted to sell crops *to be grown on designated land* may be regarded as falling within * * * this section, and he may be excused, when there is a failure of the specific crop. * * *

We have carefully considered Wickliffe's argument that the contract was one-sided or unconscionable because it contained no specific "force majeure" clause in its favor as it did in favor of Owensboro Grain and conclude the argument is without merit. We reach a like conclusion on Wickliffe's position that an "adhesion contract" resulted from the "fill in the blanks" form of the contract.

Wickliffe's principal argument is that the defense of impossibility provided by KRS 355.2-615 should be available to it due to the fact that it was contemplated by both parties that the No. 2 white corn was to be grown on its 2000 contiguous acres in Muhlenburg County and, that the adverse weather of the 1980 summer was a condition that was unforeseen and unforeseeable by the parties, and which rendered Wickliffe's performance impossible, and, pursuant to the statute, thereby excused his obligation to fully perform.

Nowhere in the contract, however, is there any reference to any specific acreage upon which the crop was to be grown. Wickliffe urges that KRS 355.2-202 [UCC 2-202] permits contradiction of the written terms of the parties' intention by admission of proof of a contemporaneous oral agreement. * * * This argument ignores the fact that to be admissible, the proof must come within the provisions of subparagraph (b) of the statute that requires the parol evidence be of additional terms consistent with the written contract. Here there is no consistency between Wickliffe's claim that the corn was to be produced off a particular part of a 2000 acre farm and a contract providing for nothing other than buying and selling 35,000 bushels of No. 2 white corn. There was no proof before the trial court, parol or otherwise, offered or proffered by Wickliffe, to establish that both parties contemplated and agreed upon a contract to sell the corn from any particularly designated acreage.

The undisputed admissible material facts before the trial court prove the ordinary "futures contract" of an agreement to buy and sell a quantity of grain at a given price per bushel, to be delivered at a future date, the purchaser thereafter arranging a "back to back" sale of the commodity. The sellers in such a transaction gamble the market price will not be greater at the time of delivery and the buyers gamble that it will not be lower. All Owensboro Grain was interested in was buying 35,000 bushels of No. 2 white corn from Wickliffe at $3.70 per bushel and nothing more. Its business was not to speculate either in the weather, crop yield or fluctuation of market price. It guaranteed its profit by selling immediately. Wickliffe's only interest was to sell it. It chose to contract to deliver the corn at a given price at a given future date and failed to do so.

* * * [T]he trial court committed no error in granting summary judgment on Owensboro Grain's counterclaims. * * *

Notes

1.   Why didn't the court analyze the case under UCC 2-613? *See* UCC 2-501. Assume the corn was planted at the time the contract for sale was made. Now is it a case for analysis under UCC 2-~~613~~?

2.   Why must the seller prove an agreement to sell the corn from designated acres? How is that relevant to the test under UCC 2-615? For example, in *Alimenta (U.S.A.), Inc. v. Gibbs Nathaniel (Canada) Ltd.*, 802 F.2d 1362 (11th Cir. 1986), a dealer in, rather than a grower of, peanuts was granted relief under UCC 2-615(a) when a drought hit the regional growing areas. The expected peanut crop was reduced by 35%. The court, among other things, held that the seller's failure to insist upon a clause relieving it from the risk of drought did not mean that it assumed, as a matter of law, a "greater obligation" by agreement under UCC 2-615(a).[*]

3.   **Adjustment after excuse.** If excuse is granted under UCC 2-613, the contract is terminated if the "loss is total." UCC 2-613(a), *compare* UCC 2A-221(a). If the loss is partial or the goods no longer conform to the contract, the buyer is given a statutory option either to terminate the contract or to accept the goods with a price adjustment. UCC 2-613(b), *compare* UCC 2A-221(b).

Under UCC 2-615, the adjustment process is more complicated. If delay or non-delivery of the entire performance is excused under UCC 2-615(a), the seller must give the buyer seasonable notification, UCC 2-615(c). The buyer then has the options set forth in UCC 2-616(1), including the right to "terminate and thereby discharge any unexecuted portion of the contract." *Compare* UCC 2A-405 and 2A-406.

In excused cases of delay or non-delivery in "part," however, the seller "must allocate production and deliveries among its customers but may at its option include

---

[*] *See also Alimenta (U.S.A.), Inc. v. Cargill, Inc.*, 861 F.2d 650 (11th Cir. 1988), where on similar facts the court granted relief under UCC 2-615(a) and excluded evidence of the size and financial responsibility of the seller. This evidence was irrelevant to the statutory question under UCC 2-615(a) whether "performance as agreed" was made impracticable by the drought. *But see Clark v. Wallace County Cooperative Equity Exchange*, 986 P.2d 391 (Kan. Ct. App. 1999) (contract must identify specified tract of land); *ConAgra, Inc. v. Bartlett Partnership*, 540 N.W.2d 333 (Neb. 1995) (contract must require corn to be grown on designated land). *See* David C. Bugg, *Crop Destruction and Forward Grain Contracts: Why Don't Sections 2-613 and 2-615 of the UCC Provide More Relief?*, 12 HAMLINE L. REV. 669 (1989).

regular customers not then under contract as well as its own requirements for further manufacture" and this may be done in "any manner which is fair and reasonable." UCC 2-615(b). Note that the seller must now notify the buyer of the delay and the "estimated quota * * * made available for the buyer," UCC 2-615(c). *Compare* UCC 2A-405.

The buyer's option under UCC 2-616(1) with regard to an allocation "justified" under UCC 2-615(b) is either to terminate the contract or to "modify the contract by agreeing to take the buyer's available quota in substitution." *But see* UCC 2-616(2), imposing a duty on the buyer to act "within a reasonable time not exceeding thirty days." A seller who fails to allocate deliveries in a fair and reasonable manner cannot assert the defense of commercial impracticability under UCC 2-615.[*] A buyer who fails to exercise the statutory options within a reasonable time loses the opportunity to preserve an adjusted contract for future performance. *See* UCC 2-616(2).[**] *Compare* UCC 2A-405 and 2A-406.

SPECIALTY TIRES OF AMERICA, INC. V. THE CIT GROUP/EQUIPMENT FINANCING, INC.
UNITED STATES DISTRICT COURT, W.D. PENNSYLVANIA, 2000
82 F. SUPP.2D 434

D. BROOKS SMITH, DISTRICT JUDGE

[Specialty sued CIT for breach of contract arising out CIT's failure to deliver eleven tire presses that it had previously contracted to sell to Specialty. CIT, in turn, has filed a third-party complaint against Condere Corporation arising out of the latter's alleged wrongful refusal to permit those presses to be removed from its factory. Specialty moved for partial summary judgment while CIT moved for full summary judgment on the ground that its performance was excused under the doctrine of impossibility or commercial impracticability. The court granted CIT's motion based on impossibility and denied all other motions as moot.] * * *

I.

The material facts of this case are simple and undisputed. In December 1993, CIT, a major equipment leasing company, entered into a sale/leaseback with

---

[*] *Roth Steel Products v. Sharon Steel Corp.*, 705 F.2d 134 (6th Cir. 1983).

[**] *Federal Pants, Inc. v. Stocking*, 762 F.2d 561 (7th Cir. 1985) (contract lapses with respect to any deliveries affected).

Condere for eleven tire presses located at Condere's tire plant in Natchez, Mississippi, under which CIT purchased the presses from Condere and leased them back to it for a term of years. CIT retained title to the presses, as well as the right to possession in the event of a default by Condere. In May 1997, Condere ceased making the required lease payments and filed for Chapter 11 bankruptcy in the Southern District of Mississippi. In September 1997, Condere rejected the executory portion of the lease agreement, and the bankruptcy court lifted the automatic stay as to CIT's claim involving the presses.

CIT thus found itself, unexpectedly, with eleven tire presses it needed to sell. Maurice "Maury" Taylor, a former minor candidate for President of the United States and the CEO of Condere and Titan International, stated his desire that the presses be removed quickly and advised CIT on how they might be sold. Later, CIT brought two potential buyers to Condere's Natchez plant, where representatives of Condere conducted them on a tour of the facility. Subsequently, Taylor and CIT negotiated concerning Condere's purchase of the presses, but negotiations fell through, after which Taylor again offered his assistance in locating another buyer.

When no buyer was found, CIT decided to advertise the presses. Specialty, a manufacturer of tires which sought to expand its plant in Tennessee, responded, and in early December 1997, representatives of Specialty, CIT and Condere met to conduct an on-site inspection of the equipment. Condere's representative discussed with CIT's personnel and in the presence of Specialty's agents the logistics concerning the removal of the presses. At that meeting, Condere's representative told CIT and Specialty that CIT had an immediate right to possession of the tire presses, and the right to sell them. At no time did any representative of Condere, whether by words or conduct, express any intent to oppose the removal of this equipment. * * * The negotiations proved fruitful, and, in late December 1997, CIT and Specialty entered into a contract for the sale of the presses for $250,000. CIT warranted its title to and right to sell the presses.

Events then took a turn which led to this lawsuit. When CIT attempted to gain access to the presses to have them rigged and shipped to Specialty, Condere refused to allow this equipment to be removed from the plant. This refusal was apparently because Condere had just tendered a check to CIT for $224,000, without the approval of the bankruptcy court, in an attempt to cure its default under the lease. * * * This unexpected change in position was rejected by CIT, which promptly filed a complaint in replevin in the Southern District of Mississippi to obtain possession. Condere then posted a bond and the replevin court removed the action from the expedited list, scheduling a case management conference for April 1998.

It became clear at that juncture that Specialty was not going to obtain its tire presses expeditiously.

[The court reviewed the status of the property in bankruptcy and noted that although Specialty demanded performance of the contract it might accept a late delivery in partial settlement of its claims. The court then stated the standards for granting summary judgment motions.] * * *

III.

In the overwhelming majority of circumstances, contractual promises are to be performed, not avoided: *pacta sunt servanda*, or, as the Seventh Circuit loosely translated it, "a deal's a deal." *Waukesha Foundry, Inc. v. Industrial Engineering, Inc.*, 91 F.3d 1002, 1010 (7th Cir. 1996) (citation omitted); *see generally* JOHN D. CALAMARI & JOSEPH M. PERILLO, THE LAW OF CONTRACTS § 13.1, at 495 (4th ed. 1998). This is an eminently sound doctrine, because typically

> a court cannot improve matters by intervention after the fact. It can only destabilize the institution of contract, increase risk, and make parties worse off.* * * Parties to contracts are entitled to seek, and retain, personal advantage; striving for that advantage is the source of much economic progress. Contract law does not require parties to be fair, or kind, or reasonable, or to share gains or losses equally.

Industrial Representatives, Inc. v. CP Clare Corp., 74 F.3d 128, 131-32 (7th Cir. 1996) (Easterbrook, J.). Promisors are free to assume risks, even huge ones, and promisees are entitled to rely on those voluntary assumptions. CALAMARI & PERILLO, *supra* § 13.16, at 522. Futures contracts, as just one example, are so aleatory that risk-bearing is their sole purpose, yet they are fully enforceable. * * *

Even so, courts have recognized, in an evolving line of cases from the common law down to the present, that there are limited instances in which unexpectedly and radically changed conditions render the judicial enforcement of certain promises of little or no utility. This has come to be known, for our purposes, as the doctrines of impossibility and impracticability.[1] Because of the unexpected nature of such occurrences, litigated cases usually involve, not interpretation of a contractual term, but the judicial filling of a lacuna in the parties agreement. *See* 2 E. ALLAN

---

[1] The reported cases on this topic, unfortunately, are not characterized by either consistency or clarity of expression. As one respected treatise puts it, "Students who have concluded a first year contracts course in confusion about the doctrine of impossibility and have since * * * found that the cases somehow slip through their fingers when they try to apply them to new situations[ ] may take some comfort in knowing that they are in good company." 1 WHITE & SUMMERS, *supra* § 3-10, at 164.

FARNSWORTH, FARNSWORTH ON CONTRACTS § 9.5, at 603 (2d ed.1998); 1 JAMES J. WHITE & ROBERT S. SUMMERS, UNIFORM COMMERCIAL CODE § 3-10, at 169 (4th ed. 1995). Such "gap- filling," however, must be understood for what it is: a court-ordered, as opposed to bargained-for, allocation of risk between the parties.* * *

Traditionally, there were three kinds of supervening events that would provide a legally cognizable excuse for failing to perform: death of the promisor (if the performance was personal), illegality of the performance, and destruction of the subject matter; beyond that the doctrine has grown to recognize that

> relief is most justified if unexpected events inflict a loss on one party and provide a windfall gain for the other or where the excuse would save one party from an unexpected loss while leaving the other party in a position no worse than it would have without the contract.[2]

CALAMARI & PERILLO, *supra* § 13.1, at 496; *see also* 2 FARNSWORTH, *supra* § 9.6, at 612. Thus, the SECOND RESTATEMENT OF CONTRACTS expresses the doctrine of impracticability this way:

> Where, after a contract is made, a party's performance is made impracticable without his fault by the occurrence of an event the non-occurrence of which was a basic assumption on which the contract was made, his duty to render that performance is discharged, unless the language or the circumstances indicate the contrary.

RESTATEMENT (SECOND) OF CONTRACTS § 261 (1981). Article 2 of the U.C.C., which applies to the sale of goods presented by the case *sub judice*, puts it similarly:

> Delay in delivery or non-delivery in whole or in part by a seller * * * is not a breach of his duty under a contract for sale if performance as agreed has been made impracticable by the occurrence of a contingency the non-occurrence of which was a basic assumption on which the contract was made.* * *

U.C.C. § 2-615(1) (codified at 13 Pa.C.S. 2615(1)).

The principal inquiry in an impracticability analysis, then, is whether there was a contingency the non-occurrence of which was a basic assumption underlying the contract. It is often said that this question turns on whether the contingency was "foreseeable," 2 FARNSWORTH, *supra* § 9.6, at 616, on the rationale that if it was,

---

[2] The second of these two grounds is what economists deem a "Pareto-optimal" move; that is, an adjustment that makes some parties better off and none worse off than they were initially. For an economic analysis of the law of impossibility, *see* HON. RICHARD A. POSNER, ECONOMIC ANALYSIS OF LAW § 4.5 (5th ed. 1998).

the promisor could have sought to negotiate explicit contractual protection * * *.[3] This, however, is an incomplete and sometimes misleading test. Anyone can foresee, in some general sense, a whole variety of potential calamities, but that does not mean that he or she will deem them worth bargaining over. *See* CALAMARI & PERILLO, *supra* § 13.18, at 526; MURRAY, *supra*, § 112, at 641 ("If 'foreseeable' is equated with 'conceivable', nothing is unforeseeable"). The risk may be too remote, the party may not have sufficient bargaining power, or neither party may have any superior ability to avoid the harm. 2 FARNSWORTH, *supra*, § 9.6, at 617. As my late colleague Judge Teitelbaum recited two decades ago in a famous case of impracticability:

> Foreseeability or even recognition of a risk does not necessarily prove its allocation. Parties to a contract are not always able to provide for all the possibilities of which they are aware, sometimes because they cannot agree, often because they are too busy. Moreover, that some abnormal risk was contemplated is probative but does not necessarily establish an allocation of the risk of the contingency which actually occurs.

Aluminum Co. of Am. v. Essex Group, Inc., 499 F. Supp. 53, 76 (W.D. Pa. 1980) (applying Indiana law) (quoting *Transatlantic Financing Corp. v. United States*, 363 F.2d 312 (D.C. Cir. 1966) (Skelly Wright, J.)) (internal ellipses omitted); *accord Opera Co. v. Wolf Trap Found.*, 817 F.2d 1094, 1101 (4th Cir. 1987) (also quoting *Transatlantic*). So, while the risk of an unforeseeable event can safely be deemed not to have been assumed by the promisor, the converse is not necessarily true. *See* RESTATEMENT (SECOND) OF CONTRACTS § 261 cmt. c. Properly seen, then, foreseeability, while perhaps the most important factor,

> is at best one fact to be considered in resolving first how likely the occurrence of the event in question was and, second, whether its occurrence, based on past experience, was of such reasonable likelihood that the obligor should not merely foresee the risk but, because of the degree of its likelihood, the obligor should have guarded against it or provided for non-liability against the risk.

Wolf Trap, 817 F.2d at 1102-03 (quoted in FARNSWORTH, *supra* § 9.6, at 617-18).[4]

---

[3] Indeed, this rationale can be traced down to the root of the impossibility doctrine at common law as expressed by *Paradine v. Jane, Aleyn 26*, 82 ENG. REP. 897 [1647]. *See* MURRAY, *supra* § 112, at 634.

[4] Another respected text defines the unforeseeable as "an event so unlikely to occur that
(continued...)

It is also commonly said that the standard of impossibility is objective rather than subjective-that the question is whether the thing can be done, not whether the promisor can do it. 2 FARNSWORTH, *supra* § 9.6, at 619. This too is more truism than test, although Pennsylvania courts have couched their decisions in this rhetoric* * *. Indeed, the FIRST RESTATEMENT took such an approach, *see* CALAMARI & PERILLO, *supra* § 13.15, at 521, but the SECOND simply applies "the rationale * * * that a party generally assumes the risk of his own inability to perform his duty."* * * This holds particularly when the duty is merely to pay money* * * It is therefore "preferable to say that such ['subjective'] risks as these are generally considered to be sufficiently within the control of one party that they are assumed by that party." 2 FARNSWORTH, *supra* § 9.6, at 619-20. It is, of course, essential that the impossibility asserted by the promisor as a defense not have been caused by the promisor. *Id.* § 9.6, at 613-14 * * *.

Generally speaking, while loss, destruction or a major price increase of fungible goods will not excuse the seller's duty to perform, the rule is different when the goods are unique, have been identified to the contract or are to be produced from a specific, agreed-upon source. In such a case, the nonexistence or unavailability of a specific thing will establish a defense of impracticability. * * * Thus, § 263 of the SECOND RESTATEMENT recites:

> If the existence of a specific thing is necessary for the performance of a duty, its failure to come into existence, destruction, or such deterioration as makes performance impracticable is an event the non-occurrence of which was a basic assumption on which the contract was made.

Moreover, the Supreme Court of Pennsylvania has interpreted this section's predecessor in the FIRST RESTATEMENT to apply to, in addition to physical destruction and deterioration, interference by third parties with a specific chattel necessary to the carrying out of the agreement. *Greenfield,* 380 A.2d at 759 (quoting *West v. Peoples First Nat'l Bank & Trust Co.*, 378 Pa. 275, 106 A.2d 427 (1954)) * * *.

[The court discussed the Pennsylvania cases.]

* * *

The situation presented here is in accord with these cases. To recapitulate, CIT

---

[4] (...continued)
reasonable parties see no need explicitly to allocate the risk of its occurrence, although the impact it might have would be of such magnitude that the parties would have negotiated over it, had the event been more likely." CALAMARI & PERILLO, *supra,* § 13.18, at 526.

contracted to supply specific tire presses to Specialty. This was not a case of fungible goods; Specialty inspected, and bid for, certain identified, used presses located at the Natchez plant operated by Condere. All parties believed that CIT was the owner of the presses and was entitled to their immediate possession; Condere's representatives stated as much during the inspection visit. Neither Specialty nor CIT had any reason to believe that Condere would subsequently turn an about-face and assert a possessory interest in the presses. The most that can be said is that CIT had a course of dealings with Condere, but nowhere is it argued that there was any history of tortious or opportunistic conduct that would have alerted CIT that Condere would attempt to convert the presses to its own use.

Thus, whether analyzed traditionally in terms of foreseeability, as courts apply that term, or by the risk-exposure methodology outlined *supra*, it is clear that this is not the sort of risk that CIT should have expected to either bear or contract against. In economic terms, which I apply as a "check" rather than as substantive law, it cannot be said with any reliability that either Specialty or CIT was able to avoid the risk of what Condere did at a lower cost. It was "a bolt out of the blue" for both parties. On the other hand, Specialty was in a better position to know what consequences and damages would likely flow from nondelivery or delayed delivery of the presses. This suggests that Specialty is the appropriate party on which to impose the risk, *See* POSNER, *supra* § 4.5, at 118; CALAMARI & PERILLO, *supra* § 13.2, at 498. Moreover, judicial discharge of CIT's promise under these circumstances leaves Specialty in no worse a position than it would have occupied without the contract; either way, it would not have these presses, and it has only been able to locate and purchase three similar used presses on the open market since CIT's failure to deliver. On the other hand, CIT is relieved of the obligation to pay damages. Accordingly, excuse for impracticability would appear to be a Pareto-optimal move, note [2], *supra*, increasing CIT's welfare while not harming Specialty. This too is a valid policy reason for imposing the risk of loss on Specialty. *See* CALAMARI & PERILLO, *supra* § 13.1, at 496. Thus, economic analysis confirms as sound policy the result suggested by the caselaw discussed *supra*.

[The court then rejected several other arguments made by Specialty.] * * *

Accordingly, I conclude on this record that CIT has made out its defense of impracticability. The ruling of the replevin court, however, indicates that CIT's performance is impracticable only in the temporary sense. Temporary impracticability only relieves the promisor of the obligation to perform as long as the impracticability lasts and for a reasonable time thereafter.* * * Once it receives possession of the presses, CIT asserts that it stands ready and willing to perform its contract with Specialty. * * * That issue is not ripe for adjudication and must await a separate lawsuit if CIT should fail to perform after obtaining possession. Suffice it to say that, to the extent Specialty seeks damages for nondelivery of the presses to date, CIT is excused by the doctrine of impracticability and is entitled to full summary judgment. * * *

[Some footnotes omitted. Those retained have been renumbered.]

Notes

1.   Surprise! The court both endorses economic analysis and grants relief from the contract. Not surprisingly, however, the court does an excellent job in collecting and analyzing the authorities and reaches a sound outcome.

2.   **Sole source suppliers under UCC 2-615(a).** The defense of "sole source" failure has been difficult to establish under UCC 2-615(a), especially in light of the risk assumption outcome suggested in Comment 8 when the event is "sufficiently foreshadowed at the time of contracting to be included among the business risks which are fairly to be regarded as part of the dickered terms, either consciously or as a matter of reasonable, commercial interpretation from the circumstances."[*]

An exception is where a particular supplier is specified in the contract, assumed by the parties to be the exclusive source of supply, and fails to perform. Here the seller is excused, provided that it (1) employed all "due measures" to assure that the agreed supplier would perform, and (2) turned over to the buyer any rights against the supplier corresponding to the seller's claim of excuse. UCC 2-615, Comment 5. In *Zidell Explorations, Inc. v. Conval International, Ltd.*, 719 F.2d 1465 (9th Cir. 1983), the court held that a failure to tender rights against the seller did not constitute a *per se* violation of the duty of good faith. Rather, the jury must determine in all the facts and circumstances whether the seller had satisfied its responsibility under Comment 5.

Should the same analysis apply under UCC 2A-405 when the lessor seeks excuse because of the failure of the lessor's source of supply? What would be the result in an international sale of goods? *See* CISG Art. 79(1).

3.   *Force Majeure* **Clauses.** Frequently, a seller will attempt to protect itself

---

[*]   *See Rockland Industries, Inc. v. E+E (US), Inc.*, 991 F. Supp. 468 (D. Md. 1998) (seller assumes the risk that sole source supplier failed).

against failures in a contemplated source of supply, whether agreed to be exclusive or not, by a *force majeure* clause. Such clauses vary in scope and content from industry to industry. A common form may look like this:

> "Neither party shall be liable for * * * loss, damage, claims or demands of any nature whatsoever due to delays or defaults in performance caused by impairment in any manner of seller's source of supply by (list causes or events) or by any other event, whether or not similar to the causes specified above * * * , which shall not be reasonably within the control of the party against whom the claim would otherwise be made."

When a *force majeure* clause is invoked, the following questions must be answered:

(1) Are the events specified and the relief sought within the scope of the clause;

(2) If so, was the event within the control or due to the fault or negligence of the party seeking relief;[*]

(3) If not, did the party seeking relief exercise reasonable efforts after the event occurred to secure performance as agreed from some source;[**] and

(4) Is relief under a *force majeure* clause restricted in any way by UCC 2-615(a)? Put differently, if the parties clearly agree to expand the scope of excuse available under UCC 2-615(a), should the agreement be enforced? In *Interpetrol Bermuda Ltd. v. Kaiser Aluminum International Corp.*, 719 F.2d 992 (9th Cir. 1983), the answer was that the parties had power to expand the scope of excuse, subject to the requirement of conscionability and the good faith duty to seek an alternative source of performance. In addition, the court held that where excuse was based upon the *force majeure* clause rather than UCC 2-615, there was no requirement that the seller assign its rights against the defaulting source of supply to the buyer. Consider this excerpt from *Interpetrol Bermuda*, 719 F.2d at 999-1001:

> We agree with the district court that comment 5 does not control in this case. Kaiser was not excused under § 2-615 and could not have been. Section 2-615 applies only when the events that made the performance of the contract impracticable were unforeseen at the time the contract was executed* * *. The extensive negotiations over the *force majeure* clause, discussed above, indicate that the parties not only foresaw the risk that Oxy Crude would default but also bargained over which party would bear the loss in that event. Accordingly, it would violate fundamental principles of

---

[*] *See PPG Indus. Inc. v. Shell Oil Co.*, 919 F.2d 17 (5th Cir. 1990).

[**] *See Nissho-Iwai Co., Ltd. v. Occidental Crude Sales, Inc.*, 729 F.2d 1530 (5th Cir. 1984).

contract law to use § 2-615 of the U.C.C to rewrite the contract to which the parties agreed. U.C.C § 2-615, comment 8 (§ 2-615 inapplicable if "contingency in question is * * * included among the business risks which are fairly to be regarded as part of the dickered terms. * * *").

Although there has been some doubt expressed as to whether the Code permits parties to bargain for exemptions broader than those available under § 2-615, at least one circuit has concluded they may. *See Eastern Airlines, Inc. v. McDonnell Douglas Corp.*, 532 F.2d 957, 990 (5th Cir. 1976)* * *. We agree with the Fifth Circuit. Comment 8 to § 2-615 plainly indicates that parties may "enlarge upon or supplant" § 2-615. While exculpatory clauses phrased in general language should not be construed to expand excuses not provided for by the Code, circumstances surrounding a particular agreement may indicate that the parties intended to accord the seller an exemption broader than is available under the UCC. *Eastern Airlines*, 532 F.2d at 990-91. We have already decided that the *force majeure* clause agreed to by Kaiser and InterPetrol was intended to excuse Kaiser prior to shipment of the crude from the Persian Gulf if Kaiser's supplier failed to deliver for any reason. We now hold that it was permissible for them to make such an agreement. Thus, if InterPetrol is to prevail on its claim that it succeeds to Kaiser's rights, it must do so on grounds apart from the Code.

California courts have read into *force majeure* clauses an implied covenant of good faith. * * * This common law covenant of good faith is applicable to *force majeure* clauses such as the one agreed to by Kaiser and InterPetrol. If the common law requirement of good faith implies a requirement that a seller turn over to its buyer the seller's rights against a defaulting supplier, then the district court erred in granting Kaiser's motion to dismiss.

InterPetrol failed to cite any instance under the common law, under circumstances similar to those of this case, where a buyer succeeded to the rights of the seller against a defaulting supplier. The common law has not provided to a disappointed buyer the rights called for by InterPetrol.

We see no reason to now create a right which has not been recognized by the common law. There is a certain amount of economic wisdom in permitting a seller, consistent with the limiting provisions of the Code, to contract out of liability. In a relatively free and fluid wholesale market, a seller should be entitled to utilize the power of his position to contract to his best advantage. That might include, as here, the extraction of a *force majeure* clause from a buyer. If the seller's supplier is not able because of market forces to require a similar provision in the agreement between seller and supplier, the result is that the seller is excused but the supplier is not. Yet we see no reason to award the windfall of recovery against the supplier to the buyer, who agreed to excuse the seller, instead of the seller, who was able to insist on better protections. When a trader is able to bargain for such favorable conditions, the natural trend will be for traders in the less favorable positions of buyer and supplier to move into the less competitive and therefore more contractually secure part of the market.

We find no reason to transfer the benefit of Kaiser's superior negotiating position to InterPetrol by giving InterPetrol Kaiser's rights against Trako and Oxy Crude. We do find that it serves the forces of natural market adjustments not to transfer Kaiser's rights. We therefore affirm the decision of the district court. [Footnotes omitted.]

Does that same rationale apply to UCC 2A-405?

D. Relief From Non-Force Majeure Events

1. Increased Costs of Performance

In volatile markets, prices may rise and fall over the course of a contract. Thus, parties to a fixed price contract will have an incentive to seek excuse when the market moves against them. Similarly, the cost to perform may increase substantially. For example, the cost of money to the buyer may increase as interest rates rise and the cost to the seller to manufacture or obtain promised goods may rise as inflation sets in. When, if ever, can a party obtain relief from these market events when no force majeure events actually prevents or hinders performance? These issues were posed in the famous (or infamous) *ALCOA* case.

In *Aluminum Company of America v. Essex Group, Inc.*, 499 F. Supp. 53 (W.D. Pa. 1980), the parties in 1967 entered into a 17 year contract under which ALCOA was to process alumina supplied by Essex into molten aluminum to be used by Essex in the manufacture of aluminum wire products. The long-term contract, called a "toll conversion service contract," was to be performed at a plant owned by ALCOA in Indiana. As part of the pricing mechanism, the parties agreed upon an escalation clause, developed by the noted economist Alan Greenspan, which varied with actual production costs at the plant. The clause was developed on the basis of past cost patterns and reflected projected cost variations that would give ALCOA a target profit of $.04 per pound.

In 1973, during the energy crisis, electricity costs at the Indiana plant began to escalate well beyond the projections in the price escalation clause. Even though the contract was profitable up to this time, it was estimated that ALCOA would lose $60 million over the balance of the contract due to a 500% variation between indexed and actual costs. At the same time, Essex was enjoying an apparent windfall gain by reselling converted aluminum for which it paid ALCOA $.364 per pound on the open market for $.733 per pound. When efforts by ALCOA to obtain an agreed price adjustment from Essex failed, ALCOA sued to obtain relief from the escalation clause and a reformation of the contract so that Essex would be required to pay the actual costs incurred at the plant. Essex counterclaimed for breach damages and the issues were joined.

In an unprecedented decision, the court concluded that ALCOA was entitled to "some relief" from the changed circumstances and that the relief should be an equitable reformation of, rather than discharge from, the contract. The court, without the agreement of the parties, devised its own adjustment formula to fill the gap in the agreement. Essex appealed but the parties settled the dispute by agreement before the case could be heard.

Since the contract between ALCOA and Essex was characterized as for services rather than the sale of goods, UCC 2-615 was not directly applicable. The court, however, blended the doctrine of mutual mistake, commercial impracticability and frustration of purpose to achieve a result that, in part, could have been reached under UCC 2-615. The court's analysis was consistent with the four steps required to deal with UCC 2-615's "basic assumption" test:

First, did the seller assume by agreement a greater obligation than the degree of excuse normally available under UCC 2-615? If so, excuse should be denied. The court's answer in *ALCOA* was no.

Second, if a greater obligation was not assumed, was the event that materialized a "contingency the non-occurrence of which was a basic assumption on which the contract was made?" If not, excuse should be denied. The court's answer was yes: both parties assumed at the time of contracting that the escalation clause was reasonable and the changed circumstances were not foreseen as likely to occur.

Third, if so, did the contingency make "performance as agreed * * * impracticable?" If the answer is yes, then the seller is entitled to "some relief." The court's answer was yes: A $60 million loss over the balance of a commercial contract made continued performance "commercially senseless and unjust," particularly where Essex was realizing "windfall" profits.

Fourth, if the seller is entitled to "some relief," should that relief take the form of discharge of the executory contract or preservation of the contract under a court-imposed price adjustment? The Code's answer is not clear. *ALCOA*'s answer was to delete the existing price escalation clause, which had failed its intended purpose, and to impose in the gap a new price term which was thought to respond to the changed circumstances.[*]

ALCOA, to date, stands as the high (or low) water mark in disputes under UCC 2-615. Under circumstances comparable to *ALCOA*, *i.e.*, rising costs of performance or sharply higher prices, other courts have denied any relief to the seller under UCC 2-615(a).[**] But the facts in *ALCOA* were compelling in that the escalation clause agreed to by the parties failed to keep pace with escalating energy costs, resulting in both dramatic cost increases to ALCOA and an unanticipated windfall to Essex.

2. Buyer's Excuse

Under the opposite circumstances, *i.e.*, a sharply reduced demand and, thus, lower prices for the product, buyers have fared no better than sellers. Although the courts, citing Comment 9, concede that UCC 2-615(a) protects buyers,[***] little mercy has been shown to the buyer who, in the light of changed circumstances, has agreed to take goods at a quantity in excess of current needs and pay a price substantially in excess of market. For example, in *Northern Illinois Gas Co. v. Energy Cooperative, Inc.*, 461 N.E.2d 1049, 1059 (Ill. Ct. App. 1984), the court stated in part: "* * * [A]s any trader knows, the only certainty of the market is that prices will change. Changing and shifting markets and prices from multitudinous causes is endemic to the economy in which we live. Market forecasts by supposed

---

[*] For more discussion, *see* Richard E. Speidel, *Court-Imposed Price Adjustments Under Long-Term Supply Contracts,* 76 Nw. U. L. Rev. 369 (1981).

[**] *See Iowa Elec. Light and Power Co. v. Atlas Corp.*, 467 F. Supp. 129, 134 (N.D. Iowa 1978), *rev'd on other grounds*, 603 F.2d 1301 (8th Cir. 1979); *Louisiana Power & Light v. Allegheny Ludlum Industries*, 517 F. Supp. 1319 (E.D. La. 1981); *Missouri Public Serv. Co. v. Peabody Coal Co.*, 583 S.W.2d 721 (Mo. Ct. App. 1979), *cert. denied*, 444 U.S. 865 (1979).

[***] *See Power Engineering v. Krug International*, 501 N.W.2d 490 (Iowa 1993).

experts are sometimes right, often wrong, and usually mixed. If changed prices, standing alone, constitute a frustrating event sufficient to excuse performance of a contract, then the law binding contractual parties to their agreements is no more." In Judge Posner's words:

> Since impossibility and related doctrines are devices for shifting risk in accordance with the parties' presumed intentions, which are to minimize the costs of contract performance, one of which is the disutility created by risk, they have no place when the contract explicitly assigns a particular risk to one party or the other. As we have already noted, a fixed-price contract is an explicit assignment of the risk of market price increases to the seller and the risk of market price decreases to the buyer, and the assignment of the latter risk to the buyer is even clearer where, as in this case, the contract places a floor under price but allows for escalation. If, as is also the case here, the buyer forecasts the market incorrectly and therefore finds himself locked into a disadvantageous contract, he has only himself to blame and so cannot shift the risk back to the buyer by invoking impossibility or related doctrines. * * * Since 'the very purpose of a fixed price agreement is to place the risk of increased costs on the promisor (and the risk of decreased costs on the promisee),' the fact that costs decrease steeply * * * cannot allow the buyer to walk away from the contract.

Northern Indiana Public Service Co. v. Carbon County Coal Company, 799 F.2d 265, 278 (7th Cir. 1986).

3. Effect of Agreement on Excuse

INTERNATIONAL MINERALS & CHEMICAL CORP. V. LLANO, INC.
UNITED STATES COURT OF APPEALS, TENTH CIRCUIT, 1985
770 F.2D 879; CERT. DENIED, 475 U.S. 1015 (1986)

[International (IMC) agreed to purchase natural gas from Llano under a ten year contract, scheduled to terminate on June 30, 1982. IMC sought a declaratory judgment that it was excused from its obligation to "take or pay" for an agreed minimum quantity of natural gas during the last eighteen months of the contract, due to more stringent regulation by the New Mexico Environmental Improvement Board of particle emissions from existing combustion evaporators in IMC's plant. Under EIB Regulation 508, IMC was ultimately required to shut down the combustion evaporators, which had consumed approximately 60% of its natural gas requirements. Llano counterclaimed for $3,564,617.12, the amount that it claimed was due under the contract for gas for which IMC should have paid.

The trial court held: (1) UCC 2-615 was not applicable to buyers unless the contract was "conditioned on a definite and specific venture or assumption. * * *"; and (2) The *"force majeure"* and "adjustment of minimum bill" clauses in the contract, Paragraphs 15 and 16 set out below, did not excuse performance unless it became absolutely impossible or illegal to purchase the minimum amount of gas. On the facts, the trial court denied relief to IMC and concluded that IMC was liable for the contract price for gas it should have taken, even though Llano had been able to sell the gas elsewhere for a higher price.

IMC appealed and the court limited its consideration to whether IMC was excused under either UCC 2-615 or Paragraphs 15 and 16 of the contract.]

BARRETT, CIRCUIT JUDGE

* * *

The pertinent portions of the contract are as follows:

NOW, THEREFORE, in consideration of the premises and of the mutual covenants and agreements hereinafter set forth, the parties do hereby bargain, contract and agree as follows:

1. *SUPPLY OF NATURAL GAS:* Subject to the terms and conditions of this Contract, Seller will sell and deliver to Buyer and Buyer will take, purchase and pay for the entire fuel requirements of Buyer's Plant, provided that Buyer may at its option procure and maintain a supply of standby fuel to be used only to such extent as may be necessary when the gas supply from Seller may be interrupted or curtailed, as hereinafter provided, and in such other amounts as may be necessary from time to time to test such standby facilities and fuel.* * *

6. *DELIVERY REQUIREMENTS:* During the term of this Contract, unless Seller agrees in writing to the contrary, the minimum daily deliveries that Seller shall make to Buyer and Buyer shall take from Seller shall be 4800 million BTU's per day except as hereafter provided. The maximum daily deliveries that Seller shall be required to make to Buyer shall be 133% of the average daily requirements of Buyer's Plant for the preceding 365 days provided, however, Seller shall at no time be required to deliver in excess of 6400 million BTU's per day unless Seller agrees in writing to the contrary.

Buyer does not contemplate reducing its operations, but on the contrary contemplates the increase thereof from the present daily requirements. In order to meet unanticipated contingencies, it is agreed that in the event Buyer during the term of this Contract reduces its operation by closing a portion of its plant, it shall have the right upon six months notice in writing to reduce the minimum requirements to a figure equal to 70% of the stated minimum of 4800 million BTU's per day. In the event of such reduction in minimum requirements, Seller's price to Buyer then in effect under the terms hereof shall be increased by ½¢ per million BTU's, but not in excess of the highest price for a like quantity of gas then being paid by any potash company in the area.

7. *MINIMUM ANNUAL PURCHASE:*   During the term of this Contract, commencing with the first year, Buyer agrees to take from Seller a volume of gas having a BTU content of not less than 355 times the minimum daily deliveries specified in Section 6 hereof. Buyer agrees to pay Seller for such minimum volume of gas at the price set forth in Section 5 hereof provided that if Buyer fails during any calendar year to take such minimum volume of gas, then the deficiency between the volume actually taken and Buyer's minimum purchase obligation shall be paid at the price in effect during the calendar year in which such deficiency occurs.

Billing for any payment due by reason of a deficiency in Buyer's takings of gas hereunder during a particular calendar year shall be included on the bill rendered to Buyer for gas delivered to Buyer during the month of December in the calendar year in which such deficiency occurred and payment therefore shall be made in the manner provided for monthly bills in Section 11 hereof. Failure on the part of Seller to so bill Buyer for any such deficiency payment shall not constitute a waiver hereof by Seller. * * *

15. *FORCE MAJEURE:* Either party shall be excused for delay or failure to perform its agreements and undertakings, in whole or in part, when and to the extent that such failure or delay is occasioned by fire, flood, wind, lightning, or other acts of the elements, explosion, act of God, act of the public enemy, or interference of civil and/or military authorities, mobs, labor difficulties, vandalism, sabotage, malicious mischief, usurpation of power, depletion of wells, freezing or accidents to wells, pipelines, permanent closing of Buyer's operations at its Eddy County mine and refinery, after not less than six (6) months notice thereof to Seller, or other casualty or cause beyond the reasonable control of the parties,

respectively, which delays or prevents such performance in whole or in part, as the case may be; provided, however, that the party whose performance hereunder is so affected shall immediately notify the other party of all pertinent facts and take all reasonable steps promptly and diligently to prevent such causes if feasible to do so, or to minimize or eliminate the effect without delay. It is understood and agreed that settlement of strikes or other labor disputes shall be at the sole discretion of the party encountering the strike or dispute.

Nothing contained herein, however, shall be construed as preventing the Buyer from discontinuing the operation of the plant for such periods of time as may be required by Buyer to perform necessary overhaul operations on plant properties or to accomplish preventative maintenance operations on such plant properties, which the Buyer may determine as necessary to safeguard its investment in the plant.

16. *ADJUSTMENT OF MINIMUM BILL:* In the event that Seller is unable to deliver or Buyer is unable to receive gas as provided in this Contract for any reason beyond the reasonable control of the parties, or in the event of force majeure as provided in Section 15 hereof, an appropriate adjustment in the minimum purchase requirements specified in Section 7 shall be made.

(Pl.Exh. 3, Def.Exh. C8b).

The contract may be characterized as a requirements contract, with an important limitation: Pursuant to paragraph 6, the buyer (IMC) is obligated to take, at a minimum, a daily average of 4800 million BTU's of gas. Pursuant to paragraph 7, if the buyer does not take this minimum amount, the buyer is obligated to pay for the minimum amount of gas anyway. These provisions are known in the industry as "take or pay" provisions, the purpose of which is to compensate the seller for being ready at all times to deliver the maximum amount of gas to the buyer and to eliminate the risk that the seller would face in a pure requirements contract were the buyer's requirements to drop too low.* * * The harshness of the "take or pay" provisions in this contract are to some extent ameliorated by the "*force majeure*" provision of paragraph 15 and the "adjustment of minimum bill" provision of paragraph 16; paragraphs 15 and 16 are discussed below. * * *

On a fundamental level, this case is one of contract construction. Our primary objective, as always, in the construction or interpretation of a contract is to ascertain the intention of the parties. * * * We assume that the parties intended a reasonable interpretation of the language.* * * Accordingly, the legal context in which the contract was made will be relevant. As mentioned above, paragraphs 15 and 16 ameliorate the harshness of the "take or pay" provisions in that either party's duty of performance may be excused upon the occurrence of certain contingencies. As we examine the language of paragraphs 15 and 16, an appropriate area to look for guidance is the common law doctrine of impossibility/impracticability, codified at Section 2-615 of New Mexico's Uniform Commercial Code (N.M. Stat. Ann. § 55-2-615 (1978)), which was the law in New Mexico at the time the parties contracted and which remains the law today. While it is a basic premise of both Section 2-615 and the Uniform Commercial Code in general that the parties may allocate risks and penalties between themselves in any manner they choose, N.M. Stat. Ann. §§ 55-1-102 and 55-2-615 (1978), the Code and the common law upon which it is based remain a significant backdrop.

We first consider the effect of paragraph 15, the *"force majeure"* provision, on IMC's duty of performance under the circumstances of this case. Specifically, Paragraph 15 provides that either party is excused from performance if failure or delay in performance is "occasioned" by such events as fire, flood, act of God, interference of civil and/or military authorities, etc. The party seeking to be excused from performance must provide the other party with immediate notice of all pertinent facts and take all reasonable steps to prevent the occurrence. It also appears that the seller is entitled to six months notice before the buyer can be excused. We agree with the trial court that paragraph 15 does not operate to excuse IMC, although our conclusion is based on a somewhat different rationale. First, IMC's notice to Llano was inadequate in that no reasons were given as to why gas consumption would be decreased. Adequate notice was required to trigger the protections of the provision. Second, even if we assume *arguendo* that Rule 508 prevented IMC from taking the gas, Rule 508 would still pose no obstacle to IMC's ability to pay. Since this is a "take or pay" contract, the buyer can perform in either of two ways. It can either (1) take the minimum purchase obligation of natural gas (and pay) or (2) pay the minimum bill. It is settled law that when a promisor can perform a contract in either of two alternative ways, the impracticability of one alternative does not excuse the promisor if performance by means of the other alternative is still practicable.* * * RESTATEMENT (SECOND) OF CONTRACTS § 261, comment f (1981). Paragraph 15 does not compel a different result; it would at most excuse IMC from its duty to "take," not from its duty to "pay."

Paragraph 16, the "minimum bill" provision, however, affords the buyer additional protection. It provides that, in the event the buyer is *"unable* to receive gas as provided in the Contract for any reason *beyond the reasonable control* of the parties * * * " (emphasis added), then "an appropriate adjustment in the minimum purchase requirements specified in Section [paragraph] 7 shall be made." Paragraph 7, in turn, provides for a minimum bill based on the difference between the buyer's minimum purchase obligation and the gas actually taken. It follows that an adjustment of the buyer's minimum purchase requirements made pursuant to paragraph 16 would have the effect of lowering the buyer's minimum bill under paragraph 7. Llano's contention that paragraph 16 provides for a reduction in IMC's minimum purchase obligation but not its minimum bill obligation (Appellee's Brief at 4) is thus quickly disposed of.

The determinative question, then, is: Did the promulgation of Rule 508 constitute an event beyond the reasonable control of IMC that rendered IMC "unable" to receive its minimum amount of gas under the contract?

A simplistic, literal interpretation of the word "unable" would, in our view, be inappropriate and lead to absurd results: IMC could never be "unable" to take Llano's gas; IMC could always take the gas and vent it into the air, even if its facilities were completely destroyed. The word "unable" appears here as a term in a contract, prepared by businessmen and attorneys; thus, it is appropriate to construe the term in light of the common law as it existed in New Mexico when the contract was entered into. For our purposes, then, "unable" is synonymous with "impracticable," as that term is used in the common law and in Section 2-615.

The term "impracticable" has, over the years, acquired a fairly specific meaning. Although earlier cases required that performance be physically impossible before the promisor would be excused, strict impossibility is no longer required. *See* RESTATEMENT (SECOND) OF CONTRACTS § 261, comment d (1981). The New Mexico Supreme Court has described the doctrine of impracticability as follows:

> Regarding the meaning of "impossibility" as used in the rules that excuse the non-performance of contracts, it is stated:

>> "As pointed out in the Restatement of Contracts, the essence of the modern defense of impossibility is that the promised performance was at the making of the contract, or thereafter became, impracticable owing to some extreme or unreasonable difficulty, expense, injury, or loss involved, rather than that it is scientifically impossible. * * * The important question is whether an unanticipated circumstance has made performance of the promise vitally different from what should reasonably have been within the contemplation of both parties when they entered into the

contract. If so, the risk should not fairly be thrown upon the promisor."

Wood v. Bartolino, 48 N.M. 175, 146 P.2d 883, 886, (1944), *quoting* 6 WILLISTON ON CONTRACTS, § 1931.* * *

Performance will be excused when made impracticable by having to comply with a supervening governmental regulation. N.M. Stat. Ann. § 55-2-615 (1978); RESTATEMENT (SECOND) OF CONTRACTS § 264 (1981). Thus, for example, in the case of *Kansas City, Missouri v. Kansas City, Kansas,* 393 F. Supp. 1 (W.D. Mo. 1975), the court held that the defendant city's obligation to accept the plaintiff city's sewage was excused by the enactment of the Federal Water Pollution Control Act Amendments of 1972. The federal act imposed new requirements with regard to the treatment of sewage that was discharged into the Missouri River; the court found that the added expense of such treatment would impose a significant, unreasonable burden on the defendant. *Accord City of Vernon v. City of Los Angeles,* 45 Cal. 2d 710, 290 P.2d 841 (1955).

Inasmuch as there was no technically suitable way for IMC to comply with the EIB's Regulation 508 without shutting down the Ozarks and changing to the SOP, with the concomitant decrease in natural gas consumption, we hold that the adjustment provision of paragraph 16 of the contract was triggered. IMC was unable, for reasons beyond its reasonable control, to receive its minimum purchase obligation of natural gas between January 1, 1981 and June 30, 1982; thus, the minimum bill should have been adjusted appropriately. IMC should not be required to pay for any natural gas it did not take under the contract.

Llano contends that there was no supervening legal impracticability in this case because IMC was not required to be in final compliance until December 31, 1984, and that IMC cooperated with the EIB and came into compliance too early. The argument here is that, notwithstanding the interim standards contained in the schedules of compliance, IMC should have stalled in its negotiations with the state regulatory agency, which would have resulted in the pollution of air until the last minute. We must reject this contention on two grounds: First, as a matter of policy, individuals and corporations who cooperate with local regulatory agencies and comply with the letter and spirit of legally proper regulations, environmental or otherwise, are to be encouraged. Stalling tactics are not regarded favorably. Second, as a matter of law, government policy need not be explicitly mandatory to cause impracticability. Thus, for example, in *Eastern Air Lines, Inc. v. McDonnell Douglas Corporation,* 532 F.2d 957 (5th Cir. 1976), an aircraft manufacturer was excused from its contractual obligation to deliver commercial jet airliners on certain scheduled dates because it had voluntarily complied with government requests to expedite production of military equipment needed for the war in Vietnam. Similarly, in the maritime context, shipowners have been excused from contractual obligations because they have anticipated governmental intrusion.* * * There is, we recognize, a limit to the extent to which an individual can seek refuge in the context of a case such as this by cooperating with the government: "any action by the party claiming excuse which causes or colludes in inducing the governmental action preventing his performance would be in breach of good faith and would destroy his exemption." Official Comment 10, N.M. Stat. Ann. § 55-2-615 (1978). Here, Regulation 508 was promulgated by the EIB as part of New Mexico's State Implementation Plan mandated by the Clean Air Act. Regulation 508's existence and its enforcement mechanism is designed to eliminate pollution of the environment, thus serving the public health and welfare. IMC's recognition of the public benefit goal and its willingness to cooperate in eliminating pollution can hardly be termed improper collusion.

For the reasons described above, the judgment of the trial court in favor of Llano is reversed. The case is remanded with direction that the court enter a declaratory judgment in accordance with this opinion.

Notes

1. **Take or Pay Contracts.** *International Minerals* featured a "take or pay" contract under which the buyer agreed to either "take" the gas when produced and pay for it or "pay" for the gas without taking it, with the producer holding it for "make up" deliveries in the future. As one court put it:

> The purpose of the take or pay clause is to apportion the risks of natural gas production and sales between the buyer and seller. The seller bears the risk of production. To compensate the seller for that risk, the buyer agrees to take, or pay for if not taken, a minimum quantity of gas. The buyer bears the risk of market demand.

Universal Resources Corp. v. Panhandle Eastern Pipe Line Co., 813 F.2d 77, 80 (5th Cir. 1987). The courts have held that such clauses are not unconscionable at the time of contracting and are agreements for alternative performance rather than liquidated damage clauses. Thus, the failure to "take" is not itself a breach of contract by the buyer. In order for a buyer to breach such an alternative performance contract, the buyer must *both* fail to take *and* fail to pay.[*] It follows that "The * * * take or pay clause is a promise [of performance] in the Agreement, not a measure of damages after breach. * * *" *Universal Resources Corp.*, 813 F.2d at 80 n.4. Where the buyer is in breach, the UCC does not allow the seller to recover the price, *i.e.*, the face amount under the "or pay" clause, because the terms of UCC 2-709 on price actions are not met, and a seller is not allowed specific performance of the price term under UCC 2-716. Rather, the seller's UCC remedy is under UCC 2-708.[**]

Depending upon the market and the exercise of bargaining power, "take or pay" contracts may also contain a *force majeure* clause similar to that in *International Minerals* or other clauses allocating risk, such as a "market out" clause. Under a "market out" clause, the buyer, usually a pipeline, can terminate the contract if a more favorable long term price for gas can be found from another source and the producer is unwilling or unable to match it.[***]

In the absence of a "market out" or similar clause, the courts have been unwilling to excuse the buyer, commonly a pipeline, in the face of dramatic declines in market prices for gas from the wellhead, even when resulting from deregulatory acts by the FERC, the Federal Energy Regulatory Commission.[****] The reasoning seems to be that the "take or pay" clause allocates such risk to the buyer, thereby foreclosing excuse under UCC 2-615(a), and that the language of the *force majeure* clause was not intended to cover shifts in market price or demand.[*****] Query whether this analysis is really applicable given the highly regulated nature of the industry, with market swings attributable to de-regulatory acts that were not really

---

[*] On alternative performance contracts, *see* 11 CORBIN ON CONTRACTS §§ 1079-87 (1993).

[**] One court has taken a different view and allowed the producer to recover the full amount of the "or pay" clause as if it were a liquidated damages clause. *See Prenalta Corp. v. Colorado Interstate Gas Co.*, 944 F.2d 677 (10th Cir. 1991).

[***] *See* Joe Caggiano, *Understanding Natural Gas Contracts,* 38 OIL & GAS TAX Q. 267, 267-278 (1989).

[****] *See Moncrief v. Williston Basin Interstate Pipeline Co.*, 880 F. Supp. 1495 (D. Wyo. 1995) (expanded government regulation neither a *force majeure* nor the failure of a basic assumption), *aff'd in part and rev'd in part*, 174 F.3d 1150 (10th Cir. 1999).

[*****] *See, e.g., Kaiser-Francis Oil Co. v. Producer's Gas Co.*, 870 F.2d 563 (10th Cir. 1980); *Golsen v. ONG Western, Inc.*, 756 P.2d 1209 (Okla. 1988).

foreseen when the parties originally entered their take-or-pay contracts many years earlier.

2.   **Effect of Subsequent Government Acts.** In a regulated economy, acts subsequent to the contract by state or the federal government may prevent or make illegal contract performance or may make performance more difficult or expensive. Or the subsequent government act may frustrate the purpose of one or both parties. A good example of prevention is the state environmental regulation in *International Minerals*, *supra*.

There is a somewhat different test for excuse in these cases.   Both the RESTATEMENT (SECOND) OF CONTRACTS 264 and UCC 2-615(a) dispense with the basic assumption test. Rather, if the seller's delay or non-delivery has been made "impracticable * * * by compliance in good faith with any applicable foreign or domestic government regulation whether or not it later proves to be invalid" there is no breach of contract. UCC 2-615(a). The parties, of course, can allocate this risk by agreement and Comment 10 to UCC 2-615 says that the governmental interference must truly "supervene" in such a manner "as to be beyond the seller's assumption of risk." But the text does not require that the basic assumption test be satisfied for excuse and substitutes a "good faith compliance test." For example, in *Harriscom Svenska, AB v. Harris Corp.*, 3 F.3d 576 (2nd Cir. 1993), the seller was excused from a contract for sale when performance was prevented by an informal government ban on sales to Iran and there was no evidence that the seller had acted in bad faith. However, in *MG Refining & Marketing, Inc. v. Knight Enterprises, Inc.*, 25 F. Supp. 2d 175 (S.D.N.Y 1998), the court held the defense was not available where the party caused the government act preventing performance regardless of the party's good faith.

3.   **Excuse in a finance lease.** As we have seen, the Article 2A provisions on excuse mirror, in most respects, the provisions from Article 2. Article 2A also recognizes excuse in the case of a supplier under a finance lease who is unable to provide the contracted-for goods. UCC 2A-221, 2A-404, and 2A-405 all refer to a supplier in addition to the lessor. What is different in UCC 2A-221 and 2A-406 from the analogous Article 2 provisions is the lessee's allowed response in the case of a non-consumer finance lease. In UCC 2A-221(b) and 2A-406(1)(b), the lessee may not agree to modify the contract to accept the damaged or allocated goods and get a reduction in the rent. To allow such a reduction would go against the "hell or high water" principle found in UCC 2A-407. However, in both cases, the lessee may opt to terminate the contract and not take the goods at all.

4.   **Excuse under CISG Article 79 and the UNIDROIT Principles of**

International Commercial Contracts. CISG Article 79 provides a limited "exemption" from performance which is available to both sellers and buyers. Read that Article, please. To what extent does Article 79 excuse a seller or buyer from *force majeure* events? How about from wild market fluctuations? There is no duty under the CISG to negotiate in good faith when disputes over exemption arise and the court or arbitrator is given no power to adjust the contract. Agreed modifications, however, are facilitated by Art. 29(1), which provides that a "contract may be modified or terminated by the mere agreement of the parties."

The UNIDROIT Principles of International Commercial Contracts provide more extensive relief from changed circumstances. Article 7.1.7, entitled *"Force majeure,"* follows CISG Art. 79. *See also* Art. 7.1.6 ("exemption" clauses). The Principles Articles 6.2.1 through 6.2.3, however, provide relief from hardship, either through a negotiated modification where good faith duties are imposed, or through judicial or arbitral action to "adapt the contract with a view to restoring its equilibrium." Art. 6.2.3. Hardship is defined as a fundamental alteration of the "equilibrium of the contract either because the cost of a party's performance has increased or because the value of the performance a party receives has diminished," unless the risk was assumed by what was foreseeable at the time of contracting or by agreement. Art. 6.2.2. Wait a minute. Aren't these principles similar to those invoked in the *ALCOA* case, *supra*?

5. **Excuse under UCITA.** In a provision modeled after UCC 2-615 and 2-616, UCITA 615 addresses excuse for either the licensor or licensee except for the obligation to make payments or the obligation to conform to contractual use terms. UCITA does not contain any analogs to UCC 2-613 or 2-614.

Problem 7-3

Softstuff, a coal producer, manufactures coke for steel production. Coke is made by subjecting coal to extreme heat in specially constructed ovens or batteries. Bitum is a steel maker. In May, 1995, the parties began to negotiate over a 10 year coke supply contract. It was agreed that Bitum was to take and pay for 20,000 tons of coke per month. This was, in effect, Softstuff's output from its coke batteries. In addition to agreements on quality, the parties agreed that Bitum was to pay a base price of $42 per ton, subject to escalation based upon externally compiled cost indices. These indices reflected the average costs incurred by coke producers rather than the actual costs of Softstuff's operation.

At the time of negotiation, the demand for coke was strong and the market price per ton was $41. The parties discussed the question of price stability over a ten year period. Softstuff "hoped" that strong demand would continue but Bitum was more pessimistic. Bitum proposed and Softstuff rejected a clause giving Bitum the option to terminate the contract at the end of any year wherein the market price of coke was 30% lower than the adjusted contract price for three or more months. There was no trade usage on price adjustment and the parties had not done business with each other before.

After further negotiations, the parties concluded a contract which, among other things, contained the following clause:

EXCUSE FOR BUYER

1. If because of Buyer's reduced blast furnace production, Buyer's requirements for coke cease or are reduced to a point where it is not practical for Buyer to purchase coke pursuant to this agreement, Buyer shall be released from its future obligations hereunder for the period of such cessation or reduction without any liability whatsoever upon Buyer giving Seller 90 days advance written notice.

2. Buyer's failure to comply or delay in compliance with the terms and conditions of this agreement shall be excused if due to any of the following which render performance commercially impracticable: act of God, fire, flood, strike, work stoppage, labor dispute, accident or mill interruption, complete or partial blast furnace relining, temporary failure of supply of iron ore, pellets or flux, any action by governmental authority, including ecological authorities, or any other cause beyond Buyer's reasonable control.

On January 15, 1996, Softstuff shipped and Bitum accepted and paid for the first 20,000 ton installment of coke at the base contract price. This pattern of performance continued until January 15, 2000, when Bitum notified Softstuff in writing that due to a "collapse in the market for coke and steel products" the contract is "hereby terminated in 90 days." At that time, the escalated contract price for coke was $50 per ton. The market price for comparable coke, however, had dropped to $25 per ton and the demand for Bitum's steel products had dropped 60% since the time of contracting. After an unsuccessful effort to negotiate a modification, Bitum reaffirmed that, after the 90 days period had expired, it would not accept any more coke under the contract.

In August, 2000, Softstuff sued Bitum for breach of contract. The sole question for you is whether Bitum is excused from performance under either paragraph of the EXCUSE FOR BUYER clause. If Bitum is not excused by virtue of the clause in the contract, does UCC 2-615 help the buyer?

SECTION 2.   MODIFICATION OF THE CONTRACT

A. Agreed Modifications

The parties to a dispute over contract performance frequently settle the matter by agreement. In one type of settlement, claims are adjusted, payments are made and the contract is discharged. A settlement of this kind is sometimes described as an accord and satisfaction. In another type of settlement, contract duties are adjusted by agreement in a bargain under which performance is to continue. These settlements are called contract modifications. In both, the enforceability of the settlement may be subsequently attacked on the grounds of fraud, lack of consideration, or duress. You have encountered both types of settlements in the course on contracts.

In this subsection we will focus on agreed modifications made in response to changed circumstances. The key provision is UCC 2-209. *Compare* UCC 2A-208. There are several questions to answer. For example, how do you show that you have an agreement to modify? If you have an agreement to modify, should that modification be enforced? *See* UCC 2-209, comment 2. Is good faith a workable tool for deciding when to enforce an agreement to modify? What would result if modifications are too readily enforced? What would result if modifications are not readily enforced? Is "good faith" the right standard for making that determination? If so, what is "good faith" in this context?[*] Does a modification need to be in a record? Read UCC 2-209(2) and (3). *Compare* UCC 2A-208(2). Article 2A does not have a provision comparable to UCC 2-209(3).

1. Agreed Modifications in Good Faith

Problem 7-4

A. Suppose, in Problem 7-3 *supra*, that before Bitum attempted to terminate

---

[*] Irma S. Russell, *Reinventing the Deal: A Sequential Approach to Analyzing Claims for Enforcement of Modified Sales Contract*, 53 FLA. L. REV. 49 (2001). For an analysis of the requirement of good faith from an economic efficiency perspective, *see* Jason Scott Johnston, *Default Rules/Mandatory Principles: A Game Theoretic Analysis of Good Faith and the Contract Modification Problem*, 3 S. CAL. INTERDISCIPLINARY L.J. 335 (1993).

the contract under the Excuse clause, Bitum explained the changing market situation and its impact on Bitum to Softstuff and requested Softstuff to consider and to negotiate over a proposed modification of the contract. Bitum suggested that the contract be adjusted in either of two ways for the remaining six years: (1) Keep the pricing structure but permit Bitum to order "requirements;" or (2) Keep the quantity term but permit Bitum to pay the market price of coke at the time of delivery. Bitum argued that Softstuff had, at a minimum, a duty to negotiate in good faith over the proposed adjustment, citing UCC 2-209, 1-304 [former 1-203], and Comments 6 & 7 to UCC 2-615. Softstuff declined, contending that unless the contract required it (and it did not), there was no duty to negotiate PERIOD. Softstuff cited *Missouri Public Serv. Co. v. Peabody Coal Co.*, 583 S.W.2d 721, 725 (Mo. Ct. App. 1979), *cert. denied*, 444 U.S. 865 (1979), where the court concluded: "Where an enforceable, untainted contract exists, refusing modification of price and seeking specific performance of valid covenants does not constitute bad faith or breach of contract . * * *" How should Bitum respond?

B. Suppose, after negotiations, Softstuff agreed to substitute "market price" for escalated price for the duration of the contract. Thereafter, Softstuff determined that market price would not cover its production costs and claimed that the modification was not enforceable, citing UCC 2-209(1). What result? See the next case which, to date, is the best decision dealing with the requirement of good faith in contract modifications.

ROTH STEEL PRODUCTS V. SHARON STEEL CORP.
UNITED STATES COURT OF APPEALS, SIXTH CIRCUIT, 1983
705 F.2D 134

[In November, 1972, Roth contracted to purchase 200 tons of "hot rolled" steel per month from Sharon through December, 1973. The price was $148 per ton. Sharon also "indicated" that it could sell "hot rolled" steel on an "open schedule" basis for $140 and discussed the "probability" that Sharon could sell 500 tons of "cold rolled" steel at prices varying with the type ordered. At that time, the steel industry was operating at 70% of capacity, steel prices were "highly competitive" and Sharon's quoted prices to Roth were "substantially lower" than Sharon's book price for steel. In early 1973, market conditions changed dramatically due to the development of an attractive export market and an increased domestic demand for steel. During 1973 and 1974, the steel industry operated at full capacity, steel prices rose and nearly every producer experienced substantial delays in filling orders. In March, 1973, Sharon notified all purchasers, including Roth, that it was discontinuing price concessions given in 1972.

After negotiations, the parties agreed that Roth would pay the agreed price until June 30, 1973 and a price somewhere between the agreed price and Sharon's published prices for the balance of 1973. Roth was initially reluctant to agree to this modification, but ultimately agreed "primarily because they were unable to purchase sufficient steel elsewhere to meet their production requirements." Sharon was supplying one-third of Roth's requirements and all other possible suppliers were "operating at full capacity and * * * were fully booked." The parties proceeded under this modification during the balance of 1973, although Sharon experienced difficulties in filling orders on time.

During 1974, the parties did business on an entirely different basis. Roth would order steel, Sharon would accept the order at the price "prevailing at the time of shipment." During 1974 and 1975, Sharon's deliveries were chronically late, thereby increasing the price to Roth in a rising market. Roth, however, acquiesced in this pattern because it believed Sharon's assurances that late deliveries resulted from shortages of raw materials and the need for equitable allocation among customers and because there was "no practical alternative source of supply." This acquiescence was jolted in May, 1974 when Roth learned that Sharon was allocating substantial quantities of rolled steel to a subsidiary for sale at premium prices. After several more months of desultory performance on both sides, Roth sued Sharon for breach of contract, with special emphasis upon the modified contract for 1973. Sharon raised several defenses, including impracticability and, in the alternative, the agreed modification. The district court, after a long trial, held, *inter alia*, that Sharon was not excused from the 1973 contract on the grounds of impracticability and that the modification was unenforceable. A judgment for $555,968.46 was entered for Roth.

On appeal, the court of appeals affirmed the district court's decision on the impracticability, modification and other issues, but remanded the case for factual findings on whether Roth gave Sharon timely notice of breach. On the impracticability defense under UCC 2-615(a), the court held that "Sharon's inability to perform was a result of its policy of accepting far more orders than it was capable of fulfilling, rather than a result of the existing shortage of raw materials." In refusing to enforce the modification of the 1973 contract, the court had this to say.]

CELEBREZZE, SENIOR CIRCUIT JUDGE

* * * C. In March, 1973, Sharon notified its customers that it intended to charge the

maximum permissible price for all of its products; accordingly, all price concessions, including those made to the plaintiffs, were to be rescinded effective April 1, 1973. On March 23, 1973, Guerin [Roth's vice pres.] indicated to Metzger [Sharon's sales manager] that the plaintiffs considered the proposed price increase to be a breach of the November, 1972 contract. In an effort to resolve the dispute, Guerin met with representatives of Sharon on March 28, 1973 and asked Sharon to postpone any price increases until June or July, 1973. Several days later, Richard Mecaskey, Guerin's replacement, sent a letter to Sharon which indicated that the plaintiffs believed that the November, 1972 agreement was enforceable and that the plaintiffs were willing to negotiate a price modification if Sharon's cost increases warranted such an action. As a result of this letter, another meeting was held between Sharon and the plaintiffs. At this meeting, Walter Gregg, Sharon's vice-president and chairman of the board, agreed to continue charging the November, 1972 prices until June 30, 1973 and offered, for the remainder of 1973, to charge prices that were lower than Sharon's published prices but higher than the 1972 prices. Although the plaintiffs initially rejected the terms offered by Sharon for the second half of 1973, Mecaskey reluctantly agreed to Sharon's terms on June 29, 1973.

Before the district court, Sharon asserted that it properly increased prices because the parties had modified the November, 1973 contract to reflect changed market conditions. The district court, however, made several findings which, it believed, indicated that Sharon did not seek a modification to avoid a loss on the contract. The district court also found that the plaintiffs' inventories of rolled steel were "alarmingly deficient" at the time modification was sought and that Sharon had threatened to cease selling steel to the plaintiffs in the second-half of 1973 unless the plaintiffs agreed to the modification. Because Sharon had used its position as the plaintiffs' chief supplier to extract the price modification, the district court concluded that Sharon had acted in bad faith by seeking to modify the contract. In the alternative, the court concluded that the modification agreement was voidable because it was extracted by means of economic duress; the tight steel market prevented the plaintiffs from obtaining steel elsewhere at an affordable price and, consequently, the plaintiffs were forced to agree to the modification in order to assure a continued supply of steel.* * * Sharon challenges these conclusions on appeal.

The ability of a party to modify a contract which is subject to Article Two of the Uniform Commercial Code is broader than common law, primarily because the modification needs no consideration to be binding. O.R.C § 1302.12 (UCC § 2-

209(1)). A party's ability to modify an agreement is limited only by Article Two's general obligation of good faith. * * * In determining whether a particular modification was obtained in good faith, a court must make two distinct inquiries: whether the party's conduct is consistent with "reasonable commercial standards of fair dealing in the trade," * * * and whether the parties were in fact motivated to seek modification by an honest desire to compensate for commercial exigencies * * * ORC § 1302.01(m)(2) (UCC § 2-103). The first inquiry is relatively straightforward; the party asserting the modification must demonstrate that his decision to seek modification was the result of a factor, such as increased costs, which would cause an ordinary merchant to seek a modification of the contract. *See* Official Comment 2, O.R.C § 1302.12 (UCC § 2-209) (reasonable commercial standards may require objective reason); J. WHITE & R. SUMMERS, HANDBOOK OF LAW UNDER THE UCC at 41. The second inquiry, regarding the subjective honesty of the parties, is less clearly defined. Essentially, this inquiry requires the party asserting the modification to demonstrate that he was, in fact, motivated by a legitimate commercial reason and that such a reason is not offered merely as a pretext. * * * Moreover, the trier of fact must determine whether the means used to obtain the modification are an impermissible attempt to obtain a modification by extortion or overreaching. * * *

Sharon argues that its decision to seek a modification was consistent with reasonable commercial standards of fair dealing because market exigencies made further performance entail a substantial loss. The district court, however, made three findings which caused it to conclude that economic circumstances were not the reason that Sharon sought a modification: it found that Sharon was partially insulated from raw material price increases, that Sharon bargained for a contract with a slim profit margin and thus implicitly assumed the risk that performance might come to involve a loss, and that Sharon's overall profit in 1973 and its profit on the contract in the first quarter of 1973 were inconsistent with Sharon's position that the modification was sought to avoid a loss. Although all of these findings are marginally related to the question whether Sharon's conduct was consistent with reasonable commercial standards of fair dealing, we do not believe that they are sufficient to support a finding that Sharon did not observe reasonable commercial standards by seeking a modification. In our view, these findings do not support a conclusion that a reasonable merchant, in light of the circumstances, would not have sought a modification in order to avoid a loss. * * *

In the final analysis, the single most important consideration in determining whether the decision to seek a modification is justified in this context is whether, because of changes in the market or other unforeseeable conditions, performance of the contract has come to involve a loss. In this case, the district court found that Sharon suffered substantial losses by performing the contract *as modified.* * * * We are convinced that unforeseen economic exigencies existed which would prompt an ordinary merchant to seek a modification to avoid a loss on the contract; thus, we believe that the district court's findings to the contrary are clearly erroneous. * * *

The second part of the analysis, honesty in fact, is pivotal. The district court found that Sharon "threatened not to sell Roth and Toledo any steel if they refused to pay increased prices after July 1, 1973" and, consequently, that Sharon acted wrongfully. Sharon does not dispute the finding that it threatened to stop selling steel to the plaintiffs. Instead, it asserts that such a finding is merely evidence of bad faith and that it has rebutted any inference of bad faith based on that finding. We agree with this analysis; although coercive conduct is evidence that a modification of a contract is sought in bad faith, that prima facie showing may be effectively rebutted by the party seeking to enforce the modification. * * * Although we agree with Sharon's statement of principles, we do not agree that Sharon has rebutted the inference of bad faith that rises from its coercive conduct. Sharon asserts that its decision to unilaterally raise prices was based on language in the November 17, 1972 letter which allowed it to raise prices to the extent of any general industry-wide price increase. Because prices in the steel industry had increased, Sharon concludes that it was justified in raising its prices. Because it was justified in raising the contract price, the plaintiffs were bound by the terms of the contract to pay the increased prices. Consequently, any refusal by the plaintiffs to pay the price increase sought by Sharon must be viewed as a material breach of the November, 1972 contract which would excuse Sharon from any further performance. Thus, Sharon reasons that its refusal to perform absent a price increase was justified under the contract and consistent with good faith.

This argument fails in two respects. First, the contractual language on which Sharon relies only permits, at most, a price increase for cold rolled steel; thus, even if Sharon's position were supported by the evidence, Sharon would not have been justified in refusing to sell the plaintiff's hot rolled steel because of the plaintiffs' refusal to pay higher prices for the product. More importantly, however, the evidence does not indicate that Sharon ever offered this theory as a justification until this matter was tried. Sharon's representatives, in their testimony, did not attempt to justify Sharon's refusal to ship steel at 1972 prices in this fashion. Furthermore, none of the contemporaneous communications contain this justification for Sharon's action. In short, we can find no evidence in the record which indicates that Sharon offered this theory as a justification at the time the modification was sought. Consequently, we believe that the district court's conclusion that Sharon acted in bad faith by using coercive conduct to extract the price modification is not clearly erroneous. Therefore, we hold that Sharon's attempt to modify the November, 1972 contract, in order to compensate for increased costs which made performance come to involve a loss, is ineffective because Sharon did not act in a manner consistent with Article Two's requirement of honesty in fact when it refused to perform its remaining obligations under the contract at 1972 prices.[1] * * *

[Some footnotes omitted. Those retained have been renumbered.]

Notes

1.   Section 89 of the RESTATEMENT (SECOND) OF CONTRACTS provides: "A promise modifying a duty under a contract not fully performed on either side is binding (a) if the modification is fair and equitable in view of circumstances not anticipated by the parties when the contract was made; or (b) to the extent provided by statute; or (c) to the extent that justice requires enforcement in view of material change of position in reliance on the promise." Is *Roth* consistent with the RESTATEMENT?

2.   Following the logic of UCC 2-209(1) and the comments, *Roth* invalidated the modification because of Sharon's bad faith rather than because of economic duress. In fact, the court, in a footnote, suggested that proof of coercive means will not necessarily invalidate a modification made in good faith. Exactly what is bad faith in the Sixth Circuit?

3.   Economic duress may be invoked to invalidate a modification where one

---

[1] The district court also found, as an alternative ground, that the modification was voidable because the plaintiffs agreed to the modification due to economic duress. *See, e.g., Oskey Gasoline & Oil Co. v. Continental Oil*, 534 F.2d 1281 (8th Cir.1976). Because we conclude that the modification was ineffective as a result of Sharon's bad faith, we do not reach the issue whether the contract modification was also voidable because of economic duress. We note, however, that proof that coercive means were used is necessary to establish that a contract is voidable because of economic duress. Normally, it cannot be used to void a contract modification which has been sought in good faith; if a contract modification has been found to be in good faith, then presumably no wrongful coercive means have been used to extract the modification.

party has made a "wrongful" threat to withhold delivery of needed goods, the threatened party can not obtain substitute goods from another source and the ordinary remedy of an action for breach of contract is not adequate.[*] Could the modification in *Roth* be invalidated for economic duress?[**]

2. Agreed Modifications and the Statute of Frauds

Assume that S and B enter into an oral contract to sell 100 units of a good for the total price of $4,000. The statute of frauds does not apply because the price is less than $5,000. UCC 2-201(1). [formerly $500]. Suppose that the parties, before any performance has occurred, modify the contract by adding 100 more units for an additional $4,000. This agreement modifying the contract is clearly enforceable under UCC 2-209(1). But now UCC 2-209(3) comes into play: "The requirements of the statute of frauds * * * (Section 2-201) must be satisfied if the contract as modified is within its provisions." Without question, the "contract as modified" is within UCC 2-201(1), even though neither the original contract nor the modification were for a price of "$5,000 or more." Thus, it would appear that the modification must meet the requirement of a writing in UCC 2-201(1) or satisfy the exceptions listed in UCC 2-201(3). In addition, the modification should be in writing if it falls within UCC 2-201(1) on its own or if it changes the quantity term of an original contract that fell within UCC 2-201. A literal reading of this somewhat murky provision does not, however, support the conclusion that if the original contract was within UCC 2-201, any modification must also be in writing.[***] Notice that UCC 2A-208 does not have a comparable provision regarding the statute of frauds. Does the reasoning of the comment to UCC 2A-208 apply equally to UCC 2-209?

The parties to a contract for sale may create their own statute of frauds requirements for agreed modifications. UCC 2-209(2) provides:

---

[*] *See Austin Instrument, Inc. v. Loral Corp.*, 272 N.E.2d 533 (N.Y. 1971). Professor Hillman, for one, favors this approach. *See* Robert A. Hillman, *Contract Modification Under the Restatement (Second) of Contracts,* 67 CORNELL L. REV. 680 (1982).

[**] *See Kelsey-Hayes Co. v. Galtaco Redlaw Castings Corp.*, 749 F. Supp. 794 (E.D. Mich. 1990) (holding that UCC 2-209(1) does not preempt the common law of economic duress).

[***] *Compare Costco Wholesale Corp. v. World Wide Licensing Corp.*, 898 P.2d 347 (Wash. Ct. App. 1995) (all modifications need not be in writing) *with Zemco Manufacturing Inc. v. Navistar Int'l Transportation Corp.*, 186 F. 3d 815 (7th Cir. 1999) (all modifications must be in writing).

An agreement in a signed record which excludes modification or rescission except by a signed record may not be otherwise modified or rescinded, but except as between merchants such a requirement in a form supplied by the merchant must be separately signed by the other party.

What is the purpose of the so-called "no oral modification" (NOM) agreement? Suppose the NOM clause is in a contract for the sale of manufactured goods and is a condition precedent to the buyer's duty to pay more than the agreed price under alleged modifications. The clause protects the buyer against, among other things, unauthorized agreements between its agent and the seller as work progresses. Thus, if the agent enters an oral agreement with the seller increasing the price by $10,000 to pay for the extra work, the oral modification is not enforceable (although the restitution principle may operate in this setting).

B. Modification or Rescission by Waiver

At common law, the concept of waiver was frequently invoked to excuse conditions precedent to a contractual duty to perform. Suppose, for example, the contract provided that before the buyer had a duty to pay for goods delivered, they must be inspected and certified by a designated third party. In theory, the buyer has no duty to pay until the condition is satisfied. But if, with knowledge that no certificate had been issued, the buyer elected to accept and pay for the goods, the condition was waived and could not be reinstated for the delivery involved. This was waiver by "election."

Suppose, however, that B, before delivery, represented to S that the certificate would not be required. Although this representation was, in a broad sense, a waiver, no election was involved. B could retract the waiver (just like retracting a repudiation) unless S relied in a material way upon that representation. If there was reliance (waiver by estoppel) the condition would be discharged. The former (election) waived conditions which had already failed and the latter (estoppel) waived conditions which had not.[*] Although both types of waiver modified or discharged conditions in the contract, they did not affect the right of the waiving party to damages for defective performance: only a modification supported by

---

[*] *See* RESTATEMENT (SECOND) OF CONTRACTS 84.

consideration or other valid reasons for enforcement could do that.[*]

With this sketchy background, look again at UCC 2-209(2), (4), and (5) and consider the following cases.[**] *Compare* 2A-208(2), (3) and (4). What is the difference between waiver of a condition and waiver of breach of a performance obligation?

BMC INDUSTRIES, INC. v. BARTH INDUSTRIES, INC.
UNITED STATES COURT OF APPEALS FOR THE ELEVENTH CIRCUIT, 1998
160 F.3D 1322, *CERT. DENIED*, 526 U.S. 1132 (1999)

TJOFLAT, CIRCUIT JUDGE

This appeal arises from a contract entered into between BMC Industries, Inc., and Barth Industries, Inc., for the design, manufacture, and installation of equipment to automate BMC's production line for unfinished eyeglass lenses. Eighteen months after the delivery date set out in the contract had passed, BMC filed suit against Barth for breach of contract. Barth, in turn, counterclaimed for breach of contract. * * * [Jury found in favor of BMC on the breach of contract claim. Barth appealed.]

I.
A.

BMC, through its Vision-Ease division, manufactures semi-finished polymer opthalmic lenses that are used in the production of eyeglasses. These lenses are created by an assembly-line process. * * *

In order to decrease labor costs, and thereby remain competitive with other lens manufacturers who were utilizing cheaper foreign labor, BMC decided to become the first company to automate portions of its lens manufacturing process. Consequently, in early 1986, BMC commissioned Barth to complete a preliminary design and feasibility study. Barth's subcontractor, Komech, finished the study in June 1986. Based on this study, Barth and BMC entered into a contract (the "Contract") which provided that Barth would "design, fabricate, debug/test and supervise field installation and start up of equipment to automate the operations of

---

[*] *See National Utility Service, Inc. v. Whirlpool Corp.*, 325 F.2d 779 (2nd Cir. 1963). *See also* UCC 1-306 [former 1-107].

[**] *See also* David V. Snyder, *The Law of Contract and the Concept of Change: Public and Private Attempts to Regulate Modification, Waiver, and Estoppel*, 1999 WIS. L. REV. 607; Douglas K. Newell, *Cleaning up UCC Section 2-209*, 27 IDAHO L. REV. 487 (1990).

mold assembly declipping, clip transport, mold assembly clipping, and mold filling." The Contract, which stated that it was governed by Florida law, listed a price of $515,200 and provided for delivery of four automated production lines by June 1987. The Contract also stated that time was of the essence.

On November 4, 1986, Barth and BMC executed a written amendment to the Contract, extending the delivery date by one month. In February 1987, Barth terminated Komech as design subcontractor, and hired another engineering company, Belcan, in its place. Belcan subsequently redesigned the automation equipment, which delayed Barth's progress and led the parties to execute the second (and last) written amendment, which extended the delivery date to "October 1987."

After this second amendment, Barth continued to experience technical problems and design difficulties that caused repeated delays. The parties did not extend the delivery date beyond October 1987 to accommodate these delays, however. Instead, Barth and BMC each demonstrated a willingness to continue performance under the Contract. * * *

This design problem was only one of many technical difficulties that developed; other problems arose with the filling nozzles and mold assembly springs, among other components. Consequently, by October 1987, the amended Contract's delivery deadline, Barth estimated that it could not deliver the equipment until April 1988. BMC executives were still anxious, however, to continue the automation project. Thus, during the spring of 1988, although they protested Barth's failure to deliver the equipment on time, these executives encouraged Barth to continue working on the project.

In June 1988, Barth completed the four automated de-clip/de-gasket machines and delivered them to BMC. Without the entire automated system, however, BMC could not fully test these machines; the whole production line had to be in place.

By August 1988, BMC's mounting apprehension about Barth's ability to perform led it to seek assurance that Barth would be able to complete performance under the Contract. In an effort to obtain such assurance, BMC executives met with Robert Tomsich, a Barth officer (and director) who also served as Nesco's president. According to these executives, Tomsich ensured them that Barth would perform the Contract, that Nesco's resources were committed to the project, and that, in the future, BMC should deal directly with Nesco.

Although BMC had considered terminating the Contract and suing Barth for breach, BMC took neither step. Instead, it continued to lead Barth and Nesco to believe that it was determined to finish the project; BMC collaborated with Barth's engineers to overcome difficulties, suggested design changes, and asked Barth whether more money (presumably provided by BMC) would help it complete the equipment in less time.

By January 1989, Barth still had not produced a functioning automation system. Due to time and cost overruns, Barth had invested over $1 million of its own money in the project. BMC previously had agreed to compensate Barth for these additional expenses; consequently, during that month, Tomsich asked BMC for $250,000 to cover some of Barth's cost overruns. One month later, BMC responded with a $100,000 payment, along with a letter stating that BMC was "insisting on Barth's adherence to the projected schedule," and was "not waiving any rights or remedies" for any breach, including "Barth's failure to meet the delivery dates specified in the contract." Barth's latest schedule called for delivery in June 1989.

Barth's delays and setbacks continued throughout the spring of 1989; but while BMC encouraged Barth to carry on, and continued to cooperate with Barth's engineers to solve problems, BMC also became increasingly impatient. In March, and again in April 1989, BMC pointed out Barth's unacceptable failure to meet deadlines.

Near the end of May 1989, Barth notified BMC that it had finally completed the mold assembly filling machine and that it would deliver the equipment F.O.B. Barth's dock in accordance with the Contract. BMC refused delivery of the mold assembly filler, and instead filed this lawsuit on June 5, 1989.

B.

* * * BMC's breach of contract count alleged that the second written amendment to the Contract established October 1987 as the deadline for Barth's performance. Because Barth failed to deliver the automated equipment by that date, Barth was in default of its contractual obligations. BMC sought damages for Barth's breach in the sum of $6.4 million. Two separate injuries suffered by BMC comprised this measure of damages. First, BMC sought to recover the labor costs that it would have saved had it been able to use the automated equipment rather than pay employees to produce the lenses manually. Because BMC executives predicted that the automated equipment would have a useful life of ten years, BMC sought these lost labor savings for the ten year period from October 1987 until October 1997. Second, BMC sought compensation for what it termed the "working capital effect." This effect is an estimate of the money BMC lost because its capital was tied up paying higher labor costs rather than being used for investment or being used to pay off the company's debt (and thus reducing the interest BMC paid to its creditors).

As an affirmative defense to BMC's breach of contract claim, Barth asserted that BMC's conduct after the October 1987 delivery date had passed amounted to a waiver of the delivery date under Article 2 of the Uniform Commercial Code ("UCC"). Although Barth failed to deliver the machines by October 1987, Barth argued, BMC executives urged Barth to keep working, BMC engineers continued to assist Barth in overcoming technical problems, and BMC executives agreed to increase the purchase price. Therefore, Barth claimed, BMC waived its entitlement to delivery of the machines in October 1987. * * *

[The Court of Appeals reversed the trial court determination that the UCC did not apply to this transaction.] * * *

Having determined that the UCC governs this case, we must next apply Article 2's waiver provision to the Contract. The UCC waiver provision states in relevant part:

(2) A signed agreement which excludes modification or recission except by a signed writing cannot be otherwise modified or rescinded.* * *

* * *

(4) Although an attempt at modification or recission does not satisfy the requirements of subsection (2) or (3) [regarding the statute of frauds] it can operate as a *waiver*.

(5) A party who has made a waiver affecting an executory portion of the contract may retract the waiver by reasonable notification received by the other party that strict performance will be required of any term waived, unless the retraction would be unjust in view of a material change of position in reliance on the waiver.

Fla. Stat. ch. 672.209 (1997) (emphasis added).* * *

Although the UCC does not specifically lay out the elements of waiver, we have stated that waiver requires "(1) the existence at the time of the waiver a right, privilege, advantage, or benefit which may be waived; (2) the actual constructive knowledge thereof; and (3) an intention to relinquish such right, privilege, advantage, or benefit."* * * Conduct may constitute waiver of a contract term, but such an implied waiver must be demonstrated by clear evidence.* * * Waiver may be implied when a party's actions are inconsistent with continued retention of the right* * *.

As an initial matter, we must determine whether, under the UCC, waiver must be accompanied by detrimental reliance. Although it is settled that waiver under Florida common law must be supported by valid consideration or detrimental reliance* * *, courts disagree on whether the UCC retains this requirement. We conclude, however, that the UCC does not require consideration or detrimental reliance for waiver of a contract term.

Our conclusion follows from the plain language of subsections 672.209(4) and (5). While subsection (4) states that an attempted modification that fails may still constitute a waiver, subsection (5) provides that the waiver may be retracted *unless* the non-waiving party relies on the waiver. Consequently, the statute recognizes that waivers may exist in the absence of detrimental reliance–these are the retractable waivers referred to in subsection (5). Only this interpretation renders meaning to subsection (5), because reading subsection (4) to require detrimental reliance for all waivers means that waivers would *never* be retractable. *See Wisconsin Knife Works v. National Metal Crafters*, 781 F.2d 1280, 1291 (7th Cir. 1986) (Easterbrook, J., dissenting) (noting that reading a detrimental reliance requirement into the UCC would eliminate the distinction between subsections (4) and (5)). Subsection (5) would therefore be meaningless.

At least one Florida court implicitly agrees with this conclusion; * * *

Although other courts have held that waiver requires reliance under the UCC, those courts have ignored the UCC's plain language. The leading case espousing this view of waiver is *Wisconsin Knife Works v. National Metal Crafters*, 781 F.2d 1280 (7th Cir. 1986) (addressing section 2-209 of the model version of the UCC, from which Florida adopted section 672.209 verbatim), in which a panel of the Seventh Circuit addressed a contract that included a term prohibiting oral modifications, and considered whether an attempted oral modification could instead constitute a waiver. Writing for the majority, Judge Posner concluded that the UCC's subsection (2), which gives effect to "no oral modification" provisions, would become superfluous if contract terms could be waived without detrimental reliance. Judge Posner reasoned that if attempted oral modifications that were unenforceable because of subsection (2) were nevertheless enforced as waivers under subsection (4), then subsection (2) is "very nearly a dead letter." *Id.* at 1286. According to Judge Posner, there must be some difference between modification and waiver in order for both subsections (2) and (4) to have meaning. This difference is waiver's detrimental reliance requirement.[1]

---

[1] Contrary to our reasoning above, Judge Posner claims that reading a reliance requirement into waiver under subsection (4) is not inconsistent with subsection (5). According to Judge Posner, subsection (5) is broader than subsection (4), covering waivers other than mere attempts at oral modification. Judge Posner argues as an example that subsection (5) covers express waivers that are written and signed. *See id.* at 1287. In dissent, however, Judge Easterbrook convincingly dissects this argument. As Judge Easterbrook explains, subsection (5) is narrower than subsection (4)–limiting the effect of waivers that are not detrimentally

(continued...)

Judge Posner, however, ignores a fundamental difference between modifications and waivers: while a party that has agreed to a contract modification cannot cancel the modification without giving consideration for the cancellation, a party may unilaterally retract its waiver of a contract term provided it gives reasonable notice. The fact that waivers may unilaterally be retracted provides the difference between subsections (2) and (4) that allows both to have meaning. We therefore conclude that waiver under the UCC does not require detrimental reliance. Consequently, without reaching the issue of detrimental reliance, we consider whether BMC waived the Contract's October 1987 delivery date. * * *

Applying the elements of waiver to the facts before us, we hold as a matter of law that BMC waived the October 1987 delivery date. The October 1987 delivery date was a waivable contract right, of which BMC had actual knowledge. We also conclude that BMC's conduct impliedly demonstrated an intent to relinquish that right.

The most cogent evidence of this waiver is BMC's own representation of its relationship with Nesco. Throughout this litigation, BMC has maintained that Nesco, beginning in August 1988, "stepped in and promised to complete the project. In doing so, Nesco expressly represented that all of its resources were committed to the project, and instructed BMC to deal solely with Nesco." According to BMC, therefore, Nesco voluntarily became liable, in the fall of 1988, for Barth's completion of the project. By that time, however, the October 1987 delivery date had already passed. If, as BMC claims, the contract was already breached, then Nesco could never have performed its obligations; Nesco was in breach of its promise as soon as that promise was made, and could have been sued by BMC the next day. For Nesco's promise to have meaning, BMC must have given Barth and Nesco additional time to perform--in other words, BMC must have waived the October 1987 delivery date.* * *

Furthermore, BMC's course of dealing with Barth evidenced BMC's waiver of the October 1987 delivery date, because BMC failed timely to demand compliance with that contract term or terminate the Contract and file suit. When a delivery date passes without the seller's delivery, the buyer must object within a reasonable time and warn the seller that it is in breach. * * *

---

[1] (...continued)
relied upon--not the reverse as Judge Posner claims. Furthermore, Judge Easterbrook demonstrates that subsection (5) cannot cover express written and signed waivers because such writings are not waivers, but rather effective written modifications under subsection (2). *See id.* at 1291 (Easterbrook, J., dissenting).

Although BMC maintained at trial that Barth breached the contract as of October 1987, BMC did not tell Barth it intended to terminate the contract and hold Barth liable for the breach until May 1989. In fact, the earliest indication from BMC that it was considering termination was August 1988, when BMC executives met with Tomsich to seek assurance that Barth would perform. As we have already stated, however, the result of that meeting was a waiver of the October 1987 delivery date, not a timely exercise of BMC's right to terminate the Contract. BMC did not warn Barth in earnest of its intent to terminate until February 1989, when BMC sent Barth a letter along with $100,000 of the $250,000 payment Tomsich had requested at the August 1988 meeting. This letter warned Barth that BMC was not waiving its rights and remedies for Barth's failure to meet contractual delivery dates. BMC warned Barth again in March when it sent a letter advising of its intent to "hold [Barth] responsible, both for the initial breach and for all failures to meet subsequently promised dates."

Until 1989, however, BMC continued to act as though both parties were bound by the Contract and that Barth was not in default of its obligations: the October 1987 delivery date passed without comment from BMC; engineers from BMC frequently provided advice or assistance to help Barth personnel overcome technical problems; BMC executives frequently visited Barth's production facilities and encouraged Barth to continue working to complete the equipment; BMC even continued to spend money on the project--in December 1987, over one month after the October 1987 delivery date had passed, BMC purchased an additional $71,075 worth of springs and tooling for the machines. In sum, rather than terminating the Contract, or at least warning Barth that it was in breach after the October 1987 delivery date had passed, BMC continued to act as though the Contract remained in effect.

This is not to say that BMC never complained that Barth had missed deadlines; BMC executives frequently expressed their concern and disappointment that the project was so far behind schedule. * * *

The UCC states that when a contractual delivery date is waived, delivery must be made within a reasonable time. * * * Consequently, because BMC waived the October 1987 delivery date, Barth was only obligated to deliver the machines within a reasonable time period. We remand this case to the district court for a new trial on the question of whether Barth tendered the machines within a reasonable time period. * * *

* * * [W]e conclude that BMC waived the October 1987 delivery date. We therefore VACATE the district court's judgment against Barth and REMAND the

case to the district court for retrial of BMC's claims against Barth as well as Barth's counterclaims in accordance with the UCC. * * *

[Some footnotes omitted. Those retained have been renumbered.]

Notes

1.   Note that the waiver by the buyer was of the agreed due date for delivery, a part of the agreed exchange. The result was that the contract then contained a "gap" in an essential term. The court used the "gap filler" found in UCC 2-309, so that the date for delivery was "a reasonable time." How does this differ from the waiver of a condition precedent, i.e. an event that must happen before a duty to perform arises but an event whose failure is not a breach of contract?

2.   Florida law apparently required either reliance or consideration for a waiver. Did the court purport to find a waiver without detrimental reliance by the seller? What language of UCC 2-209 supports that result? Exactly how does the court distinguish the conclusion of Judge Posner in *Wisconsin Knife Works*, discussed in the opinion? Are you persuaded? See the next case.

CLOUD CORPORATION V. HASBRO, INC.
UNITED STATES COURT OF APPEALS, SEVENTH CIRCUIT, 2002
314 F.3D 289

POSNER, CIRCUIT JUDGE

"Wonder World Aquarium" is a toy that Hasbro, Inc., the well-known designer and marketer of toys, sold for a brief period in the mid-1990s. The toy comes as a package that contains (we simplify slightly) the aquarium itself, some plastic fish, and, depending on the size of the aquarium (for this varies), large or small packets of a powder that when dissolved in distilled water forms a transparent gelatinous filling for the aquarium. The gel simulates water, and the plastic fish can be inserted into it with tweezers to create the illusion of a real fish tank with living, though curiously inert, fish. "Pretend blood," included in some of the packages, can be added for even greater verisimilitude. The consumer can choose among versions of Wonder World Aquarium that range from "My Pretty Mermaid" to "Piranha Attack"--the latter a scenario in which the pretend blood is doubtless a mandatory rather than optional ingredient.

Hasbro contracted out the manufacture of this remarkable product. Southern

Clay Products Company was to sell and ship Laponite HB, a patented synthetic clay, to Cloud Corporation, which was to mix the Laponite with a preservative according to a formula supplied by Hasbro, pack the mixture in the packets that we mentioned, and ship them to affiliates of Hasbro in East Asia. The affiliates would prepare and package the final product--that is the aquarium, the packet of gel, and the plastic fish (and "pretend blood")--and ship it back to Hasbro in the United States for distribution to retailers.

Beginning in mid-1995, Hasbro would from time to time issue purchase orders for a specified number of large and small packets to Cloud, which would in turn order the quantity of Laponite from Southern Clay Products that it needed in order to manufacture the specified number of packets. The required quantity of Laponite depended not only on the number of large and small packets ordered by Hasbro but also on the formula that Hasbro supplied to Cloud specifying the proportion of Laponite in each packet. The formula was changed frequently. The less Laponite per packet specified in the formula, the more packets could be manufactured for a given quantity of the ingredient.

Early in 1997 Hasbro discovered that its East Asian affiliates, the assemblers of the final package, had more than enough powder on hand to supply Hasbro's needs, which were diminishing, no doubt because Wonder World Aquarium was losing market appeal. Mistakenly believing that Hasbro's market was expanding rather than contracting, Cloud had manufactured a great many packets of powder in advance of receiving formal purchase orders for them from Hasbro. Hasbro refused to accept delivery of these packets or to pay for them. Contending that this refusal was a breach of contract, Cloud sued Hasbro in federal district court in Chicago, basing jurisdiction on diversity of citizenship and seeking more than $600,000 in damages based mainly on the price of the packets that it had manufactured and not delivered to Hasbro and now was stuck with-- for the packets, being usable only in Wonder World Aquaria, had no resale value. After a bench trial, the district judge ruled in favor of Hasbro.

Cloud does not quarrel with the district judge's findings of fact, but only with her legal conclusions. The governing law is the Uniform Commercial Code as interpreted in Illinois.

The original understanding between Hasbro and Cloud regarding Cloud's role in the Wonder World Aquarium project either was not a contract or was not broken-- probably the former, as the parties had not agreed on the price, quantity, delivery dates, or composition of the packets. These essential terms were set forth in the purchase orders that Hasbro sent Cloud, confirming discussions between employees of Cloud and Kathy Esposito, Hasbro's employee in charge of purchasing inputs for the company's foreign affiliates. Upon receipt of a purchase order, Cloud would send Hasbro an order acknowledgment and would order from Southern Clay Products the quantity of Laponite required to fill the purchase order.

In October 1995, which is to say a few months after the launch of Wonder World Aquarium, Hasbro sent a letter to all its suppliers, including Cloud, that contained a "terms and conditions" form to govern future purchase orders. One of the terms was that a supplier could not deviate from a purchase order without Hasbro's written consent. As requested, Cloud signed the form and returned it to Hasbro. Nevertheless, to make assurance doubly sure, every time Hasbro sent a purchase order to Cloud it would include an acknowledgment form for Cloud to sign that contained the same terms and conditions that were in the October letter. Cloud did not sign any of these acknowledgment forms.   The order acknowledgments that it sent Hasbro in response to Hasbro's purchase orders contained on the back of each acknowledgment Cloud's own set of terms and conditions--and the provision in Hasbro's letter and forms requiring Hasbro's written consent to any modification of the purchase order was not among them. There was a space for Hasbro to sign Cloud's acknowledgment form but it never did so. Neither party complained about the other's failure to sign the tendered forms.

Hasbro placed its last purchase orders with Cloud in February and April 1996. The orders for February specified 2.3 million small packets and 3.2 million large ones. For April the numbers were 1.5 and 1.4 million. Hasbro notified Cloud of the formula that it was to use in making the packets and Cloud ordered Laponite from Southern Clay Products accordingly.

Now as it happened Southern Clay Products was having trouble delivering the Laponite in time to enable Cloud to meet its own delivery schedule. In June 1996, amidst complaints from Hasbro's East Asian affiliates that they were running out of powder, and concerned about the lag in Laponite deliveries, Hasbro notified Cloud that it was to use a new formula in manufacturing the powder, a formula that required so much less Laponite that the same quantity would enable Cloud to produce a third again as many packets. Cloud determined that by using the new formula it could produce from the quantity of Laponite that it had on hand 4.5 million small and 5 million large packets, compared to the 3.8 and 3.9 million called for by the February and April orders but not yet delivered. Cloud had delivered 700,000 of the large packets ordered in February and April; that is why it had 7.7 million packets still to deliver under those orders rather than 8.4 million, the total number of packets ordered (2.3 + 3.2 + 1.5 + 1.4 = 8.4).

Although it had received no additional purchase orders, Cloud sent Hasbro an order acknowledgment for 4.5 million small and 5 million large packets with a delivery date similar to that for the April order, but at a lower price per packet, reflecting the smaller quantity of Laponite, the expensive ingredient in the powder, in each packet.

Cloud's acknowledgment was sent in June. Hasbro did not respond to it--at least not explicitly. It did receive it, however. And Kathy Esposito continued having e-mail exchanges and phone conversations with Cloud. These focused on delivery dates and, importantly, on the quantities to be delivered on those dates. Importantly because some very large numbers--much larger than the February and April numbers, numbers consistent however with Cloud's order acknowledgment sent to Hasbro in June--appear in these and other e-mails written by her. In two of the e-mails the quantity Cloud is to ship is described as "more or less depending on the formula," consistent with Cloud's understanding that if the formula reduced the amount of Laponite per packet Cloud should increase the number of packets it made rather than return unused Laponite to Southern Clay Products. A notation made in August by another member of Hasbro's purchasing department, Maryann Ricci-"Cloud O/S; 4,000,000 sm; 3.5 million lg."--indicates her belief that Cloud had outstanding ("O/S") purchase orders for 4 million small and 3.5 million large packets. These numbers were far in excess of the undelivered portions of the February and April orders; and since all the earlier orders had, so far as we can determine, already been filled and so were no longer outstanding, she must have been referring to the numbers in Cloud's June order acknowledgment.

The district judge, despite ruling for Hasbro, found that indeed "Hasbro intended to exceed the quantities of ... packages it had ordered from Cloud in February and April of 1996," that "Hasbro was more concerned with prompt product than with the specific terms of its order[s]," and, most important, that "given Hasbro's repeated message that it could not get enough Laponite HB to fill its needs in a timely fashion, Cloud's decision to produce as many packets as possible appeared to be a safe course of action. Cloud was trying to keep pace with Hasbro's Laponite HB needs, a task made virtually impossible by the length of time it took Southern Clay to fill Cloud's Laponite HB orders." The judge even suggested that given Hasbro's desperation, Cloud could have persuaded Hasbro to execute additional purchase orders at prices equal to those in the February and April orders. Instead, rather than trying to take advantage of Hasbro's fix, Cloud reduced its price to reflect its lower cost. A curious consequence of the reduction, unremarked by the parties, is that even if Cloud has no contract remedy, it has (unless time barred) a remedy in quantum meruit for the benefit it conferred on Hasbro by voluntarily reducing the price specified in the February and April purchase orders.

When some months later Hasbro pulled the plug on Wonder World Aquarium, Cloud had not begun delivering any of the additional quantity that it had manufactured over and above the quantities called for in the February and April purchase orders.

Was Cloud commercially unreasonable in producing the additional quantity without a purchase order? If not, should the Uniform Commercial Code, which was intended to conform sales law to the customs and usages of business people, UCC §§ 1-102(2)(b), 1-105 comment 3; * * * nevertheless condemn Cloud, as the district judge believed, for failing to request written purchase orders for the additional quantity that the change in formula enabled it to manufacture? Or was Hasbro contractually obligated to pay for that additional quantity?

The answers to these questions depend on whether there was a valid modification of the quantity specifications in the February and April purchase orders (obviously Hasbro cannot complain about the price modification!). The October letter provided that purchase orders could not be modified without Hasbro's written consent. Cloud signed the letter and so became bound by it, consideration being furnished by Hasbro's continuing to do business with Cloud. Hasbro's order acknowledgments accompanying its February and April purchase orders also provided that the orders could not be modified without Hasbro's written consent.* * *

For unexpressed reasons the district judge did not focus on the contractual provisions requiring that any modification of a purchase order be in writing. She considered only whether the UCC's statute of frauds required this, and ruled that it did. The quantity term in a contract for the sale of goods for more than $500 must be memorialized in a writing signed by the party sought to be held to that term, UCC § 2-201(1), and so, therefore, must a modification of that term. UCC § 2-209(3). However--and here we part company with the district judge--Kathy Esposito's e- mails, plus the notation that we quoted earlier signed by Maryann Ricci, another member of Hasbro's purchasing department, satisfy the statutory requirement. The UCC does not require that the contract itself be in writing, only that there be adequate documentary evidence of its existence and essential terms, which there was here. * * *

The purpose of the statute of frauds is to prevent a contracting party from creating a triable issue concerning the terms of the contract--or for that matter concerning whether a contract even exists--on the basis of his say-so alone. That purpose does not require a handwritten signature, especially in a case such as this in which there is other evidence, and not merely say-so evidence, of the existence of the contract (more precisely, the contract modification) besides the writings. The fact that Cloud produced the additional quantity is pretty powerful evidence of a contract,* * * as it would have been taking a terrible risk in doing so had it thought it would have no right to be paid if Hasbro refused to accept delivery but would instead be stuck with a huge quantity of a product that had no salvage value. Actually, in the case of a contract for goods specially manufactured by the buyer, partial performance by the seller takes the contract outside the statute of frauds, without more. UCC § 2-201(3)(a). This may well be such a case; but we need not decide.

The background to the modification--the fact that the parties had dealt informally with each other (as shown by their disregard of the form contracts), and above all that Hasbro plainly wanted more product and wanted it fast--is further evidence that had Cloud asked for a written purchase order in June 1996 for the additional quantity, Hasbro would have given it, especially since Cloud was offering a lower price.

There is more: "between merchants [a term that embraces 'any transaction with respect to which both parties are chargeable with the knowledge or skill of merchants,' UCC § 2-104(3)] if within a reasonable time a writing in confirmation of the contract and sufficient against the sender is received and the party receiving it has reason to know its contents, it satisfies the requirements of subsection 1 [the statute of frauds] ... unless written notice of objection to its contents is given within 10 days after it is received." UCC § 2-201(2). Cloud sent an order acknowledgment, reciting the increased quantity, shortly after the oral modification, and Hasbro did not object within ten days. * * *

So Hasbro's statute of frauds defense fails on a number of independent grounds. But what of the *contractual* requirement of the buyer's consent in writing to any modification? Could that stiffen the requirements of the UCC's statute of frauds? Parties are free to incorporate stronger conditions for contractual modification than the UCC provides: "A signed agreement which excludes modification or rescission except by a signed writing cannot be otherwise modified or rescinded, but except as between merchants such a requirement on a form supplied by the merchant must be separately signed by the other party." UCC § 2-209(2) * * *. The UCC's statute of frauds requires only quantity terms to be in writing. The contractual requirement that the buyer's consent be in writing was not limited to quantity terms, but this makes no difference, since those are the terms in dispute.

Could the contractual statute of frauds (to speak oxymoronically) be broader in a different sense? Specifically, could "consent in writing" require an explicit written statement of consent, missing here, rather than merely an inference of consent from a writing or series of writings? Maybe, but Hasbro does not argue that the contractual statute of frauds in this case has any different scope from the statutory, though it seems highly unlikely that a no-oral-modification clause would be subject to the exception in section 2-201(2) (quoted earlier) to the statute of frauds. Such a clause is added to a contract when the parties want to draft their own statute of frauds, as they are permitted to do; and there is no reason to suppose that they would want to adopt wholesale the limitations that the UCC imposes on its own statute of frauds. If they wanted those limitations they wouldn't need their own, customized clause.

So we may set section 2-201(2) to one side. That leaves intact, however, Cloud's argument, which we have accepted, that there was adequate evidence of written consent to the modification. And it leaves intact still *another* alternative argument by Cloud: "an attempt at modification" that does not satisfy the statute of frauds nevertheless "can operate as a waiver." § 2-209(4). The word "can" is key. To prevent the "attempt" provision from eviscerating the statute of frauds, the courts require that the attempting modifier, Cloud in this case, must show either that it reasonably relied on the other party's having waived the requirement of a writing, *Wisconsin Knife Works v. National Metal Crafters, supra,* 781 F.2d at 1286-87 (7th Cir.1986); *American Suzuki Motor Corp. v. Bill Kummer, Inc.,* 65 F.3d 1381, 1386 (7th Cir.1995); *contra, BMC Industries, Inc. v. Barth Industries, Inc.,* 160 F.3d 1322, 1333 (11th Cir.1998), or that the waiver was clear and unequivocal. * * * This exception to the statute of frauds applies equally to the "buyer's written consent" provision of the parties' contracts, UCC § 2-209(4); *Wisconsin Knife Works v. National Metal Crafters, supra,* 781 F.2d at 1284-87, because waiver is a general doctrine of contract law rather than an appendage to the statute of frauds.

The district judge erred by requiring that Cloud show *both* reasonable reliance and that the waiver was clear and unequivocal. There was no clear and unequivocal waiver, but there was reliance. The judge *found* reliance. She found that Cloud had been acting in good faith in producing the additional quantity of packets because it reasonably believed that Hasbro wanted the additional quantity. But she concluded that Cloud had been unreasonable in relying on its reasonable belief because it could so easily have insisted on a written purchase order modifying the quantity terms in the February and April orders. Reasonableness, however, is relative to commercial practices and understandings rather than to the desire of judges and lawyers, reflecting their training and professional culture, to see a deal memorialized in a form that leaves no room for misunderstanding the legal consequences. The employees of Hasbro and Cloud who were responsible for the administration of the parties' contractual undertaking were not lawyers. Doubtless because of this, the parties had, as we have noted, been casual about documentation. Cloud had treated the purchase orders as sources of information on how much Hasbro wanted when and according to what formula, but had paid no attention to them as contracts containing terms and conditions that might bind it. Hasbro had treated Cloud's purchase-order acknowledgments with similar insouciance. The parties had a smooth working relationship the details of which were worked out in informal communications. With time of the essence and the parties on good terms and therefore careless or impatient with formalities, Cloud was reasonable in believing that *if* Hasbro didn't want to be committed to buying the additional quantity that it plainly wanted in the summer and autumn of 1996, it would so advise Cloud rather than leading Cloud down the primrose path. A practice, under the rubric of "course of dealing," can be evidence of what a contract requires, see, e.g., UCC § 1-205; * * *--can even, under the rubric of "contract implied in fact," give rise to binding contractual obligations though no words are spoken. * * *

Cloud could have been more careful. But a failure to insist that every i be dotted and t crossed is not the same thing as being unreasonable. In any event, to repeat an earlier point, Hasbro did give its written consent to the modification.

We conclude that the June modification was enforceable and we therefore reverse the judgment and remand the case for a determination of Cloud's damages.

Notes

1. How do the two courts differ in their analysis of the issue of an attempted modification acting as a waiver?

2. What does the *Hasbro* case teach about the relationship between the exceptions to the record requirement in UCC 2-201 and a "no oral modification" clause?

3. **CISG.** Article 29 addresses modifications. Agreements to modify are enforceable. Although no general statute of frauds applies to modifications, Art. 11, the parties may have a "no oral modification" clause. Art. 29(2). How does the CISG address issues of waiver?

4. **UCITA.** UCITA 303 addresses modification and is modeled on UCC 2-209 and 2A-208. The analog to UCC 2-209(5) is contained in UCITA 702(a).

5. Now try your hand at the following problem.

Problem 7-5

After negotiations, B mailed S a written order for the purchase of 281,000 "spade bit blanks," for use in the manufacture of spade bits. The goods were to be delivered in installments by the dates stipulated in the purchase order. In addition, the purchase order contained, inter alia, the following "condition" of purchase: "No modification of this contract shall be binding upon Buyer unless made in writing and signed by Buyer's authorized representative. Buyer shall have the right to make changes in the Order by a notice, in writing, to seller." Seller accepted the purchase order in a written acknowledgment and commenced to manufacture the bits.

S was consistently late in tendering delivery. B, however, accepted the late deliveries without declaring a breach or invoking the written modification condition. After accepting 144,000 blanks, however, B, invoking the delivery schedule in the purchase order, canceled the contract for breach and sued S for damages. (There was some evidence that B canceled because of a dispute with a sub-purchaser of the completed spade bit rather than S's delays.)

You are clerk to the trial judge. She asks you for a memo on the following questions:

A. Was the "no modification" condition in the purchase order enforceable against Seller? *See* UCC 2-209(2).

B. If so, did B's conduct of accepting S's late deliveries "operate as a waiver" of either the contract delivery schedule or the "no modification" condition? *See* UCC 1-303 [former 2-208], 2-209(4).

C. If the conduct did operate as a waiver, how is UCC 2-209(5) relevant to the dispute?

CHAPTER EIGHT

RISK OF LOSS AND INSURANCE

SECTION 1.   GROUND RULES

There's many a slip 'twixt the cup and the lip. One is where goods that have been identified to the contract for sale are destroyed or damaged before delivery without the fault or negligence of either party. Which party bears the risk of this loss?

The question is important. If the risk of loss has passed, the buyer must, unless insured, absorb the loss and either pay the contract price, UCC 2-709(1)(a), or be liable for breach of contract, UCC 2-703. If the buyer has insured the goods, the insurance company will indemnify the buyer to the extent obligated under the policy and, through equitable or contractual subrogation, assert any claims that the buyer might have against third parties who caused the loss.

If the risk of loss has not passed, the seller, unless insured, must absorb the loss and, unless excused from performance, tender delivery of substitute goods or be liable for breach of contract. UCC 2-711. Again, if the goods are insured, the insurance company will indemnify the seller and, in all probability, assert any claims the seller may have against third parties through subrogation. When is the seller with the risk excused from performance because the goods were lost or damaged? The answer in most cases will be found in UCC 2-613 and 2-615. *See* Chapter Seven, *supra.*

When does the risk of loss pass? Section 22 of the Uniform Sales Act, which was enacted in 37 states, provided that the goods remained at the seller's risk until the "property" was transferred to the buyer. Thereafter, the risk was on the buyer "whether delivery had been made or not * * *." Section 18, however, provided that the property in "specific or ascertained goods" passed from the seller when the contract intended it to be transferred and Section 19 stated a series of five rules for ascertaining such intention when it was not otherwise made clear.

The "property" or "title" approach to risk of loss and other problems was thought both to promote confusion and to ignore commercial realities and was rejected in Article 2. UCC 2-401 provides in relevant part:

> Each provision of this Article with regard to the rights, obligations, and remedies of the seller, the buyer, purchasers, or other third parties applies irrespective of title to the goods except where the provision refers to such

title.

Thus, title may be relevant to other issues such as the scope of an insurance policy or state taxation, but not to risk of loss.[*] Property concepts, however, are still very important in Article 2 and are the subject of Chapter Nine, *infra*.[**]

The primary provisions dealing with risk of loss are UCC 2-509 and 2-510. Note that the test is flexible rather than rigid and is keyed to the agreement of the parties and the stage of performance thereunder.[***] More particularly, the risk is tied, in most cases at least, to which party has possession of or control over the goods. Two assumptions appear to underlie this approach:

(1) The party in possession or in control of the goods is in the "best" position, cost considered, to minimize or avoid loss; and

(2) The party in possession or in control of the goods is more likely to have insurance against losses that could not be avoided.

In short, parties in control of goods are thought to be what economists call the "least cost loss avoiders" and the best insurers against risk.[****] Thus, the UCC sought to minimize the cases where the risk passed to the buyer before the goods changed hands–cases where the risk of loss was not on the party with possession and control and where the one with the risk would often not be insured for the loss.

A practical note: there has been little litigation of significance under UCC 2-509 and UCC 2-510. What might explain this?

Predictably, risk of loss allocation in Article 2A follows the Article 2 model. The default rule for non-finance leases is that the risk of loss stays on the lessor.

---

[*] *See, e.g., Circuit City Stores Inc. v. Commissioner of Revenue*, 790 N.E.2d 636 (Mass. 2003); *House of Lloyd, Inc. v. Director of Revenue*, 824 S.W.2d 914 (Mo. 1992) (risk of loss and title pass at different times), *overruled on other grounds, Sipco, Inc. v. Director of Revenue*, 875 S.W.2d 539 (Mo. 1994). *See also* UCC 2-403 where title is relevant to disputes over ownership.

[**] *See* Jeanne L. Schroeder, *Death and Transfiguration: The Myth that the U.C.C. Killed "Property,"* 69 TEMP. L. REV. 1281 (1996).

[***] *See* Robert L. Flores, *Risk of Loss in Sales: A Missing Chapter in the History of the U.C.C.: Through Llewellyn to Williston and A Bit Beyond*, 27 PAC. L.J. 161 (1996).

[****] *See* Note, *Risk of Loss in Commercial Transactions: Efficiency Thrown Into the Breach*, 65 VA. L. REV. 557 (1979). A useful discussion is Margaret Howard, *Allocation of Risk of Loss Under the UCC: A Transactional Evaluation of Sections 2-509 and 2-510*, 15 UCC L.J. 334 (1983).

For finance leases and for non-finance leases where the parties so agree, the risk of loss will pass to the lessee as stated either in the agreement or in UCC 2A-219 or 2A-220. As under Article 2, location of title or possession of the goods does not affect application of the Article 2A provisions except as provided in each provision. *See* UCC 2A-302. Thus title is not relevant to passage of the risk of loss under Article 2A.

SECTION 2.   RISK OF LOSS IN THE ABSENCE OF BREACH

A. Goods in Possession of Seller

Unless otherwise agreed, the seller has no obligation to ship the goods to the buyer. The place of delivery is the "seller's place of business or if none, the seller's residence." UCC 2-308(a). What the seller must do to tender delivery to the buyer is spelled out in UCC 2-503(1). Read UCC 2-509(3) and (4). The 2003 revisions to Article 2 eliminated the default rule that a non-merchant seller could pass the risk of loss through tender of delivery. Rather, the seller will pass the risk of loss to the buyer upon the buyer's receipt of the goods unless one of the other provisions of UCC 2-509 apply. When has the buyer "received" the goods? UCC 2-103 contains a definition.

Problem 8-1

Sam purchased a new plasma screen TV for $5,000 in June. In November, Sam, pressed for cash, advertised the TV for sale. On Friday, Bob visited Sam's condo, inspected the TV and, after some negotiations, agreed to buy it for $3,000, with $500 down and the balance on delivery. Bob asked when he could take the TV. Sam said he wanted it over the weekend to watch the Bear's game and that he would call Bob at work on Monday to set up a time "after work on Monday." Bob agreed. On Sunday evening, the TV was stolen from Sam's apartment When informed, Bob stopped payment on the $500 check. Sam argued that the TV was Bob's and that he still owed Sam the entire $3,000. Neither party was insured. Who should prevail under amended UCC 2-509? Would your analysis change if former 2-509 governed the transaction?

Problem 8-2

After negotiations and inspection, B agreed in writing to purchase identified, new factory equipment for $15,000. The agreement provided, in part, that the price was due "when goods received by the purchaser" and that delivery was to be to "purchaser's truck within 4 weeks of contract date, seller to give purchaser seven days notice of delivery." Two weeks later, S notified B in writing that the goods were "in a deliverable state and at your disposal." B received the notice on a Friday. Over the weekend and before B took possession, vandals broke into S's plant and seriously damaged the machinery. B refused to take delivery, claiming that the risk of loss was on S. Neither party was insured. Who prevails?

Problem 8-3

Suppose in Problem 8-2, above, that B had told S that it could not pick up the goods during working hours and wondered if a different arrangement could be worked out. After discussions, the parties agreed that S should leave the crated goods on the plant loading dock chained and locked to an iron post after closing on Friday. S did what was agreed but the machinery was stolen from the loading dock on Friday evening before B could pick it up. The thieves had used a welding torch to burn through the chain. Who has the risk of loss? *See McKenzie v. Olmstead*, 587 N.W.2d 863 (Minn. Ct. App. 1999) (holding on similar facts that the risk of loss was on the buyer).

Problem 8-4

Suppose in Problem 8-2 above, the parties had agreed that the equipment was to be delivered to B's factory and installed by S. S delivered the equipment to B's loading dock on Monday after hours. S left the equipment on the loading dock and B did not know that the equipment had been delivered as B's factory was closed at the time of delivery. On Tuesday morning, S returned to install the equipment and it was gone (presumably stolen). Who had the risk of loss? *See In re Thomas*, 182 B.R. 347 (Bankr. S.D. Fla. 1995).

B. Goods in the Possession of a Bailee to be Delivered Without Being Moved

If at the time of contracting, identified goods are in the possession "of a bailee and are to be delivered without being moved," what the seller must do to tender delivery is spelled out in UCC 2-503(4). *See also* UCC 2-308(b). Under UCC 2-509(2), the risk of loss will pass to the buyer under the earliest of the times stated. Notice how the tender of delivery sections and the risk of loss section have certain parallels. Prior to the 2003 amendments to Article 2, UCC 2-509(2)(b) did not specify to whom the bailee must acknowledge the buyer's right to possession of the goods. The leading case holding that the bailee's acknowledgment must be to the buyer is *Jason's Foods, Inc. v. Peter Eckrich & Sons, Inc.*, 774 F.2d 214 (7th Cir. 1985). The 2003 amendments to both UCC 2-509(2) and 2-503(4) adopted that position. In order for UCC 2-509(2) to apply, the goods must be in the hands of a bailee and the parties must agree the goods are to be delivered without being moved. Who is a bailee under this section?

SILVER V. WYCOMBE, MEYER & CO., INC.
CIVIL COURT OF THE CITY OF NEW YORK, 1984
124 MISC. 2D 717, 477 N.Y.S.2D 288

DAVID B. SAXE, JUDGE

This action by an insurance company, as subrogee, to recover proceeds paid to its insured, Martin Silver, was tried before the court on stipulated facts.

Plaintiff, through his agent, Elsie Simpson, an interior decorator, ordered custom furniture from defendant Wycombe, Meyer & Co., Inc. (Wycombe). The furniture was manufactured by codefendant Jackson-Allen Upholstery Corp. (Jackson-Allen), a subsidiary of defendant Wycombe, at its factory in Catasauqua, Pennsylvania. On or about February 23, 1982, Wycombe sent invoices to plaintiff advising that the furniture was ready for shipment. Plaintiff thereupon tendered payment in full and directed Wycombe to ship one room of furniture but to hold the other until instructed further. Accordingly, one room of furniture was shipped to plaintiff. But before any instructions were received as to the second room of furniture, it was destroyed in a fire which was not due to any negligence on the part of defendants. Fireman's Fund Insurance Co. paid plaintiff for the loss and seeks to recover the proceeds from defendants on the theory that the risk of loss never passed to the buyer, its insured.

In the absence of contrary agreement by the parties, risk of loss under the Uniform Commercial Code is determined by the manner in which delivery is to be made (U.C.C. 2-509). The original order, documented by defendant Wycombe's order form, indicates a price of $7053 "+ del'y," and all invoices provide for shipment to plaintiff's home "Truck prepaid." It is clear that the provisions of U.C.C. 2-509 Subdiv. (1) govern the issue of when risk of loss passes to the buyer "where the contract requires or authorizes the seller to ship the goods by carrier * * *." Where the contract requires the seller to deliver the merchandise at a particular location, risk of loss passes upon tender of the goods at that location (U.C.C. 2-509(1)(b)) and where the contract does not require the seller to deliver the goods to a particular destination, it passes upon their delivery to the carrier (par. (a)). Where the contract provides for delivery at the seller's place of business or at the situs of the goods, risk of loss passes upon actual receipt by the buyer, if seller is a merchant, and otherwise upon tender of delivery (U.C.C. 2-509(3)).

Under the facts of the case at bar, the terms of the contract as it regards delivery are not stated. It is apparent, however, that regardless of the particular agreement between buyer and seller, defendants have set forth no facts sufficient to place the risk of loss upon plaintiff under any of the cited U.C.C. provisions. Indeed, the Official Comment 3 to U.C.C. 2-509 makes it clear that "a merchant seller cannot transfer risk of loss and it remains upon him until actual receipt by the buyer, even though full payment has been made and the buyer has been notified that the goods are at his disposal" * * *.

Defendants, however, advance the novel theory that, because of plaintiff's request that they hold the furniture subject to further instruction, they became mere bailees of the goods and that the provisions of U.C.C. 2-509(2) should govern this case. They argue that the invoices informing plaintiff that the furniture was ready for shipment constitute acknowledgment of the buyer's right to possession, transferring the risk of loss pursuant to U.C.C. 2-509(2)(b) to the buyer.

This position is entirely without merit. The provisions of U.C.C. 2-509(2) contemplate a situation in which goods are in the physical possession of a third party who will continue to hold them after consummation of the sale. Therefore, this is not a provision appropriately applied to the circumstances at bar which anticipate the passing of title *and* physical possession more or less simultaneously. Furthermore, bailment requires *delivery* of the goods to the bailee (*see* BLACK'S LAW DICTIONARY, 4th ed., p. 179, 1968). Having concluded that defendants failed to establish delivery of the furniture to plaintiff, by no stretch of the imagination may plaintiff be said to have redelivered it to defendants for safe-keeping.

Defendants cannot transform what is clearly a sale of goods into a bailment simply because they acceded to the buyer's request to postpone delivery. The agreement between buyer and seller clearly contemplates delivery at the buyer's home and, under the Uniform Commercial Code, risk of loss remains upon a merchant seller until he completes his performance with reference to the physical delivery of the goods (U.C.C. 2-401(2); U.C.C. 2-509(3) and Note 3 to U.C.C. 2-509; *Ramos v. Wheel Sports Center,* 96 Misc. 2d 646, 409 N.Y.S.2d 505, Civ. Ct., Bx.). It may be that defendant Jackson-Allen is a bailee for defendant Wycombe, but this Court is not required to rule on and makes no determination of this question.

Accordingly, judgment for plaintiff in the amount demanded in the complaint together with costs, disbursements and interest from April 13, 1982.

Notes

1.   Under what circumstances, if any, can a merchant seller become a "bailee" for purposes of UCC 2-509(2)?

2.   Note that the buyer's insurance company had indemnified the buyer for loss of the goods and sued the seller as a subrogee. Why did the insurer argue that risk of loss had not passed to the buyer? If the risk had passed, upon what theory could the insurer recover from the seller?

3.   At common law, if the goods were identified and in the possession of a bailee, title and, thus, risk of loss, passed at the time of sale even though the buyer was not entitled to take possession.[*] *Compare* UCC 2-401(3).

4.   Even though the goods are in the possession of a bailee at the time of contracting, the parties may agree that the bailee is to ship or deliver the goods to the buyer rather than simply acknowledge that the buyer is entitled to possession. If so, risk of loss is governed by either UCC 2-509(1) or (3) rather than UCC 2-509(2). In *Commonwealth Petroleum Co. v. Petrosol Int'l, Inc.,* 901 F.2d 1314 (6th Cir. 1990), the goods were propane stored in underground tanks in the possession of a bailee. After buyer paid the price and bailee acknowledged buyer's right to possession but before any tender of delivery by bailee, the propane was destroyed. The court, after extensive litigation, ultimately held that the parties had not agreed that bailee was to ship or deliver the goods to buyer and left the risk of loss on

---

[*] *See Tarling v. Baxter,* 6 B. & C. 360, 108 Eng. Rep. 484 (KB 1827).

buyer under UCC 2-509(2)(b). In short, the goods were to be delivered "without being moved."

5. If goods are damaged or lost while in the possession of a bailee or third party, UCC 2-722 specifies who is the real party in interest that may maintain an action for damages against the third party. Under Article 7, a bailee's duty is one of reasonable care of the goods. UCC 7-204, 7-309. Other federal or state law may prescribe higher standards of care.

6. UCC 2A-219(2)(b) addresses the situation where goods are held by a bailee and are to be delivered to a lessee without being moved. That section only contains one of the three provisions that are included in UCC 2-509(2). So if a supplier in a finance lease tenders to the lessee a negotiable document of title covering the goods, does the supplier retain the risk of loss until the bailee acknowledges the lessee's rights to the goods? Why does Article 2A not contain the rules concerning passage of risk of loss when the tender is made through documents of title?

Problem 8-5

Red Feather, a fine filly, won her first race. The pleased Owner (much pleased) shipped her back to the stable by common carrier, taking a non-negotiable bill of lading naming Owner as the consignee. While the horse was in transit, Owner sold her to B for $10,000. Owner accepted a check for $10,000, handed B the non-negotiable bill of lading and stated "she's all yours." Two hours later, Red Feather was killed in an accident while still in the carrier's possession.

A. B stopped payment on the check and insisted that the risk of loss remained on Owner. Is B correct?

B. Suppose that, unknown to either party, Red Feather was dead at the time of the contract. What result? *See* UCC 2-613.

C. Seller Authorized or Required to Ship Goods by Carrier

Probably the most common transaction in which risk of loss disputes will arise involves contracts that require or authorize the seller to ship the goods to the buyer by carrier. It is also likely that the agreement will use certain delivery terms which may have a bearing on the allocation of risk of loss. As indicated in Chapter Six, *supra*, the 2003 amendments to Article 2 eliminated the statutory definitions of shipping terms found in former 2-319 through 2-324. Under UCC 2-509(1), the passage of the risk of loss will depend upon whether the contract between the buyer and the seller is a shipment or a destination contract. Under amended Article 2, the parties will have to prove the commercial understanding of the shipping terms they have used.* Other than determining whether the parties have agreed to a shipment or destination contract, what else do you need to know to determine whether the risk of loss has passed to the buyer under a shipment or a destination contract?

WINDOWS, INC. V. JORDAN PANEL SYSTEMS CORP.
UNITED STATES COURT OF APPEALS, SECOND CIRCUIT, 1999
177 F.3D 114

LEVAL, CIRCUIT JUDGE

This is an appeal by a buyer from a grant of summary judgment in favor of the seller dismissing the buyer's claim for incidental and consequential damages resulting from damage suffered by the goods during shipment. The district court found that any negligence that might have caused the damage was attributable to the carrier and not the seller. It therefore concluded that the buyer's claim for incidental and consequential damages was barred by N.Y.U.C.C. § 2-613, which precludes the award of such damages when the goods are damaged "without fault of either party." We affirm, but in reliance on different provisions of the Code.

Windows, Inc. ("Windows" or "the seller") is a fabricator and seller of windows, based in South Dakota. Jordan Systems, Inc. ("Jordan" or "the buyer") is a construction subcontractor, which contracted to install window wall panels at an air cargo facility at John F. Kennedy Airport in New York City. Jordan ordered custom-made windows from Windows. The purchase contract specified that the windows were to be shipped properly packaged for cross country motor freight transit and "delivered to New York City."

Windows constructed the windows according to Jordan's specifications. It arranged to have them shipped to Jordan by a common carrier, Consolidated Freightways Corp. ("Consolidated" or "the carrier"), and delivered them to Consolidated intact and properly packaged. During the course of shipment, however, the goods sustained extensive damage. Much of the glass was broken and many of the window frames were gouged and twisted. Jordan's president signed a delivery receipt noting that approximately two-thirds of the shipment was damaged due to "load shift." Jordan, seeking to stay on its contractor's schedule,

---

* *See* Daniel E. Murray, *Risk of Loss of Goods in Transit: A Comparison of the 1990 Incoterms with Terms from Other Voices*, 23 U. MIAMI INTER-AM. L. REV. 93 (1991).

directed its employees to disassemble the window frames in an effort to salvage as much of the shipment as possible.

Jordan made a claim with Consolidated for damages it had sustained as a result of the casualty, including labor costs from its salvage efforts and other costs from Jordan's inability to perform its own contractual obligations on schedule. Jordan also ordered a new shipment from Windows, which was delivered without incident.

Jordan did not pay Windows for either the first shipment of damaged windows or the second, intact shipment. Windows filed suit to recover payment from Jordan for both shipments in the Supreme Court of the State of New York, Suffolk County. Jordan counterclaimed, seeking incidental and consequential damages resulting from the damaged shipment. Windows then brought a third-party claim against Consolidated, which removed the suit to the United States District Court for the Eastern District of New York.

Windows settled its claims against Consolidated. Windows later withdrew its claims against Jordan. The only remaining claim is Jordan's counterclaim against Windows for incidental and consequential damages.

The district court granted Windows' motion for summary judgment. It held that § 2-613 of the New York Uniform Commercial Code shields a seller from liability for such damages. That statute provides:

> Where the contract requires for its performance goods identified when the contract is made, and the goods suffer casualty *without fault of either party* before the risk of loss passes to the buyer * * * then
>
> > (a) if the loss is total then the contract is avoided; and
> >
> > (b) if the loss is partial or the goods have so deteriorated as no longer to conform to the contract the buyer may nevertheless demand inspection and at his option either treat the contract as avoided or accept the goods with due allowance from the contract price for the deterioration or the deficiency in quantity *but without further right against the seller*.

N.Y.U.C.C. § 2-613 (emphasis added).

The district court found that Windows was "without fault" within the meaning of § 2-613 on two grounds. First, the court found that there was no showing of negligence on the part of Windows or its employees. The goods were damaged during cross-country shipment because they were improperly loaded on the truck by Consolidated's employees. (Although Windows' employees assisted in the loading, the court found there was no evidence they were responsible for the negligent stowage.)

Second, the court rejected Jordan's argument that Consolidated's negligence should be attributed to Windows because Consolidated was Windows' "subcontractor." While not disputing Jordan's claim that a seller may be "at fault" for the negligence of its subcontractor, the court found that no subcontractor-principal relationship had been shown, as the contract did not require Windows to "personally deliver" the shipment to New York. "[A]ny negligence attributable to Consolidated," the court ruled, "is not the 'fault' of Windows." Because the goods suffered casualty "without fault of either party," Section 2-613(b) was found to bar Jordan's suit for incidental and consequential damages. This appeal followed.

DISCUSSION

Jordan does not contest the district court's factual finding that there was no negligence on the part of Windows' employees. However, in view of Windows' engagement of Consolidated, and Consolidated's fault in causing damage to the goods during shipment, Jordan contests the court's conclusion that Windows was "without fault" within the meaning of N.Y.U.C.C. § 2-613. We abandon inquiry into whether the terms of N.Y.U.C.C. § 2-613 were satisfied because the judgment may be affirmed on different grounds.

Jordan seeks to recover incidental and consequential damages pursuant to N.Y.U.C.C. § 2-715. Under that provision, Jordan's entitlement to recover incidental and consequential damages depends on whether those damages "result[ed] from the seller's breach." A destination contract is covered by § 2-503(3); it arises where "the seller is *required to deliver* at a particular destination." N.Y.U.C.C. § 2-503(3)(emphasis added). In contrast, a shipment contract arises where "the seller is required * * * to send the goods to the buyer and the contract *does not require him to deliver* them at a particular destination." § 2-504 (emphasis added). Under a shipment contract, the seller must "put the goods in the possession of such a carrier and make such a contract for their transportation as may be reasonable having regard to the nature of the goods and other circumstances of the case." § 2-504(a). *See also* § 2-504 official c. cmt. 1 (contrasting shipment contracts with destination contracts).

Where the terms of an agreement are ambiguous, there is a strong presumption under the U.C.C. favoring shipment contracts. Unless the parties "expressly specify" that the contract requires the seller to deliver to a particular destination, the contract is generally construed as one for shipment. 3A RONALD A. ANDERSON UNIFORM COMMERCIAL CODE §§ 2-503:24, 2-503:26; *see also Dana Debs, Inc. v. Lady Rose Stores, Inc.*, 65 Misc. 2d 697, 319 N.Y.S.2d 111, 112 (N.Y. City Civ. Ct.

1970) (no destination contract absent "explicit written understanding" that goods will be delivered to buyer at a "particular destination").

Jordan's confirmation of its purchase order, by letter to Windows dated September 22, 1993, provided, "All windows to be shipped properly crated/packaged/boxed suitable for cross country motor freight transit and delivered to New York City." We conclude that this was a shipment contract rather than a destination contract.

To overcome the presumption favoring shipment contracts, the parties must have explicitly agreed to impose on Windows the obligation to effect delivery at a particular destination. The language of this contract does not do so. Nor did Jordan use any commonly recognized industry term indicating that a seller is obligated to deliver the goods to the buyer's specified destination. *See* 3A ANDERSON § 2-503:26.

Given the strong presumption favoring shipment contracts, and the absence of explicit terms satisfying both requirements for a destination contract, we conclude that the contract should be deemed a shipment contract.[1]

Under the terms of its contract, Windows thus satisfied its obligations to Jordan when it put the goods, properly packaged, into the possession of the carrier for shipment. Upon Windows' proper delivery to the carrier, Jordan assumed the risk of loss, and cannot recover incidental or consequential damages from the seller caused by the carrier's negligence.

This allocation of risk is confirmed by the terms of N.Y.U.C.C. § 2- 509(1)(a), entitled "Risk of Loss in the Absence of Breach." It provides that where the contract "does not require [the seller] to deliver [the goods] at a particular destination, the risk of loss passes to the buyer when the goods are duly delivered to the carrier." N.Y.U.C.C. § 2-509(1)(a). As noted earlier, Jordan does not contest the court's finding that Windows duly delivered conforming goods to the carrier.

---

[1] Judge Parker suggests that the contract was not a destination contract because, while § 2-503(3) requires delivery "*at*" a particular destination, Jordan's confirmation letter said "*to* New York City." We respectfully disagree with Judge Parker's view, and do not rest our opinion on a distinction between "at" and "to." In our view, the distinction between destination and shipment contracts turns on whether the contract required the seller to deliver the goods at (or to) a destination specified by the buyer. We do not read § 2-503(3)'s use of the preposition "at" as a talismanic requirement. In our view, making liability turn on whether the parties used "to" or "at" would produce capricious results and would undermine reasonable expectations where the parties expressly agreed to place responsibility upon the seller to make delivery, but provided delivery should be made "to" the buyer's address.

Accordingly, as Windows had already fulfilled its contractual obligations at the time the goods were damaged and Jordan had assumed the risk of loss, there was no "seller's breach" as is required for a buyer to claim incidental and consequential damages under § 2-715. Summary judgment for Windows was therefore proper.

We are mindful of Jordan's concern that it not be left "holding the bag" for the damages it sustained through no fault of its own. The fact that Jordan had assumed the risk of loss under § 2-509(1)(a) by the time the goods were damaged does not mean it is without a remedy. Under the 1906 Carmack Amendment to the Interstate Commerce Act, a buyer or seller has long been able to recover directly from an interstate common carrier in whose care their goods are damaged. *See* 49 U.S.C. § 14706 (formerly 49 U.S.C. § 11707) (1998). Liability attaches unless the carrier can establish one of several affirmative defenses; for example, by showing that the damage was the fault of the shipper or caused by an Act of God. *See Missouri Pac. R.R. Co. v. Elmore & Stahl*, 377 U.S. 134, 137, 84 S. Ct. 1142, 12 L. Ed. 2d 194 (1964). Suits under the Carmack Amendment may be brought against a carrier by any person entitled to recover in the carrier's "bill of lading," including the buyer who was to receive the goods. *See* 49 U.S.C. §§ 14706(a)(1), 14706(d); * * * Relief available includes "all damages resulting from any failure to discharge a carrier's duty with respect to any part of the transportation to the agreed destination."* * *

CONCLUSION

The judgment of the district court is affirmed.

PARKER, Circuit Judge, concurring with separate opinion:

I fully concur in the result of the majority opinion and most of its reasoning. I am writing separately to make a point that I think is important but which has not been emphasized in the majority opinion.

The majority opinion analyzes whether the contract in this case was a "shipment" contract or a "destination" contract. It properly indicates that a shipment contract arises where "the seller is required * * * to send the goods to the buyer and the contract does not require him to deliver them *at* a particular destination." N.Y.U.C.C. § 2-504 (emphasis mine). On the other hand, a destination contract arises where "the seller is required to deliver *at* a particular destination." N.Y.U.C.C. § 2-503 (3)(emphasis mine).

In this case, the language of the contract provided that the windows were "to be shipped properly crated/packaged/boxed suitable for cross country motor freight transit and delivered *to* New York City." (Emphasis added.) Additionally, the contract referred to the specific job site at issue, "Nippon Cargo, JFK Airport, N.Y." To my reading, this contract unambiguously required delivery of goods to a particular location, namely the buyer's job site.

I agree with the majority opinion's conclusion that there is a strong presumption under the N.Y.U.C.C. favoring "shipment" contracts. The question then arises as to what it takes to overcome the presumption. While the opinion appropriately suggests that a commonly recognized industry term would do it,[2] it fails to emphasize the importance of the distinction between delivery *to* a destination versus delivery *at* a destination.

Every sales contract entails a "delivery." *See* N.Y.U.C.C. § 2-503. Further, to the extent that a shipment contract is one that requires or authorizes the seller to "send the goods to the buyer," N.Y.U.C.C. § 2-504, such contract contemplates "delivery," in the colloquial sense, *to* a designated location. *Accord La Casse*, 403 N.Y.S.2d at 442 (shipping instruction to deliver to buyer's residence did not create a destination contract). Accordingly, contractual language that requires goods to be "delivered to" a location does not by itself create a destination contract. This is not to say that a contract containing a term requiring delivery "to" a location is necessarily a shipment contract. The parties may, of course, create a destination contract by the use of language making it clear that the seller's obligation continues to the point of delivery at a particular destination. Rather, the point is that, standing alone, "delivered to" does not constitute a specific agreement designating where the seller will perform its obligation to deliver goods. *See* N.Y.U.C.C. § 2-503 official cmt. 5 ("The seller is not obligated to deliver at a named destination and bear the concurrent risk of loss until arrival, unless he has specifically agreed so to deliver * * *.").

By contrast, contractual language that requires the seller to "deliver at" a particular location designates a location *at* which the seller must effect delivery. Until the goods are tendered *at* that location, delivery has not occurred and the seller has not performed its duties under the contract.* * *

I do not view this distinction between "to" and "at" as technical or as a trap for the unwary. Parties should be able to create unambiguous destination contracts by employing the precise text of the controlling statute. They may also do so by using other language but should be aware that deviation from the text risks confusion. In sum, "delivered to" and "delivered at" are not, in this context, synonymous.

In my view had the contract in this case tracked the language of § 2-503 (3) by

---

[2] The term "F.O.B. buyer's job site" is an example.

specifying that Windows was required to deliver at a particular location in New York City, it would have been a destination contract. The fact that instead Windows was required to deliver *to* a particular location in New York City (absent any additional language) was insufficient to overcome the presumption.

Problem 8-6

From its mill in Fortuna, California, Seller, Raylo Lumber, received a written order for lumber sent by Buyer, Oregon Pacific Lumber, from its place of business in Portland, Oregon. The order provided in part:

> To Raylo Lbr. Co. Ship to Oregon-Pacific Lumber Co. Council Bluffs, Iowa Rate 1.20 (show on bill of lading) Routing SP UP (via Colby, Kansas) Shipment One week Terms: Regular 2% ADF 10 days Please Show Oregon-Pacific Lumber Co. as Shipper * * * Thoroughly Air Dried White Fir–WCLA Rules No. 15 Constr. & Btr., Allow. 25% standard ALS S4S EE DET–Clean Bright Stock one (1) Carload.

Two days later, Seller loaded a railroad car provided by the carrier with conforming lumber and sealed the door. Later that day, Seller prepared an invoice for Buyer as follows: "Shipped to Oregon-Pacific Lumber Company Council Bluffs, Iowa * * * F.O.B. delivered $1.20 rate. * * * 31,152' White Fir, A.D. 2 × 4 STD. & BTR. S4S at $84.00 Per M–$2,616.77." Later that day, Seller prepared a non-negotiable bill of lading naming Buyer as both Consignor and Consignee and presented it to an agent of the railroad. The agent signed the bill of lading and Seller immediately mailed the bill and the invoice to Buyer.

Before the bill and invoice were received and before Carrier picked up the load car from siding, fire broke out without the fault of Seller and the goods were destroyed. B argued that risk of loss had not passed before the fire. More specifically, B argued that the term "F.O.B. delivered" in context meant that S had agreed to deliver the goods "at a particular destination" and that risk of loss would not pass until the goods were "duly tendered" at that destination. *See* UCC 2-509(1)(b). Is that argument correct?

Note: Risk of Loss and Insurance

In shipment contracts, the risk of loss passes at the time the seller tenders delivery at the point to which the goods are to be delivered. UCC 2-509(1). In shipment contracts, the critical tender section is UCC 2-504. Although the seller must do a number of things to tender delivery, obtaining insurance for the buyer's account is not one of them.[*] Thus, where risk of loss passes to the buyer upon tender to the carrier, the buyer, not the seller, must make sure that the goods are properly insured. Nevertheless, the seller must still "promptly notify the buyer of the shipment."[**]

As previously noted, the risk of loss rules in UCC 2-509 were designed, in part, to conform to assumptions about which party, seller or buyer, was in the best position, cost considered, either to prevent or to insure against loss of or damage to the goods. As Judge Posner put it in *Jason's Foods Inc. v. Peter Eckrich & Sons, Inc.*, 774 F.2d 214, 218 (7th Cir. 1985):

> The Code sought to create a set of standard contract terms that would reflect in the generality of cases the preferences of contracting parties at the time of contract. One such preference is for assignments of liability–or, what amounts to the same thing, assignments of the risk of loss–that create incentives to minimize the adverse consequences of untoward events such as * * * a warehouse fire. There are two ways of minimizing such consequences. One is to make them less painful by insuring against them. Insurance does not prevent a loss–it merely spreads it–but in doing so it reduces (for those who are risk averse) the disutility of the loss. So if one of the contracting parties can insure at lower cost than the other, this is an argument for placing the risk of loss on him, to give him an incentive to do so. * * * The other method of minimizing the consequences of an unanticipated loss is through prevention of the loss. If one party is in a better position than the other to prevent it, this is a reason for placing the risk of loss on him, to give him an incentive to prevent it. It would be a reason for placing liability on a seller who still had possession of the goods, even though title had passed * * *.

The UCC, however, has very little to say about insurance. UCC 2-501 states some but not all the circumstances where the seller and buyer will have an insurable interest in the goods. Thus, the "buyer obtains a special property interest and an insurable interest in goods by identification of existing goods as goods to which the

---

[*] *Cook Specialty Co. v. Schrlock*, 772 F. Supp. 1532 (E.D. Pa. 1991).

[**] *See Rheinberg-Kellerei GMBH v. Vineyard Wine Co., Inc.*, 281 S.E.2d 425 (N.C. Ct. App. 1981).

contract refers even though the goods so identified are non-conforming and the buyer has an option to return or reject them * * *," UCC 2-501(1), and the "seller retains an insurable interest in the goods so long as title to or any security interest in the goods remains in the seller." UCC 2-501(2). But UCC 2-501(3) provides that "Nothing in this section impairs any insurable interest recognized under any other statute or rule of law." Thus, UCC 2-501 is a one-way ratchet provision: it can expand, but not contract, the scope of insurable interest. Beyond insurable interest and the anti-subrogation rule of UCC 2-510, however, one must look elsewhere when disputes over insurance arise.* Article 2A has a similar set of principles in UCC 2A-218.

Note: *Liability of Overland Carrier for Goods Lost or Damaged in Shipment*

As we have seen, in a shipment contract, risk of loss passes to the buyer when the seller tenders the goods to a carrier, whether that carrier be a truck, airplane, railroad or vessel. In addition, under the documents issued by the carrier, the buyer is the person "entitled" to the goods. *See* UCC 7-102 (definition of consignee) & 7-403. Thus, if the goods are lost or damaged in transit, the buyer or its insurance company as subrogee has both the standing and the incentive to bring suit against the carrier. Several things make the carrier an appealing defendant. First, it is likely that the carrier causes or has the potential for causing more loss, destruction and damage than any other party associated with a typical sales transaction. Second, the carrier is almost always solvent. Third, it is easy to prove a case against a carrier. Finally, the carrier, as a public service enterprise, is obliged to deal with all persons and cannot readily use economic pressure of withholding services to forestall a suit. *Kumar Corp. v. Nopal Lines, Ltd.*, 462 So. 2d 1178 (Fla. Ct. App. 1985) holds that plaintiffs with standing to sue the carrier include the party with the risk of loss or his agent and an insurance subrogee. *See* UCC 2-722.

The common law liability of the overland carrier has been described as follows in ARMISTEAD MASON DOBIE, BAILMENTS AND CARRIERS § 116, at 325 (1914):

---

* For the scope of insurable interest in property insurance cases, one may consult John M. Stockton, *An Analysis of Insurable Interest Under Article Two of the Uniform Commercial Code,* 17 VAND. L. REV. 815 (1964). *See also* Robert S. Pinzur, *Insurable Interest: A Search for Consistency,* 46 INS. COUNSEL J. 109 (1979). For an example of a court using Article 2 to determine if a seller retained an insurable interest after tender of the goods to a buyer who had prepaid in full, *see Spirit of Excellence, Ltd. v. Intercargo Ins. Co.*, 777 N.E.2d 660 (Ill. Ct. App. 2002).

By the common law the common carrier is, with certain exceptions, an insurer of the goods intrusted to him. According to the very early cases, the only exceptions to the common carrier's liability as an insurer of the safe delivery of the goods were: 1) The act of God; and 2) The public enemy. To these, however, native justice and the genius of our jurisprudence have added: 3) The act of the shipper; 4) public authority; and 5) the inherent nature of the goods.

The common-law liability of common carriers, however, was subject to contractual limitations and exclusions inserted by carriers in the relevant documents.

The current status of carrier liability is determined under federal and state legislation and international treaties that, in turn, depend upon the type of carrier and the scope of its operation. Thus, the liability of international air carriers is determined by the Warsaw Convention, ratified by the United States in 1934, 49 Stat. 3000 (1934), T.S. No. 876, and the liability of vessels engaged in "foreign trade" is regulated by the Carriage of Goods by Sea Act, enacted by Congress in 1936. 49 Stat. 1207 (1936), 46 U.S.C. App. 1300-15.[*]

The liability of domestic overland carriers in interstate commerce, *i.e.*, railroads and truckers, is regulated by the 1906 Carmack amendments to the Interstate Commerce Commission Act of 1887, as reenacted in 1980 without substantial change. *See* 49 U.S.C. 11707. The statute is, essentially, a codification of the carrier's insurer liability at common law with the important benefit to the shipper that efforts to exclude or modify the scope of statutory liability by agreement are void. As the statute has been interpreted by the courts, the person entitled under the document states a *prima facie* case against the carrier by showing that the goods were delivered in good condition and arrived in a damaged condition and the amount of damages. To escape liability, the carrier has what is described as a "substantial double burden:" it must show both that it was free from negligence and that the damage to the cargo was due to one of the excepted causes relieving the carrier of liability at common law, *i.e.*, act of God, public enemy, act of shipper himself, act of public authority or an inherent vice in the goods.[**]

---

[*] A general survey appears in Saul Sorkin, *Changing Concepts of Liability,* 17 FORUM 710 (1982).

[**] *See Martin Imports v. Courier-Newsom Exp., Inc.*, 580 F.2d 240, 242 (7th Cir.1978), *cert. denied*, 439 U.S. 983 (1978). The leading case in this line is *Missouri P.R. Co. v. Elmore & Stahl*, 377 U.S. 134 (1964). For an illustrative interpretation, *see Oak Hall Cap and Gown*

(continued...)

The liability of domestic overland carriers in intrastate commerce is determined by Article 7 of the UCC, more particularly, UCC 7-309.[*] Subsection 7-309 starts by imposing a duty of ordinary care on the carrier, but then states that the subsection "does not repeal or change any law or rule of law which imposes liability upon a common carrier for damages not caused by its negligence." Thus, in the many states where the common law liability of a carrier as insurer was recognized, the carrier could be liable even though exercising reasonable care. Subsection 7-309 gives effect to provisions in the bill of lading or a transportation agreement limiting liability: the carrier can limit liability to the value of the goods stated in the document but "no such limitation is effective with respect to the carrier's liability for conversion to its own use."

As one might expect, there has been no litigation of significance involving UCC 7-309.

SECTION 3. EFFECT OF BREACH ON RISK OF LOSS

UCC 2-510 modifies the risk of loss principles established by UCC 2-509 in certain circumstances where one of the parties is in breach. The consequences of this modification are twofold.

First, in some cases the breaching party will have to absorb the loss of or pay for lost, stolen or destroyed goods where, but for the breach, the risk of loss would have been on the other party. Thus, UCC 2-510 reallocates the risk of loss because one party breached the contract and negates the assumptions made *ex ante* about who was in the best position to insure. This reallocation can be questioned on policy grounds.

Second, UCC 2-510 operates, in some circumstances, as an anti-subrogation clause: it places the risk on the non-breaching party's insurance company in circumstances where but for the insurance contract the risk of loss would be on the breaching party. Thus, under UCC 2-510(2), a buyer who, because of the seller's breach, rightfully revokes acceptance may treat the risk of loss as having rested on the seller "to the extent of any deficiency in the buyer's effective insurance coverage." Because of the statute, the insurance company must pay if there is no

---

[**] (...continued)
Co. v. Old Dominion Freight Line, Inc., 899 F.2d 291 (4th Cir. 1990).

[*] *See* UCC 7-103; *Starmakers Pub. Corp. v. Acme Fast Freight, Inc.*, 615 F. Supp. 787 (S.D.N.Y. 1985) (Carmack Act preempts UCC where interstate shipments are concerned).

deficiency and, apparently, is precluded from any recovery as a subrogee against the seller. *See* Comment 3, which states: "This section merely distributes the risk of loss as stated and is not intended to be disturbed by any subrogation of an insurer."

What is the point of all this? One commentator has suggested that UCC 2-510 is of "dubious origin," has little practical impact on the way that insurance companies do business and "serves no practical purpose save the harassment of the legal mind."[*] Professor Margaret Howard questions whether a commercial breach in the absence of bad faith is important enough to undercut the importance of insurance.[**] Professor Flores, however, suggests that the provisions reflect the assumption that risk of loss should pass only when the seller has so far performed the agreement so as to justify the passage of the risk to the buyer.[***]

Problem 8-7

On June 1, S contracted to sell B 10 units of described goods for $10,000. S agreed to ship the goods "FOB point of shipment" by June 15 and B agreed to pay in full within 30 days of receipt. S had insurance on the goods until they were delivered to the carrier. B had insurance on the goods when "title" passed to him, *i.e.*, at the "time and place of shipment." UCC 2-401(2)(a). S's insurance covered the current market value of the described goods. B's insurance covered 50% of the current market value of the goods.

A. S delivered the goods to the carrier on June 16 (they were shipped on June 17) and failed to give B any notice of the shipment. Review UCC 2-504. The goods were totally destroyed in transit on June 19. B, citing UCC 2-510, argues that the risk of loss was on S. Consequently, B had no liability for the price. Is B correct? *See* UCC 2-601 (right of rejection), 2-508 (cure) and 2-606 (acceptance).

B. Suppose, in (A) above, that the goods were not destroyed in transit. Rather, they were tendered by the carrier and accepted by B and taken to its plant. *See* UCC 2-606. The next day, the goods were destroyed without B's fault or negligence. Who has the risk of loss?

---

[*] F. Carlton King, Jr., *UCC Section 2-510–A Rule Without Reason,* 77 COM. L.J. 272 (1972).

[**] Margaret Howard, *Allocation of Risk of Loss Under the UCC: A Transactional Evaluation of Sections 2-509 and 2-510,* 15 UCC L.J. 334, 355-68 (1983).

[***] *See* Robert L. Flores, *Risk of Loss in Sales: A Missing Chapter in the History of the U.C.C.: Through Llewellyn to Williston and a Bit Beyond,* 27 PAC. L.J. 161, 214 (1996).

C. Continuing this exercise, suppose in (B) above, that after B accepted the goods, inspection at the plant revealed a latent, substantial defect which justified revocation of acceptance under UCC 2-608(1). B promptly notified S of the revocation. UCC 2-608(2). The next day, before S could send instructions, the goods were destroyed without the fault or negligence of B. Assuming that B, at the time of loss, had no liability for the price, *see* UCC 2-709, comment 5, who has the risk of loss?

D. Suppose on June 14, prior to S's planned delivery of the goods to the carrier B called S and told S not to bother, B no longer wanted the goods. On June 15, the goods were destroyed by an unfortunate fire at S's warehouse. Who has the risk of loss for the goods?

Note: Risk of Loss Under the CISG

Articles 66-70 deal with the "passing of risk" in an international contract for the sale of goods. Several general points should be made.[*]

First, the passing of risk will be influenced if not determined by the delivery term selected by the parties, usually a term contained in the Incoterms of the International Chamber of Commerce. These terms usually determine the place where the seller is to deliver the goods, who pays what costs associated with the shipment, whether the seller must make the contract of carriage, who pays the costs and taxes of export, whether the seller must notify buyer of shipment, whether the seller is to obtain insurance, and the cooperation of the parties expected in furnishing documents of title or obtaining documents for importing the goods.

Second, in the unlikely absence of a delivery term, the seller's delivery obligations are set forth in Articles 30-34. For example, the seller's obligation in contracts where "carriage" of the goods are involved are stated in Art. 31(a) and Art. 32.

Third, after the seller's delivery obligations are determined from the delivery terms and/or the Convention, the risk of loss principles kick in. Review Articles 66-70, please. Note:

Art. 67 covers risk of loss when the contract involves carriage of the goods.

---

[*] For a more in depth analysis, *see* Shivbir S. Grewal, *Risk of Loss in Goods Sold During Transit: A Comparative Study of the U.N. Convention on Contracts for the International Sale of Goods, the U.C.C., and the British Sale of Goods Act*, 14 LOY. L.A. INT'L & COMP. L.J. 93 (1991).

These rules are similar to those in UCC 2-509(1).

Art. 68 covers risk of loss when goods are sold in transit. There is no comparable provision in Article 2.

Art. 69 applies when Articles 67 and 68 do not. Note that Art. 69(1) resembles UCC 2-509(3) and that Art. 69(2) seems to cover cases where the goods are in the possession of a third person (a bailee) and are to be "taken over" by the buyer at that place. *Compare* UCC 2-509(2).

Finally, Articles 68 and 70 deal with the effect of conduct of the seller that damages the goods or a fundamental breach by the seller. *Compare* UCC 2-510.

Consider the following case which discusses passage of the risk of loss under the CISG and the Incoterm "CFR."

BP OIL INTERNATIONAL, LTD. V. EMPRESA ESTATAL
PETROLEOS DE ECUADOR (PETROECUADOR)
UNITED STATES COURT OF APPEALS, FIFTH CIRCUIT, 2003
332 F.3D 333

JERRY E. SMITH, CIRCUIT JUDGE

Empresa Estatal Petroleos de Ecuador ("PetroEcuador") contracted with BP Oil International, Ltd. ("BP"), for the purchase and transport of gasoline from Texas to Ecuador. PetroEcuador refused to accept delivery, so BP sold the gasoline at a loss. BP appeals a summary judgment dismissing PetroEcuador and Saybolt, Inc. ("Saybolt"), the company responsible for testing the gasoline at the port of departure. We affirm in part, reverse in part, and remand.

I.

PetroEcuador sent BP an invitation to bid for supplying 140,000 barrels of unleaded gasoline deliverable "CFR" to Ecuador. "CFR," which stands for "Cost and FReight," is one of thirteen International Commercial Terms ("Incoterms") designed to "provide a set of international rules for the interpretation of the most commonly used trade terms in foreign trade."[1] Incoterms are recognized through their incorporation into the Convention on Contracts for the International Sale of

---

[1] INTERNATIONAL CHAMBER OF COMMERCE, INCOTERMS 1990 (1990); *see also Nuovo Pignone, SpA v. Storman Asia M/V,* 310 F.3d 374, 380 n. 5 (5th Cir.2002).

Goods ("CISG").[2] *St. Paul Guardian Ins. Co. v. Neuromed Med. Sys. & Support, GmbH,* 2002 WL 465312, at *2, 2002 U.S. Dist. LEXIS 5096, at *9-*10 (S.D.N.Y. Mar. 26, 2002).

BP responded favorably to the invitation, and PetroEcuador confirmed the sale on its contract form. The final agreement required that the oil be sent "CFR La Libertad-Ecuador." A separate provision, paragraph 10, states, "Jurisdiction: Laws of the Republic of Ecuador." The contract further specifies that the gasoline have a gum content of less than three milligrams per one hundred milliliters, to be determined at the port of departure. PetroEcuador appointed Saybolt, a company specializing in quality control services, to ensure this requirement was met.

To fulfill the contract, BP purchased gasoline from Shell Oil Company and, following testing by Saybolt, loaded it on board the M/T TIBER at Shell's Deer Park, Texas, refinery. The TIBER sailed to La Libertad, Ecuador, where the gasoline was again tested for gum content. On learning that the gum content now exceeded the contractual limit, PetroEcuador refused to accept delivery. Eventually, BP resold the gasoline to Shell at a loss of approximately two million dollars.

BP sued PetroEcuador for breach of contract and wrongful draw of a letter of guarantee. After PetroEcuador filed a notice of intent to apply foreign law pursuant to Fed.R.Civ.P. 44.1, the district court applied Texas choice of law rules and determined that Ecuadorian law governed. BP argued that the term "CFR" demonstrated the parties' intent to pass the risk of loss to PetroEcuador once the goods were delivered on board the TIBER. The district court disagreed and held that under Ecuadorian law, the seller must deliver conforming goods to the agreed destination, in this case Ecuador. The court granted summary judgment for PetroEcuador. * * *

III.

BP and PetroEcuador dispute whether the domestic law of Ecuador or the CISG applies. After recognizing that federal courts sitting in diversity apply the choice of law rules of the state in which they sit. . . the district court applied Texas law, which enforces unambiguous choice of law provisions. . . Paragraph 10, which states "Jurisdiction: Laws of the Republic of Ecuador," purports to apply Ecuadorian law. Based on an affidavit submitted by PetroEcuador's expert, Dr.

---

[2] United Nations Convention on Contracts for the International Sale of Goods, Apr. 11, 1980, S. Treaty Doc. No. 98-9 (1983), 19 I.L.M. 668 (1980), reprinted at 15 U.S.C. app. (entered into force Jan. 1, 1988).

Gustavo Romero, the court held that Ecuadorian law requires the seller to deliver conforming goods at the agreed destination, making summary judgment inappropriate for BP.

A.

Though the court correctly recognized that federal courts apply the choice of law rules of the state in which they sit, it overlooked its concurrent federal question jurisdiction that makes a conflict of laws analysis unnecessary. The general federal question jurisdiction statute grants subject matter jurisdiction over every civil action that arises, *inter alia,* under a treaty of the United States. 28 U.S.C. sec. 1331(a). The CISG, ratified by the Senate in 1986, creates a private right of action in federal court. . . . The treaty applies to "contracts of sale of goods between parties whose places of business are in different States ... [w]hen the States are Contracting States." CISG art. 1(1)(a). BP, an American corporation, and PetroEcuador, an Ecuadorian company, contracted for the sale of gasoline; the United States and Ecuador have ratified the CISG.

As incorporated federal law, the CISG governs the dispute so long as the parties have not elected to exclude its application. CISG art. 6. PetroEcuador argues that the choice of law provision demonstrates the parties' intent to apply Ecuadorian domestic law instead of the CISG. We disagree.

A signatory's assent to the CISG necessarily incorporates the treaty as part of that nation's domestic law. BP's expert witness as to Ecuadorian law, Xavier Rosales-Kuri, observed that "the following source of *Ecuadorian law* would be applicable to the present case: (i) United Nations Convention on the International Sale of Goods...." PetroEcuador's expert did not disagree with this assessment. Given that the CISG *is* Ecuadorian law, a choice of law provision designating Ecuadorian law merely confirms that the treaty governs the transaction.

Where parties seek to apply a signatory's domestic law in lieu of the CISG, they must affirmatively opt-out of the CISG. In *Asante Techs., Inc. v. PMC- Sierra, Inc.,* 164 F.Supp.2d 1142, 1150 (N.D.Cal.2001), the court held that a choice-of-law provision selecting British Columbia law did not, without more, "evince a clear intent to opt out of the CISG.... Defendant's choice of applicable law adopts the law of British Columbia, and it is undisputed that the CISG *is* the law of British Columbia."

Similarly, because the CISG is the law of Ecuador, it governs this dispute. "[I]f the parties decide to exclude the Convention, it should be expressly excluded by language which states that it does not apply and also states what law shall govern the contract." RALPH H. FOLSOM, ET AL., INTERNATIONAL BUSINESS TRANSACTIONS 12 (2d ed.2001). An affirmative opt-out requirement promotes uniformity and the observance of good faith in international trade, two principles that guide interpretation of the CISG. CISG art. 7(1).

B.

The CISG incorporates Incoterms through article 9(2), which provides:

The parties are considered, unless otherwise agreed, to have impliedly made applicable to their contract or its formation a usage of which the parties knew or ought to have known and which in international trade is widely known to, and regularly observed by, parties to contracts of the type involved in the particular trade concerned.

CISG art. 9(2). Even if the usage of Incoterms is not global, the fact that they are well known in international trade means that they are incorporated through article 9(2).[3]

PetroEcuador's invitation to bid for the procurement of 140,000 barrels of gasoline proposed "CFR" delivery. The final agreement, drafted by PetroEcuador, again specified that the gasoline be sent "CFR La Libertad- Ecuador" and that the cargo's gum content be tested pre-shipment.[4] Shipments designated "CFR" require the seller to pay the costs and freight to transport the goods to the delivery port, but pass title and risk of loss to the buyer once the goods "pass the ship's rail" at the port of shipment. The goods should be tested for conformity before the risk of loss passes to the buyer. FOLSOM, *supra,* at 41. In the event of subsequent damage or loss, the buyer generally must seek a remedy against the carrier or insurer. . . .

In light of the parties' unambiguous use of the Incoterm "CFR," BP fulfilled its contractual obligations if the gasoline met the contract's qualitative specifications when it passed the ship's rail and risk transferred to PetroEcuador. CISG art. 36(1).

---

[3] *See St. Paul Guardian Ins.,* 2002 WL 465312, at *2, 2002 U.S. Dist. LEXIS 5096, at *9-*10 (stating that "INCOTERMS are incorporated into the CISG through Article 9(2)"); RALPH H. FOLSOM, ET AL., *supra,* at 72 ("Incoterms could be made an implicit term of the contract as part of international custom. Courts in France and Germany have done so, and both treaties and the UNCITRAL Secretariat describe Incoterms as a widely- observed usage for commercial terms.").

[4] In accepting PetroEcuador's invitation, BP stated "CNF" as the condition of delivery. CNF was used in a previous version of Incoterms to specify "cost and freight" delivery. INTERNATIONAL CHAMBER OF COMMERCE, INCOTERMS 1980 (1980). In any event, the final agreement uses the term "CFR."

Indeed, Saybolt's testing confirmed that the gasoline's gum content was adequate before departure from Texas. Nevertheless, in its opposition to BP's motion for summary judgment, PetroEcuador contends that BP purchased the gasoline from Shell on an "as is" basis and thereafter failed to add sufficient gum inhibitor as a way to "cut corners."[5] In other words, the cargo contained a hidden defect.

Having appointed Saybolt to test the gasoline, PetroEcuador "ought to have discovered" the defect before the cargo left Texas. CISG art. 39(1). Permitting PetroEcuador now to distance itself from Saybolt's test would negate the parties' selection of CFR delivery and would undermine the key role that reliance plays in international sales agreements. Nevertheless, BP could have breached the agreement if it provided goods that it "knew or could not have been unaware" were defective when they "passed over the ship's rail" and risk shifted to PetroEcuador. CISG art. 40.

Therefore, there is a fact issue as to whether BP provided defective gasoline by failing to add sufficient gum inhibitor. The district court should permit the parties to conduct discovery as to this issue only.

* * *

[Some footnotes omitted, those retained are renumbered.]

Note: Risk of Loss Under UCITA

Under UCITA, the risk of loss provision is aimed at the risk of loss of a copy of computer information, not computer information itself. *See* UCITA 614. UCITA has no specific provision on risk of loss of the computer information. UCITA 614 is modeled on UCC 2-509 with only a small remnant of UCC 2-510 reflected in UCITA 614(b)(3). UCITA does not address any insurance issues.

---

[5] Under CISG article 36(1), "[t]he seller is liable in accordance with the contract ... for any lack of conformity which exists at the time when the risk passes to the buyer, even though the lack of conformity becomes apparent only after that time."

CHAPTER NINE

PROPERTY RIGHTS

SECTION 1.   TITLE AND IDENTIFICATION

Under our legal system, a person with "good" title to goods is given extensive protection against a wide range of claims to the goods by third persons. What is the scope of this protection under the UCC?

De-emphasis of title.   One approach to this question is to understand the importance (or lack of it) of title. A sale of goods is a transaction whereby title is passed "from the seller to the buyer for a price * * *." UCC 2-106(1). In an effort to clarify when title passes in a contract for sale, Article 2 prescribes the conditions which must exist before any interest in goods can pass, *see* UCC 2-105(1) [former subsection (2)], makes a careful distinction between present and future sales, *see* UCC 2-106(1), and provides an intricate set of rules to assist in transactions where the parties have not otherwise explicitly agreed. *See* UCC 2-401. To this extent, Article 2 closely follows the Uniform Sales Act.

Here, however, the resemblance ends. UCC 2-401 provides that "each provision of this Article with regard to the rights, obligations and remedies of the seller, the buyer, purchasers or other third parties applies irrespective of title to the goods except where the provision refers to such title." *See also* UCC 9-202 and 2A-302, where the same policy is announced for secured transactions and leases of goods. As stated in the comment to UCC 2-101, the "purpose is to avoid making practical issues between practical men turn on the location of an intangible something, the passing of which no man can prove by evidence and to substitute for such abstractions proof of words and actions of a tangible character."

It is clear that the rules about title contained in UCC 2-401 may be relevant in resolving controversies beyond the scope of Article 2, *e.g.*, the right of the buyer's creditors to levy on goods still in the seller's possession, the coverage of an insurance policy, the applicability of a state sales tax, the criminal responsibility of a person accused of larceny, or whether property becomes part of the buyer's estate in a bankruptcy.[*] However, when the issue is within the scope of Article 2, title

---

[*] *See ALOFS Manufacturing Co. v. Toyota Manufacturing Kentucky, Inc.*, 209 B.R. 83 (Bankr. W.D. Mich. 1997); *Concord General Mut. Ins. Co. v. Sumner*, 762 A. 2d 849 (Vt.

(continued...)

becomes relevant only when the applicable provisions specifically refer to title. Such specific reference is made in UCC 2-403 and UCC 2-312. Although Article 2 de-emphasizes the role of title in determining the rights of the buyer and seller, do not be misled into thinking property rights are irrelevant in an Article 2 transaction.[*] The range of problems emanating from these sections and their frequent overlap with Article 9 will be the subject of this Chapter.

Problem 9-1

Read UCC 2-401. In the absence of the parties' agreement otherwise, when does title to the goods pass from the seller to the buyer in a sales transaction? Now compare the default rules on title passage to the default rules on tender of delivery in UCC 2-503 and passage of the risk of loss in UCC 2-509. How are they similar to and how do they differ from the title passage rules?

Property interests in a lease transaction. Property rights issues also arise in a lease transaction. A lease is "a transfer of the right to possession and use of goods for a period in return for consideration * * *." UCC 2A-103(1)(p) [former subsection (1)(j)]. In a lease transaction, a lessee does not obtain ownership of the leased goods but rather receives only the right to possession and use of the goods. The lessor retains title.

Many cases have been litigated concerning the distinction between a "true lease" and a sale with a security interest. In a sale with a security interest, ownership passes to the buyer and the seller retains a security interest in the purchased goods to secure payment of the price. That issue was addressed in Chapter Two as it relates to determining whether the transaction is governed by Article 2 or Article 2A. That issue also is important in deciding the applicability of Article 9 to the transaction. *See* UCC 9-109, 1-201(b)(35), 1-203 [former 1-201(37)].

---

[*] (...continued)
2000).

[*] *See* Jeanne L. Schroeder, *Death and Transfiguration: The Myth That The U.C.C. Killed "Property"*, 69 TEMP. L. REV. 1281 (1996); Linda J. Rusch, *Property Concepts in the Revised U.C.C. Articles 2 and 9 Are Alive and Well*, 54 SMU L. REV. 947 (2001). *See generally* William L. Tabac, *The Unbearable Lightness of Title Under the Uniform Commercial Code*, 50 MD. L. REV. 408 (1991).

A true lease is not only a contract but also a transaction that transfers property rights of possession and use but not ownership. Assuming the transaction is a true lease, several issues relating to property rights may arise in the transaction. First, can the lessee or lessor voluntarily transfer their property rights to a third party without the other party's consent? Second, if such property rights can be transferred, what rights does the third-party transferee have as against its transferor and the other party to the lease contract? Third, can either the lessor's or lessee's property rights be involuntarily transferred through legal process such as an execution on a judgment? Fourth, if so, what property rights does the party who buys those rights through the execution process obtain? Fifth, what is the relationship between the concept of contractual assignment and delegation and those property rights issues? Article 2A has several sections which address these issues. *See* UCC 2A-301 through 2A-311.

Identification and the special property interest. In a sales transaction, the seller has title to the goods which at some point will be transferred to the buyer. Prior to that point, however, the buyer may have a property interest in the goods other than title even though the seller still has possession of the goods. Read UCC 2-501, 2-722. What is a "special property interest" and what function does it perform? Identification of goods to the contract provides the buyer with its earliest possible property interest in the goods. Identification is not the same as title passage. *See* UCC 2-401.

Article 2A follows a similar scheme in UCC 2A-217 and 2A-218. Read UCC 2-501, 2A-217 and 2A-218. In the absence of the parties' agreement otherwise, when are goods identified to a sale or lease contract? What is the effect of that identification? Does identification preclude the seller or lessor from substituting other goods for the identified goods prior to delivery? What is the relationship between the concept of identification and the idea of passage of title to the goods?

Note: Title and Identification Under the CISG

CISG applies to "contracts of sale of goods" between parties where the jurisdictional requirements are met. Art. 1(1). "Contracts of sale," however, are not defined and there is no attempt to define either title or identification. In fact, Art. 4(b) provides that "except as otherwise expressly provided in this Convention, it is not concerned with: * * * the effect which the contract may have on the property in the goods sold." Thus, "title" (and the effect of identification) are not relevant under the CISG unless there is an article expressly providing otherwise. In *Usinor*

Industeel v. Leeco Steel Products Inc., 209 F. Supp. 2d 880 (N.D. Ill 2002), the court held that because the CISG did not cover the property rights aspects of the contract for sale, the Illinois UCC provisions governed the seller's property claim to the goods which were located in Illinois.

Note: Title and Identification Under UCITA

Both Article 2 and Article 2A build upon common law concepts of property rights about goods. UCITA, on the other hand, must take into account property rights as provided by federal law in the various types of intellectual property that are the subject matter of UCITA. Of course under the supremacy clause of the United States Constitution, federal law would control in the event of a conflict.

UCITA distinguishes between ownership of a copy and ownership of the informational rights in the information that is protected under intellectual property law. UCITA 501, 102(a)(38) (definition of informational rights). A license to possess or control a copy or use information is not ownership of that information. Thus, transfer of ownership of a copy does not transfer ownership of the intellectual property. UCITA 501(b), 502. Transfer of ownership of the intellectual property is governed by federal law. A licensee of information does not obtain any property rights at all in the information and may not even have any property rights in the copy unless the license so provides. UCITA 502. The licensor's or licensee's ability to transfer its rights under the license are treated purely as contact assignments and are not a transfer of any property rights in the information. UCITA 503 through 506.

UCITA 501addresses identification of the informational rights to the contract but does not provide any definition of identification. Identification functions as part of the default rule for determining when ownership of informational rights in a computer program passes to a buyer. Generally the parties' agreement will provide that ownership will pass at a different time than identification. Given that a non-exclusive license of information does not constitute a transfer of a property right in informational rights, the identification concept has limited utility in UCITA.

SECTION 2.   SELLER OR LESSOR IN POSSESSION OF THE GOODS

A. Introduction

If the seller or lessor is in possession of the goods, can the buyer or lessee compel the seller or lessor to transfer possession of the goods to the buyer or lessee under the contract? Can this be done under Article 2 or 2A if the buyer or lessee does not have a perfected security interest in the goods under Article 9? Suppose the seller still has title to the goods but the goods are identified to the contract. That identification gives the buyer a "special property interest" in the goods under UCC 2-501(1), but does that give the buyer a right to possession of the goods? Even if title is to remain with the lessor in a non-finance lease transaction, under UCC 2A-218, the lessee obtains an insurable interest in the goods upon identification of the goods to the contract? Does this insurable interest give the lessee a right to obtain possession of the goods from the lessor?

We will first consider the buyer or lessee's ability to use that identification of the goods to the contract as a basis for compelling transfer of possession of the goods to the buyer and lessee. We will then consider whether those rights of the buyer or lessee as against the seller or lessor are also good as against other persons who may claim they have rights in the goods deriving from their interaction with the seller or lessor. This second issue presents a classic priority contest as to which of the two parties have the superior right to possession of the goods.

B. Buyer's or Lessee's Rights to Obtain the Goods From the Seller or Lessor

1. Pre-paying Buyer or Lessee

Read UCC 2-502. Article 2A has a comparable provision, UCC 2A-522. Notice that mere identification of the goods to the sales contract under UCC 2-501 or to the lease contract under UCC 2A-217 does not provide the buyer or lessee with any enforceable right to compel the seller or lessor to deliver possession of the goods to the buyer or lessee.[*] Something more is required.

Problem 9-2

A. Buyer, an individual, agreed to purchase Seller's car, putting $1,000 down and agreeing to pay the balance on delivery. Seller refused to deliver the car on the delivery date even though the car was available for delivery. Seller offered Buyer her money back. What are Buyer's rights under UCC 2-502?

---

[*] *Sam and Mac, Inc. v. Treat*, 783 N.E.2d 760 (Ind. Ct. App. 2003).

B. Buyer, a corporation, agreed to purchase a delivery truck from Dealer, putting down $1,000 and agreeing to pay the balance on delivery. Dealer refused to deliver the truck on the delivery date even though the truck was available for delivery. Dealer offered Buyer its money back. What are Buyer's rights under UCC 2-502?

C. Is there any difference in analysis if either transaction above is a lease transaction? UCC 2A-522.

D. Suppose the seller agreed to manufacture goods and the buyer agreed to pay $500,000 of the $1,000,000 purchase price in advance. After identification but before completion of the goods, the seller repudiated the contract. Can the buyer tender the remaining $500,000 due under the contract and recover the still uncompleted goods?

2. Specific Performance and Replevin

Now read UCC 2-716 and 2A-507A [former 2A-521]. These sections address the right of a buyer or lessee to obtain specific performance, or in the alternative, to replevin goods identified to the contract.

Specific performance is a remedy for breach of contract that compels a party to perform the contract but does not actually create property rights in the goods in the possession of the seller or lessor.[*] In fact, a specific performance decree may order a seller or lessor to manufacture or obtain goods not yet existing or identified to the contract. To obtain specific performance, the plaintiff must demonstrate that it is entitled to injunctive relief. An order for specific performance is a type of injunction. The party requesting specific performance must convince the court that the party has met the requirements for granting an injunction and one of those requirements is the moving party has no other adequate remedy at law. The provisions of UCC 2-716(1) and 2A-507A [former 2A-521] are designed to broaden the ability of a party to obtain this type of injunctive relief by permitting such a decree in "if the goods are unique or other proper circumstances."[**] This

---

[*] See David Frisch, *Remedies as Property: A Different Perspective on Specific Performance Clauses*, 35 WM. & MARY L. REV. 1691 (1994).

[**] A useful history of UCC 2-716 and a comparison with the RESTATEMENT (SECOND) OF CONTRACTS, is Harold Greenberg, *Specific Performance Under Section 2-716 of the Uniform Commercial Code: "A More Liberal Attitude" in the "Grand Style"*, 17 N. ENG. L. REV.
(continued...)

broadening is consistent with the arguments made by some economists that specific performance rather than damages be the preferred remedy in all cases of breach of contract. Put differently, if it were clear that specific performance: (1) best protected the promisee's subjective value in the contract; (2) minimized if not avoided consequential damages; and (3) decreased the overall costs of judicial administration or the parties' post-breach negotiations, what are the arguments for the current rule, *i.e.*, damages are preferred unless they are inadequate?*

The 2003 amendments to Articles 2 and 2A broadened the grounds for specific performance in two ways. First, the amendments permit a court to order specific performance if the parties have agreed to the remedy. Second, the amendments allow the seller or lessor to obtain specific performance against the buyer or lessee. The revision, however, provides that if the parties "agree to specific performance, specific performance may not be decreed if the breaching party's sole remaining contractual obligation is the payment of money." What is the justification for this limitation?

Replevin. The common law writ of replevin permitted the owner of goods held improperly by another party to obtain possession. Most states have statutes that implement this basic property right. Usually a writ is filed, a public official, usually a sheriff, takes possession of the goods, and a prompt hearing is held to determine whether the petitioner is entitled to the goods.

Read UCC 2-716(3) and 2A-507A(3) [former 2A-521(3)]. What are the requirements for replevin or a "similar remedy?" Note the "vesting" provision in UCC 2-716(4) (added by the 2003 amendments). As between a buyer and a seller in possession of the goods, when does the right to replevin "vest?" What is the point of stating this vesting rule? *See* UCC 2-402(1). *Compare* UCC 2-502(2). Notice that the vesting rule is not stated in UCC 2A-507A.

Security interests compared. The Article 2 and 2A sections that allow the buyer or lessee to obtain possession from the seller or lesser do not authorize self help. These are rights the buyer or lessee enforce through judicial procedures.

A buyer, however, may perfect a security interest in the goods. If the seller defaults in the obligation (usually to manufacture the goods) that is secured by the

---

** (...continued)
321, 344-53 (1982).

* An argument for specific performance "on demand" is made in Thomas S. Ulen, *The Efficiency of Specific Performance: Toward A Unified Theory of Contract Remedies,* 83 MICH. L. REV. 341 (1984).

goods, the buyer may peacefully repossess the goods by self-help under Article 9. UCC 9-609. Presumably a lessee could do the same thing under Article 9. Buyers who advance funds to finance the seller's performance under the contract for sale and create a security interest in the goods under manufacture are called "financing buyers."[*]

Problem 9-3

Return to Problem 9-2. Would the buyer or lessee be able to obtain specific performance of the contract from the seller or lessor? Would the buyer or lessee be able to obtain the goods by replevin from the seller or lessor?

Note: Rights of a Buyer to Obtain the Goods Under the CISG

Article 45(1)(a) of the CISG provides that if "the seller fails to perform any of his obligations under the contract or this Convention, the buyer may: (a) exercise the rights provided in articles 46 to 52 * * *." Article 46(1), which applies to non-delivery by the seller, provides that the "buyer may require performance by the seller of his obligations unless the buyer has resorted to a remedy which is inconsistent with this requirement." Thus, the buyer appears to have power to demand specific performance as a matter of right. If delivered goods "do not conform with the contract," Art. 46(2) provides the buyer may "require delivery of substitute goods only if the lack of conformity constitutes a fundamental breach of contract" and Art. 46(3) permits the buyer to "require the seller to remedy the lack of conformity by repair, unless this is unreasonable having regard to all the circumstances." Article 28, however, provides that a court is not bound to order specific performance "unless the court would do so under its own law in respect of similar contracts for sale not governed by this Convention." Thus, in cases where the Convention applies, a United States court would not be required to order specific performance if that remedy was not available under UCC 2-716(1).[**]

---

[*] *See generally* Thomas H. Jackson & Anthony T. Kronman, *A Plea for the Financing Buyer,* 85 YALE L.J. 1 (1975).

[**] *See* Steven Walt, *For Specific Performance Under the United Nations Sales Convention,* 26 TEX. INT'L L.J. 211 (1991).

Note: Rights of a Licensee to Obtain the Product Under UCITA

UCITA has only one section that addresses the right of a licensee to obtain the information or a copy from the licensor. UCITA 811 addresses the right of specific performance. That provision parallels UCC 2-716(1). UCITA has no provision comparable to UCC 2-502 or UCC 2-716(3) and (4).

C. The Buyer's or Lessee's Right to Obtain Possession As Against Third Persons with Claims to the Goods

While the goods are in the seller's or lessor's possession, other parties may have rights in those goods other than the buyer or lessee. For example, the seller or lessor may have granted a security interest in the goods to a secured party. A creditor of the seller or lessor may have levied on the goods. Under most state debtor-creditor laws, a creditor without a security interest does not have a lien on the goods until it has levied on the goods. Levy generally means that the relevant legal authority, like the county sheriff, has taken either actual or constructive possession of the goods. Another type of claim to the goods in the seller's or lessor's possession may arise from another lessee or buyer of the goods from the seller or lessor. When the seller or lessor has possession of the goods in these situations, does the buyer or lessee have the ability to obtain possession of the goods from the seller or lessor free of the claims of those third persons?

Read UCC 2-402, 2A-307, and 2A-308. These sections address the rights of creditors of the seller or lessor as against the buyer or lessee. Note that UCC 2-402(1) states that the rights of "unsecured creditors of the seller with respect to goods which have been identified to a contract for sale are subject to the buyer's rights to recover the goods under UCC 2-502 and UCC 2-716." How should this phrase be interpreted? Suppose, for example, the creditors were unsecured at the time of identification but became secured, either by a lien or perfected security interest, shortly thereafter?

1. Lien Creditors

Problem 9-4

A. Buyer, a consumer, made a $100 down payment on a new stereo at Dealer's store. Buyer and Dealer agreed that Buyer could take possession of the stereo when

Buyer paid the purchase price of $800 in full. Dealer marked the stereo with Buyer's name and stored the stereo in the warehouse. Dealer had several creditors with judgments against Dealer. One creditor, to enforce its judgment, levied on the Dealer's inventory, including the stereo that was marked for Buyer. Buyer returned to the store with the $700 remaining purchase price and wanted the stereo. Dealer refused to deliver the stereo because of the levy. As between the lien creditor and Buyer, who has the superior right to possession of the stereo? Is a lien creditor an "unsecured creditor" of the buyer under UCC 2-402(1)? *See* UCC 1-201(b)(13) definition of "creditor." Does the vesting rule in UCC 2-502(2) help your analysis?

B. Assume in (A) above that Dealer had kept the goods for Buyer for what is later determined to be an unreasonable length of time at the time the creditor levied. Any change in your analysis? *See* UCC 2-402(2).

C. Lessee, a consumer, made a down payment of $100 on identified household goods that Lessor will lease to Lessee for one year. The entire rent under the lease contract is $1,000. While Lessor still had possession of the goods, one of Lessor's creditors levied on the goods. As between Lessee and the levying creditor, who has the superior right of possession to the goods? *See* UCC 2A-307.

D. Assume in C above that the Lessor had possession of the goods for an unreasonable length of time after Lessee made the lease contract. Any change in your analysis? *See* UCC 2A-308.

2. Secured Creditors

The rights of a buyer or lessee as against the seller's or lessor's secured party are determined under Article 9. UCC 2-402(3) and 2A-307(3). The relevant Article 9 provisions are UCC 9-317, 9-320, and 9-321. If the security interest in the goods is perfected at the time the buyer's or lessee's special property interest arises, the secured party clearly has priority in the goods over the buyer or lessee unless the buyer or lessee is in ordinary course of business and the security interest was created by the buyer's seller or the lessee's lessor. UCC 9-320(a) and 9-321(c). The definition of a buyer in ordinary course is in UCC 1-201(b)(9) and of a lessee in ordinary course is in 2A-103. If the seller or lessor has possession of the goods, however, a buyer or a lessee will be in "ordinary course" only if they have the right to recover the goods from the seller or lessor under Article 2 or Article 2A. Those rights are given under UCC 2-502, 2-716, 2A-507A [former 2A-521] and 2A-522.

Notice that if the buyer or lessee is not a buyer or lessee in ordinary course of business, the buyer or lessee will not be able to assert rights superior to the Article

9 secured creditor of the seller or lessor unless the buyer or lessee takes delivery of the goods and gives value without knowledge of the security interest and before the security interest is perfected. UCC 9-317. Thus, when the goods are in the possession of the seller or lessor, the buyer or lessee will not have a superior right to possession of the goods as against the seller's or lessor's secured party unless the buyer or lessee qualifies as in "ordinary course" or the buyer's or lessee's rights under UCC 2-502, 2-716(3), 2A-507A, or 2A-522 vest before the seller's or lessor's creditor's security interest becomes enforceable. *See* UCC 9-203.

Problem 9-5

A. Dealer financed its retail operation by granting a security interest in its inventory to First Bank. First Bank properly perfected its security interest in the inventory under the rules of Article 9. Buyer, a consumer, made a $100 down payment on a new stereo at Dealer's store. Buyer and Dealer agreed that Buyer could take possession of the stereo when Buyer paid the purchase price of $800 in full. Dealer marked the stereo with Buyer's name and stored the stereo in the warehouse. Dealer defaulted on its obligations to First Bank and First Bank repossessed Dealer's inventory, including the stereo marked with Buyer's name. As between Buyer and First Bank, who has the superior right to possession of the stereo?

B. Dealer financed its retail operation by granting a security interest in its inventory to First Bank. First Bank properly perfected its security interest in the inventory under the rules of Article 9. Lessee, a consumer, made a down payment of $100 on identified household goods that Lessor will lease to Lessee for one year. The entire rent under the lease contract is $1,000. Dealer defaulted on its obligations to First Bank and First Bank repossessed Dealer's inventory, including the household goods identified to the lease contract with Lessee. As between First Bank and Lessee, who has a superior right of possession to those goods?

C. Suppose, on the facts above, that the buyer's rights under UCC 2-502 vest before First Bank attaches its security interest to Dealer's goods. UCC 9-203. What result? What if the security interest attaches prior to vesting of buyer's rights under UCC 2-502 but First Bank perfects its security interest subsequent to Buyer's right under UCC 2-502 vesting? Then what result? UCC 9-320, 9-317.

3. Buyers or Lessees from the Seller or Lessor

Now consider other claims to the goods while the goods are in the seller's or lessor's possession. One type of claim is that the seller or lessor does not have rights in the goods that can be transferred to a buyer or lessee because the seller or lessor has already transferred the seller's or lessor's rights in the goods to someone else.

Read UCC 2-403(1), first sentence and 2A-304(1), first sentence. A fundamental principle of property law is that a person may only transfer what rights they have in property.* This fundamental rule is subject to exceptions. One exception to this rule is the "entrustment rule." Read UCC 2-403(2). *Compare* UCC 2A-304(2) and 2A-305(2). Notice the entrustment rule only protects "ordinary course" buyers or lessees. When the seller or lessor has possession of the goods, then, that returns us again to the question of whether the buyer or lessee has a right to obtain possession from the seller or lessor in order to qualify as "ordinary course."

Another exception to the rule that a person may only transfer rights that they have in property is that, in some situations, a person with a voidable interest may transfer a good interest to a person who qualifies as a good faith purchaser for value. Read UCC 2-403(1), 2A-304(1) and 2A-305(1). When does a seller or lessor have voidable title? When does a buyer or lessee qualify as a good faith purchaser for value? Read the definition of "purchaser" and "good faith" in UCC 1-201 and "value" in UCC 1-204 [former 1-201]. Unlike the definition of buyer or lessee in ordinary course, the concept of purchaser does not entail the idea that the person must have taken possession of the goods or have a right to possession in order to be a purchaser.

Problem 9-6

A. August, the owner of a diamond necklace, left the necklace with Dealer for repair of the necklace. Dealer entered into a contract to sell the diamond necklace to Buyer who made a down payment on the necklace but did not take possession. As between August and Buyer, who would have superior right to possession of the goods before Buyer obtained possession of the necklace from Dealer?

---

* *See* Steven L. Harris, *Using Fundamental Principles of Commercial Law to Decide UCC Cases*, 26 LOY. L.A. L. REV. 637 (1993).

B. Assume Dealer had contracted to sell the necklace to August (who paid $1,000 down of the $9,000 price) and left it in Dealer's possession. Thereafter Dealer sold the same necklace to July for $10,000. Under what circumstances would July win?

C. August leased a diamond necklace from Dealer. Before August took possession of the necklace, Dealer entered into a lease contract with Lessee for the necklace. Lessee made a down payment on the necklace but did not obtain possession yet. As between August and Lessee, who has a superior right to possession of the necklace?

D. Assume in the three situations above that Dealer is not a merchant that deals in goods of the kind. Same result?

D. Seller's or Lessor's Ability to Stop or Withhold Delivery of the Goods From the Buyer or Lessee

If the goods are identified to a contract for sale, the buyer will obtain, at least, a special property interest and, at most, title. Review UCC 2-401 and 2-501. In short, the buyer could be the owner of the goods before they are delivered. A lessee may have an insurable interest in the goods prior to delivery of the goods. UCC 2A-217, 2A-219.

As between the parties, the seller may withhold or stop delivery of the goods if the buyer has become insolvent or otherwise breached the contract even though the time for delivery has arrived. UCC 2-702(1), 2-705. This seller's right is like a possessory lien to secure the buyer's performance. Similarly, the lessor may withhold or stop delivery of the goods when the lessee is insolvent or has otherwise breached the contract. UCC 2A-523, 2A-525(1), 2A-526. The 2003 amendments broadened the right of the seller or lessor to stop delivery by eliminating the requirement that only entire carloads, plane loads or other large shipments could be halted because of the buyer's or lessee's breach of contract. The revisions also broadened and clarified the catalog of seller's possessory remedies in UCC 2-703 and the lessor's possessory remedies in UCC 2A-523.

If the goods are in the hands of a bailee, the seller or lessor must take action in the prescribed time frame to enable the bailee to act to stop delivery of the goods. UCC 2-705(2), (3), 2A-526(2), (3). *See also* UCC 7-403.

The relationship between the seller's or lessor's right to withhold delivery for the buyer's or lessee's breach or insolvency and an Article 9 security interest is clarified in UCC 9-110, cmt. 5. The right to stop or withhold delivery is not a security interest arising under Article 2 or 2A. Rather the creditors of or purchasers from the buyer or lessee take subject to the seller's or lessor's right to withhold or stop delivery as long as the seller or lessor retains possession or control of the goods. UCC 2-403(1), 2A-307(1). We will explore those rights in more detail, *infra*, in Subsection F.

Problem 9-7

A. Seller sold diamonds to Buyer and the parties agreed that the Seller would send the diamonds to Buyer under a shipment contract. Upon notification of shipment, Buyer was to make a funds transfer to Seller's bank account. Seller shipped the diamonds to Buyer using Federated Shipping. Federated Shipping issued a negotiable bill of lading to Seller. Buyer failed to make the funds transfer after Seller notified Buyer the goods had been shipped. Seller contacted Federated Shipping and instructed Federated to not deliver the package to Buyer but to hold it until Seller otherwise notified Federated.

    1. Did Seller act rightfully in ordering Federated to hold the package?

    2. Does Federated have to obey Seller's instructions?

B. If this was a lease transaction, would the analysis change?

E. Security Interests Arising Under Article 2: Seller's Right to Retain Title or Ship Under Reservation

Under UCC 2-401(1) and 2-505, the seller may take an Article 2 security interest in goods that are shipped or delivered to the buyer. The retention of title term is generally contained in the sales contract between the buyer and the seller. The seller ships under reservation pursuant to the requirements of UCC 2-505. These security interests, which arise under Article 2, are subject to the provisions of Article 9. UCC 9-110. As long as the buyer does not obtain possession of the goods, the seller need not have an authenticated security agreement in order to make these security interests enforceable against the debtor.

Note: Retaining Control of the Product Under UCITA

UCITA hinges the ability to retain possession or control of the subject matter of the contract on the licensee's material breach. If the licensee has committed a material breach, the licensor may cancel the license. UCITA 802. Upon cancellation, the licensor has the right to possession or control of the information and copies. UCITA 802(c)(3), 815.

F. Claims to the Goods Asserted by the Buyer's or Lessee's Creditors or Transferees When the Seller or Lessor in Possession of the Goods

If the seller is in possession of the goods or rightfully withheld or stopped delivery of the goods from the buyer, what are the seller's rights in the goods as against creditors and transferees from the buyer? Under the principle of derivative rights (a person may only transfer the rights one has), the seller would argue that if the buyer is subject to the seller's right to keep possession of the goods or withhold or stop delivery, persons who derive their claim due to a transaction with the buyer should also be subject to those rights. UCC 2-403(1), first sentence. *See* UCC 9-110, comment 5.[*]

The second sentence of UCC 2-403(1) does not allow a good faith purchaser from a buyer to assert rights superior to the seller if the buyer has not taken delivery of the goods. Courts hold that in order for the buyer to have voidable title that it can transfer to a good faith purchaser, the buyer has to have taken delivery of the goods under a transaction of purchase. *See Inmi-Etti v. Aluisi, infra.* The entrustment rule of UCC 2-403(2) does not help potential transferees of the buyer as the seller has not entrusted possession of the goods to the buyer. *See* UCC 2-403(3) defining "entrustment." UCC 9-110 does provide that if the buyer does not receive possession of the goods, the seller's security interest under UCC 2-401 or 2-505 has priority over another security interest created by the buyer. This rule at least contemplates that a buyer could grant a security interest to a creditor that is effective before the buyer obtains possession of the goods.[**] Thus a seller who retains possession while asserting Article 2 remedies has priority in the goods over the buyer and creditors of or purchasers from the buyer.

Creditors of the lessee generally take subject to the lease contract. UCC 2A-307(1). A buyer or lessee from a lessee only takes the rights that the lessee had.

---

[*] *In re Kellstrom Industries, Inc.*, 282 B.R. 787 (Bankr. D. Del. 2002); *In re Trico Steel Co.*, 282 B.R. 318 (Bankr. D. Del. 2002), *aff'd*, 302 B.R. 489 (D. Del. 2003).

[**] *But see, Conister Trust Ltd. v. Boating Corp. of America*, 2002 WL 389864 (Tenn. Ct. App. 2002) (mere identification of goods to contract when seller in possession of goods and buyer in breach of contract insufficient to support attachment of buyer's creditor's security interest in goods.)

UCC 2A-305(1). Just as in the sales transaction, when the lessor has possession, the entrustment rule does not help a buyer or lessee from the first lessee because the lessor has not entrusted the goods to the first lessee. UCC 2A-305(2).

Problem 9-8

S agreed to manufacture factory equipment according to B's specifications for $100,000. Under the agreement, title was to pass to B when conforming goods were identified to the contract. In addition, B agreed to pay $50,000 upon delivery and to give S a promissory note, due six months after delivery, for the balance. S completed and identified conforming goods to the contract on July 1. On August 1, the date for delivery, S tendered delivery but B failed to pay the $50,000 due so S retained possession. UCC 2-703. Shortly thereafter, S was beset with the following claims by third parties who had dealt with B:

1. Bank had a perfected security interest in B's equipment, existing and after-acquired. Bank argued that B had "rights in the collateral" on July 1, the security interest attached on that date, *see* UCC 9-203, and that it was perfected with priority over S, citing UCC 9-322. *See* UCC 9-110.

2. Lien creditor argued it had priority because its judgment against B was executed by levy on July 15, citing UCC 9-317.

3. Buyer argued it had priority because it paid B $90,000 for the goods, to be delivered later, on July 20.

Which, if any, of these parties should prevail over S, the party in possession of the goods? Do you have any different analysis if S had shipped under reservation and had timely instructed the carrier to not deliver the goods to the buyer?

SECTION 3.   BUYER OR LESSEE IN POSSESSION OF THE GOODS

A. Introduction

Now we consider the situation where the buyer or lessee has obtained possession of the goods.* This occurs when the buyer takes physical possession of

---

* Determining when the buyer or lessee has obtained possession of the goods may present interesting issues. *Kunkel v. Sprague National Bank*, 128 F. 3d 636 (8th Cir. 1997) (buyer received "constructive" possession when cattle never left seller's feedlot and buyer acknowledged receipt of cattle, cattle bailed to seller to feed prior to slaughter).

the goods, UCC 2-103(1)(l), or has control of them under a negotiable document of title or otherwise.

This section will deal with three closely related questions. The first question concerns the circumstances under which the seller or lessor can regain or reclaim possession of the goods from the buyer or lessee. Given that under a lease, the goods will ultimately return to the lessor, it is not surprising that the lessor's right to regain the goods from the lessee are more expansive than the rights of a seller to regain the goods from the buyer. UCC 2A-525(1). The second question involves the priority of the seller's or lessor's rights to reclaim possession of the goods as against the rights of the buyer's or lessee's creditors or transferees. Third, we consider the ability of the buyer or lessee to retain possession of the goods as against claimants (such as an owner or secured party) who have derived their rights from a transaction with the seller or the lessor.

B. Seller's or Lessor's Right to Regain Possession of the Goods From Buyer or Lessee

1. Seller's Security Interest in Goods

A seller who delivers possession of goods sold to the buyer on credit may create and perfect a security interest in those goods under Article 9. If the buyer defaulted, *i.e.*, failed to pay the price when due, the seller, as a secured party, could enforce the security interest by repossessing the goods, UCC 9-601 and 9-609, selling them in a commercially reasonable manner, UCC 9-610, and applying the proceeds to the obligation, UCC 9-615. A seller with an Article 9 security interest may repossess the goods without judicial process as long as it does so without a breach of the peace. UCC 9-609. For a full treatment of a secured party's rights upon default by the debtor, *see* Article 9, Part 6. If a seller has "retained title" to the goods in the contract for sale and the goods are delivered to the buyer, the seller has a security interest in the goods that is fully subject to the rules of Article 9. UCC 2-401, 9-110, 1-201(b)(35) [former 1-201(37)].

2. Seller's Right to Reclaim When no Security Interest in Goods

Article 2 provides a seller with two separate rights to reclaim. UCC 2-702(2) addresses the ability of a seller to reclaim when the seller delivers on credit to an insolvent buyer. The credit seller's reclamation right is based upon the common law theory that the buyer who receives goods on credit while insolvent has engaged in fraud for which the seller's remedy is rescission of the contract for sale and reclamation of the goods.[*] The 2003 amendments expanded the right of the credit seller to reclaim by eliminating the previous limitation that the demand for reclamation must be made within 10 days of the buyer's receipt of the goods unless the buyer made a written misrepresentation of solvency to the seller in the three months prior to delivery. After the amendments, the seller must reclaim by a demand made "within a reasonable time after the buyer's receipt of goods." UCC 2-702(2).

Second, UCC 2-507(2) addresses the ability of a seller to reclaim when the seller has sold in a non-credit transaction and the payment mechanism fails. An example of this is where the seller delivers the goods in exchange for a check in payment and the check is later dishonored because of insufficient funds. The 2003 amendments codified the right that was previously set forth in the comment to UCC 2-507. Thus, if the check bounces, the seller may "reclaim the goods delivered upon a demand made within a reasonable time after the seller discovers or should have discovered that payment was not made." UCC 2-507(2).

Under both UCC 2-702(2) and 2-507(2), the seller's demand for reclamation must be made within a reasonable time. The time is measured from the time of the buyer's receipt of the goods under UCC 2-702(2) and from the time the seller discovered or should have discovered the payment mechanism failed under UCC 2-507(2).

Reclamation is not a self help remedy. If the buyer does not comply with a reclamation demand, an Article 2 seller who does not have an enforceable Article 9 security interest must use judicial process to enforce the demand. Further, as we shall see, *infra*, a right to reclaim against the buyer may be subject to the rights of creditors of or purchasers from the buyer.

3. Consignments

In a consignment, an owner of goods delivers them to an agent or "factor," who is usually a merchant with regard to goods of that kind, with power to sell them to third parties. The owner retains title and fixes the price and conditions of sale. If the goods are sold, the factor delivers possession to the buyer and the title passes

---

[*] *See* Larry T. Garvin, *Credit, Information, and Trust in the Law of Sales: The Credit Seller's Right of Reclamation*, 44 UCLA L. REV. 247 (1996).

directly from the owner to the buyer. The factor, after taking a commission, accounts to the owner for the price. If the goods are not sold, they are returned by the factor to the owner, usually without obligation. In the interim between delivery and sale, most consignment agreements permit the owner to recover the goods and obligate the factor to return them on request. A number of questions still shroud this transaction with uncertainty before and even after the enactment of Revised Article 9.

Prior to the Article 9 revision, a critical question was when is the transaction a "true" consignment and when is it a "consignment intended for security?" *See* UCC 1-201(b)(35) [former 1-201(37)]. If it was a "true" consignment, pre-revision Article 9 did not apply but the notice provisions of former 2-326(3) and former 9-114 had to be satisfied in order for the consignor to protect its ownership rights from the claims of the consignee's creditors. A consignment intended as security, however, was a secured transaction subject to Article 9. A leading case stated that the "easiest way to determine the intention of the parties is to concentrate on the *function* of the consignment." The court continued:

> (C)onsignments are used in two ways: (1) As a security consignment where the goods go to the merchant who is unwilling to risk finding a market for the goods so the "title" remains in the consignor; and (2) as a price-fixing device. Number (1) is clearly a secured transaction with the reservation of title to goods acting as collateral. Number (2) is designed only to insure resale maintenance and has nothing to do with security.

Columbia International Corp. v. Kempler, 175 N.W.2d 465, 470-71 (Wis. 1970). *But see* William A. Hawkland, *The Proposed Amendments to Article 9 of the UCC-Part 5: Consignments and Equipment Leases,* 77 COM. L.J. 108, 109 (1972), who suggests that the distinction between true and false consignments was "never clearly articulated or defined by the common law courts" and this "led to uncertain results and made consignment planning hazardous."[*] In short, the characterization process was uncertain and the anti-trust problem lurked in the background. Thus, pre-

---

[*] For example, suppose that the function of the transaction was to control resale prices and to require the consignee to pay for all or part of the price, even though there was no sale of the goods. *See also* William A. Harrington, *The Law of Consignments: Antitrust and Commercial Pitfalls,* 34 BUS. LAW. 431, 446 (1979), who claims that "any widespread consignment program aimed at resale price maintenance must be viewed as suspect, particularly if there are any elements of coercion of distributors." For identification and application of the factors in the determination, *see In re Ide Jewelry Co.,* 75 B.R. 969 (Bankr. D.C.1987).

revision Article 9 provided for optional filing of consignments (and leases) to protect against the risk that the transaction created a security interest. Former 9-408.

Under Revised Article 9, even a "true" consignment may be covered by Article 9. Read the definition of consignment in UCC 9-102(a)(20). UCC 9-109(a)(4) provides that Article 9 applies to true consignments that meet the definition in UCC 9-102. *See* UCC 9-109, cmt. 6. For included consignments, the consignor is treated as a secured party with a purchase money security interest, UCC 9-103(d), and Article 9 governs attachment, perfection, and priority of the consignor's interest in the goods in the hands of the consignee. Upon default, however, the enforcement rules in Part 6 do not apply. *See* UCC 9-601(g). A consignment that is not a "true" consignment but a consignment that creates a security interest is subject to all of the Article 9 rules, including the rules on process in event of default.

If the transaction is a true consignment and not within the scope of the definition of consignment in UCC 9-102, the transaction is a bailment for sale. The rights of the creditors and transferees of the bailee would be determined under common law principles, not Article 9 or Article 2. *See* UCC 9-109, cmt. 6. As part of the Article 9 revision process, former 2-326(3) was deleted from Article 2.

4. Lessor's Right to Possession of Goods from Lessee

Once a lessor delivers the goods to a lessee, the lessor's right to reclaim the goods is governed by UCC 2A-525(2) and (3). That section allows reclamation upon a default by the lessee. Reclamation under Article 2A follows the Article 9 model which allows the lessor to recover the goods without judicial process if it can be done without breach of the peace.

Note: Licensor Reclamation Under UCITA

A licensor has a right upon cancellation of a license for material breach to recover the information and prevent its use. UCITA 815. Following the Article 9 model, such repossession must be done without breach of the peace in order to avoid using judicial process. Allowing electronic self-help reclamation was very controversial in the drafting process.[*] *See* UCITA 816 on how the controversy was

---

[*] *See* Stephen L. Poe and Teresa L. Conover, *Pulling the Plug: The Use and Legality of*
(continued...)

eventually handled. Electronic self-help may occur in non-UCITA contexts, such as in disabling equipment with computer programs and radio signals. Revised Article 9 does not specifically address electronic self-help.

C. Priority of Seller's or Lessor's Right to Possession Against Buyer's or Lessee's Creditors or Transferees

In this subsection, let us assume that the seller or lessor has a right to regain possession of the goods from the buyer's or lessee's possession as against the buyer or lessee. But suppose the buyer's or lessee's creditors or transferees claim rights in the goods and assert that their rights are superior to the rights of the seller or lesser. What then?

1. Seller's Security Interest or a Consignor's Interest in Goods

If a seller retains title, takes a security interest in goods, or is a consignor of goods in an Article 9 consignment, the interest would be a "purchase money" security interest, *see* UCC 9-103(b). The security interest might have have priority over security interests created by the buyer if the conditions of UCC 9-324 are met. One of those conditions is perfection of the security interest under the rules of Article 9. UCC 9-308. If the secured party-seller properly perfected its security interest under the rules in Article 9, the seller would also have priority over a subsequent lien creditor who levied on the goods while the goods were in the buyer's possession. UCC 9-317. The secured party-seller's security interest would not be effective against a buyer in ordinary course of business from the buyer, UCC 9-320(a), but would be effective in the proceeds of the sale. UCC 9-315. In short, playing the Article 9 game is the route to maximum protection in this situation. A full treatment of Article 9, including the ways in which to perfect a security interest and exploration of the many priority rules awaits you in the course on secured transactions.

Problem 9-9

A. Under a "true" consignment, Consignor intends to deliver goods (textbooks)

---

* (...continued)
Technology-Based Remedies by Vendors in Software Contracts, 56 ALB. L. REV. 609 (1993).

to a Consignee who operates a university bookstore under its own name. Consignor discovers that a secured party has perfected a security interest in Consignee's "inventory, existing and after-acquired." What should Consignor do prior to delivery of the goods to Consignee to provide the maximum protection for Consignor's interest in the goods?

B. Suppose that Consignee did not maintain a place of business where he dealt with textbooks. Rather, Consignee entered into contracts with retail outlets under which Consignee would insure that textbooks were delivered in exchange for a commission on sales. Under the contract with Consignor, the books were delivered directly to the retail outlets: Consignee never had possession or control. Consignee, however, would remit the price for books sold and insure that unsold books were returned. Is this transaction subject to Article 9?

C. Suppose the transaction was a "sale or return" rather than a consignment. How does the seller protect itself against the buyer's creditors? UCC 2-326, 2-327.

2. Seller's Right to Reclaim

The priority of the seller's right to reclaim the goods as against creditors or transferees of the buyer is governed by UCC 2-702(3) and 2-507(3). The rights of buyers in ordinary course and "good faith purchasers for value" under UCC 2-403 will trump the reclamation rights of the seller. Neither section addresses the rights of a reclaiming seller as against a lien creditor of the buyer.[*]

Most of the litigation concerning reclamation has arisen in the context of the buyer's bankruptcy case. Here are the basics. Section 546(c) of the Bankruptcy Code provides that the avoidance powers of the trustee in Sections 544(a), 545, 547 and 549 are "subject to any statutory or common law right of a seller of goods that has sold goods to the debtor, in the ordinary course of such seller's business, to reclaim such goods if the debtor has received such goods while insolvent, but—(1) such a seller may not reclaim any such goods unless such seller demands in writing reclamation of such goods before ten days after receipt of such goods by the debtor * * *." 11 U.S.C. 546. This provision has been criticized as unduly restrictive, in that it (i) narrows the scope of reclamation available under UCC 2-702(2) and (ii) is the exclusive avenue of relief for the reclaiming seller under the Bankruptcy Code even if the reclamation is carried out prior to the buyer's bankruptcy filing. In short, unless the reclaiming seller satisfies both UCC 2-702(2) and Section 546(c),

---

[*] This priority dispute is resolved under common law where the reclaiming seller prevailed.

the reclamation claim will fail against the trustee.* Even then, it may still be subject to the claim of a "floating lienor"(the buyer's secured party) who qualifies as a good faith "purchaser" under UCC 2-403.** If the seller is reclaiming under UCC 2-507(2), 11 U.S.C. 546(c) does not protect the seller's reclamation right in the buyer's bankruptcy proceeding because reclamation is not based upon the buyer's insolvency.

Problem 9-10

Farmer raises cattle for beef. When the cattle are ready, Farmer sells them to Bravo, a meat processor. Bravo agrees to pay the price within 30 days after delivery. On March 1, Farmer delivered 50 head of cattle to Bravo for $35,000. Unknown to Farmer, Bravo was insolvent at that time. UCC 1-201 (definition of insolvency).

A. Assume no third parties are involved. If Farmer discovers the insolvency on March 8, what can he do to reclaim the cattle from Bravo? *See* UCC 2-702(2). Suppose the cattle have been processed and sold but the proceeds of that sale can be identified. Can Farmer reclaim the proceeds under UCC 2-702(2)? *Compare* UCC 9-315.***

B. Suppose that Farmer, on March 8, made an oral demand on Bravo for the cattle, which had not yet been slaughtered. On March 6, however, Eric, a creditor, had obtained a judicial lien on all of Bravo's personal property. Can Farmer

---

* *See* Richard A. Mann & Michael J. Phillips, *Section 546(c) of the Bankruptcy Reform Act: An Imperfect Resolution of the Conflict Between the Reclaiming Seller and the Bankruptcy Trustee,* 54 AM. BANKR. L.J. 239 (1980). *See In re Zeta Consumer Products Corp.*, 291 B.R. 336 (Bankr. D. N.J. 2003) (seller who reclaimed goods in 90 day period prior to bankruptcy unable to assert reclamation as a defense to preference action unless seller complied with section 546(c)).

** *See In re Pester Refining Co.*, 964 F.2d 842 (8th Cir. 1992), holding that the seller was "subject to" the rights of the qualifying secured party. *See also* Julian B. McDonnell, *The Floating Lienor as Good Faith Purchaser,* 50 S. CAL. L. REV. 429 (1977), who explores the equities of that result.

*** The cases disagree. An affirmative answer was given in *United States v. Westside Bank*, 732 F.2d 1258, 1263 (5th Cir. 1984), where the court stated that to "hold otherwise would in many instances render the statutory remedy a nullity." *But see In re Diversified Food Service Distributors, Inc.*, 130 B.R. 427 (Bankr. S.D.N.Y. 1991) (reclamation limited to goods).

reclaim the cattle from Bravo free from Eric's lien? *See* UCC 2-702(3). Note that UCC 2-702(3) was amended in 1966 to exclude lien creditors. What does one do next? *See* UCC 1-103. The common law rule is that lien creditors would not defeat the seller's right to reclaim when that right is based upon buyer's fraud.

C. Suppose Farmer made an oral demand on March 8. On March 6, however, Bravo had filed a voluntary case in bankruptcy. Could Farmer reclaim the cattle against the trustee? Read UCC 9-317 and Sections 544(a) and 546 of the Bankruptcy Code, 11 U.S.C. 544(a) & 546.

D. How would Farmer, who made an oral demand on March 8, fare against a buyer from Bravo who, on March 6, had paid the price but had not taken possession from Bravo on March 8? *See* UCC 2-702(3). What if the buyer has taken possession of the cattle prior to March 8?

E. The last (but not least) variation. Suppose that First Bank had created and perfected an Article 9 security interest in Bravo's "inventory, existing and after-acquired," on February 1. The effect of this is that when Bravo obtains "rights" in the cattle (upon delivery by Farmer), First Bank's security interest attaches to and becomes perfected in the cattle. Assuming that First Bank is unaware of Farmer's claim but has made no new advances between March 1 and March 8, could Farmer effectively reclaim against First Bank? Is First Bank a good faith purchaser for value? UCC 1-201, 1-204.[*]

F. Is there any change in your analysis of the above questions if Farmer's right to reclaim is because Bravo's check it gave Farmer for the price of the cattle was dishonored?

3. Lessor's Right to Reclaim Against the Lessee's Creditors or Transferees

UCC 2A-307(1) provides that creditors of the lessee take subject to the lease contract. Thus, creditors of the lessee should be subject to the lessor's ability to reclaim the goods upon the lessee's default. If the lessee is a merchant dealing in goods of the kind to whom the lessor entrusted the goods, a buyer or lessee in ordinary course can take the goods free of the lessor's rights under the lease contract. UCC 2A-305(2).

---

[*] *See In re Arlco, Inc.*, 239 B.R. 261 (Bankr. S.D.N.Y. 1999). *But see* William Louis Tabac, *Battle for the Bulge: The Reclaiming Seller vs. the Floating Lien Creditor*, 2001 COLUM. BUS. L. REV. 509.

D. Priority of Buyer's or Lessee's Claim to the Goods Against Persons Claiming Pre-existing Ownership

1. Buyer Against Persons Claiming Pre-existing Ownership of the Goods

We first consider the rights of a buyer of goods as against another person who claims an ownership interest in the goods. In a typical case, a buyer purchases goods from a seller, takes possession of the goods and pays the price. Later, a third person claiming to be the owner of the goods attempts either to recover the goods from the buyer or recover damages for conversion. The buyer's defense is that she took "good title" from her seller. Whether this defense works is determined by UCC 2-403. Review that section and the applicable definitions in UCC 1-201 and 1-204. Consider the following case and problems.

INMI-ETTI V. ALUISI
COURT OF APPEALS OF MARYLAND, 1985
63 MD. APP. 293, 492 A.2D 917

[Appellant, a resident of Nigeria, ordered a new Honda Prelude while visiting her sister in the United States. Butler, an acquaintance of her family, offered to assist. Appellant returned to Nigeria, leaving cash with the sister to complete the purchase. The sale was completed and a certificate of title was issued in appellant's name. The car, however, was delivered to Butler, who removed it from the sister without permission. The sister had an arrest warrant issued, but it was later quashed. Butler, claiming that appellant was an absconding debtor, then brought suit against her and filed an application for an attachment on the Honda. When appellant did not answer, Butler was granted a summary judgment. Thereafter, appellee, a deputy sheriff, executed the writ of attachment on the Honda but left it in Butler's possession.

Butler, representing that he was the owner, then contracted to sell the Honda to Pohanka, a dealer, for $7,200. Pohanka paid Butler $2,000 and agreed to pay the balance when Butler obtained a certificate of title. After executing a false affidavit in his application for a certificate of title, Butler was issued a certificate in his own name by the Motor Vehicle Administration. Butler then returned to Pohanka and exchanged the certificate for the balance of the contract price.

Appellant, upon returning to the United States, had Butler's summary judgment set aside. In addition, she sued Butler and Pohanka for conversion and appellee for negligent attachment. In the lower court, appellant obtained a default judgment against Butler. The court, however, granted a summary judgment to Pohanka and appellee. On appeal, the summary judgment in favor of appellee was sustained but the summary judgment in favor of Pohanka was reversed.] * * *

In order for the appellant to establish her right to summary judgment against Pohanka, we must be convinced that the record before the lower court contained undisputed facts and inferences properly deducible therefrom, demonstrating that Pohanka committed a conversion of the appellant's vehicle as a matter of law. * * * In *Interstate Ins. Co. v. Logan,* 205 Md. 583, 588-89, 109 A.2d 904 (1959), the Court of Appeals summarized the law of conversion:

> [F]orcible dispossession of personal property is not essential to constitute a conversion. A "conversion" is any distinct act of ownership or dominion exerted by one person over the personal property of another in denial of his right or inconsistent with it. * * *

* * * In the instant case it is undisputed that Pohanka exerted acts of use or ownership over the automobile in question by selling it on February 1, 1982. Nevertheless, our analysis cannot end here. We explain.

At common law the maxim was: "He who hath not cannot give (nemo dat qui non habet)." BLACK'S LAW DICTIONARY 935 (5th ed. 1979). Although at times the Uniform Commercial Code may seem to the reader as unintelligible as the Latin phrases which preceded it, we find in § 2-403 of the Code a definite modification of the above maxim. * * * *See generally* HAWKLAND UCC SERIES § 2-403:01 *et seq.* for an enlightening history of the origins of § 2-403.

In short, the answer to the appellant's claim against Pohanka depends on whether Butler had "void" or "voidable" title at the time of the purported sale to Pohanka. If Butler had voidable title, then he had the power to vest good title in Pohanka. If, on the other hand, Butler possessed void title (*i.e.*, no title at all), then Pohanka received no title and is liable in trover for the conversion of the appellant's automobile. Preliminarily, we note that there was no evidence that Butler was a "merchant who deals in goods of that kind" (*i.e.* automobiles). Md. Code, *supra,* §§ 2-403(2) and 2-104(1). Therefore the entrustment provisions of § 2-403(2)-(3) do not apply.

It has been observed that:

> Under 2-403, voidable title is to be distinguished from void title. A thief, for example, "gets" only void title and without more cannot pass any title to a good faith purchaser. "Voidable title" is a murky concept. The

Code does not define the phrase. The comments do not even discuss it. Subsections (1)(a)-(d) of 2-403 clarify the law as to particular transactions which were "troublesome under prior law." Beyond these, we must look to non-Code state law.

J. WHITE & R. SUMMERS, HANDBOOK OF THE LAW UNDER THE UNIFORM COMMERCIAL CODE § 3-11 (2d ed. 1980) (footnote omitted). White and Summers further explain that: subsection (a) of § 2-403(1) deals with cases where the purchaser *impersonates* someone else; subsection (b) deals with "rubber checks"; subsection (c) deals with "*cash sales*"; and subsection (d) deals with cases of *forged checks* and other acts fraudulent to the seller. *Id.* None of these subsections apply to the facts of the present case and we, therefore, must turn to "non-Code state law" to determine whether Butler had voidable title.

HAWKLAND, *supra*, § 403:04, suggests that "voidable title" may only be obtained when the owner of the goods makes a voluntary transfer of the goods. He reaches that conclusion from the Code definitions of the words "delivery" and "purchase" and summarizes:

> Section 2-403(1)(d) does not create a voidable title in the situation where the goods are wrongfully taken, as contrasted with delivered voluntarily because of the concepts of "delivery" and "purchaser" which are necessary preconditions. "Delivery" is defined by section 1-201(14) "with respect to instruments, documents of title, chattel paper or securities" to mean "voluntary transfer of possession." By analogy, it should be held that goods are not delivered for purposes of section 2-403 unless they are voluntarily transferred. Additionally, section 2-403(1)(d) is limited by the requirement that the goods "have been delivered under a transaction of purchase." "Purchase" is defined by section 1-201(32) to include only voluntary transactions. A thief who wrongfully takes goods is not a purchaser within the meaning of this definition, but a swindler who fraudulently induces the victim to voluntarily deliver them is a purchaser for this purpose. This distinction, reminiscent of the distinction between larceny and larceny by trick made by the common law, is a basic one for the understanding of the meaning of section 2-403(1)(d).

Hawkland later states that the above language applies generally to § 2-403(1) and not merely to subsection (1)(d). *See* HAWKLAND, *supra*, § 2-403:05. The following cases and, indeed, (a) through (d) of § 2-403(1) seem to support Hawkland's theory that only a voluntary transfer by the owner can vest "voidable title" in a "person." * * * Without attempting to specify all the situations which could give rise to a voidable title under § 2-403 of the Uniform Commercial Code, we refer to the above authorities to support our conclusion that voidable title under the Code can only arise from a voluntary transfer or delivery of the goods by the owner. If the goods are stolen or otherwise obtained against the will of the owner, only void title can result.

Under the undisputed facts of the present case Butler possessed void title when Pohanka dealt with him. Although the record simply is not sufficient for us to decide whether Butler actually stole the appellant's vehicle, it is undisputed that the appellant at no time made a voluntary transfer to Butler. Thus, Pohanka obtained no title, and its sale of the vehicle constituted a conversion of the appellant's property. We believe the above analysis sufficient to impose liability upon Pohanka. We will nevertheless answer certain of Pohanka's collateral arguments.

We reject any notion that Butler obtained voidable title to the vehicle as a result of the attachment on original process carried out pursuant to former Maryland District Rules G40-60. * * *

The only way Butler could have obtained title in the vehicle through those attachment proceedings was if he had purchased it at a judicial sale. That clearly never occurred.

Implicit in all that we have said so far is the fact that Butler did not obtain title (voidable or otherwise) merely from the fact that he was able to convince the Motor Vehicle Administration to issue a certificate of title for the automobile to him. Although "[a] certificate of title issued by the Administration is prima facie evidence of the facts appearing on it," Md. Code (1977, 1984 Repl. Vol.), § 13-107 of the Transportation Article, the erroneous issuance of such a certificate cannot divest the title of the true owner of the automobile. * * *

Likewise, we find unpersuasive Pohanka's argument that since Butler had possession of the automobile and a duly issued certificate of title in his name, Pohanka should be protected as a "good faith purchaser for value" under § 2-403 of the Commercial Law Article, *supra.* Such status under that section of the Uniform Commercial Code is relevant in situations where the seller (transferor) is possessed of voidable title. It does not apply to the situation presented by the instant case where the seller had no title at all. * * *

Finally, whether Pohanka converted the vehicle with innocent intent is immaterial. * * * "The mere receipt of the possession of the goods under such circumstances is a conversion." [quoting from RESTATEMENT (SECOND) OF TORTS § 229 comment e, Ed.]

Accordingly, we shall reverse the summary judgment in favor of Pohanka and enter judgment in favor of the appellant against Pohanka for $8,200, an amount representing the agreed fair market value of the appellant's automobile at the time of its conversion, plus interest at 10 percent per annum from February 1, 1982, the date when Pohanka sold the automobile. Md. Rule 1075. * * *

[Footnotes omitted.]

Notes

1. The classic case of "void" title is where a thief steals the goods from Owner. There is no voluntary transfer of possession. Thus a buyer of the goods from the thief or any person to whom the thief has delivered the goods gets no protection under UCC 2-403, even if she is a buyer in ordinary course of business.

2. A classic case of "voidable" title at common law is where the seller, induced by a fraudulent representation by the buyer, delivers the goods to the buyer under a contract for sale. Such a case is *Johnson & Johnson Prod. v. Dal Intern. Trading,* 798 F.2d 100 (3rd Cir. 1986), where the buyer misrepresented that the goods sold would be distributed only in Poland. In fact, they were distributed through various intermediaries in the so-called "gray market" to buyers in the United States. When the plaintiff sought an injunction against sales in the United States, the defendant claimed its seller had voidable title and that it was a "good faith purchaser for value" under UCC 2-403(1). The court agreed, holding that the buyer had no reason to suspect that there was fraud (even though it had reason to believe it had purchased "gray" goods) and, therefore, there was no duty to investigate or inquire as to whether there might have been a misrepresentation. In short, the buyer was "honest in fact" because it did not "subjectively" suspect that the title was flawed and proceed with the purchase "despite his or her suspicions."

3. A classic example of the so-called "entrustment" provision, UCC 2-403(2), is where O, the owner of a diamond necklace, delivers it to M, a merchant who both repairs and sells goods of that kind, for the purpose of having the clasp repaired. M, with intent to default, removes the stone from the necklace and sells and delivers it to B, a buyer in ordinary course of business. *See* UCC 1-201(b)(9). In this case, B wins. Do you see why? As one court put it:

> The entrustment provision of the UCC is designed to enhance the reliability of commercial sales by merchants who deal in the kind of goods sold * * *. It shifts the risk of resale to the one who leaves his property with the merchant. * * * When a person knowingly delivers his property into the

possession of a merchant dealing in goods of that kind, that person assumes the risk of the merchant's acting unscrupulously by selling the property to an innocent purchaser. The entrustment provision places the loss upon the party who vested the merchant with the ability to transfer the property with apparent good title.

DeWeldon, Ltd. v. McKean, 125 F.3d 24, 27-28 (1ˢᵗ Cir. 1997). Note that UCC 1-201(b)(9) provides that only a "buyer that takes possession of the goods or has a right to recover the goods from the seller under Article 2 may be a buyer in the ordinary course of business." Why is possession so important in this context?

Note: Certificates of Title and the BFP of Motor Vehicles

Almost all states have statutes which require motor vehicles to be "titled." Suppose that Owner, whose certificate of title is in the possession of a secured party, entrusts the motor vehicle to a car dealer (a merchant) for repairs. Suppose, further, that the dealer, without Owner's or secured party's consent, puts the car on the lot and sells it to Cal in the ordinary course of business. Cal pays cash and takes delivery of the car only, without knowledge of Owner's title or the outstanding security interest. Assume Owner pays off secured party and seeks return of the car from Cal, certificate of title in hand. May Owner replevy the car from Cal?

Under the Code the answer would appear to be no: UCC 2-403(2) protects Cal and title has passed under UCC 2-401. But the critical question is whether the particular certificate of title act involved preempts UCC 2-403(2) and, in effect, conditions passage of title upon delivery of the certificate. In some states it does,[*] but in most states it does not.[**] Even where the Code controls, however, a buyer may have some responsibility for inquiring after the required certificate.[***]

---

[*] *Saturn of Kings Automall, Inc. v. Mike Albert Leasing Inc.*, 751 N.E.2d 1019 (Ohio 2001); *Messer v. Averill*, 183 N.W.2d 802 (Mich. Ct. App. 1970).

[**] *Jones v. Mitchell*, 816 So. 2d 68 (Ala. Ct. App. 2001); *Madrid v. Bloomington Auto Co.*, 782 N.E.2d 386 (Ind. Ct. App. 2002); *Godfrey v. Gilsdorf*, 476 P.2d 3 (Nev. 1970); *Martin v. Nager*, 469 A.2d 519 (N.J. Super. Ct. Ch. Div. 1983).

[***] *See Mattek v. Malofsky*, 165 N.W.2d 406 (Wis. 1969) (merchant buyer from dealer to whom titled car had been entrusted is "unreasonable as a matter of law" in not obtaining the required certificate); *Reliance Insurance Co. v. Market Motors, Inc.*, 498 A.2d 571 (D.C. Ct. App. 1985); *Ellsworth v. Worthey*, 612 S.W.2d 396 (Mo.Ct. App. 1981). *See also*

(continued...)

The 2003 amendments to Article 2 address the interaction between certificate of title laws and the Article 2 rules on ownership interests. UCC 2-108(1)(a). The new section appears to reverse the majority rule by protecting the rights of a buyer in ordinary course of business only if the rights arise before a certificate of title covering the goods "is effective in the name of any other buyer."

Problem 9-11

Suppose that in a credit contract, S#1, a used farm implement dealer, creates and perfects a security interest in a tractor, delivered to B#1. Later B#1 returns the goods to S#1 for repairs. S#1 then sells the tractor to S#2, a merchant, who in turn sells and delivers the tractor to B#2, a BIOCOB. When B#1 discovers these events, it refuses to pay S#1 and seeks to replevin the tractor in B#2's possession. S#1, upon B#1's default, seeks to enforce the security interest by repossessing the tractor in B#2's possession. B#2 claims that it got good title to the tractor free of the claim of B#1 and free of the security interest created by S#1 under UCC 2-402(3) and UCC 2-403. Is B#2 correct?

Problem 9-12

While vacationing in Miami Beach, Ashley was approached by a middle-aged man who asked if the lovely diamond necklace was for sale. He said that his name was Boscoe and offered to pay $90,000. Ashley, who was a bit short of cash, agreed to sell but then balked when Boscoe started to write a check. She wanted cash. Boscoe assured her that he was solvent and stated that he was Mr. Fred C. Boscoe of Grosse Pointe. Ashley excused herself from the room and confirmed by a telephone call to a friend in Detroit that Mr. Fred C. Boscoe owned a large home in Grosse Pointe and was a vice-president of a well-known automobile manufacturer. Ashley returned to the room and informed the man that she would accept a check for the stone. Boscoe then drew a counter check on a Detroit bank and delivered it to Ashley in exchange for the necklace. The check, of course,

---

[***] (...continued)

Dartmouth Motor Sales, Inc. v. Wilcox, 517 A.2d 804 (N.H. 1986) (certificate of title, even though not authorized, must be "facially valid"); *Marlow v. Conley*, 787 N.E. 2d 490 (Ind. Ct. App. 2003) (certificate of title anomalies not sufficient in case to make purchaser lack good faith). *See* Christina L. Kunz, *Motor Vehicle Ownership Disputes Involving Certificate-of-Title Acts and Article Two of the UCC*, 39 BUS. LAW. 1599 (1984).

bounced and Ashley then discovered that her purchaser had no account at that bank and was not Mr. Fred C. Boscoe of Grosse Pointe. Further, before disappearing, the "rogue" had sold the diamond for $91,000 to Dimwit, who purchased the stone in good faith. May Ashley replevy the stone from Dimwit?

Would it make any difference if the transaction and the exchange of check for necklace had been completed by mail? Suppose that Ashley had met Boscoe in a "chatroom" on the Internet?

Problem 9-13

Ashley sold the necklace to Boscoe. Boscoe gave Ashley a check for the price and left with the necklace. The check was dishonored as Boscoe did not have enough funds in the bank on which the check was drawn. Boscoe sold the necklace to Casper who gave Boscoe cash for the necklace. May Ashley recover the necklace from Casper?[*] What if Boscoe granted Casper a security interest in the necklace?

Problem 9-14

Ashley agreed to purchase a unique new necklace from Casper's jewelry store. Ashley made a down payment and promised to pay the rest the following day and pick up the necklace at that time. Later that day Bessie purchased that same necklace from the store, paying in full and taking possession of the necklace. Ashley is upset and wants to recover the necklace from Bessie. What do you tell Ashley?

Problem 9-15

Suppose that Ashley owned several diamonds and was in the habit of lending the stones to her society friends for use on important occasions. She charged a good fee for this service and was, of course, fully insured against loss. Ashley leased the stone worth $60,000 to Bessie to be worn at the Muckraker's Ball. Bessie, who was short of cash, sold the diamond to Casper for $55,000. Casper, who had purchased in good faith, sold the stone to Dimwit, a buyer in ordinary course of business, for $65,000. May Ashley (or her insurance company claiming by subrogation) replevy

---

[*] *See Mitchell Motors Inc. v. Barnett*, 549 S.E. 2d 445 (Ga. Ct. App. 2001).

the necklace from Dimwit? *See* UCC 2-403(1), (2).

How should the court deal with the argument made by Dimwit that Bessie in fact had a voidable title under UCC 2-403 because she took in a transaction of "purchase" as that term is defined in UCC 2-403 and 1-201? *See* UCC 2A-305.[*]

2. Lessee Against Person Asserting Previously Created Right in the Goods Obtained from the Lessor

Now suppose the lessor leased goods to the lessee and the lessee took possession of the goods. A previous buyer or lessee from the lessor contends that it has superior rights in the goods over the lessee in possession due to a pre-existing contract. UCC 2A-304 and 2A-305 are the provisions for leases of goods that parallel UCC 2-403 for sales of goods.

Assume the lessor bought the goods from the seller with a check that bounced. Lessor took possession of the goods and leased the goods to the lessee, who took possession. The transaction between the seller and the lessor is a sale and governed by UCC 2-403. Lessor would have voidable title to the goods and could transfer good title to a good faith purchaser which includes the lessee. In a dispute between the seller and the lessee, the lessee should win under UCC 2-403.

Assume instead that Lessor leased the goods to Lessee 1 who did not take delivery. Lessor then leased the goods to Lessee 2 who did take delivery. As between Lessee 1 and Lessee 2, under UCC 2A-304(1), Lessee 1 would prevail. If Lessor was a merchant dealing in goods of the kind, however, and Lessee 2 was a lessee in ordinary course of business, UCC 2A-103, Lessee 2 would take free of the rights of Lessee 1 who has entrusted the goods to Lessor prior to the lease between Lessor and Lessee 2 becoming effective. UCC 2A-304(2).

Assume Lessor leased the goods to Lessee 1 who did not take deliver and then Lessor sold the goods to Buyer who took delivery. As between Lessee 1 and Buyer, who would prevail? UCC 2A-304 does not apply as the subsequent transaction is not a lease. In this case, return to UCC 2-403. Does Lessor have voidable title so that the second section of UCC 2-403(1) comes into play? If Lessor is a merchant and Buyer qualifies as a BIOCOB, Buyer should prevail under UCC 2-403(2) over Lessee 1.

Assume Lessor leased the goods to Lessee. Lessee then leased the goods to Sublessee. UCC 2A-305(1) provides that Sublessee will take the goods subject to

---

[*] *See McDonald's Chevrolet, Inc. v. Johnson*, 376 N.E.2d 106 (Ind. Ct. App. 1978).

the lease between Lessor and Lessee. The same is true if the transaction was a lease followed by a purported purchase. Under UCC 2A-305(1) and UCC 2-403(1), the buyer would have only those rights the Lessee had power to transfer, typically the lessee's leasehold interest.

Skip down to UCC 2A-305(2). If the lessee is a merchant dealing in goods of the kind and the buyer or lessee qualifies as a BIOCOB or a LIOCOB, does your analysis change?

Notice that both UCC 2A-304 and 2A-305 contain a subsection (3) that governs the interface of Article 2A with certificate of title statutes. What is the impact of those subsections?

Note: Ownership Claims Under UCITA and the CISG

UCITA does not contain any provision that parallels UCC 2-403 concerning property rights. Given that the subject matter of UCITA, computer information, is subject to extensive federal regulation concerning intellectual property, those provisions would not be effective as a matter of state law. Exploration of the laws governing intellectual property transfers are outside the scope of these materials.

Similarly, the CISG has no provision comparable to UCC 2-403 and is "not concerned with * * * the effect which the contract may have on the property in goods sold." Art. 4(b). Under Article 41, the "seller must deliver goods which are free from any right or claim of a third party, unless the buyer agreed to take the goods subject to that right or claim."

E. Buyer's and Lessee's Rights as Against Seller's or Lessor's Creditors

As previously noted, when the seller's or lessor's creditor is an Article 9 secured party with a security interest in the goods, a buyer in ordinary course from the seller or a lessee in ordinary course from the lessor will take free of the security interest created by the buyer's seller or the lessee's lessor even if it is perfected. UCC 9-320(a), 9-321(c). In most cases, the secured party expects a sale or lease of this sort and must rely on its security interest that continues in the proceeds of the sale or lease. UCC 9-315.

If the buyer or lessee is not in ordinary course, the buyer or lessee has to give value and take delivery of the goods without knowledge of the security interest and before it is perfected in order to prevail against the secured party. UCC 9-317(b) and (c). Review the definitions of buyer in ordinary course, UCC 1-201, and lessee in ordinary course, UCC 2A-103. Even if UCC 9-320(a) or 9-321(c) may protect a buyer or lessee in ordinary course, if the goods are covered by a certificate of title, this result is subject to any specific rule of priority contained in a preemptive certificate of title act.[*]

Notice that for the buyer or lessee in ordinary course to take free of the security interest under UCC 9-320(a) or 9-321(c), the security interest must be created by the seller or the lessor. For example, assume S granted a security interest in the goods to SP and then sold the goods to B, not a buyer in ordinary course, and then B sold the goods to C, a buyer in ordinary course. C would take the goods subject to the security interest of SP because the security interest was not created by B, C's seller, but by S. Even though C is a buyer in ordinary course, UCC 2-403(2) would only serve to transfer the rights of S to C as S was the person who entrusted the goods to B.[**] Of course, if SP entrusted the goods to M, a merchant, and then M sold the goods to a buyer in ordinary course of business, then the buyer would take free of the security interest, even though the security interest was not created by M, the buyer's seller. UCC 2-402(3) and 2-403(2).

Review the material on the rights of the buyer or lessee if the seller's or lessor's creditor is a lien creditor who has levied on the goods while the goods are in the seller's possession. If the buyer has possession of the goods and the seller's creditor attempts to levy on the goods in the buyer's possession, the question will be whether the seller has any property interest in the goods sufficient for the lien creditor to levy on. If under UCC 2-403, the buyer has good title to the goods, the seller's lien creditor would have no right to levy on the goods as the seller no longer has any title to the goods. If the lessee is in possession of the goods under a lease contract, the seller's lien creditor is subject to the lease contract. UCC 2A-307(2).

Consider the following problem.

---

[*] *Compare Williams v. Western Surety Co.*, 492 P.2d 596 (Wash. Ct. App. 1972) (buyer wins under Code) and *Hampton Bank v. River City Yachts, Inc.*, 528 N.W.2d 880 (Minn. Ct. App. 1995) (buyer wins under Code even when it does not get a certificate of title) *with Security Pacific Nat'l Bank v. Goodman*, 24 Cal. App.3d 131, 100 Cal. Rptr. 763 (1972) (buyer loses under California statute.) *See Toyota Motor Credit Corp. v. C.L. Hyman Auto Wholesale, Inc.*, 506 S.E.2d 14 (Va. 1998), holding that under Virginia law a bona fide purchaser for value without notice of a lien on the automobile was entitled to rely on a certificate of title which did not contain a notation of the lien.

[**] *See Superior Bank, FSB v. Human Services Employees Credit Union*, 556 S.E. 2d 155 (Ga. Ct. App. 2001); *Intermet Corp. v. Financial Federal Credit Inc.*, 588 S.E.2d 810 (Ga. Ct. App. 2004).

Problem 9-16

Seller contracted to sell ten lathes to Bowdin Manufacturing Inc. for $5,000 each (total $50,000). Bowdin paid $25,000 to Seller, the balance due on delivery. Seller delivered the lathes to Bowdin and Bowdin paid the Seller the balance due.

A. A creditor of Seller with a judgment executed its judgment by levying on the ten lathes in Bowdin's possession. Advise Bowdin whether the lathes are subject to the lien creditor's claim to the goods.

B. Seller finances its operation with operating loans from National Bank. National Bank has a perfected security interest in Seller's equipment and inventory. Seller defaulted on its loan and National Bank has written a demand letter to Bowdin to turn over the lathes. Advise Bowdin.

C. Seeta occasionally also leases lathes. If the above transaction was a lease to Bowdin instead of a sale, would your analysis of the above two priority disputes change?

Note: Licensee's Rights as Against Licensor's Creditors Under UCITA

UCITA does not speak to the conflict between creditors of the licensor and the rights of a licensee. UCITA 103(c) provides that Article 9 governs in the event of a conflict between UCITA and Article 9. UCC 9-317(d) protects licensees not in ordinary course and UCC 9-321 protects a licensee in ordinary course from a secured party's security interest in the licensor's rights. Under Article 9, a secured party may take a security interest in a software license that is either part of "goods" or if not, is classified as a "general intangible." UCC 9-102. Of course, if the rights being licensed are governed by federal law, federal law would control if there was a conflict between the state and federal schemes.

SECTION 4. WARRANTY OF TITLE, NON-INTERFERENCE, AND AGAINST INFRINGEMENT

A primary question addressed above was when does the buyer of goods get "good" title from a seller whose title is defective or nonexistent? Another was when does the buyer "take free" from a perfected security interest? These questions are often litigated when the "true" owner or secured party asserts claims to goods in the possession of the buyer. If the "true" owner wins, the buyer will be deprived of the goods and, of course, the benefit of his bargain. Does the buyer have any recourse against his seller? If so, what remedies are available? If the "true" owner loses, the buyer may keep the goods. However, she has been put through the stress and expense of a law suit and may have been temporarily deprived of possession. Does she have any recourse against the seller? We are here concerned with whether the seller has made and breached a warranty of title under UCC 2-312 and what the buyer must and may do to achieve adequate redress. Article 2A provides a similar warranty against interference and against infringement in UCC 2A-211.

In reading UCC 2-312 and 2A-211, consider the following questions. What is the seller or lessor warranting? Notice that several different warranties are provided in these sections. May the seller or lessor disclaim the warranty and if so, how so? Who may assert the claim for breach of warranty, that is, must the parties be in privity of contract in order to have a claim for breach of warranty or may the buyer or lessee bring its claim against a predecessor in title of the buyer's seller or the lessee's lessor? UCC 2-318, 2A-216.

Remember, the purpose of a warranty of title is to put the risk on the person who first took the goods from a thief or a person with an encumbrance. What is the purpose of the warranty against infringement?

SUMNER V. FEL-AIR, INC.
SUPREME COURT OF ALASKA, 1984
680 P.2D 1109

RABINOWITZ, JUSTICE

This appeal arises from a dispute over the sale of a Piper Navajo airplane by William Sumner, an Anchorage commercial aircraft dealer, to Fel-Air, Inc., a Barrow air taxi operator. In March 1976, Sumner and Fel-Air orally agreed to the basic terms of the sale, including the purchase price of $105,000.00. Sumner was to receive a Piper Aztec aircraft valued at $30,000 as a downpayment on the Navajo. Fel-Air was to remit the $75,000 balance of the purchase price in monthly installments of $2,000. Interest on the unpaid balance was to accrue at a rate of 12%. These terms were confirmed in a March 31, 1976, letter from Fel-Air's general manager to Sumner.

The Navajo was delivered to Fel-Air in April 1976. Sumner received the Aztec as a downpayment in accordance with the parties' agreement. The Navajo began to experience mechanical difficulties and was taken to Seattle Flight Service for repairs in the early summer of 1976. Two months later, after paying a repair bill of $20,000, Fel-Air regained use of the airplane.

Fel-Air sent the Navajo back to Seattle for repairs in October 1976. Two months later, while the plane was still in the custody of Seattle Flight Service, the president of Century Aircraft, Inc. informed Fel-Air that title to the Navajo was held by Century rather than by Sumner. Century's president had also told Seattle Flight Service that Century owned the aircraft. Sumner's interest in the Navajo was that of a lessee with an option to purchase. After the discovery that Century was the record owner of the Navajo, Seattle Flight Service filed a mechanic's lien against the Navajo for unpaid repair bills.

Fel-Air asserted that it telephoned Sumner in December 1976 and requested either a conditional sales contract or bill of sale which would provide the Federal Aviation Administration with a record of Fel-Air's authority to operate the Navajo, or a full refund of payments made to date on the Navajo, including return of the Aztec. Fel-Air contended that Sumner assured it that the contract would be prepared within three days. Sumner testified that he did not remember such a conversation.

In May of 1977, Fel-Air ceased making monthly payments on the Navajo. On May 10, 1978, Sumner sent a telegram to Fel-Air demanding satisfaction of the lien Seattle Flight Service had filed and payment of monthly installments then due. Fel-Air did not respond. Sumner discharged the $8,000 lien himself and had the plane flown back to Anchorage.

Sumner arranged to have the Navajo's documents of title held in escrow to assure Fel-Air that it would receive title upon payment of the balance of the purchase price and upon compensation of Sumner for payments made to satisfy the Seattle Flight Service lien. On August 3, 1977, the escrow arrangement was completed. The balance then due on the aircraft, including the payment made to discharge the mechanic's lien, was $64,936.47.

Fel-Air subsequently filed suit against Sumner, alleging Sumner had breached implied warranties of merchantability and title and that he was liable to Fel-Air for fraud and misrepresentation. Sumner denied these claims and alleged that Fel-Air had abandoned the Navajo, requested that consideration paid by Fel-Air be deemed an offset for rent owed to Sumner for use of the Navajo, and filed a counterclaim for the $8,000 he had paid to discharge the lien.

The case was tried to the superior court sitting without a jury. The court rejected Fel-Air's claims for breach of the warranty of merchantability and negligent and intentional misrepresentation. However, it concluded that Sumner had breached a warranty of title to the aircraft and awarded Fel-Air $51,166.82 in damages. This sum represented the value of the Aztec used as a downpayment

($30,000), and $21,700 in monthly payments made by Fel-Air to Sumner, less the $533.18 expense of transporting the plane back to Alaska saved by Fel-Air as a result of the breach. Pre-judgment interest accruing at 8% per annum from February 1, 1977, to May 1, 1980, was also awarded, and totaled $13,300.16. Judgment against Sumner was entered for $64,466.98. Fel-Air was also awarded costs and attorney's fees. This appeal followed.

BREACH OF WARRANTY OF TITLE

Title 45 of the Alaska Statutes adopts Article 2 of the Uniform Commercial Code as the applicable law of sales in Alaska. Under A.S. 45.02.312, an implied warranty of title accompanies the sale of goods in Alaska. It may expressly be disclaimed. A focal point of the parties' dispute is whether Sumner excluded or modified by specific language the warranty of title. Sumner does not claim that he had good title to the Navajo, but rather alleges that he informed Fel-Air that he leased, but did not own, the Navajo. Fel-Air denies that it was so informed.

The superior court specifically found that Sumner did not inform Fel-Air prior to the sale that he had neither title to the Navajo nor the right to sell it, and that the circumstances surrounding the transaction did not give Fel-Air any reason to know that Sumner did not claim title to the plane in himself. The court concluded that Sumner had therefore breached the warranty of title imposed by A.S. 45.02.312.

Sumner concedes that the superior court's conclusion that there was no express or implied disclaimer of the A.S. 45.02.312 warranty was a finding of fact which may be reversed only if clearly erroneous. * * * In the case at bar, the superior court's factual finding was based upon an assessment of the credibility of conflicting testimonial evidence. We have observed that "[i]t is the trial court's function, and not that of a reviewing court, to judge the credibility of the witnesses and to weigh conflicting evidence. This is especially true where the trial court's decision depends largely upon oral testimony." *Penn v. Ivey,* 615 P.2d 1, 3 (Alaska 1980) (citations omitted). Thus, particular deference must be accorded to the superior court's finding that Sumner did not disclaim the A.S. 45.02.312 warranty of title. After review of the entire record before us, and guided by these principles of appellate review, we conclude that the superior court's finding that an implied warranty of title accompanied the sale of the Navajo must be upheld. The question now becomes whether or not Sumner breached that warranty.[1]

---

[1] Sumner argues that Fel-Air should be held to have had "constructive notice" of Century's interest prior to consummation of the sale, since pertinent documents of title to the Navajo

(continued...)

Since Sumner did not have good title to the plane when he purported to convey it to Fel-Air, the answer to this question may seem obvious. Yet both parties agree that Century "entrusted" the plane to Sumner within the meaning of A.S. 45.02.403. Under the UCC a merchant to whom goods have been entrusted may give a buyer a better title than the merchant himself possessed. To quote A.S. 45.02.403(b):

> An entrusting of possession of goods to a merchant who deals in goods
> of that kind gives him power to transfer all rights of the entruster to a buyer
> in ordinary course of business.

Because Sumner had possession of the Navajo and was a dealer in airplanes, he had the power to transfer all of Century's rights, including its good title to the airplane. Given the facts as the parties have presented them, Fel-Air could have defeated any attempt by Century to regain possession of the Navajo.

It does not follow from the fact that the parties now agree that Fel-Air's title was good that Sumner did not breach the implied warranty of title. This question has divided the commentators. *Compare* 1 ANDERSON, UNIFORM COMMERCIAL CODE § 2-312:36 (3d ed. 1982) (warranty not breached) *with* 1 ALDERMAN, A TRANSACTIONAL GUIDE TO THE UNIFORM COMMERCIAL CODE § 1.53-52 (2d ed. 1983) (warranty breached, seller should have chance to cure). Alderman emphasizes the full text of UCC 2-312(a)(1), which provides:

> (a) Subject to (b) of this section there is in a contract for sale a warranty by
> the seller that
>> (1) the title conveyed shall be good, *and its transfer rightful.*

A.S. 45.02.312(a) and (a)(1) (emphasis added). As Alderman states, the entrustee's "wrongfulness (lack of right) in making the conveyance * * * is unquestionable, for the transfer of title [is] not made pursuant to any 'right' ". Alderman, *supra,* at 266-67. Here Sumner's lease-purchase arrangement with Century did not authorize him to transfer title to Fel-Air. The transfer he made to Fel-Air was wrongful, and thus we conclude that the warranty UCC 2-312(a)(1) establishes was breached.

Wright v. Vickaryous, 611 P.2d 20 (Alaska 1980), supports this conclusion.

---

[1] (...continued)
were on file at the Federal Aviation Administration (FAA) at that time. This argument is without merit. It is clear from the wording of A.S. 45.02.312 that only actual knowledge on the part of the buyer of the seller's lack of title, or of circumstances which would reasonably lead the buyer to reach such a conclusion, can defeat the statutory warranty. The official commentary to § 2-312 of the U.C.C. specifically states that "[t]he 'knowledge' referred to in subsection 1(b) is actual knowledge as distinct from notice." § 2-312 comment 1, 1 U.L.A. 303 (1976).

Wright suggests that a court attempting to determine whether or not a warranty of title was breached must consider the facts as they appeared to the buyer at the time title was called into question. If a reasonable buyer would conclude that "marketable title" had not been conveyed to him, the seller–assuming that he does not save the transaction by showing that the facts are not what the buyer believes them to be–has breached the warranty of title. A "substantial shadow" on title is enough to justify the buyer's refusal to proceed with his contractual performance.[2] Similarly in the instant case the revelation of Century's interest in the Piper Navajo cast such a shadow on the transaction between Sumner and Fel-Air.

To dispel a similar shadow, the buyer in *Wright* would have had to call all the people he believed to be lienholders; had he done so, he would have discovered that their liens had been released. To dispel the shadow of Century Aircraft, Fel-Air would have had to become an expert on the UCC and would then have had to determine that Sumner had not stolen or borrowed the Navajo from Century, that Sumner was indeed a "merchant who deals in [airplanes]" as the UCC defines "merchant," and that Fel-Air itself qualified as a "buyer in ordinary course of business." The parties' present agreement on these matters does not mean that these things were obvious at the time the transaction between Sumner and Fel-Air began to break down. Even if we decided to ignore A.S. 45.02.312's intimation that a "wrongful" transfer of title breaches the warranty which that section contains, we would be loath to conclude that a breach did not occur in this case. The superior court correctly decided that Sumner breached the implied warranty of title. * * *

For the foregoing reasons, the judgment of the superior court is affirmed.

[Some footnotes omitted. Those retained have been renumbered.]

---

[2] In *Wright* various third parties had taken security interests in the seller's cattle. All of them orally consented to the sale, thus releasing their security interests pursuant to UCC 9-306(2). However, the liens remained on the books, the buyer discovered them, and delivery of the cattle was refused, the seller all this time failing to point out that the security interests had been released. We held that this circumstance put a "substantial shadow" on the title and justified refusing to proceed with the sales contract. *Wright* explicitly recognized that the buyer could successfully have defended himself against any former lienholder's lawsuit, but reasoned that the risk of such a lawsuit was enough to excuse the buyer's refusal to accept delivery.

Note: Fifty Ways to Breach the UCC 2-312 Warranty of Title

Paradoxically, the warranty of title was broken in *Sumner v. Fel-Air*, although the buyer actually got good title. Is the result supported by any specific language in UCC 2-312? Is such a result justified?

A breach of warranty of title has been found when the seller of a motor vehicle fails to provide his purchaser with adequate proof of ownership because faulty documentation (number on title certificate did not correspond with number on frame of vehicle) raises reasonable doubts as to the validity of the title the buyer acquires. Here, because of the faulty documentation, the vehicle was seized by the police and the buyer had to incur legal expenses to resolve the matter favorably, expenses he then successfully sought from the seller.[*] *Accord Colton v. Decker*, 540 N.W.2d 172, 176 (S.D. 1995), where the court said:

> Wyoming Highway Patrol officials questioned Colton's ownership due to contradictory VINs [vehicle identification numbers] thus cast a colorable challenge to its title. This was sufficient for a breach of title warranty claim. * * * Indeed, the majority view holds that a purchaser can recover for a breach of warranty of title by merely showing the existence of a cloud on the title. * * * Once breach of good title is established, good faith is not a defense, nor is lack of knowledge of the defect. * * * Purchasers should not be required to enter into a contest on the validity of ownership over a titled motor vehicle. * * *

Beyond full adverse ownership claims, various "clouds" have been held to breach the title warranty.[**] Not just any assertion of a claim by a third party will breach the

---

[*] *Jefferson v. Jones*, 408 A.2d 1036 (Md.1979).

[**] *See Saber v. Dan Angelone Chevrolet, Inc.*, 811 A.2d 644 (R.I. 2002) (missing VIN numbers and Mylar sticker on parts of car raised suspicion of car contained stolen parts); *Frank Arnold Contractors, Inc. v. Vilsmeier Auction Co., Inc.*, 806 F.2d 462 (3rd Cir. 1986) (possible security interest); *Elias v. Dobrowolski*, 412 A.2d 1035 (N.H. 1980) (valid filed security interest of which buyer had no actual knowledge); *Wright v. Vickaryous*, 611 P.2d 20 (Alaska 1980) (security interests the prior discharge of which had not been communicated to buyer who then rejected the cattle); *National Crane Corp. v. Ohio Steel Tube Co.*, 332 N.W.2d 39 (Neb. 1983) (tax liens); *Catlin Aviation Co. v. Equilease Corp.*, 626 P.2d 857 (Okla. 1981) (repairman's lien); *Jeanneret v. Vichey*, 693 F.2d 259 (2nd Cir. 1982) (regulations of foreign country applicable to export of paintings could constitute cloud if not complied with).

warranty of title. Unfounded claims that are also not colorable will not.[*]

Whenever the buyer has reason to know that the seller does not claim title to himself or that he is purporting to sell only such right or title as he or a third person may have, there is no warranty of title. UCC 2-312(3) [former subsection (2)]. For example, where a buyer of a used car received from the seller a certificate of title listing another person as the seller, the jury could have found that the buyer had such "reason to know."[**] But under UCC 2-312(3) [former subsection (2)], a warranty of title or the like can be "excluded or modified only by specific language."[***]

Problem 9-17

In 1938, O purchased a painting by Chagall at an auction in Brussels for $250. During World War II, O was forced to abandon her apartment and the painting and, upon returning in 1945, she found that the Chagall had been removed by German authorities. A receipt for the painting was left. In 1955, K purchased the Chagall from a Paris gallery for $3,500. K knew nothing about the painting's history and made no inquiry. In 1975, K sold the painting to G, a New York gallery, for $50,000. In 1976, G sold the Chagall to L for $75,000. L was a private collector who purchased for pleasure and investment. In 1990, O noticed a reproduction of the painting in an art book, accompanied by a statement that the Chagall was in L's possession. O retained counsel in New York and demanded return of the painting. L refused. At that time the painting was valued at $250,000.

A. O brought an action to replevy the painting from L. L claimed that he was a buyer in ordinary course of business and that the action should be dismissed. Who wins?

B. Assume that O replevied the painting from L. Against whom in the distributive chain, the Paris gallery, K, G, or the New York gallery does L have a claim for breach of warranty? What defenses are available to these sellers?

C. Assuming that L has a claim for breach of warranty of title against the New

---

[*] *C.F. Sales, Inc. v. Amfert, Inc.*, 344 N.W.2d 543 (Iowa 1983).

[**] *Spoon v. Herndon*, 307 S.E.2d 693 (Ga. Ct. App. 1983).

[***] *Rockdale Cable T.V. Co. v. Spadora*, 423 N.E.2d 555 (Ill. Ct. App. 1981) (language in bill of sale purporting to transfer "all Seller's right, title, and interest, of every kind and nature, in and to" held insufficiently specific).

York gallery, what damages may be collected? *See* UCC 2-714, 2-715. If successful, most courts have held that consequential damages include expenses, including attorney fees, in defending title after having given notice to his seller that a third party is claiming adversely.[*]

Note: Title and Infringement Claims Under the CISG

CISG Art. 30 provides that the seller "must deliver the goods * * * and transfer the property in the goods, as required by the contract and this Convention." Suppose that the goods delivered are subject to a "right or claim of a third party" based upon (1) title or a security interest, or (2) industrial property or other intellectual property. Both Article 41 (the counterpart of UCC 2-312(1)), which deals with title or a security interest, and Article 42 (the counterpart of UCC 2-312(2)), which deals with industrial property and intellectual property, provide that the seller, with certain limitations, must deliver goods which are free from these claims. Failure to do so is a breach of contract for which the buyer may pursue appropriate remedies. CISG Art. 45.[**]

Remember, the CISG says nothing about how the third party may enforce its claim, whether by recovery of the goods or conversion.

Note: Title and Infringement Claims Under UCITA

UCITA provides a similar warranty in UCITA 401. A licensee who has contracted for possession and/or use of a product will face disruption in that possession or use if someone else asserts property rights in that product.

SECTION 5.   ASSIGNMENT AND DELEGATION

While this chapter has been concerned with property rights, assignment and delegation is concerned with enforcement of contracts rights and performance of contract duties. In the world of finance, assignment of contract rights is commonplace. A creditor may assign its right to another person to receive payment

---

[*] *See Universal C.I.T. Credit Corp. v. State Farm Mut. Auto. Ins. Co.*, 493 S.W.2d 385 (Mo. Ct. App. 1973).

[**] *See* Allen M. Shinn, Jr., *Liabilities Under Article 42 of the U.N. Convention on the International Sale of Goods*, 2 MINN. J. GLOBAL TRADE 115 (1993).

from a debtor. That assignment is an assignment of a right to receive performance.

Under the modern law of contracts as reflected in the RESTATEMENT (SECOND) OF CONTRACTS, a party to a contract may assign its rights under the contract to an assignee.* An assignment is effected by a manifestation of intent to transfer the rights. The effect of an assignment of rights under a contract is to extinguish the assignor's right to receive performance under the contract as that right has been transferred to the assignee. RESTATEMENT (SECOND) OF CONTRACTS 317(1). The assigned rights may be either of rights that have arisen or rights that will arise in the future under an existing contract. RESTATEMENT (SECOND) OF CONTRACTS 321(1). With limited exceptions, the assignee must assent to the assignment in order to make the assignment effective. RESTATEMENT (SECOND) OF CONTRACTS 327(1). An assignor who assigns rights under a contract for value warrants to the assignee that the right is valid and not subject to limitations or defenses other than those apparent or disclosed at the time of assignment. RESTATEMENT (SECOND) OF CONTRACTS 333(1). Compare this warranty to the warranty of title to goods found in UCC 2-312.

The assignee's rights against the obligor on the contract are the same as the assignor's rights as against the obligor and are subject to any claims or defenses the obligor would have against the assignor which accrued prior to notice to the obligor of the assignment and may be subject to claims and defenses based upon other selected grounds such as impracticability even if that defense accrued after notice of the assignment. RESTATEMENT (SECOND) OF CONTRACTS 336, 337. An obligor may waive its right to assert claims and defenses against an assignee. RESTATEMENT (SECOND) OF CONTRACTS 336, comment f. Generally this waiver takes place in the contract between the assignor and the obligor.

Whether an obligor has discharged its obligation by rendering performance depends upon when it renders its performance relative to notification of the assignment. Prior to notice of the assignment, the obligor may discharge its obligation under the contract by rendering performance to the assignor. After notice of the assignment, the obligor under the contract is required to render its

---

* Article 9 also contains rules relevant to the rights of an assignee of certain types of collateral subject to an Article 9 security interest. The Article 9 rules parallel, but are not always identical to, the rules discussed in the text. Accounts, chattel paper, and general intangibles, all forms of Article 9 collateral, may concern contract rights arising out of an Article 2, Article 2A or UCITA transaction and if those rights are assigned in a transaction that is subject to Article 9, the Article 9 rules will prevail over the common law rules discussed in the text. UCC 9-403 through 9-409.

performance to the assignee. RESTATEMENT (SECOND) OF CONTRACTS 338. If the obligor renders performance to the assignor after the obligor has received an effective notice of assignment, the obligor does not have a defense of a discharge of the performance obligation based upon performance rendered to the assignor when the assignee seeks to collect the performance from the obligor. E. ALLAN FARNSWORTH, CONTRACTS § 11.7 (4th ed. 2004).

A party to a contract may also delegate its duties to perform its obligations under the contract to another person. RESTATEMENT (SECOND) OF CONTRACTS 318. A person delegates its duties by manifesting an intent to do so. Generally the person to whom the duties are delegated is not obligated unless that person accepts the delegation. RESTATEMENT (SECOND) OF CONTRACTS 328. The effect of the delegation is that the delegatee must perform the duties under the contract but the delegation does not discharge the duty of the delegating obligor. RESTATEMENT (SECOND) OF CONTRACTS 318.[*]

A contract right is also an intangible form of personal property. E. ALLAN FARNSWORTH, CONTRACTS § 11.9 (4th ed. 2004). Thus persons other than an assignee may assert property claims to those contract rights. The common law approach is to follow a derivative title concept in most situations. A subsequent assignee is subject to the rights of a first assignee in most situations. In some situations, however, a subsequent assignee may obtain superiority over the rights of a first assignee. For example, if the first assignment is voidable or revoked, the subsequent assignee may have rights superior to the first assignee. If the subsequent assignee acquires its rights in good faith, without knowledge of the first assignee's rights, and for value and in addition, obtains payment, a judgment against the obligor, a new contract with the obligor, or possession of a writing that is customarily accepted as the evidence of the right assigned, the subsequent assignee may prevail over the first assignee. RESTATEMENT (SECOND) OF CONTRACTS 342.

Read UCC 2-210 and 2A-303. These provisions address the enforceability and effect of contract provisions prohibiting assignment of rights and delegation of duties.

---

[*] For the relationship between delegation of duties and suretyship principles, *see* Gary L. Monserud, *The Privileges of Suretyship for Delegating Parties Under UCC Section 2-210 in Light of the New Restatement of Suretyship*, 37 WM & MARY L. REV. 1307 (1996).

Problem 9-18

A. Seller agreed to sell specially manufactured goods to Buyer in return for a price. Seller assigned the contract to Manufacturer, who accepted the assignment. Does Buyer have to accept performance of the contract from Manufacturer?

B. Seller agreed to sell specially manufactured goods to Buyer in return for a price. Seller assigned its right to payment of the price to Lender. Does Buyer have grounds to object to the assignment?

C. Seller agreed to sell specially manufactured goods to Buyer in return for a price. Buyer assigned the contract to D. Does Seller have to render performance to D? Does Seller have grounds to object to the assignment?

The CISG does not address assignment and delegation. UCITA addresses the issues in UCITA 503 through 506.

PART FOUR:
BREACH OF CONTRACT
AND REMEDIES

CHAPTER TEN

REMEDIES: BREACH WHEN
PRODUCT NOT ACCEPTED

SECTION 1. INTRODUCTION

This chapter deals primarily with remedies where a party is in breach and the product has not been accepted by the buyer or lessee. For example, before the time for performance has arrived, the buyer or lessee might repudiate, commit a "total" breach of an installment contract, fail to make an advance payment when due, or the like. Alternatively, the seller or lessor may repudiate prior to the date for tender. In such circumstances, an aggrieved party will want to know (1) whether its own performance is excused and (2) to what remedies she may resort.

If the seller or lessor performs by tendering the goods to the buyer or lessee, the goods may not conform to the contract. If the buyer or lessee effectively and rightfully rejects the goods or revokes acceptance of the goods, the buyer or lessee will want to know what damages it may recover for the seller's or lessor's breach of contract. Similarly, if the seller or lessor performs by tendering conforming goods to the contract, the buyer or lessee may wrongfully but effectively reject the tendered goods. In that case, the seller or lessor will want to know what damages it may recover for the buyer's or lessee's breach of contract.

We will survey the various remedies open to the seller or lessor first and then we will reverse the position of the parties, and consider the various remedies open to the buyer or lessee when the other party breaches and the buyer or lessee has not accepted the goods. This chapter has been structured to afford the student maximum opportunity to compare remedies for each side of the transaction. Article 2 invites this kind of analysis, for it grants seller and buyer alike a wide range of parallel remedies. Thus, the seller's action for the price (UCC 2-709) or specific performance (UCC 2-716) is parallel to the buyer's action for specific performance (UCC 2-716). So too are the respective rights of seller and buyer to damages based on contract-market price differentials (UCC 2-708 and 2-713) and the respective rights of seller and buyer to enter into substitute transactions and measure their losses accordingly (UCC 2-706 and 2-712).[*] Part 5 of Article 2A follows a similar construct.

Before going further, we should note and respond to a suggestion that contract remedies are without practical significance.[**] According to some commentators, the student who knew of the infrequency of suit (parties want to preserve relations), the modesty of sums recovered (*Hadley v. Baxendale* and all that), and the increasing resort to alternative forms of dispute resolution (arbitration) might be tempted to include contract remedies among those things one has to study to get through law school but which have little relevance thereafter.[***]

Even so, we believe it hardly follows that the student can ignore the remedial side of the coin. In the first place, not all contract recoveries are inconsequential or piddling. If the contract is a large one which has a long term, even a modest contract-market differential can produce a whopping sum of money. Moreover, a modest relaxation of *Hadley v. Baxendale* and a willingness of the courts to compensate sellers for lost profits and lost volumes could cause an important change in the picture.

More important, however, is that the impact of contract remedy doctrine cannot properly be measured by the frequency of litigation. Surely, the predicted damage and specific performance awards that courts would grant play an important role in the negotiation of every contract dispute lawyers handle. In such cases we bargain

---

[*] A comprehensive analysis appears in John A. Sebert, Jr., *Remedies Under Article Two of the Uniform Commercial Code: An Agenda for Review*, 130 U. PA. L. REV. 360 (1981). The seminal article is Ellen A. Peters, *Remedies for Breach of Contracts Relating to the Sale of Goods Under the Uniform Commercial Code: A Roadmap for Article Two*, 73 YALE L.J. 199 (1963). *See also* ROY RYDEN ANDERSON, DAMAGES UNDER THE UNIFORM COMMERCIAL CODE (2nd ed 2003); Robert E. Scott, *The Case for Market Damages: Revisiting the Lost Profits Puzzle*, 57 U. CHI. L. REV. 1155 (1990); David W. Barnes, *The Meaning of Value in Contract Damages and Contract Theory*, 46 AM. U. L. REV. 1 (1996).

[**] *See generally* James J. White, *Contract Law in Modern Commercial Transactions, An Artifact of Twentieth Century Business Life?*, 22 WASHBURN L.J. 1 (1982).

[***] In support of this thesis, the studies of Professor Stewart Macaulay might be cited, *e.g.*, Stewart Macaulay, *Non-Contractual Relations in Business: A Preliminary Study*, 28 AM. SOCIOL. REV. 55 (1963), which suggest that commercial parties themselves iron out most contract disputes on their own on the basis of common sense and economics.

at least in part on the basis of the lawyer's judgment about what damages will be awarded at trial. Thus both the lawyer negotiating a settlement on behalf of an aggrieved client and the lawyer advising his client how best to extricate himself from a situation in which he or the opposing party has broken a contract need to know the variety of available remedies and the merits and drawbacks of each.

Amended Article 2 made a number of changes in the remedies of the seller and buyer and these will be discussed in some detail.[*] Before considering these damage remedies, let us examine some self-help remedies common to both parties.

SECTION 2.   INSECURITY AND REPUDIATION

A. Insecurity and Prospective Inability

UCC 2-609(1) provides that a contract for sale "imposes an obligation on each party that the other's expectation of receiving due performance will not be impaired." This obligation is breached when one party gives the other "reasonable grounds for insecurity" with regard to the promised performance. At this point, the aggrieved party "may in a record demand adequate assurance of due performance and until the party receives such assurance may if commercially reasonable suspend any performance for which it has not already received the agreed return." Comment 2 to UCC 2-609 stresses that the right to suspend performance includes "any preparation therefor." If the other party, upon receipt of a "justified" demand, fails "to provide within a reasonable time not exceeding 30 days such assurance of due performance as is adequate under the circumstances of the particular case," it has repudiated the contract and the aggrieved party may take appropriate remedial action, including cancellation. UCC 2-609(4). Between merchants, the reasonableness of grounds for insecurity and adequacy of any assurance offered "shall be determined according to commercial standards." UCC 2-609(2). Article 2A follows suit in UCC 2A-401.

Thus, an aggrieved party may suspend its performance even though the other party's conduct is short of breach or repudiation but the aggrieved party cannot cancel the contract until the mandatory communication procedure fails to produce "adequate assurance." In this process, a high incidence of consensual adjustment

---

[*] For a critique of these revisions, *see* Roy Ryden Anderson, *Of Hidden Agendas, Naked Emperors, And A Few Goods Soldiers: The Conference's Breach of Promise. . . Regarding Article 2 Damage Remedies*, 54 SMU L. REV. 795 (2001).

and continued performance is likely, particularly when the generality of the standards is taken into account. On the other hand, if adjustment does not occur and one party has suspended his performance or canceled the contract, the other may claim that such action was not justified. Within this framework, courts and lawyers will have to give some content to the phrases "reasonable grounds for insecurity" and "adequate assurance of due performance."[*]

Suppose that under a written contract for the sale of goods the seller is to deliver in a single lot on March 1 and the buyer is to pay the full contract price on April 1. The buyer's basic obligation here is to accept and pay for the goods in accordance with the contract, UCC 2-301, and it is in this regard that grounds for insecurity may arise. Except insofar as the seller has rights under UCC 2-702(2), however, once the buyer has accepted the seller's tender of delivery, the seller can reduce any insecurity she feels about subsequent payment of the price only by exercising rights under an Article 9 security interest–rights she may not have as she may not have taken an Article 9 security interest in the goods to secure payment of the price. As a practical matter, UCC 2-609 itself affords little protection to a seller who has fully performed her obligation before the alleged ground for insecurity arises.

Before delivery, however, UCC 2-609 is available and in some cases this availability is spelled out with precision for both seller and buyer alike. *See* UCC 2-210(2)(c) [former 2-210(5)] and UCC 2-611(2). From the seller's point of view, two situations are described which justify protective action. In an installment contract, when the buyer's default in past due payments is not sufficient to justify a cancellation, the seller may withhold delivery of goods then due until payment for past deliveries is received. UCC 2-612(3), cmt. 7. When the seller, in a credit transaction, discovers the buyer to be insolvent (as defined in UCC 1-201(b)(23)), the seller may "refuse delivery except for cash including payment for all goods theretofore delivered under the contract, and stop delivery" under UCC 2-705.

---

[*] For good background discussion, *see* Lawrence B. Wardrop, Jr., *Prospective Inability in the Law of Contracts,* 20 MINN. L. REV. 380 (1936); 13 CORBIN ON CONTRACTS §§ 68.4-.6 (2003); Alan G. Dowling, Note, *A Right to Adequate Assurance of Performance in All Transactions: UCC § 2-609 Beyond Sales of Goods,* 48 S. CAL. L. REV. 1358 (1975). *See also,* R. J. Robertson, Jr., *The Right to Demand Adequate Assurance of Due Performance: UCC Section 2-609 and Restatement (Second) of Contracts Section 251,* 38 DRAKE L. REV. 305 (1988-89).

UCC 2-702(1).[*] However, it has been held that insolvency alone does not justify cancellation of the contract.[**]

From the buyer's perspective, when it appears prior to delivery that the seller may not perform, UCC 2-609 is available. The buyer also has the rights to compel delivery of the goods under UCC 2-502 and 2-716 which were explored in Chapter Nine, *supra*. Notice that UCC 2-502 is keyed to seller insolvency in commercial cases and UCC 2-716 is keyed to the relative availability of the goods.

Short of the situations noted above, exactly what constitutes either reasonable grounds for insecurity or adequate assurance of due performance is less clear.[***] Consider the following case and then resolve the problems, giving careful attention to the comments to UCC 2-609.

TOP OF IOWA COOPERATIVE V. SIME FARMS, INC.
SUPREME COURT OF IOWA, 2000
608 N.W.2D 454

TERNUS, JUSTICE

The appellee, Top of Iowa Cooperative, sued the appellant, Sime Farms, Inc., for damages arising out of Sime Farms' failure to deliver corn under four hedge-to-arrive (HTA) contracts. Sime Farms claimed that the contracts were illegal and that, in any event, the Coop had repudiated the contract by making an unreasonable demand for assurances. A jury found in favor of the Coop and awarded damages against Sime Farms. We affirm.

I. *Background Facts and Proceedings*

A. *Hedge-to-arrive contracts.* Before we discuss the particular facts of this case, it is helpful to briefly review the nature of HTA contracts. "[I]n a basic HTA

---

[*] *See Maddux Supply Co. v. A-C Electric Co., Inc.*, 467 S.E.2d 448 (S.C. Ct. App. 1996) (seller had reasonable grounds to believe buyer was insolvent, demand for cash under UCC 2-702(1) proper). This remedy finds firm support in Uniform Sales Act 53(1)(a) and 54(1) and in prior case law. *See, e.g., Leopold v. Rock-Ola Mfg. Corp.*, 109 F.2d 611 (5th Cir. 1940).

[**] *Keppelon v. W.M. Ritter Flooring Corp.*, 116 A. 491 (N.J. 1922).

[***] *See* Larry T. Garvin, *Adequate Assurance of Performance: Of Risk, Duress, and Cognition*, 69 U. COLO. L. REV. 71 (1998).

contract, a farmer and grain elevator enter into a contract that contemplates delivery of a specified quantity of grain at a fixed point in time in the future." *Andersons, Inc. v. Horton Farms, Inc.,* 166 F.3d 308, 319 (6th Cir.1998). In a typical HTA contract, the elevator sets the price it is willing to pay based on the open market price on the Chicago Board of Trade (CBOT) for the delivery period, minus what is known as the basis.[1] (The basis is simply the elevator's cost of doing business, such as transportation costs, storage, labor, and utilities, plus a profit.) Upon entering into an HTA contract, the elevator hedges its purchase by simultaneously selling a futures contract on the CBOT, thereby protecting itself from any change in the cash price of corn at the date of delivery.

Although the transaction up to this point is relatively straightforward, there are several complicating factors. First, grain elevators must conduct their trading on the CBOT through licensed brokers. When the price of corn on the futures market rises, the contract with the broker typically requires the elevator to pay what is known as "margin money"--the difference between the original futures contract price and the current futures price--in order to maintain its futures position.[2] The elevator recovers the margin money when it sells the corn delivered by the farmer at a higher cash price.[3] Of course, if the farmer does not deliver, the elevator has

---

[1] In the Midwest, the market price for grain such as corn is set on the open market established by the CBOT. During trading hours on the CBOT, contracts are bought and sold for the future delivery of corn in the months of December, March, May, July, and September. Contracts bought and sold on the CBOT are known as "futures contracts." The price established by the CBOT for the buying and selling of grain is widely disseminated to the public.

[2] The requirement of margin payments arises from the nature of futures contracts. One court has explained these contracts in the following manner:

> Parties who enter futures contracts do not agree to pay the price that prevails when they buy the contracts; they agree to pay the price that prevails when the contracts expire (or the positions are closed by offsetting transactions). A contract for September corn, entered into in March, will fluctuate in price until September, when its final price is determined by the price of the cash commodity at the delivery point.

Nagel v. ADM Investor Servs., Inc., 65 F.Supp.2d 740, 753 (N.D.Ill.1999).

[3] An example will illustrate how hedging works and how it protects the elevator from any price risk. We will make the following assumptions. The Coop contracts to purchase 20,000 bushels of corn from Sime Farms for a December 1995 delivery date. The CBOT price for December 1995 corn is $2.49 at the time of contracting, so Sime Farms is entitled to receive

(continued...)

no grain to sell, and it cannot recover its margin. Thus, the elevator's hedged position remains risk-free only so long as the farmer can be counted upon to deliver the grain specified under the contract.

In addition, HTA contracts prevalent in the 1990's had two features that distinguished them from traditional grain contracts where the parties agreed on a fixed price for a specified future delivery date. In HTA contracts, the basis was not set at the time of contracting. Rather, the farmer was allowed to choose when to set the basis, provided it was done within the time period specified in the contract. This contract term introduced an element of speculation into the contract, because an elevator's basis generally fluctuated. Consequently, a farmer who delayed setting the basis was open to the risk that the elevator's basis would increase, thereby lowering the price the farmer would receive for his grain.

The second element of risk in HTA contracts is introduced when the farmer is allowed to postpone delivery to a later date. This practice is known as rolling. When the price of grain rises by or near the time set for delivery, the farmer may prefer to sell his grain on the current cash market for a higher price rather than deliver the grain to the elevator for the contract price. Under these circumstances, the parties may agree to modify the contract by delaying, or rolling, the delivery date to a date in the future. To preserve its hedged position, the elevator buys back, at the current price, the futures contract it had previously sold on the CBOT and enters into another futures contract to sell grain on the new delivery date.

The complicating factor in rolling is that the price of corn for the new date of delivery generally is not the same as the current price for the old delivery date. This difference is called the spread. If the new price is higher, the spread is positive and will result in a gain or carry. If the new price is lower, however, it will result in a loss or inverse. This gain or loss is fixed at the time of the roll and is added to or deducted from the new contract price under the rolled HTA contract. Thus, when the farmer decides to roll, he can determine at that time whether he will incur a gain

---

[3] (...continued)
$2.49 minus the basis upon delivery. The Coop hedges this transaction by selling a futures contract on the CBOT at the same price of $2.49. In the months leading to December 1995, the price of December corn rises to $3.00. As the price rises, the broker requires the Coop to pay a total of $ .51 (margin money) to preserve its futures position. Sime Farms delivers the corn in December 1995, as agreed. The Coop pays Sime Farms $2.49 less the basis, which the Coop retains. As noted, the price of December corn is $3.00. The Coop then sells the delivered corn for $3.00, thereby netting $.51 and recovering its margin money. Thus, both parties end up with the proceeds they bargained for in the original contract.

or loss. The problematic risk arises when the farmer rolls to a month when he will not have grain on hand to deliver. He has then exposed himself to an additional, unknown risk because he will have to roll again before he will be able to make the agreed-upon delivery. If the market deteriorates and the price of corn falls, the farmer may ultimately be required to deliver grain at a significant loss.

Unfortunately, this predicament is precisely the situation that faced Sime Farms in the summer of 1996, which brings us to the facts of this case. * * *

B. *Factual background.* Top of Iowa Cooperative is a farmer-owned cooperative that operates in several locations, including Lake Mills, Iowa. Prior to January 1995, the Lake Mills location was owned and operated as the Farmers Coop Elevator Company of Lake Mills. Sime Farms, Inc. is an Iowa corporation wholly owned by Mark Sime. As its name suggests, its business is farming. Sime Farms is a member of the Coop, and for many years prior to the time in question, did nearly all of its grain and agronomy business with the Coop's predecessor, Farmers Coop Elevator Company. (In the remainder of this opinion, we refer to both entities as the Coop.)

In the fall of 1994 and the spring of 1995, Sime Farms entered into three HTA contracts with the Coop. These contracts called for the delivery of a total of 40,000 bushels of corn in December 1995. This grain represented Sime Farms' entire annual corn production. One month before delivery was due under these contracts, Sime Farms contracted to sell an additional 20,000 bushels of corn for delivery in May 1996. The Coop hedged each contract by selling futures contracts on the CBOT for corresponding delivery dates.

In November 1995, Sime Farms rolled its December 1995 delivery dates to March 1996. Although the HTA contracts did not specifically address the ability of Sime Farms to roll, the contracts contemplated this possibility by providing for a fee of one cent per bushel for each roll. Handwritten modifications were made on the contracts indicating the new delivery dates. The contract price was also adjusted to reflect the spread between the current December 1995 futures price and the March 1996 futures price. This adjustment was a positive six cents, a seven-cent carry minus the one-cent roll fee. Sime Farms then sold its 1995 crop on the cash market at a price significantly higher than the December 1995 futures price it had contracted to receive under the original HTA contracts.

Although the roll to March 1996 resulted in a gain or carry, the parties were aware at the time of this roll that a roll to July 1996 or December 1996 would result in a significant inverse, or loss. The parties also knew that Sime Farms would have to roll again into at least December 1996 because it had no grain to deliver until it harvested its 1996 crop.

In February 1996, the contracts were rolled to May 1996. This roll resulted in a gain of slightly less than three cents per bushel, which was added to the contract price. In April 1996, all four contracts were rolled to July 1996. This roll resulted in a thirteen-cent-per-bushel loss or inverse, and so this amount was deducted from the price the Coop agreed to pay Sime Farms for July delivery. By late April 1996, the inverse between July 1996 and December 1996 was around $1.30 per bushel. Because Sime Farms had no corn to deliver in July 1996, it was faced with the prospect of rolling into December 1996 at a significant loss, or breaching its contracts with the Coop. If Sime Farms breached the contracts, the Coop would have to repurchase the offsetting futures it held on the CBOT, resulting in a loss of the margin money it had paid.

By May 1996, the Coop was becoming increasingly concerned about farmers' abilities and willingness to perform on the outstanding HTA contracts. The Coop's manager, Paul Nesler, spoke with Mark Sime at least once in May regarding the inverse situation and the effect of rolling into December. Sime told Nesler that he would get back to the Coop about what he planned to do, but he never did. The Coop's concerns were heightened even further when, that same month, the Iowa Attorney General's office announced that some of the HTA contracts might be "illegal."

On June 6, 1996, the Coop sent a letter to Sime Farms and similarly-situated producers in which the Coop stated that "[i]n response to recent market and non-market developments," the Coop wanted to confirm that its customers holding HTA contracts were capable of and intended to perform. The Coop stated it would consider compliance with the following two conditions as adequate assurance of Sime Farms' ability and willingness to perform: (1) payment in full of all commissions and margins previously paid by the Coop, or a binding letter of credit obligating an institutional lender to pay such commissions and margins; and (2) the return of a signed copy of the Coop's letter agreeing to delivery of the agreed-upon quantity of grain on or before the delivery dates set forth in the contracts. Finally, the Coop stated that a failure to provide the requested assurances would constitute a repudiation of the contract.

The next day Mark Sime came to the Coop to discuss the letter. Nesler informed Sime that Sime Farms could roll its contracts to December 1996 and would not be required to reimburse the Coop for the margin calls already paid. Nesler also told Sime that the Coop would consider a buy-out of the contracts by Sime Farms over a period of time at a low interest rate. Nesler called Sime a few days later to find out what Sime wanted to do. Sime told Nesler that the Coop would be receiving a letter from Sime Farms' lawyer.

The Coop did in fact receive a letter from Sime Farms' attorney later that day. In this letter Sime Farms took the position that the Coop's demand for assurances was an attempt to change the terms of the HTA contracts and that the Coop had no grounds to do so. Sime Farms also asserted the illegality of the contracts under the Commodity Exchange Act, 7 U.S.C. §§ 1-25. Sime Farms' attorney closed his letter by informing the Coop that Sime Farms did "not intend to deliver at a price which includes the losses your elevator agreed to assume in the contract relating to unfavorable margins." Upon receipt of this letter, the Coop terminated the futures positions it held in reliance on the Sime Farms HTA contracts. Sime Farms did not deliver grain under any of the contracts. This lawsuit followed.

C. *Course of the litigation.* The Coop claimed in this lawsuit that Sime Farms breached its contracts with the Coop by failing to give adequate assurances upon the Coop's reasonable demand for such assurances. *See* Iowa Code § 554.2609 (1995) (providing that party's failure to provide adequate assurance after a justified demand is a repudiation of the contract). Sime Farms asserted several counterclaims, including a request for a declaratory judgment that the contracts were illegal and unenforceable under the Commodity Exchange Act. Sime Farms also claimed as an affirmative defense that the Coop breached the contracts by making an unwarranted and unreasonable demand for assurances. * * * [At trial, the trial court held the HTA contracts were not illegal and the jury found for the Coop on the breach of contract claim.]

II. *Issues on Appeal*

Sime Farms raises four issues on appeal. First, it asserts that the district court erred in holding the HTA contracts were legal. Second, it claims that the Coop, as a matter of law, did not have reasonable grounds to be insecure concerning Sime Farms' performance of the contracts. Third, Sime Farms contends that the Coop's demand for assurances amounted to a repudiation as a matter of law, thereby excusing Sime Farms from performing. Sime Farms' final assignment of error is the trial court's admission of parol evidence with respect to the Coop's written demand for assurances. * * *

[The court found the HTA contracts legal and enforceable under the Commodity Exchange Act.]

* * *

IV. *Was The Trial Court Correct in Ruling That the Coop had Generated a Jury Question on the Issue of Whether the Coop had Reasonable Grounds for Insecurity?*

A. *Statement of issue.* One basis for the Coop's breach of contract claim was that Sime Farms failed to provide reasonable assurances upon the Coop's demand for such assurances. This claim arises from article 2 of the Iowa Uniform Commercial Code, which governs the sale of grain in Iowa. * * * Under the U.C.C., a party to a contract who has reasonable grounds to believe that the other party will be unwilling or unable to perform his contractual obligations may require the party to provide adequate assurances of performance. *See* Iowa Code § 554.2609.

Sime Farms sought a directed verdict on the basis that the Coop lacked reasonable grounds for insecurity as a matter of law and, therefore, had no right to make a demand for assurances. The trial court held that the Coop had generated a jury question on the issue of reasonable grounds for insecurity and, accordingly, denied Sime Farms' motion. This ruling is assigned as error on appeal. * * *

C. *Applicable legal principles.* Section 554.2609 of the Iowa U.C.C. provides in relevant part:

> 1. A contract for sale imposes an obligation on each party that the other's expectation of receiving due performance will not be impaired. When reasonable grounds for insecurity arise with respect to the performance of either party the other may in writing demand adequate assurance of due performance and until that party receives such assurance may if commercially reasonable suspend any performance for which that party has not already received the agreed return.
>
> 2. Between merchants the reasonableness of grounds for insecurity and the adequacy of any assurance offered shall be determined according to commercial standards.

Because the reasonableness of a party's insecurity is determined by commercial standards, there must be an objective factual basis for the insecurity, rather than a purely subjective fear that the party will not perform. *See* R.J. Robertson, Jr., *The Right to Demand Adequate Assurance of Due Performance: Uniform Commercial Code Section 2-609 and Restatement (Second) of Contracts Section 251,* 38 DRAKE L.REV. 305, 322 (1988-89).

> Generally, the existence of grounds for insecurity is a question of fact:
> Whether a party has reasonable grounds for insecurity depends upon many factors including the [party's] exact words or actions, the course of dealing or performance between the particular parties and the nature of the industry. What constitutes reasonable grounds for insecurity in one case

might not in another. Consequently, the trier of fact must normally answer whether grounds for insecurity exist.

1 JAMES J. WHITE & ROBERT S. SUMMERS, UNIFORM COMMERCIAL CODE § 6-2, at 286 (4th ed.1995) [hereinafter WHITE & SUMMERS]; * * * Nevertheless, occasions do arise where the undisputed facts establish that insecurity or the lack of insecurity existed as a matter of law. * * *

D. *Discussion.* The Coop's letter to Sime Farms reveals two grounds for insecurity: (1) the inverse in the market; and (2) statements in the press with respect to the unenforceability of HTA contracts. Because neither ground relates specifically to Sime Farms, Sime Farms asserts these facts do not provide reasonable grounds for the Coop to be concerned about Sime Farms' performance.

> "Clearly, the drafters of the Code did not intend that one party to a contract can go about demanding security for performance of the other whenever he gets nervous about a contract. Some reason for the demand for assurances must precede the demand."

Robertson, 38 DRAKE L.REV. at 323 (quoting *Cole v. Melvin,* 441 F.Supp. 193, 203 (D.S.D.1977)). In many cases, the grounds for insecurity are specifically tied to the party or the contract. *See, e.g., AMF, Inc.,* 536 F.2d at 1170 (holding that where prototype had never performed satisfactorily and evidence existed that seller was not actively working on project, buyer had reasonable grounds for insecurity); *Scott v. Crown,* 765 P.2d 1043, 1046 (Colo.Ct.App.1988) (finding fact that investigator told seller of active complaints against buyer and that buyer failed to make personal contact after seller refused to load wheat constituted grounds for insecurity). On the other hand, "[a] ground for insecurity need not arise from or be directly related to the contract in question." U.C.C. § 2-609 official cmt. 3.

> The grounds for insecurity need not arise from circumstances directly related to the parties or the contract itself. Thus, where the market price of a commodity is rising, the buyer may be justified in seeking assurances of performance from the seller *even though the seller did nothing to cause buyer's insecurity.*

WHITE & SUMMERS § 6-2, at 288 (emphasis added). Furthermore, in *Diskmakers, Inc. v. DeWitt Equipment Corp.,* 555 F.2d 1177 (3d Cir.1977), the Third Circuit Court of Appeals stated:

> "As between merchants, the test for determining when reasonable grounds for insecurity arise and what will constitute an adequate assurance of future performance is a commercial criterion. *Any facts which should indicate to a reasonable merchant that the promised performance might not be*

forthcoming when due should be considered reasonable grounds for insecurity ...."

555 F.2d at 1180 (quoting N.J. Stat. Ann. § 12A:2-609 study cmt. 1 (1962)) (emphasis added).

We think the market conditions existing in June 1996, combined with the widely-publicized statements that HTA contracts were illegal and unenforceable, are facts that would support a jury finding that the Coop had a reasonable basis to be concerned that Sime Farms may not perform under its contracts. The inverse in the market unquestionably made delivery under the contracts an unprofitable venture for Sime Farms. Although the Coop agreed in the contracts to pay all margins and commissions, both parties understood that any inverse would be deducted from the contract price if Sime Farms chose to roll the contracts. Consequently, if a future roll became necessary, the ultimate risk of an inverse market rested with the producer, not the Coop. That was precisely the situation here; another roll was inevitable because Sime Farms had no grain to deliver under the July contracts. Consequently, it would eventually have to roll at least to December 1996, at which time the inverse would reduce its price per bushel to a level at which it would not even recover its costs of production. Clearly, a producer in these circumstances would have every incentive to claim that the contracts were illegal and unenforceable, as the Iowa Attorney General's office had opined.

In addition, the jury was entitled to consider the market factors in the context of the relationship between the Coop and Sime Farms. *See* WHITE & SUMMERS § 6-2, at 286 ("Whether a party has reasonable grounds for insecurity depends upon many factors including the [party's] exact words or actions, the course of dealing or performance between the particular parties and the nature of the industry."); *see also Johnson v. Land O'Lakes,* 181 F.R.D. 388, 395 (N.D.Iowa 1998) (stating that "evidence of the context in which the demand is made is certainly relevant and admissible"). The Coop's local manager, Paul Nesler, spoke with Mark Sime in May to determine what Sime Farms intended to do about its July contracts. Sime was clearly aware of the inverse in the market and his need to roll the contracts to December; yet he did not contact the Coop to take any steps to work out a plan.

Sime Farms places great reliance on the testimony of Nesler, who when asked, "Did you ever believe that he [Sime] wouldn't deliver before June 6, 1996?" responded, "No, I thought Mark would probably deliver." Sime Farms claims that this testimony establishes as a matter of law that the Coop was never insecure about Sime Farms' performance. Although Nesler signed the demand for assurances on behalf of the Coop, he testified he did not draft it. The jury could certainly have concluded that Nesler's personal feelings did not reflect the Coop's belief as to Sime Farms' likely performance. Moreover, Nesler stated several times in his testimony that he was concerned that Sime had not come to the Coop with a plan, especially in view of Nesler's request that he do so. The jury was entitled to consider Nesler's testimony in its entirety and, in doing so, could discount some testimony and give more credit to other testimony. The weight to be given Nesler's testimony was for the jury to determine. *See Field v. Palmer,* 592 N.W.2d 347, 353 (Iowa 1999) (holding that credibility of witness's testimony is for the jury).

We hold there was sufficient evidence to generate a jury question on whether the Coop had an objectively reasonable basis for insecurity. Therefore, the trial court did not err in refusing to grant Sime Farms' motion for directed verdict on this basis.

V. *Was the Coop's Demand for Assurances Unreasonable as a Matter of Law?*

A. *Issue and scope of review.* Sime Farms claimed at trial that the Coop's demand for assurances was unreasonable as a matter of law and, as a result, constituted a repudiation of the contract. It claims that the trial court erred in failing to grant its motion for directed verdict on this issue. We apply the same scope of review as set out in the preceding division of this opinion.

B. *Applicable law.* Sime Farms' repudiation argument rests on its contention that the Coop's demand for assurances imposed conditions that went beyond the contract and that the Coop's performance was contingent upon acquiescence to these conditions. Sime Farms contends such a demand constitutes an anticipatory repudiation.

We disagree with Sime Farms' contention. The mere fact that the assurances demanded by the Coop necessitated action beyond that required by the contract does not render the demand unreasonable as a matter of law. As noted by a leading treatise on the Uniform Commercial Code,

> [a]ll demands for adequate assurance call for more than was originally promised under the contract, and that is precisely what 2-609 authorizes. If, for example, it was appropriate to sell on open credit at the outset of a contract but subsequent events cause insecurity, 2-609 calls for modification of the contract to provide greater security to the seller than the seller could have demanded, absent such insecurity. Thus it is the very purpose of 2-609 to authorize one party to insist upon more than the contract gives.

WHITE & SUMMERS § 6-2, at 288; *see also* U.C.C. § 2-610 official cmt. 2 ("[A] demand by one or both parties for more than the contract calls for in the way of counter-performance is not in itself a repudiation."); Robertson, 38 DRAKE L.REV. at 341 (noting that an insecure promisee can demand assurance in the nature of additional performances not required by the underlying contract, provided there are reasonable grounds for insecurity). * * *

In summary, the mere fact that the Coop demanded performance beyond that required by the contract did not transform its demand into a repudiation as a matter of law. Therefore, the trial court did not err in submitting the question of the reasonableness of the Coop's demands to the jury. * * *

[Discussion of 4th issue omitted.] Affirmed.

Problem 10-1

Seller agreed to manufacture special equipment for B on credit. Delivery was to be in installments, with payment for each installment within 15 days of delivery. Seller commenced performance but, before any deliveries were made, Seller began to hear unfavorable comments about B's credit. After a quick check, the following facts emerged: (1) Dun & Bradstreet had recently reduced B's credit rating; (2) B's working capital was fully stretched out and some suppliers were experiencing delays in payment; (3) B had recently changed banks, and the "word" was out that B's financial condition was "extended" and that care should be exercised before extending credit; and (4) B's overall financial condition had worsened since the date of the contract.

A. You represent Seller. On the day before the first delivery was due, Seller called you for a conference. With the credit information on the table, Seller stated that unless you could persuade it otherwise, it would refuse to deliver the goods unless B paid cash. What would you recommend? *See* UCC 1-201(b)(23), 2-702(1), 2-609. Does Seller have reasonable grounds to believe that B is insolvent?

B. Assume you persuade Seller to exercise caution and talk to B before taking action. Seller, therefore, gives B a written demand for "adequate assurance" and temporarily suspends the first delivery. UCC 2-609(1). B, in response, establishes solvency and claims that the current situation is "temporary." B, however, states that long-term viability depends upon getting prompt delivery of the equipment, which is needed in the business, on credit. If there are delays, no assurances can be given.

Does this constitute "adequate assurance" of due performance? Could Seller reasonably demand payment by letter of credit? On this last point, compare the court's decision in *Top of Iowa Cooperative, supra*, with the following opinion by Cummings, Circuit Judge, concurring in *Pittsburgh-Des Moines Steel Co. v. Brookhaven Manor Water Co.*, 532 F.2d 572, 583-84 (7th Cir. 1976):

Although I agree with the result reached in the majority opinion, I differ with the reasoning. Reasonable men could certainly conclude that PDM had legitimate grounds to question Brookhaven's ability to pay for the water tank. When the contract was signed, the parties understood that Brookhaven would obtain a loan to help pay for the project. When the loan failed to materialize, a prudent businessman would have "reasonable grounds for insecurity." I disagree that there must be a fundamental change in the financial position of the buyer before the seller can invoke the protection of UCC § 2-609. Rather, I believe that the Section was designed to cover instances where an underlying condition of the contract, even if not expressly incorporated into the written document, fails to occur. *See* Comment 3 to UCC § 2-609. Whether, in a specific case, the breach of the condition gives a party "reasonable grounds for insecurity" is a question of fact for the jury.

UCC § 2-609, however, does not give the alarmed party a right to redraft the contract. Whether the party invoking that provision is merely requesting an assurance that performance will be forthcoming or whether he is attempting to alter the contract is a mixed question of law and fact, depending in part upon the court's interpretation of the obligations imposed on the parties. In this case, PDM would have been assured only if significant changes in the contract were made, either by receiving Betke's personal guarantee, by attaining escrow financing or by purchasing an interest in Brookhaven. The district court could probably conclude as a matter of law that these requests by PDM demanded more than a commercially "adequate assurance of due performance."

C. Would your analysis change if Seller was leasing the equipment to B in a true lease? *See* UCC 2A-401.

Problem 10-2

Seller agreed to manufacture special equipment for B on credit. Delivery was to be in installments with payment for each installment 15 days after delivery. About one month before Seller was due to deliver the first installment, B began to hear unfavorable things about Seller's financial condition: (1) Dun & Bradstreet had recently reduced Seller's credit rating; (2) Seller's working capital was fully stretched out and some suppliers were experiencing delays in payment; (3) Seller had recently changed banks, and the "word" was out that seller's financial condition was "extended" and that care should be exercised before extending any credit; and (4) Seller's overall financial condition had worsened since the date of the contract.

Does B have reasonable grounds for insecurity? If so, what assurances would you suggest B request?

B. Repudiation

In the first-year course in contracts, considerable attention is usually given to the cognate problems of determining whether a contracting party has repudiated or materially broken an installment contract. Accordingly, our treatment here will be an abbreviated one, emphasizing the relevant Code provisions and the role of the lawyer called upon to advise a party on what to do in the face of the other party's conduct. The consequences of an erroneous decision by the lawyer can be catastrophic. The lawyer may advise that the other party has repudiated or materially broken an installment contract, and that the client is free to cease his own performance and seek damages. If this advice proves incorrect, the client will turn out to be the wrongdoer, and, accordingly, liable in damages.* In such a case he may just choose another lawyer to defend him. It should be added that the lawyer who renders advice in this context does not always have weeks to do research in the library. Her client may be manufacturing the goods or have to make a quick decision to avoid losing another business opportunity and may want to know *now* what course of action he is free to take in the face of the other party's conduct. The relevant sections to review are UCC 2-609(4), 2-610, 2-611, 2A-401(3), 2A-402 and 2A-403.

What constitutes a "repudiation"? The 2003 amendments to UCC 2-610 and 2A-402 provide a definition of repudiation. Read those sections and the comments. In real life, it is a lucky and unusual lawyer whose client reports that the other contracting party has repudiated by such unequivocal language as "I repudiate" or "kiss my foot." A more common circumstance finds the other party slowly slipping down that incline into bankruptcy while believing and fully expecting that he will "have the money in just a few days," or that he will "have the goods in just a week."

---

* For such a case, *see Teeman v. Jurek*, 251 N.W.2d 698 (Minn. 1977).

Another common cause for the same lawyer's headache is the chiseler–the fellow who asks for more than the contract clearly entitles him to, but not enough more to make his request outrageous. In *Thunder Basin Coal Co. v. Southwestern Public Service Co.*, 104 F.3d 1205 (10th Cir. 1997), the court held that the buyer had repudiated the contract by stating that it would perform only in accordance with its own interpretation of the contract. If either party threatens to cease performance unless the other agrees to a performance not fairly within the scope of the original agreement, a repudiation may have occurred.*

As we have seen, the client's situation (and therefore his lawyer's) in such a case is greatly eased by UCC 2-609 which gives the right to demand assurance of performance from the other party and causes failure of assurances to become a repudiation after "a reasonable time not exceeding 30 days." *See also* UCC 2A-401. In some cases clients will be unwilling to twiddle their thumbs for 30 days and the lawyer will be called upon to determine whether a communication from the other party constitutes a repudiation.

In long-term gas supply contracts, buyers have attempted to minimize the effect of fixed price provisions in sharply declining markets by invoking UCC 2-609. The buyer suspends its payment and sends a written demand for adequate assurance of due performance to the seller. The benefits of a temporary suspension, however, are over shadowed by the risk that there is, in fact, no "reasonable grounds" for insecurity. Thus, in *Universal Resources Corp. v. Panhandle Eastern Pipe Line Co.*, 813 F.2d 77 (5th Cir. 1987), *reh'g denied,* 821 F.2d 1097 (5th Cir. 1987), the court found no objective evidence from either the seller's words or conduct or the market for natural gas to justify a fear that the seller would be unable or unwilling to perform the contract. The buyer, in effect, relied upon hypothetical rather than real grounds. Similarly, in *United States v. Great Plains Gasification Assoc.*, 819 F.2d 831 (8th Cir. 1987), the buyer had no objective grounds to believe that the seller would abandon services and, in any event, demanded assurance in excess of

---

* For illustrations, *compare Louis Dreyfus Corp. v. Brown*, 709 F.2d 898 (5th Cir. 1983), where the court held that a farmer repudiated a contract to deliver grain, *with Bill's Coal Co., Inc. v. Board of Public Utilities of Springfield, Mo.*, 682 F.2d 883 (10th Cir. 1982), where the court held that a supplier's bad faith interpretation of the price term was not a repudiation and the buyer's cancellation, therefore, was a breach. *See also Kaiser-Francis Oil Co. v. Producer's Gas Co.*, 870 F.2d 563 (10th Cir. 1989) (buyer refuses to perform unless seller agrees to modify "take or pay" clause); *National Farmer's Org. v. Bartlett and Company, Grain*, 560 F.2d 1350 (8th Cir. 1977) (seller's demand for payment past due under separate contracts before delivery on another contract was a repudiation).

what the seller was required to perform under the contract. Buyers are induced to play "games" with UCC 2-609 because neither applicable contract clauses nor UCC 2-615 grant them relief from changed market circumstances. The cost of losing the game is, at a minimum, liability for the suspended payments plus interest and, at a maximum, a repudiation of the contract.

Another possibility for the buyer is to find an interpretation question in the contract and state to the seller that there will be no further performance until the interpretation question is resolved by a court. The buyer may also seek a declaratory judgment and should make it clear to the seller that the buyer will perform the contract in full in accordance with the court's interpretation. Will this provide the buyer with a "safe harbor" until the dispute is resolved?

The answer should be no if there is not a good faith dispute. The courts will have little sympathy if the buyer has manufactured the dispute in an effort to avoid the contract. Even if there is a good faith dispute, UCC 2-610 does not say whether this communication is a repudiation. There is some risk that a court will conclude that the buyer's qualified statement that it will not perform until the good faith dispute is resolved but then will perform in full is a repudiation.[*]

In the *Plotnick* case, *infra*, the court assessed the significance of the buyer's late payment partly in terms of whether it impaired the seller's capacity to continue performance. A court might ask similar questions about a seller's late delivery. *See* UCC 2-612(2). But such symmetry will not be found in all cases and there will be borderline situations.[**]

A party may retract a repudiation as long as the aggrieved party has not changed its position in reliance on the repudiation or indicated that it considers the repudiation final. The retracting party may have to provide adequate assurance of performance and the aggrieved party is entitled to some allowance if there is a delay caused by the suspension of the performance following the repudiation before it was retracted. UCC 2-611, 2A-403.

---

[*] *But see In re Chateaugay Corp.*, 104 B.R. 637 (S.D.N.Y. 1989), holding that the qualified statement was not a repudiation.

[**] For a helpful discussion, *see* Thomas H. Jackson, *"Anticipatory Repudiation" and the Temporal Element of Contract Law: An Economic Inquiry into Contract Damages in Cases of Prospective Nonperformance,* 31 STAN. L. REV. 69, 75-101 (1978). *See also* Keith A. Rowley, *A Brief History of Anticipatory Repudiation in American Contract Law,* 69 U. CINN. L. REV. 565 (2001).

Problem 10-3

In the Spring of 2004, Seller, a producer of rolled steel, contracted to sell a quantity of steel to Buyer at a fixed price. The steel was to be shipped "FOB Seller's plant" within 10 days of demand by Buyer. No time for the demand was specified in the agreement. In May, 2004, Seller inquired when the demand would be made and was informed by Buyer "within the next few weeks." At the end of June, Seller, pressed for cash and storage space, requested by letter that Buyer "help us out" by placing the order quickly. When there was no response, Seller telegraphed that "much as we hate to we must ask for some relief" and requested a conference to "straighten the matter out." Buyer replied that it would be glad to have a conference but "if it is in regard to taking any steel, we would say that we are not in a position, and do not intend to take any steel this year and probably not until next Fall." Seller telegraphed that the response was "totally unacceptable" and demanded that Buyer take immediate delivery. Two weeks passed without a response. At this time the market price for the steel was over 20% below the contract price. Seller is furious and wants to cancel the contract, resell the steel and "sue those * * * for damages." And he wants action "right now."

A. Has Buyer repudiated the contract? If you have doubts, what quick steps should be taken to minimize the risk? (Don't overlook the possibility that Buyer is in breach because a reasonable time for making the demand has expired. *See* UCC 2-309(1) & 1-205 [former 1-204].)

B. If Buyer has repudiated, what remedial options are available to Seller? *See* UCC 2-610, 2-611 & 2-703.

Problem 10-4

Buyer contracted with the Ace Supply Co. for Ace to furnish at a fixed price a large quantity of specially tooled valves for use in an improved line of equipment. Ace agreed to deliver the valves in six equal installments at three month intervals. Buyer stated that the installments were geared to a long range production schedule and a projected increase in demand for the equipment. Buyer furnished design drawings to assist Ace in "tooling up," gave Ace six months of lead time, and advanced 25% of the contract price. Two weeks before the first installment was due, Buyer appeared in your office with the following letter from Ace:

Gentlemen:

As suggested in our telephone conversation of last week, our engineers misread the design drawings which you furnished us.

We must, therefore, retool our original model value at considerable extra expense and some delay. We regret that we will be unable to meet the first installment, scheduled for delivery in two weeks. We will make every effort to meet the second installment three months hence and to deliver the quantity promised in the first installment before the contract delivery schedule is completed.

Yours sincerely,

Ace Supply Co.

Buyer states that it would like to cancel the contract and get back the 25% advance. Upon close questioning, you discover the following: (1) the delay in delivery will "wreak havoc" with Buyer's production schedule and existing contractual commitments; (2) if the contract were canceled, Buyer would purchase 50% of the valves ordered from Ace from another manufacturer who guaranteed full performance in four months; (3) Buyer's estimated demand for the valves was about 50% too high; and (4) in Buyer's judgment, Ace would "probably" meet the next installment and make up the late deliveries. What is your advice?

Even though the discussion above has focused on the Article 2 transaction, the same issues may arise in an Article 2A transaction.

Note: Insecurity and Anticipatory Repudiation under the CISG

Article 71(1) allows a party to suspend their performance if it "becomes apparent that the other party will not perform a substantial part of his obligations as a result of: (a) a serious deficiency in his ability to perform or in his creditworthiness; or (b) his conduct in preparing to perform or in performing the contract." If the grounds in Article 71(1) are established, a seller who has shipped the goods before the grounds become evident may "prevent the handing over of the goods to the buyer." The party suspending performance "must immediately give notice of the suspension to the other party" and must "continue with performance if the other party provides adequate assurance of his performance." Article 71(3). Article 71 does not state the consequences of a failure to give adequate assurance.

Article 72(1) provides that one party may "declare the contract avoided" if "prior to the date for performance of the contract it is clear that [the other party] will commit a fundamental breach." *See* Article 25 for a definition of "fundamental breach." If the other party "has declared that he will not perform his obligations," the other party may avoid the contract for fundamental breach without giving the other party an opportunity to provide adequate assurance. Article 72(3). For a repudiation by conduct, however, if time allows the party "intending to declare the contract avoided must give reasonable notice to the other party in order to permit him to provide adequate assurance of his performance." Article 72(2).

Note that if a repudiation is a fundamental breach, neither Article 49 nor 64 apply. The aggrieved party may avoid the contract by giving the notice required in Article 26.

Note: Insecurity and Repudiation under UCITA

UCITA 708, 709, and 710 follow the Article 2 provisions on adequate assurance, repudiation, and retraction.

C. Right to Cancel

1. Grounds for and Effect of Cancellation

As you have seen, the UCC gives the parties a number of useful, if not risky, "self-help" remedies. Under UCC 2-609 or 2A-401, a party may "suspend any performance for which it has not already received the agreed return." If the buyer is discovered to be insolvent, the seller may "refuse delivery except for cash * * * and stop delivery under this Article * * *." UCC 2-702(1). *Compare* UCC 2A-525(1). Similarly, the seller, under UCC 2-705, may withhold delivery or stop delivery by any bailee of goods affected by the buyer's breach. *Compare* UCC 2A-526. The buyer may tender remaining payment and obtain the goods under UCC 2-502 or 2-716. *Compare* UCC 2A-507A [former 2A-521] and 2A-522. These remedies protect the unperformed balance of the party's obligation but are not inconsistent with the ultimate completion by both parties of the exchange. The disruption may be adjusted and the contract performed.

The remedy of cancellation, however, is more drastic. Upon breach of contract, the aggrieved party has as one of its available remedies the right to cancel the contract. UCC 2-703, 2-711; *compare* UCC 2A-508, 2A-523. Cancellation occurs "when either party puts an end to the contract for breach by the other." UCC 2-106(4), 2A-103(1).

How does an aggrieved party "cancel" a contract? The Code prescribes no procedure and requires no notice to the other party. Thus, if the seller determines that the buyer has breached, decides to cancel rather than to suspend performance or negotiate, and takes action inconsistent with continued performance, *e.g.*, resells identified goods, the cancellation is effective.*

The effect of a cancellation is that the aggrieved party's obligation to perform any executory obligation is discharged but the aggrieved party "retains any remedy for breach of the whole contract or any unperformed balance." UCC 2-106(4), 2A-505(1). Thus the aggrieved party is able to sue the breaching party for damages for failure to perform the contract that has been cancelled. Presumably, a written cancellation without more would not be a renunciation of the right to sue for breach under UCC 1-306 [former 1-107].**

2. Cancellation Under Installment Contracts

UCC 2-612 and 2A-510 impose an important limitation on the aggrieved party's right to cancel in installment contracts. Under UCC 2-612(1), an installment contract "requires or authorizes the delivery of goods in separate lots to be separately accepted, even if the contract contains a clause 'each delivery is a separate contract' or its equivalent."*** We briefly considered installment contracts in Chapter Six, *supra*, in discussing rejection and acceptance.

Breach by buyer. Under an installment contract, payment is due "at the time and place at which the buyer is to receive the goods" unless "otherwise agreed." UCC 2-310(a). Suppose the buyer fails to pay for an installment when due or repudiates the duty to pay for a single installment? What are the seller's remedies? For example, can the seller cancel the contract under UCC 2-703, and sue for damages?

Consider, first, a failure to pay for a single installment of goods when payment is due. Under the 2003 amendments to Article 2, the buyer will have breached the contract. UCC 2-703(1). The buyer has breached when it fails to make a payment when due and the seller has the remedy of cancellation available to it to the "extent provided by this Act." One of the limitations on the seller's ability to cancel for the

---

* *See Mott Equity Elevator v. Svihovec*, 236 N.W.2d 900 (N.D. 1975).

** *See Goldstein v. Stainless Processing Co.*, 465 F.2d 392 (7th Cir. 1972).

*** *Compare* UCC 2-307; *Stinnes Interoil, Inc. v. Apex Oil Co.*, 604 F. Supp. 978 (S.D.N.Y.1985) (whether parties intended installment deliveries or delivery in a single lot is question of fact).

buyer's breach in an installment contract is obliquely referred to in UCC 2-612(3). Under that section, a default in respect to one or more installments does not result in a breach of the whole contract, unless the default is a "substantial impairment of the value of the whole contract." Because cancellation would only affect the seller's executory obligations, cancellation is important only if the seller does not want to make delivery of future installments to the buyer. The buyer's failure to pay must "substantially impair the value of the whole contract" before the seller would be entitled to cancel. Cancellation would not effect the seller's entitlement to the price for any goods if the requirements of UCC 2-709 are met.[*]

What about a clear repudiation by the buyer of the obligation to pay for an installment when the obligation to pay is not yet due? The buyer's repudiation is a breach of contract. UCC 2-703(1). The analysis would be the same as for a breach that occurs by failure to pay, if one considers a "default" under UCC 2-612(3) to include a "repudiation." Comment 6 to UCC 2-612 seems to distinguish a "nonconformity" as to one installment as a different situation than a repudiation. Would that same analysis apply to a "default?" Should a seller have to show that the value of the entire installment contract was substantially impaired by the buyer's repudiation in order to cancel the contract? One could argue that the analysis under UCC 2-610 requires substantial impairment of the value of the contract in the case of a repudiation in order to exercise any remedy including the remedy of cancellation.

Breach by seller. Suppose the seller delivers a non-conforming installment which the buyer rightfully and effectively rejects under UCC 2-612(2). The seller has breached the contract. UCC 2-711(1). Just as with the buyer's failure to pay situation, the seller's actual delivery of a nonconforming installment raises the issue as to whether the buyer may cancel the contract for that nonconformity. Cancellation would affect the executory obligations of the parties, that is, the obligation of the seller to deliver and the buyer to accept future conforming installments. UCC 2-612(3) and UCC 2-711(2) suggest no, unless the non-conformity substantially impairs the value of the contract as a whole, relying on the language in UCC 2-711(2) that the buyer is entitled to exercise remedies "to the extent provided for by this act."

---

[*] Under former 2-703(1), the answer as to payments due on or before delivery of an installment was that there must be a "breach of the whole" in an installment contract before the seller had a right to cancel. As to payments due after delivery, former 2-703(1) did not seem to allow cancellation of the contract but the seller would have been entitled to the price as to any installment the buyer accepts. Former 2-709.

Suppose the seller repudiates or refuses to deliver in an installment contract.

A repudiation is a breach under UCC 2-711(1). Again, by referring to the "requirements of the act" as a limitation on the availability of the remedy of cancellation, the substantial impairment standard of UCC 2-612(3) and of UCC 2-610 limits the ability of the buyer to cancel in an installment contract.*

Amended Article 2A follows a similar approach in UCC 2A-402, 2A-510(2), 2A-508, and 2A-523 except that the amended UCC 2A-508 and 2A-523 do not contain the language "to the extent provided for in this Act." Without that language and with the deletion of the language in former 2A-508 and 2A-523 referring to the substantial impairment standard in the case of installment leases as a precondition to exercising remedies, whether a lessee or lessor must demonstrate substantial impairment in an installment lease prior to cancellation is not so clear.

Efficient though it may be, there are some limitations upon the ability of an aggrieved party to engage in a "self help" remedy. In *Kelly v. Miller*, 575 P.2d 1221 (Alaska 1978), the seller, after the buyer had failed to pay the price due on goods delivered, moved in and "repossessed" them. The court, in a dispassionate opinion, found that "in repossessing the tractor without judicial process * * * " the seller had "fashioned his own remedy." Frontier ingenuity notwithstanding, no security interest had been retained under Article 9, there was no right to reclamation under UCC 2-702, and the seller was not entitled to replevin. The consequences? The seller's "failure to seek the remedy provided him under [UCC 2-709] combined with his resort to a remedy not recognized, so far as we have discovered, at either law or equity, precludes him from recovering damages for any loss he may have suffered as a result of [the] breach of contract." Yet the seller still has the goods! What recourse, if any, is available to the buyer? *Cf.* UCC 9-625.

Here, now, is one of the great cases on material breach in installment contracts.

PLOTNICK V. PENNSYLVANIA SMELTING & REFINING CO.
UNITED STATES COURT OF APPEALS, THIRD CIRCUIT, 1952
194 F.2D 859

HASTIE, CIRCUIT JUDGE

This litigation arises out of an installment contract for the sale of quantities of battery lead by a Canadian seller to a Pennsylvania buyer. The seller sued for the

---

* Under former 2-612(3) and 2-711(1), the limitation was clear; the substantial impairment standard applied whether it is a failure to deliver in one installment or several installments.

price of a carload of lead delivered but not paid for. The buyer counterclaimed for damages caused by the seller's failure to deliver the remaining installments covered by the contract. The district court sitting without a jury allowed recovery on both claim and counterclaim. This is an appeal by the seller from the judgment against him on the counterclaim. The ultimate question is whether the buyer had committed such a breach of contract as constituted a repudiation justifying rescission by the seller. * * *

[The court held that the Uniform Sales Act enacted by Pennsylvania applied to the dispute.]

Uncontested findings of fact show that the contract in question was the last of a series of agreements, several of them installment contracts, entered into by the parties between June and October, 1947. Under these contracts, numerous shipments of lead were made by the seller in Canada to the buyer in Philadelphia. The seller frequently complained, and with justification, that payments were too long delayed. On the other hand, several shipments were not made at the times required by the contracts. However, by the end of March 1948, all contracts other than the one in suit had been fully performed by both parties. In this connection, it was the unchallenged finding of the district court that both parties waived the delays which preceded the buyer's breach involved in this suit. The earlier delays are relevant only insofar as they may reasonably have influenced either party in its interpretation of subsequent conduct of the other party.

The contract in suit was executed October 23, 1947 and called for deliveries aggregating 200 tons of battery lead to be completed not later than December 25, 1947. The agreed price was 8.1 cents per pound, or better if quality warranted. The court found that it was the understanding of the parties that at least 63 percent of the price should be paid shortly after each shipment was delivered and the balance within four weeks after that delivery. This finding is not contested.

Under this contract a first carload was delivered November 7, 1947. About 75 percent of the price was paid six days later. A second carload was received January 8, and about 75 percent of the price was paid 10 days later. Final adjustments and payments of small balances due on these two carloads were completed March 30, and these shipments are not now in dispute. The earliest shipment immediately involved in this litigation, the third under the contract, was a carload of lead received by the buyer on March 23, 1948. This delivery followed a March 12 conference of the parties. They disagree on what transpired at that conference. However, about 290,000 pounds of lead were then still to be delivered under the contract which stated December 25, 1947 as the agreed time for the completion of performance. And shortly after the conference, one carload of 43,000 pounds was delivered. No part of the price of this third carload has been paid. It is not disputed that plaintiff is entitled to the price of this shipment and his recovery on his claim in this suit vindicates that right.

On April 7, the buyer, who had been prodding the seller for more lead for some time, notified the seller that unless the balance of the lead should be delivered within thirty days he would buy in the open market and charge the seller any cost in excess of 8.1 cents per pound. On April 10, the seller replied refusing to ship unless the recently delivered third carload should be paid for. On May 12, buyer's attorney threatened suit unless the undelivered lead should be shipped promptly and at the same time promised to pay on delivery 75 percent of the price of this prospective shipment together with the full price of the third installment already received. Seller's solicitor replied on May 22 that seller regarded the contract as "cancelled" as a result of buyer's failure to pay for lead already delivered. At the same time the letter stated the seller's willingness to deliver at the originally agreed price if the overdue payment should be made by return mail and a letter of credit established to cover the price of the lead not yet shipped. Buyer's attorney replied on May 25 that buyer had withheld the price of the third carload "only as a set-off by reason of the failure of your client to deliver" and that buyer would place the overdue payment in escrow and would accept the remaining lead if shipped to Philadelphia "sight draft attached for the full invoice price of each car". On May 27, seller's solicitors reiterated the position stated in their March 22 letter and on June 2 seller notified buyer that the Canadian government had imposed export control on lead. The district court found, and it is here admitted, that between October 1947 and May 1948 the market price of battery lead increased from 8.1 cents to 11 ½ cents per pound.

The court concluded that the failure of defendant to make a down payment of at least 63 percent of the price of the third carload constituted a breach of contract but "not such a material breach of the contract as to justify plaintiff in refusing to ship the balance due under the contract within the meaning of section 45 of The Sales Act". This was the decisive conclusion of law which the seller has challenged.

Section 45 of the Sales Act as in force in Pennsylvania provides in relevant part as follows: "Where there is a contract to sell goods to be delivered by stated instalments, which are to be separately paid for, and * * * the buyer neglects or refuses to * * * pay for one or more instalments, it depends in each case on the terms of the contract, and the circumstances of the case, whether the breach of

contract is so material as to justify the injured party in refusing to proceed further
* * * or whether the breach is severable, giving rise to a claim for compensation, but
not to a right to treat the whole contract as broken." Pa. Stat. Ann. Tit. 69, § 255
(Purdon, 1931).

We are dealing, therefore, with a situation in which the controlling statute
explicitly makes the circumstances of the particular case determine whether failure
to pay the price of one shipment delivered under an installment contract justifies the
seller in treating his own obligation with reference to future installments as ended.
Our problem is how to determine the legal effect of non-payment in a particular
case.

We think the key is to be found in the rational basis of the statute itself. The
flexibility of the statute reflects the impossibility of generalization about the
consequences of failure to pay promptly for installments as delivered. Yet, the
commercial sense of the statute yields two guiding considerations. First,
nonpayment for a delivered shipment may make it impossible or unreasonably
burdensome from a financial point of view for the seller to supply future
installments as promised. Second, buyer's breach of his promise to pay for one
installment may create such reasonable apprehension in the seller's mind
concerning payment for future installments that the seller should not be required to
take the risk involved in continuing deliveries. If any such consequence is proved,
the seller may rescind. Moreover, the Pennsylvania decisions indicate that these
embarrassments and apprehensions are normal consequences of non-payment; but
the cases also make it clear that they are not necessary consequences. * * *

In this case there is no evidence that the delay in payment for one carload made
it difficult to provide additional lead. To the contrary, seller admits that throughout
the period in controversy he had sufficient lead on hand for the full performance of
this contract. He could have delivered had he chosen to do so. His excuse, if any,
must be found in reasonable apprehension as to the future of the contract
engendered by buyer's behavior.

The district court's finding number 16, with which seller takes issue, is a direct
negation of the claim of reasonable apprehension upon which seller seeks to
establish under Section 45 of the Sales Act his asserted "right to treat the whole
contract as broken." It reads as follows: Plaintiff's claim of fear that the defendant
would not pay for the balance of battery lead due under Contract No. 5794 at the
contract price was without foundation and unreasonable."

In considering the propriety of this finding, it is to be borne in mind that the
point here is not the absence of legal justification for the withholding of an overdue

payment but rather whether, under the circumstances, that withholding gave the seller reason to believe that there was likelihood of continuing or additional default when and after he should deliver the rest of the lead in accordance with his promise. The substantiality of this alleged apprehension must be judged in the light of the uncontroverted finding that no impairment of buyer's credit had been shown. Moreover, the market was rising and all of the evidence indicates that buyer needed and urgently requested the undelivered lead. Indeed, as early as March 1, before the delivery of the carload for which payment was withheld, the buyer had complained quite urgently of the non-delivery of the entire balance of some 290,000 pounds overdue since December. Thereafter, when the seller shipped 43,000 pounds, about one-seventh of what was due, the buyer insisted that he was withholding payment because of the delay in delivery of the overdue balance. The court's finding that buyer had waived any claim for damages for delay up to that time does not alter this factual picture or its rational implications. In these circumstances, the trial court was justified in concluding that buyer's explanation of his conduct merited belief and that seller had no valid reason to be fearful that payment would not be forthcoming upon full delivery.

The clincher here is provided by the additional evidence concerning the possibility of delivery with sight draft attached. While there is no specific finding on the point, the evidence, including testimony tendered on behalf of seller, shows without dispute that at the beginning of this series of contracts, the seller had the privilege of shipping on sight draft but elected not to do so. And just before the collapse of the efforts of the parties to work out their difficulties amicably, the buyer specifically proposed that the seller assure himself of prompt payment by the use of sight drafts accompanying shipments. It is again important that at this time the market was substantially higher than the contract price and that seller was advised of buyer's urgent need for lead to meet his own commitments. In such circumstances it is incredible that the buyer would refuse to honor sight drafts for the contract price. These facts considered together leave no basis for reasonable apprehension concerning payment.

There is one other relevant and important fact. Throughout the controversial period the seller, with a stock of lead on hand adequate for the full performance of this contract, was using this lead in a rising market for sales to other purchasers at prices higher than agreed in the present contract. The inference was not only allowable but almost inescapable that desire to avoid a bad bargain rather than apprehension that the buyer would not carry out that bargain caused the seller to renounce the agreement and charge the buyer with repudiation. Rescission for such cause is not permissible. *See Truitt v. Guenther Lumber Co.*, 1920, 73 Pa. Super. 445, 450.

It follows that the seller has failed to establish justification for decision under Section 45 of the Sales Act and that judgment for the buyer on the counterclaim was proper. The judgment will be affirmed.

Notes

1. How should *Plotnick* be analyzed and decided under the UCC? *See Cassidy Podell Lynch, Inc. v. SnyderGeneral Corp.*, 944 F.2d 1131 (3rd Cir. 1991), holding that buyer's failure to pay one installment did not alone justify cancellation and that concerns over future payments should be resolved through a demand for adequate assurance under UCC 2-609(1).

2. As a law professor, Ellen A. Peters was highly critical of UCC 2-612, especially as it applied to the buyer's remedies upon breach by an installment seller. She called it a "law professor's delight" in that it required "wandering through a maze of inconsistent statutory standards and elliptical cross references." Ellen A. Peters, *Remedies for Breach of Contracts Relating to the Sale of Goods Under the Uniform Commercial Code: A Roadmap for Article Two,* 73 YALE L.J. 199, 223-27 (1963). Review UCC 2-612 as amended in 2003. Has any improvement been made?

3. As a Justice on the Supreme Court of Connecticut, Ellen Peters had an opportunity to apply UCC 2-612(3) to a default by the buyer in payment.

In *Cherwell-Ralli, Inc. v. Rytman Grain Co., Inc.*, 433 A.2d 984 (Conn. 1980), the buyer fell behind in payment for nineteen accepted shipments under an oral installment contract with the seller. Nevertheless, the buyer demanded adequate assurance of due performance, based upon a concern that the seller would close its plant due to product shortages. The seller gave adequate assurances, stating that deliveries would continue if the buyer paid his account. The buyer issued a check for some of the arrearage but then, because of renewed but unfounded concerns about the seller's capacity to perform, stopped payment. The parties reached an impasse in discussions over payment and performance and, ultimately, the seller closed its plant because it could not deliver the goods and canceled the contract. The seller sued for the price of goods accepted and the buyer counterclaimed for damages caused by the seller's failure to deliver the balance of the installments.

The Supreme Court affirmed the trial court's decision that the buyer, not the seller, had breached the contract. The court, speaking through Justice Peters, reached the following conclusions:

(1) On the facts, the improper order to stop payment of the check coupled with the substantial arrearages in payment was a breach which impaired the value of the "whole" contract under UCC 2-612(3);

(2) If the breach is of the "whole," the seller may cancel the contract without invoking the adequate assurance provisions of UCC 2-609;

(3) The seller did not reinstate the contract by bringing suit to recover the price of past installments: UCC 2-612(3) does not apply where the seller has canceled and sued for past installments due;

(4) The trial court was correct in concluding that the buyer had no "reasonable grounds for insecurity," either before or after the check was issued; and

(5) Implicitly, the seller could cancel the contract even though the breach related to payments due after delivery and the buyer did not repudiate its obligation to make future payments.

Note: Avoidance for Breach of Installment Contract Under the CISG

Article 73, which applies in the "case of a contract for delivery of goods by installments," follows the pattern of UCC 2-612. Subsection (1) provides that if the failure of one party to perform "any of his obligations in respect of any installment constitutes a fundamental breach of contract with respect to that installment, the other party may declare the contract avoided with respect to that installment." This subsection is not limited to avoidance by the buyer, as is UCC 2-612(2), and there is no reference to "cure," unlike former 2-612(2). Must the buyer notify the seller when an installment (as opposed to the contract) is avoided? *See* Art. 39(1). *See also* Art. 26. Would the seller have a right to cure under Article 48(1)? Does Article 46 give the buyer remedies after the installment is avoided?

Article 73(2) permits either party to avoid the contract if a breach "in respect of any installments gives [that party] good grounds to conclude that a fundamental breach of contract will occur with respect to future installments." The effect of a proper avoidance for fundamental breach is that the avoiding party has access to the remedies provided in Articles 75 and 76 and is subject to the provisions of Articles 81-84, stating the effects of avoidance.

How would a case like *Plotnick, supra*, be decided under the CISG? Is there any difference between the "substantial impairment" test in UCC 2-612(3) and the definition of "fundamental breach" in Article 25 of the CISG?

Note: Cancellation Under UCITA

UCITA provides more detail on the cancellation remedy than does either Article 2 or Article 2A. Read UCITA 802. Notice the following: (i) cancellation requires a material breach, subs. (a); (ii) a procedure for effecting cancellation is set forth in sub. (b); and (iii) the rights of the parties subsequent to a cancellation are explained in detail in subs. (c). Should Article 2 or Article 2A provide that same amount of detail? Why or why not?

SECTION 3.   REMEDIES OF SELLER AND LESSOR

A. Availability and Cumulative Effect

As we have already discussed, the seller or lessor is entitled to a remedy whenever the buyer or lessee has breached the contract. UCC 2-703, 2A-523. The remedies listed in those sections are designed to fulfill the general remedial policy of putting the aggrieved party in the position it would have been in if the contract had been performed. UCC 1-305 [former 1-106]. Although UCC 1-305 and most of the catalogued remedies seem to protect the so-called "expectation" interest, the residual power of a court to award "damages in any manner that is reasonable under the circumstances," UCC 2-703(2)(m), could cover reliance and restitution damages in proper situations.

The seller or lessor has four basic damage remedies available to it to measure the value of the buyer's or lessee's promised performance. Those four remedies are an action for the price or rent (UCC 2-709, 2A-529),[*] damages based upon a substitute transaction of resale or releasing the goods (UCC 2-706, 2A-527), damages based upon the market price of the goods (UCC 2-708(1), 2A-528(1)), and damages based upon the seller's or lessor's lost profit (UCC 2-708(2), 2A-528(2)). In addition, the seller or lessor may recover incidental damages (UCC 2-710(1), 2A-530(1)) and based upon the 2003 amendments, consequential damages except as against a consumer in a consumer contract (UCC 2-710(2) and (3), 2A-530(2) and (3)).

A constant theme is whether the seller or lessor is able to freely choose its

---

[*] Under the 2003 amendments, the seller or lessor may obtain specific performance as provided in UCC 2-716(1) or 2A-507A(1) unless the buyer's or lessee's sole remaining contractual obligation is the payment of money.

remedy or whether there are constraints on the availability of a particular remedy in a particular case. Read UCC 2-703, comment 1 which states that remedies are cumulative and the doctrine of election of remedies as a fundamental policy is rejected. However, it is clear that the seller or lessor cannot, for example, obtain both the price or rent and damages based upon the market price of the goods. Such a recovery would violate the basic remedial policy of putting the aggrieved party in the position it would have been in if the breaching party had performed. Rather, the question of choice of remedy arises in situations where there are two ways to measure expectation damages and the plaintiff selects the one with the greatest yield. For example, the seller may resell the goods and then sue for damages based on UCC 2-708(1) rather than UCC 2-706(1) or sue for lost profits rather than the contract price-market price differential. Another example is a seller attempting to recover market price based damages as that remedy results in a greater damage award than the award of lost profits.

As you work through the materials that follow keep in mind the following two questions: (i) How are damages measured under each section; and (ii) when is the seller or lessor entitled to the remedy.

B. Action for the Price, Rent, or Specific Performance

Apart from specific performance, the remedy that comes the closest to giving the seller or the lessor the value of the lessee's promised performance is the action for the price or rent. Read UCC 2-709 and 2A-529. In what circumstances may the seller or lessor recover the price of the goods or the rent for the goods? Note that the question is closely related to credit decisions made by the seller or lessor. Is there an agreement that the buyer or lessee can pay after the goods are delivered?[*] UCC 2-709(1) provides that the seller has an action for the price when the buyer "fails to pay the price as it becomes due." If the seller has agreed to let the buyer pay in installments after delivery of the goods, the seller should use an acceleration clause in order to be able to recover for all installments when one installment payment is missed. *See* UCC 1-309 [former 1-208].

The seller has an action for the price in three situations. What are they? UCC

---

[*] The action for the price or rent is not concerned with whether the seller or lessor can retrieve the goods when the buyer or lessee fails to pay after delivery of the goods. Review UCC 2-507, 2-702, 2A-525 and the material from Chapter Nine, *supra*. The surest way for the seller of goods to be able to retrieve the goods if the buyer has not paid for them is to take and perfect an Article 9 security interest.

2-709. What are the three situations when the lessor may obtain the rent from the lessee? UCC 2A-529. Obtaining the price or rent is a neat, clean and efficient remedy. The seller or lessor gets cash for the goods without the loss of any business volume and the buyer or lessee assumes the burden of taking over and disposing of the goods. It is, loosely speaking, like specific performance, although the seller or lessor must ultimately get a money judgment that is enforced against the buyer's or lessee's property. In fact, one court has said that the equitable remedy of specific performance and the Code's action for the price are "virtually identical."* Do you agree?

After the 2003 amendments, the remedy of specific performance is now available to a seller or lessor. Read UCC 2-716 and 2A-507A. Suppose that the parties agree that upon default by the buyer in payment the seller can have specific performance. The seller delivers the goods in a single lot and thereafter the buyer defaults in payment. Is that agreement enforceable? Under what circumstances can a seller or lessor obtain specific performance for the payment of money?

In one situation, the buyer or lessee is responsible is liable for the price or rent even though the seller or lessor still has the goods. UCC 2-709(1)(b), 2A-529(1)(b). Why should the seller or lessor have the burdens of possession and disposition in that situation? According to Professor Llewellyn:

> But then decently admeasured damages are all a seller needs, and are just what a seller needs, when the mercantile buyer repudiates. It is, indeed, social wisdom * * * (to require the seller) in most cases which have not involved shipment to a distant point, to dispose of whatever goods may have come into existence or into his warehouse; that is its business, and the buyer's prospective inability has already been evidenced. To force such goods on the buyer, where they are reasonably marketable by the seller, is social waste * * *.

Karl N. Llewellyn, *Through Title to Contract and A Bit Beyond*, 15 N.Y.U. L.Q. REV. 158, 176-177 (1938).

Problem 10-5

Seller, a manufacturer, agreed to sell to Buyer 100 customized lathes at $500 per lathe, delivery FOB Seller's Place of Business on November 1. Payment was due 30 days after delivery. On November 1, Seller delivered the lathes to the

---

* *Schumann v. Levi*, 728 F.2d 1141 (8th Cir.1984).

carrier.

A. On November 5, the carrier delivered the lathes to Buyer. On December 1, Buyer sent Seller a fax stating that it would not accept the lathes as they did not meet Buyer's needs. Does Seller have a viable action for the price of the lathes? What do you need to know to answer the question? UCC 2-602, 2-606, 2-608.*

B. On November 5, the carrier called Buyer to inform Buyer that the lathes had been destroyed in an unfortunate train derailment while in route to Buyer. Does Seller have a viable action for the price of the lathes? What do you need to know to answer the question? UCC 2-509, 2-510.

C. On October 30, Buyer told Seller it would not accept the lathes as Buyer no longer needed them. On November 20, Seller consulted you and wanted to know if it would be successful in an action for the price against Buyer. Seller tells you that it could possibly sell the lathes for $25,000 to $30,000 but has no knowledge of another buyer who could use the lathes as customized for Buyer. Seller will not pursue this remedy unless you give it an opinion that the odds are at least even that it will win the law suit. A Summer Associate has given you the extract, below, from *Foxco Indus., Ltd. v. Fabric World, Inc.*, 595 F.2d 976, 983-84 (5th Cir. 1979):

> UCC § 2-709(1)(b), that portion of § 2-709 which would apply here, provides that an action for the price of goods may be maintained "if the seller is unable after *reasonable* effort to resell them at a *reasonable* price or the circumstances *reasonably* indicate that such effort will be unavailing." Ala. Code tit. 7, § 2-709(1)(b) (1977) (emphasis added). The Official Comment to § 2-709 states, in pertinent part, that:

>> 2. The action for the price is now generally limited to those cases where resale of the goods is impracticable * * *

>> 3. This section substitutes an objective test by action for the former "not readily resalable" standard. An action for the price under subsection (1)(b) can be sustained only after a "reasonable effort to resell" the goods "at reasonable price" has actually been made or where the circumstances "reasonably indicate" that such an effort will be unavailing.

> Ala. Code tit. 7, § 7-2-709, Official Comment (1977). As was recognized in *Multi-Line Manufacturing, Inc. v. Greenwood Mills, Inc.*, 123 Ga. App.

---

* *See Brandeis Machinery and Supply Co. v. Capital Crane Rental, Inc.*, 765 N.E.2d 173 (Ind. Ct. App. 2002) (an effective but wrongful rejection precluded recovery of the contract price).

372, 180 S.E.2d 917 (1971), a case involving the cancellation of a contract to purchase fabric, the language of § 2-709(1)(b) "clearly evinces legislative intent that these matters ordinarily should be subject to determination by a jury * * * ." *Id.* at 373, 180 S.E.2d at 918. Thus, we will reverse only if, as a matter of law, there was no way in which the jury could find that Foxco was unable, after reasonable effort, to resell the fabric at a reasonable price or that it was reasonably clear that an effort to resell would have been fruitless.

The evidence at trial clearly established that all of Foxco's goods were specially manufactured for the customer who ordered them and that it was difficult for Foxco to resell fabric manufactured for one purchaser to another buyer. Further, it was normally very difficult to sell Foxco's spring fabric after the spring buying season had ended; the precipitous decline of the knitted fabric market presented an additional barrier to resale. It was not until the next spring buying season returned that Foxco, in September 1975, finally sold a portion of the goods identified to Fabric World's October 1974 order.

Fabric World argues that Foxco made no effort whatsoever to resell the goods during the months that intervened (between the contract breach and Foxco's eventual disposition of the fabric in September 1975) despite the presence of some market for the goods in that interim period. Thus Fabric World concludes, the requisites of § 2-709(1)(b) were not satisfied. Under § 2-709(1)(b), however, Foxco was required only to use *reasonable* efforts to resell its goods at a *reasonable* price. From the time of Fabric World's breach to September 1975 there was a 50% decline in the market price of this material. We cannot say that the jury was precluded from finding that Foxco acted reasonably under the circumstances or that there was no reasonable price at which Foxco could sell these goods. Fabric World breached its contract with Foxco, and the jury was entitled to a charge which gave Foxco the full benefit of its original bargain. * * *

Will you give Seller such an opinion?

D. If Seller is entitled to the price in (C) above, what are Seller's obligations in regard to the goods? UCC 2-709(2).

Problem 10-6

Seller, a manufacturer, agreed to sell to Buyer 100 customized lathes at $500 per lathe, delivery FOB Seller's Place of Business on November 1. Buyer agreed to pay the price of $50,000 in four equal, monthly installments of $12,500 each, starting on November 1. Buyer accepted the lathes on November 1, paid the first installment on November 1, and then failed to pay the installment due on December 1. What is Seller's remedy? Suppose Buyer failed to pay the November 1 installment and repudiated the contract and wrongfully attempted to revoke acceptance of the goods on November 15. Could Seller cancel the contract, accelerate the obligation, and sue for the price of all goods accepted? *See* UCC 2-610, 2-612, 2-709.

Note: Action for the Price Under the CISG

Article 53 of the CISG states that the buyer "must pay the price for the goods and take delivery of them as required by the contract and this Convention." The seller's remedies when the buyer "fails to perform any of his obligations under the contract" are stated in Articles 61-65. Assuming that the seller does not avoid the contract for fundamental breach, Article 62 provides that the seller "may require the buyer to pay the price. * * * unless the seller has resorted to a remedy which is inconsistent with this requirement." This remedy appears to be available even though the buyer's only obligation is payment of money.

The parties may agree that the buyer is to pay part or all of the price before, at, or after delivery of the goods. *See* Article 59. If there is no agreement as to when the price is to be paid, Article 58 provides the default rules. Review that Article, please.

To the extent that Article 62 gives the seller a specific performance remedy for the price, the effect of Article 28 must be considered. Read literally, a court in the United States is not required to enter a judgment for specific performance under the CISG "unless the court would do so under its own law in respect to similar contracts of sale not governed by the Convention." Under Article 2 prior to the 2003 amendments, there was no specific performance provision for the seller or lessor, although the remedy was available at common law. Under the 2003 amendments the remedy is now available but is limited. How would Article 62 fare under the 2003 amendments?

Note: Action for the Price Under UCITA

The contract price may be recovered under UCITA 808(b)(1)(A) for any performance the licensee has accepted or been provided under UCITA 604. If the licensee has not accepted or been provided the performance, the contract price is not the measure of damages but is the cap on the direct damages.

C. Resale, Release, or Substitute Transactions

If an action for the price is not available and the seller or lessor has the goods intended for the breached contract on hand, the next best remedy may be to resell or release those goods to a third person and fix damages under UCC 2-706 or 2A-527. Read UCC 2-706, answer the following questions about it and then work Problem 10-7.
- If the resale is proper, what is Seller's measure of damages? UCC 2-706(1).
- What conditions must be met to satisfy UCC 2-706(1)? Does it make any difference whether the resale is public or private? *See* UCC 2-706(2), (3), (4).
- Suppose at the time of the breach that the goods do not yet exist or existing goods have not yet been identified to the contract. Is resale available? UCC 2-706(2). *See* UCC 2-704(2).
- Suppose in a private resale that Seller fails to give reasonable notification to Buyer. Is the resale proper? UCC 2-706(2).
- What are the rights of the resale buyer if the resale itself is defective? UCC 2-706(5).
- Suppose the resale price exceeds the contract price. Must Seller account to Buyer for the surplus? UCC 2-706(6).
- Suppose the resale fails to satisfy the requirements of UCC 2-706. Does Seller have any other available remedies? *See* amended UCC 2-706(7) and cmt. 11.
Now read UCC 2A-527. How does it differ from the resale remedy in UCC 2-706?

If the buyer has prepaid for the goods in whole or part and then breached the contract so that the seller justifiably withholds or stops delivery of the goods, the buyer is entitled to restitution of the price subject to offset for the seller's damages. UCC 2-718(2) through (4). *Compare* UCC 2A-504(3) and (4).

Problem 10-7

Seller, a manufacturer in Chicago, agreed to sell to Buyer, located in Phoenix, 100 standard lathes at $500 per lathe, delivery in four equal installments, FOB Chicago, on November 1, December 1, January 1, and February 1. Payment was due 30 days after delivery. Seller delivered the first installment of lathes to the carrier on November 1 and received a $12,500 payment from Buyer. Buyer, however, was dissatisfied with the shipment and threatened not to pay for any more lathes. Seller withheld delivery of the remaining installments and tried to negotiate with Buyer regarding Buyer's dissatisfaction.

On December 4, Buyer repudiated the entire contract. Assume that Buyer's repudiation substantially impaired the value of the contract to Seller. UCC 2-610, 2-612(3). Seller has three installments of lathes, for which Buyer agreed to pay $37,500 ($12,500 per installment) on hand and identified to the contract. Seller would like to resell all of those lathes, either in Chicago or Phoenix, and obtain the maximum damages under UCC 2-706.

It is now December 15 and you have the following facts before you: The cost of shipping each installment of lathes from Illinois to Phoenix is $2,000. The market price of an installment of lathes on December 4 was $11,500 in Illinois and $13,000 in Phoenix. On December 1, the respective prices were $12,000 in Illinois and $12,500 in Phoenix. It is estimated that on January 1, the respective prices will be $7,500 in Illinois and $10,000 in Phoenix and that on February 1 the respective prices will be $8,000 in Illinois and $10,000 in Phoenix.

A. What must Seller do to conduct a resale that it can use to measure its damages under UCC 2-706?

B. What remedy, if any, is available if the conditions of UCC 2-706 are not satisfied? How should you plan for this contingency? Remember, some courts have held that a seller who acts in bad faith is limited to the damages that should have been recovered under UCC 2-706 if all the conditions had been met.

C. If, upon resale, you satisfy the conditions of UCC 2-706, are you foreclosed from using UCC 2-708(1)? Have you made an election of remedies? *See* UCC 2-703, cmt. 1. We will return again to this question after we consider damages based upon market price or the seller's lost profit.

D. If Seller was leasing the lathes to Buyer, how would your analysis change? Does it matter whether Seller tries to release or sell the lathes?

AFRAM EXPORT CORP. V. METALLURGIKI HALYPS, S.A.
UNITED STATES COURT OF APPEALS, SEVENTH CIRCUIT, 1985
772 F.2D 1358

POSNER, CIRCUIT JUDGE

The appeal and cross-appeal in this diversity breach of contract suit raise a variety of interesting issues, in particular of personal jurisdiction and contract damages.

Afram Export Corporation, the plaintiff, is a Wisconsin corporation that exports scrap metal. Metallurgiki Halyps, S.A., the defendant, is a Greek corporation that makes steel. In 1979, after a series of trans-Atlantic telephone and telex communications, the parties made a contract through an exchange of telex messages for the purchase by Metallurgiki of 15,000 tons of clean shredded scrap, at $135 per ton, F.O.B. Milwaukee, delivery to be made by the end of April. Metallurgiki apparently intended to use the scrap to make steel for shipment to Egypt, pursuant to a contract with an Egyptian buyer. Afram agreed to pay the expenses of an agent of Metallurgiki–Shields–to inspect the scrap for cleanliness before it was shipped.

The scrap for the contract was prepared, in Milwaukee, by Afram Metal Processing Company. Both Afram Metal Processing and the plaintiff Afram Export are wholly owned subsidiaries of Afram Brothers. All three are Wisconsin corporations, and have the same officers and directors. Unless otherwise indicated, when we say "Afram" we mean "Afram Export."

Shields arrived to inspect the scrap on April 12. He told Afram that the scrap was clean but that Metallurgiki would not accept it, because the price of scrap had fallen. Sure enough, Metallurgiki refused to accept it. Afram brought this suit after selling the scrap to other buyers. Metallurgiki unsuccessfully challenged the court's jurisdiction over it, then filed a counterclaim alleging that Afram had broken the contract and had thereby made it impossible for Metallurgiki to fulfill its contract with the Egyptian purchaser.

After a bench trial, the district judge gave judgment for Afram for $425,149 and dismissed the counterclaim. 592 F. Supp. 446 (D. Wis.1984). Metallurgiki has appealed from the judgment for Afram, and Afram has cross-appealed, contending that the judge should have given it the full damages it sought based on the difference between the contract price and the cover price–$483,750–plus incidental damages of $40,665, prejudgment interest, the costs of a so-called public sale, and attorney's fees for defending against the counterclaim. * * *

Afram claims that it sold all of the scrap rejected by Metallurgiki at a public sale on June 15, 1979, and that its damages should therefore be based on the price of that sale, which was $102.75 per ton. The district judge disagreed. He found that two-thirds of the scrap had been sold at a substantially higher price to Luria Brothers on June 4 ($118–actually somewhat less, because Afram defrayed some freight costs) and the other third to International Traders on September 15 at a price of $103. Afram points out that the sale on June 4 actually was made by its affiliate, Afram Metal Processing Company, and further argues that since all Afram scrap is sold from the same pile in Milwaukee it is arbitrary to treat the first sale after the breach of contract as the cover transaction, rather than the sale that Afram designated as that transaction.

We agree with the district judge that the sale on June 4 was a cover transaction, even though the nominal seller was a different corporation from the plaintiff. Not only are both corporations wholly owned subsidiaries of another corporation, not only do all three corporations have the same officers and directors, but the record indicates substantial commingling of assets and operation of the three corporations as a single entity. Shortly after Metallurgiki's rejection, Zeke Afram, an officer of both Afram Export (the party to the contract with Metallurgiki) and Afram Metal Processing (the nominal owner of the scrap sold on June 4), called Luria Brothers and explained that he had extra scrap for sale because of a buyer's breach; apparently he did not bother to indicate which Afram corporation he was calling on behalf of. The June 4 sale followed shortly. The conversation and the timing of the sale are powerful evidence that the breach enabled the sale–that it would not have occurred but for the breach–and hence that the revenue from the sale must be subtracted from the contract price to determine Afram's loss. * * *

But this does not dispose completely of the issue of the cover price. If the sale on June 15 was "made in good faith and in a commercially reasonable manner," it fixed Afram's damages on the remaining one-third of the scrap. UCC § 2-706(1), Wis. Stat. § 402.706(1). The question may seem less than earthshaking since the June 15 sale price and the September sale price which the district court used as the cover price for the remaining third were only 25 [cents] per ton apart. But the bona fides of the June 15 sale casts additional light on the intercorporate relations of the Afram group and hence on the proper interpretation of the sale to Luria Brothers. In any event, the district judge was entitled to find that neither condition in section 2-706(1) was satisfied. * * * The June 15 "sale" was about as pure a bookkeeping transaction–as empty of economic significance–as can be imagined. * * * It consisted of a transfer of the scrap on the books of one affiliated corporation to the books of another. The transferor and transferee were not only under common ownership but were operated as if they were limbs of a single organism. The scrap itself was not moved; it remained on the scrap heap till sold later on. No invoice or check for the sale was produced at trial. The inference that the sale was designed simply to maximize the enterprise's damages, leaving it free to resell the scrap at higher prices later on, is overpowering. The sale of the scrap three months later to International Traders at a (slightly) higher price provided better evidence of what the enterprise actually lost, so far as the scrap not sold to Luria Brothers is concerned, by Metallurgiki's breach of contract.

[Afram claimed that it borrowed $2.5 million from a bank, of which $2.025 was used to purchase junked cars which were shredded to produce the scrap for this contract. It paid $40,000 in interest on this loan between the date of breach and the date of cover. The court first held that a seller cannot recover consequential damages under Article 2, relying on the restrictive language in UCC 1-106(1). Because there was no provision authorizing specific performance for the seller, Afram's claim to the interest must be as incidental damages under UCC 2-715(1) or not at all. The court noted that the case was in the middle between two extremes, one where the buyer's failure to pay on time caused the seller to default on the loan and go into bankruptcy (consequential damages), and the other where the seller paid interest on a loan taken out after breach to dispose of the scrap (incidental damages). The court agreed with the district court, however, that the interest claimed was consequential damages. On incomplete evidence, it appeared that Afram was complaining about the loss of use of the money promised (an "opportunity cost") rather than interest as an additional expense. Since Afram was claiming the profit lost because the promised payment could not be invested in a valuable opportunity, the claim was for consequential damage and could not be recovered under UCC 2-706(1).] * * *

But a forgone profit from exploiting a valuable opportunity that the breach of contract denied to the victim of the breach fits more comfortably under the heading of consequential damages than of incidental damages. The profits that Afram might have made from using that $2.025 million elsewhere in its business are like the milling profits that Hadley [*Hadley v. Baxendale*, 156 Eng. Rep. 145 (1854) Ed.] might have made if the carrier had not delayed in delivering the mill shaft for repair. Afram has not tried to establish its lost profits from the temporary loss of the use of the $2.025 million; all it is seeking is the extra interest it had to pay. But its theory is one of opportunity cost, as it makes clear in its brief by stating that it would be entitled to interest as incidental damages even if it had not used borrowed money to pay for the junked cars. Afram is correct that it would incur an opportunity cost whether it used its own money or used money that it had borrowed; in either event it would lose the use of money that it could deploy elsewhere at a profit. But we do not think the law has evolved to the point where every time a buyer breaks a contract, the seller is entitled to the time value of the money tied up in the contract, as incidental damages. All the seller is entitled to is an out-of-pocket interest expense that would not have been incurred but for the breach. We have found no case where (so far as we are able to determine from the statement of facts in the case) the seller was able to recover interest on a general business loan not tied to the subject matter of the sale, but we have found two cases that imply he may not. *See Schiavi Mobile Homes, Inc. v. Gironda,* 463 A.2d 722, 727 (Me. 1983); *S.C. Gray, Inc. v. Ford Motor Co.,* 92 Mich. App. 789, 811-12, 286 N.W.2d 34, 43-44 (1979). * * *

Thus we affirm the judgment of the district court except with respect to the denial of prejudgment interest to Afram, as to which we remand the case for a determination of the amount of prejudgment interest to which Afram is entitled at the statutory rate of five percent. Wis. Stat. § 138.04; * * *. No costs in this court.

Affirmed in part, reversed in part, and remanded.

Notes

1. Why was the public resale on June 15 at $102.75 per ton improper? Should the September resale price of $103 per ton be used to measure damages under UCC 2-706(1)? UCC 2-708(1)? Courts tend to give leeway in favor of a resale under UCC 2-706.*

2. According to the court, Afram was not a "lost volume" seller–but for the breach, Afram could not have resold the scrap. How, then, are the proceeds from the resale to be treated under UCC 2-706(1)? The answer, on these facts, is that Buyer's liability in damages should be reduced by any loss that Seller could have reasonably avoided after the breach. Thus, if Seller did resell or could have reasonably resold, those proceeds should be credited to the buyer. But doesn't UCC 2-706(1) [and UCC 2-708(1)] do that in the damage formula? Yes, it does.

3. Exactly how did Judge Posner classify and treat the interest payments made by Afram after the breach on an obligation incurred much earlier? If they are neither incidental nor consequential damages, what are they–fixed or "overhead" costs? In *Ernst Steel Corp. v. Horn Construction Division,* 104 A.D.2d 55, 481 N.Y.S.2d 833, 839 (1984), the court stated: "In an appropriate case a seller is entitled to recover commercially reasonable finance and interest charges incurred as a result of a buyer's breach as a proper item of incidental damages. * * * For the

---

* *See, e.g., Firwood Mfg. Co. v. General Tire, Inc.,* 96 F.3d 163 (6th Cir. 1996) (resale proper even though made three years after breach and good resold contained different but functionally similar components). *Compare Apex Oil Co. v. Belcher Co. of New York, Inc.,* 855 F.2d 997 (2nd Cir. 1988) (resale of fungible goods in fluctuating market six weeks after breach not commercially reasonable).

most part, however, interest expenses have only been awarded to sellers for indebtedness specifically identified to goods intended for resale to the breaching party and who, as a result of the breaching, cannot repay the loans." We return to the distinction between incidental and consequential damages in Section 3G, *infra*.

    4. **Consequential damages for a seller or lessor.** Former 2-710 and 2A-530 did not explicitly provide that the seller or lessor may recover consequential damages caused by a buyer's breach. *Compare* UCC 2-715(2), 2A-520. But does it foreclose such a recovery? Under UCC 1-305 [former 1-106], the answer is yes unless consequential damages are available "by other rule of law." The court in *Afram* did not explore whether a seller could recover consequential damages under non-code law in Wisconsin.

    Suppose that the buyer had promised to pay $100,000 on August 1 for scrap delivered on July 1 and knew that the seller needed prompt payment to renew an advantageous contract with another supplier. Despite assurances that payment would be made, the buyer did not pay and the contract was not renewed. The seller, although making reasonable efforts, was unable to obtain alternative financing. It is clear, is it not, that this is a proper case for a consequential damage claim under general contract law? *See* UCC 1-103; RESTATEMENT (SECOND) OF CONTRACTS 351, Comment (e). Does UCC 1-305 [former 1-106] preclude access to the common law?[*] Amended Articles 2 and 2A allow the seller or lessor in non-consumer contracts to obtain consequential damages. *See* UCC 2-710(2) and (3), 2A-530(2) and (3). We will explore seller's and lessor's consequential damages in Section 3G, *infra*.

Note: Disposition by Lease of Goods under Article 2A

    A default by the lessee under Article 2A adds some wrinkles to the so-called "resale" remedy. Suppose, for example, that the lessee has possession of the goods and fails to make a payment when due. Under UCC 2A-525(2), the lessor has the right to take possession of the goods, either without judicial process if there is no breach of the peace or by an appropriate judicial action. UCC 2A-525(3). Unless there is a perfected security interest or a right to reclaim the goods, the seller does not have this remedy under Article 2.

---

[*] *See Linc Equipment Services Inc. v. Signal Medical Devices, Inc.*, 319 F.3d 288 (7th Cir. 2003) (stating in dicta that the failure to mention consequential damages in former 2A-530 does not preclude the lessor from recovering such damages).

If the lessor has or retakes possession of the goods after the lessee's breach, the lessor may then "dispose of the goods concerned or the undelivered balance thereof by lease, sale, or otherwise." UCC 2A-527(1). If the disposition is by "sale or otherwise," the damage formula in UCC 2A-528(1) applies. UCC 2A-527(3). But if the disposition is by "lease agreement substantially similar to the original lease agreement" and the new lease agreement is made in good faith and in a commercially reasonable manner, then recovery of damages as provided in UCC 2A-527(2) is allowed:

> [T]he lessor may recover from the lessee as damages (i) accrued and unpaid rent as of the date of the commencement of the term of the new lease agreement, (ii) the present value, as of the same date, of the total rent for the then remaining lease term of the original lease agreement, minus the present value, as of the same date, of the rent under the new lease agreement applicable to that period of the new lease term which is comparable to the then remaining term of the original lease agreement, and (iii) any incidental or consequential damages allowed...less expenses saved in consequence of the lessee's default.

"Present value" is defined in amended UCC 2A-103(1)(aa). If the disposition by lease does not qualify under the requirements of UCC 2A-527(2), the lessor must claim and prove damages under UCC 2A-528.

Note: Substitute Transactions Under the CISG

Article 75 of the CISG provides that "if the contract is avoided and if, in a reasonable manner and within a reasonable time after avoidance, * * * the seller has resold the goods, the party claiming damages may recover the difference between the contract price and the price in the substitute transaction as well as any further damages recoverable under Article 74." As we have seen, for a seller to avoid the contract, the buyer must have committed a fundamental breach, *see* Art. 25, 64(1)(a), and the seller must make the declaration of avoidance required by Article 26 and satisfy the procedural requirements of Article 64(2). The avoidance rules are more complicated where there is an installment contract. *See* Art. 73.

Suppose that the buyer failed to pay the price on the agreed date. Assuming that the delay would not be a fundamental breach, the seller can fix an additional period or reasonable time for performance by the buyer. Art. 63(1). Suppose the seller says "I will give you an additional five days to pay." If the buyer fails to pay by then, the seller may avoid the contract under Art. 64(1)(b) and resell the goods.

Note: Substitute Transactions Under UCITA

UCITA's damages scheme is somewhat different given that in many instances information is licensed under a non-exclusive license. Substitute transactions made possible by the licensee's breach are thus not the usual case. If a substitute transaction is made possible by the breach, UCITA 808(b)(1)(B) allows for either the substitute license price or the market price to provide the measure of direct damages. Notice that the measurement principle in UCITA 808 is subject to the remedial principles in UCITA 807 and 801.

D. Contract-Market Damages

Suppose Seller and Buyer have a contract under which Seller is to deliver equipment for Buyer's plant for the price of $20,000. If Buyer repudiates or fails to make a payment due before delivery, any one of the following situations might exist. First, the equipment may exist and be identified to the contract or be very close to that status. *See* UCC 2-704(1). As noted, Seller may be able to recover the price under UCC 2-709(1)(b) or resell them under UCC 2-706. Second, the equipment may not exist. No orders have been placed or no work commenced at the time of breach. Here, Seller is likely to stop work on the contract and seek a remedy other than the price or resale. Third, the equipment may not be finished (conform to the contract) but work may be started or orders placed and substantial costs incurred by Seller. Here UCC 2-704(2) gives Seller a choice, if "reasonable commercial judgment" is exercised, to "either complete the manufacture and wholly identify the goods to the contract or cease manufacture and resell for scrap or salvage value or proceed in any other reasonable manner." If Seller chooses to complete, an action for the price or a resale may be available. If Seller chooses to stop work and salvage, Seller must seek another remedy.

A possible other remedy is to seek damages under UCC 2-708. *See* UCC 2-703. But the measures of damages under UCC 2-708 are strikingly different: Subsection (1), an objective standard, measures loss by the difference between the market price and the contract price while subsection (2), a subjective standard, allows recovery of the "profit (including reasonable overhead) which the seller would have made from full performance by the buyer * * * " on the particular contract in dispute. Subsection (2) is available to the seller if damages under subsection (1) or UCC 2-706 are "inadequate to put the seller in as good a position as performance would have done."

These options pose two important questions: (i) What limitations, if any, are imposed upon a seller's decision to pursue the remedy in UCC 2-708 subsection (1) or subsection (2); and (ii) Once a proper remedy has been selected, how are damages to be measured?[*]

Consider, first, UCC 2-708(1). The contract price-market price measure can be fraught with impropriety and difficulty. For example, suppose Seller selects subsection (1) in each of the three situations described above. In which, if any, would subsection (1) put Seller in the position it would have occupied if there had been full performance? As you can see, UCC 2-708(1) may either over-or-under compensate the seller. Should it be explicitly limited by the "expectation" compensation policy expressed in UCC 1-305 [former 1-106]?[**] Does UCC 2A-528 raise the same issues?

Former 2-708(1) required the market price be measured at the time and place of tender. That time of tender presented difficulties in the case of repudiation in long term contracts. Former 2-723(1) addressed that issue in a somewhat bizarre manner. If the case came up for trial before the time for performance as to *any* of the goods involved in the contract, time for measuring the market price for *any* of the goods was to be at the time of the repudiation. Thus the time for measurement of the market price changed depending upon when the trial happened. The 2003 amendments address the issue of measurement of a market price in the case of an anticipatory repudiation, UCC 2-708(1)(b), and deleted former 2-723(1). Apply the 2003 amendments to the following problem and consider how former 2-708(1) and 2-723 might have lead to a different result.

How to prove market price is addressed in UCC 2-723 and 2-724. *Compare* UCC 2A-507.

Problem 10-8

Seller, a manufacturer in Chicago, agreed to sell to Buyer, located in Phoenix, 100 standard lathes at $500 per lathe, delivery in four equal installments, FOB

---

[*] Remember that a breaching buyer who has prepaid in whole or part is entitled to restitution of the price when the goods have not been delivered to the buyer. UCC 2-718(2) and (3). *Compare* UCC 2A-504(3) and (4).

[**] *See Diversified Energy Inc. v. Tennessee Valley Authority*, 339 F.3d 437 (6th Cir. 2003) (middlemen with a set profit margin is not entitled to the market price remedy when its buyer breaches).

Chicago, on November 1, December 1, January 1, and February 1. Payment was due 30 days after delivery. Assume the deal was signed on July 1. On August 3, Buyer repudiated.

A. On August 5, Seller accepted Buyer's repudiation, canceled the contract and sued for damages under UCC 2-708(1). *See* UCC 2-610. The case came to trial in January and the following evidence was introduced: (1) The aggregate market price on August 5 in Illinois of the four lots was $40,000 and that price stayed steady throughout October; (2) Also in Illinois, the market value of the November installment was $10,000, the December installment was $11,000, the January installment was $12,500 and the February installment was estimated to be $12,000; (3) In Phoenix, the prices are the same except for the January lot, which was $10,000. Assuming that Seller has not resold the goods, to what damages is Seller entitled under UCC 2-708(1)? On the time and place for tender, *see* UCC 2-503. On proof of market price, *see* UCC 2-723.

B. Assume, on August 3, Seller decided to wait to see whether Buyer would retract the repudiation. UCC 2-611. Seller waited until October 15, then canceled the contract and sued for damages under UCC 2-708(1) and the case came up for trial in July of the following year. If Seller does not resell, will its damages be the same as in (A), above?

C. What if Seller had resold all 100 lathes on August 5 for $60,000? For $30,000? Is Seller bound by this election to resell? *See* UCC 2-706.

D. What if Seller successfully recovers damages based upon UCC 2-708(1) and, subsequent to the entry of judgment against Buyer, resells the lathes for $100,000. Does Buyer have any ground for protest?

E. Does your analysis of any of the above change if instead of a repudiation before the first delivery, Buyer wrongfully but effectively rejected the first shipment of standard lathes and repudiated its obligation under the contract to take any further shipments?

Note: Market Price Damages Under the CISG

The seller's comparable remedy under the CISG is found in Article 76. Note that the seller must avoid the contract and not make a resale under Article 75 before the seller can recover "the difference between the price fixed by the contract and the current price at the time of avoidance." Article 74 damages are also available. Even so, there must be a "current price" for the goods before Art. 76(1) applies. *See* Art. 76(2) defining "current price."

Note: Market Price Damages Under UCITA

UCITA 808(b)(1)(B) allows market price based damages if the breach makes possible a substitute transaction.

E. Lost Profit

In the scheme of things, UCC 2-708(2) appears to be the seller's remedy of last resort. An assumption is that if conforming goods can be identified before or after the breach, the seller will prefer either an action for the price under UCC 2-709 or damages based upon a resale under UCC 2-706. If those remedies fail, the seller can resort to damages under UCC 2-708. But which part of UCC 2-708, subsection (1) with its contract-market price formula, or subsection (2) which awards the "profit (including reasonable overhead) that the seller would have made from full performance by the buyer? "

The UCC answer is that UCC 2-708(2) is available if the measure of damages in UCC 2-706 (cross reference added by 2003 amendments) or 2-708 is "inadequate to put the seller in as good a position as performance would have done * * *. " There are two critical questions for the lawyer and judge: (i) When are the other measures of damages inadequate so that UCC 2-708(2) should be used to measure the seller's damages; and (ii) When UCC 2-708(2) is applicable, how should those damages be measured?[*] These questions have generated a continuing flow of law review commentary, much of which attempts to apply rather complex if not sophisticated economic analysis.[**]

The 2003 amendments to UCC 2-708(2), in addition to adding a cross reference to damages inadequate under UCC 2-706, deleted the language "due allowance for costs reasonably incurred and due credit for payments or proceeds of resale." Read

---

[*] Remember the breaching buyer's right to restitution when the buyer has prepaid and the goods have not been delivered to the buyer. UCC 2-718(2) and (3). *Compare* UCC 2A-504(3) and (4).

[**] For an example, *see* Paul E. Caselton, Note, *Lost-Profits Damage Awards Under Uniform Commercial Code Section 2-708(2),* 37 STAN. L. REV. 1109 (1985). For a clear and sensible analysis, *see* John A. Sebert, *Jr., Remedies Under Article Two of the Uniform Commercial Code: An Agenda for Review,* 130 U. PA. L. REV. 360, 383-407 (1981). *See generally* Robert E. Scott, *The Case for Market Damages: Revisiting the Lost Profits Puzzle,* 57 U. CHI. L. REV. 1155, 1165-68, 1179-86 (1990).

the amended Comment 1 for an explanation for that change. Will it change the analysis of how damages are measured under this subsection?

As usual, Article 2A adopts the same approach as Article 2, UCC 2A-528(2), except that it does not contain a cross reference to the lessor's damages based upon releasing.[*]

Consider the following case which confronts the issue of if lost profit is the appropriate measure of damages when the seller has resold the goods to another buyer.

R.E. DAVIS CHEMICAL CORP. V. DIASONICS, INC.
UNITED STATES COURT OF APPEALS, SEVENTH CIRCUIT, 1987
826 F.2D 678

CUDAHY, Circuit Judge

Diasonics, Inc. appeals from the orders of the district court denying its motion for summary judgment and granting R.E. Davis Chemical Corp.'s summary judgment motion. Diasonics also appeals from the order dismissing its third-party complaint against Dr. Glen D. Dobbin and Dr. Galdino Valvassori. We affirm the dismissal of the third-party complaint, reverse the grant of summary judgment in favor of Davis and remand for further proceedings.

I.

Diasonics is a California corporation engaged in the business of manufacturing and selling medical diagnostic equipment. Davis is an Illinois corporation that contracted to purchase a piece of medical diagnostic equipment from Diasonics. On or about February 23, 1984, Davis and Diasonics entered into a written contract under which Davis agreed to purchase the equipment. Pursuant to this agreement, Davis paid Diasonics a $300,000 deposit on February 29, 1984. Prior to entering into its agreement with Diasonics, Davis had contracted with Dobbin and Valvassori to establish a medical facility where the equipment was to be used. Dobbin and Valvassori subsequently breached their contract with Davis. Davis then breached its contract with Diasonics; it refused to take delivery of the equipment or to pay the balance due under the agreement. Diasonics later resold the equipment to a third party for the same price at which it was to be sold to Davis.

Davis sued Diasonics, asking for restitution of its $300,000 down payment

---

[*] For an example of a case under former 2A-528, *see The Corner v. Pinnacle, Inc.,* 907 P.2d 1281 (Wyo. 1995).

under section 2-718(2) of the Uniform Commercial Code (the "UCC" or the "Code"). Ill. Rev. Stat. ch. 26, para. 2-718(2) (1985). Diasonics counterclaimed. Diasonics did not deny that Davis was entitled to recover its $300,000 deposit less $500 as provided in section 2-718(2)(b). However, Diasonics claimed that it was entitled to an offset under section 2-718(3). Diasonics alleged that it was a "lost volume seller," and, as such, it lost the profit from one sale when Davis breached its contract. Diasonics' position was that, in order to be put in as good a position as it would have been in had Davis performed, it was entitled to recover its lost profit on its contract with Davis under section 2-708(2) of the UCC. Ill. Rev. Stat. ch. 26, para. 2-708(2) (1985). * * *

Diasonics subsequently filed a third-party complaint against Dobbin and Valvassori, alleging that they tortiously interfered with its contract with Davis. Diasonics claimed that the doctors knew of the contract between Davis and Diasonics and also knew that, if they breached their contract with Davis, Davis would have no use for the equipment it had agreed to buy from Diasonics.

The district court dismissed Diasonics' third-party complaint for failure to state a claim upon which relief could be granted, finding that the complaint did not allege that the doctors intended to induce Davis to breach its contract with Diasonics. The court also entered summary judgment for Davis. The court held that lost volume sellers were not entitled to recover damages under 2-708(2) but rather were limited to recovering the difference between the resale price and the contract price along with incidental damages under section 2-706(1). Ill. Rev. Stat. ch. 26, para. 2-706(1) (1985). * * *

Davis was awarded $322,656, which represented Davis' down payment plus prejudgment interest less Diasonics' incidental damages. Diasonics appeals the district court's decision respecting its measure of damages as well as the dismissal of its third-party complaint.

II.

We consider first Diasonics' claim that the district court erred in holding that Diasonics was limited to the measure of damages provided in 2-706 and could not recover lost profits as a lost volume seller under 2-708(2). Surprisingly, given its importance, this issue has never been addressed by an Illinois court, nor, apparently, by any other court construing Illinois law. Thus, we must attempt to predict how the Illinois Supreme Court would resolve this issue if it were presented to it. Courts applying the laws of other states have unanimously adopted the position that a lost volume seller can recover its lost profits under 2-708(2).[1] Contrary to the result reached by the district court, we conclude that the Illinois Supreme Court would follow these other cases and would allow a lost volume seller to recover its lost profit under 2-708(2).

We begin our analysis with 2-718(2) and (3). Under 2-718(2)(b), Davis is entitled to the return of its down payment less $500. Davis' right to restitution, however, is qualified under 2-718(3)(a) to the extent that Diasonics can establish a right to recover damages under any other provision of Article 2 of the UCC. Article 2 contains four provisions that concern the recovery of a seller's general damages (as opposed to its incidental or consequential damages): 2-706 (contract price less resale price); 2-708(1) (contract price less market price); 2-708(2) (profit); and 2-709 (price). The problem we face here is determining whether Diasonics' damages should be measured under 2-706 or 2-708(2). To answer this question, we need to engage in a detailed look at the language and structure of these various damage provisions.

The Code does not provide a great deal of guidance as to when a particular damage remedy is appropriate. The damage remedies provided under the Code are catalogued in section 2-703, but this section does not indicate that there is any hierarchy among the remedies. One method of approaching the damage sections is to conclude that 2-708 is relegated to a role inferior to that of 2-706 and 2-709 and that one can turn to 2-708 only after one has concluded that neither 2-706 nor 2-709 is applicable.[2] Under this interpretation of the relationship between 2-706 and 2-

---

[1] See, e.g., Comeq, Inc. v. Mitternight Boiler Works, Inc., 456 So.2d 264, 267-69 (Ala. Sup.Ct.1984); Autonumerics, Inc. v. Bayer Ind., Inc., 144 Ariz. 181, 191, 696 P.2d 1330, 1340 (Ariz. App. Ct.1984); Capital Steel Co. v. Foster & Creighton Co., 264 Ark. 683, 689, 574 S.W.2d 256, 259-60 (Sup. Ct.1978); National Controls, Inc. v. Commodore Business Machines, Inc., 163 Cal. App.3d 688, 696-99, 209 Cal. Rptr. 636, 641-43 (1st Dist.1985); Snyder v. Herbert Greenbaum & Assocs., Inc., 38 Md. App. 144, 153-54, 380 A.2d 618, 624-25 (1977); Teradyne, Inc. v. Teledyne Ind., Inc., 676 F.2d 865, 868 (1st Cir. 1982) (applying Massachusetts law); Neri v. Retail Marine Corp., 30 N.Y.2d 393, 397-99, 334 N.Y.S.2d 165, 167-70, 285 N.E.2d 311, 313-14 (1972); Lake Erie Boat Sales, Inc. v. Johnson, 11 Ohio App. 3d 55, 56, 463 N.E.2d 70, 71-72 (1983); Famous Knitwear Corp. v. Drug Fair, Inc., 493 F.2d 251, 253-54 (4th Cir. 1974) (applying Virginia law); Islamic Republic of Iran v. Boeing Co., 771 F.2d 1279, 1289-90 (9th Cir. 1985) (applying Washington law), cert. dismissed, ___ U.S. ___, 107 S. Ct. 450, 93 L. Ed. 2d 397 (1986).

[2] Evidence to support this approach can be found in the language of the various damage sections and of the official comments to the UCC. See § 2-709(3) ("a seller who is held not
(continued...)

708, if the goods have been resold, the seller can sue to recover damages measured by the difference between the contract price and the resale price under 2-706. The seller can turn to 2-708 only if it resells in a commercially unreasonable manner or if it cannot resell but an action for the price is inappropriate under 2-709. The district court adopted this reading of the Code's damage remedies and, accordingly, limited Diasonics to the measure of damages provided in 2-706 because it resold the equipment in a commercially reasonable manner.

The district court's interpretation of 2-706 and 2-708, however, creates its own problems of statutory construction. There is some suggestion in the Code that the "fact that plaintiff resold the goods [in a commercially reasonable manner] does *not* compel him to use the resale remedy of § 2-706 rather than the damage remedy of § 2-708." Harris, *A Radical Restatement of the Law of Seller's Damages: Sales Act and Commercial Code Results Compared,* 18 STAN. L. REV. 66, 101 n.174 (1965) (emphasis in original). Official comment 1 to 2-703, which catalogues the remedies available to a seller, states that these "remedies are essentially cumulative in nature" and that "[w]hether the pursuit of one remedy bars another depends entirely on the facts of the individual case." *See also State of New York, Report of the Law Revision Comm'n for 1956,* 396-97 (1956).[3]

---

[2] (...continued)
entitled to the price under this Section shall nevertheless be awarded damages for non-acceptance under the preceding section [§ 2-708]"); UCC comment 7 to § 2-709 ("[i]f the action for the price fails, the seller may nonetheless have proved a case entitling him to damages for non-acceptance [under § 2-708]"); UCC comment 2 to § 2-706 ("[f]ailure to act properly under this section deprives the seller of the measure of damages here provided and relegates him to that provided in Section 2-708"); UCC comment 1 to § 2-704 (describes § 2-706 as the "primary remedy" available to a seller upon breach by the buyer); *see also Commonwealth Edison Co. v. Decker Coal Co.,* 653 F. Supp. 841, 844 (N.D. Ill. 1987) (statutory language and case law suggest that "§ 2-708 remedies are available only to a seller who is not entitled to the contract price" under § 2-709); Childres & Burgess, *Seller's Remedies: The Primacy of UCC 2-708(2),* 48 N.Y. U. L. REV. 833, 863-64 (1973). As one commentator has noted, 2-706
      is the Code section drafted specifically to define the damage rights of aggrieved
      reselling sellers, and there is no suggestion within it that the profit formula of
      section 2-708(2) is in any way intended to qualify or be superior to it.
Shanker, *The Case for a Literal Reading of UCC Section 2-708(2) (One Profit for the Reseller),* 24 CASE W. RES. 697, 699 (1973).

[3] UCC comment 2 to 2-708(2) also suggests that 2-708 has broader applicability than
(continued...)

Those courts that found that a lost volume seller can recover its lost profits under 2-708(2) implicitly rejected the position adopted by the district court; those courts started with the assumption that 2-708 applied to a lost volume seller without considering whether the seller was limited to the remedy provided under 2-706. None of those courts even suggested that a seller who resold goods in a commercially reasonable manner was limited to the damage formula provided under 2-706. We conclude that the Illinois Supreme Court, if presented with this question, would adopt the position of these other jurisdictions and would conclude that a reselling seller, such as Diasonics, is free to reject the damage formula prescribed in 2-706 and choose to proceed under 2-708.

Concluding that Diasonics is entitled to seek damages under 2-708, however, does not automatically result in Diasonics being awarded its lost profit. Two different measures of damages are provided in 2-708. Subsection 2-708(1) provides for a measure of damages calculated by subtracting the market price at the time and place for tender from the contract price.[4] The profit measure of damages, for which

---

[3] (...continued)
suggested by the district court. UCC comment 2 provides:
> This section permits the recovery of lost profits in all appropriate cases, which would include all standard priced goods. The normal measure there would be list price less cost to the dealer or list price less manufacturing cost to the manufacturer.

The district court's restrictive interpretation of 2-708(2) was based in part on UCC comment 1 to 2-704 which describes 2-706 as the aggrieved seller's primary remedy. The district court concluded that, if a lost volume seller could recover its lost profit under 2-708(2), every seller would attempt to recover damages under 2-708(2) and 2-706 would become the aggrieved seller's residuary remedy. This argument ignores the fact that to recover under 2-708(2), a seller must first establish its status as a lost volume seller. * * *

The district court also concluded that a lost volume seller cannot recover its lost profit under 2-708(2) because such a result would negate a seller's duty to mitigate damages. This position fails to recognize the fact that, by definition, a lost volume seller cannot mitigate damages through resale. Resale does not reduce a lost volume seller's damages because the breach has still resulted in its losing one sale and a corresponding profit.

[4] There is some debate in the commentaries about whether a seller who has resold the goods may ignore the measure of damages provided in 2-706 and elect to proceed under 2-708(1). Under some circumstances the contract-market price differential will result in overcompensating such a seller. *See* J. WHITE & R. SUMMERS, HANDBOOK OF THE LAW UNDER THE UNIFORM COMMERCIAL CODE § 7-7, at 271-73 (2d ed. 1980); Sebert, *Remedies under Article Two of the Uniform Commercial Code: An Agenda for Review,* 130 U. PA. L. REV. 360, 380-83 (1981). We need not struggle with this question here because Diasonics

(continued...)

Diasonics is asking, is contained in 2-708(2). However, one applies 2-708(2) only if "the measure of damages provided in subsection (1) is inadequate to put the seller in as good a position as performance would have done. * * * " Ill. Rev. Stat. ch. 26, para. 2-708(2)(1985). Diasonics claims that 2-708(1) does not provide an adequate measure of damages when the seller is a lost volume seller.[5] To understand Diasonics' argument, we need to define the concept of the lost volume seller. Those cases that have addressed this issue have defined a lost volume seller as one that has a predictable and finite number of customers and that has the capacity either to sell to all new buyers or to make the one additional sale represented by the resale after the breach. According to a number of courts and commentators, if the seller would have made the sale represented by the resale whether or not the breach occurred, damages measured by the difference between the contract price and market price cannot put the lost volume seller in as good a position as it would have been in had the buyer performed.[6] The breach effectively cost the seller a "profit," and the seller can only be made whole by awarding it damages in the amount of its "lost profit" under 2-708(2).

We agree with Diasonics' position that, under some circumstances, the measure of damages provided under 2-708(1) will not put a reselling seller in as good a position as it would have been in had the buyer performed because the breach resulted in the seller losing sales volume. However, we disagree with the definition of "lost volume seller" adopted by other courts. Courts awarding lost profits to a lost volume seller have focused on whether the seller had the capacity to supply the breached units in addition to what it actually sold. In reality, however, the relevant questions include, not only whether the seller could have produced the breached units in addition to its actual volume, but also whether it would have been profitable

---

[4] (...continued)
has not sought to recover damages under 2-708(1).

[5] This is also the position adopted by those courts that have held that a lost volume seller can recover its lost profits under 2-708(2). *See, e.g., Snyder,* 38 Md. App. at 153-54, 380 A.2d at 624-25.

[6] According to one commentator,
   Resale results in loss of volume only if three conditions are met: (1) the person who bought the resold entity would have been solicited by plaintiff had there been no breach and resale; (2) the solicitation would have been successful; and (3) the plaintiff could have performed that additional contract.
Harris, *supra* p. 682, at 82 (footnotes omitted).

for the seller to produce both units. Goetz & Scott, *Measuring Sellers' Damages: The Lost-Profits Puzzle,* 31 STAN. L. REV. 323, 332-33, 346-47 (1979). As one commentator has noted, under

> the economic law of diminishing returns or increasing marginal costs[,] * * * as a seller's volume increases, then a point will inevitably be reached where the cost of selling each additional item diminishes the incremental return to the seller and eventually makes it entirely unprofitable to conclude the next sale. * * *

Thus, under some conditions, awarding a lost volume seller its presumed lost profit will result in overcompensating the seller, and 2-708(2) would not take effect because the damage formula provided in 2-708(1) does place the seller in as good a position as if the buyer had performed. Therefore, on remand, Diasonics must establish, not only that it had the capacity to produce the breached unit in addition to the unit resold, but also that it would have been profitable for it to have produced and sold both. Diasonics carries the burden of establishing these facts because the burden of proof is generally on the party claiming injury to establish the amount of its damages; especially in a case such as this, the plaintiff has easiest access to the relevant data. *Finance America Commercial Corp. v. Econo Coach, Inc.,* 118 Ill. App. 3d 385, 390, 73 Ill. Dec. 878, 882, 454 N.E.2d 1127, 1131 (2d Dist. 1983) ("A party seeking to recover has the burden not only to establish that he sustained damages but also to establish a reasonable basis for computation of those damages.") (citation omitted); *see also Snyder,* 38 Md. App. at 158-59 & n.7, 380 A.2d at 627 & n.7.[7]

One final problem with awarding a lost volume seller its lost profits was raised by the district court. This problem stems from the formulation of the measure of damages provided under section 2-708(2) which is "the profit (including reasonable overhead) which the seller would have made from full performance by the buyer, together with any incidental damages provided in this Article (Section 2-710), due allowance for costs reasonably incurred and due credit for payments or *proceeds of resale.*" Ill. Rev. Stat. ch. 26, para. 2-708(2) (1985) (emphasis added). The literal language of 2-708(2) requires that the proceeds from resale be credited against the amount of damages awarded which, in most cases, would result in the seller

---

[7] As some commentators have pointed out, the cost of calculating a loss of profit may be very high. Goetz & Scott, *supra,* at 353 ("the complexity of the lost-volume problem suggests that the information costs of exposing an overcompensatory rule are relatively high").

recovering nominal damages. In those cases in which the lost volume seller was awarded its lost profit as damages, the courts have circumvented this problem by concluding that this language only applies to proceeds realized from the resale of uncompleted goods for scrap. *See, e.g., Neri,* 30 N.Y.2d at 399 & n.2, 334 N.Y.S.2d at 169 & n.2, 285 N.E.2d at 314 & n.2; *see also* J. WHITE & R. SUMMERS, HANDBOOK OF THE LAW UNDER THE UNIFORM COMMERCIAL CODE § 7-13, at 285 ("courts should simply ignore the 'due credit' language in lost volume cases") (footnote omitted). Although neither the text of 2-708(2) nor the official comments limit its application to resale of goods for scrap, there is evidence that the drafters of 2-708 seemed to have had this more limited application in mind when they proposed amending 2-708 to include the phrase "due credit for payments or proceeds of resale."[8] We conclude that the Illinois Supreme Court would adopt this more restrictive interpretation of this phrase rendering it inapplicable to this case.

We therefore reverse the grant of summary judgment in favor of Davis and remand with instructions that the district court calculate Diasonics' damages under 2-708(2) if Diasonics can establish, not only that it had the capacity to make the sale to Davis as well as the sale to the resale buyer, but also that it would have been profitable for it to make both sales. Of course, Diasonics, in addition, must show that it probably would have made the second sale absent the breach.[9]

* * *

IV.

Accordingly, we affirm the district court's dismissal of the third-party complaint, reverse the grant of summary judgment in favor of Davis and remand for further proceedings consistent with this opinion. Affirmed in part, reversed in part and remanded.

[Some footnotes omitted. Those retained have been renumbered.]

---

[8] In explaining its recommendation that 2-708 be amended to include the requirement that due credit be given for resale, the Enlarged Editorial Board stated that its purpose was "to clarify the privilege of the seller to realize junk value when it is manifestly useless to complete the operation of manufacture." Supplement No. 1 to the 1952 Official Draft (1955), *quoted in* Harris, *supra* p. 682, at 98.

[9] *See supra* p. 683 n.13; *see also* Schlosser, *Damages for the Lost-Volume Seller: Does an Efficient Formula Already Exist?* 17 U.C.C. L.J. 238, 245 & n. 20 (1985); Sebert, *supra* p. 683 n.9, at 387-88.

Notes

1. After remand and trial, R.E. Davis again appealed from a judgment of the district court in favor of Diasonics. *R.E. Davis Chemical Corp. v. Diasonics, Inc.*, 924 F.2d 709 (7th Cir. 1991). The Court of Appeals affirmed that Diasonics was a lost volume seller under the test announced in the first opinion, even though it had failed to identify the exact unit sold or the buyer to whom that unit was sold. The court also affirmed the trial court's calculation of lost profits under former 2-708(2), [$453,050, less the $300,000 deposit] but reversed and remanded with regret on the ground that the trial court erroneously excluded evidence of additional expenses that Diasonics would have incurred if Davis had fully performed its part of the bargain. The court stated that "Diasonics is entitled to the benefit of its bargain, no more, no less." There have been few cases involving the lost-volume dispute since the decision in *R. E. Davis.*[*]

2. The assumption underlying the "lost volume" problem is simple to state: If a seller had the capacity to and probably would have made a second sale regardless of the buyer's breach, the goal of UCC 1-305 [former 1-106] will be frustrated if the profit the seller would have made on the first sale is offset by the proceeds of the second sale. Embracing this assumption, *R.E. Davis* and the authorities cited therein have used UCC 2-708(2) to protect the profit on the first sale without regard to the proceeds of any resale, at least if the second sale would have been profitable.

In so doing, most courts have adopted a simple test for determining lost volume: If, in the relevant time period, the seller had the capacity to make a second sale and, after the breach, in fact made a resale, the requirement is satisfied. Rejected is the view, advocated by some commentators, that lost volume exists when the seller satisfies three conditions: (1) The buyer who purchased the resold entity would have been solicited by the seller had there been no breach; (2) The solicitation would have been successful; and (3) The seller could have performed the additional contract.[**] In refusing to "require proof of a complex economic relationship," one

---

[*] For two cases, *see Rodriguez v. Learjet, Inc.*, 946 P.2d 1010 (Kan. Ct. App. 1997); *In re El Paso Refinery, L.P.*, 196 B.R. 58 (Bankr. W.D. Tex. 1996). *See also C.I.C. Corp. v. Ragtime, Inc.*, 726 A.2d 316 (N.J. Super. App. Div. 1999) for treatment of the issue in a lease transaction.

[**] Robert A. Harris, *A Radical Restatement of the Law of Seller's Damages: Sales Act and* (continued...)

court was satisfied by proof that the seller "would have made the sale to the resale purchaser even if" the buyer had performed, that the seller "resold the parts, and that it had an existing inventory of these parts." *Islamic Republic of Iran v. Boeing Co.*, 771 F.2d 1279 (9th Cir. 1985) (Washington law).

In addition, most courts have ignored (if not rejected) the claim by some that even if a second sale could have been made, it would not, in all probability, have been profitable. *See* Charles J. Goetz & Robert E. Scott, *Measuring Seller's Damages: The Lost-Profits Puzzle,* 31 STAN. L. REV. 323 (1979). Why? The argument is summarized by Professor Sebert in John A. Sebert, *Remedies Under Article 2 of the Uniform Commercial Code: An Agenda for Review*, 130 U. PA. L. REV. 360, 389-90 (1981).

> One foundation of the Geotz and Scott argument is the accepted proposition that economically efficient entities, whether they be manufacturers or retailers, attempt to operate at a level of output where marginal cost equals marginal revenue. Economic theory also posits that these efficient sellers are likely to be producing at a level where marginal costs are rising as additional units are produced or sold, and that marginal revenue is likely to be falling, or at best remaining constant, because the increased supply caused by additional production or sales will cause the market price to fall. Based upon these traditional economic concepts, Goetz and Scott argue that, even if the seller had the capacity to do so, a seller operating at the level where marginal cost equals marginal revenue would not have produced the additional goods to sell to buyer 2 if buyer 1 had not breached. In a world of rising marginal costs and static or declining marginal revenue, it would not have been efficient for the seller to produce or obtain additional goods to sell to buyer 2 because the marginal cost of those goods would exceed the marginal revenue received from their sale and the seller would have lost money. Thus, Goetz and Scott suggest that the sale to buyer 2 is a sale that the efficient seller normally would not have made, and therefore the seller is not a lost volume seller.

Professor Sebert rejects Goetz and Scott's presumption that the seller is not a lost

---

[**] (...continued)

Commercial Code Results Compared, 18 STAN. L. REV. 66, 80-83 (1965). *See* John M. Breen, *The Lost Volume Seller and Lost Profits Under UCC § 2-708(2): A Conceptual and Linguistic Critique,* 50 U. MIAMI L. REV. 779 (1996).

volume seller, "even though a seller has the capacity to make an additional sale and even though the resale buyer probably would have bought from the seller had the original buyer not breached" without rejecting the possibility that the resale merely replaces the original sale because of the assumed rising marginal costs. He proposes the following approach: " * * * [O]nce the seller shows that he had the capacity to make an additional sale and that the resale buyer probably would have bought from him anyway, I would place the burden of proof on the breaching buyer to show that the seller would not have made an additional sale because of rising marginal costs." Sebert, *supra* at 391.

3   Other situations in which the courts have held the seller should recover lost profits in order to avoid under compensation that would take place if UCC 2-708(1) was used to measure damages are summarized in *Purina Mills, L.L.C. v. Less*, 295 F. Supp. 2d 1017, 1035-36 (N.D. Iowa 2003):

> Courts have routinely recognized that the contract/market remedy is inadequate, and that the lost profits formula is applicable, in three situations. First, where the goods to be sold, and that are the subject of the breached or repudiated contract, are specially-manufactured goods for which there is no readily accessible market. . . .The second situation is where the seller is a "lost volume seller," which is defined as: "... one who upon a buyers breach of contract, resells the article to a second purchaser at the price agreed to by the first purchaser. The second purchaser, however, would have purchased a similar article notwithstanding the first purchaser's breach. Under such circumstances, when the seller resells the article, he is still not made whole because he will have lost one sale, one profit, over the course of the year." . . .The third, and final, category of sellers recognized as *inadequately* compensated under the contract/market formula are sellers who are "jobbers." According to the Eighth Circuit Court of Appeals, to be classified as a "jobber" a seller must: (1) never acquire the contract goods; and (2) his decision not to acquire the goods after learning of the breach must be commercially reasonable. . . .

Problem 10-9

On July 1, Buyer contracted with Seller, a distributor, to purchase factory equipment to be manufactured by Dolt. The price was $90,000. Seller then placed an order for the equipment with Dolt for $80,000, with delivery to Buyer no later than October 1. On August 15, Buyer, without justification, repudiated the contract with Seller. Seller promptly canceled the order with Dolt, who had not started to work on the equipment, for a customary cancellation charge of $1,000.

Seller comes to you for advice. The market price of the equipment at the "time and place for tender," October 1, under UCC 2-708(1) was estimated to be $90,000. Seller had incurred $2,000 in expenses preparing to perform between July 1 and August 15. Seller would have paid Dolt $80,000 for the lathes and spent another $1,500 to prepare the goods for delivery if Buyer had not repudiated. These expenditures, however, were not made.

A. Neither UCC 2-709 or 2-706 are available on these facts. Do you see why? As between UCC 2-708(1) and (2), which section should be used to determine Seller's damages? Why? What would Seller's damages be under UCC 2-708(1)?

B. If UCC 2-708(2) is applicable, how does a court determine Seller's damages? Would that amount fully compensate Seller?

Note: Lost Profits Under the CISG

What about the CISG? See Art. 74 which provides, in part, that "damages for breach of contract by one party consist of a sum equal to the loss, including loss of profit, suffered by the other party as a consequence of the breach." This remedy, which is available regardless of whether the seller has avoided the contract, contains a foreseeability limitation.

Note: Lost Profits Under UCITA

UCITA provides for lost profit recovery in UCITA 808(b)(1)(C).

F. Remedial Choice

Reread UCC 2-703 and its comments. When will the seller or lessor be precluded from recovering based upon the damage remedy it selects? One can assume for a moment that in any given case, at the point it gets to litigation, that the seller or lessor wants to put in its damages case to result in the highest possible recovery of damages. Similarly, one can assume the buyer or lessee will make all possible arguments in an attempt to reduce the recoverable damages in the event it loses on the issue of liability for breach of contract. Given those competing perspectives, which of the four remedies we have studied should a seller or lessor be allowed to use to recover its damages?

TRANS WORLD METALS, INC. V. SOUTHWIRE CO.
UNITED STATES COURT OF APPEALS, SECOND CIRCUIT, 1985
769 F.2D 902

[In April, 1981 the parties entered into a contract for the sale of 12,000 metric tons of primary aluminum, to be delivered in monthly installments of 1,000 metric tons from January through December, 1982. The contract price was $.77 per pound, or a total price of $20.4 million. Seller shipped 750 metric tons in January, 1982 and the balance of the first installment in early February. Between April, 1981 and March, 1982, the market price of aluminum dropped "dramatically." On March 4, 1982, Buyer, without discussing the late first installment or issuing additional delivery instructions, cancelled the contract because of Seller's default. In Seller's suit for damages, the jury concluded that Buyer had accepted all deliveries and even if late, there was no substantial impairment of the value of either the first installment or the whole contract. Thus, Buyer had repudiated the contract. This conclusion was affirmed on appeal.

The jury awarded Seller damages of $7,122,141.84, consisting of $6,702,529 for Buyer's repudiation of the balance of the contract and $419,232.84 for the installment accepted. The district court added prejudgment interest of $1,304,804.88 and entered a judgment for $8,426,946.72. The propriety of this damage award under the UCC was attacked on appeal.]

NEWMAN, J.

* * *

II.

Southwire complains that the damage award, calculated by the difference between contract and market prices, gave Trans World an unwarranted windfall. Southwire favors an alternative measure of damages based on the rate of profit earned by Trans World on the first month's completed shipments projected over the twelve-month life of the contract. Such a measure, Southwire argues, would better estimate the amount Trans World would have made had the contract been completed. We reject this alternative as contrary to the Uniform Commercial Code.

Seller's damages for repudiation are governed by section 2-708 of the Uniform Commercial Code. Subsection 1 of this section sets forth the general rule that damages are to be calculated by the difference between the contract and market prices:

(1) Subject to subsection (2) and to the provisions of this Article with

respect to proof of market price (Section 2-723), the measure of damages for non-acceptance or repudiation by the buyer is the difference between the market price at the time and place for tender and the unpaid contract price together with any incidental damages provided in this Article (Section 2-710), but less expenses saved in consequence of the buyer's breach.

N.Y. U.C.C. Law § 2-708(1). The drafters of the Uniform Commercial Code recognized that this measure would not adequately compensate certain types of sellers, generally referred to as "lost volume sellers." *See* J. WHITE & R. SUMMERS, UNIFORM COMMERCIAL CODE § 7-9, at 274-76 (2d ed. 1980) ("WHITE & SUMMERS"). Therefore, an alternative measure of damages was provided for those sellers who would be *inadequately* compensated by the standard contract/market price differential:

> (2) If the measure of damages provided in subsection (1) is inadequate to put the seller in as good a position as performance would have done then the measure of damages is the profit (including reasonable overhead) which the seller would have made from full performance by the buyer, together with any incidental damages provided in this Article (Section 2-710), due allowance for costs reasonably incurred and due credit for payments or proceeds of resale.

N.Y.U.C.C. Law § 2-708(2). This measure of damages is often preferred by sellers who have not acquired the goods to be sold prior to the buyer's repudiation because such sellers often would be undercompensated by the contract/market price measure of damages.[1]

Southwire argues that the "lost profits" measure should also apply when the seller would be *overcompensated* by section 2-708(1). We disagree. We do not doubt that the contract/market price differential "will seldom be the same as the

---

[1] Professors White and Summers refer to such sellers as "jobbers."

By "jobber" we refer to a seller who satisfies two conditions. First, he is a seller who never acquires the contract goods. Second, his decision not to acquire those goods after learning of the breach is commercially reasonable under 2-704. * * * Since he has no goods on hand to resell, he cannot even resell on the market at the time of tender and so recoup the amount necessary to make him whole by adding such proceeds to his 2-708(1) recovery. Thus the only recovery which grossly approximates the "jobber's" economic loss is a recovery based on lost profits.

WHITE & SUMMERS § 7-10, at 278. In a case involving a commodity like aluminum that fluctuates rapidly in price–as compared to standard-priced goods like cars, *see* 67 Am. Jur. 2d *Sales* § 1129–the lost profits of a selling jobber may well be adequately reflected by the contract/market price differential.

seller's actual economic loss from breach." WHITE & SUMMERS § 7-7, at 269; *see* Peters, *Remedies for Breach of Contracts Relating to the Sale of Goods Under the Uniform Commercial Code: A Roadmap for Article Two*, 73 YALE L.J. 199, 259 (1963). However, nothing in the language or history of section 2-708(2) suggests that it was intended to apply to cases in which section 2-708(1) might overcompensate the seller. *See* WHITE & SUMMERS § 7-12, at 283. Nor has Southwire cited any New York case that interprets section 2-708(2) as Southwire urges us to interpret it. As a federal court sitting in diversity, we will not extend the application of this state law.

Nor are we convinced that Trans World has been overcompensated. No measure other than the contract/market price differential will award Trans World the "benefit of its bargain," that is, the "amount necessary to put [it] in as good a position as [it] would have been if the defendant had abided by the contract." *Western Geophysical Co. of America, Inc. v. Bolt Associates, Inc.*, 584 F.2d 1164, 1172 (2d Cir. 1978) (quoting *Perma Research & Development Co. v. Singer Co.*, 402 F. Supp. 881, 898 (S.D.N.Y.1975), *aff'd*, 542 F.2d 111 (2d Cir.), *cert. denied*, 429 U.S. 987, 97 S. Ct. 507, 50 L. Ed. 2d 598 (1976)). The contract at issue in this case is an aluminum supply contract entered into eight months prior to the initial deliveries called for by its terms. The last of the anticipated deliveries of aluminum would not have been completed until a full twenty months after the negotiations took place. It simply could not have escaped these parties that they were betting on which way aluminum prices would move. Trans World took the risk that the price would rise; Southwire took the risk that the price would fall. Under these circumstances, Trans World should not be denied the benefit of its bargain, as reflected by the contract/market price differential.[2] *Cf. Apex Oil Co. v. Vanguard Oil & Service Co.*, 760 F.2d 417 (2d Cir. 1985) (defaulting seller obliged to pay damages based on contract/market price differential).

The decision primarily relied upon by Southwire is distinguishable from this case. *Nobs Chemical, U.S.A., Inc. v. Koppers Co., Inc.*, 616 F.2d 212 (5th Cir. 1980), involved a seller acting as a middleman. The seller in Nobs had entered into a second fixed-price contract with its own supplier for purchase of the goods to be sold under the contract sued upon; its "market price" thus had been fixed in advance

---

[2] Southwire presented no evidence and made no claim concerning any expenses saved by Trans World as a result of Southwire's breach. Such expenses, if established, would have reduced the recoverable damages. N.Y. U.C.C. Law § 2-708(1); *see Katz Communications, Inc. v. The Evening News Association*, 705 F.2d 20, 26-27 (2d Cir. 1983).

by contract. Because the seller had contractually protected itself against market price fluctuation, the Fifth Circuit concluded that it would have been unfair to permit the seller to reap a riskless benefit. As that Court noted, "the difference between the fallen market price and the contract price is [not] necessary to compensate the plaintiffs for the breach. Had the transaction been completed, their 'benefit of the bargain' would not have been affected by the fall in the market price. * * * " *Id.* at 215. Whether or not we would have reached the same result in *Nobs,* here the benefit of the bargain under a completed contract would have been affected by the fall in aluminum prices.[3] Because Trans World accepted the risk that prices would rise, it is entitled to benefit from their fall.

III.

[The court held that since the trial for this action based on anticipatory repudiation was held after the agreed time for performance, the time for measuring market price was not the date the seller "learned of the repudiation." Former 2-723(1). Rather, market price should be measured at the time each installment was delivered.] * * *

We therefore conclude that when calculating damages for a buyer's repudiation of an installment contract by the contract/market price differential, "time * * * for tender" under section 2-708(1) is the date for each successive tender of an installment, as specified in the contract. * * * In this case the successive dates for tender were the last day of each month in 1982, at which time Trans World was authorized to invoice that month's shipments even if such shipments had not been "released" by Southwire's delivery instructions. A contract/market price differential should have been calculated for each month during 1982. * * *

We have considered Southwire's remaining claims and find them to lack merit. The judgment of the District Court is affirmed.

[Some footnotes omitted. Those retained have been renumbered.]

---

[3] Although Trans World had available to it about 78,000 tons of aluminum at the time of the breach, Trans World had corresponding obligations to deliver about 76,000 tons of aluminum to buyers other than Southwire. Absent any indication that Trans World had "identified" any of this metal to the Southwire contract, *see* N.Y. U.C.C. Law § 2-501(b), we cannot say, as could the court in *Nobs,* that a change in the market price would not affect the seller's "benefit of the bargain."

Notes

1. Given the remedial objectives of UCC 1-305 [former 1-106] and the general duty of good faith in the "enforcement" of the contract, UCC 1-304 [former 1-203], was the seller overcompensated under UCC 2-708(1)? Retrace the statutory steps to the seller's victory: UCC 2-610(b) and former 2-703(e), 2-708(2) (rejected by the court), and 2-708(1).

Relying on *Nobs Chemical,* which was distinguished in the principal case, the court in *Union Carbide Corporation v. Consumers Power Co.*, 636 F. Supp. 1498 (E.D. Mich. 1986), held that a seller who was a middleman and who did not, under the pricing arrangement, bear the risk of fluctuations in the market price, could not use UCC 2-708(1) when that measure resulted in overcompensation. The court interpreted the word "inadequate" in UCC 2-708(2) to mean "incapable or inadequate to accomplish the stated purpose of the UCC remedies of compensating the aggrieved person but not overcompensating that person or specifically punishing the other person." In short, where the measure of damages in UCC 2-708(1) fails fairly to measure the damages suffered by the plaintiff, that formula is "inadequate" and, to avoid a penalty, UCC 2-708(2) should be applied. Does this result undercut the risk allocated at the time of contracting by a fixed price? Some have argued that if the parties knew *ex ante* contract that UCC 2-708(2) rather than UCC 2-708(1) would be applied, there would be a different price for the goods.

In Purina Mills, L.L.C. v. Less, 295 F. Supp. 2d 1017 (N.D. Iowa 2003), the court found that the seller should be limited to its lost profit instead of market price based damages because even though the seller took the risk of market fluctuations by agreeing to purchase the goods for resale in a fixed price contract to supply the breaching buyer, who also agreed to a fixed price contract, the seller inexplicably turned down the ability to buy out of its supply contract to which it had committed. Because of this failure to mitigate, the court allowed the seller only its profit and not the difference between the contract price and market price when the buyer repudiated the contract to buy.

2. Suppose Seller, in a falling market, resells goods intended for the contract at Price $X and, later, sues Buyer under UCC 2-708(1) for the difference between the contract price and an even lower market price, Price $X-Y, at the time and place of tender. Can Seller recover under UCC 2-708(1) or may Buyer limit damages to those that would be available for a proper resale under UCC 2-706(1)? In *Tesoro Petroleum Corp. v. Holborn Oil Co., Ltd*, 547 N.Y.S.2d 1012 (N.Y. Sup. Ct. 1989), where there was a $3,000,000 difference, the court held the seller to damages under

UCC 2-706: "If plaintiff's damages are measured in accordance with § 2-706, it would be receiving the benefit reasonably to be expected when it entered the alleged contract with defendant. Granting it the approximately $3,000,000 additional recovery that it seeks would result in a windfall which cannot be said to have been in the contemplation of the parties at the time of their negotiations, and would be inconsistent with the policy of the Code as expressed in § 1-106."

3. In *Trans World Metals* the case came to trial *after* the time for performance had passed. Thus, former 2-723(1), which measures damages at the time when the seller "learns of the repudiation," did not apply. As such, the court felt free to measure market damages at the "time and place for tender," former 2-708(1), even though that time was significantly after the seller learned of the breach. Amended UCC 2-708(1)(b) would have measured the market price at the end of a commercially reasonable time after the repudiation as long as that was not later than the time of tender. On the facts of *Trans World Metals*, what was that date and what difference would it have made in the calculation of damages?

4. A risk of pursuing a particular remedy and failing is, apparently, one of evidence: will the record support a claim for damages under a remedy other than the remedy that is the primary theory of the case? A case in point is *B & R Textile Corp. v. Paul Rothman Indus. Ltd.*, 101 Misc. 2d 98, 420 N.Y.S.2d 609 (1979), *aff'd*, 27 UCC Rep. Serv. 994 (N.Y. Sup. Ct. 1979), where the buyer argued that the seller's reliance upon the price received in a resale where the required notice was not given constituted an election of remedies. This argument was rejected by the court, which held that the seller's prompt resale generated a price which, when supported by evidence of other sales contemporaneously made by the seller, established the "market price" under UCC 2-708(1). *See also Cole v. Melvin*, 441 F. Supp. 193 (D.S.D. 1977), where a defective resale left a thin but adequate record from which to establish the market price. The point for the litigator is clear: develop, if possible, the "fall back" evidence necessary to satisfy an alternative remedy.

5. Some policy questions lurk on the fringes. Suppose the seller pursues the resale remedy and complies fully with UCC 2-706. If, thereafter, it sues for higher damages under UCC 2-708(1), will damages be limited by UCC 2-706(1)? At least one court has so held.[*] Does the same issue arise under UCC 2A-527 and 2A-528? Or, suppose the seller arguably should have resold under UCC 2-706 but failed to

---

[*] *See Tesoro Petroleum Corp. v. Holborn Oil Co., Ltd.*, 145 Misc. 2d 715, 547 N.Y.S.2d 1012 (Sup. Ct. N.Y. 1989).

do so. Will a recovery under UCC 2-708(1) be reduced by what could have been obtained on a resale? At least one court, has held that if the seller is *not* a "lost volume" seller and has conducted a commercially unreasonable resale under UCC 2-706(1), the recovery under UCC 2-708(1) will be limited by what the seller *should* have received in damages if the resale had been proper. The seller's apparent bad faith in the resale limited the recovery to "actual losses" and precluded any windfall gains permitted under the formula in UCC 2-708(1).[*] Does the same issue arise in an Article 2A transaction? Does the general principle of UCC 1-305 [former 1-106] help govern this type of issue?[**] Does the 2003 amendment which adds UCC 2-706(7) change the result?

Read UCC 2-704 and consider the following problem. *Compare* UCC 2A-524 and UCITA 812.

Problem 10-10

On March 1, Seller contracted to manufacture custom lathes for Buyer for $80,000, delivery F.O.B. Illinois no later than November 1. On May 1, Buyer repudiated without justification. Seller had commenced to manufacture the lathes but no item was completed. The market price of the lathes in Chicago was $60,000. The market price in Phoenix was $55,000. The economy was in a mild recession, and the respective market prices in November were expected to be $40,000 in Chicago and $35,000 in Phoenix.

A. A summer associate has given you the following memo:

It is clear that Seller could complete the manufacture, UCC 2-704(2), and attempt to resell the custom lathes. *See* UCC 2-706(2), stating that it is 'not necessary that the goods be in existence or that any or all of them have been identified to the contract before the breach.' If a resale can be made, damages can be recovered under UCC 2-706(1), or, if there is lost volume, under UCC 2-708(2). If a resale cannot be made, Seller can recover the price from Buyer. UCC 2-709(1)(b). I recommend that we advise Seller to complete the manufacturing process.

Do you agree?

---

[*] *See Coast Trading Co. v. Cudahy Co.*, 592 F.2d 1074 (9th Cir. 1979).

[**] *See* David W. Barnes, *The Net Expectation Interest in Contract Damages*, 48 EMORY L.J. 1137 (1999).

B. Suppose, in the exercise of reasonable commercial judgment, Seller stopped the manufacturing process. UCC 2-704(2). Seller had components on hand purchased for the contract which cost $20,000. These components were scrapped for $15,000. Seller had incurred other performance costs ("variable" costs) of $10,000 which could not be salvaged. Because of the breach, Seller did not have to incur other performance of "variable" costs, estimated to be $25,000. What damages would Seller recover under UCC 2-708(1)? What damages would Seller recover under UCC 2-708(2)? Which is the better remedy for Seller?

C. Suppose Seller completed manufacture of the lathes in October and resold the lathes for an above market price of $50,000 to Dolt. Seller did not comply with the requirements of UCC 2-706 because it did not give notice of the sale to Buyer. Seller sued Buyer for the difference between the market price of $40,000 and the contract price. Buyer argued that Seller is only entitled to $30,000, the difference between the resale price and the contract price. Is Buyer correct?

G. Incidental and Consequential Damages

In former Article 2 and 2A, a seller or lessor (arguably) was not entitled to consequential damages, only incidental damages. *See* former 2-710, 2A-530.[*] As already stated above, the 2003 amendments to UCC 2-710 and 2A-530 allow a seller to recover consequential damages in non-consumer contracts. These damages are in addition to the direct damages computed under the four formulas discussed above and incidental damages under UCC 2-710(1).

Remember in the *Afram* case *supra*, the court found that the seller's interest expense incurred because it did not receive payment of the price from the buyer was not an incidental damage but rather a consequential damage and unrecoverable. Under the 2003 amendments, a court would have to consider whether such expense, assuming it is in fact a consequential damage, is recoverable from the buyer under the test stated in UCC 2-710(2).

What is that test? It is comparable to the test for consequential damages for a buyer or lessee under UCC 2-715(2) and 2A-520(2). In order to recover consequential damages from a buyer or lessee, the seller or lessor will have to prove: (i) that the seller or lessor suffered a loss as a consequence of the buyer's breach; (ii) that the buyer or lessee had reason to know at the time of contracting of the

---

[*] *But see* Roy Ryden Anderson, *In Support of Consequential Damages for Sellers*, 11 J.L. & COM. 123 (1992).

seller's or lessor's general or particular requirements and needs that resulted in that loss; (iii) that the seller or lessor could not have reasonably prevented the loss by appropriate mitigating activity; and (iv) the amount of the loss. Given that this provision has yet to be enacted, only time will tell whether the prediction in the new comment 2 to UCC 2-710 will be born out: "Sellers rarely suffer compensable consequential damages."

For review, suppose that the buyer has defaulted in the payment of the price. How would you classify the follow interest costs in an action by a seller against the buyer for breach of contract:

(1) interest on a loan obtained before the breach to finance the operation of the plant and to purchase equipment;

(2) interest on a loan obtained before the breach to finance performance of the particular contract;

(3) interest on a loan obtained after the breach to make a profitable investment that was to be financed by payment of the price;

(4) interest on a loan obtained after the breach to finish work and obtain a commercially reasonable resale.

Note: Consequential Damages Under the CISG

Sellers under the CISG can recover consequential damages. *See* Art. 74. In addition, the seller is entitled to interest if the buyer fails to pay the price "without prejudice to any claim for damages recoverable under article 74." Interest other than that on the unpaid price would be recoverable if a foreseeable loss "suffered by the other party as a consequence of the breach" and the seller took reasonable measures to "mitigate the loss * * * resulting from the breach." Art. 77.

Note: Consequential Damages Under UCITA

UCITA allows a licensor to recover consequential and incidental damages. UCITA 808(b)(2). *See* the definitions in UCITA 102.

SECTION 4.   REMEDIES OF BUYER OR LESSEE

A. Introduction

There are three garden varieties of breach by a seller or lessor: repudiation, failure to deliver, and tender of delivery which does not conform to the contract. In the last situation, the buyer or lessee may have effectively rejected or revoked acceptance of the goods. This section will feature damage remedies that the buyer or lessee has when the buyer or lessee does not receive delivery of or accept the goods from the seller or lessor. For a review of the buyer's "goods orientated" remedies, including specific performance, *see* Chapter Nine, Section 2, *supra*.

The buyer or lessee may base damages on its "cover" under UCC 2-712 or 2A-518 or upon market price under UCC 2-713 or 2A-519. In addition, the buyer or lessee is also entitled to incidental and consequential damages. UCC 2-715, 2A-520. We have deferred until Chapter Eleven, *infra*, more extensive treatment of the non-conformity called breach of warranty and the remedies available to a buyer or lessee who has accepted a defective product and, for one reason or another, does not revoke acceptance.

Read UCC 2-711 and 2A-508. If the buyer or lessee does not accept the goods because of a breach by the seller or lessor, the seller or lessor has the obligation to refund the price or rent that has been paid. Notice that if the buyer or lessee has effectively and rightfully rejected the goods or effectively and justifiably revoked acceptance of the goods, the buyer or lessee has a security interest in the goods in its possession to secure any prepayments of the price or rent and some types of incidental damages. This possessory security interest is governed by Article 9, UCC 9-110. However, as long as the seller or lessor does not obtain possession of the goods, the buyer's or lessee's security interest is considered perfected and has priority over other security interests created by the seller or lessor. The buyer or lessee may resell the goods using the provisions of Article 2, UCC 2-706, or Article 2A, UCC 2A-527. If the goods bring more than the amount secured by the security interest, the buyer or lessee must account to the seller or lessor for any surplus. UCC 2-706(6), 2A-527(5). The buyer's or lessee's rights to enforce its security interest is in addition to the ability of the buyer or lessee to recover damages based upon either cover or market price.

In an Article 2 transaction although the buyer like the seller, is in business to make a profit (and, undoubtedly, most buyers are also sellers), the purchase contract is designed to obtain goods that will be used in the overall business enterprise. The better the price, the quicker the delivery, and the higher the quality, the more likely that the overall business will be profitable. Consequently, unless the buyer's plans have changed, an immediate concern upon breach by the seller will be replacing the goods or inducing the seller to perform. Higher costs and delays in this replacement process both deprive the buyer of the benefit of her bargain and affect overall profitability. Thus, if the goods have not been tendered, the most important remedies will be specific performance, UCC 2-716, or cover, UCC 2-712, and, if delay is involved, recovery of consequential damages under UCC 2-715(2).

The "formula" in UCC 2-713(1) is a residual remedy which is used when specific performance is not available and relief for "cover" in UCC 2-712(1) is, for whatever reason, not pursued.[*] Whatever the value of this "residual" remedy, one thing is clear: since the buyer's contract, unlike the seller's, is not complicated by "lost volume" problems, there is, perhaps, a sounder basis for concluding that a buyer who did cover or should have covered is foreclosed from using UCC 2-713(1) when that would provide a higher recovery. Even if this option is preserved, the buyer cannot recover consequential damages caused by the breach which could have been "reasonably * * * prevented by cover or otherwise." UCC 2-715(2)(a). In the balance of this Chapter we will consider these possibilities and whether the same considerations are true in a lease of goods or a license of information.

B. Cover

Cover is an important UCC innovation. It is an intelligent legal response to the legitimate needs of the ordinary buyer who, when faced with the seller's breach, must look elsewhere for the goods. Under the standard contract-market differential formula, an aggrieved buyer who repurchased to fulfill his needs was taking a real risk. If, as was likely to be the case, the court measured the market at a time or place other than those at which he purchased, the contract-market paid too much or too little. UCC 2-712 changes all of that.

The conditions which one must meet to comply with UCC 2-712 are like those of UCC 2-706: at least superficially simple and unspecific. One must purchase: (1) reasonably and in good faith; (2) without unreasonable delay; and (3) in substitution for the goods due under the contract. On reflection a few problems appear. The first is the recurring problem: what is the reasonable time and what is a commercially reasonable purchase?[**] Second, if the buyer routinely purchases separate lots of goods and now seeks to allocate one of those routinely purchased

---

[*] Some have urged that UCC 2-713 be repealed. *See* Robert Childres, *Buyer's Remedies: The Danger of Section 2-713,* 72 Nw. U. L. Rev. 837 (1978).

[**] *See Hessler v. Crystal Lake Chrysler-Plymouth, Inc.,* 788 N.E. 2d 405 (Ill. Ct. App. 2003) (paying approximately $30,000 more than the contract price with seller was reasonable when seller refused to sell car to buyer and buyer located a similar car from another dealer)

lots to this contract's cover, what result? A third problem is the question whether cover, if made, is the exclusive measure of damages. A fourth is how one adjusts . for the difference between cover items and those contracted for–what if the contract calls for AM radios but AM-FM radios are procured as cover?[*]

Article 2A allows a lessee to engage in a substitute transaction and then use the price of that substitute transaction to measure damages. UCC 2A-518. What type of substitute transaction is permissible under UCC 2A-518 to set the lessee's damages?

Problem 10-11

Seller, a manufacturer in Chicago, agreed to sell to Buyer, located in Phoenix, 100 standard lathes at $500 per lathe, delivery in four equal installments, FOB Chicago, on November 1, December 1, January 1, and February 1. Payment was due 30 days after delivery. Shipping costs were $1,000 per installment. Assume that Seller missed the first delivery of lathes and, on November 15, mailed an unequivocal repudiation of the entire contract. On March 1, Buyer replaced, from a supplier in Denver, all of the lathes for $75,000. The shipment was F.O.B. destination, Phoenix. If shipment had been priced separately from the price of the goods, shipping would have been $6,000. Buyer claims $25,000 damages under UCC 2-712. Seller's lawyer has responded with the following arguments:

1. UCC 2-712 is not available, since there was an unreasonable delay in the repurchase. The time starts running from the date of repudiation, not from the date upon which the contract would have been performed.

2. Even so, the $25,000 damages should be reduced by the transportation cost which the second seller paid from Denver to Phoenix. Buyer would have had to pay those costs under the repudiated F.O.B. contract.

3. In fact, the market for the standard lathes was $50,000. The goods which Buyer purchased in Denver were of higher quality than that required by the contract. What damages?

Problem 10-12

Seller, a manufacturer in Chicago, agreed to sell to Buyer, located in Phoenix,

---

[*] See *Ctkovic v. Boch, Inc.*, 2003 WL 139779 (Mass. App. Div. 2003) (court held a new 2000 Nissan Maxima was not a reasonable substitute for a used 1998Mitsubishe Diamante).

100 standard lathes at $500 per lathe, delivery in four equal installments, FOB Chicago, on November 1, December 1, January 1, and February 1. Payment was due 30 days after delivery. Seller repudiates on November 15. A series of negotiations considering possible alternatives are conducted between Buyer and Seller, and these eventually break down in January. At that time the market price was $100,000 for nearly identical replacement lathes. Buyer, a good negotiator, was able to procure substitute lathes from another seller in February for $90,000. Buyer now sues Seller under UCC 2-713 for the contract-market differential which the court finds was $50,000.

Seller's counsel has argued that the February purchase constituted a cover and that such cover is the exclusive measure of damages. In support of his argument Seller's counsel cites Comment 5 to UCC 2-713. What should Buyer receive?

FERTICO BELGIUM S.A. V. PHOSPHATE CHEMICALS EXPORT ASSOCIATION, INC.
NEW YORK COURT OF APPEALS, 1987
70 N.Y.2D 76, 517 N.Y.S.2D 465, 510 N.E.2D 334

BELLACOSA, J.

A seller (Phoschem) breached its contract to timely deliver goods to a buyer-trader (Fertico) who properly sought cover (under the Uniform Commercial Code that means acquiring substitute goods) from another source (Unifert) in order to avoid breaching that buyer-trader's obligation to a third-party buyer (Altawreed). The sole issue involves the applicable principles and computation of damages for breach of the Phoschem-to-Fertico contract.

We hold that under the exceptional circumstances of this case plaintiff Fertico, as a buyer-trader, is entitled to damages from seller Phoschem equal to the increased cost of cover plus consequential and incidental damages minus expenses saved (UCC § 2-712[2]). In this case, expenses saved as a result of the breach are limited to costs or expenditures which would have arisen had there been no breach. Thus, the seller Phoschem is not entitled to a credit from the profits of a subsequent sale by the first buyer-trader Fertico to a fourth party (Janssens) of nonconforming goods from Phoschem. Fertico's letter of credit had been presented by Phoschem and honored so, under the specific facts of this case, Fertico had no commercially reasonable alternative but to retain and resell the fertilizer. This is so despite Fertico's exercise of cover in connection with the first set of transactions, *i.e.*, Phoschem to Fertico to Altawreed. The covering buyer-trader may not, however, as in this case, recover other consequential damages when the third party to which it made its sale provides increased compensation to offset additional costs arising as a consequence of the breach.

In October 1978 appellant Fertico Belgium S.A. (Fertico), an international trader of fertilizer, contracted with Phosphate Chemicals Export Association, Inc. (Phoschem), a corporation engaged in exporting phosphate fertilizer, to purchase two separate shipments of fertilizer for delivery to Antwerp, Belgium. The first shipment was to be 15,000 tons delivered no later than November 20, 1978 and the second was to be 20,000 tons delivered by November 30, 1978. Phoschem knew that Fertico required delivery on the specified dates so that the fertilizer could be bagged and shipped in satisfaction of a secondary contract Fertico had with Altawreed, Iraq's agricultural ministry. Fertico secured a letter of credit in a timely manner with respect to the first shipment. After Phoschem projected a first shipment delivery date of December 4, 1978, Fertico advised Phoschem, on November 13, 1978, that the breach as to the first shipment presented "huge problems" and cancelled the second shipment which had not as of that date been loaded, thus ensuring its late delivery. The first shipment did not actually arrive in Antwerp until December 17 and was not off loaded until December 21, 1978. Despite the breach as to the first shipment, Fertico retained custody and indeed acquired title over that first shipment because, as its president testified, "[w]e had no other choice" (Rec. on App., at 597-598) as defendant seller Phoschem had presented Fertico's $1.7 million letter of credit as of November 17, 1978, and the same had been honored by the issuer (*see*, UCC § 5-114).

Fertico's predicament from the breach by delay of even the first shipment, a breach which Phoschem does not deny, was that it, in turn, would breach its contract to sell to Altawreed unless it acquired substitute goods. In an effort to avoid that secondary breach, Fertico took steps in mid-November to cover (UCC § 2-712) the goods by purchasing 35,000 tons of the same type fertilizer from Unifert, a Lebanese concern. The cost of the fertilizer itself under the Phoschem-to-Fertico contract was $4,025,000, and under the Unifert-to-Fertico contract $4,725,000, a differential of $700,000. On the same day Fertico acquired cover, November 15, 1978, Fertico's president traveled to Baghdad, Iraq to renegotiate its contract with Altawreed. In return for a postponed delivery date and an additional payment of $20.50 per ton, Fertico agreed to make direct inland delivery rather than delivery to the seaport of Basra. Fertico fulfilled its renegotiated Altawreed contract with the substitute fertilizer purchased as cover from Unifert.

In addition to the problems related to its Altawreed contract, Fertico was left with 15,000 tons of late-delivered fertilizer which it did not require but which it had been compelled to take because Phoschem had received payment on Fertico's letter of credit. This aggrieved international buyer-seller was required to store the product and seek out a new purchaser. Fertico sold the 15,000 tons of the belatedly delivered Phoschem fertilizer to another buyer, Janssens, on March 19, 1979, some three months after the non-conforming delivery, and earned a profit of $454,000 based on the cost to it from Phoschem and its sale price to Janssens.

In 1981 Fertico commenced this action against Phoschem seeking $1.25 million in damages for Phoschem's breach of the October 1978 agreement. A jury returned a verdict of $1.07 million which the trial court refused to overturn on a motion for judgment notwithstanding the verdict. The Appellate Division vacated the damage award, ordered a new trial on the damages issue only and ruled, as a matter of law, (1) that the increased transportation costs on the Altawreed contract were not consequential damages; (2) that the higher purchase price paid by Altrawreed to Fertico was an expense saved as a consequence of the Phoschem breach; and (3) that the Fertico damages had to be reduced by the profits from the Janssens' sale (*Fertico Belgium S.A. v. Phosphate Chemicals Export Assoc. Inc.*, 120 A.D.2d 401, 501 N.Y.S.2d 867). Fertico appealed to this court on a stipulation for judgment absolute. We disagree with propositions (2) and (3) in the Appellate Division ruling, and conclude that the Uniform Commercial Code and our analysis support a modification and reinstatement of $700,000 of the damage award in a final judgment resolving this litigation between the parties.

Failure by Phoschem to make delivery on the contract dates concededly constituted a breach of the contract (WHITE AND SUMMERS, UNIFORM COMMERCIAL CODE § 6-2, at 207 [2d ed.]). THE UNIFORM COMMERCIAL CODE, § 2-711, gives the non-breaching party the alternative of either seeking the partial self-help of cover along with recovery of damages (UCC § 2-712), or of recovering damages only for the differential between the market price and the contract price, together with incidental and consequential damages less expenses saved (UCC § 2-713; *see also, Productora e Importadora de Papel, S.A. de C.V. v. Fleming*, 376 Mass. 826, 383 N.E.2d 1129). Fertico exercised its right as the wronged buyer-trader to cover in order to obtain the substitute fertilizer it required to meet its obligation under its Altawreed contract (*see*, UCC § 2-712, Comment 1).

A covering buyer's damages are equal to the difference between the presumably higher cost of cover and the contract price, plus incidental or consequential damages suffered on account of the breach, less expenses saved (UCC § 2-712[2]). Fertico is thus entitled to a damage remedy under this section because its cover purchase was made in good faith, without unreasonable delay, and the Unifert fertilizer was a reasonable substitute for the Phoschem fertilizer (UCC § 2-712[1]; *Reynolds v. Underwriters Bank*, 44 N.Y.2d 568, 572-573, 406 N.Y.S.2d 743, 378 N.E.2d 106).

Fertico's additional costs for delivering the fertilizer inland rather than at a seaport would usually constitute consequential damages because they resulted from Phoschem's breach, because Phoschem knew that Fertico would incur damages under its separate contract obligation and because the damages were not prevented by the cover (UCC § 2-715[2]). The increased costs attendant to the Altawreed contract are consequential damages because they did not "arise within the scope of the immediate [Phoschem-Fertico] transaction, but rather stem from losses incurred by [Fertico] in its dealings [with Altawreed] which were a proximate result of the breach, and which were reasonably foreseeable by the breaching party at the time of contracting" (*Petroleo Brasileiro, S.A. Petrobras v. Ameropan Oil Co.*, 372 F. Supp. 503, 508). Ordinarily, an award for consequential damages occasioned by the seller's breach would be necessary to put a buyer like Fertico in as good a position as it would have been had there been no breach (UCC § 1-106; *see, Neri v. Retail Marine Corporation*, 30 N.Y.2d 393, 334 N.Y.S.2d 165, 285 N.E.2d 311; 3 HAWKLAND, UNIFORM COMMERCIAL CODE SERIES § 2-715:01, at 389). Inasmuch as Altawreed compensated Fertico for the additional delivery costs, Fertico was insulated from any loss in that respect as a result of Phoschem's breach, thereby eliminating this category of potential damages. On this question of consequential damages, the appellate division was correct.

The additional compensation to Fertico, an international trader, from Altawreed is not, however, an expense saved as a consequence of the seller Phoschem's breach for which Phoschem is entitled to any credit (UCC § 2-712[2]). In most instances, and particularly in this case, saved expenses must be costs or expenditures which would be anticipated had there been no breach (*see, Productora e Importadora de Papel, S.A. de C.V. v. Fleming*, 376 Mass. 826, 839, 383 N.E.2d 1129, 1137, *supra*). For example, if a seller were to breach a contract to deliver an unpackaged product to the buyer and the buyer were to cover with the same product prepackaged, the cost of packaging which the buyer would have had to perform is an expense saved as a consequence of the breach (*see*, 3 HAWKLAND, UNIFORM COMMERCIAL CODE SERIES § 2-712:02, at 362). The increased remuneration from Altawreed was compensation for the additional shipment responsibilities incurred by Fertico, not a cost or expenditure anticipated in the absence of a breach, and therefore was erroneously analyzed and credited in Phoschem's favor by the Appellate Division.

[On the third prong of damages, the majority reversed the Appellate Division and held that Fertico did not have to account for the profit made "from the independent sale of the Phoschem fertilizer to Janssens." Treating the fertilizer as if it were in Fertico's inventory, the court analogized the sale to the lost-volume problem, discussed previously. Fertico could have made the sale and earned the profit regardless of Phoschem's breach. To deduct gains that could have been made regardless of the breach would "perversely enrich the wrongdoer at the expense of the wronged party." The dissent rejected the lost-volume analogy and in an elaborate analysis preferred to treat the fertilizer as if it had been rightfully rejected for breach of contract and held by Fertico as a bailee for Phoschem. As such, Fertico must account to Phoschem for the proceeds of the sale of Phoschem's goods, with an appropriate deduction for reasonable costs incurred in storage and arranging the sale.]

Note: Other Sources of Cover

UCC 2-712(1) provides that upon breach by the seller "the buyer may 'cover' by making in good faith and without unreasonable delay any reasonable purchase of or contract to purchase goods in substitution for those due from the seller." Must that purchase be from a third party selling substitute goods in the open market, or can the buyer cover by making a purchase from the breaching seller or by manufacturing the goods itself?

In *Kelsey-Hayes Co. v. Galtaco Redlaw Castings Corp.*, 749 F. Supp. 794 (E.D. Mich. 1990), the court held without much discussion that the breaching seller was a proper source for cover under UCC 2-712(1). The seller had repudiated because of financial considerations but offered to continue production at a slightly higher price until the buyer could find an alternative source of supply. The buyer accepted the offer without reserving any rights under the breached contract. The court concluded that the purchase may be viewed as a "successful effort" to cover, even though the buyer bought the same goods from the same seller on different terms. On balance, the decision favored the seller more than the buyer because the court rejected the buyer's claim that the agreed cover contract was entered under duress. Thus, the "cover" contract, in the form of a modification, was enforced and the buyer's damages were limited to the difference between the contract price and the higher price in the "cover" contract.

In *Dura-Wood Treating Co. v. Century Forest Indus., Inc.*, 675 F.2d 745 (5th Cir. 1982), the court held that under proper circumstances the "cover" remedy was satisfied when the buyer manufactured the goods itself. Upon seller's breach of a contract to deliver creosote treated hardwood cross-ties, the buyer obtained price quotations from other suppliers and concluded that it could produce the ties internally at a lower price than it could purchase substitutes on the open market. That price, however, was higher than the contract price and the seller objected that UCC 2-712(1) required a "cover" from a third party. The court, recognizing that UCC 2-712(1) "read literally" appears to require cover from an outside source, nevertheless held that an internal cover was sufficient where it put the buyer in the same position as full performance would have done and enabled the buyer to obtain needed goods. The court then affirmed the district court's finding that the buyer acted in good faith, covered within a reasonable time and provided a reasonable substitute. Although the factual questions raised by an internal cover are complex, other courts are in accord with the *Dura-Wood* decision.[*]

Would these same arguments apply to an Article 2A transaction?

Note that the cases discussed above support unique covers actually undertaken by the buyer. But suppose the buyer had failed to follow these interesting paths? One consequence is that damages under UCC 2-712(2) are not available. The buyer must sue under UCC 2-713(1). More importantly, the failure to cover may effect the buyer's ability to recover consequential damages under UCC 2-715(2)(a), which provides that consequential damages are recoverable "which could not reasonably be prevented by cover or otherwise." Do you think that a refusal by the buyer to cover from the breaching seller or by internal production would be reasonable?

Note: Cover Under the CISG

If the seller has committed a fundamental breach by repudiation, *see* Art. 72, or otherwise and the buyer has avoided the contract for fundamental breach under Article 49, a remedy based upon cover is then available. *See* Art. 75. If "in a reasonable manner and within a reasonable time after avoidance, the buyer has bought goods in replacement * * * the party claiming damages may recover the difference between the contract price and the price in the substitute transaction as well as any further damages recoverable under article 74." There is no requirement that the buyer replace in good faith. *See* UCC 2-712(1).

---

[*] *See, e.g., Cives Corp. v. Callier Steel Pipe & Tube, Inc.*, 482 A.2d 852, 858 (Me. 1984).

Note: Cover Under UCITA

UCITA also allows the licensee to engage in a substitute transaction and use that transaction to measure damages. UCITA 809(a)(1)(B)(iii).

C. Market-Contract Damages

Former 2-713 instructed the court to use the market price "at the time when the buyer learned of the breach." Amended UCC 2-713(1)(a) provides that market price be determined at the time of tender except in the cases of anticipatory repudiation. In the case of an anticipatory repudiation, the time for measuring the market price will be a commercially reasonable time after the repudiation but no later than the time of tender. UCC 2-713(1)(b). *Compare* UCC 2-708(1). *Compare* UCC 2A-519 which does not distinguish between repudiations and other types of breaches. The place for measuring market price is addressed in UCC 2-713(2).

Prior to the 2003 amendments, the courts attempted to determine "when the buyer learned of the breach" in the case of an anticipatory repudiation.* After the amendments the question of what is a "commercially reasonable" time after repudiation will be the subject of litigation. *See* Comment 4 to amended UCC 2-713.

Problem 10-13

Seller, a manufacturer in Chicago, agreed to sell to Buyer, located in Phoenix, 100 standard lathes at $500 per lathe, delivery in four equal installments, FOB Chicago, on November 1, December 1, January 1, and February 1. Payment was due 30 days after delivery. Cost of shipment of each installment was $1,000. Buyer had to pay the carrier $1,000 in shipment costs in order to retrieve the first shipment from the carrier. Seller delivered the first installment which the Buyer rightfully and effectively rejected due to nonconformity to the contract. Seller then repudiated on November 5 and Buyer did not cover. Buyer requested instructions as to what to do with the rejected shipment of lathes and received no response. Buyer stored the lathes for 2 months for a cost of $500 and then notified Seller it

---

* *Compare Hess Energy Inc. v. Lightning Oil Co.*, 338 F.3d 357 (4th Cir. 2003) (date of tender) *with Cosden Oil v. Karl O. Helm Aktiengesellschaft*, 736 F.2d 1064 (5th Cir. 1984) *rehearing denied*, 750 F.2d 69 (1984) (commercially reasonable time after the repudiation).

was going to sell the lathes. Buyer sold the lathes in a commercially reasonable manner for $12,000 and gave notice of the sale to Seller. Buyer incurred $100 costs in conducting the resale. Buyer sued Seller for damages under UCC 2-713. Buyer submitted the following proof on market prices for each installment when the case went to trial the following July:
1. November 1: Chicago, $13,500; Phoenix, $13,000.
2. December 1: Chicago, $14,000; Phoenix, $13,500.
3. January 1: Chicago, $14,000; Phoenix, $13,500.
4. February 1: Chicago, $14,500; Phoenix, $14,000.

Seller asserted a counterclaim for the price for the lathes from the first shipment. How much in damages, if any, should the court award to Buyer?

Problem 10-14

In April, 2003, Buyer, a cooperative, contracted to buy Seller's seasonal output of sunflower seeds at $13 per hundred pounds. It was estimated that Seller would grow between 80 and 85 thousand pounds, with delivery in three installments between December, 2003 and March, 2004. Buyer resold the seeds to Dealer for $13 per hundred pounds, and was to retain a $.55 per hundred pound handling charge for each pound received from Seller and delivered to Dealer. Due to bad weather, the market price began to escalate. Seller, without delivering anything, repudiated in January, 2003. The market price had nearly doubled and by February 28, 2004, Seller had sold 80,000 pounds of sunflower seeds to another dealer for the prevailing market price of $26 per hundred pound.

Buyer sued seller for damages under UCC 2-713(1), measured by the difference between the contract price and the market price, some $13 per pound. Seller argued that Buyer's recovery should be limited to $.55 per hundred pound, the fee that would have been earned upon full performance by Seller. Seller relied upon UCC 1-305 [former 1-106] as a limitation on UCC 2-713(1) and stressed that since Buyer's profit was fixed, it assumed no risk on fluctuating market prices. There was no evidence on how the dispute, if any, between Buyer and Dealer was resolved.

After trial, a judgment was entered for Buyer. The trial judge's memo, relying on *Tongish v. Thomas*, 840 P.2d 471 (Kan. 1992) provided the following.

First, in interpreting Article 2, if general and specific provisions cannot be harmonized, the specific should prevail. Since UCC 1-305 [former 1-106(1)] and UCC 2-713(1) are arguably inconsistent, UCC 2-713(1) controls as a matter of statutory interpretation.

Second, the clear language of UCC 2-713's compensation scheme directs a court to award expectation damages in accordance with the parties' allocation of risk as measured by the difference between contract price and market price on the date set for performance.

Third, damages based upon the profit lost on a resale are inappropriate in cases where the seller has repudiated and the buyer has protected itself against market fluctuations. Since lost profits reflect the value of a completed exchange, they create instability before delivery and give the seller an incentive to breach the contract if the market fluctuates to its advantage. Damages under UCC 2-713, on the other hand, tend to discourage breach by the seller.

Fourth, Buyer elected not to cover and fix its loss. Thus, it saved an amount equal to the difference between the market price and the contract price. The UCC formula reflects a policy judgment that it makes more sense to award the amount of that saving to the buyer than to permit the non-performing and non-covering seller to retain it.

You represent Seller. On appeal, what arguments should you make? How should the case be decided?*

Note: Market Price Damages Under the CISG

Like the "cover" remedy, availability of damages to the CISG buyer based upon the difference between the contract price and the market price is conditioned upon a proper avoidance of the contract for fundamental breach. *See* Art. 49(1), Art. 76. Suppose that Seller in New York repudiated a contract with Buyer in Frankfurt on May 1. Buyer learned of the repudiation on May 5 and the repudiation was reaffirmed by Seller on May 7. On these facts, Buyer must avoid the contract "within a reasonable time * * * after he knew or ought to have known of the breach." Art. 49(2)(b)(i). If Buyer avoided on May 9 (within a reasonable time), damages where there is a current price for the goods are "the difference between the price fixed by the contract and the current price at the time of avoidance as well as any further damages recoverable under article 74." Art. 76(1). If Buyer has avoided the contract after taking over the goods (not the facts here), the current price is determined at the "time of such taking." As to the place where the current price is determined, *see* Art. 76(2).

---

* *See TexPar Energy, Inc. v. Murphy Oil USA, Inc.*, 45 F.3d 1111 (7th Cir. 1995).

How well does this approach work in long-term, installment contracts of sale? Suppose Buyer avoided the contract after an unreasonable time has passed?

Note: Market Price Damages Under UCITA

UCITA 809(a)(1)(B)(ii) allows the licensee's damages to be calculated using the market price.

D. Consequential and Incidental Damages

A commercial buyer may have different objectives in contracting to buy goods: (1) As a jobber or distributor, to resell goods in the same condition as delivered by the seller; (2) As a manufacturer, to use the goods as part of a product to be manufactured and resold; and (3) As a manufacturer, to use the goods as equipment to maintain or expand its capacity to produce goods for resale. Thus, a jobber would purchase, say, a completed wood stove for resale to consumers while a manufacturer would purchase either steel to be incorporated into a stove to be manufactured or equipment with which to manufacture the stove.

In each case, an unexcused delay or a failure to deliver by the seller results in three potential sources of damages, "direct" damages measured by the contract price and either the market price, UCC 2-713, or the cost to cover, UCC 2-712, "consequential" damages, measured by the buyer's loss from being unable to use the goods, UCC 2-715(2)(a), and "incidental" damages, UCC 2-715(1). Frequently, the buyer claims as consequential damages the net profits that would have been made if the goods had been delivered on time. *Compare* UCC 2A-520.

There are four traditional limitations upon the recovery of consequential damages.[*] Three limitations are explicit in UCC 2-715(2)(a): (i) The loss must result from or be caused by the breach; (ii) The loss must result from "general or particular requirements and needs" of the buyer "of which the seller at the time of contracting had reason to know "; and (iii) The loss must be one "which could not

---

[*] Why should these limitations arise at all? For one view of the "forseeability" requirement, *see* Barry E. Adler, *The Questionable Ascent of Hadley v. Baxendale*, 51 STAN. L. REV. 1547 (1999). Should there be more limitations on the recovery of consequential damages? *See* RESTATMENT (SECOND) OF CONTRACTS 351(3) and Larry T. Garvin, *Disproportionality and the Law of Consequential Damages: Default Theory and Cognitive Reality*, 59 OHIO ST. L.J. 339 (1998).

reasonably be prevented by cover or otherwise."" A fourth limitation, applicable to all claims for damages, is that the loss must be proved by the plaintiff with reasonable certainty. To prevail in a claim for consequential damages, the plaintiff must satisfy all four limitations. *Compare* UCC 2A-520.

Consider the following problem. We will return to the consequential damages problem in connection with the claim for damages with regard to accepted products.

Problem 10-15

On May 1, F, a farmer, sold B, a dealer, 2,000 bushels of # 1 yellow corn, just planted in F's fields, for $3.00 a bushel. Delivery was promised no later than October 15. On May 15, B resold the corn to C, a cereal manufacturer, for $4.00 a bushel. Due to a drought in other parts of the country, the market price for # 1 yellow at the time of delivery was $5.00 per bushel. F failed to deliver and C demanded delivery from B of 2,000 bushels at $4.00 per bushel.

A. Assume B purchased corn on the market at $5.00 per bushel to satisfy C. What are B's damages against F?

B. Assume B did not purchase corn and thus breached the contract with C. What are B's damages against F?

C. Suppose, after negotiations, C agreed to release B from the contract upon payment of $500. B paid the $500. What are B's damages against F?

D. Suppose on May 15, B had been able to resell the corn to C for $6.00 a bushel even though the prevailing market price for futures was $4.00. What damages?

E. Suppose B was going to use the corn purchased from F to make livestock feed instead of reselling to C. Due to F's breach, B was unable to supply enough feed to its buyers. What are B's damages against F?

Note: Consequential Damages Under the CISG

Article 74 allows for damages for the sum equal to the loss including consequential loss. Article 74 imposes a foreseeability limitation on damages.

---

* Who bears the burden of proof on whether the consequential loss could have been mitigated is an interesting question. *See Glen Distributors Corp. v. Carlisle Plastics, Inc.*, 297 F.3d 294 (3rd Cir. 2002) (burden to prove buyer could have mitigated and did not do so is on the breaching seller).

Damages "suffered" by a party "as a consequence of the breach * * * may not exceed the loss which the party in breach foresaw or ought to have foreseen at the time of the conclusion of the contract, in the light of the facts and matters of which he then knew or ought to have known, as a possible consequence of the breach of contract."

Note: Consequential Damages Under UCITA

UCITA also provides for a licensee's incidental and consequential damages. UCITA 809. *See* UCITA 102 for the definitions of both types of damages.

Note: Punitive Damages for Breach by Repudiation or Non-delivery

Under what circumstances, if any, can a plaintiff recover punitive damages for breach of a contract for sale?

UCC 1-305 [former 1-106] provides that "penal damages" may not be recovered "except as specifically provided in [the UCC] or by other rule of law." There is nothing in the UCC which "specifically" authorizes punitive damages for any breach of a contract for sale. What about "other" rules of law? UCC 1-103.

In the absence of legislation preempting the UCC, an accepted starting place is the RESTATEMENT (SECOND) OF CONTRACTS 355: "Punitive damages are not recoverable for a breach of contract unless the conduct constituting the breach is also a tort for which punitive damages are recoverable." Thus, if the breach is not "also" a tort, punitives are not recoverable. Even so, the breach which is a tort must, in the view of some courts, be "wilful" and "accompanied by fraud, malice, wantoness or oppression." *McIntosh v. Magna Systems, Inc.*, 539 F. Supp. 1185, 1190 (N.D. Ill. 1982). In most cases, this exacting test will not capture a breach that is simply negligent or a breach that is wilful where the objective is to recapture a gain that was foregone in the bargaining at the time of contracting. Moreover, the duty of good faith imposed by general contract law, *see* RESTATEMENT (SECOND) OF CONTRACTS 205, is classified as a term of the contract. Thus, bad faith in the performance or enforcement of the contract, however defined, is a breach of the bargain for which contract rather than tort remedies are available. *See* RESTATEMENT (SECOND) OF CONTRACTS 5(2), 235(2) and Comment (b).

A court could, however, decide that a "bad faith" breach was a tort which, if egregious, would support an award of punitive damages. California courts have done so in the context of insurance, and this result has been accepted in many states.

Insurance contracts, however, contain elements not normally present in a commercial contract for sale between professional sellers and buyers. *See* Charles M. Louderbach & Thomas W. Jurika, *Standards for Limiting the Tort of Bad Faith Breach of Contract,* 16 U.S.F. L. REV. 187 (1982), who note the existence of a "special" relationship, with elements of unequal capacity, dependence, and trust between the individual insured and a corporate insurer. The absence of these special dimensions in commercial transactions has lead most courts to conclude that tort damages, including punitives, are not appropriate, regardless of the nature or purpose of the breach. A leading case is *Freeman & Mills, Inc. v. Belcher Oil Co.,* 900 P.2d 669, 679-80 (Cal. 1995), adopting a "general rule precluding tort recovery for noninsurance contract breach, at least in the absence of violation of an 'independent duty arising from principles of tort law' * * * other than the bad faith denial of the existence of, or liability under, the breached contract."

CHAPTER ELEVEN

NON-CONFORMING PERFORMANCE AND ACCEPTED PRODUCTS: DAMAGES FOR BREACH

SECTION 1. REPRISE OF REJECTION, ACCEPTANCE AND REVOCATION OF ACCEPTANCE

First, some words in summary. If the commercial buyer or lessee can establish that a warranty was made and breached, the timing of that discovery will be critical to the available remedy choices. If the breach was discovered before acceptance, rejection of the goods may be a proper remedy. UCC 2-601, 2-612, 2A-509, 2A-510. The buyer or lessee must timely notify the seller or lessor and take proper care of the goods after rejection, UCC 2-602, 2A-512, or in some circumstances follow instructions as to disposing of the goods. UCC 2-603, 2A-511. If the breach was discovered after acceptance and the buyer or lessee acts fast, a revocation of acceptance may be proper under UCC 2-608 or 2A-517. Again the buyer or lessee must timely notify the seller or lessor and must take proper care of the goods. In both cases, the goods are "thrown back" at the seller or lessor. Unless there is a right to cure under UCC 2-508, 2A-513, or the contract, the seller or lessor is responsible for disposing of the goods and the buyer or lessee may shoot for the remedies contained in UCC 2-711 or 2A-508. The remedies of rejection and revocation of acceptance were explored more fully in Chapter Six, *supra.*

But our buyer or lessee may never reach this position, either because it wants to accept the goods despite any defects, or because it is unable to reject or revoke acceptance, or because the breach may have rendered the goods worthless. What then? When a buyer or lessee accepts a nonconforming performance, she is obligated to pay the contract price for that performance. UCC 2-607(1), 2A-516(1). Setoff of damages from the price or rent still owed under that contract is allowed in some circumstances. *See* UCC 2-717, 2A-508(5) [former subs. (6)]. If the buyer or lessee has given proper notice under UCC 2-607(3) or 2A-516(3), initiated suit before the statute of limitations expires, UCC 2-725, 2A-506, and established that the seller or lessor breached the contract, the remedies for breach with regard to accepted goods are available. *See* UCC 2-714 , 2-715, 2A-519(3) and (4). In this Chapter, we will explore the scope of protection under these sections.

SECTION 2.   ACCEPTING A NON-CONFORMING PERFORMANCE; NOTICE

In order to pursue remedies for breach when the product has been accepted, the buyer or lessee must give notice of the breach. Under former Articles 2 and 2A, the failure to give timely notice barred the buyer or lessee from pursuing any remedy. Under the 2003 amendments, the buyer or lessee that fails to give timely notice of breach will be barred from any remedy only if the seller or lessor is prejudiced by the failure to give timely notice. UCC 2-607(3), 2A-516(3).

A number of questions surround the interpretation of these sections:

(1) What purposes are served by notice in commercial cases?

(2) When "should" the buyer or lessee have discovered the breach?

(3) When does a "reasonable time" expire?

(4) Does a buyer or lessee have to give notice to a remote seller or lessor?

(5) What should the form and content of the notice be?

(6) When is a seller or lessor prejudiced by the failure to get timely notice?

Regardless of how these questions are answered from case to case, two things are clear: (1) The plaintiff must, at the very least, plead and prove that adequate notice was given to state a cause of action for breach of warranty, and (2) The notice condition does not apply to actions grounded in strict tort liability, *i.e.*, where a defective product has caused damage to person or property.[*] Consider the following leading case decided before the 2003 amendments to Articles 2 and 2A. Would the analysis be the same under the amended UCC 2-607(3) and 2A-516(3)?

AQUALON COMPANY V. MAC EQUIPMENT, INC.
UNITED STATES COURT OF APPEALS, FOURTH CIRCUIT, 1998
149 F.3D 262

MURNAGHAN, CIRCUIT JUDGE

Aqualon Company, a chemical manufacturer, asked MAC Equipment, Incorporated, to produce rotary valves, also called airlocks, for use in a pneumatic conveying system. The system was designed by C.W. Nofsinger Company to move

---

[*] *See Cole v. Keller Industries, Inc.*, 132 F.3d 1044 (4th Cir. 1998); RESTATEMENT (SECOND) OF TORTS 402A, Comment m. *See* RESTATEMENT (THIRD) OF TORTS: PRODUCTS LIABILITY 18. *But see American Bumper & Manufacturing Co. v. Transtechnology Corp.*, 652 N.W.2d 252 (Mich. Ct. App. 2002) (per curium) (failure to give timely notice barred indemnity action).

a chemical, blended carboxymethyl cellulose. Before MAC was awarded a contract to produce the valves, it provided estimates of how much air its valves would leak. However, once the valves were actually constructed, they leaked much more than expected.

After almost a year of complaints and negotiations between Aqualon and MAC, it became apparent that the valves could not be made to leak any less. Aqualon modified its system design so that it would still be able to move the chemical despite the leakage. In the spring of 1993 Aqualon reissued a purchase order for the leaky valves; Aqualon accepted the valves in June; and Aqualon paid for them in full as of December 19, 1993. MAC did not conceal, and Aqualon knew, the valves' air leakage rate.

Three years thereafter Aqualon served MAC with a complaint for breach of contract and warranty. The district court granted summary judgment to MAC, holding that Aqualon had not given MAC notice within a reasonable time of its claim for breach. Aqualon appeals.

[The court first held that it had jurisdiction.] * * *

II.

As this appeal arises from a grant of summary judgment, we view the facts in the light most favorable to the non-moving party, deciding matters of law de novo. * * * Here the relevant facts are essentially agreed upon. Aqualon, after repeatedly stressing its right to reject nonconforming valves, reissued purchase orders for the valves knowing full well that they leaked more than MAC had estimated, accepted delivery and paid for the valves in full, all without notifying MAC that it found the transaction *still* troublesome. The first such notice Aqualon gave MAC that it intended to pursue a claim of breach was the complaint served on MAC three years after acceptance. The district court dismissed Aqualon's breach of contract and breach of warranty claims on the ground that such notice was not given within a reasonable time after acceptance, as section 2-607(3) of the Uniform Commercial Code requires. We are asked to review the application of the U.C.C. section 2-607(3) as a matter of law.

Section 2-607(3) provides:

> (3) Where a tender has been accepted
>
> (a) the buyer must within a reasonable time after he discovers or should have discovered any breach notify the seller of breach or be barred from any remedy* * *

U.C.C. § 2-607(3). The notice required by section 2-607(3) "need merely be sufficient to let the seller know that the transaction is still troublesome and must be watched." U.C.C. § 2-607, cmt. 4.

Aqualon makes four related arguments: 1) section 2-607(3) does not apply to the circumstance presented here; 2) Aqualon's pre-acceptance complaints that the valves leaked more than it had estimated constituted reasonable notice of the breach; 3) MAC's actual knowledge that the valves leaked more than MAC had estimated fulfilled the purposes of the U.C.C. notice requirement; and 4) Aqualon's serving MAC with a complaint three years after acceptance constituted notice within a reasonable time. We address each contention in turn.

A. U.C.C. Section 2-607(3) Does Apply

By its terms, U.C.C. section 2-607(3) applies to this case because this is a situation "[w]here a tender [of goods, *i.e.*, the valves] has been accepted." Section 2-607(3) bars a breach of contract claim by a buyer, such as Aqualon, who has accepted the seller's, such as MAC's, tender of goods unless Aqualon gave MAC notice of the alleged breach within a reasonable time.

Section 2-607(3) is based on section 49 of the Uniform Sales Act. *See* U.C.C. § 2-607, cmt. (Prior Uniform Statutory Provision). Professor Williston, the author of the Uniform Sales Act, has explained that section 49 ameliorated the harsh rule that acceptance of a tender of goods acted as a release by the buyer of any claim that the goods did not conform to the contract. *See* 5 WILLISTON ON CONTRACTS § 714 (3d ed.1961). But the Uniform Sales Act did not go entirely to the other extreme by allowing the buyer to accept goods without objection and then assert claims for breach of contract at any time within the statute of limitations period. *See id.* Instead, the Act "allow[ed] the buyer to accept the offer without waiving any claims, provided the buyer gave the seller prompt notice of any claimed breach." *Southeastern Steel Co. v. W.A. Hunt Constr. Co.*, 301 S.C. 140, 390 S.E.2d 475, 478 (1990). Courts have held that the same understanding applies to section 2-607(3) of the U.C.C. * * *

Aqualon has argued that the U.C.C. provision does not apply to this case because MAC had actual knowledge that its valves were inadequate long before Aqualon's acceptance. Requiring further notice after acceptance would be pointless, Aqualon argues. In support, Aqualon cites *Jay V. Zimmerman Co. v. General Mills, Inc.*, 327 F. Supp. 1198 (E.D. Mo. 1971). In *Jay V. Zimmerman Co.*, the seller was unable to deliver the goods by the date specified in the contract. The seller clearly knew that it was in breach of the contract when it delivered the goods late, and the buyer did not formally notify the seller of its intent to sue for breach after accepting the late goods. The court found that section 2-607(3) did not apply in the situation where the seller had actual knowledge of the breach at the time of delivery, holding that "[i]t would be an unreasonable, if not absurd, construction of the statute to require a renewed notice of breach *after* acceptance of the goods" in those circumstances. *Id.* at 1204.

Both previous and subsequent cases have rejected the reasoning of *Jay V. Zimmerman Co.* Under the Uniform Sales Act predecessor to section 2- 607(3) "it was irrelevant whether a seller had actual knowledge of a nonconforming tender. Instead, the critical question was whether the seller had been informed that the buyer considered him to be in breach." [citing *Eastern Air Lines, Inc. v. McDonnell Douglas Corp.*, 532 F.2d 957, 972 (5th Cir. 1976) (*rejecting Jay V. Zimmerman Co.*); * * * As the *Southeastern Steel Co.* court noted, Judge Learned Hand "eloquently disposed of this imaginative, but fallacious, argument," 390 S.E.2d at 480, that a seller's knowledge of a defective tender was sufficient notice of breach:

> The plaintiff replies that the buyer is not required to give notice of what the seller already knows, but this confuses two quite different things. The notice "of the breach" required is not of the facts, which the seller presumably knows quite as well as, if not better than, the buyer, but of buyer's claim that they constitute a breach. The purpose of the notice is to advise the seller that he must meet a claim for damages, as to which, rightly or wrongly, the law requires that he shall have early warning.

American Mfg. Co. v. United States Shipping Bd. Emergency Fleet Corp., 7 F.2d 565, 566 (2d Cir.1925); * * * [N]umerous courts have applied Judge Hand's reasoning to cases involving U.C.C. section 2-607(3). * * * The reasoning is persuasive, and it produces no "harsh results" in this case. Aqualon was required by section 2-607(3) to give formal notice to MAC, after accepting the valves, that it still found the transaction troublesome. Only then would MAC know not to assume a position of repose, but that it should attempt either to cure the defect, negotiate a settlement or prepare for litigation.

[The court distinguished cases and concluded that MAC did not know that Aqualon "would claim that the valves' excessive leakage rate constituted a breach of contract or breach of warranty."] * * *

B. Aqualon's Pre-Acceptance Complaints Did Not Satisfy the Requirements of U.C.C. Section 2-607(3)

[The court held that Section 2-607(3)(a) was not satisfied where MAC knew that Aqualon considered the valves to be non-conforming but Aqualon did not inform MAC that it still believed that there was a breach after acceptance. At a minimum, Aqualon should have notified MAC after acceptance that it still considered the transaction to be "troublesome."] * * *

C. The Purposes of the Notice Requirement Were Not Met

Acknowledging that it gave no additional notice after it accepted the valves that the transaction was "still troublesome," Aqualon asserts that the *purposes* of the notice requirement were met by MAC's actual knowledge that its valves were inadequate. Aqualon argues that where those purposes have been satisfied, its failure to comply with the technical requirements of the U.C.C. should not bar it from litigating the case on the merits. * * *

Aqualon contends that three purposes of the notice requirement were met in this case. The three purposes that Aqualon identifies for the U.C.C.'s notice requirement are:

(1) to prevent surprise and allow the seller the opportunity to make recommendations on how to cure the nonconformance;

(2) to permit the seller the fair opportunity to investigate and prepare for litigation; and

(3) to open the way for normal settlement of claims through negotiation.

Aqualon, however, neglects to include a further purpose identified by the district court:

(4) to protect the seller from stale claims and provide certainty in contractual arrangements.

Cf. 1 JAMES J. WHITE & ROBERT S. SUMMERS, UNIFORM COMMERCIAL CODE § 11-10, at 612-13 (4th ed.1995) (listing these purposes, as well as the purpose of recognizing a general disbelief of tardy claims). Assuming, without deciding, that satisfaction of these four purposes would obviate the need to comply with the terms of the statute, Aqualon cannot demonstrate that the purposes were satisfied.

First, the notice requirement provides an opportunity for the seller to cure the defect. * * * MAC knew in August of 1992 that its valves would leak far more than stated in its original proposal. Both MAC and Aqualon worked together for the next six months to try to modify Aqualon's system design to use those valves, because both parties knew that nothing more could be done to improve the performance of the valves. Because MAC had in excess of six months to effect a cure and was unable to do so, Aqualon contends that the first purpose of the notice requirement was satisfied.

Second, the notice requirement is intended to give the seller a fair chance to prepare for litigation, for example by gathering documents and taking depositions while the evidence is still available and memories are still fresh. * * * Aqualon asserts that this purpose was fulfilled because MAC knew of the possibility of litigation by virtue of its knowledge that the system as originally designed did not work with the leaky valves. However, as explained above, the aforementioned knowledge demonstrates that MAC knew the facts, but not that MAC knew that Aqualon would consider these facts to constitute a breach of warranty. Aqualon's acceptance of and full payment for the valves without further complaint, knowing their leakage rates, communicated to MAC that the valves were acceptable.

Third, the notice requirement prompts negotiation and settlement of claims. * * * If MAC had been notified more promptly after Aqualon's acceptance of the valves that Aqualon intended to sue MAC (specifically, before Aqualon filed its complaint), it might have settled the underlying claim. Because MAC would not have had to undertake the expenses of litigation that arose when it had to respond to Aqualon's complaint, MAC would likely have offered more money in settlement of the claim. And because Aqualon would not yet have invested in litigation by paying lawyers to prepare and file the complaint, Aqualon would presumably have agreed to receive less money in settlement of its claim. In this way, earlier notice would have led to a greater chance of settlement. Aqualon's bare assertion that "MAC has suffered no detriment with respect to the options of settlement," just because settlement efforts were unsuccessful, is mistaken.

Finally, the notice requirement is intended to protect the seller from stale claims and provide certainty in contractual arrangements. *See id.* Aqualon argues that using a notice requirement to give peace of mind to a defendant and to protect against stale claims is inappropriate and unnecessary because that purpose is served by a statute of limitations. It is true that a state may decide to serve these policies through a strict statute of limitations. But a state may also choose to enact a notice requirement in addition to a longer statute of limitations. Such a two-part scheme preserves claims of which the defendant has *not* been notified for only a short period of time, but if the defendant *has* been notified, it preserves those claims for a longer period. The Delaware equivalent of U.C.C. section 2-607(3) combines with Delaware's statute of limitations to create just such a scheme. Because Aqualon made no complaints to MAC for three years after accepting the valves, MAC was *entitled* to assume a position of repose.

D. Aqualon's Delay of Three Years Was Not
Notification Within a Reasonable Time

Finally, Aqualon argues that even if its pre-acceptance complaints did not serve to notify MAC that it found the transaction "still troublesome," Aqualon's service of a civil complaint on MAC approximately three years after accepting the valves was notification within a "reasonable time," satisfying U.C.C. section 2-607(3). The district court found that such a delay was unreasonable, relying on our statement in *Hebron* that "[i]n the circumstances of this case, we hold that a two-year delay in giving notice under [the Virginia equivalent of U.C.C. section 2-607(3)] is unreasonable as a matter of law where no explanation for the delay is provided and actual prejudice is sustained." 60 F.3d at 1098.

Aqualon asserts that, unlike the plaintiff in *Hebron*, it had good reasons for delay. The reasons it provides boil down to simply that Aqualon was slow in figuring out that it wanted to blame MAC for the cost over-run in designing its system. Furthermore, Aqualon offers no explanation whatsoever for the delay of a year after filing its complaint against MAC before Aqualon served MAC with the complaint.

Aqualon also asserts that the delay was not unreasonable because MAC has not suffered any prejudice from the delay. MAC claims that there was prejudice to its case because of faded memories and lost documents, and gives an example of a lost document. Aqualon argues in rebuttal that the named document would have been irrelevant to MAC's case. We cannot tell whether the document would have been helpful because, it being lost, we cannot know exactly what information it contained. Furthermore, we cannot tell whether there may have been other pertinent documents available three years before MAC was served that were lost and have been forgotten during its period of repose. These considerations demonstrate why, although prejudice is relevant to whether a delay was reasonable, no showing of prejudice is required to make section 2- 607(3) applicable.

III.

The district court correctly denied Aqualon's motion to remand the case and correctly dismissed Aqualon's contract and warranty claims because of Aqualon's failure to notify MAC of those claims within a reasonable time after accepting tender of the valves. The district court's judgment is

Affirmed.

[Footnotes omitted.]

Notes

1. The "prejudice" standard was adopted under former 2-607(3) in the case of a consumer buyer in *Wal-Mart Stores, Inc. v. Wheeler*, 586 S.E.2d 83 (Ga. Ct. App. 2003). The consumer buyer had not given notice to Wal-Mart until 2 years after the injury occurred. The court relied on the former comment to former 2-607 stating that the notice provision should not be applied to "deprive a good faith consumer

of his remedy."

2.   Should the buyer or lessee have to give notice to sellers or lessors who are not in privity of contract with the buyer or lessee in order to recover for breach of a warranty? Several cases, relying on former comment 5 to former 2-607, so held.[*] Will purchasers attempting to enforce the remote obligations under UCC 2-313A and 2-313B have to give timely notice to the remote seller in order to enforce the obligations set forth in those sections? The comments to those sections and the new comments to UCC 2-607 give no direction.

3.   UCC 2-607(5) addresses another type of notice in a process referred to as "vouching in." If a buyer is sued for an obligation that the buyer's seller is liable for, the buyer notifies the seller to come in and defend. If the seller does not do so after notice, the seller is bound by the factual findings in the first suit.[**]

Problem 11-1

Bristow, the holder of a McDonalds franchise, contracted with Stiko, a manufacturer, for 17 dozen pans expressly designed for the preparation of Big Mac sandwiches. A December 1 shipment date was agreed. On November 28, Stiko telephoned Bristow to say that they were having "a bit of trouble" and that the pans "could not be delivered until late January." Bristow replied that timely delivery was important and if the pans were not shipped by December 1, "we will consider that you have breached the contract." The pans were shipped on January 17. Bristow accepted the pans and there was no further communication until Stiko sued for the contract price in May. Bristow claimed an offset from the contract price based upon damages for late delivery. The trial court, relying on UCC 2-607(3), denied the offset and entered judgment for the contract price. In his memorandum opinion, the trial judge held that UCC 2-607(3) required notice after acceptance. Here none was given. Further, even if the answer were treated as a notice, "the delay was unreasonable as a matter of law."

What arguments will you make on appeal? Would your argument be any different if it was a lease transaction?

---

[*] *See e.g. U.S. Tire-Tech, Inc. v. Boeran, B.V.*, 110 S.W.3d 194 (Tex. Ct. App. 2003).

[**] For a rare case discussing the process, *see Old Kent Bank v. Kal Kustom, Inc.*, 660 N.W.2d 384 (Mich. Ct. App. 2003) (buyer not obligated to 'vouch in' seller).

Problem 11-2

Your client entered into a contract to purchase a specified quantity of yarn. The expected quality was spelled out in some detail. As part of the contract, the client agreed to the following clauses in the sales contract:

    2. No claims relating to excessive moisture content, short weight, count variations, twist, quality or shade shall be allowed *if made after weaving, knitting, or processing,* or more than 10 days after receipt of shipment. * * * The buyer shall within 10 days of the receipt of the merchandise by himself or agent examine the merchandise for any and all defects. * * *

    4. This instrument constitutes the entire agreement between the parties, superseding all previous communications, oral or written, and no changes, amendments or additions hereto will be recognized unless in writing signed by both seller and buyer or buyer's agent. It is expressly agreed that no representations or warranties, express or implied, have been or are made by the seller except as stated herein, and the seller makes no warranty, express or implied, as to the fitness for buyer's purposes of yarn purchased hereunder, seller's obligations, except as expressly stated herein, being limited to the *delivery of good merchantable yarn of the description stated herein.*

The yarn was tendered on March 1 and, after an inspection, accepted by your client on March 2. Thereafter the yarn was cut and knitted into sweaters and the finished product was washed. During the washing, which took place on March 15 and 16, your client discovered that the color of the yarn had "shaded," that is, there was a variation in color from piece to piece and within the pieces. This was clearly a defect that made the yarn unmerchantable and could not have been discovered by a reasonable inspection. Your client promptly gave notice to the seller of the defect. Since revocation of acceptance was not possible (do you see why?), your client asserted a claim for damages under UCC 2-714(2) and 2-715(2). The seller, pointing to the contract, denied any liability.

    Your client comes to you for advice. Is the clause enforceable? *See* UCC 1-205 [former 1-204], 2-302 and 2-719. After you have completed your analysis, you may wish to compare it with *Wilson Trading Corp. v. David Ferguson, Ltd.*, 244 N.E.2d 685 (N.Y. 1968).

Note: Notice of Breach Under the CISG

Under Article 39(1) of the CISG, the buyer "loses the right to rely on a lack of conformity of the goods if he does not give notice to the seller specifying the nature of the lack of conformity within a reasonable time after he has discovered it or ought to have discovered it." Even if the buyer ought not to have discovered a "latent" defect, the buyer loses the right to rely on the nonconformity unless notice is given to the seller "at the latest within a period of two years from the date on which the goods were actually handed over to the buyer, unless this time-limit is inconsistent with a contractual period of guarantee." Art. 39(2). What happens if the seller knew or had reason to know of the defect and did not disclose it to the buyer? *See* Art. 40. For the seller's right to cure, *see* Art. 37 & Art. 48.

Note: Notice of Breach Under UCITA

UCITA 610(c) provides that if the performance is provision of a copy of computer information and the copy is accepted, the licensee must give notice of certain claims to the licensor within a reasonable time after it discovered or should have discovered the breach or be barred from any remedy. Those claims are claims for breach of contract other than for a breach of the warranty of noninfringement, a breach of an express warranty concerning misappropriation, or libel or slander or similar claims. If the claim is a breach of the warranty of noninfringment, a breach of an express warranty concerning misappropriation, libel or slander or similar claims and the licensee is sued by a third party for those claims, the licensee must give notice to the licensor within a reasonable time after receiving notice of the litigation or be precluded from any remedy against the licensor on those claims.

SECTION 3.   DAMAGES FOR ACCEPTED PERFORMANCE

A. Direct Damages

Under the Article 2 scheme, all damages that do not qualify as incidental damages, UCC 2-715(1), or consequential damages, UCC 2-715(2) are lumped rather ingloriously under the label of "direct" damages. UCC 2-714 is included under that label and is a functional counterpart of UCC 2-712 and UCC 2-713. All three sections attempt to preserve the benefit of the bargained for benefit of buyer's agreement with the seller. *See* UCC 1-305 [former 1-106]. Remember the buyer still has the goods and is liable for their price, UCC 2-607(1), subject to the power, upon notice to the seller, to "deduct all or any part of the damages resulting from any breach of the contract from any part of the price still due under the same contract." UCC 2-717. UCC 2-714 is somewhat open-ended and difficult to apply with precision. Several questions arise.

UCC 2-714(2) provides the measure of damages for breach of warranty. To what disputes does UCC 2-714(1) apply? How does one determine what losses resulted "in the ordinary course of events from the seller's breach as determined in any manner which is reasonable"? To illustrate, suppose the seller was ten days late in delivery or delivered only 90% of the goods and the buyer accepted the goods. How would loses resulting from those breaches be measured? In UCC 2-714(2), how does the buyer prove the "difference at the time and place of acceptance between the value of goods accepted and the value they would have had if they had been as warranted"? Why does the UCC adopt a diminished value test rather than a market test for accepted goods? In UCC 2-714(2), what "special circumstances" show proximate damages of a different amount? How is the line between "direct" damages under UCC 2-714(2) and "incidental and consequential damages" under UCC 2-715 to be drawn?

The damage remedy for accepted leased goods is the same as for a sales transaction. *See* UCC 2A-519(3) and (4). The lessee has possession of the goods and must pay the contract rent, UCC 2A-516(1), subject to the ability to deduct damages from the rent yet due, UCC 2A-508(5) [former subsection (6)].

Problem 11-3

A. Sunshine Cannery contracted on May 1 to purchase 10,000 bushels of # 1 grade tomatoes for $10 a bushel from Seller, a grower. The market price at that time was $8 a bushel. On August 10, the time for delivery, Seller tendered 10,000 bushels of # 2 grade tomatoes. Caught at the end of the canning season, Sunshine accepted the goods. The market value of the tomatoes accepted was $7 per bushel. The market value of # 1 grade tomatoes was $9 per bushel. Seller claims the contract price of $100,000. What damages may Sunshine deduct under UCC 2-714(2)? What is the value of the goods as warranted?*

B. Assume in (A) above, that at the time of acceptance # 1 tomatoes had risen

---

* *See JHC Ventures, L.P. v. Fast Trucking, Inc.*, 94 S.W.3d 762 (Tex. Ct. App. 2003) (contract price some evidence of value of goods as warranted).

in value to $12 per bushel and # 2 tomatoes were worth $9 per bushel. What damages?

C. Suppose, in (A) above, the Seller tendered and Sunshine accepted what passed in the trade as # 1 tomatoes. Upon unpacking, however, the entire lot was found to be decayed and suffering from the notorious Veggie Rot. Sunshine salvaged the lot for $1,000 and replaced it from another grower for $13 per bushel. What damages? Should Sunshine recover the difference between the replacement cost and the salvage value? Or should Sunshine get the difference in value between the tomatoes as warranted and the tomatoes received (that value measured by the salvage value)?

Problem 11-4

Seller agreed to manufacture, sell and deliver 500 railroad hopper cars to Railroad for the approximate price of $10,000,000, or $20,000 per car. After delivery, Railroad discovered cracks in the structure and weld of many cars. Seller refused to repair, claiming it had no responsibility for the alleged defects, and Railroad implemented its own program of repair at a total cost of $5,000,000, or $10,000 per car. Railroad brought suit under UCC 2-714(2) and alleged (1) the value of each car as warranted was $20,000, (2) the cost to repair each car was $10,000, and (3) the value of the car as repaired was $19,000. Therefore, the "difference in value" under UCC 2-714(2) is $11,000 per car, the cost to repair plus the difference in value between the car as warranted and the car as repaired.

A. Is Railroad correct?[*] What arguments should Seller make in defense?

B. Suppose Railroad spent $10,000 per car to repair and the value of each car as repaired was $22,000. How much should Railroad recover?

C. Suppose Railroad spent $10,000 per car to repair and the value of each car repaired was $12,000. How much should Railroad recover? Does it make any difference what the value of the cars were prior to repair?

Problem 11-5

In July, CRN Corporation sold Burgess Industries a computer system for $85,000, including a three-year service contract. The system, called a CRN 400, consisted of computer hardware valued at $50,000 and six computer software

---

[*] *See Forest River, Inc. v. Posten*, 847 So.2d 957 (Ala. Ct. App. 2002).

programs, valued at $20,000. The sale followed an extensive analysis of Burgess's computer needs and was induced by CRN's written representation that the CRN 400 would meet all of Burgess's needs.

By December it was clear that the CRN 400 met only 40% of those needs and that CRN would be unable to improve its performance. Frustrated, Burgess consulted a computer expert who concluded that the CRN 400 was not capable of meeting those computer needs. In her opinion, the only system with that capability was a CRN 1500 or a comparable system made by others for a price of $250,000. Burgess, after consulting with counsel, offered to settle the dispute by exchanging the CRN 400, which had hardly been used, for a CRN 1500. CRN refused. Next, Burgess presented a claim for damages under UCC 2-714(2), measured by the difference in value between the CRN 400 and a CRN 1500 or equal. Burgess claimed that this amount was $210,000, since the value of a CRN 1500 was $250,000 and the value of the CRN 400, which could only meet 40% of Burgess's needs, was $40,000.

CRN rejected this claim for the following reasons: (1) The value of the CRN as warranted cannot exceed the contract price; (2) Burgess must value the "goods as warranted," not another or a hypothetical computer system; and (3) The award of $210,000 in damages would put Burgess in a better position than if CRN had fully performed and, therefore, constitute improper punitive damages. *See* UCC 1-305 [former 1-106].

What arguments should Burgess make in reply? *See* UCC 2-315. How should the court decide?

Note: Damages for Breach When Goods Accepted Under the CISG

Under the CISG, a buyer who has taken delivery of goods owes the contract price unless the contract is avoided for fundamental breach under Article 49(1). The word "accepted" is not used. If the proper notice is given under Article 39, the remedies in Articles 48 and 49 are not pursued, and the seller does not cure under Article 48, the buyer may resort to a remedy provided in Article 50 which bears a superficial resemblance to UCC 2-714(2) and 2-717.

> If the goods do not conform with the contract and whether or not the price has already been paid, the buyer may reduce the price in the same proportion as the value that the goods actually delivered had at the time of the delivery bears to the value that conforming goods would have had at that time.

CISG Art. 50. Assume that the contract price was $100, the value of the goods actually delivered was $50 and the value of conforming goods (at the time of delivery) was $90. How much should the price be reduced? Is this an exclusive remedy or can the buyer also recover damages under Article 74?

Note: Damages for Breach When Product Accepted Under UCITA

The damage remedy for accepted copies of information follows the same pattern as Article 2 in UCITA 809(a)(1)(A). *See also* UCITA 610(a) (contract price for accepted performance) and 810 (setoff allowed from price yet due).

B. Incidental and Consequential Damages

Commercial parties purchase or lease products for use, perhaps to resell to customers or to consume in the business. If accepted products fail to conform to warranties made, the planned use of the products may be impaired. Put differently, a result of the breach may be that the buyer or lessee is deprived of the use of the products during the time when they are being repaired or replaced. *See* Chapter Ten, Section 4D, *supra*.

Damages resulting from loss of use are called consequential damages and are recoverable under UCC 2-714(3), 2-715(2) or 2A-519(3) and (4), 2A-520(2). They may be recovered without proof of either "special circumstances" or a "tacit agreement" of the seller, lessor or licensor to assume them[*] if four conditions are satisfied:

(1) The loss results "from general or particular requirements and needs of which the [seller or lessor] at the time of contracting had reason to know." UCC 2-715(2)(a), 2A-520(2)(a).

(2) The buyer or lessee has mitigated damages, *i.e.*, the loss "could not reasonably be prevented by cover or otherwise." UCC 2-715(2)(a), 2A-520(2)(a). The burden is usually on the seller or lessor to prove that the buyer or lessee failed to mitigate.[**]

---

[*] *See R.I. Lampus Co. v. Neville Cement Products Corp.*, 378 A.2d 288 (Pa. 1977),

[**] *Cates v. Morgan Portable Building Corp.*, 780 F.2d 683 (7th Cir. 1985). *But see International Petroleum Services, Inc. v. S & N Well Service, Inc.*, 639 P.2d 29, 38 (Kan. 1982) (burden of proving mitigation on buyer).

(3) The breach was the substantial cause in fact of the loss.[*]

(4) The type and amount of loss is proved with reasonable certainty.[**]

The conditions are easy to state. Applying them is another matter.[***]

Incidental damages are damages that the buyer or lessee incurs in dealing with the non-conforming goods. Read UCC 2-715(1) and 2A-520(1). When the buyer or lessee has accepted non-conforming goods, what are the likely incidental damages that will be incurred?

HYDRAFORM PRODUCTS CORP. V. AMERICAN STEEL & ALUMINUM CORP.
SUPREME COURT OF NEW HAMPSHIRE, 1985
127 N.H. 187, 498 A.2D 339

SOUTER, JUSTICE[1]

The defendant, American Steel & Aluminum Corporation, appeals from the judgment entered on a jury verdict against it. The plaintiff, Hydraform Products Corporation, brought this action for direct and consequential damages based on claims of negligent misrepresentation and breach of a contract to supply steel to be used in manufacturing woodstoves. American claims that prior to trial, the Superior Court (Nadeau, J.) erroneously held that a limitation of damages clause was ineffective to bar the claim for consequential damages. American further claims, *inter alia*, that the Trial Court (Dalianis, J.) erred (a) in allowing the jury to calculate lost profits on the basis of a volume of business in excess of what the contract disclosed and for a period beyond the year in which the steel was to be supplied; (b) in allowing the jury to award damages for the diminished value of the woodstove division of Hydraform's business; (c) in failing to direct a verdict for the

---

[*] *Overstreet v. Norden Laboratories, Inc.*, 669 F.2d 1286 (6th Cir. 1982) (no proof that allegedly defective vaccine caused mares to abort foals).

[**] *Horizons, Inc. v. Avco Corp.*, 714 F.2d 862 (8th Cir. 1983).

[***] For a discussion of various policies that might factor into the ability to recover consequential damages for economic loss, *see* Thomas A. Diamond & Howard Foss, *Consequential Damages for Commercial Loss: An Alternative to Hadley v. Baxendale*, 63 FORDHAM L. REV. 665 (1994) (recognizing the policies of compensation, deterrence, reliability of contracts, reducing subsidization of loss by buyer's customer, predictability, disclosure of information, likely risk allocation).

[1] Now Associate Justice of the United States Supreme Court.

defendant on the misrepresentation claim; and (d) in allowing Hydraform's president to testify as an expert witness. We hold that the trial court properly refused to enforce the limitation of damages clause, but we sustain the other claims of error and reverse the judgment.

Hydraform was incorporated in 1975 and began manufacturing and selling woodstoves in 1976. During the sales season of 1977-78 it sold 640 stoves. It purchased steel from a number of suppliers until July 1978, when it entered into a "trial run" contract with American for enough steel to manufacture 40 stoves. Upon delivery of the steel, certain of Hydraform's agents and employees signed a delivery receipt prepared by American, containing the following language:

"Seller will replace or refund the purchase price for any goods which at the time of delivery to buyer were damaged, defective or not in conformance with the buyer's written purchase order, provided that the buyer gives seller written notice by mail of such damage, defect or deviation within 10 days following its receipt of the goods. *In no event shall seller be liable for labor costs expended on such goods or other consequential damages.*"

(Emphasis added.)

When some of the deliveries under this contract were late, Hydraform's president, J.R. Choate, explained to an agent of American that late deliveries of steel during the peak season for manufacturing and selling stoves could ruin Hydraform's business for a year. In response, American's agent stated that if Hydraform placed a further order, American would sheer and stockpile in advance, at its own plant, enough steel for 400 stoves, and would supply further steel on demand. Thereafter Hydraform did submit a purchase order for steel sufficient to manufacture 400 stoves, to be delivered in four equal installments on the first days of September, October, November and December of 1978.

American's acceptance of this offer took the form of deliveries accompanied by receipt forms. The forms included the same language limiting American's liability for damages that had appeared on the receipts used during the trial run agreement. Hydraform's employees signed these receipts as the steel was delivered from time to time, and no one representing Hydraform ever objected to that language.

Other aspects of American's performance under the trial run contract reoccurred as well. Deliveries were late, some of the steel delivered was defective, and replacements of defective steel were tardy. Throughout the fall of 1978 Mr. Choate protested the slow and defective shipments, while American's agent continually reassured him that the deficient performance would be corrected. Late in the fall,

Mr. Choate finally concluded that American would never perform as agreed, and attempted to obtain steel from other suppliers. He found, however, that none could supply the steel he required in time to manufacture stoves for the 1978-79 sales season. In the meantime, the delays in manufacturing had led to canceled orders, and by the end of the season Hydraform had manufactured and sold only 250 stoves. In September, 1979, Hydraform sold its woodstove manufacturing division for $150,000 plus royalties.

In December, 1979, Hydraform brought an action for breach of contract, which provoked a countersuit by American. In January, 1983, American moved to dismiss Hydraform's claims for consequential damages to compensate for lost profits and for loss on the sale of the business. American based the motion on the limitation of damages clause and upon its defense that Hydraform had failed to mitigate its damages by cover or otherwise. In February, 1983, Hydraform's pretrial statement filed under Superior Court Rule 62 disclosed that it claimed $100,000 as damages for lost profits generally and $220,000 as a loss on the sale of the business. Later in February, 1983, the superior court permitted Hydraform to amend its writ by adding further counts, which included claims for fraudulent and negligent misrepresentation. Hydraform did not, however, proceed to trial on the claim of fraud.

In April, 1983, Nadeau, J., denied American's motion to dismiss the claims for consequential damages. He relied on the Uniform Commercial Code as adopted in New Hampshire, RSA chapter 382-A, in ruling that the limitation of damages clause was unenforceable on the alternative grounds that the clause would have been a material alteration of the contract, *see* RSA 382-A:2-207(2)(b), or was unconscionable or was a term that had failed of its essential purpose, *see* RSA 382-A:2-719(2) and (3). He further concluded that, under the circumstances of the case, the failure to cover, if proven, would not bar consequential damages.

The case was tried to a jury before Dalianis, J. American's exceptions at trial are discussed in detail below. At the close of the evidence, American objected to the use of a verdict form with provision for special findings, and the case was submitted for a general verdict, which the jury returned for Hydraform in the amount of $80,245.12. * * *

Since the clause was not enforceable, the trial court allowed the jury to consider Hydraform's claims for lost profits in the year of the contract, 1978, and for the two years thereafter, as well as its claim for loss in the value of the stove manufacturing business resulting in a lower sales price for the business in 1979. American argues that the court erred in submitting such claims to the jury, and rests its position on three requirements governing the recovery of consequential damages.

First, under RSA 382-A:2-715(2)(a) consequential damages are limited to compensation for "loss resulting from general or particular requirements and needs of which the seller at the time of contracting had reason to know * * *." This reflection of *Hadley v. Baxendale,* 156 Eng. Rep. 145 (1854) thus limits damages to those reasonably foreseeable at the time of the contract. * * * To satisfy the foreseeability requirement, the injury for which damages are sought "must follow the breach in the natural course of events, or the evidence must specifically show that the breaching party had reason to foresee the injury." *Salem Engineering & Const. Corp. v. Londonderry School Dist.,* 122 N.H. 379, 384, 445 A.2d 1091, 1094 (1982). Thus, peculiar circumstances and particular needs must be made known to the seller if they are to be considered in determining the foreseeability of damages. * * *

Second, the damages sought must be limited to recompense for the reasonably ascertainable consequences of the breach. *See* RSA 382-A:2-715, comment 4. While proof of damages to the degree of mathematical certainty is not necessary, * * * a claim for lost profits must rest on evidence demonstrating that the profits claimed were "reasonably certain" in the absence of the breach. * * * Speculative losses are not recoverable.

Third, consequential damages such as lost profits are recoverable only if the loss "could not reasonably be prevented by cover or otherwise." § 2-715(2)(a). *See* § 2-712(1) (*i.e.,* by purchase or contract to purchase goods in substitution for those due from seller). In summary, consequential damages must be reasonably foreseeable, ascertainable and unavoidable.

Applying these standards, we look first at the claim for lost profits for the manufacturing season beginning in September, 1978. There is no serious question that loss of profit on sales was foreseeable up to the number of 400 stoves referred to in the contract, and there is a clear evidentiary basis for a finding that Hydraform would have sold at least that number. There was also an evidentiary basis for the trial court's ruling that Hydraform acted reasonably even though it did not attempt to cover until the season was underway and it turned out to be too late. American had led Hydraform on by repeatedly promising to take steps to remedy its failures, and the court could find that Hydraform's reliance on these promises was reasonable up to the time when it finally and unsuccessfully tried to cover.

Lost profits on sales beyond the 400 stoves presents a foreseeability issue, however. Although American's agent had stated that American would supply steel beyond the 400 stove level on demand, there is no evidence that Hydraform indicated that it would be likely to make such a demand to the extent of any reasonably foreseeable amount. Rather, the evidence was that Mr. Choate had told American's agent that the business was seasonal with a busy period of about four months. The contract referred to delivery dates on the first of four separate months and spoke of only 400 stoves. Thus, there appears to be no basis on which American should have foreseen a volume in excess of 400 for the season beginning in 1978. Lost profits for sales beyond that amount therefore were not recoverable, and it was error to allow the jury to consider them.

Nor should the claims for profits lost on sales projected for the two subsequent years have been submitted to the jury. The impediment to recovery of these profits was not total unforeseeability that the breach could have effects in a subsequent year or years, but the inability to calculate any such loss with reasonable certainty. In arguing that a reasonably certain calculation was possible, Hydraform relies heavily on *Van Hooijdonk v. Langley,* 111 N.H. 32, 274 A.2d 798 (1971), a case that arose from a landlord's cancellation of a business lease. The court held that the jury could award damages for profits that a seasonal restaurant anticipated for the three years that lease should have run. It reasoned that the experience of one two-month season provided sufficient data for a reasonably certain opinion about the extent of future profits. The court thus found sufficient certainty where damages were estimated on the basis of one year of operation and profit, as compared with no operation and hence no profit in the later years.

Hydraform's situation, however, presents a variable that distinguishes it from *Van Hooijdonk.* In our case the evidence did not indicate that American's breach had forced Hydraform's stove manufacturing enterprise out of business, and therefore the jury could not assume that there would be no profits in later years. Without that assumption the jury could not come to any reasonably certain conclusion about the anticipated level of sales absent a breach by American. The jury could predict that Hydraform would obtain steel from another source and would be able to manufacture stoves; but it did not have the evidence from which to infer the future volume of manufacturing and sales. Thus, it could not calculate anticipated lost profits with a reasonable degree of certainty.

There is, moreover, a further reason to deny recovery for profits said to have been lost in the later years. Although Hydraform's pretrial statement disclosed that Hydraform claimed $100,000 in lost profits, it did not indicate that the claim related to the seasons beginning in 1979 and 1980. Since the pretrial statement also listed a claim for loss of the value of the business at the time of its sale in 1979, we believe that the statement could reasonably be read as claiming lost profit only for the one year before the business was sold. Therefore the claim for profits in 1979 and 1980 should have been disallowed for failure to disclose the claim as required by Superior Court Rule 62.

We consider next the claim for loss in the value of the business as realized at the time of its sale in 1979. As a general rule, loss in the value of a business as a going concern, or loss in the value of its good will, may be recovered as an element of consequential damages. * * *

In this case, however, it was error to submit the claim for diminished value to the jury, for three reasons. First, to the extent that diminished value was thought to reflect anticipated loss of profits in future years, as a capitalization of the loss, it could not be calculated with reasonable certainty for the reasons we have just discussed. Second, even if such profits could have been calculated in this case, allowing the jury to consider both a claim for diminished value resting on lost profits and a claim for the lost profits themselves would have allowed a double recovery. * * * Third, to the extent that diminished value was thought to rest on any other theory, there was no evidence on which it could have been calculated. There was nothing more than Mr. Choate's testimony that he had sold the business in September of 1979 for $150,000 plus minimum royalties, together with his opinion that the sales price was less than the business was worth. This testimony provided the jury with no basis for determining what the business was worth or for calculating the claimed loss, and any award on this theory rested on sheer speculation.

In summary, we hold that the jury should not have been allowed to consider any contract claim for consequential damages for lost profits beyond those lost on the sale of 150 stoves, the difference between the 400 mentioned in the contract and the 250 actually sold. Nor should the trial court have allowed the jury to consider the claim for loss in the value of the business. * * *

Reversed.

Notes

1. How are consequential lost profits proved with reasonable certainty? Assuming the requirements of foreseeability, mitigation, and causation are satisfied (they may overlap with the proof problem), there are several steps.

First, establish the relevant time period for measurement. In *Hydraform* it was one year. It could be shorter or longer. For example, suppose Seller refused to deliver goods needed for a business expansion and it took Buyer four months to obtain substitute goods from another supplier. Assuming Buyer made reasonable efforts to cover, the relevant time period is at least four months.

Second, establish what profits would have been made during that period if there had been no breach. Here the buyer must prove what the gross income would have been during the relevant period and subtract from that the total variable costs that would have been incurred to earn that income. The result is the net profit prevented plus allocated overhead. Both elements should be recovered. *Compare* UCC 2-708(2). This task is easier in cases like *Hydraform* where the buyer had a fixed capacity and could have sold all of that capacity during the year involved. If the buyer is a going business concern, proof for a particular time period can be aided by proof of profits made before the breach and after the relevant time period.

Third, if lost profits cannot be proved with reasonable certainty, the buyer may be able to recover wasted reliance invested in preparing to use the goods.

2. Suppose Buyer is a jobber who buys completed goods from Seller for resale to other customers. Or suppose Buyer buys components to be manufactured into a product that will be sold to other customers. If Seller fails to deliver, Buyer will be concerned that the profits expected on a resale will be impaired. This is especially true if Buyer has arranged resale contracts with customers before the breach. How should Buyer respond in this situation?

3. The problems become more complicated where Seller has delivered defective goods or components, Buyer actually resells to customers, and the problems first emerge as the customer uses or attempts to resell. For example, if Seller manufactures and sells to Buyer an emulsion for bags designed to hold fresh vegetables and the emulsion fails while in use by Buyer's customers, the potential scope of liability is broader than simple lost profits. The customers may have consequential damages and seek indemnification from Buyer. How should Buyer respond in this situation?

NEZPERCE STORAGE CO. V. ZENNER
SUPREME COURT OF IDAHO, 1983
105 IDAHO 464, 670 P.2D 871

[In March, 1976, Zenner, a wheat farmer, sold Nezperce 2,000 bushels of "spring" wheat. Nezperce resold a portion of the wheat for seed to eight farmers. Six weeks after planting, it became obvious that some of the wheat was not maturing and that the seed had been a mixture of spring and winter wheat. Since winter wheat requires several weeks of freezing weather to mature, the farmers suffered a crop failure. Nezperce settled the farmer's claims for $84,000 and brought suit against Zenner for indemnification.

Zenner, who grew both winter and spring wheat, had harvested his crop in August, 1975 and, according to his testimony, stored it in different bins over the winter. The Winter of 1975-76 was severe and much of the winter wheat planted in the previous fall was killed. A shortage of spring wheat developed, of which Zenner was aware at the time of the sale to Nezperce. Zenner also knew that Nezperce was purchasing his wheat to meet the shortage of spring wheat seed in the Camas Prairie area.

Nezperce cleaned and bagged the wheat seed without mixing it with another variety. Nezperce performed a successful "germination" to determine if the seed would grow but did not conduct other tests, *i.e.*, a "grow out" test or an electrofloresis test, to determine if the seed was in fact spring wheat. The evidence was conflicting as to whether either test was available or practical.

The jury returned a verdict that Zenner had made and breached an express warranty and that Nezperce should recover the amount of the settlement made with the farmers.] * * *

Although many of the allegations of the Nezperce complaint and the Zenners' counterclaim were disputed at trial, the essential arguments upon this appeal are the Zenners' assertions of error relating to the findings of the jury that Joseph Zenner was aware of the shortage of spring wheat seed in the Camas Prairie area and that he knew or had reason to know that Nezperce was purchasing his wheat for processing into spring wheat seed for resale to its customers; that the award of consequential damages was improper and that Nezperce did not reasonably mitigate its damages by testing the seed.

The propriety of awarding consequential damages in the instant case is governed by I.C. § 28-2-715(2)(a), which provides in pertinent part:

"(2) Consequential damages resulting from the seller's breach include

(a) Any loss resulting from general or particular requirements and needs of which the seller at the time of contracting had reason to know and which could not reasonably be prevented by cover or otherwise. * * * "

Clearly, Nezperce sustained a "loss" in reimbursing its customers for the damages they suffered by purchasing and planting seed which was not spring wheat. In a breach of warranty action, indemnification for this kind of a loss is proper when a seller such as Nezperce receives a warranty from a supplier such as Zenner and passes that warranty on to customers. * * *

As stated in *Clark v. International Harvester Co.*, 99 Idaho 326, 346, 581 P.2d 784, 804 (1978), "there are certain limitations on the right to recover consequential damages under § 28-2-715(2)(a). First, the losses must have resulted from needs which the seller knew or had reason to know at the time of contracting." Here the special interrogatories returned by the jury indicate that Zenner was aware of the shortage of spring wheat seed in the Camas Prairie area and that Zenner had reason to realize that "Nezperce Storage Company's purpose in purchasing MP-1 wheat was to meet an apparent shortage of spring wheat seed on the Camas Prairie," and that Zenner had reason to know that Nezperce was buying the wheat from Zenner to process it into spring wheat seed for resale. Those findings are supported by substantial, albeit conflicting, evidence, and therefore they will not be disturbed on appeal. * * * Hence, the foreseeability requirement of I.C. § 28-2-715(2)(a) has been satisfied.

The propriety of an award of consequential damages must also satisfy the second condition of I.C. § 28-2-715(2)(a), *i.e.*, that they could not have been *reasonably* prevented by cover or otherwise. As to this condition, the Court in *Clark v. International Harvester Co.*, 99 Idaho 326, 347, 581 P.2d 784, 805 (1978), held that "the plaintiffs were only required to take reasonable efforts to mitigate their damages, [citation] and the burden of proving that the damages could have been minimized was on the defendants." In *S.J. Groves & Sons Co. v. Warner Co.*, 576 F.2d 524, 528 (3rd Cir. 1978), it was held that, in an action to recover consequential damages under the same UCC provision, "[t]he requirement of * * * mitigation of damages is not an absolute, unyielding one, but is subject to the circumstances," and "[t]he test for plaintiff's efforts [to mitigate damages] is reasonableness * * *." *Id.*, at n.5. In the instant case the Zenners presented testimony attempting to convince the jury that Nezperce could have mitigated or avoided its consequential damages by subjecting the seed to tests to determine seed variety prior to the time it resold the seed to its customers. As indicated in *West v. Whitney-Fidalgo Seafoods, Inc.*, 628 P.2d 10 (Alaska 1981), and *AES Technology Systems, Inc. v. Coherent Radiation*, 583 F.2d 933 (7th Cir. 1978), the question of whether Nezperce acted properly to mitigate its damages is a factual matter to be determined by the trier of the fact. Here the jury specifically found:

> "it [was] reasonable for plaintiff Nezperce Storage to sell the seed it manufactured from the Zenner wheat to its customers without doing any more than the facts show it did do to determine whether or not such seed was actually of a spring wheat variety."

That finding is supported by substantial, albeit conflicting, testimony and will not be disturbed on appeal. * * *

The Zenners argue that the finding of the jury should be disregarded because the jury was not properly instructed as to what a "reasonable man" would have done in that the court failed to give Zenners' submitted instructions regarding negligence per se. We disagree and find no error in the refusal of the trial court to give Zenners' requested instructions. In the instant case we need not decide whether negligence per se can ever be used to limit a party's consequential damages under I.C. § 28-2-715(2)(a). While a court may adopt the requirements of a legislative enactment as the standard of conduct of a reasonable man, * * * that doctrine is ordinarily applied in negligence actions where a plaintiff has suffered injury by a defendant who was in violation of a statute or ordinance. However,

> "In order for the violation of a statute to be pertinent in a particular case, the statute must be * * * designed to protect (1) the class of persons in which the plaintiff is included (2) against the type of harm which has in fact occurred as a result of its violation."

Kinney v. Smith, 95 Idaho 328, 331, 508 P.2d 1234, 1237 (1973); * * *

The statute at issue, I.C. § 22-417(3), imposes penalties upon one who sells seeds which are incorrectly labeled when the person selling the seed "has failed to obtain an invoice or growers declaration giving kind, or kind and variety * * * and to take such other precautions as may be necessary to insure the identity to be that stated." We deem it clear and obvious that, in the instant case, the statute was designed to protect the following class of persons: those customers who purchased the seed from Nezperce. Cases construing similar seed laws, *e.g., Agr. Services Ass'n, Inc. v. Ferry-Morse Seed Co., Inc.,* 551 F.2d 1057 (6th Cir. 1977), and *Klein v. Asgrow Seed Co.,* 246 Cal. App. 2d 87, 54 Cal. Rptr. 609 (1966), have so held. Equally clearly, the statute was not designed to provide protection to the Zenners, who can best be described as suppliers of mislabeled seed. Hence, we deem the statute and the doctrine of negligence per se in the instant case irrelevant. *See also S.J. Groves & Sons Co. v. Warner, supra,* which states:

> "Where both the plaintiff and the defendant have had equal opportunity to reduce the damages by the same act and it is equally reasonable to expect the defendant to minimize damages, the defendant is in no position to contend that the plaintiff failed to mitigate. Nor will the award be reduced on account of damages the defendant could have avoided as easily as the plaintiff."

At page 530; *See also Shea-S & M Ball v. Massman-Kiewit-Early,* 606 F.2d 1245 (D.C. Cir. 1979). * * *

The judgment of the district court is affirmed. Costs to respondents. No attorney fees allowed.

Notes

1. Suppose Zenner warranted the wheat to be spring wheat and knew that Nezperce intended to resell it to his customers, but was unaware of the shortage of spring wheat seed in the Camas Prairie area. Should that alter the result in this case?

2. Suppose Zenner sold and delivered grain described as "spring wheat" to Nezperce in the Fall of 1975 at $5.00 per bushel. Nezperce immediately resold 50% to customers for April, 1976 delivery at $6.00 per bushel. All of the Zenner wheat was stored together. In March, after the big chill, the price of spring wheat had risen to $20. Nezperce resold the balance to customers for $22 per bushel. Nezperce then had an electrofloresis test performed on a sample of Zenner wheat and discovered that it was mixed substantially with winter wheat. Nezperce promptly purchased replacement spring wheat in the open market for $22 per bushel, which was delivered to customers, and sold the Zenner wheat for $5 per bushel. What damages should Nezperce recover for Zenner's breach of warranty?

3. How does the Code treat expenditures made by the buyer after the breach is discovered? If they are made to repair or replace the non-conforming goods, they may be recoverable as "direct" damages under UCC 2-714(2): Repair or replacement costs are frequently used to measure difference between the value of the goods as warranted and the value as accepted.[*] If expenditures are made to avoid losses or to pursue permissible remedies, they may be "incidental" damages under UCC 2-715(1). Or, expenditures may be "consequential" damages under UCC 2-715(2)(a). *Compare* UCC 2A-520. How is the line to be drawn between incidental and consequential damages? The question is important, for incidental damages need not satisfy all the conditions for the recovery of consequential damages and will not be covered by clauses in the contract purporting to exclude the seller's liability for consequential damages. *See* Chapter Ten, Section 4D, *supra*.

---

[*] *See Soo Line Railroad Company v. Fruehauf Corp.*, 547 F.2d 1365 (8th Cir. 1977); *Vista St. Clair, Inc. v. Landry's Commercial Furnishings, Inc.*, 643 P.2d 1378 (Or. Ct. App. 1982).

DELANO GROWER'S CO-OP. WINERY V. SUPREME WINE CO.
SUPREME JUDICIAL COURT OF MASSACHUSETTS, 1985
393 MASS. 666, 473 N.E.2D 1066

[The court's decision on the liability issue is printed *supra* in Chapter Five.]

* * *

6. *Calculation of damages for lost good will.* Delano argues that there is no basis in the record for the conclusion that it caused injury to Supreme's business reputation. The master found that the primary reason for Supreme's decline in sales after 1973 was the defective Delano wine. This finding was prima facie evidence of the causal connection between Delano's acts and the damage to Supreme's business reputation. At trial, Delano presented the testimony of several former Supreme customers to rebut the evidence of a causal connection. Supreme presented testimony of its former officers to support the evidence that Delano caused the injury to Supreme's business reputation. This record is hardly one, as Delano argues, that is totally devoid of any basis for finding a causal connection between Delano's acts and Supreme's damages. Rather, it exhibits an instance where the judge was required to weigh the credibility of the evidence before him and to determine whether a causal connection existed. The judge's finding that Supreme had proved a causal connection between its loss of business reputation and Delano's breach is not clearly erroneous.

Delano contends that the record contains scant evidence supporting a valuation of Supreme's good will. However, it did not produce any direct evidence at trial before the judge which rebutted Supreme's evidence of the good will value. At trial, Supreme presented the testimony of an expert in business appraising. This expert had over eight years' experience as a business broker engaged in buying and selling businesses in and around Boston. In this connection he was required to appraise a business's value, including the value of its good will. The judge's acceptance of the expert testimony implies that he found this expert sufficiently qualified to render an opinion. * * * A finding that this expert possessed sufficient knowledge, skill, and experience to render an opinion was neither an abuse of discretion nor erroneous as matter of law. * * *

The expert valued the business at $593,700, including assets and good will. The assets were valued at $237,092. This valuation was based on the business records introduced in evidence and certain other facts. This was a sufficient basis for his opinion. * * * Supreme's president and its treasurer testified that Supreme's value was $500,000.

The judge found that Supreme's loss of good will attributable to Delano's breach was $100,000. He based this on the evidence in the record and an examination of valuation methods. He rejected Supreme's theories supporting its valuation as lacking factual grounding. In determining the value of Supreme's good will, the judge was not bound by the expert testimony. * * *

Delano argues that the trial judge relied on extraneous materials, not admitted at trial, in determining good will. Specifically, he discussed certain statistics from Business Week, indicating an increased consumption of wine and a growth in the wine industry. This reference occurred in a lengthy discussion of various methods used in valuing good will. This same discussion specifically refers to evidence introduced at trial which sufficiently supported a valuation of the lost good will. There is no clear indication to what degree, if any, the discussion of the extraneous material influenced the good will valuation. The judge found sufficient grounds to reduce the value from that given by Supreme. Where there was sufficient evidence to warrant a valuation of lost good will and the causal connection of that loss, we will not upset this finding. It was not clearly erroneous and was based on the judge's weighing the credibility of the evidence before him. The weight given this evidence was then used in accepted formulations of good will to determine the damage. We do not require that such damages be proved with mathematical certainty. * * * The judge did not err in calculating the damages for good will.

Neither party has addressed the issue whether lost good will is a proper consequential damage under G.L. c. 106, § 2-715. This court has stated that prospective profits are recoverable in the appropriate case. * * * In examining whether good will is also recoverable, we note that Pennsylvania, in disallowing such recovery, based its decision on the interpretation of its prior law, which did not allow recovery for good will. *Harry Rubin & Sons v. Consolidated Pipe Co. of America,* 396 Pa. 506, 153 A.2d 472 (1959). Other cases in which recovery for good will has been denied are based on the speculative nature of damages in the particular case or on a failure of proof. * * * Under our law as it was before the enactment of the Uniform Commercial Code, "[l]oss of good will [was] recognized as an element of damages flowing from the use of unfit material received from one who warranted it to be fit." *Royal Paper Box Co. v. Munro & Church Co.,* 284 Mass. 446, 452, 188 N.E. 223 (1933) (interpreting G.L. [Ter. Ed.] c. 106, § 17[1]). Where a seller of goods reasonably knows that substantially impaired goods provided for resale could affect continued operations and established good will, the buyer's loss of good will caused by the seller's breach is properly recoverable as consequential damages unless the loss could have been prevented by cover or otherwise. G.L. c. 106, § 2-715(2)(a). This is not a harsh result as the seller may contractually limit this remedy. Uniform Commercial Code § 2-715, comment 3 1A U.L.A. 446 (1976). In this case, Supreme's loss of good will was found to be a direct consequence of Delano's breach. Once sufficiently ascertained, the award of damages for lost good will was properly allowed. * * *

[Footnotes omitted.]

Problem 11-6

Assume the following facts from *Delano Grower's*. Delano delivered 8,000 cases of defective wine. Supreme agreed to pay Delano $8 per case and sold 8,000 cases of wine to its customers for $13 per case. Supreme has not yet paid Delano for the wine. Supreme's customers returned 5,000 cases as defective, receiving a refund of the price paid, and Supreme reprocessed the 5,000 cases of wine into 4,000 cases and resold it for $10 per case. The cost of reprocessing was $1,000. Supreme can prove that it lost customers because of the bad wine experience and estimates a $50,000 loss in sales in addition to the loss it sustained on the bad wine by giving refunds to its customers. Calculate Supreme's damage claim against Delano under UCC 2-714 and 2-715.

Problem 11-7

S is a manufacturer of heart valves. In 2002, S manufactured 10,000,000 valves and sold them to five medical supply corporations for an average price of $15 each. In June, 2003, it was discovered that 5% of the heart valves were not fit for ordinary purposes. After insertion in a patient, they would fail within 18 months. A merchantable heart valve would last for at least 10 years. It was estimated that 500,000 of the valves had already been inserted in patients. The others were in the possession of either the medical supply corporations (the original buyers) or resale buyers, such as hospitals and clinics. With the approval of the Food and Drug Administration, all of the heart valves were recalled by the original buyers and doctors who had inserted heart valves in patients were warned of the problem. When the news hit the press, S's other customers canceled or refused to make orders for the product, and business dropped 85% from 2002 levels.

A. What is the potential scope of S's potential liability on these facts? Is that potential "disproportionate" to the amount invested in the heart valves?

B. In your judgment, does Article 2 adequately protect a buyer under these circumstances?

Problem 11-8

Farmer purchased 10 cans of herbicide from a dealer for $250. The herbicide was produced by BWC Corp. On each can in conspicuous print was the following language:

> BWC WARRANTS THAT THIS PRODUCT CONFORMS TO THE CHEMICAL DESCRIPTION ON THE LABEL AND IS REASONABLY FIT FOR THE PURPOSES REFERRED TO IN THE DIRECTIONS FOR USE. IN NO CASE SHALL BWC OR ANY RETAIL SELLER BE LIABLE FOR CONSEQUENTIAL, SPECIAL OR INDIRECT DAMAGES RESULTING FROM THE USE OR HANDLING OF THIS PRODUCT.

Farmer was aware of this language at the time of purchase.

Farmer properly applied the herbicide to 1,450 acres. The herbicide failed to work (all agree it was unmerchantable) and farmer lost 80% of the crop that would have been produced if the herbicide had been as warranted. In the trial court, Farmer sued BWC and the retailer, proved that the difference between the crop that would have been harvested and the crop actually produced was $200,000, and argued that this amount should be awarded under UCC 2-714(2). BWC, to the contrary, argued that the value of the lost crop was actually consequential damages which had been validly excluded by the language on the can, citing UCC 2-719(3), and that Farmer's recovery is limited to the difference in value between the herbicide as warranted, $250, and the herbicide actually delivered, $0, plus incidental damages. The trial court submitted the case to the jury, which returned a verdict of $200,000 in favor of Farmer. The trial court's analysis and basic charge to the jury were as follows:

> The formula in subsection (2) of 2-714 up to the "unless" clause is inapplicable to a herbicide failure case. This formula is most appropriate where the nonconforming goods can be repaired or replaced and value can be defined with certainty.
>
> A herbicide failure is a latent defect in the product. There is no reasonable way that Farmer can determine in advance whether the herbicide will perform as warranted. Discovery of the problem must await the development of the crop at which time it is usually too late to correct.
>
> The value of a herbicide as warranted is difficult to define. Price and

value are not equivalents. From Farmer's perspective, the value of the herbicide is a healthy crop at maturity. In the manufacturer's viewpoint, the value is its selling price. The value as accepted is equally uncertain and difficult to define. There is no market for such goods and thus no market price. If anything, it has a negative value.

In our view, the inability of a court to ascertain with certainty the value of goods both as warranted and as accepted creates a special circumstances within the meaning of the "unless" clause in UCC 2-714(2). Thus, the formula in subsection (2) does not apply and the general measurement principle in subsection (1) does.

The court will charge the jury that the measure of actual damages in cases like this is the value the crop would have had if the product had conformed to the warranty less the value of the crop actually produced, less the expense of preparing for market the portion of the probable crop prevented from maturing.

On appeal, what arguments should BWC make? Will they succeed? Consider the following case, summarized by your able Summer Associate.

In *Martin v. Joseph Harris Co., Inc.*, 767 F.2d 296 (6th Cir. 1985) *overruled on other grounds, Salve Regina College v. Russell*, 499 U.S. 225 (1991), the plaintiffs purchased and planted cabbage seed infected with "black leg" fungus from the defendant. When the condition was discovered, plaintiffs took action to minimize the damage but still lost a "large portion" of their cabbage crop. Because of the high demand for cabbage, caused by the "black leg" epidemic, plaintiffs were able to sell the smaller cabbage crop at a profit equal to or higher than in previous years. Defendant argued that there is "no breach of the implied warranty of merchantability where there is no economic loss." Although "black leg" was damaging the plaintiffs' cabbage, the "law of supply and demand was making them * * * whole."

The court of appeals affirmed the district court's conclusion that the defendant's attempt to disclaim warranties and exclude liability for consequential damages was unconscionable. The court also affirmed the district court's decision to uphold a jury verdict of $52,000 for the plaintiffs:

(W)e are persuaded by the district court's finding that the defendant's sale of diseased seed to *these two* plaintiffs did not create the increased market price. Similarly, we note that [they] purchased some healthy seed from other companies and some other farmers produced completely healthy crops. To further complicate the problem, there was evidence to the effect

that the black leg epidemic was partially caused by the sale of diseased seed by other merchants and, thus, the rise in the market price of cabbage did not result entirely from Harris Seed's breach. Therefore, following the dictates of U.C.C. 1-106(1) * * * in order to put Martin and Rick in the same position as many of their neighboring farmers who purchased healthy seed, we hold that the proper measure of damages as applied by the district court is the difference in value between the cabbage crops actually raised by these plaintiffs and the cabbage crops that they would have raised if their seed had not been diseased.
767 F.2d at 302-03.

Note: Consequential and Incidental Damages Under the CISG

Under the CISG, both the seller and the buyer can recover consequential damages under Article 74. *See* Art. 45(1)(b), Art. 61(1)(b). There is no need to first avoid the contract for fundamental breach before these damages are recoverable. Read Article 74. Can either party recover incidental damages under Article 74? Article 77 of CISG deals with the responsibility of a party who relies on a breach to "take such measures as are reasonable in the circumstances to mitigate the loss, including loss of profit, resulting from the breach." *Compare* UCC 2-715(2)(a).*

Note: Consequential and Incidental Damages Under UCITA

A licensee's damages for breach in terms of accepted products include consequential and incidental damages. UCITA 809(a)(2). The definitions of each parallel the Article 2 provision. UCITA 102(a)(13) and (a)(34).

SECTION 4.   PRODUCTS LIABILITY LAW

A. Injury to Person and Property

Injury to person and property for breach of warranty is another type of consequential damage. When there is personal injury to person or property other

---

* For an illustration of these principles at work in a case under the CISG, *see Delchi Carrier, SpA v. Rotorex Corp.*, 71 F.3d 1024 (2nd Cir. 1995).

then the product itself, principles from both tort and contract law are involved. We will take up those issues in this Section.

Warranty as we have studied it under Article 2 or Article 2A is a theory of strict but limited liability. Warranties arise when the seller or lessor makes representations, express or implied, about the quality of the goods sold or leased which become part of the agreement. Disputes involving warranties are resolved within the respective statutory scheme which has a set of limitations and policies associated primarily with exchange transactions. In addition to limitations which have been noted, these statutory schemes also permit the parties by agreement to disclaim or limit warranties and limit remedies for breach of warranty. A number of recurring problems, however, have tested the nature of warranty theory and, perforce, the limitations of contract law. In contracts for the sale of goods, they usually arise after the goods have been accepted and take the form of consequential damage claims. *See* UCC 2-715(2).

Suppose a seller sells unmerchantable goods which cause damage to the person or property of a buyer. Suppose, further, that the buyer would be foreclosed from recovery by one or more limitations upon warranty liability found in the UCC, *e.g.*, failure to give notice of the breach, lack of contractual privity, an enforceable disclaimer, or expiration of the statute of limitations. Does Article 2 preempt the dispute or may the buyer also pursue the claim in strict products liability or negligence, where tort rather than contract limitations apply?

Although Article 2 explicitly covers personal injury and property damage claims, *see* UCC 2-715(2)(b), 2-719(3) and 2-318, the usual answer to the question is no: neither the original drafters of Article 2 nor the state legislatures which enacted it intended to preempt the then developing theory of strict liability restated in 1965 in 402A of the RESTATEMENT (SECOND) OF TORTS.[*] The upshot is that a plaintiff who is injured in person or property by a defective product may escape contract law for the more favorable law of tort, if he so elects.

Suppose, however, that a person who is injured while using goods sues in tort

---

[*] *See Phipps v. General Motors Corp.*, 363 A.2d 955 (Md. 1976); John E. Murray, Jr., *Products Liability vs. Warranty Claims: Untangling the Web,* 3 J.L. & COM. 269 (1983); John W. Wade, *Tort Liability for Products Causing Physical Injury and Article 2 of the U.C.C.,* 48 MO. L. REV. 1 (1983). For contrary opinions, *see Cline v. Prowler Industries of Maryland,* 418 A.2d 968 (Del. 1980); Morris G. Shanker, *A Reexamination of Prosser's Products Liability Crossword Game: The Strict or Stricter Liability of Commercial Code Sales Warranty,* 29 CASE W. RES. L. REV. 550 (1979) (Article 2 applies to physical damage claims).

claiming that the goods were defective and sues in warranty claiming that the goods were unmerchantable. Because of historical origins and some common policies, a few courts have concluded that the tort and warranty claims merge in these cases.[*] Thus, if the goods are unmerchantable in warranty they are defective in tort and vice versa. More importantly, if the goods are not defective in tort they cannot be unmerchantable in warranty. Not all courts agree with that perspective. Review *Castro v. QVC Network, Inc.*, 139 F.3d 114 (2nd Cir. 1998) in Chapter Five, *supra*.

At issue here is whether there is any difference between the concept of merchantability that a product should be "fit for its ordinary purpose" including operating with the requisite degree of safety, and the concept of product defect in tort law.[**] As stated in the *Castro* case:

---

[*] *See Larsen v. Pacesetter Systems, Inc.*, 837 P.2d 1273 (Haw. 1992); *Piotrowski v. Southworth Products Corp.*, 15 F.3d 748 (8th Cir. 1994) (Minnesota law).

[**] Consider the use of product defect from the RESTATEMENT (SECOND) OF TORTS 402A (1965):

402A. SPECIAL LIABILITY OF SELLER OF PRODUCT FOR PHYSICAL HARM TO USER OR CONSUMER
(1) One who sells any product in a defective condition unreasonably dangerous to the user or consumer or to his property is subject to liability for physical harm thereby caused to the ultimate user or consumer, or to his property, if
(a) the seller is engaged in the business of selling such a product, and
(b) it is expected to and does reach the user or consumer without substantial change in the condition in which it is sold.
(2) The rule stated in Subsection (1) applies although
(a) the seller has exercised all possible care in the preparation and sale of his product, and
(b) the user or consumer has not bought the product from or entered into any contractual relation with the seller.
Now compare the definition of product defect from the RESTATEMENT (THIRD) OF TORTS: PRODUCTS LIABILITY 2 (1998):
2. CATEGORIES OF PRODUCT DEFECT
A product is defective when, at the time of sale or distribution, it contains a manufacturing defect, is defective in design, or is defective because of inadequate instructions or warnings. A product:
(a) contains a manufacturing defect when the product departs from its intended design even though all possible care was exercised in the preparation and marketing of the product;
(b) is defective in design when the foreseeable risks of harm posed by the product could have been reduced or avoided by the adoption of a reasonable

(continued...)

Over the years, both in the cases and in the literature, two approaches have come to predominate. The first is the risk/utility theory, which focuses on whether the benefits of a product outweigh the dangers of its design. The second is the consumer expectations theory, which focuses on what a buyer/user of a product would properly expect that the product would be suited for . . . . The imposition of strict liability for an alleged design "defect" is determined by a risk-utility standard, * * *. The notion of "defect" in a U.C.C.-based breach of warranty claim focuses, instead, on consumer expectations. * * *

139 F.3d 114, 116, 118. What arguments can you make that the concept of product defect in tort law should be the same or different from the concept of merchantability in contract law?

Problem 11-9

Defendant manufactured a four-wheel drive "Utility" vehicle designed primarily for off-road use on unpaved trails and rugged terrain. The vehicle was not intended to be sold as a conventional passenger automobile. Nevertheless, defendant produced a marketing manual for dealers that noted the fashion appeal of utility vehicles in suburban areas and suggested that the sales presentation should take into account the suitability for "commuting and for suburban and city driving" and the added safety of four-wheel drive when driving in ice and snow. Plaintiff, a research scientist, was aware of the apparent safety benefits of four-wheel drive and bought a Utility Vehicle to commute to and from work, a round trip of 50 miles. She had no interest in off-road use.

Plaintiff was injured and the vehicle was destroyed when it rolled over after Plaintiff slammed on the brakes to avoid a deer that had run onto the highway. It was a sunny day and there was no ice or snow on the highway. Plaintiff sued

---

** (...continued)
alternative design by the seller or other distributor, or a predecessor in the commercial chain of distribution, and the omission of the alternative design renders the product not reasonably safe;

(c) is defective because of inadequate instructions or warnings when the foreseeable risks of harm posed by the product could have been reduced or avoided by the provision of reasonable instructions or warnings by the seller or other distributor, or a predecessor in the commercial chain of distribution, and the omission of the instructions or warnings renders the product not reasonably safe.

Defendant in strict tort liability and for breach of the implied warranty of merchantability. After a proper charge on strict tort liability by the trial judge, the jury found that the vehicle was not defective: there was neither a manufacturing nor a design defect because there was no evidence that the vehicle would not perform with safety off-road. The trial judge also charged the jury that if they found there was no defect in tort they must rule for the defendant. In essence, the trial court charged that "if it is not defective in tort, it must be merchantable in warranty."

Plaintiff had introduced evidence that the Utility Vehicle was not reasonably fit for use on the road and wants to appeal the trial court's ruling. Would you take this appeal? What arguments should you make under Article 2? *See Denny v. Ford Motor Co.*, 662 N.E.2d 730 (N.Y. 1995), holding, in part, that in personal injury cases goods that are not defective in tort may still be unmerchantable for purposes of warranty.

The revision of Article 2 and the completion by the American Law Institute of the RESTATEMENT (THIRD) OF TORTS: PRODUCTS LIABILITY (1998) provided an opportunity to revisit the "usual answer" to the question. After extended discussions, the following consensus emerged which is reflected in the new comment to amended UCC 2-314.

First, to the extent that the plaintiff claims that the injury to person or property resulted from breach of an implied warranty of merchantability, tort law should control. If the goods are defective under tort law, *i.e.,* contain a design or manufacturing defect, then Plaintiff must sue in tort. If the goods are not defective under tort law, Plaintiff cannot sue for breach of the implied warranty of merchantability under the UCC.

Second, if Plaintiff claims that a breach of an express warranty or an implied warranty of fitness resulted in personal injury or property damage, a suit under the UCC can proceed regardless of whether a suit in tort is possible, subject to the usual limitations upon claims for breach of warranty. Why this difference? The concept of merchantability, with its emphasis upon implied duties, is closer to duties imposed in tort than the concept of express warranties, with its concern about reasonable expectations created. A contract theory works well when duties are created by affirmations of fact or bargained for fitness expectations. Do you agree with the proposed reconciliation between the concepts?[*]

---

[*] *See* James A. Henderson, Jr. & Aaron D. Twerski, *Achieving Consensus on Defective*

(continued...)

B. The "Economic Loss" Doctrine

Suppose that B, an electric utility, buys a generator from S, a manufacturer. Due to defects in components that S purchased from C, a manufacturer, and installed in the generator, the generator broke down. Moreover, the defective components caused substantial damage to the generator itself. If the defects had been discovered before the break down, the cost to repair and replace would have been $5,000. B, however, claims the following damages and sues both S and C in warranty and in tort: (1) $250,000 for damage to the generator, measured by the difference in value between the generator as warranted and the generator after the accident; and (2) $1,000,000 in lost profits while the generator was under repair. S and C argue that B cannot sue in tort because it has suffered only "economic loss." Since B can sue only in warranty, C moves to dismiss on the grounds that there was no privity of contract and S moves to dismiss on the grounds that the contract between S and B excluded all liability for consequential damages. B counters by arguing that the components were both defective and unmerchantable (a "manufacturing" defect) and that the defect created a substantial risk that when the inevitable accident occurred there would be damage to property other than the generator and injury to workers in the plant. B concedes, however, that because of a prompt response during the accident that damage was contained to the generator. Who wins?

In most states, S and C win under the so-called "economic loss" rule. In commercial cases where damages are limited to lost profits and damages to the goods sold, Article 2 of the UCC rather than tort is the proper framework for decision. The problem arises on the contract side of the line, and Article 2 provides the appropriate principles for allocating risk by agreement and determining liability if there is no agreement.[*] On the other hand, if the generator had exploded and

---

[*] (...continued)

Product Design, 83 CORNELL L. REV. 867 (1998); Marshall S. Shapo, *In Search of the Law of Products Liability: The ALI Restatement Project*, 48 VAND. L. REV. 631 (1995); Thomas C. Galligan, *Contortions Along the Boundary Between Contracts and Torts*, 69 TUL. L. REV. 457 (1994); William L. Prosser, *The Implied Warranty of Merchantable Quality*, 27 MINN. L. REV. 117 (1943).

[*] *See Alloway v. General Marine Industries, L.P.*, 695 A.2d 264 (N.J. 1997), reviewing authorities and holding that the economic loss rule applied to claims by commercial and consumer buyers.

damaged surrounding property or injured an employee, a suit in tort for damage to person and property some types of economic loss could be brought. *See* RESTATEMENT (THIRD) OF TORTS: PRODUCTS LIABILITY 1, 21 (1998), stating that "harm to persons or property includes economic loss if caused by harm to: (a) the plaintiff's person; * * * (c) the plaintiff's property other than the defective product itself."* Why is tort law not appropriate in cases where only economic loss occurs? Hear the words of the Court of Appeals of New York.

> Tort recovery in strict products liability and negligence against a manufacturer should not be available to a downstream purchaser where the claimed losses flow from damage to the property that is the subject of the contract. Transforming manufacturers into insurers with the empty promise that they can guarantee perpetual and total public safety, by making them liable in tort for all commercial setbacks and adversities is not prudent or sound tort public policy. In such instances, no directly related or commensurate public interest is served or protected by holding manufacturers liable. Tort law should not be bent so far our of its traditional progressive path and discipline by allowing tort lawsuits where the claims at issue are, fundamentally and in all relevant respects, essentially contractual, product-failure controversies. Tort law is not the answer for this loss of commercial bargain.

Bocre Leasing Corp. v. General Motors Corp., 645 N.E.2d 1195, 1199 (N.Y. 1995). However, if the contract at issue is not a contract for the sale of goods but rather a contract for services, some courts hold that the fact that a party to the contract suffered only economic loss does not matter, that party may still bring an action for its loss in tort, if the loss is normally compensated through tort law. *Paramount Aviation Corp. v. Agusta*, 288 F.3d 67 (3rd Cir. 2002). The *Paramount* court reasoned that the UCC provides a comprehensive scheme for allocating economic losses from defective goods but the absence of such scheme for a contract for

---

* *See* Linda J. Rusch, *Products Liability Trapped by History: Our Choice of Rules Rules Our Choices*, 76 TEMP. L. REV. 739 (2003); Steven C. Tourek, et al., *Bucking the "Trend": The Uniform Commercial Code, The Economic Loss Doctrine, and Common Law Causes of Action for Fraud and Misrepresentation*, 84 IOWA L. REV. 875 (1999); Eileen Silverstein, *On Recovery in Tort for Pure Economic Loss*, 32 U. MICH. J. OF L. REFORM 403 (1999); Christopher Scott D'Angelo, *The Economic Loss Doctrine: Saving Contract Warranty Law From Drowning in a Sea of Torts*, 26 U. TOL. L. REV. 591 (1995); Richard E. Speidel, *Warranty Theory, Economic Loss, and the Privity Requirement: Once More Into the Void*, 67 B.U. L. REV. 9 (1987).

services supported allowing a claim for negligence when the losses for which recovery was sought were only economic losses. The court remanded to determine what damages were actually recoverable in a negligence action under the applicable state law.[*]

Note: Leases and Licenses

Should the same analysis apply to contracts involving the lease of goods and the license of software? One could argue that given the parallels between Articles 2 and 2A, to the extent a leased good is defective, the same analysis should apply. As to licenses of software, consider a defective computer program that is part of the flight control for an airplane. That defective software has the potential for causing harm to the plane's computer systems, to the plane itself by causing it to crash and, needless to say, personal injury to passengers and crew. Should the economic loss doctrine which has developed in the context of sales of goods be imported into the software licensing paradigm?[**]

Note: The CISG

Article 5 provides that the Convention "does not apply to the liability of the seller for death or personal injury caused by the goods to any person." Thus, the classic personal injury products liability case would be governed by other law. What about economic loss, whether simply lost profits or damage to any personal property? These losses are protected under Article 74, which states that damages for "breach of contract by one party consist of a sum equal to the loss, including loss of profit, suffered by the other party as a consequence of the breach." But even if there is a breach of contract in the tender of non-conforming goods under Article 35, the CISG appears to be limited to direct contractual relations between the seller and the buyer. *See* CISG Art. 1(1), which states that the CISG "applies to contract

---

[*] *See also Quest Diagnostics, Inc. v. MCI Worldcom, Inc.*, 656 N.W.2d 858 (Mich. Ct. App. 2003), *appl. denied*, 671 N.W.2d 886 (Mich. 2003).

[**] *See* David W. Lannetti, *Toward a Revised Definition of "Product" Under the Restatement (Third) of Torts: Product Liability*, 55 BUS. LAW 799 (2000); Reed R. Kathrein, *Class Actions in Year 2000 Defective Software and Hardware Litigation*, 18 REV. LITIG. 487 (1999); Peter A. Alces, *W(h)ither Warranty: The B(l)oom of Products Liability Theory in Cases of Deficient Software Design*, 87 CALIF. L. REV. 269 (1999).

of sale of goods between parties whose places of business are in different states" and Article 35(1) which states that the seller must deliver goods that are of the quality and description "required by the contract."

Suppose a French seller delivers non-conforming goods to an American buyer who resells them to an American business. The goods contain a defect that makes them unfit for ordinary purposes, Art. 35(2)(a), and they break apart in operation causing damage to the goods themselves and surrounding personal property. Are there any legitimate arguments that the American resale buyer can sue the French seller under the CISG? Suppose that amended UCC 2-313A was enacted law. Would that help? Would the French seller under the CISG ever be treated as a seller under the UCC?

Note: Status of Consumers

Suppose the buyer is a consumer, *i.e.*, a person who purchased the goods for personal, family or household purposes, who has suffered only economic loss. Should the "ordinary" consumer with less overall capacity than the professional seller be entitled to greater protection for breach of warranty than a commercial buyer and, if so, what and why? More extended treatment is provided in Chapter Twelve, Section 2, *infra*, but here are some tentative conclusions.

1. In most states, the consumer buyer's claim for economic loss must be pursued under the UCC. The mere status of being a consumer does not a tort claim make.

2. Article 2 has no special rules for consumers in economic loss cases.[*] The consumer's claim is treated just like a commercial buyer's claim, unless the court is persuaded to develop some exceptions. These exceptions usually result in rejection of the privity requirement.

3. The federal Magnuson-Moss Warranty Act offers some protection to consumer buyers against sellers or lessors who sell or lease goods in commerce and make express warranties. This protection is minimized when the seller makes a "limited" as opposed to a "full" warranty, but lack of privity is not a defense under

---

[*] Whether the amended Article 2 should have contained any consumer protection principles in this area was a matter of great debate. *See* Michael M. Greenfield, *The Role of Assent in Article 2 and Article 9*, 75 WASH. U. L.Q. 289 (1997). For an argument that the UCC could provide sufficient remedies for this type of harm with some amendments, *see* Richard C. Ausness, *Replacing Strict Liability with a Contract-Based Products Liability Regime*, 71 TEMP. L. REV. 171 (1998).

Mag-Moss. Most sellers elect to make a "limited" warranty. *See* 15 U.S.C. 2301 *et seq.*

4. Most states have enacted some consumer protection legislation, such as "lemon" laws or statutes that protect against deceptive practices or excessive consumer credit charges. The "lemon" laws deal with new car warranties and vary in scope and effect. In short, there are major gaps in warranty protection from state to state. We return to these issues in Chapter Twelve, Section 2, *infra.*

Now consider the following California decision covering many of the issues raised in this Chapter.

FIELDSTONE CO. V. BRIGGS PLUMBING PRODUCTS, INC.
COURT OF APPEAL, FOURTH DISTRICT, DIVISION 1, CALIFORNIA, 1997
54 CAL. APP. 4TH 357, 62 CAL. RPTR.2D 701

HUFFMAN, ACTING PRESIDING JUSTICE

Briggs Plumbing Products, Inc., doing business as Briggs Industries; Verson Allsteel Press, the predecessor of Allied Products Corporation (together Allied); and CR/PL, Inc., manufactured inexpensive bathroom sinks, hundreds of which the Fieldstone Company installed in residential developments throughout San Diego County in the 1980's. Fieldstone, which brought this action to recoup costs of replacing sinks prematurely rusting and chipping, appeals from summary judgments in favor of the manufacturers. We affirm.

I
FACTUAL AND PROCEDURAL BACKGROUND

The manufacturers produced low-cost enameled steel bathroom sinks; they carried written one-year warranties. Pursuant to Fieldstone's specification, plumbing subcontractors installed the sinks in numerous Fieldstone residential developments. Instead of lasting twenty-five or more years as expected, unsightly rusting and porcelain chipping, or "popping," occurred within one to five years, due to spot welding and inadequate coating around steel overflow outlets.

In response to homeowner complaints, Fieldstone spent more than $250,000 replacing 1,900 of the enameled steel sinks with ones made of vitreous china. When the manufacturers refused to reimburse Fieldstone, it filed this suit for breach of express and implied warranties, strict liability, implied equitable indemnity and declaratory relief. The manufacturers brought motions for summary judgment, arguing the products liability claims were meritless because there was no requisite property damage. Rather, the sinks only damaged themselves, and thus damages were purely noncompensable economic ones. With regard to warranty issues, the manufacturers argued among other things that Fieldstone failed to give timely notice of breach of any express warranties created by their promotional materials, and lack of privity abrogated implied warranty claims. After oral argument, the trial court granted the motions. On appeal, Fieldstone contends the court erred as there are triable issues of material fact on all issues.

II

DISCUSSION

A. Standard of Review

* * * [The court reviewed the record *de novo* to determine whether there were triable issues of material fact.]

B. Strict Liability Claims

Under California law, a manufacturer may be strictly liable for physical injuries caused to person or property, but not for purely economic losses. (*Seely v. White Motor Co.* (1965) 63 Cal. 2d 9, 18-19, 45 Cal. Rptr. 17, 403 P.2d 145 (Seely); *San Francisco Unified School Dist. v. W.R. Grace & Co.* (1995) 37 Cal. App. 4th 1318, 1327-1329, 44 Cal. Rptr. 2d 305; *Sacramento Regional Transit Dist. v. Grumman Flxible* (1984) 158 Cal. App. 3d 289, 298, 204 Cal. Rptr. 736.) "[T]he line between physical injury to property and economic loss reflects the line of demarcation between tort theory and contract theory. [Citation.] ' "Economic" loss or harm has been defined as "damages for inadequate value, costs of repair and replacement of the defective product or consequent loss of profits--without any claim of personal injury or damages to other property.* * *" ' [Citations.]" (*Id.* at p. 294, 204 Cal. Rptr. 736; * * *.)

Fieldstone argues the economic loss rule does not foreclose tort recovery here because the sink defects–spot welding and insufficient coating–caused injuries–rusting and chipping–to other, nondefective portions of the sinks, and thus the requisite damage to "other property" occurred. The essential facts are undisputed; the issue of whether Fieldstone suffered "property damage" or merely "economic loss" related to the sinks presents a question of law. * * *

Jurisdictions differ as to whether tort recovery is available where the sole physical injury is to the product itself. (2 SHAPO, THE LAW OF PRODUCTS LIABILITY (3d ed. 1994)) 72 A.L.R.4th 12. A number of courts have allowed such recovery, finding the rationales behind the adoption of strict liability apply whether damages are to the same or other property; a large number of other courts have ruled otherwise, reasoning that warranty theories provide the exclusive remedy; and, yet "[o]ther courts have recognized that there may be particular exceptions to the rule of nonrecovery for mere economic damage to the product itself, based on an analysis of the nature of the defect and the risks involved. Accordingly, these courts have ruled that strict liability in tort could serve as a basis of recovery where the damage occurred in a sudden or calamitous manner, since this was akin to ordinary tort claims which ordinarily involve sudden injuries or damage, as opposed to mere deterioration over a length of time." (72 A.L.R.4th at p. 16.)

California courts, with little or no analysis of the issue, have indicated that manufacturers may be strictly liable for physical injury to the product itself. [citing cases] . * * *

Relying on the above cases, in *Sacramento Regional Transit Dist. v. Grumman Flxible, supra*, 158 Cal. App. 3d at page 293, 204 Cal. Rptr. 736, the court broadly stated that for purposes of strict liability, the "damaged property may consist of the product itself." However, it cautioned that tort recovery in such a situation is precluded absent " * * * physical injury to the property apart from the manifestation of the defect itself. * * * The rule imposing strict liability in tort for damage to property presupposes (1) a defect and (2) *further* damage to plaintiff's property caused by the defect. When the defect and the damage are one and the same, the defect may not be considered to have caused physical injury. [Citation.]" * * * There, plaintiff was denied tort recovery where it, "* * * pled that it purchased busses from defendant, that the busses are latently defective in that the fuel tank support members are prone to cracking; [and] that the fuel tank support members of certain of its busses are already cracked. * * * " (*Id.* at p. 294, fn. 3, 204 Cal. Rptr. 736.)

We conclude that here there was no injury to "other property" for purposes of imposing tort liability. The spot welding and inadequate coating were latent defects which made the sinks prone to rusting, chipping and premature deterioration. In other words, this case presents a routine situation in which a purchaser seeks replacement costs because a poorly designed and built product failed to meet its expectations. The doctrine of strict liability, however, is not a substitute for contract and warranty law where the purchaser's loss is the benefit of the bargain, and unless the parties specifically agree the product will perform in a certain way, the manufacturer is not responsible for its failure. * * * Certainly, Fieldstone is a sophisticated consumer and could have specified a higher quality product; but, whether or not it is a "merchant" as defined by the Uniform Commercial Code, there is no justification here for imposing tort liability on manufacturers that guaranteed their products for only one year. We reject Fieldstone's analysis, under which virtually every defective product evidencing deterioration of any nature would constitute "other property" for purposes of tort recovery. Such is not the law.

C. Equitable Indemnity Claims

[The court held that the manufacturers could not be liable for indemnity, because they were not liable for Fieldstone's economic damages under either a strict liability or negligence theory as a matter of law. The court also discussed and distinguished *J'Aire Corp. v. Gregory* (1979) 24 Cal.3d 799, 806, 157 Cal. Rptr. 407, 598 P.2d 60, where the court held economic damages are recoverable in a negligence action, despite the absence of physical or personal injury, if the parties have a "special relationship." * * *] * * *

The determination whether a special relationship exists is a matter of policy and involves the balancing of various factors, including "(1) the extent to which the transaction was intended to affect the plaintiff, (2) the foreseeability of harm to the plaintiff, (3) the degree of certainty that the plaintiff suffered injury, (4) the closeness of the connection between the defendant's conduct and the injury suffered, (5) the moral blame attached to the defendant's conduct and (6) the policy of preventing future harm." * * *

In an attempt to meet the *J'Aire* test, Fieldstone asserts it submitted evidence in opposition to the motions for summary judgment, establishing: (1) the manufacturers "knew that their bathroom sinks would be installed in middle-class homes * * * [t]he sinks were specifically made for that purpose"; (2) the manufacturers "also knew that defects causing rusting and chipping would render the lavatories unserviceable and the homeowners would be harmed"; (3) "[t]here is no doubt here that the homeowners were damaged because the sinks had to be replaced for both aesthetic and functional reasons"; (4) "[t]he defective design and workmanship of the lavatories directly caused the unsightly, debilitating damage"; (5) "Briggs and [Allied] both knew their lavatories leaked, rusted and chipped, but warned no one"; and, (6) "[h]olding [the manufacturers] responsible for damages caused by the defective lavatories will encourage them to produce more sound products in the future, and discourage them from placing unsuitable products into the stream of commerce which flows straight into the laps of very unhappy consumers."

Fieldstone's analysis fails because the evidence does not suggest the transactions in question were intended to affect Fieldstone or the homeowners "in any way particular to [them], as opposed to all potential purchasers of the equipment. The absence of this foundation precludes a finding of 'special relationship' as required by *J'Aire*: to the extent the [product] was intended to affect [Fieldstone or the homeowners] in the same way as all retail buyers, this becomes a traditional products liability or negligence case in which economic damages are not available. * * *" We need not consider the remaining parts of the *J'Aire* test. "Even if [they] weighed in favor of finding a duty of care, we would still conclude that no duty existed. If a duty of care to avoid economic injury existed in the circumstances of the present case, every manufacturer would become an insurer, potentially forever, against economic loss from negligent defects in a product used for its intended purpose. *J'Aire* neither requires nor supports such a radical departure from traditional notions of liability." * * *

D. Express Warranty Claims

In opposition to the manufacturers' motions, Fieldstone argued they breached express warranties created by their promotional literature. The trial court, however, found that as a matter of law Fieldstone failed to give reasonable notice as required by Commercial Code section 2607, subdivision (3)(A). It provides, "[t]he buyer must, within a reasonable time after he or she discovers or should have discovered any breach, notify the seller of breach or be barred from any remedy. * * *" (*Ibid.*) On appeal, Fieldstone contends the notice requirement is inapplicable because there was no privity of contract between it and the manufacturers.[1]

Fieldstone relies on *Greenman v. Yuba Power Products, Inc.* (1963) 59 Cal.2d 57, 61, 27 Cal. Rptr. 697, 377 P.2d 897, in which the court held the notice requirement "is not an appropriate one for the court to adopt in actions by injured consumers against manufacturers with whom they have not dealt. [Citations.]" The court further explained, however, that " '[a]s applied to personal injuries, and notice to a remote seller, it becomes a booby-trap for the unwary. The injured consumer is seldom "steeped in the business practice which justifies the rule," [citation] and at least until he has had legal advice it will not occur to him to give notice to one with whom he has had no dealings.' [Citation.]" (*Ibid.*)

That is hardly the situation where, as here, plaintiff is a sophisticated development company which has built many thousands of homes over the last two decades. In fact, after *Greenman*, the court held the notice requirement applied to an implied warranty claim against a developer. It stated: "In treating common law warranties, it has been recognized that statutory standards should be utilized where appropriate. [Citations.] The requirement of notice of breach is based on a sound commercial rule designed to allow the defendant opportunity for repairing the defective item, reducing damages, avoiding defective products in the future, and

---

[1] Interestingly, with regard to its implied warranty cause of action, Fieldstone contends it was in privity with the manufacturers.

negotiating settlements. The notice requirement also protects against stale claims. [Citation.] These considerations are as applicable to builders and sellers of new construction as to manufacturers and dealers of chattels." * * *

Alternatively, Fieldstone contends it gave the manufacturers reasonable notice. It submitted evidence of the following: Fieldstone's sink replacements "began in January 1988. The lavatory replacements were 66 for the year in 1988, with a slowly increasing frequency of replacement in 1989 (158 for the year) and 1990 (209 for the year). However, in 1991, replacements more than equaled what they had been in 1988, 1989 and 1990 combined–replacements in 1991 were 460 for the year." Initially, Fieldstone believed the sink problems were associated with homeowner abuse; however, by 1989 it "believed the rusting and chipping to be a problem with the lavatories," but it was unaware "of the origin or cause of the problem." Fieldstone only learned of the specific nature of the sink defects after it filed this action in September 1993. On March 14, 1991, Fieldstone's then customer service manager, Robert Chappell, sent Briggs a letter notifying it of the sink problems. It also sent a letter to a person at Delco Products whom Chappell "vaguely recall[ed] * * * was a [CR/PL] representative." There is no evidence Fieldstone apprised Allied of any problem before it filed this action.

The question of whether notice was reasonable must be determined from the particular circumstances and, where but one inference can be drawn from undisputed facts, the issue may be determined as a matter of law. * * * Here, we conclude from the undisputed facts that Fieldstone failed to give the manufacturers reasonable notice of breach of any express warranties. * * * Although perhaps not aware of the specific causes, Fieldstone knew the sinks were defective for three years before giving notice to Briggs and CR/PL; it gave Allied no indication of a problem for five years, until it filed this lawsuit. * * *

E. Implied Warranty Claims

The trial court determined as a matter of law, Fieldstone's implied warranty claims were meritless because it had no privity with the manufacturers. We conclude there was no error.

"Vertical privity is a prerequisite in California for recovery on a theory of breach of the implied warranties of fitness and merchantability. [Citations.]" (*U.S. Roofing, Inc. v. Credit Alliance Corp.* (1991) 228 Cal. App. 3d 1431, 1441, 279 Cal. Rptr. 533.) "[T]here is no privity between the original seller and a subsequent purchaser who is in no way a party to the original sale. [Citations.]" (*Burr v. Sherwin Williams Co., supra*, 42 Cal.2d at p. 695, 268 P.2d 1041.)

While conceding it did not contract with the manufacturers, Fieldstone argues that because at least Briggs and CR/PL "make sales calls on developers such as Fieldstone," and "Fieldstone's plumbers special ordered shipments of lavatories for use in Fieldstone's specifically designated projects," "Fieldstone is a purchaser from respondent as much as it is from its plumbers * * * within the overall context of the relationships among the parties." We reject such a notion. * * * As discussed above, privity is not required where plaintiff relied on defendant's promotional materials. * * *

DISPOSITION

The judgments are affirmed. Fieldstone to bear the manufacturers' costs on appeal.

[Some footnotes omitted. Those retained have been renumbered.]

Notes

1. The scope of the economic loss doctrine was clarified and narrowed somewhat by the Supreme Court of California in *Jimenez v. The Superior Court of San Diego County*, 58 P.3d 450 (Cal. 2002). In this case, the defendants manufactured windows which were installed by others in mass-produced homes. The defendants did not own or control the homes under construction. The windows were defective with the result that physical damage to other parts of the homes occurred. The court in a long opinion with a strong dissent held: (i) the manufacturer was strictly liable in tort to the purchaser of the homes for harm resulting from the defects; and (ii) strict liability extended to physical damage to other parts of the houses in which the windows were installed. In rejecting an argument that recovery was barred by the economic loss rule, the court held that the "economic loss rule allows a plaintiff to recover in strict products liability in tort when a product defect causes damage to 'other property' that is property other than the product itself." *Id.* at 483. According to the court, the "law of contractual warranty governs damage to the product itself." *Id.*

In concurring, Judge Kennard would require that an installed defective component not lose its separate identity for strict liability to apply. If identity was lost (the component became part of the whole), the economic loss doctrine would bar recovery in tort. According to Judge Kennard, the windows were "not so integrated into houses as to lose their separate identity." *Id.* at 487. Thus, damage to other parts of the house was not damage to the product itself.

In dissenting, Judge Brown argued that the economic loss doctrine should apply under what he called a "product sold" test:

> Here plaintiff bought their homes as single integrated products complete with windows and other constituent parts one would expect in a home. They allege the windows were defective and caused damage to the other parts of their homes, but plaintiffs suffered no personal injury from these defects, nor was any property, other than the homes themselves, damaged. In other words, the product they bought–their homes–did not meet the quality standard they expected at the time of purchase. In those circumstances, the economic loss rule limits their recovery to the bargain. If for some reason, such as a limited warranty, they find their contractual remedies inadequate, that fact is a function of their bargain with the other; it is not a loss the general public should have to subsidize.

Id. at 496.

2.   What do you think of the lines drawn by the court? If the *Fieldstone* case had been decided after the *Jimenez* case, would the result have changed?

CHAPTER TWELVE

LIMITATIONS ON REMEDIES
FOR BREACH OF CONTRACT

SECTION 1.   AGREED LIMITATIONS ON REMEDIES

A. Liquidated Damages

One way to control risk arising from potential breach of contract is to have a clause in the contract liquidating damages. Under current law, liquidated damages provisions that are agreed to by the parties are not enforced if the provision is a "penalty." Read UCC 2-718 and 2A-504. What factors are used in deciding whether a liquidated damages clause should be enforceable? Consider this discussion of liquidated damages clauses generally.

METLIFE CAPITAL FINANCIAL CORP. V.
WASHINGTON AVENUE ASSOCIATES L.P.
SUPREME COURT OF NEW JERSEY, 1999
159 N.J. 484, 732 A.2D 493

GARIBALDI, J.

This appeal involves a $1.5 million dollar loan made by MetLife Capital Corporation, predecessor in interest to plaintiff MetLife Capital Financial Corporation ("MetLife"), to defendant Washington Avenue Associates, L.P. ("Washington Avenue"). The loan was secured by a Mortgage and Security Agreement on a commercial property in Belleville, New Jersey. Numerous payments on the loan were delinquent, and Washington Avenue ultimately defaulted on the final "balloon payment." We now consider whether the five percent late charge assessed against each delinquent payment, and the default rate of interest, constitute reasonable stipulated damages provisions. * * *

II.

Historically, courts have closely scrutinized contract provisions that provided for the payment of specific damages upon breach. *Wasserman's Inc. v. Middletown*, 137 N.J. 238, 248, 645 A.2d 100 (1994). The need for close scrutiny arises from the possibility that stipulated damages clauses may constitute an oppressive penalty. Enforceable stipulated damages clauses are referred to as "liquidated damages," while unenforceable provisions are labeled "penalties." *Ibid.* (*quoting* Kenneth W. Clarkson, et al., *Liquidated Damages v. Penalties: Sense or Nonsense?*, 1978 WISC. L. REV. 351, 351 n.1).

The common law distinction between a provision authorizing liquidated damages and a provision authorizing a penalty was set forth in the RESTATEMENT OF CONTRACTS more than 60 years ago:

> An agreement, made in advance of breach, fixing the damages therefore, is not enforceable as a contract and does not affect the damages recoverable for the breach, unless (a) the amount so fixed is a reasonable forecast of just compensation for the harm that is caused by the breach, and (b) the harm that is caused by the breach is one that is incapable or very difficult of accurate estimation.

RESTATEMENT OF CONTRACTS § 339 (1932).

New Jersey adopted the RESTATEMENT method for evaluating stipulated damage clauses in *Westmount Country Club v. Kameny*, 82 N.J. Super. 200, 197 A.2d 379 (App.Div.1964). In *Westmount*, the Appellate Division considered the validity of a contract clause requiring full payment for a country club membership, even if the membership was canceled mid-year. *Westmount, supra*, 82 N.J. Super. at 203, 197 A.2d 379. That court concluded that there was no evidence that the full contract price was a reasonable estimate of damages or that the actual damages were difficult to estimate and declined to enforce the stipulated damages clause. *Id.* at 206-07, 197 A.2d 379.

The law, however, has not remained static. Courts began to treat the two-pronged *Westmount* test as a continuum; the more uncertain the damages caused by a breach, the more latitude courts gave the parties on their estimate of damages. Charles J. Goetz & Robert E. Scott, *Liquidated Damages, Penalties and the Just Compensation Principle: Some Notes on an Enforcement Model and a Theory of Efficient Breach*, 77 COLUM. L. REV. 554, 560 (1977). The Uniform Commercial Code provision on liquidated damages, adopted in New Jersey as N.J.S.A. 12A:2-718, incorporated this more flexible test. N.J.S.A. 12A:2-718 treats the prongs of the *Westmount* test as elements of "reasonableness" in evaluating a stipulated damages provision. *Id.* at 560 n.25; *see also* N.J.S.A. 12A:2-718(1) ("[d]amages for breach by either party may be liquidated in the agreement but only at an amount which is reasonable in light of the anticipated or actual harm caused by the breach, the difficulties of proof of loss, and the inconvenience or non-feasibility of otherwise obtaining an adequate remedy. A term fixing unreasonably large liquidated damages is void as a penalty."). The SECOND

RESTATEMENT "redrafted" the liquidated damages provision "to harmonize with Uniform Commercial Code § 2-718(1)." RESTATEMENT (SECOND) OF CONTRACTS § 356 (Reporter's Note) (1981). That provision endorsed the "reasonableness" approach employed by the Uniform Commercial Code:

> Damages for breach by either party may be liquidated in the agreement but only at an amount that is reasonable in light of the anticipated or actual loss caused by the breach and the difficulties of proof of loss. A term fixing unreasonably large liquidated damages is unenforceable on grounds of public policy as a penalty.

Id. at § 356.

The Appellate Division tacitly acknowledged this more flexible approach in *Stuchin v. Kasirer*, 237 N.J. Super. 604, 568 A.2d 907 (App.Div.1990), *cert. denied*, 121 N.J. 660, 583 A.2d 346 (1990). In *Stuchin*, the defendants in a foreclosure case challenged the application of an enhanced default rate, which increased the contract interest rate by fifteen percent. *Id.* at 610, 568 A.2d 907. Despite reciting the strict two-pronged test of *Westmount*, the Appellate Division remanded the issue to the trial court to receive "appropriate evidence of the reasonableness or unreasonableness of the 15% rate increase * * *." *Id.* at 614, 568 A.2d 907.

Subsequently, this Court expressly addressed the proper method for evaluating stipulated damages clauses. *Wasserman's Inc. v. Middletown, supra*, 137 N.J. at 249-54, 645 A.2d 100. In that case we considered the validity of a stipulated damages clause that provided that if Middletown canceled a lease of commercial property Middletown would pay damages equal to twenty-five percent of Wasserman's gross annual receipts. *Id.* at 242, 645 A.2d 100. After reviewing the history and development of stipulated damages provisions, we concluded that "[s]o viewed, 'reasonableness' emerges as the standard for deciding the validity of stipulated damages clauses." *Id.* at 249, 645 A.2d 100. Treating reasonableness "as the touchstone," we noted that the difficulty in assessing damages, intention of the parties, the actual damages sustained, and the bargaining power of the parties all affect the validity of a stipulated damages clause. *Id.* at 250-54, 645 A.2d 100. We did not, however, consider any of those factors dispositive, and remanded the case, leaving "to the sound discretion of the trial court the extent to which additional proof is necessary on the reasonableness of the clause." *Id.* at 258, 645 A.2d 100. * * *[W]e find that the five percent late charge and 12.55 percent default rate set by the trial court are reasonable liquidated damages.

Notes

1. The court characterizes former 2-718(1) as adopting the "reasonableness" approach. At what time is reasonableness determined, the time of contracting or the time of breach? Compare amended UCC 2-718(1). How does that change the answer to the question? *See* UCC 1-305(a) [former 1-106] which states that "no penal damages may be had except as specifically provided in the [UCC] or by other rule of law."

2. Suppose that a contract for sale contains a provision that provides: "If the buyer breaches the contract at any time the seller may recover the agreed contract price as liquidated damages and not as a penalty." Is this clause enforceable under UCC 2-718(1)? If not, can you draft an enforceable clause where the seller is entitled to a stated percentage of the contract price if the buyer breaches? *Compare* the comment to UCC 2A-504.

3. Should there be any limitations on the enforceability of a liquidated damages clause? In light of a legal structure that allows for significant freedom of contract, what is the policy reason supporting judicial scrutiny of these clauses?*

IN RE BALDWIN RENTAL CENTERS, INC.
UNITED STATES BANKRUPTCY COURT, S.D. GEORGIA, 1998
228 B.R. 504

JAMES D. WALKER, JR., BANKRUPTCY JUDGE

* * *

Findings of Fact

Baldwin Rental Centers, Inc. ("Debtor") entered into fourteen equipment leasing agreements with Case. It was Debtor's practice to sublease this equipment to its customers at a higher price than that paid under its agreement with Case, thereby generating profit. Debtor, however, was unable to generate enough profit to stay current on the lease payments owed to Case, and on August 20, 1997, Debtor filed a voluntary petition under Chapter 11 of the Bankruptcy Code.

Baldwin Rental, as Debtor-in-Possession ("DIP"), continued to possess and sublease the leased equipment post-petition. On January 7, 1998, after a hearing on

---

* *See* Larry A. Dimatteo, *A Theory of Efficient Penalty: Eliminating the Law of Liquidated Damages*, 38 AM. BUS. L. J. 633 (2001) (arguing that liquidated damages clauses should be presumed enforceable subject to the being declared unenforceable only if unconscionable).

October 12, 1997, this Court entered a consent order allowing DIP to assume five of the fourteen unexpired leases ("assumed leases") and reject the remaining nine leases ("rejected leases"). At the time of the October hearing, the rejected leases had accrued unpaid rent post-petition in an amount totaling $20,823.32, and they had produced revenue totaling $35,260.17.

On January 30, 1998, DIP rejected the assumed leases. Each of the assumed leases contained a liquidated damages clause which provided:

> I [Debtor] agree that you [Case] may sell the Equipment (including at wholesale), re-lease it or otherwise dispose of it in a commercially reasonable manner. I agree to pay you, as liquidated damages, an amount equal to (a) any unpaid rent, plus (b) the present value as of the date of default of the rent for the remainder of the term (using the Present Value Rate), plus (c) the Purchase Option Price, plus, (d) any excess hour charges, plus (e), to the extent permitted by law, reasonable attorney fees and legal expenses incurred by you in connection with this Agreement, plus (f) any other liabilities under this Agreement, minus the present value of the net proceeds resulting from the disposition of the Equipment (whether by sale or re-lease).

In aggregate, the unpaid rent on the leases totaled $31,586.84; the present value of the future rent for the remaining term under each of the leases totaled $76,302.88; and the purchase option price (*i.e.* residual value) of the equipment under the leases totaled $148,717.39. Debtor initially requested the equipment be disposed of by public auction. However, Debtor withdrew this request and Case sold the equipment at a private sale for wholesale value. The aggregate price received for the five pieces of equipment was $151,600.00.[1] Therefore, the liquidated damages provision results in total damages of $105,007.11 for rejection of the assumed leases.

Case requests that $125,830.43 ($20,823.32 in accrued post-petition rent for the rejected leases, plus the $105,007.11 in liquidated damages for the assumed leases) be given administrative expense priority and be paid in full prior to or at the time of confirmation of Debtor's Chapter 11 plan of reorganization. Debtor disputes both the amount due for rejecting the assumed leases and the amount qualified for

---

[1] The assumed leases covered four backhoes and one wheel loader. The wheel loader sold for $43,000.00. Three of the backhoes sold for $27,150.00 apiece. The fourth backhoe was stolen before the sale. Case is seeking to recover the value of the backhoe from its insurance company. However, for purposes of this opinion, the Court finds that the fourth backhoe would likely have also been sold for $27,150.00.

administrative expense priority. Debtor first argues that the liquidated damages provision is unenforceable as a penalty. Thus, Debtor claims damages resulting from breach of the assumed leases should be computed under state law. Next, Debtor claims that any future rents that may be due under the assumed leases, and the rent accrued post-petition under the rejected leases, conferred no benefit on the estate and, therefore, do not qualify for administrative expense priority, but rather should be treated as general unsecured claims. The Court finds 1) that the liquidated damages provision is enforceable, 2) that in this case, the plain language of the Bankruptcy Code requires a finding that all damages resulting from rejection of the assumed leases, including future rents, are administrative expenses, and 3) that the rent accrued post-petition on the rejected leases did confer a benefit on the estate and is, therefore, an administrative expense.

Conclusions of Law

I. Liquidated Damages

The assumed leases each contain a formula to be used to liquidate damages in the event of breach. "[A]ll lease contracts for 'goods' * * * first made or first effective on or after July 1, 1993, are governed by Article 2A of the Uniform Commercial Code." *Colonial Pacific Leasing Corp. v. McNatt*, 268 Ga. 265, 268, 486 S.E.2d 804, 807 (1997). These lease agreements were first effective in 1995. Therefore, Article 2A governs the enforceability of the liquidated damages provisions.

O.C.G.A. § 11-2A-504(1) provides:

Damages payable by either party for default * * * may be liquidated in the lease agreement but only at an amount or by a formula that is reasonable in light of the then anticipated harm caused by the default* * *.

In creating this rule, the drafters of the UCC made this comment:

Many leasing transactions are predicated on the parties' ability to agree to an appropriate amount of damages or formula for damages in the event of default or other act or omission. The rule with respect to sales of goods (Section 2-718) may not be sufficiently flexible to accommodate this practice. Thus, consistent with the common law emphasis upon freedom to contract with respect to bailments for hire, this section has created a revised rule that allows greater flexibility with respect to leases of goods. * * * By deleting the reference to unreasonably large liquidated damages [contained in Section 2-718(1)] the parties are free to negotiate a formula, restrained by the rule of reasonableness in this section. These changes should invite the parties to liquidate damages.

UCC § 2A-504(1), Official Comment.[2] Thus, parties to a lease are encouraged to liquidate their damages subject only to the rule of reasonableness. Whether a liquidated damages clause is enforceable is a question of law. *Carter v. Tokai Fin. Servs., Inc.*, 231 Ga.App. 755, 758, 500 S.E.2d 638, 641 (1998). In Georgia, three factors must be present for the clause to be enforceable:

> First, the injury caused by the breach must be difficult or impossible of accurate estimation; second, the parties must intend to provide for damages rather than for a penalty; and, third, the sum stipulated must be a reasonable pre-estimate of the probable loss.

This constitutes a two-part test: 1) difficulty of estimation, and 2) reasonable pre-estimation of probable loss. Whether the clause is a penalty is determined by the second part of the test. The moment of inquiry to determine reasonableness is at the time the parties entered into the agreement, and a reasonable provision that in hindsight contains an inaccurate estimation of the probable loss should not be rendered unenforceable. *See Coastal Leasing Corp. v. T-Bar S Corp.*, 128 N.C. App. 379, 496 S.E.2d 795, 798 (N.C. Ct. App. 1998).

In the only Georgia case to interpret section 11-2A-504(1), the Georgia Court of Appeals struck down the liquidated damages provision at issue as an unenforceable penalty. *Carter*, 231 Ga. App. at 759, 500 S.E.2d at 641. The clause provided that upon default, the lessor could recover 1) accrued and unpaid rent, plus 2) the present value of all future rent plus one percent, plus 3) the present value of the equipment's residual value. In addition, the lessor could sell the equipment subject to the lease without having to account to the lessee for any of the sale proceeds. *Id.* at 758, 500 S.E.2d at 641. The court found that reducing the future rent to present value indicated the clause was a reasonable estimate of probable loss. *Id.* at 759, 500 S.E.2d at 641. However, the fact that the clause allowed the lessor to retain the value of the equipment as well as the value of all future rental payments put the lessor in a better position following default than he would have been in had the lease been fully performed. Therefore, the liquidated damages provision was found to be an unenforceable penalty. *Id.* [The court discussed two cases.] * * *

The above cases illustrate that so long as the liquidated damages formula puts

---

[2] When a section of the Uniform Commercial Code is adopted verbatim by the Georgia Legislature, as section 11-2A-504(1) was here, "the intentions of the drafters of the Uniform Commercial Code as evidenced in the official comments to the Uniform Commercial Code should be given due consideration." *Warren's Kiddie Shoppe, Inc. v. Casual Slacks, Inc.*, 120 Ga.App. 578, 580, 171 S.E.2d 643, 645 (1969).

the lessor in no better position than it would otherwise be in had the lease been fully performed, the provision is likely to be a reasonable pre-estimate of probable loss. The formula is likely to put the lessor in such a position if it contains two elements in its calculation: 1) the balance of the lease payments reduced to present value, and 2) a credit to the lessee for the amount the lessor receives, or would receive, upon selling or re-leasing the property subject to the lease.

The Court now turns to the liquidated damages provision in the case at hand. The formula provides that Case is entitled to 1) any accrued, unpaid rent at the time of breach, plus 2) the present value of the rent for the remainder of the lease term, plus 3) the residual value of the equipment, minus 4) the present value of the net proceeds resulting from disposition of the equipment.[3] Debtor argues that the formula's inclusion of the residual value of the equipment, which Debtor was never obligated to pay, makes the provision a penalty. While Case's inclusion of this amount in the formula seems misplaced,[4] it does not render the provision unenforceable.

Initially, the Court notes that this formula does provide for reducing the future rent to present value and crediting Debtor with the proceeds from Case's disposition of the equipment. In addition, the Court finds that the formula leaves Case in no better position than it would have been in had the lease been fully performed by Debtor.

Had the lease been fully performed, Case would have received from Debtor, at present value, $107,889.72 (accrued rent plus the present value of future rent). Plus, at the end of the lease term, Case would have had possession of five pieces of equipment with an estimated combined value of $148,717.39 that it could sell to Debtor or a third party. Thus, Case could have potentially received $256,607.11 if Debtor had fully performed its obligations under the lease. Under the liquidated damages formula, Case received $151,600 for the sale of the equipment. This was $2,882.61 more than the estimated value of the equipment one year later. The $107,889.72 in rent owed to Case under the lease agreement, and provided for in the liquidated damages provision, was reduced by this $2,882.61 difference, thus requiring Debtor to pay the remaining $105,007.11 in damages. Therefore, under

---

[3] The clause provided for certain other damages that the lessor chose not to include in its determination of damages.

[4] The Court notes that the formula calls for reducing proceeds from the disposition of the equipment to present value, while not reducing the residual value to present value. However, such an oversight does not give rise to a finding that the provision is a penalty.

the liquidated damages provision, Case receives $256,607.11 (accrued rent and the present value of future rent due under the lease from Debtor, plus the proceeds from the sale of the equipment), the same amount Case would have received under the lease if Debtor had fully performed. Because the liquidated damages provision leaves Case in no better position that it would be in had the lease been fully performed, the Court finds that the liquidated damages provision is reasonable.

Further evidence that the liquidated damages provision contained in these leases is reasonable is the fact that it is just such a provision contemplated by the drafters of section 2A-504. The Official Comment to section 2A-504 notes that a common liquidated damages formula in leasing practice

> provides that the sum of lease payments past due, accelerated future lease payments, and the lessor's estimated residual interest, less the net proceeds of disposition (whether by sale or re-lease) of the leased goods is the lessor's damages. Tax indemnities, costs, interest and attorney's fees are also added to determine the lessor's damages.

UCC § 2A-504(1), Official Comment. This provision is identical to the provisions in the assumed leases with the only difference being that none of the figures in the Comment are reduced to present value. The Comment goes on to state that "[w]hether these formulae are enforceable will be determined in the context of each case by applying a standard of reasonableness in light of the harm anticipated when the formula was agreed to." *Id.* Considering that the formula in the assumed leases provides for damages equal to what Case would have received had the lease been fully performed, this Court finds that the liquidated damages provisions are reasonable in this case. Therefore, Debtor is liable for $105,007.11 in liquidated damages flowing from the breach of the assumed leases.

The Court now turns its attention to Case's claim that the liquidated damages provided under the assumed leases and the rent accrued post-petition on the rejected leases qualify as administrative expenses. * * *

ORDER

In accordance with the memorandum opinion entered on this date, it is hereby ordered that the liquidated damages provision contained in the assumed leases are reasonable and enforceable pursuant to O.C.G.A. § 11-2A-504(1); * * *

Notes

1. Should proof of the actual damages suffered influence the enforceability of

a liquidated damages clause? The 2003 amendments to UCC 2-718(1) changed the test for non-consumer contracts by focusing on reasonableness in light of actual or anticipated harm, dropping the factors of difficulty of proof of loss and inconvenience or non-feasibility of obtaining an adequate remedy.[*] The test for reasonableness in a consumer contract remains as under prior law. What difference is the amendment likely to make in determining whether a liquidated damages clause is enforceable?

2. The effect of an enforceable liquidated damages clause is that the damages stipulated in that clause take the place of the damages the aggrieved party would otherwise be entitled to under the damage provisions we studied in Chapters Ten and Eleven, *supra.*

3. **Restitution for a breaching buyer or lessee.** Notice that in UCC 2-718(3) and 2A-504(3), a buyer or lessee that is in breach of contract is entitled to return of the price paid with an offset for liquidated or other damages to which the seller or lessor is entitled. Former Articles 2 and 2A had a statutory "liquidated damages" provision that could be used as an offset if there was no enforceable liquidated damages clause. The 2003 amendments eliminated the statutory "liquidated damages." Thus, the breaching buyer or lessee will be entitled to restitution of the price paid to the extent that amount is more than either the seller's or lessor's liquidated damages or alternatively, if no enforceable liquidated damages clause, the amount of the seller's or lessor's damages.

Problem 12-1

B, a baker, planned to expand its capacity by 30%. Accordingly, on March 1, it ordered a custom-made oven from S, a manufacturer, to be delivered not later than September 1. B informed S of its planned expansion and stated that "time was of the essence." B had developed a new bread for hotels and restaurants and wanted to be in production for the Fall convention season. S and B negotiated over how to deal with the risk of delay in delivery.

After discussing B's current profit margin and the probabilities that an expansion would be profitable, S agreed, in a clause labeled LIQUIDATED DAMAGES, to pay B $1,000 for every day of a non-excusable delay in delivery.

---

[*] *See* Debora L. Threedy, *Liquidated and Limited Damages and the Revision of Article 2: An Opportunity to Rethink the U.C.C.'s Treatment of Agreed Remedies*, 27 IDAHO L. REV. 427 (1990/91).

S did not deliver the oven until October 1. B claimed liquidated damages in the amount of $30,000. S, however, can establish that the convention business during September was very slow and that, at best, B would have made only $2,500 in net profits if the oven had been delivered on time. Is the agreed damage clause enforceable under UCC 2-718?

Note: Liquidated Damages Under the CISG

The CISG does not deal specifically with liquidated damage clauses. Suppose the parties agree to liquidate damages arising under Article 74 and, later, the buyer claims that the seller was grossly overcompensated. Should the clause be enforced? *See* Art. 6. At what point does the buyer's argument involve the "validity of the contract or any of its provisions"? *See* Art. 4(a).

Note: Liquidated Damages Under UCITA

UCITA 804 provides liquidated damages clauses are enforceable if reasonable based upon the anticipated loss, the actual loss, or the difficulties of proving loss. That section also provides for a breaching licensee's restitution of the price paid for copies withheld due to breach of contract subject to offset by the liquidated damages clause amount or the licensor's actual damages.

B. Limited Remedies

Limited remedies, as opposed to liquidated damages, are governed by UCC 2-719 or 2A-503. These sections raise several questions.

First, what is the difference between a limited monetary remedy and a liquidated damages clause and how do the tests of enforceability for each differ? The 2003 amendments to UCC 2-718(1) provide that the enforceability of a limited remedy clause is determined under UCC 2-719. *Compare* UCC 2A-504 and 2A-503. Second, when can the contract terms bar consequential damage recovery? Does the same rule apply to incidental damages?[*] Third, what does it mean for a limited remedy to "fail of its essential purpose"? What is the consequence of such a failure on the remedial package contained in the contract including the clause

---

[*] *See McNally Wellman Co. v. New York State Elec. & Gas Corp.*, 63 F.3d 1188 (2nd Cir. 1995) (noting that courts routinely apply the same test to incidental damages).

excluding recovery of consequential and incidental damages?

Problem 12-2

A. Suppose that the clause in Problem 12-1 was labeled LIMITATION OF DAMAGES and S agreed to pay "no more than $500 for each day of un-excused delay." The oven was delivered on October 1. B is prepared to establish that the convention market boomed during September and that the delay in delivery deprived it of at least $2,500 in net profits per day. B claims that the limitation clause was unreasonable. Is B correct? *See* UCC 2-718 & 2-719.

B. Suppose that B, citing UCC 2-719(3), claimed that the clause was unconscionable. B conceded that it was fully aware of and agreed to the clause at the time of contracting, but that it operated in an unconscionable manner by depriving B of a minimum adequate remedy. Will this argument succeed?

CAYUGA HARVESTER, INC. v. ALLIS-CHALMERS CORP.
SUPREME COURT OF NEW YORK, APPELLATE DIVISION, 1983
95 A.D.2D 5, 465 N.Y.S.2D 606

HANCOCK, JUSTICE

Under the Uniform Commercial Code, the parties to a sale may, within certain limitations, allocate the risks of their bargain by limiting the remedy of the buyer (Uniform Commercial Code, § 2-719, subd. 1, par. a). When, however, a limited remedy such as an exclusive repair and replacement warranty fails of its essential purpose, the buyer is relieved of its restrictions and may resort to other remedies as provided in section 2-719 (subd. 2). The Code also permits the parties to agree to exclude consequential damages unless the exclusion is unconscionable (Uniform Commercial Code, § 2-719, subd. 3). Here the contract in issue contains both an exclusive repair and replacement warranty and an exclusion of consequential damages; plaintiff claiming that the limited remedy failed of its essential purpose seeks to recover consequential as well as other damages for breach of warranty. A major question arises from plaintiff's contention that proof of the failure of the limited repair and replacement warranty would free it not only from the restrictions of that clause but also from the clause excluding consequential damages.

The action arises out of the sale of an N-7 harvesting machine manufactured by defendant Allis-Chalmers Corporation ("Allis"). Plaintiff, the operator of an extensive corn-growing business in Cato, New York, purchased the machine for

$142,213 from defendant R.C. Church & Sons, Inc. ("Church"), a farm machinery dealer, under a written purchase order containing a limited repair and replacement warranty and an exclusion of consequential damages. The balance of the purchase price, after a down payment of $36,989.80, was financed through defendant Allis-Chalmers Credit Corporation ("Allis Credit"). Plaintiff alleges that the machine did not operate or function properly and that it suffered numerous failures and breakdowns preventing it from making a timely and effective harvest of its 1981 corn crop.

The issues considered concerning various sections of the Uniform Commercial Code are as follows:

I.   A.   whether the limited repair and replacement warranty failed of its essential purpose (§ 2-719, subd. 2);

B.   if so, whether, despite the failure, the consequential damages exclusion remains in effect; and

C.   whether the clause excluding consequential damages is unconscionable (§§ 2-719, subd. 3; 2-302, subds. 1, 2). * * *

I

We consider first the grant of summary judgment dismissing the first two causes of action against Allis alleging breaches of express warranties. In the purchase order under the "Allis-Chalmers New Farm Equipment Warranty", Allis gave an express warranty limited to the repair or replacement of defective parts in the following provisions which we quote in part:

WHAT IS WARRANTED

Allis-Chalmers Corporation ("Company") warrants new farm equipment sold by it to be merchantable and free of defects in workmanship and material at the time of shipment from the Company's factory. THERE ARE NO WARRANTIES WHICH EXTEND BEYOND THOSE EXPRESSLY STATED HEREIN. The warranty is made to the original purchaser or lessee from an authorized Allis-Chalmers Dealer of each item of new Allis-Chalmers farm equipment.

1. *Equipment Warranty.* Parts which are defective in workmanship and material as delivered will be repaired or replaced as follows: * * *

(There follow several paragraphs detailing the terms and conditions of Allis' obligation to make repairs and replacements and the periods during which the warranty is effective.)

I. REMEDIES EXCLUSIVE.

THE COMPANY'S LIABILITY, WHETHER IN CONTRACT OR IN

TORT, ARISING OUT OF WARRANTIES, REPRESENTATIONS, INSTRUCTIONS, OR DEFECTS FROM ANY CAUSE SHALL BE LIMITED EXCLUSIVELY TO REPAIRING OR REPLACING PARTS UNDER THE CONDITIONS AS AFORESAID, AND IN NO EVENT WILL THE COMPANY BE LIABLE FOR CONSEQUENTIAL DAMAGES, INCLUDING BUT NOT LIMITED TO LOSS OF CROPS, LOSS OF PROFITS, RENTAL OR SUBSTITUTE EQUIPMENT, OR OTHER COMMERCIAL LOSS.

In granting Allis' motions Special Term held that the provision excluding consequential damages in Paragraph "I", above, was, as a matter of law, not unconscionable under Uniform Commercial Code (§§ 2-719, subd. 3; 2-302, subd. 1) and that it acted as a total bar to plaintiff's express warranty claims. The court did not find it necessary to reach the issues before us concerning the alleged failure of the essential purpose of the repair and replacement warranty under the Uniform Commercial Code (§ 2-719, subd. 2) and the effect of that failure on the exclusion of consequential damages.

A

Ordinarily, whether circumstances have caused a "limited remedy to fail of its essential purpose" (Uniform Commercial Code, § 2-719, subd. 2) is a question of fact for the jury and one necessarily to be resolved upon proof of the circumstances occurring after the contract is formed. * * * It should be noted that in order to establish a failure of a limited remedy under section 2-719 (subd. 2) it is not necessary to show that the warrantor's conduct in failing to effect repairs was wilfully dilatory or even negligent. Rather, the section is to apply "whenever an exclusive remedy, which may have appeared fair and reasonable at the inception of the contract, as a result of later circumstances operates to deprive a party of a substantial benefit of the bargain" (*Clark v. International Harvester Co.,* 99 Idaho 326, 340, 581 P.2d 784; *see* Uniform Commercial Code, § 2-719, Official Comment 1; WHITE & SUMMERS, HANDBOOK OF THE LAW UNDER THE UNIFORM COMMERCIAL CODE, (2d ed.), § 12-10). The damage to the buyer is the same whether the seller diligently but unsuccessfully attempts to honor his promise or acts negligently or in bad faith. * * * Moreover, a "delay in supplying the remedy can just as effectively deny the purchaser the product he expected as can the total inability to repair. In both instances the buyer loses the substantial benefit of his purchase" (*Chatlos Systems, Inc. v. National Cash Register Corp.,* 635 F.2d 1081, 1085 (3d Cir. 1980)). Thus, if it is found at trial that plaintiff, because of defendant Allis' failure to repair or replace parts within a reasonable time, has been deprived of a substantial benefit of its bargain, it may prevail even though, as is the case here, there is no claim of bad faith or wilfully dilatory conduct and the record demonstrates that defendant made extensive efforts to comply.

The precise question here is whether plaintiff has made a prima facie showing that the limited remedy failed of its essential purpose. On our review of the record we hold that plaintiff has made such a showing and that Special Term was in error in granting summary judgment dismissing the first two causes of action against Allis in their entirety (C.P.L.R. 3212, subd. b). Mr. Sheckler, plaintiff's president, states in an affidavit "that the N-7 combine purchased by plaintiff suffered over 100 mechanical failures and over 100 parts replacements resulting in over 640 actual hours of machine down-time. Because of the inoperability of the N-7 combine a full eight months were required for plaintiff to complete the process of driving the combine over all the acres of corn." Annexed to plaintiff's affidavits are a detailed log of the numerous machine failures and a lengthy list of warranty claims totaling many thousands of dollars submitted by Church to Allis covering work performed and parts supplied from the delivery of the machine in July of 1981 through February, 1982.

It is settled that a finding that a limited warranty has failed of its essential purpose frees the buyer to pursue his remedies under other provisions of the Uniform Commercial Code as if the clause did not exist * * *. Plaintiff would, therefore, not be precluded by the exclusive remedy clause from recovering under the usual measure of damages in warranty cases; *i.e.*, "the difference at the time and place of acceptance between the value of the goods accepted and the value they would have had if they had been as warranted" (Uniform Commercial Code, § 2-714, subd. 2) * * *.

The order granting summary judgment to defendant Allis should be reversed to the extent that it dismisses the first and second causes of action in their entirety.

B

We come next to the legal question whether the consequential damage exclusion in Paragraph "I" would survive a finding that the limited repair and replacement warranty in that paragraph had failed of its essential purpose. We have found no controlling authority on the point in this state, and the numerous decisions in federal courts and the courts of other states are in conflict.

As we view it, the problem requires a two-step analysis: first, construing Paragraph "I" in its context as one clause in a contract concerning a substantial commercial transaction in order to ascertain the allocation of the risks as intended by the parties; and, second, determining whether that agreed-upon allocation of the risks leaves "at least a fair quantum of remedy for breach of the obligations or duties outlined in the contract" (McKINNEY'S CONS.LAWS OF N.Y., Book 62 ½, Part 1, Uniform Commercial Code, § 2-719, Official Comment 1, p. 691). Paragraph "I" states:

> THE COMPANY'S LIABILITY, WHETHER IN CONTRACT OR IN TORT, ARISING OUT OF WARRANTIES, REPRESENTATIONS, INSTRUCTIONS, OR DEFECTS FROM ANY CAUSE SHALL BE LIMITED EXCLUSIVELY TO REPAIRING OR REPLACING PARTS UNDER THE CONDITIONS AS AFORESAID, AND IN NO EVENT WILL THE COMPANY BE LIABLE FOR CONSEQUENTIAL DAMAGES, INCLUDING BUT NOT LIMITED TO LOSS OF CROPS, LOSS OF PROFITS, RENTAL OR SUBSTITUTE EQUIPMENT, OR OTHER COMMERCIAL LOSS.

Preliminarily, it may be helpful to set forth two factors which are material to our analysis and, we think, significant: (1) this is not a case involving bad faith or wilfully dilatory conduct on the part of the defendant (*compare, e.g., Jones & McKnight Corp. v. Birdsboro Corp.,* 320 F. Supp. 39, 43 (D.C. Ill. 1970); *Adams v. J.I. Case Co.,* 125 Ill. App. 2d 388, 402, 261 N.E.2d 1; and (2) plaintiff, if it should succeed in proving that the limited warranty has failed, would, regardless of a contrary ruling on the survivability of the consequential damages exclusion, be permitted to recover damages allowed by Uniform Commercial Code (§ 2-714, subd. 2) (*see* subpart A, *supra*).

Plaintiff argues that the promise of defendant to repair and replace defective parts in the first part of Paragraph "I" and the clause exempting defendant from the assessment of consequential damages in the second part are mutually dependent, *i.e.*, that a failure on the part of defendant to perform its obligations under the first, as a matter of law, deprives it of its exemption under the second part and frees plaintiff from its limitations. Defendant, on the other hand, maintains that the two provisions are unrelated and independent.

In our view defendant has the better of the argument. Certainly, no wording in Paragraph "I", itself, indicates that the provisions are interrelated or that the failure of defendant to perform under the repair and replacement warranty deprives it of the protection of the consequential damages exclusion. The purposes of the two clauses are totally discrete: that of the first is to restrict defendant's obligations under the transaction to repairing or replacing defective parts while that of the second is to rule out a specific type of damage. Each clause stands on its own and may be given effect without regard to the other. Thus, the plain meaning of Paragraph "I" appears to favor defendant.

Nor, given the larger context of Paragraph "I" as one term in a transaction involving the sale of an expensive piece of farm machinery to a large commercial grower, would it be reasonable to give it a different construction. Adopting plaintiff's interpretation, defendant's failure to repair and replace defective parts would, despite its good-faith efforts to fulfill its obligations, subject it to a lawsuit for consequential damages and loss of profits which, in view of the size of plaintiff's operation, could result in a recovery many times the value of the N-7 combine. It defies reason to suppose that defendant could have intended to assume such risks. The contrary construction urged by defendant entails a more plausible allocation of the risks and one that the parties could reasonably have had in mind: *i.e.*, that a failure of the repair and replacement warranty, despite defendant's good faith efforts to comply, would permit plaintiff to recover the ordinary breach of warranty damages (Uniform Commercial Code, § 2-714, subd. 2) but not loss of profits or other consequential damages.

We find nothing in the Uniform Commercial Code that rules out defendant's construction. On the contrary, under Uniform Commercial Code (§ 2-719) the "parties are left free to shape their remedies to their particular requirements and reasonable agreements limiting or modifying remedies are to be given effect" (MCKINNEY'S CONS. LAWS OF N.Y., Book 62, Part 1, Uniform Commercial Code, § 2-719, Official Comment 1, p. 691), provided that the remedy limitations are not unconscionable and that "there be at least a fair quantum of remedy for breach of the obligations or duties outlined in the contract" (MCKINNEY'S CONS. LAWS OF N.Y., Book 621/2, Part 1, Uniform Commercial Code, § 2-719, Official Comment 1, p. 691). Moreover, Uniform Commercial Code (§ 2-719, subd. 3) provides specifically that consequential damages "may be limited or excluded unless the limitation or exclusion is unconscionable." In a similar vein, the Official Comment 3 to section 2-719 states: "Subsection (3) recognizes the validity of clauses limiting or excluding consequential damages but makes it clear that they may not operate in an unconscionable manner. Actually such terms are merely an allocation of unknown or undeterminable risks. The seller in all cases is free to disclaim warranties in the manner provided in Section 2-316" (MCKINNEY'S CONS. LAWS OF N.Y., Book 62,1/2, Part 1, Uniform Commercial Code, § 2-719, Official Comment 3, p. 691). In sum, plaintiff has offered no good reason why the consequential damage exclusion clause should not be given effect in these circumstances, where the failure of the repair and replacement warranty is not due to bad faith or wilfully dilatory conduct. That the clause be given effect here would be an allocation of the risks which leaves the buyer a fair quantum of remedy as required by the Code and one that the parties to this commercial contract could reasonably have intended. We conclude, therefore, that if plaintiff succeeds in establishing that the repair and replacement warranty failed of its essential purpose (Uniform Commercial Code, § 2-719, subd. 2), the exclusion of consequential damages provided by Paragraph "I" remains in effect.

As stated, the decisions are in conflict but the proper rule, we think, is that set forth in *Chatlos Systems, Inc. v. National Cash Register Corp.,* 635 F.2d 1081, 1086 (3d Cir. 1980), *supra*: "The limited remedy of repair and a consequential damages exclusion are two discrete ways of attempting to limit recovery for breach of warranty. (Citations omitted.) The Code, moreover, tests each by a different standard. The former survives unless it fails of its essential purpose, while the latter is valid unless it is unconscionable. We therefore see no reason to hold, as a general proposition, that the failure of the limited remedy provided in the contract, without more, invalidates a wholly distinct term in the agreement excluding consequential damages." * * *

The leading cases cited as supporting the opposite view are *Jones & McKnight Corp. v. Birdsboro Corp.,* 320 F. Supp. 39 (D.C. Ill. 1970), *supra*, and *Adams v. J.I. Case Co.,* 125 Ill. App. 2d 388, 261 N.E.2d 1, *supra* * * *.

On analysis, however, neither *Jones & McKnight* nor *Adams* is inconsistent with our holding. Each case involves outright repudiation of the repair and replacement warranty or conduct by the seller that was wilfully dilatory. Thus, in *Jones & McKnight* the court held that the buyer was entitled to assume that the seller "would not be unreasonable or wilfully dilatory in making good their warranty in the event of defects in the machinery and equipment" and refused to allow the defendant "to shelter itself behind one segment of the warranty when it has allegedly repudiated and ignored its very limited obligations under another segment of the same warranty" (*Jones & McKnight Corp. v. Birdsboro Corp., supra*, p.43). Similarly, in *Adams* the court, in holding that the repair and replacement warranty and the consequential damages exclusion were "not separable" held that "plaintiff could not have made [its] bargain and purchase with knowledge that defendant [ ] would be unreasonable, or, * * * wilfully dilatory or careless and negligent in making good [its] warranty in the event of its breach" (*Adams v. J.I. Case Co., supra*, 125 Ill. App. 2d at p. 402, 261 N.E.2d 1).

We need not decide whether we would follow *Jones & McKnight* and *Adams* if plaintiff could contend, as did the buyers in those cases, that in agreeing to the consequential damages exclusion it never contemplated that defendant would not make good-faith efforts to effect repairs. That issue is not before us.

While not all of the cases following the *Jones & McKnight* and *Adams* rule involve bad faith or wilful repudiation of the repair and replacement warranty, several arise from non-commercial sales where the purchaser was an individual consumer. * * * Moreover, in *Clark v. International Harvester Co.* (*supra*), which entailed a purchase of a tractor by an individual custom farmer, the court points to a factor not present in the case at bar, *i.e.*, that there "was a significant disparity in bargaining power between the parties in this case" (*Clark v. International Harvester Co., supra*, 99 Idaho at p. 343, 581 P.2d 784).

Although we hold that plaintiff may not recover consequential damages, it will, if successful at trial, be entitled to other damages (Uniform Commercial Code, § 2-714, subd. 2). The order granting summary judgment should, therefore, be modified to a grant of partial summary judgment dismissing only those elements of the first two causes of action against Allis which seek consequential damages. * * *

Finally, we analyze plaintiff's contentions that Paragraph "I" is unconscionable under sections 2-719 (subd. 3) and 2-302 (subds. 1, 2) of the Code. A determination as to the conscionability of a contract relates to the circumstances existing at the time of its formation (Uniform Commercial Code, § 2-302, subd. 1). As a practical matter, however, the determination is inevitably made after a dispute has arisen. Thus, the agreement must be tested as to conscionability as it is applied to the particular breach which has occurred. Here, there is no claim of bad faith or that the failure to repair was wilfully dilatory, and we have held that the parties did not intend in Paragraph "I" that defendant's good faith but unsuccessful efforts to repair would negate the consequential damages exclusion. We have also held that such an agreed upon allocation of the risks does not offend the Code requirement that there be at least a fair quantum of remedy for breach of defendant's obligations. We must now decide whether this agreed upon allocation of the risks is unconscionable. * * *

On this record, in view of the nature of plaintiff's business as a large commercial grower, the size of the transaction involved, the fact that plaintiff had available other sources for purchasing similar equipment, the experience of its president and his familiarity with similar damage exclusion clauses, we agree with Special Term that plaintiff was not put in a bargaining position where it lacked a meaningful choice; nor was the agreement allocating the risk of crop loss and other consequential damages to the plaintiff, provided that good faith efforts be made to fulfill the repair warranty, unreasonably favorable to the defendant. * * *

The significant facts germane to the conscionability issue were essentially undisputed and we hold that Special Term correctly determined, as a legal question, that Paragraph "I" was not unconscionable and properly did so on the affidavits and other documents before it without the aid of a hearing (see Uniform Commercial Code, § 2-302). * * *

[Footnotes omitted.]

Notes

1. *Cayuga Harvester* involved a fairly typical risk allocation package with four parts:

(a) A limited express warranty, *i.e.*, that the goods were "merchantable and free of defects in material and workmanship at the time of shipment. * * *;

(b) A disclaimer of all other warranties, express or implied plus a "merger" clause;

(c) An agreed, exclusive limited remedy for breach, *i.e.*, the "repair or replacement" of parts which are "defective in workmanship and material as delivered" within a stated period of time; and

(d) An exclusion in any event of liability for consequential damages for liability, "whether in contract or tort, arising out of any warranties made."

These packages vary from industry to industry, but the thrust is essentially the same.[*] The problem arises when, after a defect is discovered, the seller is unable or unwilling to repair it within the stated time.

> This rosy picture of the limited repair warranty, however, rests upon at least three assumptions: that the warrantor will diligently make repairs, that such repairs will indeed 'cure' the defects, and that consequential loss in the interim will be negligible. So long as these assumptions hold true, the limited remedy appears to operate fairly and * * * will usually withstand contentions of 'unconscionability.' But when one of these assumptions proves false in a particular case, the purchaser may find that the substantial benefit of the bargain has been lost.

Jonathon A. Eddy, *On the "Essential" Purposes of Limited Remedies: The Metaphysics of U.C.C. Section 2-719(2)*, 65 CALIF. L. REV. 28, 63 (1977).

---

[*] *See Transamerica Oil Corp. v. Lynes, Inc.*, 723 F.2d 758 (10th Cir. 1983), where the court concluded that a similar limitation was so "pervasive" in the trade that the parties must have contracted with reference to it.

2.   If, as Jonathon Eddy suggested, failure of the agreed remedy deprives the buyer of the "substantial benefit" of the bargain, why should the buyer be bound by any part of the agreed remedy limitation?   Should your answer depend upon whether there was a commercial or a consumer buyer?

Section 2-810(b) of the May 1999 draft of Revised Article 2 distinguished between commercial and consumer contracts when an agreed limited remedy failed of its essential purpose. In the former case, the buyer was entitled to pursue "all remedies available" except that a clause expressly excluding consequential damages was enforceable unless it operated in an unconscionable manner. In the latter case, the consumer buyer could "reject the goods or revoke acceptance and ... pursue all remedies available under this article including the right to recover consequential damages, despite any term purporting to exclude or limit consequential damages." This proposal was ultimately rejected.

Note: Effect When Agreed Remedy Fails of its Essential Purpose

When a disappointed buyer attacks the limited remedy, the cases tend to agree on the questions which must be asked and answered. The answers, however, may vary from case to case. Here is a brief sample:

1.   Was the limited remedy "expressly agreed to be exclusive"? UCC 2-719(1)(b). If not, resort to it by the buyer is optional. If so, it is "the sole remedy."[*]

2.   Did the "circumstances cause an exclusive or limited remedy to fail of its essential purpose"? UCC 2-719(2). If not, it is enforceable. If so, "remedy may be had as provided in this Act." The most common "circumstances" are the seller's failure to "cure" the defect within the time stated or a reasonable time. As Judge Aspen put it: "A limited remedy of repair and replacement fails of its essential purposes when it is inadequate to provide the buyer with goods which conform to the contract within a reasonable time. * * * It is irrelevant to this standard whether the seller's failure to correct the defect is willful or not." *Custom Automated Machinery v. Penda Corp.*, 537 F. Supp. 77, 83 (N.D. Ill. 1982).[**]

---

[*] *See, e.g., Leininger v. Sola*, 314 N.W.2d 39 (N.D. 1981). *Compare Figgie Intern., Inc. v. Destileria Serralles, Inc.*, 190 F.3d 252 (4th Cir. 1999).

[**] *See also, Employers Ins. of Wausau v. Suwanee River SPA Lines, Inc.*, 866 F.2d 752 (5th Cir. 1989) (good faith failure to repair); *Rudd Construction Equipment Co., Inc. v. Clark Equipment Co.*, 735 F.2d 974 (6th Cir. 1984) (limited remedy fails essential purpose when

(continued...)

3. If the limited remedy of repair or replacement failed its essential purpose, what is the effect on the total risk allocation package? More particularly, if the failure enables the buyer to pursue normal remedies for "direct" damages under UCC 2-714, what about the clause excluding consequential damages?[*] There are several closely related subquestions.

First, did the parties intend the exclusion clause to be an integral part of the risk allocation package? If so, the failure of one part dooms the entire package, with the result that the buyer can pursue consequential damages under UCC 2-715(2).[**]

Second, if the parties did not so intend, does the separate exclusion clause drop out because UCC 2-719(2) provides that "remedy may be had as provided in this Act" and "this Act" permits consequential damages? Some courts have answered "yes," but the majority have answered "no."[***] Under the majority interpretation, the separate consequential damages exclusion clause must be evaluated under UCC 2-719(3).

Third, is the consequential damages exclusion clause unconscionable? There is no certain answer, even in commercial cases. A number of factors are relevant to the inquiry. Was there a prior course of dealing between the parties; was the exclusion clause conspicuous or brought to the buyer's attention; did the parties bargain in good faith; did the buyer have any realistic choices other than to deal with the seller; did the parties intend to allocate unknown or indeterminate risks? Is unconscionability tested as of the making of the agreement or at the time the

---

[**] (...continued)
defect causes fire which destroyed goods before seller had opportunity to cure).

[*] *See* Daniel C. Hagen, *Note, Sections 2-719(2) and 2-719(3) of the Uniform Commercial Code: The Limited Warranty Package & Consequential Damages*, 31 VAL. U. L. REV. 111 (1996).

[**] *See Bishop Logging Co. v. John Deere Indus. Equip.*, 455 S.E.2d 183 (S.C. App. 1995); *Waters v. Massey-Ferguson, Inc.*, 775 F.2d 587 (4th Cir. 1985); *Milgard Tempering, Inc. v. Selas Corp. of America*, 761 F.2d 553 (9th Cir. 1985) (whether clause separate is question of intent). *See also Hawaiian Telephone Co. v. Microform Data Systems, Inc.*, 829 F.2d 919 (9th Cir. 1987) (operation of exclusion clause dependent upon delivery of goods).

[***] Holding the exclusion drops out is *Fidelity & Deposit Co. of Maryland v. Krebs Engineers*, 859 F.2d 501 (7th Cir. 1988) (Wisconsin). The following cases rejected that analysis, *Rheem Manuf. Co. v. Phelps Heating & Air Conditioning Co.*, 746 N.E.2d 941 (Ind. 2001); *Smith v. Navistar Intern. Transp. Corp.*, 957 F.2d 1439 (7th Cir. 1992) (Illinois); *Pierce v. Catalina Yachts, Inc.*, 2 P.3d 618 (Ala. 2000).

remedies are sought? *See* comment 3 to UCC 2-719. *Compare* UCC 2-302.* In most cases, however, the exclusion clause is upheld against an unconscionability attack.**

Fourth, are there any equitable considerations that should prompt a court to invalidate the entire package, including the exclusion clause? For example, suppose the seller suspected that the goods were defective and knew that the limited remedy would not correct them. Or, suppose that the seller made no effort to cure or engaged in a careless or unprofessional effort. Or, suppose that the agreed remedy limited the buyer to less than the contract price if a cure was not forthcoming. In any of these cases, should the court conclude that the operation of the failed remedy package was unconscionable and the buyer should have the full remedies provided by Article 2?

Where does *Cayuga Harvester* fit in this range of possibilities? Should the analysis of UCC 2A-503 be any different?

Neither the enforceability of clauses limiting liability and remedy nor the result when a limited remedy fails to work are specifically covered in the CISG. UCITA 803 governs limited remedies modeled after the Article 2 provision except that the statute states a presumption that if the limited remedy fails, the consequential damage exclusion also fails, unless the agreement "expressly" provides the limited remedy and the consequential damage exclusion are independent. UCITA 803(c).

Note: Contracting Out of Tort Liability

In *Cayuga Harvester,* the seller attempted to exclude or "contract out" of "liability * * * in tort, arising out of warranties, representations, instructions, or defects from any cause," at least to the extent consequential damages were involved. What is the effect of these provisions?***

If a defect in the product caused personal injuries, strict products liability would apply and the clause would be unenforceable (against public policy) against the

---

* *See Cognitest Corp. v. Riverside Publishing Co.*, 107 F.3d 493 (7th Cir. 1997).

** *See, e.g., Lindemann v. Eli Lilly & Co.*, 816 F.2d 199 (5th Cir. 1987); *Island Creek Coal Co. v. Lake Shore, Inc.*, 832 F.2d 274 (4th Cir. 1987); *American Nursery Products, Inc. v. Indian Wells Orchards*, 797 P.2d 477 (Wash. 1990).

*** *See* William J. McNichols, *Who Says That Strict Tort Disclaimers Can Never Be Effective? The Courts Cannot Agree*, 28 Okla. L. Rev. 494 (1975).

plaintiff.[*] Between commercial parties ("extraordinary" consumers) where only economic loss is involved, that is harm to the product sold or consequential economic harm, the seller is, in most states, not liable in either strict products liability or negligence. In short, the buyer can pursue a warranty but not a tort theory. Thus, the disclaimer would be tested under the UCC in most cases, not in tort. However, if property damage is confined to the goods sold, some courts have concluded that strict tort liability applies if the nature of the defect, the risk created and the manner in which the accident occurred raised an issue of product safety. The emphasis is upon the nature of the risk created to person and property, not upon the type of damage actually caused.[**]

But suppose a defect in the product caused both economic loss and damage to property other than the product sold, *e.g.*, a defective product caused extensive damage to nearby property. Does warranty or tort theory apply and, if the latter, is the exclusion clause enforceable outside of the Code?[***]

If governed by the tort side of the line, the UCC does not apply to test the enforceability of disclaimers of liability. Nevertheless, commercial parties can agree to exculpate the seller from tort liability or from consequential damages if high standards insuring the quality of bargaining have been met. Thus, in *Salt River Project Agr. v. Westinghouse Electric Co.*, 694 P.2d 198 (Ariz. 1984), a turbine case, the court upheld an exculpation clause where the parties dealt in a commercial setting from positions of relatively equal bargaining strength, bargained over the specifications of the product and negotiated concerning the risk of loss from defects in the product.

SECTION 2.   CONSUMER PROTECTION LAW

Assume an individual purchases a car, stereo, furniture or even a mobile home

---

[*] *See* RESTATEMENT (THIRD) OF TORTS: PRODUCTS LIABILITY 18 (1998); Peter M. Kincaid and William J. Stuntz, Note, *Enforcing Waivers in Products Liability,* 69 VA. L. REV. 1111 (1983).

[**] *But see* RESTATEMENT (THIRD) OF TORTS: PRODUCTS LIABILITY 21, cmt. d (1998) (stating that the RESTATEMENT does not address this type of harm).

[***] *See* RESTATEMENT (THIRD) OF TORTS: PRODUCTS LIABILITY 21, cmt. f (1998) (leaving the issue to case law). Richard C. Ausness, *"Waive" Goodbye to Tort Liability: A Proposal to Remove Paternalism from Product Sales Transactions*, 37 SAN DIEGO L. REV. 293 (2000).

from a dealer for personal, family or household purposes. In short, they are consumer goods. *See* amended UCC 2-103(1)(c), 9-102(a)(23). A common assumption is that consumer buyers, as a class, have less capacity than the professional seller to protect themselves in the bargain. They are at a disadvantage in assessing risk, evaluating quality, obtaining adequate information, bargaining over contract provisions and pursuing remedies if problems arise. They are "ordinary" consumers who are more susceptible to exploitation or unprovable fraud by the seller than a commercial or "extraordinary" buyer. The distinction between "ordinary" and "extraordinary" consumers was advanced by Justice Peters, dissenting in *Seely v. White Motor Co.*, 403 P.2d 145 (Cal. 1965), to draw the line between warranty and tort in products liability cases. According to Peters, the test should depend upon the "relative roles played by the parties to the purchase contract and the nature of the transaction" rather than the type of loss caused and ask whether, at the time of contracting, the goods were sold to a commercial party or to an "ordinary consumer who is usually unable to protect himself * * *" or a commercial buyer who possessed "more bargaining power than does the usual individual who purchases * * * on the retail level." 403 P.2d at 152-58. The conclusion from this is that consumers need more legal protection than commercial buyers.[*]

When the losses are solely economic, the consumer buyer's or lessee's legal protection from breach of warranty by the seller or lessor is, without more, governed by the UCC. Additional, albeit uneven, protection is provided by the Magnuson-Moss Warranty Act on the federal level and, in some states, consumer protection legislation, including the so-called "lemon" laws.[**] In this Section, we

---

[*] This conclusion is sometimes disputed, *see, e.g.*, Alan Schwartz & Louis L. Wilde, *Imperfect Information in Markets for Contract Terms: The Examples of Warranties and Security Interests,* 69 VA. L. REV. 1387 (1983); *compare* Anthony T. Kronman, *Paternalism and the Law of Contracts,* 92 YALE L.J. 763, 766-74 (1983) (assessing risk of unprovable fraud by seller).

[**] *See* CURTIS R. REITZ, CONSUMER PRODUCT WARRANTIES UNDER FEDERAL AND STATE LAWS (2nd ed. 1987). Courts are in conflict whether the protections of the Magnuson Moss Warranty-Federal Trade Commission Improvement Act protect consumer lessees. *Compare DiCintio v. Daimler Chrysler Corp.*, 768 N.E.2d 1121 (N.Y. 2002) (holding no) *with Dekelaita v. Nissan Motor Corp.*, 799 N.E.2d 367 (Ill. Ct. App. 2003) (holding yes). The Federal Consumer Leases Act, codified at 15 U.S.C. 1667 *et. seq.*, provides for disclosures to consumers regarding the cost of leasing, regulation of lease advertising, and some

(continued...)

will see how the consumer buyer or lessee of a "big ticket" item, a new car, might fare under this mix of federal and state law.* As we explore the protections for buyers of consumer goods, consider whether similar protection should apply to consumer lessees of goods and consumer licensees of computer information.

A. Federal Law: FTC and the Magnuson-Moss Warranty Act

The Magnuson-Moss Warranty-Federal Trade Commission Improvement Act, 15 U.S.C. 2301 *et. seq.*, and the Act's implementing regulations, 16 CFR Parts 700-703, provide some federal protection to consumers who buy non-conforming goods from sellers in interstate commerce. Here is a brief overview of the Act and Regulations.

1. Section 101 [15 U.S.C. 2301] defines terms. Terms like "consumer product," "consumer," "warrantor," and "written warranty" determine the scope of the Act. *See* 16 CFR 700.1, 700.3.

2. Section 102 [15 U.S.C. 2302] requires certain disclosures by the warrantor. *See* 16 CFR 701, 702.

3. Section 103 [15 U.S.C. 2303] requires the warrantor to designate a written warranty, if made, as a "full" warranty which must meet the standards of Section 104 or a "limited" warranty which need not meet the standards of Section 104.

4. Section 104 [15 U.S.C. 2304] states what a warrantor must do to meet the requirements of a "full warranty." Read, in particular, subsection (a).

5. Section 108 [15 U.S.C. 2308] states limitations on disclaimers that apply

---

** (...continued)
protection against excessive termination costs. NCCUSL recently promulgated the Uniform Consumer Leases Act which provides some additional protections for consumer lessees. For a description of that act and its interface with Article 2A, *see* Ralph J. Rohner, *Leasing Consumer Goods: The Spotlight Shifts to the Uniform Consumer Leases Act*, 35 CONN. L. REV. 647 (2003).

* For general background and more detail, we recommend David A. Rice, *Product Quality Laws and the Economics of Federalism,* 65 B.U. L. REV. 1 (1985). *See also* Jean Braucher, *An Informal Resolution Model of Consumer Product Warranty Law,* 1985 WIS. L. REV. 1405; Joan Vogel, *Squeezing Consumers: Lemon Laws, Consumer Warranties, and a Proposal for Reform,* 1985 ARIZ. ST. L.J. 589; Richard E. Coffinberger & Linda B. Samuels, *Legislative Responses to the Plight of New Car Purchasers,* 18 U.C.C. L.J. 168 (1985); Rachel Miller & Lawrence Kanter, *Litigation Under Magnuson-Moss: New Opportunities in Private Actions,* 13 U.C.C. L.J. 10 (1980).

regardless of how the written warranty is designated. Note that a warrantor cannot disclaim "any implied warranty to a consumer with respect to such consumer product" but may limit the duration of an implied warranty to the duration of a written warranty of "reasonable duration, if such limitation is conscionable and is set forth in clear and unmistakable language and prominently displayed on the face of the warranty."

6.   Section 110 [15 U.S.C. 2310] provides private remedies for violation of the Act. Subsection (a) deals with the establishment of informal dispute settlement procedures. *See* 16 CFR, Part 703.   Subsections (c) and (d) state available remedies, define the jurisdiction of the court , and regulate class actions.

Keep this overview in mind as you study the following case.

VENTURA V. FORD MOTOR CORP.
SUPERIOR COURT OF NEW JERSEY, APPELLATE DIVISION, 1981
180 N.J. SUPER. 45, 433 A.2D 801

[Marino Auto sold Ventura a new 1978 Ford. The car was substantially impaired due to persistent and continual stalling and hesitation. Ventura sued both Marino Auto and Ford, the manufacturer, for damages and Marino Auto cross-claimed against Ford for indemnification. At the conclusion of the non-jury trial, the trial judge concluded that Ford had breached a warranty to Ventura, made through Marino Auto, but that Ventura had not proven damages against Ford. Ventura, however, could recover attorney's fees in the amount of $5,165 from Ford under the Magnuson-Moss Warranty Act, 15 U.S.C.A. § 2310(d)(2). In addition, despite an attempt by the dealer to disclaim all warranties, express or implied, Ventura could revoke its acceptance against and recover the purchase price less an allowance for use, a total of $6,745.59, from Marino Auto. Finally, the trial court entered a judgment in favor of Marino Auto against Ford for $2,910.59 and rejected Ventura's claims for interest, punitive damages and treble damages.

On appeal, the judgment was affirmed. The court assumed that Marino Auto's disclaimer of the implied warranty of merchantability was valid under the UCC, and concluded that the judgment was supported by the Magnuson-Moss Warranty Act.]

* * *

The Magnuson-Moss Warranty-Federal Trade Commission Improvement Act, *supra,* was adopted on January 4, 1975, 88 Stat. 2183. Its purpose was to make "warranties on consumer products more readily understandable and enforceable." Note, 7 RUTGERS-CAMDEN L.J. 379 (1976). The act enhances the consumer's position by allowing recovery under a warranty without regard to privity of contract between the consumer and warrantor, by prohibiting the disclaimer of implied warranties in a written warranty, and by enlarging the remedies available to a consumer for breach of warranty, including the award of attorneys' fees. *Id.* The requirement of privity of contract between the consumer and the warrantor has been removed by assuring consumers a remedy against all warrantors of the product.[1] A consumer is defined in 15 U.S.C.A. § 2301(3) as follows:

> (3) The term 'consumer' means a buyer (other than for purposes of resale) of any consumer product, any person to whom such product is transferred during the duration of an implied or written warranty (or service contract) applicable to the product, and any other person who is entitled by the terms of such warranty (or service contract) or under applicable State law to enforce against the warrantor (or service contract) the obligations of the warranty (or service contract).

A "supplier" is defined as any person engaged in the business of making a consumer product directly or indirectly available to consumers, § 2301(4), and a "warrantor" includes any supplier or other person who gives or offers to give a written warranty or who is obligated under an implied warranty. § 2301(5). The term "written warranty" is defined in § 2301(6) to include:

> (A) any written affirmation of fact or written promise made in connection with the sale of a consumer product by a supplier to a buyer which relates to the nature of the material or workmanship and affirms or promises that such material or workmanship is defect free or will meet a specified level of performance over a specified period of time, or
>
> (B) any undertaking in writing in connection with the sale by a supplier of a consumer product to refund, repair, replace or take other remedial action with respect to such product in the event that such product fails to meet the specifications set forth in the undertaking.

The Magnuson-Moss Warranty Act provides for two types of written warranties on consumer products, those described as "full" warranties and those described as "limited" warranties. 15 U.S.C.A. § 2303. The nature of the "full" warranty is prescribed by § 2304. It expressly provides in subsection (a)(4) that a consumer must be given the election to receive a refund or replacement without charge of a

---

[1] In Miller and Kanter, *Litigation Under Magnuson-Moss: New Opportunities in Private Actions*, 13 UCC L.J. 10, 21-22 (1980), the authors discuss the broad definition of a consumer and state that "an assumption is now created that no privity restriction exists."

product or part which is defective or malfunctions after a reasonable number of attempts by the warrantor to correct such condition. For the breach of any warranty, express or implied, or of a service contract (defined in 15 U.S.C.A. § 2301(8)), consumers are given the right to sue for damages and "other legal and equitable relief" afforded under state or federal law, 15 U.S.C.A. § 2310(d); 15 U.S.C.A. § 2311(b)(1).

Appellant Ford contends that the trial judge improperly invoked § 2304 of the act as a basis for allowing "rescission" in the case since the warranty given by Ford was a limited warranty and not a full warranty. 15 U.S.C.A. § 2303(a)(2) provides that all warranties that do not meet federal minimum standards for warranty contained in § 2304 shall be conspicuously designated a "limited warranty." "Limited" warranties protect consumers by prohibiting disclaimers of implied warranties, § 2308, but are otherwise not described in the act. Note, *supra,* 7 RUT.-CAM. L.J. at 381. Clearly, Ford's warranty, which is quoted later in this opinion, was a limited warranty.

15 U.S.C.A. § 2308 provides as follows:

(a) No supplier may disclaim or modify (except as provided in subsection (b) of this section) any implied warranty to a consumer with respect to such consumer product if (1) such supplier makes any written warranty to the consumer with respect to such consumer product, or (2) at the time of sale, or within 90 days thereafter, such supplier enters into a service contract with the consumer which applies to such consumer product.

(b) For purposes of this chapter (other than section 2304(a)(2) of this title), implied warranties may be limited in duration to the duration of a written warranty of reasonable duration, if such limitation is conscionable and is set forth in clear and unmistakable language and prominently displayed on the face of the warranty.

(c) A disclaimer, modification, or limitation made in violation of this section shall be ineffective for purposes of this chapter and State law.

We will first consider the application of this act to the dealer, Marino Auto. As quoted above, paragraph 7 of the purchase order-contract provides that there are no warranties, express or implied, made by the selling dealer or manufacturer except, in the case of a new motor vehicle, "the warranty expressly given to the purchaser upon delivery of such motor vehicle. * * *" This section also provides: "The selling dealer also agrees to promptly perform and fulfill all terms and conditions of the owner service policy." Ford contended in the trial court that Marino Auto had "a duty" to properly diagnose and make repairs, that such duty was "fixed both by the express warranty * * * which they passed on * * * and by the terms of [paragraph 7 of the contract with plaintiff]" by which Marino Auto expressly undertook "to perform its obligations under the owner service policy." *See* 15 U.S.C.A. § 2310(f); 16 C.F.R. § 700.4 (1980). The provision in paragraph 7 in these circumstances is a "written warranty" within the meaning of § 2301(6)(B) since it constitutes an undertaking in connection with the sale to take "remedial action with respect to such product in the event that such product fails to meet the specifications set forth in the undertaking. * * *" In our view the specifications of the undertaking include, at the least, the provisions of the limited warranty furnished by Ford, namely:

LIMITED WARRANTY (12 MONTHS OR 12,000 MILES/19,312 KILOMETRES) 1978 NEW CAR AND LIGHT TRUCK

Ford warrants for its 1978 model cars and light trucks that the Selling Dealer will repair or replace free any parts, except tires, found under normal use in the U.S. or Canada to be defective in factory materials or workmanship within the earlier of 12 months or 12,000 miles/19,312 km from either first use or retail delivery. All we require is that you properly operate and maintain your vehicle and that you return for warranty service to your Selling Dealer or any Ford or Lincoln-Mercury Dealer if you are traveling, have moved a long distance or need emergency repairs. Warranty repairs will be made with Ford Authorized Service or Remanufactured Parts.

THERE IS NO OTHER EXPRESS WARRANTY ON THIS VEHICLE.[2]

The record does not contain a written description of the "owner service policy"

---

[2] The warranty also provided:

TO THE EXTENT ALLOWED BY LAW:

1. ANY IMPLIED WARRANTY OF MERCHANTABILITY OR FITNESS IS LIMITED TO THE 12 MONTH OR 12,000-MILE/19,312-KM DURATION OF THIS WRITTEN WARRANTY.

2. NEITHER FORD NOR THE SELLING DEALER SHALL HAVE ANY RESPONSIBILITY FOR LOSS OF USE OF THE VEHICLE, LOSS OF TIME, INCONVENIENCE, COMMERCIAL LOSS OR CONSEQUENTIAL DAMAGES. Some states do not allow limitations on how long an implied warranty lasts or the exclusion or limitation of incidental or consequential damages, so the above limitations may not apply to you.

This warranty gives you specific legal rights, and you also may have other rights which vary from state to state.

which the dealer agreed to perform. Nevertheless, since Ford is the appellant here, we take its contentions at trial and documents in the record to establish the dealer's obligation to Ford and to plaintiff to make the warranty repairs on behalf of Ford (subject to the right of reimbursement or other terms that may be contained in their agreement). For the purpose of this appeal we are satisfied that the dealer's undertaking in paragraph 7 constitutes a written warranty within the meaning of 15 U.S.C.A. § 2301(6)(B). Accordingly, having furnished a written warranty to the consumer, the dealer as a supplier may not "disclaim or modify [except to limit in duration] any implied warranty to a consumer. * * *" The result of this analysis is to invalidate the attempted disclaimer by the dealer of the implied warranties of merchantability and fitness.[3] Being bound by those implied warranties arising under state law, N.J.S.A. 12A:2-314 and 315, Marino Auto was liable to plaintiff for the breach thereof as found by the trial judge, and plaintiff could timely revoke his acceptance of the automobile and claim a refund of his purchase price. N.J.S.A. 12A:2-608 and N.J.S.A. 12A:2-711. *Zabriskie Chevrolet, Inc. v. Smith,* 99 N.J. Super. 441, 240 A.2d 195 (Law Div. 1968). In this connection we note that the trial judge found that plaintiff's attempted revocation of acceptance was made in timely fashion, and that finding has adequate support in the evidence.

As the trial judge noted, 15 U.S.C.A. § 2310(d)(1) provides that a consumer who is damaged by the failure of a warrantor to comply with any obligation under the act, or under a written warranty or implied warranty or service contract, may bring suit "for damages and other legal and equitable relief. * * *" Although the remedy of refund of the purchase price is expressly provided by the Magnuson-Moss Warranty Act for breach of a full warranty, granting this remedy under state law for breach of a limited warranty is not barred by or inconsistent with the act. 15 U.S.C.A. § 2311(b)(1) provides that nothing in the act restricts "any right or remedy of any consumer under State law or other Federal law." *See also* 15 U.S.C.A. § 2311(c)(2). Thus, for breach of the implied warranty of merchantability, plaintiff was entitled to revoke acceptance against Marino Auto, and a judgment for the purchase price less an allowance for the use of the vehicle was properly entered against Marino Auto. N.J.S.A. 12A:2-608 and 711. *Cf.* 15 U.S.C.A. § 2301(12) which defines "refund" as the return of the purchase price "less reasonable depreciation based on actual use where permitted" by regulations.

Plaintiff also could have recovered damages against Ford for Ford's breach of

---

[3] The same holding would apply if the undertaking by Marino Auto to perform the "owner service policy" is construed as a "service contract." 15 U.S.C.A. § 2308(a), *supra.*

its written limited warranty. Marino Auto was Ford's representative for the purpose of making repairs to plaintiff's vehicle under the warranty. * * * The limited warranty expressly required the purchaser to return the vehicle "for warranty service" to the dealer or to any Ford or Lincoln-Mercury dealer if the purchaser is traveling or has moved a long distance or needs emergency repairs. Ford contends that it put purchasers on notice that they should advise Ford's district office if they have problems with their cars that a dealer is unable to fix. The record contains a document listing "frequently asked warranty questions" which states:

> The Dealership where you purchased your vehicle has the responsibility for performing warranty repairs; therefore, take your vehicle to that Dealership.
> * * * If you encounter a service problem, refer to the service assistance section of your Owner's Guide for suggested action.

We do not read these provisions as requiring notice to Ford as a condition of relief against Ford when Ford's dealer has failed after numerous attempts to correct defects under warranty.

Normally, the measure of damages for a breach of warranty is the difference between the price paid by the purchaser and the market value of the defective product. *Santor v. A & M Karagheusian, Inc., supra,* 44 N.J. at 63, 68-69, 207 A.2d 305; *see Herbstman v. Eastman Kodak Co., supra,* 68 N.J. at 11, 342 A.2d 181. However, as Judge Conford said in his concurring opinion in *Herbstman, supra,* 68 N.J. at 15-16, 342 A.2d 181, under principles of strict liability in tort a purchaser may be entitled to rescind the transaction and receive the return of the purchase price from the manufacturer without privity if the defect causes substantial impairment of value of the product. The strict liability in tort doctrine as developed in this state in the *Santor* case, *supra,* eliminated the need for privity of contract between the purchaser and the manufacturer as a condition for the purchaser's claim for his loss of bargain caused by a defect in the product. As noted above, the Magnuson-Moss Warranty Act accomplished the same result.

One question posed by this case is whether recovery of the purchase price from the manufacturer was available to plaintiff for breach of the manufacturer's warranty. If the warranty were a full warranty plaintiff would have been entitled to a refund of the purchase price under the Magnuson-Moss Warranty Act. Since Ford's warranty was a limited warranty we must look to state law to determine plaintiff's right to damages or other legal and equitable relief. 15 U.S.C.A. § 2310(d)(1). Once privity is removed as an obstacle to relief we see no reason why a purchaser cannot also elect the equitable remedy of returning the goods to the manufacturer who is a warrantor and claiming a refund of the purchase price less an allowance for use of the product. * * *

We are dealing with the breach of an express contractual obligation. Nothing prevents us from granting an adequate remedy under state law for that breach of contract, including rescission when appropriate. Under state law the right to revoke acceptance for defects substantially impairing the value of the product (N.J.S.A. 12A:2-608) and to receive a refund of the purchase price (N.J.S.A. 12A:2-711) are rights available to a buyer against a seller in privity. Where the manufacturer gives a warranty to induce the sale it is consistent to allow the same type of remedy as against that manufacturer. * * *. Only the privity concept, which is frequently viewed as a relic these days, * * * has interfered with a rescission-type remedy against the manufacturer of goods not purchased directly from the manufacturer. If we focus on the fact that the warranty creates a direct contractual obligation to the buyer, the reason for allowing the same remedy that is available against a direct seller becomes clear. Although the manufacturer intended to limit the remedy to the repair and replacement of defective parts, the failure of that remedy, see N.J.S.A. 12A:2-719(2); *Goddard v. General Motors Corp.,* 60 Ohio St. 2d 41, 396 N.E.2d 761 (Sup. Ct. 1979); *Seely v. White Motor Co., supra,* and the consequent breach of the implied warranty of merchantability which accompanied the limited warranty by virtue of the Magnuson-Moss Warranty Act, make a rescission-type remedy appropriate when revocation of acceptance is justified. * * *

Lastly, we consider Ford's contention that a counsel fee was improperly granted to plaintiff since no judgment was entered in favor of plaintiff against Ford and Ford contends it was not given adequate notice of the defects in the car. 15 U.S.C.A. § 2310(d)(2) provides that a consumer who "prevails in any action brought [in any court] under paragraph (1) of this subsection * * * may be allowed by the court to recover as part of the judgment * * * expenses (including attorney's fees based on the actual time expended). * * *" This section is subject to the provisions contained in § 2310(e). Subsection (e) provides that, with certain exceptions, no action based upon breach of a written or implied warranty or service contract may be prosecuted unless a person obligated under the warranty or service contract "is afforded a reasonable opportunity to cure such failure to comply." Here that opportunity was given to Ford's designated representative to whom the purchaser was required to bring the car. A direct employee of Ford, Bednarz, also met with plaintiff or his wife and was made aware of some difficulty with the car. We are not certain of the extent of Ford's knowledge of those difficulties. However, in our view the opportunities given to Marino Auto to repair the vehicle satisfied the requirements of 15 U.S.C.A. § 2310(e) in this case.

As noted, Ford also contends that a counsel fee could not be awarded against Ford because plaintiff did not recover a judgment against Ford. The Magnuson-Moss Warranty Act permits a prevailing consumer to recover attorney's fees "as part of the judgment." The trial judge found that Ford had breached its warranty and that the car's value was substantially impaired. He entered no damage judgment against Ford. However, in the absence of proof of actual damages, plaintiff was entitled to a judgment against Ford for nominal damages. * * * Ford was not prejudiced by the failure of the trial judge to enter a judgment for nominal damages to which the award of attorney's fees could be attached. * * * The award of counsel fees fulfills the intent of the Magnuson-Moss Warranty Act. Without such an award consumers frequently would be unable to vindicate warranty rights accorded by law.

As to the amount of counsel fees allowed by the trial judge, we find no abuse of discretion. The allowance was for actual time spent at an hourly rate of $75. Consideration could properly be given to the fact that plaintiff's attorney undertook this claim on a contingency basis with a relatively small retainer. DR 2-106(A)(8). The normal breach of warranty case ought not require four separate appearances before the trial court. To some extent this was not in the control of plaintiff's attorney, and plaintiff might have obtained all the relief required against Ford on the first day of trial. But it did not work out that way. In other cases it may be possible to stipulate damages and simplify the issues, thus limiting the cost of this type of litigation for consumers and suppliers alike. But the issues raised in this case were novel in this State, and no one can be faulted for the difficulty and time consumed in this litigation.

We have stated that in an appropriate case a consumer could recover the purchase price from a manufacturer for breach of a limited warranty causing a substantial impairment of the value of the product. The application of the Magnuson-Moss Warranty Act is one distinction between this case and *Herbstman v. Eastman Kodak Co., supra,* 68 N.J. at 9-12, n.1, 342 A.2d 181. However, we need not determine whether plaintiff had the right to such relief in this case. Ordinarily, a purchaser seeking such relief after unsuccessful repairs should be required to give timely notice to the manufacturer of revocation of acceptance of defective goods and of his demand for a refund of the purchase price. *See Dwarf v. Rod Baxter Imports, Inc., supra,* 262 N.W.2d at 353. Plaintiff's complaint alleges that such notice and demand were given to Ford in this case, but no finding was made by the trial judge on plaintiff's claim against Ford. Having determined that plaintiff was entitled to a judgment for nominal damages and counsel fees against

Ford, and that judgments against Marino Auto and for indemnification by Ford were properly entered, it makes no difference in this case whether plaintiff was also entitled to a refund of his purchase price from Ford.

The result in this case differs from that reached in *Edelstein v. Toyota Motors Distributors, supra.* However, the differences in the cases, the absence there of proof of any warranty from defendants, and the apparent failure of the purchaser to rely on the Magnuson-Moss Warranty Act make it unnecessary for us to comment on that holding. Affirmed.

[Some footnotes omitted. Those retained have been renumbered.]

Notes

1. The court assumes in *Ventura* that the Dealer had effectively disclaimed all warranties under the UCC. How does the Magnuson-Moss Warranty Act support the court's conclusion that, nevertheless, the dealer breached an implied warranty of merchantability? Note that the dealer failed to "cure" the problem and that the buyer's remedy included revocation of acceptance, UCC 2-608(1), and a refund of the price, UCC 2-711, adjusted for the value of buyer's use after the revocation. Consequential damages were not claimed.*

2. Suppose the dealer made no "written warranty," *see* 15 U.S.C. 2301(6), and effectively disclaimed all warranties under UCC 2-316. Would the buyer have any claims against the dealer under either the Magnuson-Moss Act or the UCC?

3. The manufacturer, Ford Motor Company, made a written, "limited" warranty to Ventura. The express warranty was breached and the dealer failed to "cure." What was the maximum protection, liability and remedy, to which Ventura was entitled against Ford under the Magnuson-Moss Act? Read the entire statute, please. Why was Ventura's recovery limited to the recovery of attorney's fees?

4. Suppose that Ford (or the Dealer) had made a written, "full" warranty to Ventura. To what additional protection would Ventura be entitled? *See,* particularly, 15 U.S.C. 2304(a). How does this differ from protection available

---

* *Compare Bogner v. General Motors Corp.*, 117 Misc. 2d 929, 459 N.Y.S.2d 679 (N.Y. Civ. Ct. 1982) (although consequential damages excluded, court awards damages for emotional distress). *See also Ramirez v. Autosport*, 440 A.2d 1345 (N.J. 1982) (buyer properly rejects camper-van for defects, cancels contract and recovers price); *Jacobs v. Rosemount Dodge-Winnebago South*, 310 N.W.2d 71 (Minn. 1981) (limited remedy fails essential purpose, buyer permitted to revoke acceptance and recover consequential damages).

under the UCC when a limited remedy "fails" its essential purpose? As a matter of practice, few manufacturers or sellers are willing to make "full" written warranties, and there is no penalty imposed for that omission under Magnuson-Moss.

5. **Privity Revisited.** Suppose a manufacturer makes a "limited" express warranty on a product and this warranty is passed on by the dealer to the consumer. The product has several substantial defects which neither the manufacturer nor the dealer are able to cure. Clearly, the consumer is not entitled under a "limited" warranty to either a refund or a new product under Magnuson-Moss. In *Gochey v. Bomardier, Inc.*, 572 A.2d 921 (Vt. 1990), however, the court permitted the consumer to invoke UCC 2-608, revoke his acceptance against the manufacturer and recover the purchase price under former 2-711(1). The court stated:

> We agree with the rationale expressed in *Ventura* that when a manufacturer expressly warrants its goods, it, in effect, creates a direct contract with the ultimate buyer. Accordingly, in an action pursuant to the Magnuson-Moss Warranty Act, the consumer may collect reasonable attorneys' fees, 15 U.S.C. § 2310(d)(2), and secure any available state remedies, including a refund of the purchase price along with incidental and consequential damages and interest, directly from the manufacturer when the manufacturer's defect substantially impairs the product. * * * When the manufacturer's defect results in revocation by the consumer, the manufacturer must assume the liability it incurred when it warranted the product to the ultimate user.

572 A.2d at 924. Suppose the manufacturer made a "limited" express warranty to the consumer but did not breach it. The goods, however, were unmerchantable under UCC 2-314. In *Rothe v. Maloney Cadillac, Inc.*, 518 N.E.2d 1028 (Ill. 1988), the Illinois Supreme Court, elaborating on its earlier decision in *Szajna v. General Motors Corp.*, 503 N.E.2d 760 (Ill. 1986), held that the consumer could sue the manufacturer for breach of implied warranty under the Magnuson-Moss Act even though lack of privity would bar the suit under state law. The court concluded that Magnuson-Moss imposed the same implied warranties on the manufacturer that would be imposed under state law, with the differences that they could not be disclaimed and lack of privity was no defense.

6. In *Walton v. Rose Mobile Homes LLC*, 298 F.3d 470 (5th Cir. 2002), the Court of Appeals held that a clause in the written warranty, governed by Magnuson-Moss, which provided for binding arbitration was enforceable. The court rejected the FTC interpretation that such binding arbitration clauses are not enforceable under the Magnuson-Moss regime.

7. A few states have passed special consumer legislation to deal with perceived shortcomings in the UCC. *See*, for example, Mass. Gen. Laws Ann. 106 2-316A, enacted in 1973:

2-316A. Limitation of Exclusion or Modification of Warranties

(1) The provisions of section 2-316 shall not apply to [sales of consumer goods, services or both.]

(2) Any language, oral or written, used by a seller or manufacturer of consumer goods and services, which attempts to exclude or modify any implied warranties of merchantability and fitness for a particular purpose or to exclude or modify the consumer's remedies for breach of those warranties, shall be unenforceable.

(3) Any language, oral or written, used by a manufacturer of consumer goods, which attempts to limit or modify a consumer's remedies for breach of such manufacturer's express warranties, shall be unenforceable, unless such manufacturer maintains facilities within the commonwealth sufficient to provide reasonable and expeditious performance of the warranty obligations. * * *

(5) The provisions of this section may not be disclaimed or waived by agreement.

Now try your hand at the following problem.

Problem 12-3

S, an authorized dealer of Wanderer Motor Homes, sold to B a Wanderer Luxury II motor home for $80,000. In the discussion prior to the sale, S told B that the motorhome was an energy efficient model and should get at least 15 miles per gallon in a normal mix of city and highway driving. B was intending to take the motorhome across the United States, stopping to golf at every public course B could find as research for a book on public golf courses. S knew what B intended since B told S in the course of looking at various models of motor homes. The document that B signed when B agreed to buy the motorhome provided the following:

The Wanderer Luxury II motorhome is warranted by the manufacturer to be free of defects in materials or workmanship at the time of delivery. B's sole remedy is that an authorized dealer will repair or replace any defective parts for 1 year from the date of delivery. DEALER AND MANUFACTURER MAKE NO OTHER WARRANTIES, EXPRESS OR IMPLIED, INCLUDING THE WARRANTY OF MERCHANTABILITY AND

FITNESS FOR A PARTICULAR PURPOSE. Dealer or Manufacturer are not liable for any consequential or incidental damages. This writing is the complete, exclusive and final statement of all terms of the sale.

B took delivery of the motor home on March 1, 2003. On March 5, 2003, B returned the motorhome to the dealership due to whistling sounds in the windows. S resealed the windows and B took the motorhome back on March 10, 2003. From April through November, B returned the motorhome to S four separate times to fix various items such as a leak in the roof, a malfunctioning refrigerator, a cracked sewage hose, and an overheating engine. B's trouble with the motorhome continued throughout the winter (December through February) including a propane leak in the stove resulting in a short hospital stay for B and her spouse due to gas inhalation and a leaky shower stall resulting in ruined carpeting. Each time B took the motorhome to S, the problem was successfully repaired. However, each time, B had to drive from wherever B was on B's golf odyssey to S's dealership. As a result, B only got to play about half of the golf courses B had planned on, resulting in a delay in B's book project.

On March 1, 2004, B drove the motorhome to S's location and told S that B was returning the motor home due to the many problems that B had experienced and that over the course of the year, the motor home averaged 10 miles per gallon. B demanded B's money returned. S refused to take the motor home back and told B the year warranty period was up and B was on her own with the motor home. The manufacturer did not respond to B's complaint. Advise B. Include in your analysis all parties' likely arguments.

B. State Law: "Lemon" Laws

To fill in the gaps between the Magnuson-Moss Warranty Act, which does not go far enough, and Article 2 of the UCC, which says nothing about consumers or consumer protection, every state has enacted so-called "lemon laws" to regulate the relationship between a consumer buyer and a merchant seller (dealer) of automobiles.[*] Many states also have consumer protection acts that supplement the

---

[*] Phillip R. Nowicki, *State Lemon Law Coverage Terms: Dissecting the Differences*, 11 LOY. CONSUMER L. REP. 39 (1999). *See* Bruce Mann and Thomas J. Holdych, *When Lemons are Better Than Lemonade: The Case Against Mandatory Used Car Warranties*, 15 YALE L. & POL'Y REV. 1 (1996).

UCC's warranty provisions.[*] The European Union has been an international leader in the consumer protection area.[**]

Please read the following description of state lemon laws. Read the "Lemon Law" in the state where you intend to practice. How does it conform to Vogel's description? Should there be lemon laws that apply to leased automobiles? Should there be lemon laws that apply to goods other than automobiles or licenses of computer information? Should lemon laws protect buyers other than consumer buyers? What is the relationship between a state's lemon law and the provisions of Article 2? Does the fact that every state has enacted lemon laws to apply to new automobiles tell us anything about what Article 2 should provide? If you were going to be involved in revising the lemon laws of your state, what policy choices would you make?

JOAN VOGEL

Squeezing Consumers: Lemon Laws, Consumer Warranties,
and a Proposal for Reform
1985 ARIZ. ST. L.J. 589, 615, 644-47

* * * Acting on consumer complaints, legislatures in 37 states [The count is now 50 states and the District of Columbia. Ed] have passed lemon laws to help car owners. Although the laws vary in many important respects, they still have a number of features in common. First, the lemon laws apply only to new cars and generally only to cars purchased for noncommercial purposes. Second, the laws require the manufacturer to conform the vehicle to the terms of the warranty upon receiving notice of the problem from the consumer. If the manufacturer is unable to correct the defect within a stated period of time or after a certain number of attempts, the lemon laws allow purchasers to return defective cars and to receive either a refund of the purchase price or a replacement vehicle. However, the refund or replacement remedy may not be available to a consumer unless he or she gives the manufacturer notice that efforts to repair the car have failed. Finally, a number

---

[*] For an analysis of the Texas statute, which has historically been very protective of consumers, *see* A. Michael Ferrill & Charles A. Japhet, *Deceptive Trade Practices–Consumer Protection Act*, 52 SMU L. REV. 971 (1999).

[**] *See* Frances E. Zollers, et al., *Consumer Protection in the European Union: An Analysis of the Directive on the Sale of Consumer Goods and Associated Guarantees*, 20 U. PENN. J. OF INT'L ECON. L. 97 (1999).

of lemon laws also restrict the resale of returned vehicles to other purchasers.* * *

As has been seen, the lemon laws by themselves do not provide consumers with an effective remedy. In many respects, they simply restate the present law. In other respects they are more restrictive than alternative legal remedies. Consequently, if a consumer has a warranty problem, it may be necessary to bring an action under the UCC, the Magnuson-Moss Warranty Act, and the lemon law. Generally, the lemon laws allow for this. With the exception of Arizona, Florida, Illinois, New Mexico, North Dakota, and Tennessee, all the lemon laws contain a provision which states that the lemon law does not limit rights or remedies under other law.

If lawmakers wish to provide increased protection to purchasers of automobiles, there are certain modifications which would make the lemon laws more effective: (1) clear rules or standards; (2) presumptions which ease the burden of proof, (3) a minimum of technicalities; and (4) a choice between a refund and other damages or a replacement vehicle. They could also publicize consumers' rights under the improved laws.

For consumers and manufacturers to know their rights under the lemon laws, the laws must contain clear rules or standards specifying when the consumer may return the defective car and seek a refund or a replacement vehicle. The lemon laws make strides in this direction by spelling out the number of repair attempts and the number of days a car must be in the shop for repair before the consumer can invoke the refund and replacement provision. However, the standard is often stricter than that governing failure of essential purpose under the UCC. Consumers need a clear rule that does not grant an unreasonable amount of time to repair the car. There is little reason to require that the consumer give the manufacturer more than one repair attempt or one week in the shop. The consumer should not have to suffer through numerous trips to the dealer or long delays in repair.

Specification of a time for repair can significantly ease the burden of the consumer. The easier it is for the consumer to prove that he or she is entitled to the remedies under the lemon laws, the more likely that the consumer will seek redress and reach an equitable agreement with the manufacturer. A short, but reasonable, statutory period should suffice. If the consumer is able to show that the defect was not repaired within the period (perhaps a week), the presumption would apply. The manufacturer would then have the burden of establishing that more time was necessary and reasonable under the circumstances.

The typical lemon law contains other provisions which are unclear. For example, the laws do not define what constitutes substantial impairment of value, safety, or use. As a result, consumers will often not know what they are entitled to, even if the lemon law applies. These terms can be defined and clarified, as has been done in some cases interpreting UCC section 2-608. Specific provision should be made for taking account of the consumer's individual circumstances, as well as of clusters or groups of defects that substantially impair the value of the car.

Having clear rules and presumptions that ease the burden of proof will not mean much if other technical requirements deprive a consumer of the ability to use the lemon law. The notice requirements are especially troublesome. Consumers rarely know about notice requirements and often fail to comply with them. The only notice requirement the lemon laws should contain is the requirement that the consumer notify the dealer of the problem with the car. As was mentioned, the manufacturer will find out about the problem when the dealer seeks reimbursement for the warranty work. The manufacturer should have the responsibility of seeing to it that the dealer supplies it with this information promptly.

Once the consumer establishes that the car was not or could not be fixed, the lemon laws should provide that the consumer can choose between a refund or a replacement vehicle. If the consumer opts for a replacement vehicle, the manufacturer should be required to supply one of equal value. If the consumer chooses a refund, the lemon law should allow the recovery of the purchase price, collateral charges, and incidental and consequential damages when appropriate. If the manufacturer is allowed an offset for use, it should only cover use before the defects occurred and the manufacturer should have the burden of establishing its right to any offset and its amount.

All such changes will have little effect, however, if consumers do not fully understand them. The usual approach to informing consumers is to require the dealers and the manufacturers to supply a written statement which explains consumers' rights under the lemon law. The experience with the Magnuson-Moss Warranty Act indicates that this approach is ineffective. Consequently, legislators should consider using the broadcast media and newspapers to present information concerning consumer remedies. Public service ads on radio and television could greatly increase awareness of consumer warranty rights. Certainly, there is enough talent and knowledge available to structure such a campaign and the expense of conducting it is not likely to be much more than that of printing forms. A number of state and federal consumer protection agencies already conduct such campaigns, and there is no reason why similar efforts cannot be mounted to inform consumers of their rights under automobile lemon laws. [Footnotes omitted.]

Note: Informal Dispute Resolution

Most state Lemon Laws deny consumers the statutory remedies unless the consumer has first resorted to an informal settlement procedure applicable to disputes to which the subsection would apply, where the manufacturer has established a procedure that conforms substantially with 16 CFR, Part 703 and there has been adequate disclosure. If, however, the consumer is dissatisfied with the decision reached in an informal dispute settlement procedure or the results of such a decision, the consumer may sue to enforce rights created by the statute. *See* 16 CFR 703.5(j) (although decisions of the process are not legally binding "on any person," the warrantor shall act in good faith and any decision from the process shall be admissible in evidence).

Is an established informal settlement procedure an arbitration procedure to which the Federal Arbitration Act applies? According to the Third Circuit, the answer is no, at least under the Pennsylvania "Lemon" law. The fly in the arbitration ointment is 16 CFR 703.5(i) which provides that a "requirement that a consumer resort to the Mechanism prior to the commencement of an action * * * shall be satisfied 40 days after notification to the Mechanism of the dispute or when the Mechanism completes all of its duties* * *." [Mechanism is defined as the informal dispute resolution process, 16 CFR 703.1(e).] If the procedure can be terminated without a decision of the dispute by the Mechanism, the procedure is not arbitration which, at the very least, requires an agreement that some decision on the merits be made. *See Harrison v. Nissan Motor Corp. in U.S.A.*, 111 F.3d 343 (3rd Cir. 1997).

SECTION 3.   THE STATUTE OF LIMITATIONS

Another major limitation on the availability of remedies under Articles 2 or 2A is the statute of limitations. Read UCC 2-725 and 2A-506. The 2003 amendments to Article 2 significantly rewrote UCC 2-725 to provide for several different accrual rules, lengthen the possible limitations period, and prevent shortening the limitations period in a consumer contract. Only the last change was made to UCC 2A-506. These sections bear careful reading. Note the following:

1.   Each provides rules on when the cause of action accrues. Notice there are different accrual rules depending upon what type of action is involved.

2.   Each provides for a limitation period that starts to run from the time the cause of action accrued.

3. Each provides that the parties may by agreement in some cases alter the limitation period.

4. Each provides that conduct that "tolls" (or stops the running of) the limitation period is governed by other law.[*]

The former statute of limitations in Article 2 has generated much litigation on a host of issues.[**] Whether the amended statute of limitations will fare better remains to be seen.

Problem 12-4

On May 1, 2000, Seller and Buyer, a grain dealer, entered a written contract for the sale of three prefabricated metal grain bins, each 30 feet tall, for a total price of $50,000. The bins were to be shipped to Buyer FOB Point of Destination and Seller agreed to erect and install them at Buyer's place of business. The contract provided, inter alia, that "the above described bins will, if properly installed, withstand winds up to 90 MPH."

The bins were shipped on June 1, 2000 and arrived on June 5, 2000. The buyer removed the disassembled parts from the carrier and notified the Seller, who completed the installation by July 1, 2000. On June 15, 2004, a severe storm with winds up to 80 MPH hit the area where Buyer did business. Two of the bins were toppled by the wind, resulting in damage to the bins and the stored grain. An expert will testify that the internal support seams had gradually and imperceptibly deteriorated since installation.

Buyer's attorney has asked you, his associate, whether the statute of limitations has run. First analyze this problem under former 2-725 and then analyze the problem under amended UCC 2-725. Do you get a different result?[***]

---

[*] *See, e.g., Evens ex rel. Husted v. General Motors Corp.*, 732 N.E.2d 79 (Ill. Ct. App. 2000) (limitations period tolled due to plaintiff's status as a minor).

[**] Larry T. Garvin, *Uncertainty and Error in the Law of Sales: The Article Two Statute of Limitations*, 83 B.U. L. REV. 345 (2003). *See also* Chris Williams, *The Statute of Limitations, Prospective Warranties, and Problems of Interpretation in Article Two of the UCC,* 52 GEO. WASH. L. REV. 67 (1983); Keven D. Lyles, Note, *UCC Section 2-725: A Statute Uncertain in Application and Effect,* 46 OHIO ST. U. L. J. 755 (1985).

[***] *See Baker v. DEC International*, 580 N.W.2d 894 (Mich. 1998), holding that if the contract required installation by the seller the buyer's cause of action accrued when the

(continued...)

STANDARD ALLIANCE INDUS., INC. V. BLACK CLAWSON CO.
UNITED STATES COURT OF APPEALS, SIXTH CIRCUIT, 1978
587 F.2D 813

[Defendant sold Plaintiff a 175-ton "horizontal automatic radial forging facility," known as the "green monster." After extensive negotiations where Plaintiff persuaded Defendant to manufacture the machine to meet Plaintiff's special needs, Defendant made a series of express performance warranties and agreed to repair or replace defective parts for one year after acceptance. Implied warranties were disclaimed and consequential damages were excluded in the agreement. There were problems with the machine from the start. For five months, Defendant, with Plaintiff's assistance, attempted to remedy the difficulties. Defendant then ceased working on the machine. Thereafter, efforts by Plaintiff, under new ownership, to resolve the problems were unsuccessful and the machine was dismantled and sold for scrap. Just over eleven months after Defendant ceased efforts to repair the machine, Plaintiff brought suit on various warranty theories, claiming damages in excess of $525,000. After trial, the trial court submitted two questions to the jury: 1) did Defendant breach the negotiated performance warranties; and 2) did Defendant breach the express warranty to repair and replace defective parts? The jury found for Plaintiff on both questions. On appeal, Defendant argued that the claim based upon breach of performance warranties was barred by the statute of limitations. Defendant also argued that the claim based upon breach of the warranty to repair and replace was barred because Plaintiff failed to give notice as required by UCC 2-607(3). The court first held that the claim based upon breach of the warranty to repair and replace was barred under UCC 2-607(3) and then turned to the statute of limitations defense.] * * *

A. The Statute of Limitations and Count I

Chronology is important to a precise understanding of the issues. The machine was delivered and assembled at Standard Alliance's plant in the fall of 1967. The machine proved defective, and Standard Alliance wrote Black Clawson on December 27, 1967, delineating exactly what was wrong with the machine and requesting that Black Clawson fix it. Black Clawson worked on the machine until June 21, 1968, when it abandoned repair efforts. This suit was filed on May 29, 1969.

*** (...continued)
component parts were fully installed.

The original contract contained a one-year limitations period;[1] the minimum allowable under UCC § 2-725(1). UCC § 2-725(1) also provides that the limitations period begins to run when the cause of action accrues. UCC § 2-725(2) explains that a cause of action accrues when a breach occurs. A breach of warranty is deemed to occur upon tender of delivery "except that where a warranty explicitly extends to future performance of the goods and discovery of the breach must await the time of such performance the cause of action accrues when the breach is or should have been discovered." UCC § 2-725(2). Black Clawson argues that the machine was tendered in the fall of 1967 and that, even granting that the warranty extends to future performance, the cause of action under Count I accrued no later than December 27, 1967, when Standard Alliance wrote its letter claiming that the machine was defective. Standard Alliance makes numerous arguments in reply. Primarily, we must consider the question of when breach occurred. This involves analysis of two separate issues: when tender of delivery was made; whether the warranty extended to future performance. In addition, we must consider various estoppel and policy arguments.

Standard Alliance first contends, with some support in the record, that novel machines like the one here often have long "shakedown" periods before they can be made to function properly. The import of its argument is that "tender" of a defective machine should not be deemed to take place until the machine is made to run properly. Since the machine in the instant case did not function properly when initially installed in October of 1967, Standard Alliance argues, tender of delivery was never really made until June 21, 1968, when Black Clawson halted its efforts to get the machine going. Thus, even assuming that the warranty did not extend to future performance, the earliest a breach could have occurred and a cause of action accrued, on Standard Alliance's theory, was June 21, 1968.

This argument is plausible, but withers upon proper examination of the Uniform Commercial Code. UCC § 2-503(1) defines "tender of delivery" as requiring " * * * that the seller put and hold conforming goods at the buyer's disposition * * *." Comment 1 to UCC § 2-503 explains that at times "tender" means "due tender" meaning " * * * an offer coupled with a present ability to fulfill all the conditions resting on the tendering party [which must be] followed by actual performance if

---

[1] [Based upon information provided by counsel, the editors of the Callaghan Uniform Commercial Code Reporting Service state that the exact language of the "limitation" clause was as follows: "Any action or arbitration proceeding for breach of this agreement must be brought within one year after the cause of action has accrued." Ed.]

the other party shows himself ready to proceed." "At other times [tender] is used to refer to an offer of goods or documents under a contract as if in fulfillment of its conditions even though there is a defect when measured against the contract obligation." *Id.* We think that "tender" as used in UCC § 2-725(2) is the latter and not the former. A contrary interpretation would extend the statute of limitations indefinitely into the future since a defect at the time of delivery would prevent proper "due tender" from taking place until it was corrected. Under section 2-725, a cause of action accrues upon initial installation of the product regardless whether it functions properly or not so long as the warranty does not extend to future performance. *See Val Decker Packing Co. v. Corn Products Sales Co.*, 411 F.2d 850 (6th Cir. 1969).

Secondly, Standard Alliance argues that the page twelve warranties[2] did extend to future performance under section 2-725(2), and that the statute of limitations thus ran from the date of discovery of the defect. It particularly points to the phrase, "Black Clawson warrants that the subject machinery *will* perform the following mechanical functions." Plaintiff's argument proves too much. Since all contracts contain future promises, words of futurity such as "will" are common. When the contract at issue here was signed, the machine was not yet built; the word "will"

---

[2] The negotiated performance or "page twelve warranties" provided:

"The following express warranties, which relate to mechanical function only become an adjunct to our contract clause # 1 page 11 and supersede all references to warranties that may be contained in the description of the machine pages 2-7, either expressed or implied.

"Black Clawson warrants that the subject machinery will perform the following mechanical functions:

"1. Press will deliver 1000 ton ram capacity at 150 strokes per minute @ 1/4" from bottom dead center.

"2. Press will have a maximum speed of 250 strokes per minute—with a range of 10 to 250 SPM.

"3. Rams at bottom of stroke will have a parallelism of within .005".

"4. Peel and press will trace template within plus or minus .015".

"5. Feed adjustments will have a range up to 0.375" per second.

"6. Peel rotation will have a range of 5 to 100 RPM and will be designed to lock at the 90° positions.

"7. Peel traverse speed will have a range of 1 ft/minute to 45 ft/minute, and will be designed to lock in position.

"8. The mechanical functions can be programmed to operate in automatic sequence in the specified capacities and accuracies or may be operator interrupted and/or commanded as required.

"The quality and quantity of production is not the responsibility of the seller."

was necessarily used. The proper question is whether the statute of limitations is meant to run from the day of delivery or from the day when a defect is found sometime in the future.

Most courts have been very harsh in determining whether a warranty explicitly extends to future performance. Emphasizing the word "explicitly," they have ruled that there must be specific reference to a future time in the warranty. As a result of this harsh construction, most express warranties cannot meet the test and no implied warranties can since, by their very nature, they never "explicitly extend to future performance." * * *

Two rare examples where express warranties were found to explicitly extend to future performance are *Rempe v. General Electric Co.*, 28 Conn. Super. 160, 254 A.2d 577 (1969) (product was to "work properly for a lifetime") and *Mittasch v. Seal Lock Burial Vault, Inc.*, 42 A.D.2d 573, 344 N.Y.S.2d 101 (1973) (warranty that vault "will give satisfactory service at all times").

It is clear that a buyer and a seller can freely negotiate to extend liability into the future; that is why specific allowance was made for warranties "explicitly" extending to future performance. * * * In the absence of explicit agreement, however, UCC § 2-725(2) reflecting the drafters' intention to establish a reasonable period of time, four years,[3] beyond which business persons need not worry about stale warranty claims is applicable. This policy consideration underlying § 2-725 makes it acceptable to bar implied warranty claims brought more than a specified number of years after the sale; otherwise merchants could be forever liable for breach of warranty on any goods which they sold. * * * Similarly, an express warranty which makes no reference at all to any future date should not be allowed to extend past the limitations period. Thus, where a manufacturer warrants that a welder will meet certain performance warranties, but makes no mention of how long the warranties are meant to last; the statute of limitations begins to run at delivery. * * *

Where, however, an express warranty is made which extends for a specific period of time, *i.e.* one year, the policy reasons behind strict application of the limitations period do not apply. If a seller expressly warrants a product for a specified number of years, it is clear that, by this action alone, he is explicitly

---

[3] We are aware that some states have adopted a limitations period greater than four years, e.g. Wis. Stat. § 402.725 (6 years); Okla. Stat. tit. 12A § 2-725 (5 years). Ohio, however, follows the majority of the states in establishing a four year period. Ohio Rev. Code § 1302.98 [UCC § 2-725]. The parties agree that Ohio law governs this diversity action.

warranting the future performance of the goods for that period of time. As J. WHITE & R. SUMMERS UNIFORM COMMERCIAL CODE 342 (1972), points out, if an automobile is warranted to last for twenty-four thousand miles or four years, the warranty should extend to future performance. If the car fails within the warranty period, the limitations period should begin to run from the day the defect is or should have been discovered.

In the case at bar, Black Clawson expressly warranted the machine for a period of one year. Thus, we hold that the warranties explicitly extended to future performance for a period of one year. Therefore, under § 2-725(2) the cause of action accrued when Standard Alliance discovered or should have discovered that the machine was defective, so long as the defect arose within the warranty period.

Unfortunately, this holding does not assist the plaintiff. Under the contractual limitations period, Standard Alliance had one year from the date of discovery of defect to bring suit. Standard Alliance reported the machine's problems to Black Clawson by letter on December 27, 1967. At least as of this date, Standard Alliance had discovered the breach. Since suit was not brought until over a year later, on May 29, 1969, this action is barred by section 2-725(2). * * *

Plaintiff thirdly argues that Black Clawson should be estopped from asserting the statute of limitations as a defense because it promised to repair the defects and spent over five months attempting to do so. In effect, plaintiff contends that it reasonably relied on the repair efforts, to its detriment. Decisions in other jurisdictions are split. * * *

We must determine what the Ohio courts would do if confronted with this issue. Although we have been unable to find direct case authority, an examination of the statute is illuminative. UCC § 2-725(4), as promulgated by the drafters of the Uniform Commercial Code, states:

> "This section does not alter *the law* on tolling of the statute of limitations nor does it apply to causes of action which have accrued before this Act becomes effective." (Emphasis added)

Ohio's version of UCC § 2-725(4) is codified at Ohio Rev. Code § 1302.98(D). That section provides:

> "This section does not alter *sections 2305.15 and 2305.16 of the [Ohio] Revised Code* on tolling of the statute of limitations nor does it apply to causes of action which have accrued before this Act becomes effective." (Emphasis added)

Thus, when the Ohio legislature adopted the Uniform Commercial Code, it substituted "sections 2305.15 and 2305.16 of the [Ohio] Revised Code" for "the law" in the text of UCC § 2-725(4). This significant change in the UCC's wording requires that we limit our analysis to the two Ohio statutes cited.

An examination of these statutes reveals that the limitation period is tolled if a defendant has removed himself from the state, Ohio Rev. Code § 2305.15, or if a plaintiff has suffered from some type of disability. Ohio Rev. Code § 2305.16. Neither is applicable here.

It is, of course, quite possible that the Ohio courts would apply the doctrine of equitable estoppel in a case where an innocent purchaser has relied to his detriment on a seller's promises to repair. "The principle that ' * * * no man may take advantage of his own wrong' prevents a defendant whose actions have induced a plaintiff to delay filing a suit until after the running of the limitation period from asserting the statute of limitations as a defense to the action." *Ott v. Midland-Ross Corp.*, 523 F.2d 1367, 1370 (6th Cir. 1975). *See Markese v. Ellis*, 11 Ohio App. 2d 160, 229 N.E.2d 70 (1967). Here, however, we have two corporate behemoths, well able to look out for themselves, and no evidence that one lulled the other into not suing on time. * * *

Standard Alliance's two remaining arguments, unsupported by any authority, merit only brief mention. Standard Alliance argues that this court should toll the running of the limitations period or otherwise find timely filing because the limitations period was contractually reduced from four years to one year. It would also find significant that approximately one-half the one-year limitations period was spent in attempted repairs.

The one-year limitations period is specifically allowed by UCC § 2-725(1). We see nothing unfair about this provision in a negotiated contract between two parties of equal bargaining power. Similarly, we find no prejudice to plaintiff resulted from the lengthy repair time. Standard Alliance still had time to file suit on the original breach of warranty claim even after termination of the repair efforts; it also had a cause of action under Count II for failure to fulfill the repair or replacement warranty. * * *

[Some footnotes omitted. Those retained have been renumbered.]

Notes

1. Seller, in furnishing spandrel and visions panels for a building, represented that the goods would be free from defects in material and workmanship for a "period of twenty years." The exclusive remedy for breach was limited to

replacement of defective panels. The panels, which were delivered between 1974 and 1976, were defective. The buyer sued for damages in 1981 and the district court granted the seller's motion to dismiss based upon the statute of limitations: the court held that seller had only made replacement commitments, not warranties explicitly extending to future performance. *Held,* reversed. The warranties, by explicitly stating a time beyond delivery when the condition would exist, extended the warranty to "future" performance of the goods, with a limitation of the remedy to replacement in the event of a breach. The buyer filed suit within four years of the time the breach was or "should have been discovered." *R.W. Murray Co. v. Shatterproof Glass Corp.*, 697 F.2d 818 (8th Cir. 1983).

Despite the *Shatterproof Glass* decision, there is still some unease in the cases about when a "warranty explicitly extends to future performance of the goods." UCC 2-725(2). For example, suppose there is an express warranty that goods are "free from defects in material and workmanship" and that seller will repair any such defects discovered during the first twelve months after delivery. Is this simply a limited agreement to "cure" defects existing at the time of delivery or an affirmation that the goods will function properly for 12 months after delivery? Unless there is some clear language stating, in effect, that these goods will conform to the warranty for a stated post-delivery period, the probability is that an explicit extension will not be found.* An alternative line of analysis is that the seller's promise to provide a remedy if the goods are defective is not a warranty of the goods' performance but rather a promise about the seller's performance. As such it would not be subject to the special accrual rule for breach of warranty but rather subject to the regular accrual rule, that a cause of action accrues when the seller fails to perform the promise.**

2. Note that UCC 2A-506 provides a discovery accrual rule for breach of warranty actions. Is that preferable to the more complicated approach in UCC 2-725?

3. When does the statute of limitations start to run on a claim for breach of the

---

* *Compare Tittle v. Steel City Oldsmobile, Inc.*, 544 So. 2d 883 (Ala. 1989); *Nowalski v. Ford Motor Co.*, 781 N.E.2d 578 (Ill. Ct. App. 2002) (no explicit extension) *with Poli v. Daimler Chrysler Corp.*, 793 A.2d 104 (N.J. App. Div. 2002) *and Krieger v. Nick Alexander Imports, Inc.*, 234 Cal. App. 3d 205, 285 Cal. Rptr. 717 (1991) (extension).

** *See Mississippi Chemical Corp. v. Dresser-Rand Co.*, 287 F.3d 359 (5th Cir. 2002) (cause of action accrued when repair or replace remedy failed of its essential purpose).

warranty of title and against infringement?* Amended UCC 2-725(3)(d) states a discovery rule for both. But a breach of the warranty against infringement may not be brought more then six years after tender of delivery to the aggrieved party.

4. Tolling concepts are not covered by Article 2 but rather common law concepts are incorporated into Article 2 by virtue of UCC 2-725(5) [former subsection (4)] and UCC 1-103. A common issue is whether the breaching party has engaged in some conduct that justifies estopping it from contending that the statute of limitation period bars recover. For example, assume the seller in good faith takes several months to attempt repairs which ultimately prove unsuccessful. Does the attempted repair toll the running of the limitations period?

5. The United States has ratified the Convention on the Limitation Period in the International Sale of Goods (1974, as amended in 1980), 60 Fed. Reg. 3484 (1995). The limitation "shall be four years." Art. 8. The scope of the Convention tracks the provisions of the CISG, *see* Art. 1-7. In addition, there are provisions on "tolling" of the statute, Art. 13-21, modification of the period by agreement, Art. 22, the general limit of the limitation period (i.e., 10 years), and the consequences of the expiration of the limitation period. Art. 24-27. There is a bit of complexity here, so careful attention must be given to the text.

6. UCITA 805 is modeled on the Article 2 approach with specific types of causes of action having their own separately stated accrual rules.

Problem 12-5

B contracted to purchase factory equipment from S on June 1, 2000. S warranted that the goods were free from defects in material and workmanship and agreed to repair or replace defective parts or work within that one year period. The equipment was delivered and installed on July 1, 2000. On June 1, 2001, B notified S that the machine had stopped working. S, on June 5, arrived at B's plant and attempted to "cure" the problem. After three weeks of effort, the equipment still did not work. S left the premises on June 26, 2001 insisting that he would repair the machine. "Don't worry," he said. In August, 2001, B notified S that the cure had not worked and that he considered S in breach. Again, S assured B that a cure

---

* *See Huff v. Hobgood*, 549 So.2d 951 (Miss. 1989). *See also Rosen v. Spanierman*, 894 F.2d 28 (2nd Cir. 1990) (warranty of title did not extended to future performance). For a holding that an art dealer's express warranty that a painting was a "genuine" Dali did "explicitly" extend the warranty to future performance, *see Balog v. Center Art Gallery-Hawaii, Inc.*, 745 F. Supp. 1556 (D. Haw. 1990).

would be forthcoming. S never returned to the plant and B removed the equipment from the floor and put it in storage. In July, 2004, B consults you, his attorney, about the matter. Has the statute of limitations run on B's claim for breach of warranty?[*] What are B's best arguments that its claim is not barred by the statute of limitations? If this is a lease of equipment, would B's claims be barred by the statute of limitations?

---

[*] *See Joswick v. Chesapeake Mobile Homes, Inc.*, 765 A.2d 90 (Md. Ct. App. 2001); *Nebraska Popcorn, Inc. v. Wing*, 602 N.W.2d 18 (Neb. 1999); *Painter v. General Motors Corp.*, 974 P.2d 924 (Wyo. 1999).

INDEX

ACCELERATION OF OBLIGATION
Action for price, 528-30

ACCEPTANCE OF PRODUCT
See also Revocation of Acceptance
Buyer, 334-48, 581
Leases, 581
Post-acceptance remedies,
591-612
UCITA, 319-20

ACCESS TO PRODUCT
See also Tender of Delivery
Article 2, UCC, 305-20
CISG, 317
Leases, 317
UCITA, 319-20

ADEQUATE ASSURANCE OF DUE PERFORMANCE
Buyer's insolvency, 497-511
Grounds, 495-97
Leases, 497-511
Non-material breach, 519-26
Relationship to repudiation, 511-16
UCITA, 516

AFTER-ACQUIRED PROPERTY
Credit seller's reclamation, 463-64

AGENCY
Auctioneer's warranty, 222-23

AGREEMENT
Cornerstone of Article 2, 78-79, 147-48
Course of dealing, 181-89
Course of performance, 181-89
Contracting out of tort, 36-40, 651-52
Disclaimer of warranties, 292-301
Elements, 147-48
Force majeure clauses, 365-80
Leases, 147-48
Limiting remedies, 639-52
Liquidating damages, 629-39
Modifications, 395-420
Power to vary UCC, 24-36
Price adjustment clauses, 383-95
Reducing statute of limitations, 672-79
Remedies, 629-52
Supplemental terms, 148-53
Usage of trade, 181-89

ANALOGICAL EXTENSION
Scope of Article 2, 82-93

ARBITRATION
See also Dispute Resolution
Battle of forms, 121-23
International, 75
Unconscionable term, 93

ARTICLE 1, UCC
Scope, 9
Passim

ARTICLE 2, UCC
See also Article 2 (Amended), UCC
Agreement in fact, 147-48
Agreement varying effect, 24-26
Access to goods, 305-14
Basic concepts, 76-94, 147-48, 447
"Gap fillers", 148-53
History, 9, 76-78

Mixed transactions, 65-73
Overview, 43-56
Relationship to Article 2A, 60-64
Relationship to Article 3,
Relationship to Article 9, 61-64
Relationship to common law, 99-105
Roadmap to, 43-56
Scope, 57-64
Supplemental principles, 76-93
Supplemental terms, 148-53

ARTICLE 2 (AMENDED), UCC
Background, 9
Battle of forms, 124-25
Consignments, 465-66
Cure, 352-55
Disclaimers, 292, 298
Electronic contracting, 96-98
Extension of express warranty, 301-04
"Gateway" problem, 127-28
Information excluded, 57-58, 72
Lost profits, 543-44
Risk of loss, 425
Repudiation, 511
Repudiation damages, 540-41
Seller's consequential damages, 538
Seller's specific performance, 526
Shipping terms, 149
Statute of frauds, 129-30
Statute of limitations, 670-71, 679

ARTICLE 2A, UCC
See also Leases of Goods
Overview, 9-10
Relationship to Article 9, 60-64
Roadmap, 43-56
Scope, 60-64

ARTICLE 3, UCC
Documentary sales, 314-15
Overview, 10-11

Payment by check, 53-55
Relationship to Article 2, 53-55

ARTICLE 4, UCC
Documentary sales, 314-15
Overview, 11

ARTICLE 4A, UCC
Documentary sales, 314-15
Overview, 11-12

ARTICLE 5, UCC
Letters of credit in general, 315-17
Overview, 12

ARTICLE 6, UCC
Overview, 12

ARTICLE 7, UCC
Carrier liability, 36-41, 437-39
Documentary sales, 314-15
Overview, 12
Waiver of liability, 38-40

ARTICLE 8, UCC
Overview, 12-13

ARTICLE 9, UCC
See also Security Interests
Consignments, 464-66
Overview, 12-13
Priority over buyer's right to goods sold, 456-57
Relationship to Article 2, 60-64
Relationship to Article 2A, 60-64
Security interest arising under Article 2, 311-12, 460
Security interest in goods sold, 463-67
Seller's possessory interest, 463-67

ASSIGNEE
See Assignment

ASSIGNMENT
Rights, 493-95

BAILEE
Consignee as, 464-66
Buyer after rejection, 344-48
Law governing warehouse receipts, 36-40
Liability of carrier, 437-39
Liability of warehouse, 36-41
Risk of loss, 425-28
Sale of goods in warehouse, 425-28

BAILMENT
See also Bailee
Consignment compared, 464-66

BANK
Documentary sales, 314-15
Letter of credit, 315-17

BANKRUPTCY
Reclamation right, 463-64, 468-70

BASIS OF BARGAIN
See also Express Warranty
Test for inclusion, 212-39

BATTLE OF FORMS
See Contract Formation

BEST EFFORTS
In general, 165-66

BILL OF LADING
Documentary sales, 314-15
Law governing, 315-16
Liability of carrier, 437-39

BONA FIDE PURCHASER
See also Buyer in Ordinary Course of Business
Elements, 482-89
Leases, 483-88
Priority over security interest, 455-59
Priority over true owner, 471-79

BREACH OF CONTRACT
See also Default
Accepted goods, 591-95
Effect on risk of loss, 439-46
Excusable nonperformance, 363-64
Issuer of letter of credit, 315-17
Nature in general, 495-97
Repudiation, 411-16

BULK SALES LAW
See Article 6, UCC

BURDEN OF PROOF
Accepted goods, 581-82
Breach of warranty, 283-92
Consequential damages, 595-612
Interpretation of terms, 199-201
Non-conforming goods, 320-34
Trade usage, 181-89

BUYER IN ORDINARY COURSE OF BUSINESS
Documentary transactions, 314-15
Leases, 479-80, 538
Priority over seller's creditors, 463-67
Priority over true owner, 479-80

BUYER'S REMEDIES
See also Lessee's Remedies, Seller's Remedies
Accepted goods, 591-95
Cancellation, 516-26
Consequential damages, 563-64,

595-612
Contract-market damages, 574-77
Cover, 566-74
Failure of essential purpose, 639-52
Incidental damages, 563-65, 595-612
In general, 495-97
Pre-paying buyer, 451-52
Rejection, 320-48
Replevin, 452-55
Revocation of acceptance, 348-52
Specific performance, 452-55
Suspend performance, 459-60

BUYER'S RIGHTS
See also Buyer's Remedies
Rejection, 320-34
Good title, 471-79
Inspection of documents, 313-14
Inspection of goods, 305-14
Priority over seller's creditors, 455-59
Revocation of acceptance, 348-52
Obtaining possession, 450-55

CANCELLATION OF CONTRACT
Breach by buyer, 516-17
Breach by lessee, 516-17
Breach by seller, 324-33
Installment contracts, 517-25
CISG, 356-58
UCITA, 526

CARRIER
Conflicts between insurance companies, 435-37
Documentary transactions, 314-15
Liability for damaged goods, 36-41, 437-39
Risk of loss, 428-35

CASH SELLER
Reclamation rights, 463-64

CASUALTY TO GOODS
See also Risk of Loss
Excusable non-performance, 364
Proof of defect, 283-92
Risk of loss, 421-39

CERTIFICATE OF TITLE
Good faith purchaser, 476-77

CHECK
Documentary sales, 314-15
Payment, 53-55

CHOICE OF LAW AND FORUM
CISG, 74-75
Under UCC, 24-26

CISG
Access to products, 317-19
Battle of forms, 121-22
Choice of law and forum, 74-75
Contract formation, 108, 121-23
Default rules, 153
Excusable nonperformance, 392-93
Formalities, 198-99
Fundamental breach, 356-58
Good faith, 93-94
Identification, 449-50
In general, 22-24
Infringement, 490
Insecurity, 515-16
Inspection, 317-19
Installment contracts, 525
Modifications, 418
Notice of breach, 591
Ownership claims, 480
Parol evidence, 198-99
Product liability, 619

Property rights, 449-50
Risk of loss, 441-46
Remedies
    Accepted goods, 594-95
    Action for price, 531
    Avoidance, 356-58
    Consequential damages, 564, 578-79, 612
    Contract-Market damages, 542-43, 579
    Cover, 539
    Lost profits, 555
    Resale, 539
    Specific performance, 454-55, 531
Repudiation, 515-16
Scope, 73-74
Statute of limitations, 23-24, 679
Title, 449-50, 480
Usage and practice, 201-02
Validity exemption, 93-94
Warranties, 204-14, 273, 300-01

CODIFICATION
See also Commercial law
UCC as code, 6-8

COMMERCIAL LAW
Antecedents, 6-8
Codification of, 6-8
Functions, 1-5
Law not covered in UCC, 20-21
Role of lawyer, 5-6
Transactions, 1, 14

COMMERCIAL PAPER
See Article 3, UCC

COMMERCIAL REASONABLENESS
Article 2 policy, 76-78
Modification of contract, 403-20

Resale, 532-40

COMMISSIONERS ON UNIFORM STATE LAWS
Role in codification movement, 6-8

COMMON LAW
Contract formation, 95
Relation to UCC, 25-26, 99-105

CONDUCT
Acceptance of goods, 336-44
Contract formation, 98-108

CONFLICT OF LAWS
See Choice of law

CONSEQUENTIAL DAMAGES
See also, Damages
Agreed exclusion, 639-52
Buyer, 563-64, 595-612
Good will, 607-09
Injury to person or property, 612-17
Litigation costs, 482-90
Limitations on recovery, 595-612
Lost profits, 596-608
Proof, 595-612
Seller, 563-64

CONSIGNMENT
Rights against creditors of consignee, 464-66
Secured transaction compared, 464-66

CONSUMER CONTRACTS
See also Unconscionability
Basis for special rules, 652-54
Cure, 352-58
Disclaimer of warranty, 292-301
Economic loss doctrine, 292-301
Finance lease, 275-82

Holder in due course, 275-82
"Lemon" laws, 666-70
Manguson-Moss Warranty Act, 654-66

CONSUMER GOODS
See Consumer Contracts

CONTRACT FOR SALE OF GOODS
See Article 2, UCC

CONTRACT FORMATION
Acceptance, 98-108
Battle of forms, 108-127
CISG, 108
Electronic contracting, 96-98, 105
Firm offers, 105-06
General principles, 95-96, 99-108
Leases, 98-108
Offer, 98-108, 110-119
Statute of frauds, 26-36, 128-46
Terms after payment, 127-28
UCITA, 108

CONTRACT LAW
Functions, 1-5

CONTRACT RIGHTS
See Assignments

CONVERSION
Warranty of title, 482-90

COURSE OF DEALING
See Agreement

COURSE OF PERFORMANCE
See Agreement

CREDITOR'S RIGHTS
Buyer in possession, 462-71

Documentary transactions, 314-15
Leases, 450-71
Letters of credit, 315-17
Seller in possession, 455-59, 461-62

CURE
After rejection, 323-33, 355
After revocation of acceptance, 352-58
Before acceptance, 352-58
CISG, 356-58
Consumer goods, 354-55
Scope of right, 355

DAMAGES
See also Buyer's Remedies, CISG, Leases, Seller's Remedies, UCITA
Agreed limitations, 639-52
Breach by buyer,
Action for price, 527-32
Contract-market, 574-77
Lost profits, 543-55
Resale, 532-40
Breach by seller,
Accepted goods, 591-95
Contract-market, 574-77
Cover, 566-74
Lost profits, 577-64,
Consequential, 563-64, 577-79, 595-612
Incidental, 563-64, 577-79, 595-612
Interest, 533-38, 595-612
In general, 526-27
Liquidated, 629-39
Punitive, 579-80
Remedial choices, 526-27, 555-63

DECEPTIVE TRADE PRACTICES
Termination clauses, 82-93

DEFAULT
See Breach of Contract

DEFAULT RULES
See also Terms
Article 2 as source, 147-53

DEFECTIVE GOODS
See Warranty; Products Liability

DELEGATION OF DUTIES
Effect, 490-94

DELIVERY
See Access to Product; Tender of
Delivery

DESCRIPTION
Goods, 57-65, 209-41

DISCLAIMER OF WARRANTY
Commercial sales, 292-302
Consumer contracts, 652-70
Leases, 274-83
Warranty of title, 482-90

DISHONOR
Letter of credit, 315-17

DISPUTE SETTLEMENT
See also, Accord and Satisfaction,
Arbitration
Lemon laws, 670
Modification, 403-20

DOCUMENTARY SALE
Letter of credit, 315-17
Sale of goods, 314-15

DOCUMENTS OF TITLE
Documentary sale, 314-15

DURESS
Modifications, 395-402

DUTY TO PAY
Documentary sales, 314-15
Letter of credit, 315-17

ECONOMIC LOSS DOCTRINE
See also Products Liability, Tort
Nature and effect, 617-28

ELECTION OF REMEDIES
Buyer's choices, 564-79
Election, 526-27, 555-63
Seller's choices, 527-64

ELECTRONIC CONTRACTING
Contract formation, 96-98, 105
Legislative background, 96-98

ESTOPPEL
Statute of frauds, 26-36, 130-38
Statute of limitations, 670-79

EXCUSABLE NON-PERFORMANCE
In general, 363
Basic assumption test,
    Failure of agreed delivery or
        payment mechanisms, 364-65
    Finance leases, 392
    Force majeure events, 365-77
    Force majeure clauses,
        377-80
    Government action, 383-90, 392
    Identified goods, 364
    Increased costs of performance,
        380-82
    Sources of supply, 377
Buyer's excuse, 382-83
CISG, 392-93
Relief after excuse, 370

Unidroit principles, 392-93

EXPRESS WARRANTY
See also Implied Warranty, Warranty of Title
Basis of bargain test, 212-39
History, 203-07
Knowledge of buyer, 226-33
Leases, 209
Magnuson-Moss Warranty Act, 654-66
Modification of contract, 233-39
Opinion, 212-22
Privity, 239, 621-29

FEDERAL COMMERCIAL LAW
See also Federal Consumer Law
Carriers, 437-39
CISG, 22-24
Federal Bill of Lading Act, 437-39
Magnuson-Moss Warranty Act, 654-66
Overview, 20-21

FEDERAL CONSUMER LAW
See also Consumer Contracts; Federal Commercial Law
Magnuson-Moss Warranty Act, 654-66
Overview, 652-54

FINANCE LEASE
See also Article 2A, UCC
In general, 55-56, 274-83

F.O.B.
See Tender of Delivery

FRAUD
Buyer's insolvency, 468-70
Retention of goods by seller, 459-62

GOOD FAITH
CISG, 93-94
Definition, 91-92
Enforcement of contract, 82-93
Modification agreements, 395-403
Purchaser for value, 471-99
Price determination, 166-78
Rejection remedy, 320-34
Requirements contracts, 154-65
Termination clauses, 82-91

GOOD FAITH PURCHASER
Elements, 471-76
Leases, 483-88
Rights against cash seller, 463-64, 468-69
Rights against credit seller, 463-64, 468-69
Rights against true owner, 471-78

GOODS
Definition of, 57-65

HISTORICAL DEVELOPMENT
Article 2, 9, 76-78
Article 2A, 9-10
Basis of the bargain, 223-26
Interpreting codes, 15-20
Rejection remedy, 320
Statute of frauds, 128-30
Uniform Commercial Code, 6-8
Warranty, 203-09

IDENTIFICATION OF PRODUCT
Importance, 447-50
Remedies of buyer, 451-59

IMPLIED WARRANTY OF FITNESS
Disclaimer, 292-301
Scope and effect, 266-74
Leases, 274-82

Privity, 302-04, 619-28

IMPLIED WARRANTY OF MER-CHANTABILITY
Auctions, 482-90
Disclaimer, 254-57
In general, 242-58
   Description of goods,
     243-45
   Food, 254-57
     Merchant requirement, 245-50
   Ordinary purposes, 245-50
   Used goods, 257-58
Leases, 274-82
Policy, 244-45
Privity, 65-73, 301-03
Tort compared, 258-66

IMPLIED WARRANTY OF TITLE
In general, 482-90
Statute of limitations, 670-71, 679

IMPOSSIBILITY OF PERFORMANCE
See Excusable Nonperformance

IMPRACTICABILITY
See Excusable Nonperformance

INDEFINITE QUANTITY
See also Requirements Contracts
Enforceability, 153-66

INSOLVENCY
Demand for adequate assurance, 497-511
Party to documentary sale, 314-15
Pre-paying buyer, 451-52
Seller's reclamation rights, 464-66, 468-69

INSPECTION OF DOCUMENTS
Documentary sales, 314-15
Letter of credit transaction, 315-17

INSPECTION OF GOODS
See also Access to Product, Delivery, Payment
Buyer's right, 306
CISG, 317-19
Documentary sales, 314-15
Leases, 317
Letter of credit transaction, 315-17
Third party inspection, 442-46
UCITA, 319-20

INSTALLMENT CONTRACTS
Cure after rejection, 323-332
In general, 323, 516-17
Rejection under, 323-33
Seller's cancellation, 517-26

INTEREST
See also Damages
Recovery for breach, 533-38

INTERPRETATION
See also Terms
Commercial codes, 15-20
Letter of credit, 315-17
Written agreement,
   Burden of proof, 199-201
   Parol evidence, 189-99
   Terms, 199-201
   Trade usage, 181-89

INSURANCE
Risk of loss, 435

INTERNATIONAL COMMERCIAL TRANSACTIONS
See also CISG

Letter of credit, 315-17
Overview, 22-24

JUDICIAL LIEN
See Lien Creditor

LEASE OF GOODS
See also Article 2A, UCC
Agreement in fact, 147-48
Acceptance, 334-48
Access to product, 317
Consequential damages, 538
Excusable non-performance, 392
Finance lease, 55-56, 274-82
Formation, 95-108
History, 6-14
Inspection, 317
Liquidated damages, 629-39
Open price term, 177
Ownership claims, 471-80
Priority disputes, 447-50
Property rights, 447-50
Reclamation, 470
Remedies
    In general, 495-97
    Lessee, 455-58, 564-77
    Lessor, 459-62, 463-66, 526-64
Revocation of acceptance, 352
Risk of loss, 422-23
Roadmap, 43-56
Sale compared, 60-61
Scope, 60-64
Security interest compared, 60-61
Supplemental terms, 148-53
"True" lease, 60-61
Third party rights, 56, 479-80
Warranties, 209
Warranty of title, 483-89

LESSEE OF GOODS
See also Article 2A, UCC, Lease of

Goods,
Finance lessee, 274-82
Priority, 461-62, 467-79
Remedies, Chapter 10, *passim*

LESSOR OF GOODS
See also Article 2A, UCC, Lease of
    Goods,
Finance lease, 274-82
Priority, 461-62, 467-79
Remedies, Chapter 10, *passim*

LETTER OF CREDIT
Description and function, 315-17

LICENSES
See UCITA

LIEN CREDITOR
Claims to goods sold, 455-62, 466-70
Limited remedies, 639-51

LIQUIDATED DAMAGES
See also Damages
Article 2, UCC, 632, 638-39
Enforceability of clause, 629-31
Leases, 632-38

LOST VOLUME DAMAGES
See Seller's Remedies

MAGNUSON MOSS WARRANTY ACT
See Consumer Contracts

MERCHANT
Definition and scope, 79-81
Implied warranty of merchantability, 245-58
Statute of frauds, 80-81
UCITA, 79

MODIFICATION OF CONTRACT
After excuse, 370
Agreement, 395-402
Express warranty, 233-39
Statute of frauds, 402-03
Rescission, 403-20
Waiver, 403-20

MOTOR VEHICLES
See Certificate of Title

NONCONFORMITY
Letter of credit documents, 315-17
Tender of delivery, 320-34

NOTICE
Accepted goods, 581-91
Agreed limitations, 639-52
Documentary sales, 314-15
Rejection, 333-34
Resale by seller, 532-38
Revocation of acceptance, 348-52

OFFER AND ACCEPTANCE
See Contract Formation

OPEN PRICE TERM
See also Price, Terms
Enforceability, 166-79

OPEN QUANTITY TERM
See Requirements Contracts

OPINION
Express warranty compared, 212-22

PAROL EVIDENCE RULE
In general, 179-81, 189-201
Course of dealing, 181-89
Interpretation exception, 189-96
Partial integration, 189-96
Consistent additional terms, 189-97
Merger clauses, 197-98
Trade usage, 181-89

PASSAGE OF TITLE
See also Warranty of Title
Claims of owner to goods sold, 482-90
Relevance in UCC, 447-50

PAYMENT
Check, 53-55
Documentary sales, 310-11, 314-15
Letter of credit, 315-17

POSSESSION
Claims of creditors,
Goods delivered, 463-71
Goods retained, 455-58
Consignments, 464-66
Identification, 447-50
Right to, 451-55
Title, 447-50, 471-78

PRICE
See also Open Price Term, Terms
Action for, 527-32
Delivery terms, 179
Effect open price, 166-68
Fixing price in good faith, 168-78
Price adjustment clauses, 383-93

PRIVATE SALE
Resale by seller, 532-38

PRIVITY
Commercial warranties, 239, 301-02, 617-29
Consumer warranties, 654-70
Finance lease, 274-83

Products liability, 612-17
Revised Article 2, UCC, 352
Special statutes, 301-04

PRODUCT LIABILITY
Economic loss doctrine, 617-28
Injury to person and property, 612-17
Privity, 612-17
Warranty compared, 258-66

PROMISSORY ESTOPPEL
Statute of frauds, 26-36, 130-38

PROOF
See Burden of Proof

PUBLIC SALE
Resale by seller, 532-40

PURCHASER
Buyer in ordinary course of business, 462-70
Creditor claims, 455-62
Documentary transactions, 315-17
Warranty of title, 482-90
Finance lease, 274-83
Good faith for value, 471-78

RECLAMATION
In general, 463-64

REJECTION OF GOODS
In general, 320-34, 581
Acceptance precludes, 334-40
Buyer's duties after rejection, 344-48
Consumer goods, 340-41
Cure limitation, 352-56
Good faith, 320-33
Installment contracts, 324-33
Procedural requirements, 333-34

Fundamental breach, 356-58
Leases, 317
UCITA, 358

REMEDIES
See Buyer's Remedies, CISG, Damages, Leases, Seller's Remedies, UCITA

REPLEVIN
Buyer's right, 452-55

REPUDIATION
See also Breach of Contract
Damage measure, 540-43, 574-77
Definition and effect, 511-16
Relationship to demand for assurance, 497-511

REQUIREMENTS CONTRACTS
See also Indefinite Quantity; Terms
In general, 154-66

RESTITUTION
Buyer in default, 544-55
Price term fails, 166-68
Use of goods after revocation, 348-52

REVERSIONARY INTEREST
Lease of goods, 60-65

REVISED ARTICLE 2, UCC
See Article 2 (Amended), UCC

REVOCATION OF ACCEPTANCE
Cure after, 352-59
Leases, 352
Right in general, 348-52, 581
UCITA, 358-59
Use of goods after revocation, 350-52

RISK OF LOSS
Carrier liability, 437-38
CISG, 441-46
Delivery terms,
    Domestic, 429-35
    INCO terms, 442-46
Effect of breach, 439-46
Goods in possession of bailee, 425-28
In general, 421-23
Insurance, 435
Leases, 422-23
No obligation to ship, 423-25
Seller authorized to ship, 428-39
UCITA, 446

ROADMAPS
Article 2A, 43-56
Article 2, 43-56

SALE OF GOODS
Consignment compared, 464-66
Documentary sales, 314-15
Bailment compared, 313-14
Lease compared, 57-65

SCOPE
Article 1, 57
Article 2A, 60-64
Article 2,
    Analysis, 57-60
    Computer software, 61-64, 70-72
    Economic loss, doctrine, 617-29
    Extension by analogy, 82-93
    Leases, 61-64
    Mixed transactions, 65-73
Article 9, 57-65
CISG, 73-74
UCITA, 71-73

SECURITY INTERESTS
See also Article 9, UCC

Arising under Article 2, 460
Buyer's right to goods, 453
Consignments, 464-66
Priority over buyer's right to goods, 456-57
Seller's security interest in goods, 463, 467
Shipment under reservation, 311-12

SELLER'S REMEDIES
See also Buyer's Remedies, Damages
Buyer's repudiation, 511-16
Cancellation, 516-17
Choices, 526-29, 555-62
Damages,
    Action for price, 527-32
    Consequential, 563-64
    Contract-Market, 540-43, 556-59
    Incidental, 563-64
    Interest, 533-58
    Lost profits, 543-55
    Resale, 532-40
Demand for adequate assurance, 497-511
Installment contracts, 517-26
Reclamation rights, 463-64
Retention of possession, 459-62
Specific performance, 527-32
Stoppage in transit, 459-60

SHIPMENT
See also Tender of Delivery
Delivery terms, 305-14, 439-47
Documentary sales, 314-15
Law governing bill of lading, 437-39
Risk of loss, 428-35
Under reservation, 311-12

SIGHT DRAFT
Documentary sales, 314-15
Letter of credit, 315-17

SPECIFIC PERFORMANCE
Buyer's remedy, 452-55
Seller's remedy, 527-32

STANDBY LETTER OF CREDIT
See Letter of Credit

STATUTE OF FRAUDS
Article 2,
Admission in pleading, 130-38
Confirmations, 138-44
Electric contracting, 96-98
Evaluation, 128-30
History, 128-30
Merchant exception, 80-81
Modifications, 402-11
Multiple writings, 144-46
No oral modification clause, 404-11
Part performance, 26-36, 130-35
Promissory estoppel, 26-36, 130-38
UCITA, 629

STATUTE OF LIMITATIONS
Agreed limitation, 672-77
CISG, 679
In general, 670-79
Scope and effect, 670-71
Tolling, 672-77, 679
UCITA, 679
Warranty of title, 678-79

STOPPAGE IN TRANSIT,
By seller, 459-60

STRICT TORT LIABILITY
See Products Liability

TENDER OF DELIVERY
See also Access to Product

Documentary sales, 314-15
In general, 305-20
Risk of loss,
Goods in possession of bailee, 425-28
No obligation to ship, 423-24
Obligation to ship, 428-39

TERMINATION
Franchise agreements, 82-93
In general, 359

TERMS
See also Agreement, Interpretation
Additional or different, 108-28
Delivery, 179
Flexible quantity, 154-66
Open price, 166-78
Supplemental, 145-53

THIRD PARTY BENEFICIARY
Extension of warranties, 301-04

THIRD PERSON RIGHTS
Goods in possession of bailee, 425-28
Leases, 56
Lien creditors to goods sold, 455-56, 461-62, 467-71
Secured party to goods sold, 456-58, 467-71
True owner to goods sold, 471-78

TITLE TO GOODS
See also Passage of Title
Relevance under UCC, 447-50
Owner's claim to good sold, 471-78
Retained as security, 460-61

TORT LAW
See also Products Liability
Contracting out, 36-40, 651-52

Economic loss doctrine, 416-29
Restatement (Third) of Torts, 265
Role under UCC, 258-66

TRADE USAGE
See also Interpretation, Terms
Admissibility, 181-89
Effect of parol evidence rule, 181-89
Proof, 199-200

UNCONSCIONABILITY
CISG, 93-94
Consumer contracts, 82-93, 652-66
Definition, 92-93
Disclaimers of warranty, 292-301
Exclusion of consequential damages, 639-52
Finance leases, 274-82
Termination clauses, 82-86

UNIDROIT PRINCIPLES ON INTERNATIONAL COM-MERCIAL CONTRACTS
Adjustment of contract, 396-402
Battle of forms, 125-26
In general, 23-24

UNIFORM COMMERCIAL CODE
Antecedents, 6-8
Comments, 15-17
Commercial law not covered, 20-21
History of Article 2A, 9-10
Interpretation, 15-19, 24-26
Legislative history, 17-19
Overview of Articles, 9-13
Methodology in use, 24-36
Pitfalls in using, 20-21
Recent revisions, 9-12
Scope, 9-13
Variation of effect, 24-26

UNIFORM COMPUTER INFOR-MATION TRANSACTIONS ACT (UCITA)
Acceptance, 352-53
Access to products, 319, 455, 460
Assignment and delegation, 493
Cancellation, 526
Consequential and incidental damages, 612
Contract formation, 108
Cure, 358
Default rules, 153
Drafting history, 10
Inspection, 319
Licensee's rights against Lessor's creditors, 482
Licensor's right to control, 460
Merchant concept, 79-80
Ownership claims, 480, 490
Reclamation, 466
Remedies,
Licensee, 574, 577, 595, 612
Licensor, 531, 540, 543, 555, 564
Repudiation, 516
Rejection, 358
Revocation of acceptance, 358
Risk of loss, 446
Scope, 70-72
"Shrink wrap" license, 126-27
Title, 450
Warranties, 209, 241, 273-74

UNIFORM CUSTOMS AND PRACTICES
Role in documentary credit, 314-17

UNITED NATIONS CONVENTION ON CONTRACTS FOR THE INTERNATIONAL SALE OF GOODS
See CISG

…S ACT
contract, 519-25
remedy, 320
oss, 421-23

od faith purchaser, 471-79

…VER
Liability, 36-40
Modifications, 403-20

WAREHOUSE RECEIPTS
See Collateral, Documents of Title

WAREHOUSEMAN
See Bailee

WARRANTY
See also Express Warranty, Implied
Warranty
Against infringement, 471-79
Conforming documents in letter of
credit, 315-17
Consumer products, 652-70
Defenses, 283-92
Disclaimers, 292-301
Extension to third persons, 301-04,
617-28
Express warranty, 209-41
Finance leases, 274-83
Fitness, 266-74
History, 203-07
In General, 203-07
Leases, 209
Merchantability, 242-58
Proof of breach, 283-92
Title, 482-90
UCITA, 209

WRITING
Effect of trade usage, 181-89
Electronic contracting, 95-98
Interpretation, 199-201
Statute of frauds, 130-47

ISBN 0–314–15478–7